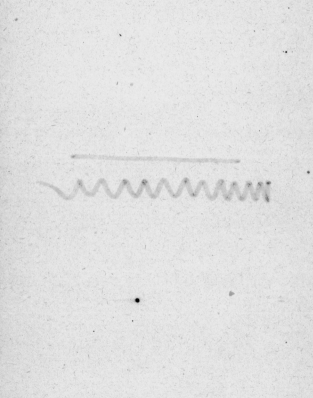

THE

HISTORY OF ENGLAND

FROM

THE INVASION OF JULIUS CÆSAR

TO

THE ABDICATION OF JAMES THE SECOND,

1688.

By DAVID HUME, Esq.,

A NEW EDITION,

WITH THE AUTHOR'S LAST CORRECTIONS AND IMPROVEMENTS.

TO WHICH IS PREFIXED

A SHORT ACCOUNT OF HIS LIFE,

WRITTEN BY HIMSELF.

VOL. I.

PHILADELPHIA:
PORTER & COATES.

MY OWN LIFE.

It is difficult for a man to speak long of himself without vanity; therefore I shall be short. It may be thought an instance of vanity that I pretend at all to write my life; but this narrative shall contain little more than the history of my writings; as, indeed, almost all my life has been spent in literary pursuits and occupations. The first success of most of my writings was not such as to be an object of vanity.

I was born the 26th of April, 1711, old style, at Edinburgh. I was of a good family, both by father and mother: my father's family is a branch of the Earl of Home's or Hume's; and my ancestors had been proprietors of the estate which my brother possesses for several generations. My mother was daughter of Sir David Falconer, President of the College of Justice: the title of Lord Halkerton came by succession to her brother.

My family, however, was not rich; and being myself a younger brother, my patrimony, according to the mode of my country, was of course very slender. My father, who passed for a man of parts, died when I was an infant, leaving me, with an elder brother and a sister, under the care of our mother, a woman of singular merit, who, though young and handsome, devoted herself entirely to the rearing and educating of her children. I passed through the ordinary course of education with success, and was seized very early with a passion for literature, which has been the ruling passion of my life and the great source of my enjoyments. My studious disposition, my sobriety, and my industry gave my family a notion that the law was a proper profession for me; but I found an unsurmountable aversion to everything but the pursuits of philosophy and general learning; and while they fancied I was poring upon Voet and Vinnius, Cicero and Virgil were the authors which I was secretly devouring.

My very slender fortune, however, being unsuitable to this plan of life, and my health being a little broken by my ardent application, I was tempted, or rather forced, to make a very feeble trial for entering into a more active scene of life. In 1734 I went to Bristol, with some recommendations to several merchants; but in a few months found that scene totally unsuitable to me. I went over to France with a view of prosecuting my studies in a country retreat; and I there laid that plan of life which I have steadily and successfully pursued. I resolved to make a very rigid frugality supply my deficiency of fortune, to maintain unimpaired my independency, and to regard every object as contemptible except the improvement of my talents in literature.

During my retreat in France, first at Rheims, but chiefly at La Flèche, in Anjou, I composed my Treatise of Human Nature. After passing three years very agreeably in that country, I came over to London in 1737. In the end of 1738 I published my Treatise, and immediately went down to my mother and my brother, who lived at his country-house, and employed himself very judiciously and successfully in the improvement of his fortune.

Never literary attempt was more unfortunate than my Treatise of Human Nature. It fell *dead-born from the press*, without reaching such distinction as even to excite a murmur among the zealots. But being naturally of a cheerful and sanguine temper, I very soon recovered the blow, and prosecuted with greater ardor my studies in the country. In 1742 I printed at Edinburgh the first part of my Essays: the work was favorably received, and soon made me entirely forget my former disappointment. I continued with my mother and brother in the country, and in that time recovered the knowledge of the Greek language, which I had too much neglected in my early youth.

In 1745 I received a letter from the Marquis of Annandale, inviting me to come and live with him in England; I found, also, that the friends and family of that young nobleman were desirous of putting him under my care and direction, for the state of his mind and health required it. I lived with him a twelvemonth. My appointments during that time made a considerable accession to my small fortune. I then received an invitation from General St. Clair to attend him as a secretary to his expedition, which was at first meant against Canada, but ended in an incursion on the coast of France. Next year—to wit, 1747—I received an invitation from the general to attend him in the same station in his military embassy to the courts of Vienna and Turin. I then wore the uniform of an officer, and was introduced at these courts as aide-de-camp to the general along with Sir Harry Erskine and Captain Grant, now General Grant. These two years were almost the only interruptions which my studies have received during the course of my life. I passed them agreeably and in good company; and my appointments, with my frugality, had made me reach a fortune which I called independent, though most of my friends were inclined to smile when I said so : in short, I was now master of near a thousand pounds.

I had always entertained a notion that my want of success in publishing the Treatise of Human Nature had proceeded more from the manner than the matter, and that I had been guilty of a very usual indiscretion in going to the press too early. I therefore cast the first part of that work anew in the Enquiry concerning Human Understanding, which was published while I was at Turin. But this piece was at first little more successful than the Treatise of Human Nature. On my return from Italy, I had the mortification to find all England in a ferment on account of Dr. Middleton's Free Enquiry, while my performance was entirely overlooked and neglected. A new edition which had been published in London, of my Essays, moral and political, met not with a much better reception.

Such is the force of natural temper, that these disappointments made little or no impression on me. I went down in 1749, and lived two years with my brother at his country-house, for my mother was now dead. I there composed the second part of my Essay, which I called Political Discourses, and also my Enquiry concerning the Principles of Morals, which is another part of my treatise that I cast anew. Meanwhile my bookseller, A. Miller, informed me that my former publications (all about the unfortunate Treatise) were beginning to be the subject of conversation; that the sale of them was gradually increasing; and that new editions were demanded. Answers by Reverends and Right Reverends came out two or three in a year; and I found, by Dr. Warburton's railing, that the books were beginning to be esteemed in good company. However, I had a fixed resolution, which I inflexibly maintained, never to reply to anybody; and not being very irascible in my temper, I have easily kept myself clear of all literary squabbles. These symptoms of a rising reputation gave me encouragement, as I was ever more disposed to see the favorable than the unfavorable side of things; a turn of mind which it is more happy to possess than to be born to an estate of ten thousand a year.

In 1751 I removed from the country to the town, the true scene for a man of letters. In 1752 were published at Edinburgh, where I then lived, my Political Discourses, the only work of mine that was successful on the first publication. It was well received at home and abroad. In the same year was published, in London, my Enquiry concerning the Principles of Morals; which, in my own opinion (who ought not to judge on that subject), is of all my writings, historical, philosophical, or literary, incomparably the best. It came unnoticed and unobserved into the world.

In 1752 the Faculty of Advocates chose me their librarian; an office from which I received little or no emolument, but which gave me command of a large library. I then formed the plan of writing the History of England; but being frightened with the notion of continuing a narrative through a period of one thousand seven hundred years, I commenced with the accession of the house of Stuart, an epoch when, I thought, the misrepresentations of faction began chiefly to take place. I was, I own, sanguine in my expectations of the success of this work. I thought that I was the only historian that had at once neglected present power, interest, and authority, and the cry of popular prejudices; and as the subject was suited to every capacity, I expected proportional applause. But miserable was my disappointment: I was assailed by one cry of reproach, disapprobation, and even detestation; English, Scotch, and Irish, Whig and Tory, churchman and sectary, freethinker and religionist, patriot and courtier, united in their rage against the man who had presumed to shed a generous tear for the fate of Charles I. and the Earl of Strafford; and after the first ebullitions of their fury were over, what was still more mortifying, the book seemed to sink into oblivion. Mr. Miller told me that in a twelvemonth he sold only forty-five copies of it. I scarcely, indeed, heard of one man in the three kingdoms, considerable for rank or letters, that could endure the book. I must only except the Primate of England, Dr. Herring, and the Primate of Ireland, Dr. Stone, which seem two odd exceptions. These ignified prelates separately sent me a message not to be iscouraged.

I was, however, I confess, discouraged; and had not the war at that time been breaking out between France and England, I had certainly retired to some provincial town of the former kingdom, have changed my name, and never more have returned to my native country. But as this scheme was not now practicable, and the subsequent volume was considerably advanced, I resolved to pick up courage and to persevere.

In this interval I published at London my Natural History of Religion, along with some other small pieces: its public entry was rather obscure, except only that Dr. Hurd wrote a pamphlet against it, with all the illiberal petulance, arrogance, and scurrility which distinguish the Warburtonian school. This pamphlet gave me some consolation for the otherwise indifferent reception of my performance.

In 1756, two years after the fall of the first volume, was published the second volume of my History, containing the period from the death of Charles I. till the Revolution. This performance happened to give less displeasure to the Whigs, and was better received. It not only rose itself, but helped to buoy up its unfortunate brother.

But though I had been taught by experience that the Whig party were in possession of bestowing all places, both in the state and in literature, I was so little inclined to yield to their senseless clamor that in above a hundred alterations, which further study, reading or reflection engaged me to make in the reigns of the two first Stuarts, I have made all of them invariably to the Tory side. It is ridiculous to consider the English constitution before that period as a regular plan of liberty.

In 1759 I published my history of the House of Tudor. The clamor against this performance was almost equal to that against the History of the two first Stuarts. The reign of Elizabeth was particularly obnoxious. But I was now callous against the impressions of public folly, and continued very peacefully and contentedly in my retreat at Edinburgh, to finish, in two volumes, the more early part of the English History, which I gave to the public in 1761, with tolerable, and but tolerable, success.

But notwithstanding this variety of winds and seasons to which my writings had been exposed, they had still been making such advances that the copy-money given me by the booksellers much exceeded anything formerly known in England : I was become not only independent, but opulent. I retired to my native country of Scotland, determined never more to set my foot out of it, and retaining the satisfaction of never having preferred a request to one great man, or even making advances of friendship to any one of them. As I was now turned of fifty, I thought of passing all the rest of my life in this philosophical manner, when I received, in 1763, an invitation from the Earl of Hertford, with whom I was not in the least acquainted, to attend him on his embassy to Paris, with a near prospect of being appointed secretary to the embassy, and, in the mean while, of performing the functions of that office. This offer, however inviting, I at first declined, both because I was reluctant to begin connections with the great, and because I was afraid that the civilities and gay company of Paris would prove disagreeable to a person of my age and humor; but on his lordship's repeating the invitation, I accepted of it. I have every reason, both of pleasure and interest, to think myself happy in my connections with that nobleman, as well as afterwards with his brother, General Conway.

Those who have not seen the strange effects of modes will never imagine the reception I met with at Paris, from men and women of all ranks and stations. The more I resiled from their excessive civilities, the more I was loaded with them. There is, however, a real satisfaction in living at Paris, from the great number of sensible, knowing, and polite company with which that city abounds above all places in the universe. I thought once of settling there for life.

I was appointed secretary to the embassy; and in summer, 1765, Lord Hertford left me, being appointed Lord Lieutenant of Ireland. I was *chargé d'affaires* till the arrival of the Duke of Richmond, towards the end of the year. In the beginning of 1766 I left Paris, and next summer went to Edinburgh, with the same view as formerly of burying myself in a philosophical retreat. I returned to that place, not richer, but with much more money, and a much larger income, by means of Lord Hertford's friendship, than I left it ; and I was desirous of trying what superfluity could produce, as I had formerly made an experiment of a competency. But in 1767 I received from Mr. Conway an invitation to be under-secretary ; and this invitation both the character of the person and my connections with Lord Hertford prevented me from declining. I returned to Edinburgh in 1769, very opulent (for I possessed a revenue of £1000 a year), healthy, and, though somewhat stricken in years, with the prospect of enjoying long my ease, and of seeing the increase of my reputation.

In spring, 1775, I was struck with a disorder in my bowels, which at first gave me no alarm, but has since, as I apprehend it, become mortal and incurable. I now reckon upon a speedily dissolution. I have suffered very little pain from my disorder; and, what is more strange, have, notwithstanding the great decline of my person, never suffered a moment's abatement of my spirits; inasmuch that were I to name a period of my life which I should most choose to pass over again, I might be tempted to point to this later period. I possess the same ardor as ever in study, and the same gayety in company. I consider, besides, that a man of sixty-five, by dying, cuts off only a few years of infirmities; and though I see many symptoms of my literary reputation's breaking out at last with additional lustre, I know that I could have but a few years to enjoy it. It is difficult to be more detached from life than I am at present.

To conclude historically with my own character. I am, or rather was (for that is the style I must now use in speaking of myself, which emboldens me the more to speak my sentiments)—I was, I say, a man of mild disposition, of command of temper, of an open, social, and cheerful humor, capable of attachment, but little susceptible of enmity, and of great moderations in all my passions. Even my love of literary fame, my ruling passion, never soured my temper, notwithstanding my frequent disappointments. My company was not unacceptable to the young and careless, as well as to the studious and literary; and as I took a particular pleasure in the company of modest women, I had no reason to be displeased with the reception I met with from them. In a word, though most men anywise eminent have found reason to complain of calumny, I never was touched or even attacked by her baleful tooth; and though I wantonly exposed myself to the rage of both civil and religious factions, they seemed to be disarmed in my behalf of their wonted fury. My friends never had occasion to vindicate any one circumstance of my character and conduct; not but that the zealots, we may well suppose, would have been glad to invent and propagate any story to my disadvantage, but they could never find any which they thought would wear the face of probability. I cannot say there is no vanity in making this funeral oration of myself, but I hope it is not a misplaced one ; and this is a matter of fact which is easily cleared and ascertained.

April 18, 1776.

LETTER

FROM

ADAM SMITH, LL.D.,

TO

WILLIAM STRAHAN, Esq.

KIRKALDY, FIFESHIRE, *November 9, 1776.*

DEAR SIR,—It is with a real though a very melancholy pleasure that I sit down to give you some account of the behavior of our late excellent friend, Mr. Hume, during his last illness.

Though in his own judgment his disease was mortal and incurable, yet he allowed himself to be prevailed upon, by the entreaty of his friends, to try what might be the effects of a long journey. A few days before he set out, he wrote that account of his own life which, together with his other papers, he has left to your care. My account, therefore, shall begin where his ends.

He set out for London towards the end of April, and at Morpeth met with Mr. John Home and myself, who had both come down from London on purpose to see him, expecting to have found him at Edinburgh. Mr. Home returned with him, and attended him, during the whole of his stay in England, with that care and attention which might be expected from a temper so perfectly friendly and affectionate. As I had written to my mother that she might expect me in Scotland, I was under the necessity of continuing my journey. His disease seemed to yield to exercise and change of air; and when he arrived in London, he was apparently in much better health than when he left Edinburgh. He was advised to go to Bath to drink the waters, which appeared for some time to have so good an effect upon him that even he himself began to entertain, what he was not apt to do, a better opinion of his own health. His symptoms, however, soon returned with their usual violence, and from that moment he gave up all thoughts of recovery, but submitted with the utmost cheerfulness, and the most perfect complacency and resignation. Upon his return to Edinburgh, though he found himself much weaker, yet his cheerfulness never abated, and he continued to divert himself, as usual, with correcting his own works for a new edition, with reading books of amusement, with the conversation of his friends, and sometimes in the evening with a party at his favorite game of whist. His cheerfulness was so great, and his conversation and amusements ran so much in their usual strain, that, notwithstanding all bad symptoms, many people could not believe he was dying. "I shall tell your friend, Colonel Edmonstone," said Doctor Dundas to him one day, "that I left you much better, and in a fair way of recovery." "Doctor," said he, "as I believe you would not choose to tell anything but the truth, you had better tell him that I am dying as fast as my enemies, if I have any, could wish, and as easily and cheerfully as my best friends could desire." Colonel Edmonstone soon afterwards came to see him and take leave of him; and on his way home he could not forbear writing him a letter, bidding him once more an eternal adieu, and applying to him, as to a dying man, the beautiful French verses in which the Abbé Chaulieu, in expectation of his own death, laments his approaching separation from his friend the Marquis de la Fare. Mr. Hume's magnanimity and firmness were such that his most affectionate friends knew that they hazarded nothing in talking or writing to him as to a dying man, and that, so far from being hurt by his frankness, he was rather pleased and flattered by it. I happened to come into his room while he was reading this letter, which he had just received, and which he immediately showed me. I told him that though I was sensible how very much he was weakened, and that appearances were in many respects very bad, yet his cheerfulness was still so great, the spirit of life seemed still to be so very strong in him, that I could not help entertaining some faint hopes. He answered, "Your hopes are groundless. An habitual diarrhœa of more than a year's standing would be a very bad disease at any age: at my age it is a mortal one. When I lie down in the evening I feel myself weaker than when I rose in the morning, and when I rise in the morning weaker than when I lay down in the evening. I am sensible, besides, that some of my vital parts are affected, so that I must soon die." " Well," said I, " if it must be so, you have at least the satisfaction of leaving all your friends, your brother's family in particular, in great prosperity." He said that he felt that satisfaction so sensibly that when he was reading, a few days before, Lucian's Dialogues of the Dead, among all the excuses which are alleged to Charon for not entering readily into his boat, he could not find one that fitted him; he had no house to finish, he had no daughter to provide for, he had no enemies upon whom he wished to revenge himself. "I could not well imagine," said he, " what excuse I could make to Charon in order to obtain a little delay. I have done everything of consequence which I ever meant to do, and I could at no time expect to leave my relations and friends in a better situation than that in which I am now likely to leave them : I therefore have all reason to die contented." He then diverted himself with inventing several jocular excuses, which he supposed he might make to Charon, and with imagining the very surly answers which it might suit the character of Charon to return to them. "Upon further consideration," said he, " I thought I might say to him, ' Good Charon, I have been correcting my works for a new edition. Allow me a little time, that I may see how the public receives the alterations.' But Charon would answer, " When you have seen the effect of these, you will be for making other alterations. There will be no end of such excuses ; so, honest friend, please step into the boat." But I might still urge, ' Have a little patience, good Charon : I have been endeavoring to open the eyes of the public. If I live a few years longer, I may have the satisfaction of seeing the downfall of some of the prevailing systems of superstition.' But Charon would then lose all temper and decency—' You loitering rogue, that will not happen these many hundred years. Do you fancy I will grant you a lease for so long a term. Get into the boat this instant, you lazy, loitering rogue!' "

But though Mr. Hume always talked of his approaching dissolution with great cheerfulness, he never affected to make any parade of his magnanimity. He never mentioned the subject but when the conversation naturally led to it, and never dwelt longer upon it than the course of the conversation happened to require. It was a subject, indeed, which occurred pretty frequently, in consequence of the inquiries which his friends, who came to see him, naturally made concerning the state of his health. The conversation which I mentioned above, and which passed on Thursday, the 8th of August, was the last, except one, that I ever had with him. He had now become so very weak that the company of his most intimate friends fatigued him; for his cheerfulness was still so great, his complaisance and social disposition were still so entire, that when any friend was with him he could not help talking more, and with greater exertion, than suited the weakness of his body. At his own desire, therefore, I agreed to leave Edinburgh, where I was staying partly upon his account, and returned to my mother's house here, at Kirkaldy, upon condition that he would send for me whenever he wished to see me; the physician who saw him most frequently, Dr. Black, undertaking in the meantime to write me occasionally an account of the state of his health.

On the 22d of August, the doctor wrote me the following letter:

"Since my last, Mr. Hume has passed his time pretty easily, but is much weaker. He sits up, goes down stairs once a day, and amuses himself with reading, but seldom sees anybody. He finds that the conversation of his most intimate friends fatigues and oppresses him; and it is happy that he does not need it, for he is quite free from anxiety, impatience, or low spirits, and passes his time very well with the assistance of amusing books."

I received the day after a letter from Mr. Hume himself, of which the following is an extract:

EDINBURGH, *August* 23, 1776.

"MY DEAREST FRIEND,—I am obliged to make use of my nephew's hand in writing to you, as I do not rise to-day.

*   *   *   *   *   *   *   *   *   *   *

"I go very fast to decline, and last night had a small fever, which I hoped might put a quicker period to this tedious illness; but, unluckily, it has in a great measure gone off. I cannot submit to your coming over here on my account, as it is possible for me to see you so small a part of the day; but Dr. Black can better inform you concerning the degree of strength which may from time to time remain with me.

"Adieu, etc."

Three days after I received the following letter from Dr. Black:

EDINBURGH, *Monday, August* 26, 1776.

" DEAR SIR,—Yesterday, about four o'clock, afternoon, Mr. Hume expired. The near approach of his death became evident in the night between Thursday and Friday, when his disease became excessive, and soon weakened him so much that he could no longer rise out of his bed. He continued to the last perfectly sensible, and free from much pain or feelings of distress. He never dropped the smallest expression of impatience; but when he had occasion to speak to the people about him, always did it with affection and tenderness. I thought it improper to write to bring you over, especially as I heard that he had dictated a letter to you, desiring you not to come. When he became very weak, it cost him an effort to speak, and he died in such a happy composure of mind that nothing could exceed it."

Thus died our most excellent and never-to-be-forgotten friend; concerning whose philosophical opinions men will no doubt judge variously, every one approving or condemning them according as they happen to coincide or disagree with his own, but concerning whose character and conduct there can scarce be a difference of opinion. His temper, indeed, seemed to be more happily balanced, if I may be allowed such an expression, than that perhaps of any other man I have ever known. Even in the lowest state of his fortune, his great and necessary frugality never hindered him from exercising, upon proper occasions, acts both of charity and generosity. It was a frugality founded not upon avarice, but upon the love of independency. The extreme gentleness of his nature never weakened either the firmness of his mind or the steadiness of his resolutions. His constant pleasantry was the genuine effusion of good-nature and good-humor, tempered with delicacy and modesty, and without even the slightest tincture of malignity, so frequently the disagreeable source of what is called wit in other men. It never was the meaning of his raillery to mortify; and therefore, far from offending, it seldom failed to please and delight even those who were the objects of it. To his friends, who were frequently the objects of it, there was not perhaps one of all his great and amiable qualities which contributed more to endear his conversation. And that gayety of temper so agreeable in society, but which is so often accompanied with frivolous and superficial qualities, was in him certainly attended with the most severe application, the most extensive learning, the greatest depth of thought, and a capacity in every respect the most comprehensive. Upon the whole, I have always considered him, both in his lifetime and since his death, as approaching as nearly to the idea of a perfectly wise and virtuous man as perhaps the nature of human frailty will permit.

> I ever am, dear sir,
>   Most affectionately yours.
>   ADAM SMITH.

CONTENTS OF THE FIRST VOLUME.

CHAPTER I.

THE BRITONS. — ROMANS. — SAXONS. — THE HEPTARCHY. — THE KINGDOM OF KENT. — OF NORTHUMBERLAND. — OF EAST ANGLIA. — OF MERCIA. — OF ESSEX. — OF SUSSEX. — OF WESSEX.

A. D.		PAGE.
	Introduction	25
	The first Inhabitants of Britain	26
	Their Manners and Government	26
	The Authority and Superstition of the Druids	27
	Invasion of Julius Cæsar (Ant. C. 55)	28
52.	Caractacus defeated and carried to Rome	29
62.	Boadicea's Rebellion and Death	31
78.	Julius Agricola establishes the Dominion of the Romans	31
411.	The Romans leave Britain	34
	Invasion of the Picts and Scots	34
	The Britons apply to Rome for help	34
	The Saxons invited to England	36
	Their Manners and Customs	36
449.	Hengist and Horsa repel the Picts and Scots	38
450.	Found the Kingdom of Kent	40
477.	Ælla establishes the Kingdom of the South Saxons	41
495.	Cerdic, that of the West Saxons	42
	THE HEPTARCHY	44
	The Kingdom of Kent	46
568	Ethelbert defeats Ceaulin	46
596.	Introduction of Christianity by Gregory the Great	48
597.	Augustine arrives in Britain	50
603.	Adelfrid King of Northumberland	55
616.	Succeeded by Edwin, one of the greatest Princes of the Age	56
	His Marriage and Conversion	57
	Other Princes of Northumberland	57
616.	The Kingdom of East Anglia	59
	The Kingdom of Mercia	59
	Various Kings of Mercia	59
755.	Offa, a considerable Prince in the Heptarchy, forms an alliance with Charlemagne	61
	Kingdom of Essex	63
	Kingdom of Sussex	63
495.	Kingdom of Wessex, founded by Cerdic	64
	His various Successors	64
800.	Egbert ascends the Throne of Wessex	67
	His Conquest of the other Kingdoms of the Heptarchy	68
827.	Unites them into one Kingdom	69
	The Superstition of the Saxon Christians	69

CHAPTER II.

THE ANGLO-SAXONS.

A. D.		PAGE.
827.	EGBERT	74
	Invasion of the Danes	74
838.	Death of Egbert	76
	ETHELWOLF, Reign of	76
	Continued Ravages of the Danes	76
	Ecclesiastics attain great Power and Grandeur	78
857.	ETHELBALD AND ETHELBERT	79
866.	ETHERED	80
	Kingdom greatly infested by the Danes	80
	Death of Ethered	81
871.	ALFRED	81
	His Birth and Education	82
	Combats with the Danes	82
875.	A new Swarm come over	83
	Compel him to leave the Throne	84
	He defeats a Party of Danes	85
	Enters the Danish Camp in Disguise	86
	His Successes over them	86
	Forms an English Fleet	88
901.	Death and Character	92
	His Laws	93
	Encouragement of Learning	96
	EDWARD THE ELDER	99
	Rebellion of Ethelwald	99
	Who perishes in Battle	100
	Success of Edward in various Engagements	100
	His Death	101
225.	ATHELSTAN, Succession of	101
	Conspiracy of Alfred	101
	His sudden Death after taking a false Oath	102
	Defeat of the Scots	103
	Stratagem of Anlaf defeated	103
941.	Athelstan dies at Gloucester	105
	EDMUND defeats the Northumbrians	105
946.	Killed by Leolf	105
	EDRED	106
	Incursions of the Northumbrian Danes	106
	Benedictines arrive in England	107
	Dunstan's Superstitions	108
	Death of Edred	110
955.	EDWY	110
	Controversy with the Monks	110
	Marries Elgiva	110
	Quarrels with Dunstan	111
	His Excommunication and Death	111
959.	EDGAR	112
	His excellent Capacity	112
	Pays Court to the Monks	113
	His Amours	115
	Marriage with Elfrida	116
	His Death	119
975.	EDWARD THE MARTYR'S Accession	119
	Miracles by Dunstan	121
978.	Murder of the King	121

CHAPTER III.

978.	ETHELRED succeeds his Brother	122
	Bribes the Danes to depart	123
	Treachery of Alfric	123
993.	The northern Invaders, Sweyn and Olave	124
997.	Other Invasions	125
1001.	Ethelred marries Emma, a Norman Princess	126
1002.	Massacre of the Danes	130

A. D.		PAGE
1003.	Sweyn's second Invasion, and further Treacheries of Alfric	131
	Ravages of the Danes	132
1013.	The King flies to Normandy	133
1014.	Death of Sweyn, and the King's Return	133
	Invasion of Canute	133
1016.	Death of the King	134
	EDMOND IRONSIDE succeeds	134
	Battle at Scoerston	134
	Compromise with Canute	135
1017.	Edmond murdered at Oxford	135
	CANUTE succeeds to the Throne	135
	Sends Edmund's Sons to Sweden	136
	Puts to Death the Traitor Edric and other English Noblemen	136
	His impartial Administration	137
	Marries Emma	137
1028.	Visits Denmark	138
	Pilgrimage to Rome	139
	Reproves his Flatterers	139
1031.	Expedition against Malcolm, King of Scotland	139
1035.	Dies at Shaftesbury	140
	HAROLD HAREFOOT	140
	Treaty with Hardicanute	141
1039.	His Death	142
	HARDICANUTE succeeds	142
1041.	His Death	143
	Edward the Confessor takes the Crown	143
	His Popularity	145
	Introduces many Normans	146
	Jealousy of Earl Godwin	146
1048.	Fracas at Dover	147
1052.	Godwin's Rebellion	148
	His Death	150
	Harold succeeds to his Father's Power and Projects	150
1055.	Siward's Expedition against Macbeth	151
	Duke William's Pretensions to the Crown of England	152
1066.	Death of King Edward	158
	HAROLD, Succession of	159
	Hostile Intrigues of his Brother Tosti	159
	William claims the Crown	160
	William prepares to invade Engiand	161
	Halfagar and Tosti make a Descent upon England, and are defeated and killed	165
	Lands in England	167
	Conduct of Harold	168
Oct. 14.	Battle of Hastings	168
	Death of Harold	171

APPENDIX I.

THE ANGLO-SAXON GOVERNMENT AND MANNERS.

First Saxon Government	172
Succession of the Kings	173
The Witenagemote	174
The Aristocracy	177
The several Orders of Men	180
Courts of Justice	183
Criminal Law	185
Rules of Proof	190
Military Force	193
Public Revenue	193
Value of Money	194
Manners	196

CHAPTER IV.

WILLIAM THE CONQUEROR.

A. D.		PAGE.
1066.	Consequences of the Battle of Hastings	197
	Submission of the English	199
1067.	Settlement of the Government	201
	King's Return to Normandy	203
	Discontents of the English	204
	Their Insurrections	205
1068.	Rigors of the Norman Government	209
1069.	New Insurrections	210
1070.	New Rigors of the Government	212
	Introduction of the Feudal Law	214
	Innovation in ecclesiastical Government	216
1074.	Insurrection of the Norman Barons	221
1076.	Dispute about Investitures	225
	Revolt of Prince Robert	228
1081.	Domesday-Book	231
	The new Forest	232
1087.	War with France	233
Sept. 9.	Death and Character of William the Conqueror	234
	His Family	237

CHAPTER V.

THE REIGN OF WILLIAM RUFUS.

1087.	Accession of William Rufus	238
	Conspiracy to dethrone him	239
1090.	Invasion of Normandy	241
1091.	War with Scotland	242
1093.	Malcolm invades England	242
1096.	The Crusades	244
	Acquisition of Normandy	248
	Quarrel with Anselm the Primate	250
1100.	Death of William (August 2)	254
	His Character	257

CHAPTER VI.

HENRY I.

1100.	The Crusades	257
	Accession of Henry	260
	Marriage of the King	264
1101.	Invasion by Duke Robert	265
	Accommodation with Robert	266
1103.	Attack of Normandy	267
1106.	Conquest of Normandy	268
1107.	Continuation of the Quarrel with Anselm the Primate	269
	Compromise with him	274
1110.	Wars abroad	276
1120.	Death of Prince William	279
1121.	King's second Marriage	280
1131.	Visits Normandy	283
1135.	Dec. 1. Death and Character of Henry	284

CHAPTER VII.

STEPHEN.

	Descent of Stephen	287
1135.	His Accession to the Throne	289
Dec. 22.	His Coronation	289
1136.	Matilda and Geoffrey unfortunate in Normandy	290

A. D.		PAGE.
1138.	War with Scotland	293
	Battle of the Standard (August 22)	293
1139.	Insurrection in favor of Matilda	294
1141.	Stephen taken Prisoner	296
	Matilda crowned	297
	Stephen released, and Matilda flies	299
1153.	Prince Henry invades England	301
	Compromise between him and the King	301
1154.	Death of King Stephen (October 25)	302

CHAPTER VIII.

HENRY II.

	State of Europe	303
	State of France	304
	Possessions of Henry on the Continent	305
1155.	First Acts of Henry's Government	307
1156.	Goes abroad to oppose Geoffrey	308
1162.	Disputes between the civil and ecclesiastical Powers	312
	Thomas à Becket made Chancellor (1145)	313
	His Preferments and Life	313
June 3.	Elected Archbishop of Canterbury	315
	Entirely changes his Conduct	315
1163.	Quarrel with the King	315
	Henry determines to make the Clergy amenable to the Civil Authorities	318
1164.	Council of Clarendon	320
	Constitutions of Clarendon	320
	Becket opposes them	322
	The King's Measures to crush him	323
	Becket escapes to France	328
1165.	His Conduct abroad	328
1166.	The King's unhappy Situation	331
1170.	Compromise with Becket	334
	Becket's Return from Banishment	336
Dec. 29.	Murdered at Canterbury	338
	The King's Grief and Submission	339

CHAPTER IX.

1172.	State of Ireland	344
	Conquest of that Island	347
	The King's Accommodation with the Pope	350
	His Children	351
1173.	Their Rebellion	352
	Joined by the King of France, etc.	355
	Wars and Insurrections	356
	War with Scotland	358
1174.	The Scots invade England	358
July 8.	Henry's Penance for Becket's Murder	359
	William, King of Scots, defeated and taken Prisoner	360
	The King's Accommodation with his Sons	361
1175.	The King of Scots does Homage to Henry for his Kingdom	362
1176.	The equitable Administration of Henry	363
1183.	Death of young Henry	367
1185.	Crusades	368
1187.	Saladin takes Jerusalem	369
1188.	Henry and Phillip of France make Preparations for a Crusade	369
1189.	Revolt of Prince Richard	370
	His Confederacy with the King of France	371
July 6.	Death and Character of Henry	373
	Miscellaneous Transactions of this Reign	375

CHAPTER X.

RICHARD I.

A. D.		PAGE.
1189.	The King's Compunction for his undutiful Behavior towards his Father	380
	Preparation for the Crusade	381
	Great Slaughter of the Jews	381
	The King's Method of raising Money	382
1190.	June 29. Joins Philip of France at Vezelay	385
	Sets out on the Crusade	385
	Transactions in Sicily	386
1191.	Jealousies between Richard and Philip	387
	Richard's Fleet driven on the Coast of Cyprus	388
May 12.	He marries Berengaria	389
	Arrives in Palestine	389
	State of that Country	390
	Philip returns to Europe	390
	Disorders in England	391
1192.	The King's heroic Actions in Palestine	393
	Marches towards Ascalon	394
	Great Victory over the Saracens	394
	A Truce concluded with Saladin	395
	The King leaves Palestine	396
1193.	Captivity in Germany	396
	War with France	397
	Treachery of John	397
	Philip invades Normandy	398
	Richard's Sufferings in Germany	398
	Accused before the Diet at Worms	390
	His Defence and Delivery	400
1194.	His Return to England	401
	War with France	402
	John returns to his allegiance	402
1199.	The King wounded near Limoges	404
April 6.	His Death and Character	405
	Miscellaneous Transactions of this Reign	406

CHAPTER XL.

JOHN.

1199.	His Accession	409
1200.	Success against Philip	410
	Marriage	412
1201.	War with France	413
1203.	Prince Arthur joins Philip	414
	Murder of Arthur	415
	The King expelled from the French Provinces	416
1204.	Siege of Chateau Gaillard	418
1205.	Philip's Conquest of Normandy	420
1207.	The King's Quarrel with the Pope	422
	Cardinal Langton appointed Archbishop of Canterbury	424
	Interdict of the Kingdom	426
	Its Consequences	426
1209.	Artful Conduct of the Court of Rome	429
	Excommunication of the King	430
1213.	His Submission to the Pope	433
May 15.	Does Homage to him for his Crown	433
1214.	Discontents of the Barons	438
1215.	Insurrection of the Barons	441
June 15.	MAGNA CHARTA	443
	Conduct of John	448
	Renewal of the Civil Wars	449
1216.	Prince Lewis called over	450
	Death and Character of the King	453

APPENDIX II.

THE FEUDAL AND ANGLO-NORMAN GOVERNMENT AND MANNERS.

A. D.   PAGE.
Origin of the Feudal Law... 455
Progress of the Feudal Law 457
The Feudal Government of England...................................... 460
The Feudal Parliament... 465
The Commons... 466
Judicial Power... 470
Revenue of the Crown... 473
Commerce 482
The Church—Civil Laws.. 484
Manners 485

CHAPTER XII.

HENRY III.

1216.   Settlement of the Government................................... 488
Oct. 28. Henry crowned at Gloucester................................... 488
         Earl of Pembroke made Protector.............................. 489
         Henry grants a new Charter................................... 489
         The French defeated at Lincoln............................... 492
         General Pacification... 493
         Death of the Protector....................................... 494
         Commotions by the Barons.................................... 494
1222.   Riot in London... 495
         Henry carries on a War in France............................. 498
1227.   Hubert de Burgh displaced.................................... 499
1231.   Bishop of Winchester Minister................................ 500
1236.   The King marries... 502
         His Partiality to Foreigners 502
         The Resentment of the Barons thereat......................... 503
         Other Grievances.. 503
1253.   Ecclesiastical Grievances.................................... 506
1255.   Sicilian Crusade... 508
         Earl of Cornwall elected King of the Romans.................. 511
         Discontents of the Barons.................................... 512
1258.   Earl of Leicester attempts an Innovation in the Government.... 515
         Calls a Meeting of the most considerable Barons.............. 516
         Provisions of Oxford... 517
         Usurpations of the Barons.................................... 519
1261.   Situation of Henry more favorable............................ 523
         Prince Edward... 525
         The King re-assumes the Government 525
1263.   Civil Wars of the Barons..................................... 526
         Violence of Leicester's Faction.............................. 529
         Reference to the King of France.............................. 530
1264.   Renewal of the civil Wars 531
May 14. Battle of Lewes 533
         The King taken Prisoner...................................... 534
         Leicester usurps the Government.............................. 535
1265.   Calls a Parliament... 538
         House of Commons 538
         Prince Edward escapes 540
         Battle of Evesham, and Death of Leicester.................... 542
         Settlement of the Government................................. 543
1272.   Death and Character of the King.............................. 546
         Miscellaneous Transactions of this Reign..................... 547

CHAPTER XIII.

EDWARD I.

A. D.		PAGE.
1272.	Edward proclaimed King	554
1274.	His Coronation	555
	His civil Administration	555
1276.	Conquest of Wales	559
1284.	Massacre of the Welsh Bards	561
1289.	Affairs of Scotland	563
1291.	Competitors for the Crown thereof	566
	Reference to Edward	567
	Homage of Scotland	568
1292.	Award of Edward in Favor of Baliol	573
1293.	War with France	574
1295.	Digression concerning the Constitution of Parliament	579
1296.	Scotland subdued	591
	War with France	592
	Dissensions with the Clergy	593
1297.	Arbitrary Measures	595
	Dissensions with the Barons	598
	Settlement of the Charters	599
1298.	Peace with France	602
	Revolt of Scotland	603
	William Wallace	604
July 22.	Battle of Falkirk	608
1300.	Scotland again subdued	610
1302.	Scotland again revolts	612
1303.	Scotland is again subdued	613
1305.	Execution of Wallace	614
1306.	Robert Bruce	614
	Third Revolt of Scotland	618
1307.	July 7. Death and Character of the King	618
	Miscellaneous Transactions of this Reign	619

HISTORY OF ENGLAND.

CHAPTER I.

THE BRITONS.—ROMANS.—SAXONS.—THE HEPTARCHY.—THE KINGDOM OF KENT.—OF NORTHUMBERLAND.—OF EAST ANGLIA.—OF MERCIA.—OF ESSEX.—OF SUSSEX.—OF WESSEX.

THE curiosity, entertained by all civilized nations, of inquiring into the exploits and adventures of their ancestors commonly excites a regret that the history of remote ages should always be so much involved in obscurity, uncertainty, and contradiction. Ingenious men possessed of leisure are apt to push their researches beyond the period in which literary monuments are framed or preserved; without reflecting that the history of past events is immediately lost or disfigured when intrusted to memory or oral tradition; and that the adventures of barbarous nations, even if they were recorded, could afford little or no entertainment to men born in a more cultivated age. The convulsions of a civilized state usually compose the most instructive and most interesting part of its history; but the sudden, violent, and unprepared revolutions incident to barbarians are so much guided by caprice, and terminate so often in cruelty, that they disgust us by the uniformity of their appearance; and it is rather fortunate for letters that they are buried in silence and oblivion. The only certain means by which nations can indulge their curiosity in researches concerning their remote origin is to consider the language, manners, and customs of their ancestors, and to compare them with those of the neighboring nations. The fables which are commonly employed to supply the place of true history ought entirely to be disregarded; or if any exception be admitted to this general rule, it can only be in favor of the

ancient Grecian fictions, which are so celebrated and so
agreeable that they will ever be the objects of the attention
of mankind. Neglecting, therefore, all traditions, or rather
tales, concerning the more early history of Britain, we shall
only consider the state of the inhabitants as it appeared to
the Romans on their invasion of this country; we shall
briefly run over the events which attended the conquest
made by that empire, as belonging more to Roman than
British story; we shall hasten through the obscure and uninteresting period of Saxon annals; and shall reserve a more
full narration for those times when the truth is both so well
ascertained and so complete as to promise entertainment
and instruction to the reader.

All ancient writers agree in representing the first inhabitants of Britain as a tribe of the Gauls or Celtæ, who peopled
that island from the neighboring continent. Their language
was the same; their manners, their government, their superstition, varied only by those small differences which time or
communication with the bordering nations must necessarily
introduce. The inhabitants of Gaul, especially in those
parts which lie contiguous to Italy, had acquired, from a
commerce with their southern neighbors, some refinement
in the arts, which gradually diffused themselves northwards,
and spread but a very faint light over this island. The
Greek and Roman navigators or merchants (for there were
scarcely any other travellers in those ages) brought back the
most shocking accounts of the ferocity of the people, which
they magnified, as usual, in order to excite the admiration
of their countrymen. The southeast parts, however, of
Britain had already, before the age of Cæsar, made the
first and most requisite step towards a civil settlement; and
the Britons, by tillage and agriculture, had there increased
to a great multitude.[1] The other inhabitants of the island
still maintained themselves by pasture: they were clothed
with skins of beasts. They dwelt in huts, which they
reared in the forests and marshes, with which the country
was covered; they shifted easily their habitation, when
actuated either by the hopes of plunder or the fear of an
enemy; the convenience of feeding their cattle was even a
sufficient motive for removing their seats; and as they were
ignorant of all the refinements of life, their wants and their
possessions were equally scanty and limited.

The Britons were divided into many small nations or

[1] Cæsar, lib. 4.

tribes; and being a military people, whose sole property was their arms and their cattle, it was impossible, after they had acquired a relish for liberty, for their princes or chieftains to establish any despotic authority over them. Their governments, though monarchical,[2] were free, as well as those of all the Celtic nations; and the common people seem even to have enjoyed more liberty among them[3] than among the nations of Gaul,[4] from whom they were descended. Each state was divided into factions within itself;[5] it was agitated with jealousy or animosity against the neighboring states; and while the arts of peace were yet unknown, wars were the chief occupation, and formed the chief object of ambition among the people.

The religion of the Britons was one of the most considerable parts of their government; and the Druids, who were their priests, possessed great authority among them. Besides ministering at the altar and directing all religious duties, they presided over the education of youth; they enjoyed an immunity from wars and taxes; they possessed both the civil and criminal jurisdiction; they decided all controversies among states as well as among private persons; and whoever refused to submit to their decree was exposed to the most severe penalties. The sentence of excommunication was pronounced against him; he was forbidden access to the sacrifices or public worship; he was debarred all intercourse with his fellow-citizens, even in the common affairs of life; his company was universally shunned, as profane and dangerous. He was refused the protection of law;[6] and death itself became an acceptable relief from the misery and infamy to which he was exposed. Thus, the bands of government, which were naturally loose among that rude and turbulent people, were happily corroborated by the terrors of their superstition.

No species of superstition was ever more terrible than that of the Druids. Besides the severe penalties which it was in the power of the ecclesiastics to inflict in this world, they inculcated the eternal transmigration of souls; and thereby extended their authority as far as the fears of their timorous votaries. They practised their rites in dark groves or other secret recesses;[7] and in order to throw a greater mystery over their religion, they communicated their doc-

[2] Diod. Sic. lib. 4.   Mela, lib. 3, cap. 6.   Strabo. lib. 4.
[3] Dion. Cassius, lib. 75.   [4] Cæsar, lib. 6.   [5] Tacit. Agr.
[6] Cæsar, lib. 6.   Strabo, lib. 4.   [7] Plin. lib. 12, cap. 1.

trines only to the initiated, and strictly forbade the committing of them to writing, lest they should at any time be exposed to the examination of the profane vulgar. Human sacrifices were practised among them; the spoils of war were often devoted to their divinities; and they punished with the severest tortures whoever dared to secrete any part of the consecrated offering; these treasures they kept in woods and forests, secured by no other guard than the terrors of their religion;[8] and this steady conquest over human avidity may be regarded as more signal than their prompting men to the most extraordinary and most violent efforts. No idolatrous worship ever attained such an ascendant over mankind as that of the ancient Gauls and Britons; and the Romans, after their conquest, finding it impossible to reconcile those nations to the laws and institutions of their masters while it maintained its authority, were at last obliged to abolish it by penal statutes; a violence which had never, in any other instance, been practised by those tolerating conquerors.[9]

The Britons had long remained in this rude but independent state, when Cæsar, having overrun all Gaul by his victories, first cast his eye on their island. He was not allured either by its riches or its renown; but being ambitious of carrying the Roman arms into a new world, then mostly unknown, he took advantage of a short interval in his Gaulic wars, and made an invasion on Britain. The natives, informed of his intention, were sensible of the unequal contest, and endeavored to appease him by submissions, which, however, retarded not the execution of his design. [Anno Ante C. 55.] After some resistance, he landed, as is supposed, at Deal; and having obtained several advantages over the Britons, and obliged them to promise hostages for their future obedience, he was constrained, by the necessity of his affairs and the approach of winter, to withdraw his forces into Gaul. The Britons, relieved from the terror of his arms, neglected the performance of their stipulations; and that haughty conqueror resolved next summer to chastise them for this breach of treaty. He landed with a greater force; and though he found a more regular resistance from the Britons, who had united under Cassivelaunus, one of their petty princes, he discomfited them in every action. He advanced into the country; passed the Thames in the face of the enemy; took and burned the capital of

8 Cæsar, lib. 6.   9 Sueton., in vita Claudii.

Cassivelaunus; established his ally, Mandubratius, in the sovereignty of the Trinobantes; and having obliged the inhabitants to make him new submissions, he again returned with his army into Gaul, and left the authority of the Romans more nominal than real in this island.

The civil wars which ensued, and which prepared the way for the establishment of monarchy in Rome, saved the Britons from that yoke which was ready to be imposed upon them. Augustus, the successor of Cæsar, content with the victory obtained over the liberties of his own country, was little ambitious of acquiring fame by foreign wars: and being apprehensive lest the same unlimited extent of dominion which had subverted the republic might also overwhelm the empire, he recommended it to his successors never to enlarge the territories of the Romans. Tiberius, jealous of the fame which might be acquired by his generals, made this advice of Augustus a pretence for his inactivity.[10] The mad sallies of Caligula, in which he menaced Britain with an invasion, served only to expose himself and the empire to ridicule; and the Britons had now, during almost a century, enjoyed their liberty unmolested; when the Romans, in the reign of Claudius, began to think seriously of reducing them under their dominion. Without seeking any more justifiable reasons of hostility than were employed by the late Europeans in subjugating the Africans and Americans, they sent over an army under the command of Plautius, an [A. D. 43.] able general, who gained some victories, and made a considerable progress in subduing the inhabitants. Claudius himself, finding matters sufficiently prepared for his reception, made a journey into Britain, and received the submission of several British states, the Cantii, Atrebates, Regni, and Trinobantes, who inhabited the southeast part of the island, and whom their possessions and more cultivated manner of life rendered willing to purchase peace at the expense of their liberty. The other Britons, under the command of Caractacus, still maintained an obstinate resistance, and the Romans made little progress against them, till Ostorius Scapula was sent over to command their armies. [A. D. 50.] This general advanced the Roman conquests over the Britons; pierced into the country of the Silures, a warlike nation who inhabited the banks of the Severn; defeated Caractacus in a great battle; took him prisoner, and sent him to Rome, where his magnanimous

[10] Tacit. Agr.

behavior procured him better treatment than those conquerors usually bestowed on captive princes.[11]

Notwithstanding these misfortunes, the Britons were
not subdued; and this island was regarded by the ambitious
Romans as a field in which military honor might still be acquired. [A. D. 59.] Under the reign of Nero, Suetonius
Paulinus was invested with the command, and prepared to
signalize his name by victories over those barbarians. Finding that the island of Mona, now Anglesey, was the chief
seat of the Druids, he resolved to attack it, and to subject a
place which was the centre of their superstition, and which
afforded protection to all their baffled forces. The Britons
endeavored to obstruct his landing upon this sacred island,
both by the force of their arms and the terrors of their religion. The women and priests were intermingled with the
soldiers upon the shore; and, running about with flaming
torches in their hands, and tossing their dishevelled hair,
they struck greater terror into the astonished Romans by
their howlings, cries, and execrations than the real danger
from the armed forces was able to inspire. But Suetonius,
exhorting his troops to despise the menaces of a superstition
which they despised, impelled them to the attack, drove the
Britons off the field, burned the Druids in the same fires
which those priests had prepared for their captive enemies,
destroyed all the consecrated groves and altars; and, having thus triumphed over the religion of the Britons, he
thought his future progress would be easy in reducing the
people to subjection. But he was disappointed in his expectations. The Britons, taking advantage of his absence,
were all in arms; and, headed by Boadicea, Queen of the
Iceni, who had been treated in the most ignominious manner by the Roman tribunes, had already attacked with success several settlements of their insulting conquerors. Suetonius hastened to the protection of London, which was already a flourishing Roman colony; but he found, on his arrival, that it would be requisite for the general safety to
abandon that place to the merciless fury of the enemy.
London was reduced to ashes; such of the inhabitants as
remained in it were cruelly massacred; the Romans and all
strangers, to the number of 70,000, were everywhere put
to the sword without distinction; and the Britons, by rendering the war thus bloody, seemed determined to cut off
all hopes of peace or composition with the enemy. But

[11] Tacit. Ann. lib. 12.

this cruelty was revenged by Suetonius in a great and decisive battle, where 80,000 of the Britons are said to have perished; and Boadicea herself, rather than fall into the hands of the enraged victor, put an end to her own life by poison.[12] Nero soon after recalled Suetonius from a government, where, by suffering and inflicting so many severities, he was judged improper for composing the angry and alarmed minds of the inhabitants. After some interval, Cerealis received the command from Vespasian, and by his bravery propagated the terror of the Roman arms. Julius Frontinus succeeded Cerealis both in authority and in reputation; but the general who finally established the dominion of the Romans in this island was Julius Agricola, who governed it in the reigns of Vespasian, Titus, and Domitian, and distinguished himself in that scene of action.

This great commander formed a regular plan for subduing Britain, and rendering the acquisition useful to the conquerors. He carried his victorious arms northwards, defeated the Britons in every encounter, pierced into the inaccessible forests and mountains of Caledonia, reduced every state to subjection in the southern part of the island, and chased before him all the men of fiercer and more intractable spirits, who deemed war and death itself less intolerable than servitude under the victors. He even defeated them in a decisive action, which they fought under Galgacus, their leader; and having fixed a chain of garrisons between the friths of Clyde and Forth, he thereby cut off the ruder and more barren parts of the island, and secured the Roman province from the incursions of the barbarous inhabitants.[13]

During these military enterprises, he neglected not the arts of peace. He introduced laws and civility among the Britons, taught them to desire and raise all the conveniences of life, reconciled them to the Roman language and manners, instructed them in letters and science, and employed every expedient to render those chains which he had forged both easy and agreeable to them.[14] The inhabitants, having experienced how unequal their own force was to resist that of the Romans, acquiesced in the dominion of their masters, and were gradually incorporated as a part of that mighty empire.

This was the last durable conquest made by the Romans; and Britain, once subdued, gave no further inquie-

[12] Tacit. Ann. lib. 14. [13] Tacit. Agr. [14] Ibid.

tude to the victor. Caledonia alone, defended by its barren
mountains and by the contempt which the Romans entertained for it, sometimes infested the more cultivated parts
of the island by the incursions of its inhabitants. The better to secure the frontiers of the empire, Adrian, who visited this island, built a rampart between the river Tyne and
the frith of Solway; Lollius Urbicus, under Antonius Pius,
erected one in the place where Agricola had formerly established his garrisons; Severus, who made an expedition
into Britain, and carried his arms to the more northern
extremity of it, added new fortifications to the walls of
Adrian; and, during the reigns of all the Roman emperors, such a profound tranquillity prevailed in Britain that
little mention is made of the affairs of that island by any
historian. The only incidents which occur are some sedi-
tions or rebellions of the Roman legions quartered there,
and some usurpations of the imperial dignity by the Roman
governors. The natives, disarmed, dispirited, and submissive had lost all desire, and even idea, of their former liberty and independence.

But the period was now come when that enormous fabric
of the Roman empire which had diffused slavery and oppression, together with peace and civility, over so considerable a
part of the globe was approaching towards its final dissolution. Italy and the centre of the empire, removed during so
many ages from all concern in the wars, had entirely lost the
military spirit; and were peopled by an enervated race, equally disposed to submit to a foreign yoke or to the tyranny of
their own rulers. The emperors found themselves obliged
to recruit their legions from the frontier provinces, where
the genius of war, though languishing, was not totally extinct; and these mercenary forces, careless of laws and civil
institutions, established a military government, no less dangerous to the sovereign than to the people. The further
progress of the same disorders introduced the bordering
barbarians into the service of the Romans; and those fierce
nations, having now added discipline to their native bravery,
could no longer be restrained by the impotent policy of the
emperors, who were accustomed to employ one in the destruction of the others. Sensible of their own force, and
allured by the prospect of so rich a prize, the northern barbarians, in the reign of Arcadius and Honorius, assailed at
once all the frontiers of the Roman empire; and, having
first satiated their avidity by plunder, began to think of

fixing a settlement in the wasted provinces. The more distant barbarians, who occupied the deserted habitations of the former, advanced in their acquisitions, and pressed with their incumbent weight the Roman state, already unequal to the load which it sustained. Instead of arming the people in their own defence, the emperors recalled all the distant legions, in whom alone they could repose confidence; and collected the whole military force for the defence of the capital and centre of the empire. The necessity of self-preservation had superseded the ambition of power; and the ancient point of honor—never to contract the limits of the empire—could no longer be attended to in this desperate extremity.

Britain, by its situation, was removed from the fury of these barbarous incursions; and, being also a remote province not much valued by the Romans, the legions which defended it were carried over to the protection of Italy and Gaul. But that province, though secured by the sea against the inroads of the greater tribes of barbarians, found enemies on its frontiers, who took advantage of its present defenceless situation. The Picts and Scots, who dwelt in the northern parts, beyond the wall of Antoninus, made incursions upon their peaceable and effeminate neighbors; and, besides the temporary depredations which they committed, these combined nations threatened the whole province with subjection, or, what the inhabitants more dreaded, with plunder and devastation. The Picts seem to have been a tribe of the native British race, who, having been chased into the northern parts by the conquest of Agricola, had there intermingled with the ancient inhabitants: the Scots were derived from the same Celtic origin, had first been established in Ireland, had migrated to the northwest coasts of this island, and had long been accustomed, as well from their old as their new seats, to infest the Roman province by piracy and rapine.[15] These tribes, finding their more opulent neighbors exposed to invasion, soon broke over the Roman wall, no longer defended by the Roman arms; and, though a contemptible enemy in themselves, met with no resistance from the unwarlike inhabitants. The Britons, accustomed to have recourse to the emperors for defence as well as government, made supplications to Rome; and one legion was sent over for their protection. This force was an overmatch for the barbarians, repelled their invasion, routed them in every engagement, and having chased them into their ancient limits, returned in triumph to the defence of the southern provinces of the empire. [16] Their retreat brought on a new invasion of the enemy. The Britons made again an application to Rome, and again obtained the assistance of a legion, which proved effectual for their relief; but the Romans, reduced to extremities at home, and fatigued with those distant expeditions, informed the Britons that they must no longer look to them for succor, exhorted them to arm in their own defence, and urged that, as they were now their own masters, it became them to protect by their valor that independence which their ancient lords had conferred upon them. [17] That they might leave the island with the better grace, the Romans assisted them in erecting anew the wall of Severus, which was built entirely of stone, and which the Britons had not at that time artificers skilful enough to repair.[18] And having done this last good office to the inhabitants, they bade a final adieu to Britain, about the year 448, after being masters of the more considerable part of it during the course of near four centuries.

The abject Britons regarded this present of liberty as fatal to them; and were in no condition to put in practice the prudent counsel given them by the Romans to arm in their own defence. Unaccustomed both to the perils of war and to the cares of civil government, they found themselves incapable of forming or executing any measures for resisting the incursions of the barbarians. Gratian also and Constantine, two Romans who had a little before assumed the purple in Britain, had carried over to the continent the flower of the British youth, and, having perished in their unsuccessful attempts on the imperial throne, had despoiled the island of those who, in this desperate extremity, were best able to defend it. The Picts and Scots, finding that the Romans had finally relinquished Britain, now regarded the whole as their prey, and attacked the northern wall with redoubled forces. The Britons, already subdued by their own fears, found the ramparts but a weak defence for them, and, deserting their station, left the country entirely open to the inroads of the barbarous enemy. The invaders carried devastation and ruin along with them, and exerted to the utmost their native ferocity, which was not mitigated

---

[16] Gildas. Bede, lib. 1, cap. 12. Paul. Diacon.   [17] Bede, lib., 1, cap. 12.
[18] Ibid.

by the helpless condition and submissive behavior of the inhabitants. [19] The unhappy Britons had a third time recourse to Rome, which had declared its resolution forever to abandon them. Aëtius, the patrician, sustained at that time, by his valor and magnanimity, the tottering ruins of the empire, and revived for a moment, among the degenerate Romans, the spirit as well as discipline of their ancestors. The British ambassador carried to him the letter of their countrymen, which was inscribed *the Groans of the Britons.* The tenor of the epistle was suitable to its superscription. "The barbarians," say they, "on the one hand, chase us into the sea; the sea, on the other, throws us back upon the barbarians; and we have only the hard choice left us, of perishing by the sword or by the waves." [20] But Aëtius, pressed by the arms of Attila, the most terrible enemy that ever assailed the empire, had no leisure to attend to the complaints of allies, whom generosity alone could induce him to assist. [21] The Britons thus rejected were reduced to despair, deserted their habitations, abandoned tillage, and, flying for protection to the forests and mountains. suffered equally from hunger and from the enemy. The barbarians themselves began to feel the pressure of famine in a country which they had ravaged; and, being harassed by the dispersed Britons, who had not dared to resist them in a body, they retreated with their spoils into their own country.[22]

The Britons, taking advantage of this interval, returned to their usual occupations; and the favorable seasons which succeeded seconded their industry, made them soon forget their past miseries, and restored to them great plenty of all the necessaries of life. No more can be imagined to have been possessed by a people so rude, who had not, without the assistance of the Romans, art of masonry sufficient to raise a stone rampart for their own defence; yet the monkish historians [23] who treat of those events complain of the luxury of the Britons during this period, and ascribe to that vice—not to their cowardice or improvident counsels—all their subsequent calamities.

The Britons, entirely occupied in the enjoyment of the present interval of peace, made no provision for resisting the enemy, who, invited by their former timid behavior,

[19] Gildas. Bede, lib. 1. Ann. Beverl. p. 45.
[20] Gildas. Bede, lib. 1, cap. 13. Malmesbury, lib. 1, cap. 1. Ann. Beverl. p. 45.
[21] Chron. Sax. p. 11, edit. 1692.
[22] Ann. Beverl. p. 45. [23] Gildas. Bede, lib. 1, cap. 14.

soon threatened them with a new invasion. We are not exactly informed what species of civil government the Romans on their departure had left among the Britons; but it appears probable that the great men in the different districts assumed a kind of regal though precarious authority, and lived in a great measure independent of each other.[24] To this disunion of counsels were also added the disputes of theology; and the disciples of Pelagius, who was himself a native of Britain, having increased to a great multitude, gave alarm to the clergy, who seem to have been more intent on suppressing them than on opposing the public enemy.[25] Laboring under these domestic evils, and menaced with a foreign invasion, the Britons attended only to the suggestions of their present fears; and, following the counsels of Vortigern, Prince of Dumnonium, who, though stained with every vice, possessed the chief authority among them,[26] they sent into Germany a deputation to invite over the Saxons for their protection and assistance.

Of all the barbarous nations, known either in ancient or modern times, the Germans seem to have been the most distinguished both by their manners and political institutions, and to have carried to the highest pitch the virtues of valor and love of liberty; the only virtues which can have place among an uncivilized people, where justice and humanity are commonly neglected. Kingly government, even when established among the Germans (for it was not universal), possessed a very limited authority; and though the sovereign was usually chosen from among the royal family, he was directed in every measure by the common consent of the nation over whom he presided. When any important affairs were transacted, all the warriors met in arms; the men of greatest authority employed persuasion to engage their consent; the people expressed their approbation by rattling their armor, or their dissent by murmurs; there was no necessity for a nice scrutiny of votes among a multitude who were usually carried with a strong current to one side or the other; and the measure thus suddenly chosen by general agreement was executed with alacrity and prosecuted with vigor. Even in war the princes governed more by example than by authority; but in peace the civil union was in a great measure dissolved, and the inferior leaders ad

---

24 Gildas. Usher, Ant. Brit. p. 248, 347.
25 Gildas. Bede, lib. 1, cap. 17. Constant. in vita Germ.
26 Gildas. Gul. Malm. p. 8.

ministered justice after an independent manner, each in his particular district. These were elected by the votes of the people in their great councils; and though regard was paid to nobility in the choice, their personal qualities, chiefly their valor, procured them, from the suffrages of their fellow-citizens, that honorable but dangerous distinction. The warriors of each tribe attached themselves to their leader with the most devoted affection and most unshaken constancy. They attended him as his ornament in peace, as his defence in war, as his council in the administration of justice. Their constant emulation in military renown dissolved not that inviolable friendship which they professed to their chieftain and to each other: to die for the honor of their band was their chief ambition; to survive its disgrace, or the death of their leader, was infamous. They even carried into the field their women and children, who adopted all the martial sentiments of the men; and being thus impelled by every human motive, they were invincible, where they were not opposed either by the similar manners and institutions of the neighboring Germans, or by the superior discipline, arms, and numbers of the Romans.[27]

The leaders and their military companions were maintained by the labor of their slaves, or by that of the weaker and less warlike part of the community, whom they defended. The contributions which they levied went not beyond a bare subsistence; and the honors, acquired by a superior rank, were the only reward of their superior dangers and fatigues. All the refined arts of life were unknown among the Germans: tillage itself was almost wholly neglected; they even seem to have been anxious to prevent any improvements of that nature; and the leaders, by annually distributing anew all the land among the inhabitants of each village, kept them from attaching themselves to particular possessions, or making such progress in agriculture as might divert their attention from military expeditions, the chief occupation of the community.[28]

The Saxons had been for some time regarded as one of the most warlike tribes of this fierce people, and had become the terror of the neighboring nations.[29] They had diffused themselves from the northern parts of Germany and the Cimbrian Chersonesus, and had taken possession of all the sea-coast from the mouth of the Rhine to Jutland,

[27] Cæsar, lib. 6. Tacit. de Mor. Germ.   [28] Ibid.
[29] Amm. Marcell. lib. 28. Orosius.

whence they had long infested by their piracies all the eastern and southern parts of Britain, and the northern of Gaul.[30] In order to oppose their inroads, the Romans had established an officer whom they called *Count of the Saxon shore;* and as the naval arts can flourish among a civilized people alone, they seem to have been more successful in repelling the Saxons than any of the other barbarians by whom they were invaded. The dissolution of the Roman power invited them to renew their inroads; and it was an acceptable circumstance that the deputies of the Britons appeared among them, and prompted them to undertake an enterprise to which they were of themselves sufficiently inclined.[31]

Hengist and Horsa, two brothers, possessed great credit among the Saxons, and were much celebrated both for their valor and nobility. They were reputed, as most of the Saxon princes, to be sprung from Woden, who was worshipped as a god among those nations, and they are said to be his great-grandsons;[32] a circumstance which added much to their authority. We shall not attempt to trace any higher the origin of those princes and nations. It is evident what fruitless labor it must be to search, in those barbarous and illiterate ages, for the annals of a people, when their first leaders, known in any true history, were believed by them to be the fourth in descent from a fabulous deity, or from a man exalted by ignorance into that character. The dark industry of antiquaries, led by imaginary analogies of names, or by uncertain traditions, would in vain attempt to pierce into that deep obscurity which covers the remote history of those nations.

These two brothers, observing the other provinces of Germany to be occupied by a warlike and necessitous people, and the rich provinces of Gaul already conquered or overrun by other German tribes, found it easy to persuade their countrymen to embrace the sole enterprise which promised a favorable opportunity of displaying their valor and gratifying their avidity. They embarked their troops in three vessels, and, about the year 449 or 450,[33] carried over 1600 men, who landed in the Isle of Thanet, and immediately marched to the defence of the Britons against the northern invaders. The Scots and Picts were unable to resist the valor of these auxiliaries; and the Britons, applauding their

[30] Amm. Marcel. lib. 27, cap. 7 ; lib. 28, cap. 7.   [31] Will. Malm. p. 8.
[32] Bede, lib. 1. cap. 15.   Chron. Sax. p. 13.   Nennius, cap. 28.
[33] Chron. Sax. p. 12.   Gul. Malm. p. 11.   Huntington, lib. 2, p. 306.   Ethelwerd. Brompton, p. 728.

own wisdom in calling over the Saxons, hoped thenceforth to enjoy peace and security under the powerful protection of that warlike people.

But Hengist and Horsa, perceiving, from their easy victory over the Scots and Picts, with what facility they might subdue the Britons themselves, who had not been able to resist those feeble invaders, were determined to conquer and fight for their own grandeur, not for the defence of their degenerate allies. They sent intelligence to Saxony of the fertility and riches of Britain; and represented as certain the subjection of a people so long disused to arms, who, being now cut off from the Roman Empire, of which they had been a province during so many ages, had not yet acquired any union among themselves, and were destitute of all affection to their new liberties, and of all national attachments and regards.[34] The vices and pusillanimity of Vortigern, the British leader, were a new ground of hope; and the Saxons in Germany, following such agreeable prospects, soon reinforced Hengist and Horsa with 5000 men, who came over in seventeen vessels. The Britons now began to entertain apprehensions of their allies, whose numbers they found continually augmenting; but thought of no remedy, except a passive submission and connivance. This weak expedient soon failed them. The Saxons sought a quarrel by complaining that their subsidies were ill paid and their provisions withdrawn;[35] and, immediately taking off the mask, they formed an alliance with the Picts and Scots, and proceeded to open hostility against the Britons.

The Britons, impelled by these violent extremities, and roused to indignation against their treacherous auxiliaries, were necessitated to take arms; and, having deposed Vortigern, who had become odious from his vices and from the bad event of his rash counsels, they put themselves under the command of his son, Vortimer. They fought many battles with their enemies; and, though the victories in these actions be disputed between the British and Saxon annalists, the progress still made by the Saxons proves that the advantage was commonly on their side. In one battle, however, fought at Eaglesford, now Ailsford, Horsa, the Saxon general, was slain, and left the sole command over his countrymen in the hands of Hengist. This active general, continually reinforced by fresh numbers from Germany,

---

[34] Chron. Sax. p. 12. Ann. Beverl. p. 49.
[35] Bede, lib. 1, cap. 15. Nennius, cap. 35. Gildas, § 23.

carried devastation into the most remote corners of Britain and, being chiefly anxious to spread the terror of his arms, he spared neither age, nor sex, nor condition, wherever he marched with his victorious forces. The private and public edifices of the Britons were reduced to ashes; the priests were slaughtered on the altars by those idolatrous ravagers; the bishops and nobility shared the fate of the vulgar; the people, flying to the mountains and deserts, were intercepted and butchered in heaps: some were glad to accept of life and servitude under their victors; others, deserting their native country, took shelter in the province of Armorica, where, being charitably received by a people of the same language and manners, they settled in great numbers, and gave the country the name of Brittany.

The British writers assign one cause which facilitated the entrance of the Saxons into this island—the love with which Vortigern was at first seized for Rovena, the daughter of Hengist, and which that artful warrior made use of to blind the eyes of the imprudent monarch.[87] The same historians add that Vortimer died, and that Vortigern, being restored to the throne, accepted of a banquet from Hengist, at Stonehenge, where three hundred of his nobility were treacherously slaughtered, and himself detained captive.[38] But these stories seem to have been invented by the Welsh authors, in order to palliate the weak resistance made at first by their countrymen, and to account for the rapid progress and licentious devastation of the Saxons.[39]

After the death of Vortimer, Ambrosius, a Briton, though of Roman descent, was invested with the command over his countrymen, and endeavored, not without success, to unite them in their resistance against the Saxons. Those contests increased the animosity between the two nations, and roused the military spirit of the ancient inhabitants, which had before been sunk into a fatal lethargy. Hengist, however, notwithstanding their opposition, still maintained his ground in Britain; and, in order to divide the forces and attention of the natives, he called over a new tribe of Saxons, under the command of his brother Octa, and of Ebissa, the son of Octa; and he settled them in Northumberland. He himself remained in the southern parts of the island, and laid the foundation of the kingdom of Kent, comprehending the

· Bede, lib. 1, cap. 15.   Usher, p. 226.   Gildas, § 24.
[27] Nennius. Galfr. lib. 6, cap. 12.   [38] Nennius, cap. 47. Galfr.
[39] Stillingfleet's Orig. Brit. pp. 324, 325.

county of that name, Middlesex, Essex, and part of Surrey. He fixed his royal seat at Canterbury, where he governed about forty years; and he died in or near the year 488, leaving his new-acquired dominions to his posterity.

The success of Hengist excited the avidity of the other northern Germans; and, at different times and under different leaders, they flocked over in multitudes to the invasion of this island. These conquerors were chiefly composed of three tribes—the Saxons, Angles, and Jutes [40]—who all passed under the common appellation, sometimes of Saxons, sometimes of Angles; and, speaking the same language and being governed by the same institutions, they were naturally led, from these causes as well as from their common interest, to unite themselves against the ancient inhabitants. The resistance, however, though unequal, was still maintained by the Britons, but became every day more feeble; and their calamities admitted of few intervals till they were driven into Cornwall and Wales, and received protection from the remote situation or inaccessible mountains of those countries.

The first Saxon state, after that of Kent, which was established in Britain was the kingdom of South Saxony. In the year 477,[41] Ælla, a Saxon chief, brought over an army from Germany, and, landing on the southern coast, proceeded to take possession of the neighboring territory. The Britons, now armed, did not tamely abandon their possessions; nor were they expelled till defeated in many battles by their warlike invaders. The most memorable action mentioned by historians is that of Meacredes Burn,[42] where, though the Saxons seem to have obtained the victory, they suffered so considerable a loss as somewhat retarded the progress of their conquests. But Ælla, reinforced by fresh numbers of his countrymen, again took the field against the Britons, and laid siege to Andred-Ceaster, which was defended by the garrison and inhabitants with desperate valor.[43] The Saxons, enraged by this resistance, and by the fatigues and dangers which they had sustained, redoubled their efforts against the place; and, when masters of it, put all their enemies to the sword without distinction.

[40] Bede, lib 1, cap. 15. Ethelwerd, p. 833, edit. Camdeni. Chron. Sax. p. 12. Ann. Beverl. p. 78. The inhabitants of Kent and the Isle of Wight were Jutes. Essex, Middlesex, Sussex, Surrey, and all the southern counties of Cornwall, were peopled by Saxons; Mercia and other parts of the kingdom were inhabited by Angles.
[41] Chron. Sax. p. 14. Ann. Beverl. p. 81.
[42] Chron. Sax. A. D. 485. Flor. Wigorn.   [43] Hen. Hunting. lib. 2.

This decisive advantage secured the conquests of Ælla, who assumed the name of king, and extended his dominion over Sussex and a great part of Surrey. He was stopped in his progress to the east by the kingdom of Kent; in that to the west by another tribe of Saxons, who had taken possession of that territory.

These Saxons, from the situation of the country in which they settled, were called the West Saxons, and landed in the year 495, under the command of Cerdic and of his son Kenric.[44] The Britons were, by past experience, so much on their guard, and so well prepared to receive the enemy, that they gave battle to Cerdic the very day of his landing; and, though vanquished, still defended, for some time, their liberties against the invaders. None of the other tribes of Saxons met with such vigorous resistance, or exerted such valor and perseverance in pushing their conquests. Cerdic was even obliged to call for the assistance of his countrymen from the kingdoms of Kent and Sussex, as well as from Germany, and he was thence joined by a fresh army under the command of Porte, and of his sons Bleda and Megla.[45] Strengthened by these succors, he fought, in the year 508, a desperate battle with the Britons, commanded by Nazan-Leod, who was victorious in the beginning of the action, and routed the wing in which Cerdic himself commanded; but Kenric, who had prevailed in the other wing, brought timely assistance to his father, and restored the battle, which ended in a complete victory gained by the Saxons.[46] Nazan-Leod perished with 5000 of his army, but left the Britons more weakened than discouraged by his death. The war still continued, though the success was commonly on the side of the Saxons, whose short swords and close manner of fighting gave them great advantage over the missile weapons of the Britons. Cerdic was not wanting to his good fortune; and, in order to extend his conquests, he laid siege to Mount Badon, or Banesdowne, near Bath, whither the most obstinate of the discomfited Britons had retired. The southern Britons, in this extremity, applied for assistance to Arthur, Prince of the Silures, whose heroic valor now sustained the declining fate of his country.[47] This is that Arthur so much celebrated in the songs of Thaliessin and the other British bards, and whose

---

[44] Will. Malm. lib. 1, cap. 1, p. 12.   Chron. Sax. p. 15.   [45] Chron. Sax. p. 17.
[46] H. Hunting. lib. 2.   Ethelwerd, lib. 1.   Chron. Sax. p. 17.
[47] Hunting. lib. 2.

military achievements have been blended with so many fables as even to give occasion for entertaining a doubt of his real existence. But poets, though they disfigure the most certain history by their fictions, and use strange liberties with truth where they are the sole historians, as among the Britons, have commonly some foundation for their wildest exaggerations. Certain it is that the siege of Badon was raised by the Britons in the year 520, and the Saxons were there discomfited in a great battle.[48] This misfortune stopped the progress of Cerdic, but was not sufficient to wrest from him the conquest which he had already made. He and his son Kenric, who succeeded him, established the kingdom of the West Saxons, or of Wessex, over the counties of Hants, Dorset, Wilts, Berks, and the Isle of Wight, and left their new-acquired dominions to their posterity. Cerdic died in 534, Kenric in 560.

While the Saxons made this progress in the south, their countrymen were not less active in other quarters. In the year 527 a great tribe of adventurers, under several leaders, landed on the east coast of Britain; and, after fighting many battles of which history has preserved no particular account, they established three new kingdoms in this island. Uffa assumed the title of King of the East Angles in 575; Crida, that of Mercia in 585; [49] and Erkenwin, that of East Saxony, or Essex, nearly about the same time, but the year is uncertain. This latter kingdom was dismembered from that of Kent, and comprehended Essex, Middlesex, and part of Hertfordshire. That of the East Angles, the counties of Cambridge, Suffolk, and Norfolk; Mercia was extended over all the middle counties, from the banks of the Severn to the frontiers of these two kingdoms.

The Saxons, soon after the landing of Hengist, had been planted in Northumberland; but, as they met with an obstinate resistance, and made but small progress in subduing the inhabitants, their affairs were in so unsettled a condition that none of their princes for a long time assumed the appellation of king. At last, in 547,[50] Ida, a Saxon prince of great valor,[51] who claimed a descent, as did all the other princes of that nation, from Woden, brought over a reinforcement from Germany, and enabled the Northumbrians to carry on their conquests over the Britons. He entirely

[48] Gildas. Chron. Sax. H. Hunting. lib. 2.
[49] Math. West. Huntington, lib. 2.
[50] Chron. Sax. p. 19.
[51] Will. Malm. p. 19.

subdued the county now called Northumberland, the bishopric of Durham, as well as some of the southeast counties of Scotland; and he assumed the crown under the title of King of Bernicia. Nearly about the same time, Ælla, another Saxon prince, having conquered Lancashire and the greater part of Yorkshire, received the appellation of King of Deïri.[52] These two kingdoms were united in the person of Ethilfrid, grandson of Ida, who married Acca, the daughter of Ælla; and, expelling her brother Edwin, established one of the most powerful of the Saxon kingdoms, by the title of Northumberland. How far his dominions extended into the country now called Scotland is uncertain; but it cannot be doubted that all the lowlands, especially the east coast of that country, were peopled in a great measure from Germany, though the expeditions made by the several Saxon adventurers have escaped the records of history. The language spoken in those countries, which is purely Saxon, is a stronger proof of this event than can be opposed by the imperfect, or rather fabulous, annals which are obtruded on us by the Scottish historians.

Thus was established, after a violent contest of near a hundred and fifty years, the Heptarchy, or seven Saxon kingdoms in Britain; and the whole southern part of the island, except Wales and Cornwall, had totally changed its inhabitants, language, customs, and political institutions. The Britons, under the Roman dominion, had made such advances towards arts and civil manners that they had built twenty-eight considerable cities within their province, besides a great number of villages and country-seats.[53] But the fierce conquerors, by whom they were now subdued, threw everything back into ancient barbarity, and those few natives who were not either massacred or expelled their habitations were reduced to the most abject slavery. None of the other northern conquerors, the Franks, Goths, Vandals, or Burgundians, though they overran the southern provinces of the empire like a mighty torrent, made such devastations in the conquered territories, or were inflamed into so violent an animosity against the ancient inhabitants. As the Saxons came over at intervals in separate bodies, the Britons, however at first unwarlike, were tempted to make resistance; and hostilities, being thereby prolonged, proved more destructive to both parties, especially to the vanquished. The first invaders from Germany, instead of ex-

[52] Ann. Beverl. p. 78   [53] Gildas. Bede, lib. 1.

cluding other adventurers, who must share with them the spoils of the ancient inhabitants, were obliged to solicit fresh supplies from their own country; and a total extermination of the Britons became the sole expedient for providing a settlement and subsistence to the new planters. Hence there have been found in history few conquests more ruinous than that of the Saxons, and few revolutions more violent than that which they introduced.

So long as the contest was maintained with the natives, the several Saxon princes preserved a union of counsels and interests; but after the Britons were shut up in the barren counties of Cornwall and Wales, and gave no further disturbance to the conquerors, the band of alliance was in a great measure dissolved among the princes of the Heptarchy. Though one prince seems still to have been allowed, or to have assumed, an ascendant over the whole, his authority, if it ought ever to be deemed regular or legal, was extremely limited; and each state acted as if it had been independent and wholly separate from the rest. Wars, therefore, and revolutions and dissensions were unavoidable among a turbulent and military people; and these events, however intricate or confused, ought now to become the objects of our attention. But, added to the difficulty of carrying on at once the history of seven independent kingdoms, there is great discouragement to a writer, arising from the uncertainty, at least barrenness, of the accounts transmitted to us. The monks, who were the only annalists during those ages, lived remote from public affairs, considered the civil transactions as entirely subordinate to the ecclesiastical, and, besides partaking of the ignorance and barbarity which were then universal, were strongly infected with credulity, with the love of wonder, and with a propensity to imposture—vices almost inseparable from their profession and manner of life. The history of that period abounds in names, but is extremely barren of events; or the events are related so much without circumstances and causes, that the most profound or most eloquent writer must despair of rendering them either instructive or entertaining to the reader. Even the great learning and vigorous imagination of Milton sank under the weight; and this author scruples not to declare that the skirmishes of kites or crows as much merited a particular narrative as the confused transactions and battles of the Saxon Heptarchy.[54] In order, however, to con-

[54] Milton in Kennet, p. 50.

nect the events in some tolerable measure, we shall give a succinct account of the succession of kings, and of the more remarkable revolutions in each particular kingdom, beginning with that of Kent, which was the first established.

Escus succeeded his father Hengist in the kingdom of Kent, but seems not to have possessed the military genius of that conqueror, who first made way for the entrance of the Saxon arms into Britain. All the Saxons, who sought either the fame of valor or new establishments by arms, flocked to the standard of Ælla, King of Sussex, who was carrying on successful war against the Britons, and laying the foundations of a new kingdom. Escus was content to possess in tranquillity the kingdom of Kent, which he left in 512 to his son Octa, in whose time the East Saxons established their monarchy, and dismembered the provinces of Essex and Middlesex from that of Kent. His death, after a reign of twenty-two years, made room for his son Hermenric in 534, who performed nothing memorable during a reign of thirty-two years, except associating with him his son Ethelbert in the government, that he might secure the succession in his family, and prevent such revolutions as are incident to a turbulent and barbarous monarchy.

Ethelbert revived the reputation of his family, which had languished for some generations. The inactivity of his predecessors, and the situation of his country, secured from all hostility with the Britons, seem to have much enfeebled the warlike genius of the Kentish Saxons; and Ethelbert, in his first attempt to aggrandize his country and distinguish his own name, was unsuccessful.[55] He was twice discomfited in battle by Ceaulin, King of Wessex, and obliged to yield the superiority in the Heptarchy to that ambitious monarch, who preserved no moderation in his victory, and, by reducing the kingdom of Sussex to subjection, excited jealousy in all the other princes. An association was formed against him; and Ethelbert, intrusted with the command of the allies, gave him battle, and obtained a decisive victory.[56] Ceaulin died soon after; and Ethelbert succeeded as well to his ascendant among the Saxon states as to his other ambitious projects. He reduced all the princes, except the King of Northumberland, to a strict dependence upon him; and even established himself by force on the throne of Mercia, the most extensive of the Saxon kingdoms. Apprehensive, however, of a dangerous league against him, like that by

[55] Chron. Sax. p. 21.   [56] H. Hunting. lib. 2.

which he himself had been enabled to overthrow Ceaulin, he had the prudence to resign the kingdom of Mercia to Webba, the rightful heir, the son of Crida, who had first founded that monarchy. But, governed still by ambition more than by justice, he gave Webba possession of the crown on such conditions as rendered him little better than a tributary prince under his artful benefactor.

But the most memorable event which distinguished the reign of this great prince was the introduction of the Christian religion among the English Saxons. The superstition of the Germans, particularly that of the Saxons, was of the grossest and most barbarous kind; and being founded on traditional tales received from their ancestors, not reduced to any system, nor supported by political institutions like that of the Druids, it seems to have made little impression on its votaries, and to have easily resigned its place to the new doctrine promulgated to them. Woden, whom they deemed the ancestor of all their princes, was regarded as the god of war, and, by a natural consequence, became their supreme deity and the chief object of their religious worship. They believed that if they obtained the favor of this divinity by their valor (for they made less account of the other virtues), they should be admitted after their death into his hall, and, reposing on couches, should satiate themselves with ale from the skulls of their enemies whom they had slain in battle. Incited by this idea of paradise, which gratified at once the passion of revenge and that of intemperance, the ruling inclinations of barbarians, they despised the dangers of war, and increased their native ferocity against the vanquished by their religious prejudices. We know little of the other theological tenets of the Saxons: we only learn that they were polytheists; that they worshipped the sun and moon; that they adored the god of thunder under the name of Thor; that they had images in their temples; that they practised sacrifices, believed firmly in spells and enchantments, and admitted in general a system of doctrines which they held as sacred, but which, like all other superstitions, must carry the air of the wildest extravagance if propounded to those who are not familiarized to it from their earliest infancy.

The constant hostilities which the Saxons maintained against the Britons would naturally indispose them for receiving the Christian faith, when preached to them by such inveterate enemies; and perhaps the Britons, as is objected

to them by Gildas and Bede, were not over-fond of com-
municating to their cruel invaders the doctrine of eternal
life and salvation. But as a civilized people, however subdued by arms, still maintain a sensible superiority over barbarous and ignorant nations, all the other northern conquerors of Europe had been already induced to embrace
the Christian faith, which they found established in the empire ; and it was impossible but the Saxons, informed of
this event, must have regarded with some degree of veneration a doctrine which had acquired the ascendant over all
their brethren. However limited in their views, they could
not but have perceived a degree of cultivation in the southern countries beyond what they themselves possessed : and
it was natural for them to yield to that superior knowledge
as well as zeal by which the inhabitants of the Christian
kingdoms were even at that time distinguished.

But these causes might long have failed of producing
any considerable effect, had not a favorable incident prepared the means of introducing Christianity into Kent.
Ethelbert, in his father's lifetime, had married Bertha, the
only daughter of Caribert, King of Paris,[57] one of the descendants of Clovis, the conqueror of Gaul ; but before he
was admitted to this alliance he was obliged to stipulate
that the princess should enjoy the free exercise of her religion—a concession not difficult to be obtained from the
idolatrous Saxons.[58] Bertha brought over a French bishop
to the court of Canterbury; and being zealous of the propagation of her religion, she had been very assiduous in her
devotional exercises, had supported the credit of her faith
by an irreproachable conduct, and had employed every art
of insinuation and address to reconcile her husband to her
religious principles. Her popularity in the court, and her
influence over Ethelbert, had so well paved the way for the
reception of the Christian doctrine that Gregory, surnamed
the Great, then Roman pontiff, began to entertain hopes of
effecting a project which he himself, before he mounted the
papal throne, had once embraced, of converting the British
Saxons.

It happened that this prelate, at that time in a private
station, had observed in the market-place of Rome some
Saxon youth exposed to sale, whom the Roman merchants,
in their trading voyages to Britain, had bought of their mer-

[57] Greg. of Tours, lib. 9, cap. 26.   H. Hunting. lib. 2.
[58] Bede, lib. 1, cap. 25.   Brompton, p. 729.

cenary parents. Struck with the beauty of their fair complexions and blooming countenances, Gregory asked to what country they belonged; and being told they were *Angles*, he replied that they ought more properly to be denominated *angels;* it were a pity that the prince of darkness should enjoy so fair a prey, and that so beautiful a frontispiece should cover a mind destitute of internal grace and righteousness. Inquiring further concerning the name of their province, he was informed that it was Deïri, a district of Northumberland. *Deïri!* replied he, *that is good! They are called to the mercy of God from his anger;* De ira. *But what is the name of the king of that province?* He was told it was *Ælla or Alla. Alleluia!* cried he, *we must endeavor that the praises of God be sung in their country.* Moved by these allusions, which appeared to him so h ppy, he determined to undertake himself a mission into Britain; and, having obtained the pope's approbation, he prepared for that perilous journey. But his popularity at home was so great that the Romans, unwilling to expose him to such dangers, opposed his designs; and he was obliged for the present to lay aside all further thoughts of executing that pious purpose.[59]

The controversy between the pagans and the Christians was not entirely cooled in that age; and no pontiff before Gregory had ever carried to greater excess an intemperate zeal against the former religion. He had waged war with all the precious monuments of the ancients, and even with their writings, which, as appears from the strain of his own wit, as well as from the style of his compositions, he had not taste or genius sufficient to comprehend. Ambitious to distinguish his pontificate by the conversion of the British Saxons, he pitched on Augustine, a Roman monk, and sent him with forty associates to preach the Gospel in this island. These missionaries, terrified with the dangers which might attend their proposing a new doctrine to so fierce a people, of whose language they were ignorant, stopped some time in France, and sent back Augustine to lay the hazards and difficulties before the pope, and crave his permission to desist from the undertaking. But Gregory exhorted them to persevere in their purpose, advised them to choose some interpreters from among the Franks, who still spoke the same language with the Saxons;[60] and recommended them to the good offices of Queen Brune-

[59] Bede, lib. 2, cap. 1. Spell. Conc. p. 91.   [60] Bede, lib. 1, cap. 23.

4

haut, who had at this time usurped the sovereign power in
France.   This princess, though stained with every vice of
treachery and cruelty, either possessed or pretended great
zeal for the cause ; and Gregory acknowledged that to her
friendly assistance was in a great measure owing the success
of that undertaking.[61]

Augustine, on his arrival in Kent, in the year 597,[62]
found the danger much less than he had apprehended.
Ethelbert, already well disposed towards the Christian faith,
assigned him a habitation in the Isle of Thanet, and soon
after admitted him to a conference.   Apprehensive, however, lest spells or enchantments might be employed against
him by priests who brought an unknown worship from a
distant country, he had the precaution to receive them in
the open air, where he believed the force of their magic
would be more easily dissipated.[63]   Here Augustine, by
means of his interpreters, delivered to him the tenets of the
Christian faith, and promised him eternal joys above, and a
kingdom in heaven without end, if he would be persuaded to
receive that salutary doctrine.[64]   " Your words and promises," replied Ethelbert, " are fair ; but because they are
new and uncertain I cannot entirely yield to them, and relinquish the principles which I and my ancestors have so
long maintained.   You are welcome, however, to remain
here in peace ; and as you have undertaken so long a journey solely, as it appears, for what you believe to be for our
advantage, I will supply you with all necessaries, and permit you to deliver your doctrine to my subjects." [65]

Augustine, encouraged by this favorable reception, and
seeing now a prospect of success, proceeded with redoubled
zeal to preach the Gospel to the Kentish Saxons.   He attracted their attention by the austerity of his manners, by
the severe penances to which he subjected himself, by the
abstinence and self-denial which he practised ; and having
excited their wonder by a course of life which appeared so
contrary to nature, he procured more easily their belief of
miracles, which, it was pretended, he wrought for their conversion.[66]   Influenced by these motives, and by the declared
favor of the court, numbers of the Kentish men were bap-

[61] Greg. Epist. lib. 9, epist. 56.   Spell. Conc. p. 82.
[62] Higden, Polychron. lib. 5.   Chron. Sax. p. 23.
[53] Bede, lib. 1, cap. 25. H. Hunting. lib. 3.   Brompton, p. 729.   Parker. Antiq.
Brit. Eccl., p. 61.
[64] Bede, lib. 1, cap. 25.   Chron. W. Thorn. p. 1759.
[65] Bede, lib. 1. cap. 25. H. Hunting. lib. 3.   Brompton, p. 729.
[66] Bede, lib. 1, cap. 26.

tized; and the king himself was persuaded to submit to that rite of Christianity. His example had great influence with his subjects; but he employed no force to bring them over to the new doctrine. Augustine thought proper, in the commencement of his mission, to assume the appearance of the greatest lenity. He told Ethelbert that the service of Christ must be entirely voluntary, and that no violence ought ever to be used in propagating so salutary a doctrine.[67]

The intelligence received of these spiritual conquests afforded great joy to the Romans, who now exulted as much in those peaceful trophies as their ancestors had ever done in their most sanguinary triumphs and most splendid victories. Gregory wrote a letter to Ethelbert, in which, after informing him that the end of the world was approaching, he exhorted him to display his zeal in the conversion of his subjects, to exert rigor against the worship of idols, and to build up the good work of holiness by every expedient of exhortation, terror, blandishment, or correction[68]—a doctrine more suitable to that age, and to the usual papal maxims, than the tolerating principles which Augustine had thought it prudent to inculcate. The pontiff also answered some questions which the missionary had put concerning the government of the new church of Kent. Besides other queries, which it is not material here to relate, Augustine asked, *Whether cousins-german might be allowed to marry?* Gregory answered that that liberty had indeed been formerly granted by the Roman law; but that experience had shown that no issue could ever come from such marriages; and he therefore prohibited them. Augustine asked, *Whether a woman pregnant might be baptized?* Gregory answered that he saw no objection. *How soon after the birth the child might receive baptism?* It was answered, Immediately, if necessary. *How soon a husband might have commerce with his wife after her delivery?* Not till she had given suck to her child—a practice to which Gregory exhorts all women. *How soon a man might enter the church, or receive the sacrament, after having had commerce with his wife?* It was replied that unless he had approached her without desire, merely for the sake of propagating his species, he was not without sin: but in all cases it was requisite for him, before he entered the church, or communicated,

[67] Bede, lib. 1, cap. 26. H. Hunting. lib. 3.
[68] Bede, lib. 1, cap. 32. Brompton, p. 732. Spell. Conc. p. 86.

to purge himself by prayer and ablution; and he ought not, even after using these precautions, to participate immediately of the sacred duties.[69] There are some other questions and replies still more indecent and more ridiculous.[70] And, on the whole, it appears that Gregory and his missionary, if sympathy of manners have any influence, were better calculated than men of more refined understandings for making a progress with the ignorant and barbarous Saxons.

The more to facilitate the reception of Christianity, Gregory enjoined Augustine to remove the idols from the heathen altars, but not to destroy the altars themselves; because the people, he said, would be allured to frequent the Christian worship, when they found it celebrated in a place which they were accustomed to revere. And as the Pagans practised sacrifices, and feasted with the priests on their offerings, he also exhorted the missionary to persuade them, on Christian festivals, to kill their cattle in the neighborhood of the church, and to indulge themselves in those cheerful entertainments to which they had been habituated.[71] These political compliances show that, notwithstanding his ignorance and prejudices, he was not unacquainted with the arts of governing mankind. Augustine was consecrated archbishop of Canterbury, was endowed by Gregory with authority over all the British churches, and received the pall, a badge of ecclesiastical honor, from Rome.[72] Gregory also advised him not to be too much elated with his gift of working miracles;[73] and as Augustine, proud of the success of his mission, seemed to think himself entitled to extend his authority over the bishops of Gaul, the Pope informed him that they lay entirely without the bounds of his jurisdiction.[74]

The marriage of Ethelbert with Bertha, and much more his embracing Christianity, begat a connection of his subjects with the French, Italians, and other nations on the continent, and tended to reclaim them from that gross igno-

[69] Bede, lib. 1, cap. 27. Spell. Conc. pp. 97, 98, 99, etc.
[70] Augustine asks, *Si mulier menstrua consuetudine tenetur, an ecclesiam intrare ei licet, aut sacræ communionis sacramenta percipere?* Gregory answers, *Sanctæ communionis mysterium in eisdem diebus percipere non debet prohiberi. Si autem ex veneratione magna percipere non præsumitur, laudanda est.* Augustine asks, *Si post illusionem quæ per somnum solet accidere, vel corpus Domini quilibet accipere valeat; vel, si sacerdos sit, sacra mysteria celebrare?* Gregory answers this learned question by many learned distinctions.
[71] Bede, lib. 1, cap. 30. Spell. Conc. p. 89. Greg. Epist. lib. 9, Epist. 71.
[72] Chron. Sax. pp. 23, 24.
[73] H. Hunting. lib. 3. Spell. Conc. p. 83. Bede, lib. 1. Greg. Epist. lib. 9, epist. 60.   [74] Bede, lib. 1, cap. 27.

rance and barbarity in which all the Saxon tribes had been hitherto involved.[75] Ethelbert also enacted,[76] with the consent of the states of his kingdom, a body of laws, the first written laws promulgated by any of the northern conquerors; and his reign was in every respect glorious to himself and beneficial to his people. He governed the kingdom of Kent fifty years, and dying in 616, left the succession to his son, Eadbald. This prince, seduced by a passion for his mother-in-law, deserted for some time the Christian faith, which permitted not these incestuous marriages: his whole people immediately returned with him to idolatry. Laurentius, the successor of Augustine, found the Christian worship wholly abandoned, and was prepared to return to France, in order to escape the mortification of preaching the Gospel without fruit to the infidels. Melitus and Justus, who had been consecrated bishops of London and Rochester, had already departed the kingdom,[77] when Laurentius, before he should entirely abandon his dignity, made one effort to reclaim the king. He appeared before that prince, and, throwing off his vestments, showed his body all torn with bruises and stripes, which he had received. Eadbald, wondering that any man should have dared to treat in that manner a person of his rank, was told by Laurentius that he had received this chastisement from St. Peter, the Prince of the Apostles, who had appeared to him in a vision, and, severely reproving him for his intention to desert his charge, had inflicted on him these visible marks of his displeasure.[78] Whether Eadbald was struck with the miracle, or influenced by some other motive, he divorced himself from his mother-in-law, and returned to the profession of Christianity:[79] his whole people returned with him. Eadbald reached not the fame or authority of his father, and died in 640, after a reign of twenty-five years, leaving two sons, Erminfred and Ercombert.

Ercombert, though the younger son, by Emma, a French princess, found means to mount the throne. He is celebrated by Bede for two exploits: for establishing the fast of Lent in his kingdom, and for utterly extirpating idolatry, which, notwithstanding the prevalence of Christianity, had hitherto been tolerated by the two preceding monarchs. He reigned twenty-four years, and left the crown to Egbert,

[75] Will. Malm. p. 10. [76] Wilkins, Leges Sax. p. 13.
[77] Bede, lib. 2, cap. 5.
[78] Bede, lib. 2, cap. 6. Chron. Sax. p. 26. Higden, lib. 5.
[79] Brompton, p. 739.

his son, who reigned nine years. This prince is renowned for his encouragement of learning, but infamous for putting to death his two cousins-german, sons of Erminfred, his uncle. The ecclesiastical writers praise him for bestowing on his sister, Domnona, some lands in the Isle of Thanet, where she founded a monastery.

The bloody precaution of Egbert could not fix the crown on the head of his son, Edric. Lothaire, brother of the deceased prince, took possession of the kingdom; and, in order to secure the power in his family, he associated with him Richard, his son, in the administration of the government. Edric, the dispossessed prince, had recourse to Edilwach, King of Sussex, for assistance, and, being supported by that prince, fought a battle with his uncle, who was defeated and slain. Richard fled into Germany, and afterwards died in Lucca, a city of Tuscany. William of Malmesbury ascribes Lothaire's bad fortune to two crimes —his concurrence in the murder of his cousins, and his contempt for relics.[80]

Lothaire reigned eleven years; Edric, his successor, only two. Upon the death of the latter, which happened in 686, Widrid, his brother, obtained possession of the crown. But as the succession had been of late so much disjointed by revolutions and usurpations, faction began to prevail among the nobility, which invited Ceodwalla, King of Wessex, with his brother Mollo, to attack the kingdom. These invaders committed great devastations in Kent; but the death of Mollo, who was slain in a skirmish,[81] gave a short breathing-time to that kingdom. Widred restored the affairs of Kent, and, after a reign of thirty-two years,[82] left the crown to his posterity. Eadbert, Ethelbert, and Alric, his descendants, successively mounted the throne. After the death of the last, which happened in 794, the royal family of Kent was extinguished, and every factious leader who could entertain hopes of ascending the throne threw the state into confusion.[83] Egbert, who first succeeded, reigned but two years; Cuthred, brother to the King of Mercia, six years; Baldred, an illegitimate branch of the royal family, eighteen: and, after a troublesome and precarious reign, he was, in the year 827, expelled by Egbert, King of Wessex, who dissolved the Saxon Heptarchy, and united the several kingdoms under his dominion.

[80] Will. Malm. p. 11.
[82] Chron. Sax. p. 52.
[81] Higden, lib. 5.
[83] Will. Malm. lib. 1, cap. 1, p. 11.

Adelfrid, King of Bernicia, having married Acca, the daughter of Ælla, King of Deïri, and expelled her infant brother, Edwin, had united all the countries north of Humber into one monarchy, and acquired a great ascendant in the Heptarchy. He also spread the terror of the Saxon arms to the neighboring people, and by his victories over the Scots and Picts as well as Welsh, extended on all sides the bounds of his dominions. Having laid siege to Chester, the Britons marched out with all their forces to engage him, and they were attended by a body of 1250 monks from the monastery of Bangor, who stood at a small distance from the field of battle in order to encourage the combatants by their presence and exhortations. Adelfrid, inquiring the purpose of this unusual appearance, was told that these priests had come to pray against him. "Then they are as much our enemies," said he, "as those who intend to fight against us;" [84] and he immediately sent a detachment, who fell upon them, and did such execution that only fifty escaped with their lives.[85] The Britons, astonished at this event, received a total defeat. Chester was obliged to surrender; and Adelfrid, pursuing his victory, made himself master of Bangor, and entirely demolished the monastery—a building so extensive that there was a mile's distance from one gate of it to another, and it contained two thousand one hundred monks, who are said to have been there maintained by their own labor.[86]

Notwithstanding Adelfrid's success in war, he lived in inquietude on account of young Edwin, whom he had unjustly dispossessed of the crown of Deïri. This prince, now grown to man's estate, wandered from place to place in continual danger from the attempts of Adelfrid, and received at last protection in the court of Redwald, King of the East Angles, where his engaging and gallant deportment procured him general esteem and affection. Redwald, however, was strongly solicited by the king of Northumberland to kill or deliver up his guest. Rich presents were promised him if he would comply, and war denounced against him in case of his refusal. After rejecting several messages of this kind, his generosity began to yield to the motives of interest, and he retained the last ambassador till he should come to a resolution in a case of such importance. Edwin, informed of his friend's perplexity, was yet determined at all hazards

84 Brompton. p. 779.   85 Trivet, apud Spell. Conc. p. 111.
86 Bede, lib. 2, cap. 2.   Will. Malm. lib. 1, cap. 3.

to remain in East Anglia, and thought that if the protection of that court failed him, it were better to die than prolong a life so much exposed to the persecutions of his powerful rival. This confidence in Redwald's honor and friendship, with his other accomplishments, engaged the queen on his side, and she effectually represented to her husband the infamy of delivering up to certain destruction their royal guest, who had fled to them for protection against his cruel and jealous enemies.[87]   Redwald, embracing more generous resolutions, thought it safest to prevent Adelfrid, before that prince was aware of his intention, and to attack him while he was yet unprepared for defence. He marched suddenly with an army into the kingdom of Northumberland, and fought a battle with Adelfrid, in which that monarch was defeated and killed, after avenging himself by the death of Regner, son of Redwald.[88]   His own sons, Eanfrid, Oswald, and Oswy, yet infants, were carried into Scotland, and Edwin obtained possession of the crown of Northumberland.

Edwin was the greatest prince of the Heptarchy in that age, and distinguished himself, both by his influence over the other kingdoms [89] and by the strict execution of justice in his own dominions. He reclaimed his subjects from the licentious life to which they had been accustomed; and it was a common saying that during his reign a woman or child might openly carry everywhere a purse of gold without any danger of violence or robbery. There is a remarkable instance transmitted to us of the affection borne him by his servants. Cuichelme, King of Wessex, was his enemy; but finding himself unable to maintain open war against so gallant and powerful a prince, he determined to use treachery against him, and he employed one Eumer for that criminal purpose. The assassin, having obtained admittance by pretending to deliver a message from Cuichelme, drew his dagger and rushed upon the king. Lilla, an officer of his army, seeing his master's danger, and having no other means of defence, interposed with his own body between the king and Eumer's dagger, which was pushed with such violence that, after piercing Lilla, it even wounded Edwin. But before the assassin could renew his blow he was despatched by the king's attendants.

The East Angles conspired against Redwald, their king; and, having put him to death, they offered their crown to

87 Will. Malm. lib. 1, cap. 3.   H. Hunting. lib. 3.   Bede.
88 Bede, lib. 2, cap. 12.   Brompton, p. 781.   89 Chron. Sax. p. 27.

Edwin, of whose valor and capacity they had had experience while he resided among them. But Edwin, from a sense of gratitude towards his benefactor, obliged them to submit to Earpwold, the son of Redwald; and that prince preserved his authority, though on a precarious footing, under the protection of the Northumbrian monarch.[90]

Edwin, after his accession to the crown, married Ethelburga, the daughter of Ethelbert, King of Kent. This princess, emulating the glory of her mother, Bertha, who had been the instrument for converting her husband and his people to Christianity, carried Paullinus, a learned bishop, along with her;[91] and besides stipulating a toleration for the exercise of her own religion, which was readily granted to her, she used every reason to persuade the king to embrace it. Edwin, like a prudent prince, hesitated on the proposal, but promised to examine the foundations of that doctrine; and declared that if he found them satisfactory he was willing to be converted.[92] Accordingly, he held several conferences with Paullinus; canvassed the arguments propounded with the wisest of his counsellors; retired frequently from company, in order to revolve alone that important question; and, after a serious and long inquiry, declared in favor of the Christian religion.[93] The people soon after imitated his example. Besides the authority and influence of the king, they were moved by another striking example. Coifi, the high-priest, being converted after a public conference with Paullinus, led the way in destroying the images which he had so long worshipped, and was forward in making his atonement for his past idolatry.[94]

This able prince perished with his son, Osfrid, in a great battle which he fought against Penda, King of Mercia, and Cædwalla, King of the Britons.[95] That event, which happened in the forty-eighth year of Edwin's age, and seventeenth of his reign,[96] divided the monarchy of Northumberland, which that prince had united in his person. Eanfrid, the son of Adelfrid, returned with his brothers, Oswald and Oswy, from Scotland, and took possession of Bernicia, his paternal kingdom. Osric, Edwin's cousin-german, established himself at Deïri, the inheritance of his family, but to which the sons of Edwin had a preferable

90 Will. Malm. lib. 1, cap. 3.
91 H. Hunting. lib. 3.
92 Bede, lib. 2, cap. 9.
93 Ibid. Will. Malm. lib. 1, cap. 3.
94 Bede, lib. 2, cap. 13. Brompton, Higden, lib. 5.
95 Matt. West. p. 114. Chron. Sax. p. 29.
96 Will. Malm. lib. 1. cap. 3.

title. Eanfrid, the elder surviving son, fled to Penda, by whom he was treacherously slain. The younger son, Vuscfræa, with Yffi, the grandson of Edwin by Osfrid, sought protection in Kent; and, not finding themselves in safety there, retired into France to King Dagobert, where they died.[97]

Osric, King of Deïri, and Eanfrid, of Bernicia, returned to paganism, and the whole people seem to have returned with them; since Paullinus, who was the first archbishop of York, and who had converted them, thought proper to retire with Ethelburga, the queen dowager, into Kent. Both these Northumbrian kings perished soon after—the first in battle against Cædwalla, the Briton; the second by the treachery of that prince. Oswald, the brother of Eanfrid, of the race of Bernicia, united again the kingdom of Northumberland in the year 634, and restored the Christian religion in his dominions. He gained a bloody and well-disputed battle against Cædwalla, the last vigorous effort which the Britons made against the Saxons. Oswald is much celebrated for his sanctity and charity by the monkish historians, and they pretend that his relics wrought miracles, particularly the curing of a sick horse which had approached the place of his interment.[98]

He died in battle against Penda, King of Mercia, and was succeeded by his brother Oswy, who established himself in the government of the whole Northumbrian kingdom by putting to death Oswin, the son of Osric, the last king of the race of Deïri. His son Egfrid succeeded him, who, perishing in battle against the Picts, without leaving any children, because Adelthrid, his wife, refused to violate her vow of chastity, Alfred, his natural brother, acquired possession of the kingdom, which he governed for nineteen years, and he left it to Osred, his son, a boy of eight years of age. This prince, after a reign of eleven years, was murdered by Kenred, his kinsman, who, after enjoying the crown only a year, perished by a like fate. Osric, and after him Celwulph, the son of Kenred, next mounted the throne, which the latter relinquished in the year 738 in favor of Eadbert, his cousin-german, who, imitating his predecessor, abdicated the crown, and retired into a monastery. Oswolf, son of Eadbert, was slain in a sedition a year after his accession to the crown; and Mollo, who was not of the royal family, seized the crown. He perished by

[97] Bede, lib. 2, cap. 20.   [98] Bede, lib. 3, cap. 9.

the treachery of Ailred, a prince of the blood; and Ailred, having succeeded in his design upon the throne, was soon after expelled by his subjects. Ethelred, his successor, the son of Mollo, underwent a like fate. Celwold, the next king, the brother of Ailred, was deposed and slain by the people, and his place was filled by Osred, his nephew, who, after a short reign of a year, made way for Ethelbert, another son of Mollo, whose death was equally tragical with that of almost all his predecessors. After Ethelbert's death a universal anarchy prevailed in Northumberland, and the people having, by so many fatal revolutions, lost all attachment to their government and princes, were well prepared for subjection to a foreign yoke, which Egbert, King of Wessex, finally imposed upon them.

The history of this kingdom contains nothing memorable except the conversion of Earpwold, the fourth king, and great-grandson of Uffa, the founder of the monarchy. The authority of Edwin, King of Northumberland, on whom that prince entirely depended, engaged him to take this step; but soon after, his wife, who was an idolatress, brought him back to her religion, and he was found unable to resist those allurements which had seduced the wisest of mankind. After his death, which was violent, like that of most of the Saxon princes that did not early retire into monasteries, Sigebert, his successor and half-brother, who had been educated in France, restored Christianity, and introduced learning among the East Angles. Some pretend that he founded the University of Cambridge, or rather some schools in that place. It is almost impossible, and quite needless, to be more particular in relating the transactions of the East Angles. What instruction or entertainment can it give the reader to hear a long beadroll of barbarous names—Egric, Annas, Ethelbert, Etherwald, Aldulf, Elfwald, Beorne, Ethelred, Ethelbert—who successively murdered, expelled, or inherited from each other, and obscurely filled the throne of that kingdom? Ethelbert, the last of these princes, was treacherously murdered by Offa, King of Mercia, in the year 792, and his state was thenceforth united with that of Offa, as we shall relate presently.

Mercia, the largest if not the most powerful kingdom of the Heptarchy, comprehended all the middle counties of England; and as its frontiers extended to those of all the other six kingdoms as well as to Wales, it received its name from that circumstance. Wibba, the son of Crida, founder of the monarchy, being placed on the throne by Ethelbert, King of Kent, governed his paternal dominions by a precarious authority; and, after his death, Ceorl, his kinsman, was, by the influence of the Kentish monarch, preferred to his son Penda, whose turbulent character appeared dangerous to that prince. Penda was thus fifty years of age before he mounted the throne, and his temerity and restless disposition were found nowise abated by time, experience, or reflection. He engaged in continual hostilities against all the neighboring states, and, by his injustice and violence, rendered himself equally odious to his own subjects and to strangers. Sigebert, Egric, and Annas, three kings of East Anglia, perished successively in battle against him, as did also Edwin and Oswald, the two greatest princes that had reigned over Northumberland. At last Oswy, brother to Oswald, having defeated and slain him in a decisive battle, freed the world from this sanguinary tyrant. Peada, his son, mounted the throne of Mercia in 655, and lived under the protection of Oswy, whose daughter he had espoused. This princess was educated in the Christian faith, and she employed her influence with success in converting her husband and his subjects to that religion. Thus the fair sex have had the merit of introducing the Christian doctrine into all the most considerable kingdoms of the Saxon Heptarchy. Peada died a violent death.[99] His son, Wolfhere, succeeded to the government, and, after having reduced to dependence the kingdoms of Essex and East Anglia, he left the crown to his brother Ethelred, who, though a lover of peace, showed himself not unfit for military enterprises. Besides making a successful expedition into Kent, he repulsed Egfrid, King of Northumberland, who had invaded his dominions; and he slew in battle Elfwin, the brother of that prince. Desirous, however, of composing all animosities with Egfrid, he paid him a sum of money as a compensation for the loss of his brother. After a prosperous reign of thirty years he resigned the crown to Kendred, son of Wolfhere, and retired into the monastery of Bardney.[100] Kendred returned the present of the crown to Ceolred, the son of Ethelred, and making a pilgrimage to Rome, passed his life there in penance and devotion. The place of Ceolred was supplied by Ethelbald, great-grandnephew to

---

[99] Hugo Candidus, p. 4, says that he was treacherously murdered by his queen, by whose persuasion he had embraced Christianity; but this account of the matter is found in that historian alone.　　　　[100] Bede, lib. 5.

Penda, by Alwy, his brother and this prince, being slain in a mutiny, was succeeded by Offa, who was a degree more remote from Penda, by Eawa, another brother.

This prince, who mounted the throne in 775,[101] had some great qualities, and was successful in his warlike enterprises against Lothaire, King of Kent, and Kenwulph, King of Wessex. He defeated the former in a bloody battle at Otford upon the Darent, and reduced his kingdom to a state of dependence; he gained a victory over the latter at Bensington, in Oxfordshire, and, conquering that county, together with that of Gloucester, annexed both to his dominions. But all these successes were stained by his treacherous murder of Ethelbert, King of the East Angles, and his violent seizing of that kingdom. This young prince, who is said to have possessed great merit, had paid his addresses to Elfrida, the daughter of Offa, and was invited, with all his retinue, to Hereford, in order to solemnize the nuptials. Amid the joy and festivity of these entertainments, he was seized by Offa and secretly beheaded; and though Elfrida, who abhorred her father's treachery, had time to give warning to the East-Anglian nobility, who escaped into their own country Offa, having extinguished the royal family, succeeded in his design of subduing that kingdom.[102] The perfidious prince, desirous of re-establishing his character in the world, and perhaps of appeasing the remorses of his own conscience, paid great court to the clergy, and practised all the monkish devotion so much esteemed in that ignorant and superstitious age. He gave the tenth of his goods to the church,[103] bestowed rich donations on the cathedral of Hereford, and even made a pilgrimage to Rome, where his great power and riches could not fail of procuring him the papal absolution. The better to ingratiate himself with the sovereign pontiff, he engaged to pay him a yearly donation for the support of an English college at Rome; [104] and in order to raise the sum, he imposed the tax of a penny on each house possessed of thirty pence a year. This imposition, being afterwards levied on all England, was commonly denominated Peter's pence,[105] and, though conferred at first as a gift, was afterwards claimed as a tribute by the Roman pontiff. Carrying his hypocrisy still further, Offa, feigning to be directed by

[101] Chron. Sax. p. 59.
[102] Brompton, p. 750, 751, 752.
[103] Spell. Conc. p. 308.   Brompton, p. 776.
[104] Spell. Conc. p. 230, 310, 312.
[105] Higden, lib. 5.

a vision from heaven, discovered at Verulam the relics of St. Alban, the martyr, and endowed a magnificent monastery in that place.[106]   Moved by all these acts of piety, Malmesbury, one of the best of the old English historians, declares himself at a loss to determine [107] whether the merits or crimes of this prince preponderated.   Offa died, after a reign of thirty-nine years, in 794.[108]

This prince was become so considerable in the Heptarchy that the emperor Charlemagne entered into an alliance and friendship with him—a circumstance which did honor to Offa, as distant princes at that time had usually little communication with each other.   That emperor being a great lover of learning and learned men, in an age very barren of that ornament, Offa, at his desire, sent him over Alcuin, a clergyman much celebrated for his knowledge, who received great honors from Charlemagne, and even became his preceptor in the sciences.   The chief reason why he had at first desired the company of Alcuin was that he might oppose his learning to the heresy of Felix, Bishop of Urgel, in Catalonia, who maintained that Jesus Christ, considered in his human nature, could more properly be denominated the adoptive than the natural son of God.[109]   This heresy was condemned in the Council of Frankfort, held in 794, and consisting of three hundred bishops.   Such were the questions which were agitated in that age, and which employed the attention not only of cloistered scholars, but of the wisest and greatest princes.[110]

Egfrith succeeded to his father Offa, but survived him only five months,[111] when he made way for Kenulph, a descendant of the royal family.   This prince waged war against Kent, and taking Egbert the king prisoner, he cut off his hands and put out his eyes, leaving Cuthred, his own brother, in possession of the crown of that kingdom. Kenulph was killed in an insurrection of the East Anglians, whose crown his predecessor, Offa, had usurped.   He left his son, Kenelm, a minor, who was murdered the same year by his sister, Quendrade, who had entertained the ambitious views of assuming the government.[112]   But she was supplanted by her uncle Ceolulf, who, two years after, was de-

---

[106] Ingulph. p. 5.   Will. Malm. lib. 1, cap. 4.   [107] Lib. 1, cap. 4.
[108] Chron. Sax. p. 65.   [109] Dupin, cent. 8. ch. 4.
[110] Offa, in order to protect his country from Wales, drew a rampart or ditch of a hundred miles in length, from Basinwerke, in Flintshire, to the south sea, near Bristol.   See Speed's Description of Wales.
[111] Ingulph. p. 6.   [112] Ingulph. p. 7.   Brompton, p. 776.

throned by Beornulf. The reign of this usurper, who was not of the royal family, was short and unfortunate: he was defeated by the West Saxons, and killed by his own subjects, the East Angles.[113] Ludican, his successor, underwent the same fate;[114] and Wiglaff, who mounted this unstable throne, and found everything in the utmost confusion, could not withstand the fortune of Egbert, who united all the Saxon kingdoms into one great monarchy.

This kingdom made no great figure in the Heptarchy, and the history of it is very imperfect. Sleda succeeded to his father, Erkinwin, the founder of the monarchy, and made way for his son, Sebert, who, being nephew to Ethelbert, King of Kent, was persuaded by that prince to embrace the Christian faith.[115] His sons and conjunct successors, Sexted and Seward, relapsed into idolatry, and were soon after slain in a battle against the West Saxons. To show the rude manner of living in that age, Bede tells us [116] that these two kings expressed great desire to eat the white bread distributed by Mellitus, the bishop, at the [117] communion. But on his refusing them, unless they would submit to be baptized, they expelled him their dominions. The names of the other princes who reigned successively in Essex are Sigebert the Little, Sigebert the Good (who restored Christianity), Swithelm, Sigheri, Offa. This last prince, having made a vow of chastity, notwithstanding his marriage with Keneswitha, a Mercian princess, daughter to Penda, went in pilgrimage to Rome, and shut himself up during the rest of his life in a cloister. Selred, his successor, reigned thirty-eight years, and was the last of the royal line; the failure of which threw the kingdom into great confusion, and reduced it to dependence under Mercia.[118] Switherd first acquired the crown by the concession of the Mercian princes, and his death made way for Sigeric, who ended his life in a pilgrimage to Rome. His successor, Sigered, unable to defend his kingdom, submitted to the victorious arms of Egbert.

The history of this kingdom, the smallest in the Heptarchy, is still more imperfect than that of Essex. Ælla, the founder of the monarchy, left the crown to his son Cissa, who is chiefly remarkable for his long reign of seventy-six years. During his time, the South Saxons fell almost into

[113] Ingulph. p. 7.   [114] Ann. Beverl. p. 87.   [115] Chron. Sax. p. 24.
[116] Lib. 2, cap. 5.   [117] H. Hunting. lib. 3. Brompton, pp. 738, 743. Bede.
[118] Will. Malm. lib. 1, cap. 6.

a total dependence on the kingdom of Wessex, and we scarcely know the names of the princes who were possessed of this titular sovereignty. Adelwalch, the last of them, was subdued in battle by Ceodwalla, King of Wessex, and was slain in the action, leaving two infant sons, who, falling into the hand of the conqueror, were murdered by him. The Abbot of Redford opposed the order for this execution, but could only prevail on Ceodwalla to suspend it till they should be baptized. Bercthun and Audhun, two noblemen of character, resisted some time the violence of the West Saxons, but their opposition served only to prolong the miseries of their country, and the subduing of this kingdom was the first step which the West Saxons made towards acquiring the sole monarchy of England.[119]

The kingdom of Wessex, which finally swallowed up all the other Saxon states, met with great resistance on its first establishment; and the Britons, who were now inured to arms, yielded not tamely their possessions to those invaders. Cerdic, the founder of the monarchy, and his son, Kenric, fought many successful, and some unsuccessful, battles against the natives; and the martial spirit, common to all the Saxons, was, by means of these hostilities, carried to the greatest height among this tribe. Ceaulin, who was the son and successor of Kenric, and who began his reign in 560, was still more ambitious and enterprising than his predecessors, and by waging continual war against the Britons he added a great part of the counties of Devon and Somerset to his other dominions. Carried along by the tide of success, he invaded the other Saxon states in his neighborhood, and, becoming terrible to all, he provoked a general confederacy against him. This alliance proved successful under the conduct of Ethelbert, King of Kent; and Ceaulin, who had lost the affections of his own subjects by his violent disposition, and had now fallen into contempt from his misfortunes, was expelled the throne,[120] and died in exile and misery. Cuichelme and Cuthwin, his sons, governed jointly the kingdom, till the expulsion of the latter (in 591) and the death of the former (in 593) made way for Cealric, to whom succeeded Ceobald in 593, by whose death, which happened in 611, Kynegils inherited the crown. This prince embraced Christianity,[121] through the persuasion of Oswald, King of Northumberland, who had married his daughter,

[119] Brompton, p. 800.   [120] Chron. Sax. p. 22.
[121] Higden, lib. 5.   Chron. Sax. p. 15.   Ann. Beverl. p. 94.

and who had attained a great ascendant in the Heptarchy.
Kenwalch next succeeded to the monarchy, and, dying in
672, left the succession so much disputed that Sexburga,
his widow, a woman of spirit,[122] kept possession of the government till her death, which happened two years after.
Escwin then peaceably acquired the crown, and after a
short reign of two years made way for Kentwin, who governed nine years. Ceodwalla, his successor, mounted not
the throne without opposition, but proved a great prince
according to the ideas of those times; that is, he was enterprising, warlike, and successful. He entirely subdued the
kingdom of Sussex, and annexed it to his own dominions.
He made inroads into Kent, but met with resistance from
Widred, the king, who proved successful against Mollo,
brother to Ceodwalla, and slew him in a skirmish. Ceodwalla, at last, tired with wars and bloodshed, was seized
with a fit of devotion; bestowed several endowments on the
Church; and made a pilgrimage to Rome, where he received
baptism, and died in 689. Ina, his successor, inherited the
military virtues of Ceodwalla, and added to them the more
valuable ones of justice, policy, and prudence. He made
war upon the Britons in Somerset, and, having finally subdued that province, he treated the vanquished with a humanity hitherto unknown to the Saxon conquerors. He
allowed the proprietors to retain possession of their lands,
encouraged marriages and alliances between them and his
ancient subjects, and gave them the privilege of being governed by the same laws. These laws he augmented and
ascertained, and, though he was disturbed by some insurrections at home, his long reign of thirty-seven years may
be regarded as one of the most glorious and most prosperous of the Heptarchy. In the decline of his age he made a
pilgrimage to Rome, and, after his return, shut himself up
in a cloister, where he died.

Though the kings of Wessex had always been princes of
the blood, descended from Cerdic, the founder of the monarchy, the order of succession had been far from exact, and
a more remote prince had often found means to mount the
throne in preference to one descended from a nearer branch
of the royal family. Ina, therefore, having no children of
his own, and lying much under the influence of Ethelburga,
his queen, left by will the succession to Adelard, her brother,
who was his remote kinsman; but this destination did not

take place without some difficulty. Oswald, a prince more nearly allied to the crown, took arms against Adelard; but he being suppressed, and dying soon after, the title of Adelard was not any further disputed, and, in the year 741, he was succeeded by his cousin, Cudred. The reign of this prince was distinguished by a great victory, which he obtained by means of Edelhun, his general, over Ethelbald, King of Mercia. His death made way for Sigebert, his kinsman, who governed so ill that his people rose in an insurrection and dethroned him, crowning Cenulph in his stead. The exiled prince found a refuge with Duke Cumbran, governor of Hampshire, who, that he might add new obligations to Sigebert, gave him many salutary counsels for his future conduct, accompanied with some reprehensions for the past. But these were so much resented by the ungrateful prince that he conspired against the life of his protector, and treacherously murdered him. After this infamous action, he was forsaken by all the world, and, skulking about in the wilds and forests, was at last discovered by a servant of Cumbran's, who instantly took revenge upon him for the murder of his master.[123]

Cenulph, who had obtained the crown on the expulsion of Sigebert, was fortunate in many expeditions against the Britons of Cornwall, but afterwards lost some reputation by his ill success against Offa, King of Mercia.[124] Kynehard also, brother to the deposed Sigebert, gave him disturbance, and, though expelled the kingdom, he hovered on the frontiers, and watched an opportunity for attacking his rival. The king had an intrigue with a young woman who lived at Merton, in Surrey, whither having secretly retired, he was on a sudden environed, in the night-time, by Kynehard and his followers, and, after making a vigorous resistance, was murdered with all his attendants. The nobility and people of the neighborhood, rising next day in arms, took revenge on Kynehard for the slaughter of their king, and put every one to the sword who had been engaged in that criminal enterprise. This event happened in 784.

Brithric next obtained possession of the government, though remotely descended from the royal family; but he enjoyed not that dignity without inquietude. Eoppa, nephew to King Ina, by his brother Ingild, who died before that prince, had begot Eta, father to Alchmond, from whom

[123] Higden, lib. 5.   Will. Malm. lib. 1, cap. 22.   [124] Will. Malm., lib. cap. 1.

sprang Egbert,[125] a young man of the most promising hopes, who gave great jealousy to Brithric, the reigning prince, both because he seemed by his birth better entitled to the crown, and because he had acquired, to an eminent degree, the affections of the people. Egbert, sensible of his danger from the suspicions of Brithric, secretly withdrew into France,[126] where he was well received by Charlemagne. By living in the court, and serving in the armies of that prince, the most able and most generous that had appeared in Europe during several ages, he acquired those accomplishments which afterwards enabled him to make such a shining figure on the throne; and, familiarizing himself to the manners of the French, who, as Malmesbury observes,[127] were eminent both for valor and civility above all the western nations, he learned to polish the rudeness and barbarity of the Saxon character; his early misfortunes thus proved of singular advantage to him.

It was not long ere Egbert had opportunities of displaying his natural and acquired talents. Brithric, King of Wessex, had married Eadburga, natural daughter of Offa, King of Mercia, a profligate woman, equally infamous for cruelty and for incontinence. Having great influence over her husband, she often instigated him to destroy such of the nobility as were obnoxious to her; and where this expedient failed, she scrupled not being herself active in traitorous attempts against them. She had mixed a cup of poison for a young nobleman who had acquired her husband's friendship, and had on that account become the object of her jealousy; but, unfortunately, the king drank of the fatal cup along with his favorite, and soon after expired.[128] This tragical incident, joined to her other crimes, rendered Eadburga so odious that she was obliged to fly into France, whence Egbert was at the same time recalled by the nobility, in order to ascend the throne of his ancestors.[129] He attained that dignity in the last year of the eighth century.

In the kingdoms of the Heptarchy, an exact rule of succession was either unknown or not strictly observed, and thence the reigning prince was continually agitated with jealousy against all the princes of the blood, whom he still considered as rivals, and whose death alone could give him entire security in his possession of the throne. From this

[125] Chron. Sax. p. 16.   [126] H. Hunting. lib. 4.   [127] Lib. 2, cap. 11
[128] Higden, lib. 5. Matt. West. p. 152. Asser. in vita Alfredi, p. 3, ex edit. Camdeni.   [129] Chron. Sax. A. D. 800. Brompton, p. 801.

fatal cause, together with the admiration of the monastic life, and the opinion of merit attending the preservation of chastity even in a married state, the royal families had been entirely extinguished in all the kingdoms except that of Wessex; and the emulations, suspicions, and conspiracies which had formerly been confined to the princes of the blood alone were now diffused among all the nobility in the several Saxon states. Egbert was the sole descendant of those first conquerors who subdued Britain, and who enhanced their authority by claiming a pedigree from Woden, the supreme divinity of their ancestors. But that prince, though invited by this favorable circumstance to make attempts on the neighboring Saxons, gave them for some time no disturbance, and rather chose to turn his arms against the Britons in Cornwall, whom he defeated in several[130] battles. He was recalled from the conquest of that country by an invasion made upon his dominions by Bernulf, King of Mercia.

The Mercians, before the accession of Egbert, had very nearly attained the absolute sovereignty in the Heptarchy; they had reduced the East Angles under subjection, and established tributary princes in the kingdoms of Kent and Essex. Northumberland was involved in anarchy; and no state of any consequence remained but that of Wessex, which, much inferior in extent to Mercia, was supported solely by the great qualities of its sovereign. Egbert led his army against the invaders, and, encountering them at Ellandun, in Wiltshire, obtained a complete victory, and by the great slaughter which he made of them in their flight gave a mortal blow to the power of the Mercians. While he himself, in prosecution of his victory, entered their country on the side of Oxfordshire, and threatened the heart of their dominions, he sent an army into Kent, commanded by Ethelwolf, his eldest son,[131] and, expelling Baldred, the tributary king, soon made himself master of that country. The kingdom of Essex was conquered with equal facility; and the East Angles, from their hatred to the Mercian government, which had been established over them by treachery and violence, and probably exercised with tyranny, immediately rose in arms, and craved the protection of Egbert.[132] Bernulf, the Mercian king, who marched against them, was defeated and slain; and two

[130] Chron. Sax. p. 69.
[131] Ethelward, lib. 3, cap. 2.
[132] Ethelward, lib. 3, cap. 3.

years after, Ludican, his successor, met with the same fate. These insurrections and calamities facilitated the enterprises of Egbert, who advanced into the centre of the Mercian territories, and made easy conquests over a dispirited and divided people. In order to engage them more easily to submission, he allowed Wiglef, their countryman, to retain the title of king, while he himself exercised the real powers of sovereignty.[133] The anarchy which prevailed in Northumberland tempted him to carry still farther his victorious arms; and the inhabitants, unable to resist his power, and desirous of possessing some established form of government, were forward, on his first appearance, to send deputies, who submitted to his authority, and swore allegiance to him as their sovereign. Egbert, however, still allowed to Northumberland, as he had done to Mercia and East Anglia, the power of electing a king, who paid him tribute, and was dependent on him.

Thus were united all the kingdoms of the Heptarchy in one great state, near four hundred years after the first arrival of the Saxons in Britain; and the fortunate arms and prudent policy of Egbert at last effected what had been so often attempted in vain by so many princes.[134] Kent, Northumberland, and Mercia, which had successively aspired to general dominion, were now incorporated in his empire, and the other subordinate kingdoms seemed willingly to share the same fate. His territories were nearly of the same extent with what is now properly called England; and a favorable prospect was afforded to the Anglo-Saxons of establishing a civilized monarchy, possessed of tranquillity within itself and secure against foreign invasion. This great event happened in the year 827.[135]

The Saxons, though they had been so long settled in the island, seem not as yet to have been much improved beyond their German ancestors, either in arts, civility, knowledge, humanity, justice, or obedience to the laws. Even Christianity, though it opened the way to connections between them and the more polished states of Europe, had not hitherto been very effectual in banishing their ignorance or softening their barbarous manners. As they received that doctrine through the corrupted channels of Rome, it carried along with it a great mixture of credulity and superstition, equally destructive to the understanding and to morals. The reverence towards saints and relics seems to have

[133] Ingulph. pp. 7, 8, 10.   [134] Chron. Sax. p. 71.   [135] Ibid.

almost supplanted the adoration of the Supreme Being. Monastic observances were esteemed more meritorious than the active virtues; the knowledge of natural causes was neglected from the universal belief of miraculous interpositions and judgments; bounty to the Church atoned for every violence against society; and the remorses for cruelty, murder, treachery, assassination, and the more robust vices were appeased, not by amendment of life, but by penances, servility to the monks, and an abject and illiberal devotion.[136] The reverence for the clergy had been carried to such a height that wherever a person appeared in a sacerdotal habit, though on the highway, the people flocked around him, and, showing him all marks of profound respect, received every word he uttered as the most sacred oracle. [137] Even the military virtues, so inherent in all the Saxon tribes, began to be neglected; and the nobility, preferring the security and sloth of the cloister to the tumults and glory of war, valued themselves chiefly on endowing monasteries, of which they assumed the government.[138] The several kings, too, being extremely impoverished by continual benefactions to the Church, to which the states of their kingdoms had weakly assented, could bestow no rewards on valor or military services, and retained not even sufficient influence to support their government.[139]

Another inconvenience which attended this corrupt species of Christianity was the superstitious attachment to Rome, and the gradual subjection of the kingdom to a foreign jurisdiction. The Britons, having never acknowledged any subordination to the Roman pontiff, had conducted all ecclesiastical government by their domestic synods and councils; [140] but the Saxons, receiving their religion from Roman monks, were taught at the same time a profound reverence for that see, and were naturally led to regard it as the capital of their religion. Pilgrimages to Rome were represented as the most meritorious acts of devotion. Not only noblemen and ladies of rank undertook this tedious journey,[141]

---

[136] These abuses were common to all the European churches; but the priests in Italy, Spain, and Gaul made some atonement for them by other advantages which they rendered society. For several ages they were almost all Romans, or, in other words, the ancient natives; and they preserved the Roman language and laws, with some remains of the former civility. But the priests in the Heptarchy, after the first missionaries, were wholly Saxons, and almost as ignorant and barbarous as the laity. They contributed, therefore, little to the improvement of society in knowledge or the arts.
[137] Bede, lib. 3, cap. 26.   [138] Bede, lib. 5, cap. 23.   Bedæ Epist. ad Egbert.
[139] Bedæ Epist. ad Egbert.
[140] Append. to Bede, No. 10, ex edit. 1722. Spell. Conc. pp. 108, 109.
[141] Bede, lib. 5, cap. 7.

but kings themselves, abdicating their crowns, sought for a secure passport to heaven at the feet of the Roman pontiff; new relics, perpetually sent from that endless mint of superstition, and magnified by lying miracles, invented in convents, operated on the astonished minds of the multitude; and every prince has attained the eulogies of the monks, the only historians of those ages, not in proportion to his civil and military virtues, but to his devoted attachment towards their order, and his superstitious reverence for Rome.

The sovereign pontiff, encouraged by this blindness and submissive disposition of the people, advanced every day in his encroachments on the independence of the English churches. Wilfrid, Bishop of Lindisferne, the sole prelate of the Northumbrian kingdom, increased this subjection in the eighth century by his making an appeal to Rome against the decisions of an English synod which had abridged his diocese by the erection of some new bishoprics.[142] Agatho, the pope, readily embraced this precedent of an appeal to his court; and Wilfrid, though the haughtiest and most luxurious prelate of his age,[143] having obtained with the people the character of sanctity, was thus able to lay the foundation of this papal pretension.

The great topic by which Wilfrid confounded the imaginations of men was that St. Peter, to whose custody the keys of heaven were intrusted, would certainly refuse admittance to every one who should be wanting in respect to his successor. This conceit, well suited to vulgar conceptions, made great impression on the people during several ages, and has not even at present lost all influence in the Catholic countries.

Had this abject superstition produced general peace and tranquillity, it had made some atonement for the ills attending it; but, besides the usual avidity of men for power and riches, frivolous controversies in theology were engendered by it, which were so much the more fatal as they admitted not, like the others, of any final determination from established possession. The disputes excited in Britain were of the most ridiculous kind, and entirely worthy of those ignorant and barbarous ages. There were some intricacies, observed by all the Christian churches, in adjusting the day of keeping Easter, which depended on a complicated consideration of the course of the sun and moon; and it hap-

---

[142] See Append. to Bede, No. 19. Higden, lib. 5.
[143] Eddius, Vita Vilfr. § 24, 60.

pened that the missionaries who had converted the Scots and Britons had followed a different calendar from that which was observed at Rome in the age when Augustine converted the Saxons. The priests also of all the Christian churches were accustomed to shave part of their head; but the form given to this tonsure was different in the former from what was practised in the latter. The Scots and Britons pleaded the antiquity of *their* usages; the Romans, and their disciples, the Saxons, insisted on the universality of *theirs*. That Easter must necessarily be kept by a rule which comprehended both the day of the year and age of the moon was agreed by all; that the tonsure of a priest could not be omitted without the utmost impiety was a point undisputed; but the Romans and Saxons called their antagonists schismatics, because they celebrated Easter on the very day of the full moon in March, if that day fell on a Sunday, instead of waiting till the Sunday following; and because they shaved the forepart of their head from ear to ear, instead of making that tonsure on the crown of the head, and in a circular form. In order to render their antagonists odious, they affirmed that once in seven years they concurred with the Jews in the time of celebrating that festival;[144] and that they might recommend their own form of tonsure, they maintained that it imitated symbolically the crown of thorns worn by Christ in his passion, whereas the other form was invented by Simon Magus, without any regard to that representation.[145] These controversies had, from the beginning, excited such animosity between the British and Romish priests that, instead of concurring in their endeavors to convert the idolatrous Saxons, they refused all communion together, and each regarded his opponent as no better than a pagan.[146] The dispute lasted more than a century, and was at last finished, not by men's discovering the folly of it, which would have been too great an effort for human reason to accomplish, but by the entire prevalence of the Romish ritual over the Scotch and British.[147] Wilfrid, Bishop of Lindisferne, acquired great merit, both with the court of Rome and with all the Southern Saxons, by expelling the quartodeciman schism, as it was called, from the Northumbrian kingdom, into which the neighborhood of the Scots had formerly introduced it.[148]

144 Bede, lib. 2, cap. 19.   145 Bede, lib. cap. 5, 21. Eddius, § 24.
146 Bede, lib. 2, cap. 2, 4, 20.   Eddius, § 12.   147 Bede, lib. 5, cap. 16, 22.
148 Bede, lib. 3, cap. 25.   Eddius, § 12.

Theodore, Archbishop of Canterbury, called, in the year 680, a synod at Hatfield, consisting of all the bishops in Britain,[149] where was accepted and ratified the decree of the Lateran Council, summoned by Martin, against the heresy of the Monothelites. The council and synod maintained, in opposition to these heretics, that though the divine and human nature in Christ made but one person, yet they had different inclinations, wills, acts, and sentiments, and that the unity of the person implied not any unity in the consciousness.[150] This opinion it seems somewhat difficult to comprehend; and no one unacquainted with the ecclesiastical history of those ages could imagine the height of zeal and violence with which it was then inculcated. The decree of the Lateran Council calls the Monothelites impious, execrable, wicked, abominable, and even diabolical; and curses and anathematizes them to all eternity.[151]

The Saxons, from the first introduction of Christianity among them, had admitted the use of images; and perhaps that religion, without some of those exterior ornaments, had not made so quick a progress with these idolaters. But they had not paid any species of worship or address to images; and this abuse never prevailed among Christians till it received the sanction of the Second Council of Nice.

[149] Spell. Conc. vol. i. p. 168.　　　[150] Spell. Conc. vol. i. p. 171.
[151] Spell. Conc. vol. i. pp. 172, 173, 174.

CHAPTER II.

EGBERT. — ETHELWOLF. — ETHELBALD AND ETHELBERT.—
ETHERED.—ALFRED THE GREAT.—EDWARD THE ELDER.—
ATHELSTAN.—EDMUND.—EDRED.—EDWY.—EDWARD THE
MARTYR.

THE kingdoms of the Heptarchy, though united by so
recent a conquest, seemed to be firmly cemented into one
state under Egbert; [827.] and the inhabitants of the
several provinces had lost all desire of revolting from that
monarch, or of restoring their former independent governments. Their language was everywhere nearly the same—
their customs, laws, institutions, civil and religious; and as
the race of the ancient kings was totally extinct in all the
subjected states, the people readily transferred their allegiance to a prince who seemed to merit it by the splendor
of his victories, the vigor of his administration, and the superior nobility of his birth. A union also in government
opened to them the agreeable prospect of future tranquillity ;
and it appeared more probable that they would henceforth
become more formidable to their neighbors than be exposed
to their inroads and devastations. But these flattering
views were soon overcast by the appearance of the Danes,
who, during some centuries, kept the Anglo-Saxons in perpetual inquietude, committed the most barbarous ravages
upon them, and at last reduced them to grievous servitude.

The Emperor Charlemagne, though naturally generous
and humane, had been induced by bigotry to exercise great
severities upon the pagan Saxons in Germany, whom he subdued ; and, besides often ravaging their country with fire
and sword, he had in cool blood decimated all the inhabitants for their revolts, and had obliged them, by the most
rigorous edicts, to make a seeming compliance with the
Christian doctrine. That religion, which had easily made
its way among the British Saxons by insinuation and address, appeared shocking to their German brethren when
imposed upon them by the violence of Charlemagne, and
the more generous and warlike of these pagans had fled

northwards into Jutland, in order to escape the fury of his persecutions. Meeting there with a people of similar manners, they were readily received among them; and they soon stimulated the natives to concur in enterprises which both promised revenge on the haughty conqueror and afforded subsistence to those numerous inhabitants with which the northern countries were now overburdened.[1] They invaded the provinces of France, which were exposed by the degeneracy and dissensions of Charlemagne's posterity; and being there known under the general name of Normans, which they received from their northern situation, they became the terror of all the maritime and even of the inland countries. They were also tempted to visit England in their frequent excursions; and being able, by sudden inroads, to make great progress over a people who were not defended by any naval force, who had relaxed their military institutions, and who were sunk into a superstition which had become odious to the Danes and ancient Saxons, they made no distinction in their hostilities between the French and English kingdoms. Their first appearance in this island was in the year 787,[2] when Brithric reigned in Wessex. A small body of them landed in that kingdom, with a view of learning the state of the country; and when the magistrate of the place questioned them concerning their enterprise, and summoned them to appear before the king and account for their intentions, they killed him, and, flying to their ships, escaped into their own country. The next alarm was given to Northumberland in the year 794,[3] when a body of these pirates pillaged a monastery; but their ships being much damaged by a storm, and their leader slain in a skirmish, they were at last defeated by the inhabitants, and the remainder of them put to the sword. Five years after Egbert had established his monarchy over England, the Danes landed in the Isle of Sheppey, and having pillaged it, escaped with impunity.[4] They were not so fortunate in their next year's enterprise, when they disembarked from thirty-five ships, and were encountered by Egbert at Charmouth, in Dorsetshire. The battle was bloody; but though the Danes lost great numbers, they maintained the post they had taken, and thence made good their retreat to their ships.[5] Having learned by experience that they must expect a vigorous re-

[1] Ypod. Neustria, p. 414.　　　　　　　[2] Chron. Sax. p. 64.
[3] Chron. Sax. p. 66.　Alur. Beverl. p. 108.
[4] Chron. Sax. p. 72.　　　[5] Chron. Sax. p. 72.　Ethelward, lib. 3, cap. 2.

sistance from this warlike prince, they entered into an alliance with the Britons of Cornwall, and, landing two years after in that country, made an inroad with their confederates into the county of Devon, but were met at Hengesdown by Egbert, and totally defeated.[6] While England remained in this state of anxiety, and defended itself more by temporary expedients than by any regular plan of administration, [838.] Egbert, who alone was able to provide effectually against this new evil, unfortunately died, and left the government to his son Ethelwolf.

This prince had neither the abilities nor the vigor of his father, and was better qualified for governing a convent than a kingdom.[7] He began his reign with making a partition of his dominions, and delivering over to his eldest son, Athelstan, the new-conquered provinces of Essex, Kent, and Sussex. But no inconveniences seem to have risen from this partition, as the continual terror of the Danish invasions prevented all domestic dissension. A fleet of these ravagers, consisting of thirty-three sail, appeared at Southampton, but were repulsed with loss by Wolfhere, governor of the neighboring county.[8] The same year, Æthelhelm, governor of Dorsetshire, routed another band which had disembarked at Portsmouth, but he obtained the victory after a furious engagement, and he bought it with the loss of his life.[9] Next year the Danes made several inroads into England, and fought battles, or rather skirmishes, in East Anglia and Lindesey and Kent, where, though they were sometimes repulsed and defeated, they always obtained their end of committing spoil upon the country and carrying off their booty. They avoided coming to a general engagement, which was not suited to their plan of operations. Their vessels were small, and ran easily up the creeks and rivers, where they drew them ashore; and having formed an intrenchment round them, which they guarded with part of their number, the remainder scattered themselves everywhere; and carrying off the inhabitants and cattle and goods, they hastened to their ships and quickly disappeared. If the military force of the county were assembled (for there was no time for troops to march from a distance), the Danes either were able to repulse them, and to continue their ravages with impunity, or they betook themselves to their vessels, and, set-

6 Chron. Sax. p. 72.   7 Will. Malm. lib. 2, cap. 2.
8 Chron. Sax. p. 73.   Ethelward, lib. 3, cap. 3.
9 Chron. Sax. p. 73.   H. Hunting. lib. 5.

ting sail, suddenly invaded some distant quarter, which was not prepared for their reception. Every part of England was held in continual alarm, and the inhabitants of one county durst not give assistance to those of another, lest their own families and property should in the meantime be exposed by their absence to the fury of these barbarous ravagers.[10] All orders of men were involved in this calamity, and the priests and monks, who had been commonly spared in the domestic quarrels of the Heptarchy, were the chief objects on which the Danish idolaters exercised their rage and animosity. Every season of the year was dangerous, and the absence of the enemy was no reason why any man could esteem himself a moment in safety.

These incursions had now become almost annual, when the Danes, encouraged by their successes against France as well as England [851.] (for both kingdoms were alike exposed to this dreadful calamity), invaded the last in so numerous a body as seemed to threaten it with universal subjection. But the English, more military than the Britons, whom a few centuries before they had treated with like violence, roused themselves with a vigor proportioned to the exigency. Ceorle, governor of Devonshire, fought a battle with one body of the Danes at Wiganburgh,[11] and put them to rout with great slaughter. King Athelstan attacked another at sea near Sandwich, sank nine of their ships, and put the rest to flight.[12] A body of them, however, ventured, for the first time, to take up winter-quarters in England ; and receiving in the spring a strong reinforcement of their countrymen in 350 vessels, they advanced from the Isle of Thanet, where they had stationed themselves, burned the cities of London and Canterbury, and, having put to flight Brichtric, who now governed Mercia under the title of king, they marched into the heart of Surrey, and laid every place waste around them. Ethelwolf, impelled by the urgency of the danger, marched against them at the head of the West Saxons, and, carrying with him his second son, Ethelbald, gave them battle at Okely, and gained a bloody victory over them. This advantage procured but a short respite to the English. The Danes still maintained their settlement in the Isle of Thanet, and being attacked by Ealher and Huda, governors of Kent and Surrey, though defeated in the beginning of

---

[10] Alur. Beverl. p. 108.
[11] H. Hunting. lib. 5. Ethelward, lib. 3, cap. 3. Simeon Dunelm. p. 120.
[12] Chron. Sax. p. 74. Asserius, p. 2.

the action, they finally repulsed the assailants, and killed both the governors. [853.] They removed thence to the Isle of Sheppey, where they took up their winter-quarters, that they might further extend their devastation and ravages.

This unsettled state of England hindered not Ethelwolf from making a pilgrimage to Rome, whither he carried his fourth and favorite son, Alfred, then only six years of age.[13] He passed there a twelvemonth in exercises of devotion, and failed not in that most essential part of devotion, liberality to the Church of Rome. Besides giving presents to the more distinguished ecclesiastics, he made a perpetual grant of three hundred mancuses[14] a year to that see; one-third to support the lamps of St. Peter's, another those of St. Paul's, a third to the pope himself.[15] In his return home he married Judith, daughter of the Emperor Charles the Bald; but on his landing in England he met with an opposition which he little looked for.

His eldest son, Athelstan, being dead, Ethelbald, his second, who had assumed the government, formed, in concert with many of the nobles, the project of excluding his father from a throne which his weakness and superstition seemed to have rendered him so ill qualified to fill. The people were divided between the two princes, and a bloody civil war, joined to all the other calamities under which the English labored, appeared inevitable, when Ethelwolf had the facility to yield to the greater part of his son's pretensions. He made with him a partition of the kingdom, and, taking to himself the eastern part, which was always at that time esteemed the least considerable as well as the most exposed,[16] he delivered over to Ethelbald the sovereignty of the western. Immediately after, he summoned the states of the whole kingdom, and with the same facility conferred a perpetual and important donation on the Church.

The ecclesiastics, in those days of ignorance, made rapid advances in the acquisition of power and grandeur; and, inculcating the most absurd and most interested doctrines —though they sometimes met, from the contrary interests of the laity, with an opposition which it required time and address to overcome—they found no obstacle in their reason

---

[13] Asserius, p. 2.   Chron. Sax. p. 76.   H. Hunting. lib. 5.
[14] A mancus was about the weight of our present half-crown. See Spellman's Glossary, *in verbo* Mancus.
[15] Will. Malm. lib. 2, cap. 2.
[16] Asserius, p. 3.   Will. Malm. lib. 2, cap. 2.   Matt. West. pp. 1, 8.

or understanding. Not content with the donations of land made them by the Saxon princes and nobles, and with temporary oblations, from the devotion of the people, they had cast a wishful eye on a vast revenue, which they claimed as belonging to them by a sacred and indefeasible title. However little versed in the Scriptures, they had been able to discover that, under the Jewish law, a tenth of all the produce of land was conferred on the priesthood; and, forgetting, what they themselves taught, that the moral part only of that law was obligatory on Christians, they insisted that this donation conveyed a perpetual property, inherent by divine right in those who officiated at the altar. During some centuries, the whole scope of sermons and homilies was directed to this purpose, and one would have imagined, from the general tenor of these discourses, that all the practical parts of Christianity were comprised in the exact and faithful payment of tithes to the clergy.[17] Encouraged by their success in inculcating these doctrines, they ventured further than they were warranted even by the Levitical law, and pretended to draw the tenth of all industry, merchandise, wages of laborers, and pay of soldiers;[18] nay, some canonists went so far as to affirm that the clergy were entitled to the tithe of the profits made by courtesans in the exercise of their profession.[19] Though parishes had been instituted in England by Honorius, Archbishop of Canterbury, near two centuries before,[20] the ecclesiastics had never yet been able to get possession of the tithes; they therefore seized the present favorable opportunity of making that acquisition, when a weak, superstitious prince filled the throne, and when the people, discouraged by their losses from the Danes, and terrified with the fear of future invasions, were susceptible of any impression which bore the appearance of religion.[21] So meritorious was this concession deemed by the English, that, trusting entirely to supernatural assistance, they neglected the ordinary means of safety, and agreed, even in the present desperate extremity, that the revenues of the Church should be exempted from all burdens, though imposed for national defence and security.[22]

Ethelwolf lived only two years after making this grant,

[17] Padre Paolo, sopra beneficii ecclesiastici, pp. 51, 52, edit. Colon. 1675.
[18] Spell. Conc. vol. i. p. 208.   [19] Padre Paolo, p. 132.
[20] Parker, p. 77.   [21] Ingulph. p. 862. Selden's Hist. of Tithes, ch. 8.
[22] Asserius, p. 2. Chron. Sax. p. 76. Will. Malm. lib. 2, cap. 2. Ethelward, lib. 3, cap. 3. Matt. West. p. 158. Ingulph. p. 17. Alur. Beverl. p. 95.

and by his will he shared England between his two eldest sons [857.], Ethelbald and Ethelbert; the west being assigned to the former, the east to the latter. Ethelbald was a profligate prince, and, marrying Judith, his mother-in-law, gave great offence to the people; but, moved by the remonstrances of Swithin, Bishop of Winchester, he was at last prevailed on to divorce her. [860.] His reign was short; and Ethelbert, his brother, succeeding to the government, behaved himself, during a reign of five years, in a manner more worthy of his birth and station. The kingdom, however, was still infested by the Danes, who made an inroad and sacked Winchester, but were there defeated. A body also of these pirates, who were quartered in the Isle of Thanet, having deceived the English by a treaty, unexpectedly broke into Kent, and committed great outrages.

Ethelbert was succeeded by his brother Ethered, who, though he defended himself with bravery, enjoyed, during his whole reign, no tranquillity from those Danish irruptions. [866.] His younger brother, Alfred, seconded him in all his enterprises, and generously sacrificed to the public good all resentment which he might entertain on account of his being excluded by Ethered from a large patrimony which had been left him by his father.

The first landing of the Danes in the reign of Ethered was among the East Angles, who, more anxious for their present safety than for the common interest, entered into a separate treaty with the enemy, and furnished them with horses, which enabled them to make an irruption by land into the kingdom of Northumberland. They there seized the city of York, and defended it against Osbricht and Ælla, two Northumbrian princes, who perished in the assault.[23] Encouraged by these successes, and by the superiority which they had acquired in arms, they now ventured, under the command of Hinguar and Hubba, to leave the sea-coast; and, penetrating into Mercia, they took up their winter-quarters at Nottingham, where they threatened the kingdom with a final subjection. The Mercians, in this extremity, applied to Ethered for succor, and that prince, with his brother Alfred, conducting a great army to Nottingham, obliged the enemy to dislodge, and to retreat into Northumberland. [870.] Their restless disposition, and their avidity for plunder, allowed them not to remain long in those

[23] Asserius, p. 6. Chron. Sax. p. 79.

quarters; they broke into East Anglia, defeated and took prisoner Edmund, the king of that country, whom they afterwards murdered in cool blood; and, committing the most barbarous ravages on the people, particularly on the monasteries, they gave the East Angles cause to regret the temporary relief which they had obtained by assisting the common enemy.

The next station of the Danes was at Reading, whence they infested the neighboring country by their incursions. [871.] The Mercians, desirous of shaking off their dependence on Ethered, refused to join him with their forces; and that prince, attended by Alfred, was obliged to march against the enemy with the West Saxons alone, his hereditary subjects. The Danes, being defeated in an action, shut themselves up in their garrison; but, quickly making thence an irruption, they routed the West Saxons, and obliged them to raise the siege. An action soon after ensued at Aston, in Berkshire, where the English, in the beginning of the day, were in danger of a total defeat. Alfred, advancing with one division of the army, was surrounded by the enemy in disadvantageous ground; and Ethered, who was at that time hearing mass, refused to march to his assistance till prayers should be finished; [24] but as he afterwards obtained the victory, this success, not the danger of Alfred, was ascribed by the monks to the piety of that monarch. This battle of Aston did not terminate the war: another battle was a little after fought at Basing, where the Danes were more successful; and being reinforced by a new army from their own country, they became every day more terrible to the English. Amid these confusions, Ethered died of a wound which he had received in an action with the Danes, and left the inheritance of his cares and misfortunes, rather than of his grandeur, to his brother, Alfred, who was now twenty-two years of age.

This prince gave very early marks of those great virtues and shining talents by which, during the most difficult times, he saved his country from utter ruin and subversion. [871.] Ethelwolf, his father, the year after his return with Alfred from Rome, had again sent the young prince thither with a numerous retinue; and a report being spread of the king's death, the pope (Leo III.) gave Alfred the royal unc-

<hr>

[24] Asserius, p. 7. Will. Malm. lib. 2, cap. 3. Simeon Dunelm. p. 125. Anglia Sacra, vol. i. p. 205.

tion ; [25] whether prognosticating his future greatness from the appearances of his pregnant genius, or willing to pretend, even in that age, to the right of conferring kingdoms. Alfred, on his return home, became every day more the object of his father's affections; but being indulged in all youthful pleasures, he was much neglected in his education ; and he had already reached his twelfth year, when he was totally ignorant of the lowest elements of literature. His genius was first roused by the recital of Saxon poems, in which the queen took delight; and this species of erudition, which is sometimes able to make a considerable progress even among barbarians, expanded those noble and elevated sentiments which he had received from nature.[26] Encouraged by the queen, and stimulated by his own ardent inclination, he soon learned to read those compositions; and proceeded thence to acquire the knowledge of the Latin tongue, in which he met with authors that better prompted his heroic spirit and directed his generous views. Absorbed in these elegant pursuits, he regarded his accession to royalty rather as an object of regret than of triumph ; [27] but being called to the throne, in preference to his brother's children, as well by the will of his father (a circumstance which had great authority with the Anglo-Saxons) [28] as by the vows of the whole nation and the urgency of public affairs, he shook off his literary indolence, and exerted himself in the defence of his people. He had scarcely buried his brother, when he was obliged to take the field in order to oppose the Danes, who had seized Wilton, and were exercising their usual ravages on the countries around. He marched against them with the few troops which he could assemble on a sudden ; and, giving them battle, gained at first an advantage, but by his pursuing the victory too far, the superiority of the enemy's numbers prevailed and recovered them the day. Their loss, however, in the action, was so considerable that, fearing Alfred would receive daily reinforcement from his subjects, they were content to stipulate for a safe retreat, and promised to depart the kingdom. For that purpose they were conducted to London, and allowed to take up winter-quarters there; but, careless of their engagements, they immediately set themselves to the committing of spoil on the neighboring country. Burrhed, king of Mercia, in

[25] Asserius, p. 2. Will. Malm. lib. 2, cap. 2. Ingulph. p. 869. Simeon Dunelm. p. 120, 139.   [26] Asserius, p. 5. Matt. West. p. 167.
[27] Asserius, p. 7.   [28] Asserius, p. 22. Simeon Dunelm. p. 121.

whose territories London was situated, made a new stipulation with them, and engaged them, by presents of money, to remove to Lindesey, in Lincolnshire, a country which they had already reduced to ruin and desolation. Finding therefore no object in that place either for their rapine or violence, they suddenly turned back upon Mercia, in a quarter where they expected to find it without defence; and fixing their station at Repton, in Derbyshire, they laid the whole country desolate with fire and sword. Burrhed, despairing of success against an enemy whom no force could resist and no treaties bind, abandoned his kingdom, and, flying to Rome, took shelter in a cloister.[29] He was brother-in-law to Alfred, and the last who bore the title of king in Mercia.

The West Saxons were now the only remaining power in England; and, though supported by the vigor and abilities of Alfred, they were unable to sustain the efforts of those ravagers who from all quarters invaded them. [875.] A new swarm of Danes came over this year under three princes, Guthrum, Oscitel, and Amund; and, having first joined their countrymen at Repton, they soon found the necessity of separating, in order to provide for their subsistence. Part of them, under the command of Haldene, their chieftain,[30] marched into Northumberland, where they fixed their quarters; part of them took quarters at Cambridge, whence they dislodged in the ensuing summer, and seized Wereham, in the county of Dorset, the very centre of Alfred's dominions. That prince so straitened them in these quarters that they were content to come to a treaty with him, and stipulated to depart his country. Alfred, well acquainted with their usual perfidy, obliged them to swear upon the holy relics to the observance of the treaty; [31] not that he expected they would pay any veneration to the relics; but he hoped that, if they now violated this oath, their impiety would infallibly draw down upon them the vengeance of Heaven. But the Danes, little apprehensive of the danger, suddenly, without seeking any pretence, fell upon Alfred's army; and having put it to rout, marched westward, and took possession of Exeter. The prince collected new forces, and exerted such vigor that he fought in one year eight battles with the enemy,[32] and reduced them to the utmost extremity. He hearkened, however, to new pro-

[29] Asserius, p. 8. Chron. Sax. p. 82. Ethelward, lib. 4. cap. 4.
[30] Chron. Sax. p. 83.
[31] Asserius, p. 8.   [32] Ibid. The Saxon Chronicle, p. 82, says nine battles.

posals of peace, and was satisfied to stipulate with them that they would settle somewhere in England,[33] and would not permit the entrance of more ravagers into the kingdom. But while he was expecting the execution of this treaty, which it seemed the interest of the Danes themselves to fulfil, he heard that another body had landed, and, having collected all the scattered troops of their countrymen, had surprised Chippenham, then a considerable town, and were exercising their usual ravages all around them.

The last incident quite broke the spirit of the Saxons, and reduced them to despair. Finding that, after all the miserable havoc which they had undergone in their persons and in their property, after all the vigorous actions which they had exerted in their own defence, a new band, equally greedy of spoil and slaughter, had disembarked among them, they believed themselves abandoned by Heaven to destruction, and delivered over to those swarms of robbers which the fertile north thus incessantly poured forth against them. Some left their country and retired into Wales, or fled beyond sea; others submitted to the conquerors, in hopes of appeasing their fury by a servile obedience.[34] And every man's attention being now engrossed in concern for his own preservation, no one would hearken to the exhortations of the king, who summoned them to make, under his conduct, one effort more in defence of their prince, their country, and their liberties. Alfred himself was obliged to relinquish the ensigns of his dignity, to dismiss his servants, and to seek shelter in the meanest disguises from the pursuit and fury of his enemies. He concealed himself under a peasant's habit, and lived some time in the house of a neat-herd who had been intrusted with the care of some of his cows.[35] There passed here an incident which has been recorded by all the historians, and was long preserved by popular tradition, though it contains nothing memorable in itself, except so far as every circumstance is interesting which attends so much virtue and dignity reduced to such distress. The wife of the neat-heard was ignorant of the condition of her royal guest; and observing him one day busy by the fireside in trimming his bows and arrows, she desired him to take care of some cakes which were toasting, while she was employed elsewhere in some other domestic affairs. But Alfred, whose thoughts were otherwise engaged, neglected this

[33] Asserius, p. 9. Alur. Beverl. p. 104.
[34] Chron. Sax. p. 84. Alur. Beverl. p. 105.
[35] Asserius, p. 9.

injunction; and the good woman, on her return, finding her cakes all burned, rated the king very severely, and upbraided him that he always seemed very well pleased to eat her warm cakes, though he was thus negligent in toasting them.[36]

By degrees, Alfred, as he found the search of the enemy become more remiss, collected some of his retainers, and retired into the centre of a bog, formed by the stagnating waters of the Thone and Parret, in Somersetshire. He here found two acres of firm ground; and, building a habitation on them, rendered himself secure by its fortifications, and still more by the unknown and inaccessible roads which led to it, and by the forests and morasses with which it was every way environed. This place he called Æthelingay, or the Isle of Nobles;[37] and it now bears the name of Athelney. He thence made frequent and unexpected sallies upon the Danes, who often felt the vigor of his arm, but knew not from what quarter the blow came. He subsisted himself and his followers by the plunder which he acquired; he procured them consolation by revenge; and from small successes he opened their minds to hope that, notwithstanding his present low condition, more important victories might at length attend his valor.

Alfred lay here concealed, but not inactive, during a twelvemonth, when the news of a prosperous event reached his ears, and called him to the field. Hubba, the Dane, having spread devastation, fire, and slaughter over Wales, had landed in Devonshire from twenty-three vessels, and laid siege to the castle of Kenwith, a place situated near the mouth of the small river Tau. Oddune, Earl of Devonshire, with his followers, had taken shelter there; and, being ill supplied with provisions, and even with water, he determined, by some vigorous blow, to prevent the necessity of submitting to the barbarous enemy. He made a sudden sally on the Danes before sunrising; and, taking them unprepared, he put them to rout, pursued them with great slaughter, killed Hubba himself, and got possession of the famous *Reafen*, or enchanted standard, in which the Danes put great confidence.[38] It contained the figure of a raven, which had been inwoven by the three sisters of Hinguar and Hubba, with many magical incantations, and which, by its

[36] Asserius. Matt. West. p. 170.

[37] Chron. Sax. p. 85. Will. Malm. lib. 2, cap. 4. Ethelward, lib. 4, cap. 4. Ingulph. p. 26.

[38] Asserius, p. 10. Chron. Sax. p. 84. Abbas Rieval. p. 395. Alur. Beverl p. 105.

different movements, prognosticated, as the Danes believed, the good or bad success of any enterprise.[39]

When Alfred observed this symptom of successful resistance in his subjects, he left his retreat; but before he would assemble them in arms, or urge them to any attempt, which, if unfortunate, might, in their present despondency, prove fatal, he resolved to inspect himself the situation of the enemy, and to judge of the probability of success. For this purpose he entered their camp under the disguise of a harper, and passed unsuspected through every quarter. He so entertained them with his music and facetious humors that he met with a welcome reception; and was even introduced to the tent of Guthrum, their prince, where he remained some days.[40] He remarked the supine security of the Danes, their contempt of the English, their negligence in foraging and plundering, and their dissolute wasting of what they gained by rapine and violence. Encouraged by these favorable appearances, he secretly sent emissaries to the most considerable of his subjects, and summoned them to a rendezvous, attended by their warlike followers, at Brixton, on the borders of Selwood forest.[41] The English, who had hoped to put an end to their calamities by servile submission, now found the insolence and rapine of the conqueror more intolerable than all past fatigues and dangers; and, at the appointed day, they joyfully resorted to their prince. On his appearance, they received him with shouts of applause;[42] and could not satiate their eyes with the sight of this beloved monarch, whom they had long regarded as dead, and who now, with voice and looks expressing his confidence of success, called them to liberty and to vengeance. He instantly conducted them to Eddington, where the Danes were encamped; and, taking advantage of his previous knowledge of the place, he directed his attack against the most unguarded quarter of the enemy. The Danes, surprised to see an army of English, whom they considered as totally subdued, and still more astonished to hear that Alfred was at their head, made but a faint resistance, notwithstanding their superiority of number, and were soon put to flight with great slaughter. The remainder of the routed army, with their prince, was besieged by Alfred in a fortified camp to which they had fled; but being reduced to extremity by

[39] Asserius, p. 10.   [40] Will. Malm. lib. 2, cap. 4.   [41] Chron. Sax. p. 85.
[42] Asserius, p. 10. Chron. Sax. p. 85. Simeon Dunelm. p. 128. Alur. Beverl.
p. 105. Abbas Rieval. p. 354.

want and hunger, they had recourse to the clemency of the victor, and offered to submit on any conditions. The king, no less generous than brave, gave them their lives; and even formed a scheme for converting them from mortal enemies into faithful subjects and confederates. He knew that the kingdoms of East Anglia and Northumberland were totally desolated by the frequent inroads of the Danes, and he now proposed to repeople them by settling there Guthrum and his followers. He hoped that the new planters would at last betake themselves to industry, when, by reason of his resistance and the exhausted condition of the country, they could no longer subsist by plunder; and that they might serve him as a rampart against any future incursions of their countrymen. But before he ratified these mild conditions with the Danes, he required that they should give him one pledge of their submission, and of their inclination to incorporate with the English, by declaring their conversion to Christianity.[43] Guthrum and his army had no aversion to the proposal; and, without much instruction, or argument, or conference, they were all admitted to baptism. The king answered for Guthrum at the font, gave him the name of Athelstan, and received him as his adopted son.[44]

The success of this expedient seemed to correspond to Alfred's hopes. [880.] The greater part of the Danes settled peacefully in their new quarters: some smaller bodies of the same nation, which were dispersed in Mercia, were distributed into the five cities of Derby, Leicester, Stamford, Lincoln, and Nottingham, and were thence called the Fif or Five-burghers. The more turbulent and unquiet made an expedition into France, under the command of Hastings;[45] and except by a short incursion of Danes, who sailed up the Thames and landed at Fulham, but suddenly retreated to their ships on finding the country in a posture of defence, Alfred was not for some years infested by the inroads of those barbarians.[46]

The king employed this interval of tranquillity in restoring order to the state, which had been shaken by so many violent convulsions; in establishing civil and military institutions; in composing the minds of men to industry and justice; and in providing against the return of like calamities. He was, more properly than his grandfather, Egbert,

[43] Chron. Sax. p. 85. [44] Asserius, p. 10. Chron. Sax. p. 90.
[45] Will. Malm. lib. 2, cap. 4. Ingulph. p. 26. [46] Asserius, p. 11.

the sole monarch of the English (for so the Saxons were now universally called), because the kingdom of Mercia was at last incorporated in his state, and was governed by Ethelbert, his brother-in-law, who bore the title of Earl; and though the Danes who peopled East Anglia and Northumberland were for some time ruled immediately by their own princes, they all acknowledged a subordination to Alfred, and submitted to his superior authority. As equality among subjects is the great source of concord, Alfred gave the same laws to the Danes and English, and put them entirely on a like footing in the administration both of civil and criminal justice. The fine for the murder of a Dane was the same with that for the murder of an Englishman— the great symbol of equality in those ages.

The king, after rebuilding the ruined cities, particularly London, [47] which had been destroyed by the Danes in the reign of Ethelwolf, established a regular militia for the defence of the kingdom. He ordained that all his people should be armed and registered; he assigned them a regular rotation of duty; he distributed part into the castles and fortresses which he built at proper places; [48] he required another part to take the field on any alarm, and to assemble at stated places of rendezvous; and he left a sufficient number at home, who were employed in the cultivation of the land, and who afterwards took their turn in military service.[49] The whole kingdom was like one great garrison; and the Danes could no sooner appear in one place than a sufficient number was assembled to oppose them, without leaving the other quarters defenceless or disarmed.[50]

But Alfred, sensible that the proper method of opposing an enemy who made incursions by sea was to meet them on their own element, took care to provide himself with a naval force,[51] which, though the most natural defence of an island, had hitherto been totally neglected by the English. He increased the shipping of his kingdom both in number and strength, and trained his subjects in the practice as well of sailing as of naval action. He distributed his armed vessels in proper stations around the island, and was sure to meet the Danish ships either before or after they had landed their troops, and to pursue them in all their incursions. Though

---

[47] Asserius, p. 15.   Chron. Sax. p. 88.   Matt. West. p. 171.   Simeon Dunelm. p. 131.   Brompton, p. 812.   Alur. Beverl. ex edit. Hearne, p. 106.
[48] Asserius, p. 18.   Ingulph. p. 27.   [49] Chron. Sax. pp, 92, 93.
[50] Spellman's Life of Alfred, pp. 147, edit. 1709.
[51] Asserius, p. 9.   Matt. West. p. 179.

the Danes might suddenly, by surprise, disembark on the coast, which was generally become desolate by their frequent ravages, they were encountered by the English fleet in their retreat; and escaped not, as formerly, by abandoning their booty, but paid, by their total destruction, the penalty of the disorders which they had committed.

In this manner Alfred repelled several inroads of these piratical Danes, and maintained his kingdom, during some years, in safety and tranquillity. A fleet of 120 ships of war was stationed upon the coast; and, being provided with warlike engines as well as with expert seamen, both Frisians and English (for Alfred supplied the defects of his own subjects by engaging able foreigners in his service), maintained a superiority over those smaller bands with which England had so often been infested.[52] [893.] But at last, Hastings, the famous Danish chief, having ravaged all the provinces of France, both along the sea-coast and the Loire and Seine, and being obliged to quit that country, more by the desolation which he himself had occasioned than by the resistance of the inhabitants, appeared off the coast of Kent with a fleet of 330 sail. The greater part of the enemy disembarked in the Rother, and seized the fort of Apuldore. Hastings himself, commanding a fleet of 80 sail, entered the Thames, and, fortifying Milton, in Kent, began to spread his forces over the country, and to commit the most destructive ravages. But Alfred, on the first alarm of this descent, flew to the defence of his people, at the head of a select band of soldiers, whom he always kept about his person;[53] and, gathering to him the armed militia from all quarters, appeared in the field with a force superior to the enemy. All straggling parties, whom necessity or love of plunder had drawn to a distance from their chief encampment, were cut off by the English;[54] and these pirates, instead of increasing their spoil, found themselves cooped up in their fortifications, and obliged to subsist by the plunder which they had brought from France. Tired of this situation, which must in the end prove ruinous to them, the Danes at Apuldore rose suddenly from their encampment, with an intention of marching towards the Thames and passing over into Essex; but they escaped not the vigilance of Alfred, who encountered them at Farnham,

[52] Asserius, p. 11.   Chron. Sax. pp. 86, 87.   Matt. West. pp. 176.
[53] Asserius, p. 19.   [54] Chron. Sax. p. 92.

put them to rout,[55] seized all their horses and baggage, and chased the runaways on board their ships, which carried them up the Colne to Mersey, in Essex, where they intrenched themselves. Hastings, at the same time, and probably by concert, made a like movement; and, deserting Milton, took possession of Bamflete, near the Isle of Canvey, in the same county,[56] where he hastily threw up fortifications for his defence against the power of Alfred.

Unfortunately for the English, Guthrum, prince of the East-Anglian Danes, was now dead, as was also Guthred, whom the king had appointed governor of the Northumbrians; and those restless tribes, being no longer restrained by the authority of their princes, and being encouraged by the appearance of so great a body of their countrymen, broke into rebellion, shook off the authority of Alfred, and, yielding to their inveterate habits of war and depredation,[57] embarked on board 240 vessels, and appeared before Exeter, in the west of England. Alfred lost not a moment in opposing this new enemy. Having left some forces at London to make head against Hastings and the other Danes, he marched suddenly to the west,[58] and, falling on the rebels before they were aware, pursued them to their ships with great slaughter. These ravagers, sailing next to Sussex, began to plunder the country near Chichester; but the order which Alfred had everywhere established sufficed here, without his presence, for the defence of the place; and the rebels, meeting with a new repulse, in which many of them were killed and some of their ships taken,[59] were obliged to put again to sea, and were discouraged from attempting any other enterprise.

Meanwhile, the Danish invaders in Essex, having united their force under the command of Hastings, advanced into the inland country, and made spoil of all around them; but soon had reason to repent of their temerity. The English army left in London, assisted by a body of the citizens, attacked the enemy's intrenchments at Bamflete, overpowered the garrison, and, having done great execution upon them, carried off the wife and two sons of Hastings.[60] Alfred generously spared these captives, and even restored them to Hastings,[61] on condition that he should depart the kingdom.

But though the king had thus honorably rid himself of this dangerous enemy, he had not entirely subdued or ex-

[55] Chron. Sax. p. 93.　Flor. Wigorn. p. 595.　　　　[56] Chron. Sax. p. 93.
[57] Chron. Sax. p. 92.
[58] Chron. Sax. p. 93.　　　　[59] Chron. Sax. p. 96.　Flor. Wigorn. p. 596.
[60] Chron. Sax. p. 94.　Matt. West. p. 178.　　　　[61] Matt. West. p. 179.

pelled the invaders. The piratical Danes willingly followed in an excursion any prosperous leader who gave them hopes of booty; but were not so easily induced to relinquish their enterprise, or submit to return, baffled and without plunder, into their native country. Great numbers of them, after the departure of Hastings, seized and fortified Shobury, at the mouth of the Thames; and, having left a garrison there, they marched along the river till they came to Boddington, in the county of Gloucester, where, being reinforced by some Welsh, they threw up intrenchments and prepared for their defence. The king here surrounded them with the whole force of his dominions; [62] and, as he had now a certain prospect of victory, he resolved to trust nothing to chance, but rather to master his enemies by famine than assault. They were reduced to such extremities that, having eaten their own horses, and having many of them perished with hunger,[63] they made a desperate sally upon the English; and, though the greater number fell in the action, a considerable body made their escape.[64] These roved about for some time in England, still pursued by the vigilance of Alfred; they attacked Leicester with success, defended themselves in Hartford, and then fled to Quatford, where they were finally broken and subdued. The small remains of them either dispersed themselves among their countrymen in Northumberland and East Anglia,[65] or had recourse again to the sea, where they exercised piracy, under the command of Sigefert, a Northumbrian. This freebooter, well acquainted with Alfred's naval preparations, had framed vessels of a new construction, higher and longer and swifter than those of the English; but the king soon discovered his superior skill by building vessels still higher and longer and swifter than those of the Northumbrians; and, falling upon them while they were exercising their ravages in the west, he took twenty of their ships, and, having tried all the prisoners at Winchester, he hanged them as pirates, the common enemies of mankind.

The well-timed severity of this execution, together with the excellent posture of defence established everywhere, restored full tranquillity to England, and provided for the future security of the government. The East-Anglian and Northumbrian Danes, on the first appearance of Alfred upon

[62] Chron. Sax. p. 94.
[63] Chron. Sax. p. 94.   Matt. West. p. 179.   Flor. Wigorn. p. 596.
[64] Chron. Sax. p. 95.   [65] Chron. Sax. p. 97.

their frontiers, made anew the most humble submissions to him; and he thought it prudent to take them under his immediate government, without establishing over them a viceroy of their own nation.[66]　The Welsh also acknowledged his authority; and this great prince had now, by prudence and justice and valor, established his sovereignty over all the southern parts of the island, from the English Channel to the frontiers of Scotland, when he died, in the vigor of his age and the full strength of his faculties, after a glorious reign of twenty-nine years and a half,[67] [901] in which he deservedly attained the appellation of Alfred the Great, and the title of Founder of the English Monarchy.

The merit of this prince, both in private and public life, may with advantage be set in opposition to that of any monarch or citizen which the annals of any age or any nation can present to us. He seems, indeed, to be the model of that perfect character which, under the denomination of a sage or wise man, philosophers have been fond of delineating, rather as a fiction of their imagination than in hopes of ever seeing it really existing: so happily were all his virtues tempered together, so justly were they blended, and so powerfully did each prevent the other from exceeding its proper boundaries. He knew how to reconcile the most enterprising spirit with the coolest moderation; the most obstinate perseverance with the easiest flexibility; the most severe justice with the gentlest lenity; the greatest vigor in commanding with the most perfect affability of deportment;[68] the highest capacity and inclination for science with the most shining talents for action. His civil and his military virtues are almost equally the objects of our admiration, excepting only that the former, being more rare among princes, as well as more useful, seem chiefly to challenge our applause. Nature, also, as if desirous that so bright a production of her skill should be set in the fairest light, had bestowed on him every bodily accomplishment— vigor of limbs, dignity of shape and air, with a pleasing, engaging, and open countenance.[69] Fortune alone, by throwing him into that barbarous age, deprived him of historians worthy to transmit his fame to posterity; and we wish to see him delineated in more lively colors and with more particular strokes, that we may at least perceive some of those

[66] Flor. Wigorn. p. 598.
[68] Asserius, p. 13.

[67] Asserius, p. 21.　Chron. Sax. p 99.
[69] Asserius, p. 5.

small specks and blemishes from which, as a man, it is impossible he could be entirely exempted.

But we should give but an imperfect idea of Alfred's merit were we to confine our narration to his military exploits, and were not more particular in our account of his institutions for the execution of justice, and of his zeal for the encouragement of arts and sciences.

After Alfred had subdued and had settled or expelled the Danes, he found the kingdom in the most wretched condition—desolated by the ravages of those barbarians, and thrown into disorders which were calculated to perpetuate its misery. Though the great armies of the Danes were broken, the country was full of straggling troops of that nation, who, being accustomed to live by plunder, were become incapable of industry, and who, from the natural ferocity of their manners, indulged themselves in committing violence, even beyond what was requisite to supply their necessities. The English themselves, reduced to the most extreme indigence by these continued depredations, had shaken off all bands of government; and those who had been plundered to-day betook themselves next day to a like disorderly life, and, from despair, joined the robbers in pillaging and ruining their fellow-citizens. These were the evils for which it was necessary that the vigilance and activity of Alfred should provide a remedy.

That he might render the execution of justice strict and regular, he divided all England into counties; these counties he subdivided into hundreds, and the hundreds into tithings. Every householder was answerable for the behavior of his family and slaves, and even of his guests if they lived above three days in his house. Ten neighboring householders were formed into one corporation, who, under the name of a tithing, decennary, or fribourg, were answerable for each other's conduct, and over whom one person, called a tithingman, headbourg, or borsholder, was appointed to preside. Every man was punished as an outlaw who did not register himself in some tithing. And no man could change his habitation without a warrant or certificate from the borsholder of the tithing to which he formerly belonged.

When any person in any tithing or decennary was guilty of a crime, the borsholder was summoned to answer for him; and if he were not willing to be surety for his appearance, and his clearing himself, the criminal was committed to prison, and there detained till his trial. If he fled, either before or after finding sureties, the borsholder and decennary became liable to inquiry, and were exposed to the penalties of law. Thirty-one days were allowed them for producing the criminal ; and if that time elapsed without their being able to find him, the borsholder, with two other members of the decennary, was obliged to appear, and, together with three chief members of the three neighboring decennaries (making twelve in all), to swear that his decennary was free from all privity both of the crime committed and of the escape of the criminal. If the borsholder could not find such a number to answer for their innocence, the decennary was compelled by fine to make satisfaction to the king, according to the degree of the offence.[70] By this institution, every man was obliged, from his own interest, to keep a watchful eye over the conduct of his neighbors, and was in a manner surety for the behavior of those who were placed under the division to which he belonged : whence these decennaries received the name of frank-pledges.

Such a regular distribution of the people, with such a strict confinement in their habitation, may not be necessary in times when men are more inured to obedience and justice, and it might perhaps be regarded as destructive of liberty and commerce in a polished state ; but it was well calculated to reduce that fierce and licentious people under the salutary restraint of law and government. But Alfred took care to temper these rigors by other institutions favorable to the freedom of the citizens ; and nothing could be more popular and liberal than his plan for the administration of justice. The borsholder summoned together his whole decennary to assist him in deciding any lesser difference which occurred among the members of this small community. In affairs of greater moment, in appeals from the decennary, or in controversies arising between members of different decennaries, the cause was brought before the hundred, which consisted of ten decennaries, or a hundred families of freemen, and which was regularly assembled once in four weeks for the deciding of causes.[71] Their method of decision deserves to be noted, as being the origin of juries—an institution admirable in itself, and the best calculated for the preservation of liberty and the administration of justice that ever was devised by the wit of man. Twelve freeholders were chosen, who, having sworn, together with the hundreder, or presiding magistrate of that

[70] Leges St. Edw. cap. 20, apud Wilkins, p. 202.
[71] Leges St. Edw. cap. 2.

division, to administer impartial justice,[72] proceeded to the examination of that cause which was submitted to their jurisdiction. And besides these monthly meetings of the hundred, there was an annual meeting, appointed for a more general inspection of the police of the district—for the inquiry into crimes, the correction of abuses in magistrates, and the obliging of every person to show the decennary in which he was registered. The people, in imitation of their ancestors, the ancient Germans, assembled there in arms; whence a hundred was sometimes called a wapentake, and its court served both for the support of military discipline and for the administration of civil justice.[73]

The next superior court to that of the hundred was the county court, which met twice a year, after Michaelmas and Easter, and consisted of the freeholders of the county, who possessed an equal vote in the decision of causes. The bishop presided in this court, together with the alderman; and the proper object of the court was the receiving of appeals from the hundreds and decennaries, and the deciding of such controversies as arose between men of different hundreds. Formerly, the alderman possessed both the civil and military authority; but Alfred, sensible that this conjunction of powers rendered the nobility dangerous and independent, appointed also a sheriff in each county, who enjoyed a co-ordinate authority with the former in the judicial function.[74] His office also empowered him to guard the rights of the crown in the county, and to levy the fines imposed, which in that age formed no contemptible part of the public revenue.

There lay an appeal, in default of justice, from all these courts to the king himself in council; and as the people, sensible of the equity and great talents of Alfred, placed their chief confidence in him, he was soon overwhelmed with appeals from all parts of England. He was indefatigable in the despatch of these causes;[75] but finding that his time must be entirely engrossed by this branch of duty, he resolved to obviate the inconvenience by correcting the ignorance or corruption of the inferior magistrates from which it arose.[76] He took care to have his nobility instructed in letters and the laws.[77] He chose the earls and sheriffs from

---

[72] Fœdus Alfred. and Gothurn apud Wilkins, cap. 3, p. 47 Leges Ethelstani, cap. 2, apud Wilkins, p. 58. Leges Ethelr. § 4. Wilkins, p. 117.
[73] Spellman, in voce Wapentake. [74] Ingulph. p. 870. [75] Asserius, p. 20.
[76] Asserius, pp. 18, 21. Flor. Wigorn. p. 594. Abbas Rieval. p. 355.
[77] Flor. Wigorn. p. 594. Brompton, p. 814.

among the men most celebrated for probity and knowledge; he punished severely all malversation in office; [78] and he removed all the earls whom he found unequal to the trust, [79] allowing only some of the more elderly to serve by a deputy, till their death should make room for more worthy successors.

The better to guide the magistrates in the administration of justice, Alfred framed a body of laws, which, though now lost, served long as the basis of English jurisprudence, and is generally deemed the origin of what is denominated the COMMON LAW. He appointed regular meetings of the states of England twice a year in London, [80] a city which he himself had repaired and beautified, and which he thus rendered the capital of the kingdom. The similarity of these institutions to the customs of the ancient Germans, to the practice of the other northern conquerors, and to the Saxon laws during the Heptarchy prevents us from regarding Alfred as the sole author of this plan of government, and leads us rather to think that, like a wise man, he contented himself with reforming, extending, and executing the institutions which he found previously established. But, on the whole, such success attended his legislation that everything bore suddenly a new face in England. Robberies and iniquities of all kinds were repressed by the punishment or reformation of the criminals; [81] and so exact was the general police that Alfred, it is said, hung up, by way of bravado, golden bracelets near the highways, and no man dared to touch them. [82] Yet, amid these rigors of justice, this great prince preserved the most sacred regard to the liberty of his people; and it is a memorable sentiment preserved in his will, that it was just the English should forever remain as free as their own thoughts [83]

As good morals and knowledge are almost inseparable in every age, though not in every individual, the care of Alfred for the encouragement of learning among his subjects was another useful branch of his legislation, and tended to reclaim the English from their former dissolute and ferocious manners. But the king was guided in this pursuit less by political views than by his natural bent and propensity towards letters. When he came to the throne, he found the nation sunk into the grossest ignorance and

[78] Le Miroir de Justice, ch. 2.   [79] Asserius, p. 20.
[80] Le Miroir de Justice.   [81] Ingulph. p. 27.
[82] Will. Malm. lib. 2, cap. 4.   [83] Asserius, p. 24.

barbarism, proceeding from the continued disorders in the government and from the ravages of the Danes. The monasteries were destroyed, the monks butchered or dispersed, their libraries burned; and thus the only seats of erudition in those ages were totally subverted. Alfred himself complains that on his accession he knew not one person south of the Thames who could so much as interpret the Latin service, and very few in the northern parts who had reached even that pitch of erudition. But this prince invited over the most celebrated scholars from all parts of Europe; he established schools everywhere for the instruction of his people; he founded, at least repaired, the University of Oxford, and endowed it with many privileges, revenues, and immunities; he enjoined by law all freeholders possessed of two hides [84] of land or more to send their children to school for their instruction; he gave preferment both in Church and State to such only as had made some proficiency in knowledge. And by all these expedients he had the satisfaction, before his death, to see a great change in the face of affairs; and in a work of his, which is still extant, he congratulates himself on the progress which learning, under his patronage, had already made in England.

But the most effectual expedient employed by Alfred for the encouragement of learning was his own example, and the constant assiduity with which, notwithstanding the multiplicity and urgency of his affairs, he employed himself in the pursuits of knowledge. He usually divided his time into three equal portions: one was employed in sleep and the refection of his body by diet and exercise; another in the despatch of business; a third in study and devotion, and that he might more exactly measure the hours, he made use of burning tapers of equal length, which he fixed in lanterns [85]—an expedient suited to that rude age, when the geometry of dialling and the mechanism of clocks and watches were totally unknown. And by such a regular distribution of his time, though he often labored under great bodily infirmities, [86] this martial hero, who fought in person fifty-six battles by sea and land, [87] was able, during a life of no extraordinary length, to acquire more knowledge, and

---

[84] A hide contained land sufficient to employ one plough. See H. Hunting. lib. 6, in A. D. 1008. Annal. Waverl. in A. D. 1083. Gervase of Tilbury says it commonly contained about 100 acres.

[85] Asserius, p. 20. Will. Malm. lib. 2, cap. 4. Ingulph. p. 870.

[86] Asserius, pp. 4, 12, 13, 17.   [87] Will. Malm. lib. 4, cap. 4.

even to compose more books, than most studious men, though blessed with the greatest leisure and application, have, in more fortunate ages, made the object of their uninterrupted industry.

Sensible that the people at all times, especially when their understandings are obstructed by ignorance and bad education, are not much susceptible of speculative instruction, Alfred endeavored to convey his morality by apologues, parables, stories, apophthegms, couched in poetry; and besides propagating among his subjects former compositions of that kind which he found in the Saxon tongue,[88] he exercised his genius in inventing works of a like nature,[89] as well as in translating from the Greek the elegant fables of Æsop. He also gave Saxon translations of Orosius's and Bede's histories, and of Boëthius concerning the consolation of philosophy.[90] And he deemed it nowise derogatory from his other great characters of sovereign, legislator, warrior, and politician thus to lead the way to his people in the pursuits of literature.

Meanwhile this prince was not negligent in encouraging the vulgar and mechanical arts, which have a more sensible, though not a closer, connection with the interests of society. He invited, from all quarters, industrious foreigners to repeople his country, which had been desolated by the ravages of the Danes.[91] He introduced and encouraged manufactures of all kinds; and no inventor or improver of any ingenious art did he suffer to go unrewarded.[92] He prompted men of activity to betake themselves to navigation, to push commerce into the most remote countries, and to acquire riches by propagating industry among their fellow-citizens. He set apart a seventh portion of his own revenue for maintaining a number of workmen, whom he constantly employed in rebuilding the ruined cities, castles, palaces, and monasteries.[93] Even the elegancies of life were brought to him from the Mediterranean and the Indies;[94] and his subjects, by seeing those productions of the peaceful arts, were taught to respect the virtues of justice and industry, from which alone they could arise. Both living and dead, Alfred was regarded by foreigners, no less than by his own subjects, as the greatest prince after Charlemagne that had appeared

---

[88] Asserius, p. 13.   [89] Spellman, p. 124.   Abbas Rieval. p. 355.
[90] Will. Malm. lib. 2, cap. 4.   Brompton, p 814.
[91] Asserius, p. 13.   Flor Wigorn. p. 5·8.   [92] Asserius, p. 20.
[93] Asserius, p. 20.   Will. Malm. lib. 2, cap. 4.   [94] Will. Malm. lib. 2, cap. 4

in Europe during several ages, and as one of the wisest and best that had ever adorned the annals of any nation.

Alfred had, by his wife, Ethelswitha, daughter of a Mercian earl, three sons and three daughters. The eldest son, Edmund, died without issue, in his father's lifetime. The third, Ethelward, inherited his father's passion for letters, and lived a private life. The second, Edward, succeeded to his power, and passes by the appellation of Edward the Elder, being the first of that name who sat on the English throne.

This prince, who equalled his father in military talents, though inferior to him in knowledge and erudition,[95] found, immediately on his accession, [901.] a specimen of that turbulent life to which all princes, and even all individuals, were exposed in an age when men, less restrained by law or justice, and less occupied by industry, had no aliment for their inquietude but wars, insurrections, convulsions, rapine, and depredation. Ethelwald, his cousin-german, son of King Ethelbert, the elder brother of Alfred, insisted on his preferable title;[96] and, arming his partisans, took possession of Winburne, where he seemed determined to defend himself to the last extremity, and to await the issue of his pretensions.[97] But when the king approached the town with a great army, Ethelwald, having the prospect of certain destruction, made his escape, and fled first into Normandy, thence into Northumberland, where he hoped that the people, who had been recently subdued by Alfred, and who were impatient of peace, would, on the intelligence of that great prince's death, seize the first pretence or opportunity of rebellion. The event did not disappoint his expectations. The Northumbrians declared for him;[98] and Ethelwald, having thus connected his interests with the Danish tribes, went beyond sea, and collecting a body of these freebooters, he excited the hopes of all those who had been accustomed to subsist by rapine and violence.[99] The East-Anglian Danes joined his party. The Five-burghers, who were seated in the heart of Mercia, began to put themselves in motion; and the English found that they were again menaced with those convulsions from which the valor and policy of Alfred had so lately rescued them. The rebels, headed by Ethel-

[95] Will. Malm. lib. 2, cap. 5.   Hoveden, p. 421.   [96] Chron. Sax. pp. 99, 100.
[97] Chron. Sax. p. 100.   H. Hunting. lib. 5, p. 352.
[98] Chron. Sax. p. 100.   H. Hunting. lib. 5, p. 352.
[99] Chron. Sax. p. 100.   Chron. Abb. St. Petri de Burgo, p. 24.

wald, made an incursion into the counties of Gloucester, Oxford, and Wilts; and having exercised their ravages in these places, they retired with their booty, before the king, who had assembled an army, was able to approach them. Edward, however, who was determined that his preparations should not be fruitless, conducted his forces into East Anglia, and retaliated the injuries which the inhabitants had committed by spreading the like devastation among them. Satiated with revenge, and loaded with booty, he gave orders to retire. But the authority of those ancient kings, which was feeble in peace, was not much better established in the field; and the Kentish men, greedy of more spoil, ventured, contrary to repeated orders, to stay behind him, and to take up their quarters in Bury. This disobedience proved in the issue fortunate to Edward. The Danes assaulted the Kentish men; but met with so vigorous a resistance that, though they gained the field of battle, they bought that advantage by the loss of their bravest leaders, and, among the rest, by that of Ethelwald, who perished in the action.[100] The king, freed from the fear of so dangerous a competitor, made peace on advantageous terms with the East Angles.[101]

In order to restore England to such a state of tranquillity as it was then capable of attaining, naught was wanting but the subjection of the Northumbrians, who, assisted by the scattered Danes in Mercia, continually infested the bowels of the kingdom. Edward, in order to divert the force of these enemies, prepared a fleet to attack them by sea; hoping that, when his ships appeared on their coast, they must at least remain at home and provide for their defence. But the Northumbrians were less anxious to secure their own property than greedy to commit spoil on their enemy; and, concluding that the chief strength of the English was embarked on board the fleet, they thought the opportunity favorable, and entered Edward's territories with all their forces. The king, who was prepared against this event, attacked them on their return at Tetenhall, in the county of Stafford, put them to rout, recovered all the booty, and pursued them with great slaughter into their own country.

All the rest of Edward's reign was a scene of continued and successful action against the Northumbrians, the East Angles, the Five-burghers, and the foreign Danes, who invaded him from Normandy and Brittany. Nor was he

100 Chron. Sax. p. 101. Brompton, p. 832.
101 Chron. Sax. p. 102 Brompton, p. 832. Matt. West. p. 181.

less provident in putting his kingdom in a posture of defence than vigorous in assaulting the enemy. He fortified the towns of Chester, Eddesbury, Warwick, Cherbury, Buckingham, Towcester, Maldon, Huntingdon, and Colchester. He fought two signal battles at Temsford and Maldon.[102] He vanquished Thurketill, a great Danish chief, and obliged him to retire with his followers into France, in quest of spoil and adventures. He subdued the East Angles, and forced them to swear allegiance to him; he expelled the two rival princes of Northumberland, Reginald and Sidroc, and acquired, for the present, the dominion of that province. Several tribes of the Britons were subjected by him; and even the Scots, who, during the reign of Egbert, had, under the conduct of Kenneth, their king, increased their power by the final subjection of the Picts, were nevertheless obliged to give him marks of submission.[103] In all these fortunate achievements he was assisted by the activity and prudence of his sister Ethelfleda, who was widow of Ethelbert, Earl of Mercia, and who, after her husband's death, retained the government of that province. This princess, who had been reduced to extremity in childbed, refused afterwards all commerce with her husband; not from any weak superstition, as was common in that age, but because she deemed all domestic occupations unworthy of her masculine and ambitious spirit.[104] She died before her brother; and Edward, during the remainder of his reign, took upon himself the immediate government of Mercia, which before had been intrusted to the authority of a governor.[105] The Saxon Chronicle fixes the death of this prince in 925: [106] his kingdom devolved to Athelstan, his natural son.

The stain in this prince's birth was not, in those times, deemed so considerable as to exclude him from the throne; [925.] and Athelstan, being of an age as well as of a capacity fitted for government, obtained the preference to Edward's younger children, who, though legitimate, were of too tender years to rule a nation so much exposed both to foreign invasion and to domestic convulsions. Some discontents, however, prevailed on his accession; and Alfred, a nobleman of considerable power, was thence encouraged to enter into a conspiracy against him. This incident is related by historians

[102] Chron. Sax. p. 108. Flor. Wigorn. p. 601.
[103] Chron. Sax. p. 110. Hoveden, p. 421.
[104] Will. Malm. lib. 2, cap. 5. Matt. West. p. 182. Ingulph. p. 28. Higden, p. 261.
[105] Chron. Sax. p. 110. Brompton, p. 831.   [106] Page 110.

with circumstances which the reader, according to the degree of credit he is disposed to give them, may impute either to the invention of monks who forged them, or to their artifice who found means of making them real. Alfred, it is said, being seized upon strong suspicions, but without any certain proof, firmly denied the conspiracy imputed to him; and, in order to justify himself, he offered to swear to his innocence before the pope, whose person, it was supposed, contained such superior sanctity that no one could presume to give a false oath in his presence and yet hope to escape the immediate vengeance of Heaven. The king accepted of the condition, and Alfred was conducted to Rome, where, either conscious of his innocence or neglecting the superstition to which he appealed, he ventured to make the oath required of him before John, who then filled the papal chair. But no sooner had he pronounced the fatal words than he fell into convulsions, of which, three days after, he expired. The king, as if the guilt of the conspirator were now fully ascertained, confiscated his estate, and made a present of it to the monastery of Malmesbury,[107] secure that no doubts would ever thenceforth be entertained concerning the justice of his proceedings.

The dominion of Athelstan was no sooner established over his English subjects than he endeavored to give security to the government by providing against the insurrections of the Danes, which had created so much disturbance to his predecessors. He marched into Northumberland; and, finding that the inhabitants bore with impatience the English yoke, he thought it prudent to confer on Sithric, a Danish nobleman, the title of king, and to attach him to his interests by giving him his sister, Editha, in marriage. But this policy proved by accident the source of dangerous consequences. Sithric died in a twelvemonth after; and his two sons by a former marriage, Anlaf and Godfrid, founding pretensions on their father's elevation, assumed the sovereignty without waiting for Athelstan's consent. They were soon expelled by the power of that monarch; and the former took shelter in Ireland, as the latter did in Scotland, where he received, during some time, protection from Constantine, who then enjoyed the crown of that kingdom. The Scottish prince, however, continually solicited, and even menaced, by Athelstan, at last promised to deliver up his guest; but, secretly detesting this treachery, he gave God-

107 Will. Malm. lib. 2, cap. 6.   Spell. Conc. p. 407.

frid warning to make his escape; [108] and that fugitive, after subsisting by piracy for some years, freed the king by his death from any further anxiety. Athelstan, resenting Constantine's behavior, entered Scotland with an army; and, ravaging the country with impunity,[109] he reduced the Scots to such distress that their king was content to preserve his crown by making submissions to the enemy. The English historians assert [110] that Constantine did homage to Athelstan for his kingdom; and they add that the latter prince, being urged by his courtiers to push the present favorable opportunity and entirely subdue Scotland, replied that it was more glorious to confer than conquer kingdoms.[111] But those annals, so uncertain and imperfect in themselves, lose all credit when national prepossessions and animosities have place; and on that account the Scotch historians, who, without having any more knowledge of the matter, strenuously deny the fact, seem more worthy of belief.

Constantine, whether he owed the retaining of his crown to the moderation of Athelstan, who was unwilling to employ all his advantages against him, or to the policy of that prince, who esteemed the humiliation of an enemy a greater acquisition than the subjection of a discontented and mutinous people, thought the behavior of the English monarch more an object of resentment than of gratitude. He entered into a confederacy with Anlaf, who had collected a great body of Danish pirates whom he found hovering in the Irish seas; and with some Welsh princes, who were terrified at the growing power of Athelstan; and all these allies made by concert an irruption with a great army into England. Athelstan, collecting his forces, met the enemy near Brunsbury, in Northumberland, and defeated them in a general engagement. This victory was chiefly ascribed to the valor of Turketul, the English chancellor; for in those turbulent ages no one was so much occupied in civil employments as wholly to lay aside the military character.[112]

There is a circumstance not unworthy of notice, which historians relate, with regard to the transactions of this war. Anlaf, on the approach of the English army, thought

[108] Will. Malm. lib. 2, cap. 6.
[109] Chron. Sax. p. 111. Hoveden, p. 422. H. Hunting. lib. 5, p. 354.
[110] Hoveden, p. 422.
[111] Will. Malm. lib. 2, cap. 6. Anglia Sacra, vol. i. p. 212.
[112] The office of chancellor among the Anglo-Saxons resembled more that of a secretary of state than that of our present chancellor. See Spellman, *in voce* Cancellarius.

that he could not venture too much to insure a fortunate event; and, employing the artifice formerly practised by Alfred against the Danes, he entered the enemy's camp in the habit of a minstrel. The stratagem was for the present attended with like success. He gave such satisfaction to the soldiers who flocked about him that they introduced him to the king's tent; and Anlaf, having played before that prince and his nobles during their repast, was dismissed with a handsome reward. His prudence kept him from refusing the present; but his pride determined him, on his departure, to bury it, while he fancied that he was unespied by all the world. But a soldier in Athelstan's camp, who had formerly served under Anlaf, had been struck with some suspicion on the first appearance of the minstrel, and was engaged by curiosity to observe all his motions. He regarded this last action as a full proof of Anlaf's disguise; and he immediately carried the intelligence to Athelstan, who blamed him for not sooner giving him information, that he might have seized his enemy. But the soldier told him that, as he had formerly sworn fealty to Anlaf, he could never have pardoned himself the treachery of betraying and ruining his ancient master; and that Athelstan himself, after such an instance of his criminal conduct, would have had equal reason to distrust his allegiance. Athelstan, having praised the generosity of the soldier's principles, reflected on the incident, which he foresaw might be attended with important consequences. He removed his station in the camp; and as a bishop arrived that evening with a reinforcement of troops (for the ecclesiastics were then no less warlike than the civil magistrates), he occupied with his train that very place which had been left vacant by the king's removal. The precaution of Athelstan was found prudent; for no sooner had darkness fallen than Anlaf broke into the camp, and, hastening directly to the place where he had left the king's tent, put the bishop to death before he had time to prepare for his defence.[113]

There fell several Danish and Welsh princes in the action of Brunsbury;[114] and Constantine and Anlaf made their escape with difficulty, leaving the greater part of their army on the field of battle. After this success, Athelstan enjoyed his crown in tranquillity; and he is regarded as one of the ablest and most active of those ancient princes. He passed

[113] Will. Malm. lib. 2, cap. 6. Higden, p. 263.
[114] Brompton, p. 839. Ingulph. p. 29.

a remarkable law, which was calculated for the encouragement of commerce, and which it required some liberality of
mind in that age to have devised—that a merchant who had
made three long sea-voyages on his own account should be
admitted to the rank of a Thane or Gentleman. This
prince died at Gloucester in the year 941,[115] after a reign of
sixteen years, and was succeeded by Edmund, his legitimate
brother.

Edmund, on his accession, met with disturbance from
the restless Northumbrians, who lay in wait for every opportunity of breaking into rebellion. [941.] But marching suddenly with his forces into their country, he so overawed the rebels that they endeavored to appease him by
the most humble submissions.[116] In order to give him the
surer pledge of their obedience, they offered to embrace
Christianity, a religion which the English Danes had frequently professed when reduced to difficulties, but which,
for that very reason, they regarded as a badge of servitude,
and shook off as soon as a favorable opportunity offered.
Edmund, trusting little to their sincerity in this forced submission, used the precaution of removing the Five-burghers
from the town of Mercia, in which they had been allowed
to settle; because it was always found that they took advantage of every commotion, and introduced the rebellious, or
foreign Danes, into the heart of the kingdom. He also conquered Cumberland from the Britons; and conferred that
territory on Malcolm, King of Scotland, on condition that
he should do him homage for it, and protect the north from
all further incursions of the Danes.

Edmund was young when he came to the crown; yet
was his reign short as his death was violent. One day as
he was solemnizing a festival in the county of Gloucester,
he remarked that Leolf, a notorious robber whom he had
sentenced to banishment, had yet the boldness to enter the
hall where he himself dined, and to sit at table with his attendants. Enraged at this insolence, he ordered him to
leave the room; but on his refusing to obey, the king, whose
temper, naturally choleric, was inflamed by this additional
insult, leaped on him himself, and seized him by the hair;
but the ruffian, pushed to extremity, drew his dagger, and
gave Edmund a wound of which he immediately expired.
This event happened in the year 946, and in the sixth year
of the king's reign. Edmund left male issue, but so young

[115] Chron. Sax. p. 114.   [116] Will. Malm. lib. 2, cap. 7.   Brompton, p. 857.

that they were incapable of governing the kingdom; and his brother, Edred, was promoted to the throne.

The reign of this prince, as those of his predecessors, was disturbed by the rebellions and incursions of the Northumbrian Danes, who, though frequently quelled, were never entirely subdued, nor had ever paid a sincere allegiance to the crown of England. [946.] The accession of a new king seemed to them a favorable opportunity for shaking off the yoke; but on Edred's appearance with an army they made him their wonted submissions; and the king having wasted the country with fire and sword as a punishment for their rebellion, obliged them to renew their oaths of allegiance; and he straight retired with his forces. The obedience of the Danes lasted no longer than the present terror. Provoked at the devastations of Edred, and even reduced by necessity to subsist on plunder, they broke into a new rebellion, and were again subdued; but the king, now instructed by experience, took greater precautions against their future revolt. He fixed English garrisons in their most considerable towns, and placed over them an English governor, who might watch all their motions, and suppress any insurrection on its first appearance. He obliged also Malcolm, King of Scotland, to renew his homage for the lands which he held in England.

Edred, though not unwarlike, nor unfit for active life, lay under the influence of the lowest superstition, and had blindly delivered over his conscience to the guidance of Dunstan, commonly called St. Dunstan, Abbot of Glastonbury, whom he advanced to the highest offices, and who covered, under the appearance of sanctity, the most violent and most insolent ambition. Taking advantage of the most implicit confidence reposed in him by the king, this churchman imported into England a new order of monks, who much changed the state of ecclesiastical affairs, and excited, on their first establishment, the most violent emotions.

From the introduction of Christianity among the Saxons, there had been monasteries in England; and these establishments had extremely multiplied by the donations of the princes and nobles, whose superstition, derived from their ignorance and precarious life, and increased by remorse for the crimes into which they were so frequently betrayed, knew no other expedient for appeasing the Deity than a profuse liberality towards the ecclesiastics. But the monks had hitherto been a species of secular priests, who

lived after the manner of the present canons or prebenda-
ries, and were both intermingled, in some degree, with the
world, and endeavored to render themselves useful to it.
They were employed in the education of youth; [117] they had
the disposal of their own time and industry; they were not
subjected to the rigid rules of an order; they had made no
vows of implicit obedience to their superiors; [118]; and they
still retained the choice, without quitting the convent, either
of a married or a single life.[119] But a mistaken piety had
produced in Italy a new species of monks called Benedictines, who, carrying further the plausible principles of mortification, secluded themselves entirely from the world,
renounced all claim to liberty, and made a merit of the most
inviolable chastity. These practices and principles, which
superstition at first engendered, were greedily embraced
and promoted by the policy of the court of Rome. The
Roman pontiff, who was making every day great advances
towards an absolute sovereignty over the ecclesiastics, perceived that the celibacy of the clergy alone could break off
entirely their connection with the civil power, and, depriving them of every other object of ambition, engage them to
promote, with unceasing industry, the grandeur of their
own order. He was sensible that so long as the monks
were indulged in marriage, and were permitted to rear families, they never could be subjected to strict discipline, or
reduced to that slavery under their superiors which was
requisite to procure to the mandates issued from Rome a
ready and zealous obedience. Celibacy, therefore, began
to be extolled as the indispensable duty of priests; and the
pope undertook to make all the clergy throughout the western world renounce at once the privilege of marriage—a
fortunate policy, but at the same time an undertaking the
most difficult of any, since he had the strongest propensities
of human nature to encounter, and found that the same connections with the female sex, which generally encourage
devotion, were here unfavorable to the success of his project. It is no wonder, therefore, that this master-stroke of
art should have met with violent contradiction, and that
the interests of the hierarchy and the inclinations of the
priests, being now placed in this singular opposition, should,
notwithstanding the continued efforts of Rome, have re-

[117] Osberne, in Anglia Sacra, vol. ii. p. 92.   [118] Osberne, p. 91.
[119] See Wharton's notes to Anglia Sacra, vol. ii. p. 91. Gervase, p. 1645.
Chron. Wint. MS. apud Spell. Conc. p. 434.

tarded the execution of that bold scheme during the course of near three centuries.

As the bishops and parochial clergy lived apart with their families, and were more connected with the world, the hopes of success with them were fainter, and the pretence for making them renounce marriage was much less plausible. But the pope, having cast his eye on the monks as the basis of his authority, was determined to reduce them under strict rules of obedience, to procure them the credit of sanctity by an appearance of the most rigid mortification, and to break off all their other ties which might interfere with his spiritual policy. Under pretence, therefore, of reforming abuses, which were, in some degree, unavoidable in the ancient establishments, he had already spread over the southern countries of Europe the severe laws of the monastic life, and began to form attempts towards a like innovation in England. The favorable opportunity offered itself (and it was greedily seized), arising from the weak superstition of Edred, and the violent, impetuous character of Dunstan.

Dunstan was born of noble parents in the west of England; and being educated under his uncle Aldhelm, then Archbishop of Canterbury, had betaken himself to the ecclesiastical life, and had acquired some character in the court of Edmund. He was, however, represented to that prince as a man of licentious manners;[120] and finding his fortune blasted by these suspicions, his ardent ambition prompted him to repair his indiscretions by running into an opposite extreme. He secluded himself entirely from the world; he framed a cell so small that he could neither stand erect in it nor stretch out his limbs during his repose; and he here employed himself perpetually either in devotion or in manual labor.[121] It is probable that his brain became gradually crazed by these solitary occupations, and that his head was filled with chimeras, which, being believed by himself and his stupid votaries, procured him the general character of sanctity among the people. He fancied that the devil, among the frequent visits which he paid him, was one day more earnest than usual in his temptations; till Dunstan, provoked at his importunity, seized him by the nose with a pair of red-hot pincers, as he put his head into the cell; and he held him there till that malignant spirit made the whole neighborhood resound with his bel-

[120] Osberne, p. 95.   Matt. West. p. 187.   [121] Osberne, p. 96.

lowings. This notable exploit was seriously credited and extolled by the public; it is transmitted to posterity by one who, considering the age in which he lived, may pass for a writer of some elegance;[122] and it insured to Dunstan a reputation which no real piety, much less virtue, could, even in the most enlightened period, have ever procured him with the people.

Supported by the character obtained in his retreat, Dunstan appeared again in the world; and gained such an ascendant over Edred, who had succeeded to the crown, as made him not only the director of that prince's conscience, but his counsellor in the most momentous affairs of government. He was placed at the head of the treasury,[123] and being thus possessed both of power at court and of credit with the populace, he was enabled to attempt with success the most arduous enterprises. Finding that his advancement had been owing to the opinion of his austerity, he professed himself a partisan of the rigid monastic rules; and after introducing that reformation into the convents of Glastonbury and Abingdon, he endeavored to render it universal in the kingdom.

The minds of men were already well prepared for this innovation. The praises of an inviolable chastity had been carried to the highest extravagance by some of the first preachers of Christianity among the Saxons: the pleasures of love had been represented as incompatible with Christian perfection; and a total abstinence from all commerce with the sex was deemed such a meritorious penance as was sufficient to atone for the greatest enormities. The consequence seemed natural that those, at least, who officiated at the altar should be clear of this pollution; and when the doctrine of transubstantiation, which was now creeping in,[124] was once fully established, the reverence to the real body of Christ in the eucharist bestowed on this argument an additional force and influence. The monks knew how to avail themselves of all these popular topics, and to set off their own character to the best advantage. They affected the greatest austerity of life and manners; they indulged themselves in the highest strains of devotion; they inveighed bitterly against the vices and pretended luxury of the age; they were particularly vehement against the dissolute lives of the secular clergy, their rivals; every instance

of libertinism in any individual of that order was represented as a general corruption; and where other topics of
defamation were wanting, their marriage became a sure subject of invective, and their wives received the name of *concubine*, or other more opprobrious appellation. The secular
clergy, on the other hand, who were numerous and rich,
and possessed of the ecclesiastical dignities, defended themselves with vigor, and endeavored to retaliate upon their
adversaries. The people were thrown into agitation; and
few instances occur of more violent dissensions, excited by
the most material differences in religion, or rather by the
most frivolous, since it is a just remark that the more affinity there is between theological parties, the greater commonly is their animosity.

The progress of the monks, which was become considerable, was somewhat retarded by the death of Edred, their
partisan, who expired after a reign of nine years.[125] He left
children; but as they were infants, his nephew, Edwy, son
of Edmund, was placed on the throne.

Edwy, at the time of his accession, was not above sixteen or seventeen years of age, was possessed of the most
amiable figure, and was even endowed, according to authentic accounts, with the most promising virtues.[126] [955]. He
would have been the favorite of his people, had he not unhappily, at the commencement of his reign, been engaged in
a controversy with the monks, whose rage neither the graces
of the body nor virtues of the mind could mitigate, and who
have pursued his memory with the same unrelenting vengeance which they exercised against his person and dignity
during his short and unfortunate reign. There was a beautiful princess of the royal blood, called Elgiva, who had
made impression on the tender heart of Edwy; and as he
was of an age when the force of the passions first begins
to be felt, he had ventured, contrary to the advice of his
gravest counsellors and the remonstrances of the more dignified ecclesiastics,[127] to espouse her, though she was within
the degrees of affinity prohibited by the canon law.[128] As
the austerity affected by the monks made them particularly
violent on this occasion, Edwy entertained a strong prepossession against them; and seemed, on that account, determined not to second their project of expelling the seculars
from all the convents and of possessing themselves of those

125 Chron. Sax. p. 115.   125 H. Hunting. lib. 5. p. 356.
127 Will. Malm. lib. 2, cap. 7.   128 Ibid.

rich establishments. War was therefore declared between the king and the monks; and the former soon found reason to repent his provoking such dangerous enemies. On the day of his coronation, his nobility were assembled in a great hall, and were indulging themselves in that riot and disorder which, from the example of their German ancestors, had become habitual to the English,[129] when Edwy, attracted by softer pleasures, retired into the queen's apartment, and in that privacy gave reins to his fondness towards his wife, which was only moderately checked by the presence of her mother. Dunstan conjectured the reason of the king's retreat; and carrying along with him Odo, Archbishop of Canterbury, over whom he had gained an absolute ascendant, he burst into the apartment, upbraided Edwy with his lasciviousness, probably bestowed on the queen the most opprobrious epithet that can be applied to her sex, and tearing him from her arms, pushed him back, in a disgraceful manner, into the banquet of the nobles.[130] Edwy, though young, and opposed by the prejudices of the people, found an opportunity of taking revenge for this public insult. He questioned Dunstan concerning the administration of the treasury during the reign of his predecessor;[131] and when that minister refused to give any account of money expended, as he affirmed, by orders of the late king, he accused him of malversation in his office and banished him the kingdom. But Dunstan's cabal was not inactive during his absence; they filled the public with high panegyrics on his sanctity; they exclaimed against the impiety of the king and queen; and having poisoned the minds of the people by these declamations, they proceeded to still more outrageous acts of violence against the royal authority. Archbishop Odo sent into the palace a party of soldiers, who seized the queen, and having burned her face with a red-hot iron, in order to destroy that fatal beauty which had seduced Edwy, they carried her by force into Ireland, there to remain in perpetual exile.[132] Edwy, finding it in vain to resist, was obliged to consent to his divorce, which was pronouced by Odo;[133] and a catastrophe still more dismal awaited the unhappy Elgiva. That amiable princess, being cured of her wounds, and having even obliterated the scars with which Odo had hoped to deface her beauty, returned into England,

---

[129] Wallingford, p. 542.
[130] Will. Malm. lib 2, cap. 7. Osberne, pp. 83, 105. Matt. West. pp. 195, 196.
[131] Wallingford, p. 542. Alur. Beverl. p. 112.
[132] Osberne, p. 84. Gervase, p. 1644.   [133] Hoveden, p. 425.

and was flying to the embraces of the king, whom she still regarded as her husband, when she fell into the hands of a party whom the primate had sent to intercept her. Nothing but her death could now give security to Odo and the monks; and the most cruel death was requisite to satiate their vengeance. She was hamstringed, and expired a few days after at Gloucester, in the most acute torments.[134]

The English, blinded with superstition, instead of being shocked with this inhumanity, exclaimed that the misfortunes of Edwy and his consort were a just judgment for their dissolute contempt of the ecclesiastical statutes. They even proceeded to rebellion against their sovereign; and having placed Edgar at their head, the younger brother of Edwy, a boy of thirteen years of age, they soon put him in possession of Mercia, Northumberland, East Anglia, and chased Edwy into the southern counties That it might not be doubtful at whose instigation this revolt was undertaken, Dunstan returned into England, and took upon him the government of Edgar and his party. He was first installed in the see of Worcester, then in that of London,[135] and on Odo's death and the violent expulsion of Brithelm, his successor, in that of Canterbury; [136] of all which he long kept possession. Odo is transmitted to us by the monks under the character of a man of piety; Dunstan was even canonized, and is one of those numerous saints of the same stamp who disgrace the Romish calendar. Meanwhile the unhappy Edwy was excommunicated,[137] and pursued with unrelenting vengeance; but his death, which happened soon after, freed his enemies from all further inquietude, and gave Edgar peaceable possession of the government.[138]

This prince, who mounted the throne in such early youth, soon discovered an excellent capacity in the administration of affairs; and his reign is one of the most fortunate that we meet with in the ancient English history. He showed no aversion to war, he made the wisest preparations against invaders; and by his vigor and foresight he was enabled, without any danger of suffering insults, to indulge his inclination towards peace, and to employ himself in supporting and improving the internal government of his kingdom. He maintained a body of disciplined troops, which he quartered in the north in order to keep the mutinous Northumbrians

[134] Osberne, p. 84.   Gervase, pp. 1645, 1646
[135] Chron. Sax. p. 117.   Flor. Wigorn. p. 605.   Wallingford, p. 544.
[136] Hoveden, p. 425.   Osberne, p. 109.
[137] Brompton, p. 863.   [138] See note [B] at the end of the volume.

in subjection and to repel the inroads of the Scots. He built and supported a powerful navy; [139] and that he might retain the seamen in the practice of their duty, and always present a formidable armament to his enemies, he stationed three squadrons off the coast, and ordered them to make from time to time the circuit of his dominions.[140] The foreign Danes dared not to approach a country which appeared in such a posture of defence. The domestic Danes saw inevitable destruction to be the consequence of their tumults and insurrections. The neighboring sovereigns, the King of Scotland, the Princes of Wales, of the Isle of Man, of the Orkneys, and even of Ireland,[141] were reduced to pay submission to so formidable a monarch. He carried his superiority to a great height, and might have excited a universal combination against him had not his power been so well established as to deprive his enemies of all hope of shaking it. It is said that, residing once at Chester, and having proposed to go by water to the abbey of St. John the Baptist, he obliged eight of his tributary princes to row him in a barge upon the Dee.[142] The English historians are fond of mentioning the name of Kenneth III., King of Scots, among the number. The Scottish historians either deny the fact, or assert that their king, if ever he acknowledged himself a vassal to Edgar, did him homage, not for his crown, but for the dominions which he held in England.

But the chief means by which Edgar maintained his authority and preserved public peace was the paying of court to Dunstan and the monks, who had at first placed him on the throne, and who, by their pretensions to superior sanctity and purity of manners, had acquired an ascendant over the people. He favored their scheme for dispossessing the secular canons of all the monasteries; [143] he bestowed preferment on none but their partisans; he allowed Dunstan to resign the see of Worcester into the hands of Oswald, one of his creatures,[144] and to place Ethelwold, another of them, in that of Winchester; [145] he consulted these prelates in the administration of all ecclesiastical and even in that of many civil affairs; and though the vigor of his own genius prevented

[139] Higden, p. 265. [140] See note [C] at the end of the volume.
[141] Spell. Conc. p. 32.
[142] Will. Malm. lib. 2, cap. 8. Hoveden, p. 406. H. Hunting. lib. 5, p. 356.
[143] Chron. Sax. pp. 117, 118. Will. Malm. lib. 2, cap. 8. Hoveden, pp. 425, 426. Osberne, p. 112.
[144] Will. Malm. lib. 2, cap. 8. Hoveden, p. 425.
[145] Gervase, pp. 1646. Brompton, p. 864. Flor. Wigorn. p. 606. Chron. Abb. St. Petri de Burgo, pp. 27, 28.

him from being implicitly guided by them, the king and the
bishops found such advantages in their mutual agreement
that they always acted in concert, and united their influence
in preserving the peace and tranquillity of the kingdom.

In order to complete the great work of placing the new
order of monks in all the convents, Edgar summoned a general council of the prelates and the heads of the religious
orders.   He here inveighed against the dissolute lives of the
secular clergy; the smallness of their tonsure, which, it is probable, maintained no longer any resemblance to the crown of
thorns ; their negligence in attending the exercise of their
function ; their mixing with the laity in the pleasures of
gaming, hunting, dancing, and singing ; and their openly
living with concubines, by which it is commonly supposed
he meant their wives.   He then turned himself to Dunstan,
the primate ; and in the name of King Edred, whom he supposed to look down from heaven with indignation against all
those enormities, he thus addressed him : "It is you, Dunstan, by whose advice I founded monasteries, built churches,
and expended my treasure in the support of religion and religious houses.   You were my counsellor and assistant in all
my schemes ; you were the director of my conscience ; to
you I was obedient in all things.   When did you call for
supplies which I refused you?   Was my assistance ever
wanting to the poor?   Did I deny support and establishments to the clergy and the convents?   Did I not hearken
to your instructions, who told me that these charities were,
of all others, the most grateful to my Maker, and fixed a
perpetual fund for the support of religion ?   And are all our
pious endeavors now frustrated by the dissolute lives of the
priests ?   Not that I throw any blame on you ; you have
reasoned, besought, inculcated, inveighed ; but it now behooves you to use sharper and more vigorous remedies ; and,
conjoining your spiritual authority with the civil power, to
purge effectually the temple of God from thieves and in-
truders." [146]   It is easy to imagine that this harangue had
the desired effect ; and that, when the king and prelates
thus concurred with the popular prejudices, it was not long
before the monks prevailed, and established their new discipline in almost all the convents.

We may remark that the declamations against the secular
clergy, are, both here and in all the historians, conveyed in
general terms ; and as that order of men are commonly re-

[146] Abbas Rieval. pp. 360, 361.   Spell. Conc. pp. 476, 477, 478.

strained by the decency of their character, it is difficult to believe that the complaints against their dissolute manners could be so universally just as is pretended. It is more probable that the monks paid court to the populace by an affected austerity of life ; and, representing the most innocent liberties taken by the other clergy as great and unpardonable enormities, thereby prepared the way for the increase of their own power and influence. Edgar, however, like a true politician, concurred with the prevailing party ; and he even indulged them in pretensions which, though they might, when complied with, engage the monks to support royal authority during his own reign, proved afterwards dangerous to his successors, and gave disturbance to the whole civil power. He seconded the policy of the court of Rome in granting to some monasteries an exemption from episcopal jurisdiction ; he allowed the convents, even those of royal foundation, to usurp the election of their own abbot ; and he admitted their forgeries of ancient charters, by which, from the pretended grant of former kings, they assumed many privileges and immunities.[147]

These merits of Edgar have procured him the highest panegyrics from the monks, and he is transmitted to us not only under the character of a consummate statesman and an active prince, praises to which he seems to have been justly entitled, but under that of a great saint and a man of virtue. But nothing could more betray both his hypocrisy in inveighing against the licentiousness of the secular clergy, and the interested spirit of his partisans in bestowing such eulogies on his piety, than the usual tenor of his conduct, which was licentious to the highest degree, and violated every law, human and divine. Yet those very monks who, as we are told by Ingulf, a very ancient historian, had no idea of any moral or religious merit, except chastity and obedience, not only connived at his enormities, but loaded him with the greatest praises. History, however, has preserved some instances of his amours, from which, as from a specimen, we may form a conjecture of the rest.

Edgar broke into a convent, carried off Editha, a nun, by force, and even committed violence on her person.[148] For this act of sacrilege he was reprimanded by Dunstan ; and that he might reconcile himself to the Church, he was obliged

[147] Chron. Sax. p. 118. Will. Malm. lib. 2, cap. 8. Seldeni Spicileg. ad Eadm. p. 149, 157.
[148] Will. Malm. lib. 2, cap. 8. Osberne, p. 3. Diceto, p. 457. Higden, pp. 265, 267, 268. Spell. Conc. p. 481.

not to separate from his mistress, but to abstain from wearing
his crown during seven years, and to deprive himself so long
of that vain ornament [149]—a punishment very unequal to that
which had been inflicted on the unfortunate Edwy, who, for
a marriage which, in the strictest sense, could only deserve
the name of irregular, was expelled his kingdom, saw his
queen treated with singular barbarity, was loaded with
calumnies, and has been represented to us under the most
odious colors.   Such is the ascendant which may be attained
by hypocrisy and cabal over mankind.

There was another mistress of Edgar, with whom he first
formed a connection by a kind of accident.   Passing one day
by Andover, he lodged in the house of a nobleman, whose
daughter, being endowed with all the graces of person and
behavior, inflamed him at first sight with the highest desire,
and he resolved by any expedient to gratify it.   As he had
not leisure to employ courtship or address for attaining his
purpose, he went directly to her mother, declared the violence of his passion, and desired that the young lady might
be allowed to pass that very night with him.   The mother
was a woman of virtue, and determined not to dishonor her
daughter and her family by compliance ; but being well acquainted with the impetuosity of the king's temper, she
thought it would be easier, as well as safer, to deceive than
refuse him.   She feigned therefore a submission to his will ;
but secretly ordered a waiting-maid, of no disagreeable figure,
to steal into the king's bed, after all the company should be
retired to rest.   In the morning before daybreak, the damsel,
agreeably to the injunctions of her mistress, offered to retire ;
but Edgar, who had no reserve in his pleasures, and whose
love to his bedfellow was rather inflamed by enjoyment,
refused his consent, and employed force and entreaties, to
detain her.   Elfleda (for that was the name of the maid),
trusting to her own charms and to the love with which she
hoped, she had now inspired the king, made probably but a
faint resistance ; and the return of light discovered the deceit to Edgar.   He passed a night so much to his satisfaction that he expressed no displeasure with the old lady on
account of her fraud.   His love was transferred to Elfleda ;
she became his favorite mistress, and maintained her ascendant over him till his marriage with Elfrida.[150]

The circumstances of his marriage with this lady were
more singular and more criminal.   Elfrida was daughter and

[149] Osborne, p. 111.   •   [150] Will. Malm. lib. 2, cap 8.   Higden, p. 268.

heir of Olgar, Earl of Devonshire; and though she had been educated in the country, and had never appeared at court, she had filled all England with the reputation of her beauty. Edgar himself, who was indifferent to no accounts of this nature, found his curiosity excited by the frequent pane-gyrics which he heard of Elfrida; and, reflecting on her noble birth, he resolved, if he found her charms answerable to their fame, to obtain possession of her on honorable terms. He communicated his intention to Earl Athelwold, his favor-ite; but used the precaution, before he made any advances to her parents, to order that nobleman, on some pretence, to pay them a visit, and to bring him a certain account of the beauty of their daughter. Athelwold, when introduced to the young lady, found general report to have fallen short of the truth; and being actuated by the most vehement love, he determined to sacrifice to this new passion his fidelity to his master and to the trust reposed in him. He returned to Edgar, and told him that the riches alone and high quality of Elfrida had been the ground of the admiration paid her; and that her charms, far from being anywise extraordinary, would have been overlooked in a woman of inferior station. When he had, by this deceit, diverted the king from his purpose, he took an opportunity, after some interval, of turning again the conversation on Elfrida; he remarked that though the parentage and fortune of the lady had not produced on him, as on others, any illusion with regard to her beauty, he could not forbear reflecting that she would, on the whole, be an advantageous match for him, and might, by her birth and riches, make him sufficient compensation for the homeliness of her person. If the king, therefore, gave his approbation, he was determined to make proposals in his own behalf to the Earl of Devonshire, and doubted not to obtain his as well as the young lady's consent to the marriage. Edgar, pleased with an expedient for establish-ing his favorite's fortune, not only exhorted him to execute his purpose, but forwarded his success by his recommenda-tions to the parents of Elfrida; and Athelwold was soon made happy in the possession of his mistress. Dreading, however, the detection of the artifice, he employed every pretence for detaining Elfrida in the country, and for keep-ing her at a distance from Edgar.

The violent passion of Athelwold had rendered him blind to the necessary consequences which must attend his con-duct, and the advantages which the numerous enemies that always pursue a royal favorite would, by its means, be able to make against him. Edgar was soon informed of the truth; but before he would execute vengeance on Athelwold's treachery, he resolved to satisfy himself with his own eyes of the certainty and full extent of his guilt. He told him that he intended to pay him a visit in his castle and be introduced to the acquaintance of his new-married wife; and Athelwold, as he could not refuse the honor, only craved leave to go before him a few hours, that he might the better prepare everything for his reception. He then discovered the whole matter to Elfrida; and begged her, if she had any regard either to her own honor or his life, to conceal from Edgar, by every circumstance of dress and behavior, that fatal beauty which had seduced him from fidelity to his friend and had betrayed him into so many falsehoods. Elfrida promised compliance, though nothing was further from her intentions. She deemed herself little beholden to Athelwold for a passion which had deprived her of a crown; and, knowing the force of her own charms, she did not despair even yet of reaching that dignity of which her husband's artifice had bereaved her. She appeared before the king with all the advantages which the richest attire and the most engaging airs could bestow upon her, and she excited at once in his bosom the highest love towards herself and the most furious desire of revenge against her husband. He knew, however, how to dissemble these passions; and, seducing Athelwold into a wood, on pretence of hunting, he stabbed him with his own hand, and soon after publicly espoused Elfrida.[151]

Before we conclude our account of this reign, we must mention two circumstances which are remarked by historians. The reputation of Edgar allured a great number of foreigners to visit his court, and he gave them encouragement to settle in England.[152] We are told that they imported all the vices of their respective countries, and contributed to corrupt the simple manners of the natives.[153] But as this simplicity of manners, so highly and often so injudiciously extolled, did not preserve them from barbarity and treachery—the greatest of all vices, and the most incident to a rude, uncultivated people—we ought perhaps to deem their acquaintance with foreigners rather an advan-

[151] Will. Malm. lib. 2, cap. 8.   Hoveden. p. 426.   Brompton, pp. 865, 866. Flor. Wigorn. p. 606.   Higden, p. 268.
[152] Chron. Sax. p. 116.   H. Hunting. lib. 5, p. 356.   Brompton, p. 865.
[153] Will. Malm. lib. 2, cap. 8.

tage, as it tended to enlarge their views and to cure them of those illiberal prejudices and rustic manners to which islanders are often subject.

Another remarkable incident of this reign was the extirpation of wolves from England. This advantage was attained by the industrious policy of Edgar. He took great pains in hunting and pursuing those ravenous animals; and when he found that all that escaped him had taken shelter in the mountains and forests of Wales, he changed the tribute of money imposed on the Welsh princes by Athelstan, his predecessor,[154] into an annual tribute of three hundred heads of wolves, which produced such diligence in hunting them that the animal has been no more seen in this island.

Edgar died after a reign of sixteen years, and in the thirty-third of his age. He was succeeded by Edward, whom he had by his first marriage with the daughter of Earl Ordmer.

The succession of this prince, who was only fifteen years of age at his father's death, did not take place without much difficulty and opposition. [957.] Elfrida, his stepmother, had a son, Ethelred, seven years old, whom she attempted to raise to the throne: she affirmed that Edgar's marriage with the mother of Edward was exposed to insuperable objections; and as she had possessed great credit with her husband, she had found means to acquire partisans, who seconded all her pretensions. But the title of Edward was supported by many advantages He was appointed successor by the will of his father;[155] he was approaching to man's estate, and might soon be able to take into his own hands the reigns of government; the principal nobility, dreading the imperious temper of Elfrida, were averse to her son's government, which must enlarge her authority, and probably put her in possession of the regency; above all, Dunstan, whose character of sanctity had given him the highest credit with the people, had espoused the cause of Edward, over whom he had already acquired a great ascendant;[156] and he was determined to execute the will of Edgar in his favor. To cut off all opposite pretensions, Dunstan resolutely anointed and crowned the young prince at Kingston; and the whole kingdom, without further dispute, submitted to him.[157]

[154] Will. Malm. lib. 2, cap. 6.   Brompton, p. 838.
[155] Hoveden, p. 427.   Eadmer, p. 3.   [156] Eadmer, ex. edit. Seldeni, p. 3.
[157] Will. Malm. lib. 2, cap. 9.   Hoveden, p. 427.   Osberne, p. 113.

It was of great importance to Dunstan and the monks to place on the throne a king favorable to their cause : the secular clergy had still partisans in England, who wished to support them in the possession of the convents, and of the ecclesiastical authority. On the first intelligence of Edgar's death, Alfere, Duke of Mercia, expelled the new orders of monks from all the monasteries which lay within his jurisdiction ; [158] but Elfwin, Duke of East Anglia, and Brithnot, Duke of the East Saxons, protected them within their territories, and insisted upon the execution of the late laws enacted in their favor. In order to settle this controversy, there were summoned several synods, which, according to the practice of those times, consisted partly of ecclesiastical members, partly of the lay nobility. The monks were able to prevail in these assemblies, though, as it appears, contrary to the secret wishes, if not the declared inclination, of the leading men in the nation ; [159] they had more invention in forging miracles to support their cause ; or, having been so fortunate as to obtain, by their pretended austerities, the character of piety, their miracles were more credited by the populace.

In one synod, Dunstan, finding the majority of votes against him, rose up and informed the audience that he had that instant received an immediate revelation in behalf of the monks. The assembly was so astonished at this intelligence, or probably so overawed by the populace, that they proceeded no further in their deliberations. In another synod, a voice issued from the crucifix, and informed the members that the establishment of the monks was founded on the will of Heaven, and could not be opposed without impiety. [160] But the miracle performed in the third synod was still more alarming : the floor of the hall in which the assembly met sank of a sudden, and a great number of the members were either bruised or killed by the fall. It was remarked that Dunstan had that day prevented the king from attending the synod, and that the beam on which his own chair stood was the only one that did not sink under the weight of the assembly. [161] But these circumstances, in-

---

[158] Chron. Sax. p. 123. Will. Malm. lib. 2, cap. 9. Hoveden, p. 427. Brompton, p. 870. Flor. Wigorn. p. 607.
[159] Will. Malm. lib. 2, cap. 9.
[160] Will. Malm. lib. 2, cap. 9. Osberne, p. 112. Gervase, p. 1647. Brompton, p. 870. Higden, p. 269.
[161] Chron. Sax. p. 124. Will. Malm. lib. 2, cap. 9. Hoveden, p. 427. H. Hunting. lib. 5, p. 357. Gervase, p. 1617. Brompton, p. 870. Flor. Wigorn. p. 607. Higden, p. 269. Chron. Abb. St. Petri de Burgo, p. 29.

stead of begetting any suspicion of contrivance, were regarded as the surest proof of the immediate interposition of Providence in behalf of those favorites of Heaven.

Edward lived four years after his accession, and there passed nothing memorable during his reign. His death alone was memorable and tragical.[162] This young prince was endowed with the most amiable innocence of manners; and as his own intentions were always pure, he was incapable cf entertaining any suspicion against others. Though his step-mother had opposed his succession, and had raised a party in favor of her own son, he always showed her marks of regard, and even expressed on all occasions the most tender affection towards his brother. He was hunting one day in Dorsetshire; and being led by the chase near Corfe-castle, where Elfrida resided, he took the opportunity of paying her a visit, unattended by any of his retinue, and he thereby presented her with the opportunity which she had long wished for. After he had mounted his horse, he desired some liquor to be brought him. While he was holding the cup to his head, a servant of Elfrida approached him, and gave him a stab behind. The prince, finding himself wounded, put spurs to his horse; but becoming faint by loss of blood, he fell from the saddle, his foot stuck in the stirrup, and he was dragged along by his unruly horse till he expired. Being tracked by the blood, his body was found, and was privately interred at Wareham by his servants.

The youth and innocence of this prince, with his tragical death, begat such compassion among the people that they believed miracles to be wrought at his tomb; and they give him the appellation of Martyr, though his murder had no connection with any religious principle or opinion. Elfrida built monasteries and performed many penances, in order to atone for her guilt, but could never, by all her hypocrisy or remorses, recover the good opinion of the public, though so easily deluded in those ignorant ages.

[162] Chron. Sax. p. 124.

CHAPTER III.

ETHELRED.— SETTLEMENT OF THE NORMANS.— EDMUND
IRONSIDE.— CANUTE.— HAROLD HAREFOOT.— HARDICA-
NUTE.—EDWARD THE CONFESSOR.—HAROLD.

THE freedom which England had so long enjoyed from
the depredations of the Danes seems to have proceeded
partly from the establishments which that piratical nation
had obtained in the north of France, and which employed
all their superfluous hands to people and maintain them;
partly from the vigor and warlike spirit of a long race of
English princes, who preserved the kingdom in a posture of
defence by sea and land, and either prevented or repelled
every attempt of the invaders. [978.] But a new genera-
tion of men being now sprung up in the northern regions
who could no longer disburden themselves on Normandy,
the English had reason to dread that the Danes would again
visit an island to which they were invited both by the memory of their past successes and by the expectation of assistance from their countrymen, who, though long established
in the kingdom, were not yet thoroughly incorporated with
the natives, nor had entirely forgotten their inveterate
habits of war and depredation. And as the reigning prince
was a minor, and even when he attained to man's estate
never discovered either courage or capacity sufficient to
govern his own subjects, much less to repel a formidable
enemy, the people might justly apprehend the worst calamities from so dangerous a crisis.

The Danes, before they durst attempt any important enterprise against England, made an inconsiderable descent
by way of trial; and having landed from seven vessels near
Southampton, they ravaged the country, enriched themselves
by spoil, and departed with impunity. [981.] Six years
after, they made a light attempt in the west, and met with
like success. The invaders, having now found affairs in a
very different situation from that in which they formerly appeared, encouraged their countrymen to assemble a greater

force, and to hope for more considerable advantages. They landed in Essex, under the command of two leaders ; and, having defeated and slain, at Malden, Brithnot, duke of that county, who ventured, with a small body, to attack them, they spread their devastations over all the neighboring provinces. [991.] In this extremity, Ethelred, to whom historians give the epithet of the *Unready*, instead of rousing his people to defend with courage their honor and their property, hearkened to the advice of Siricius, Archbishop of Canterbury, which was seconded by many of the degenerate nobility ; and paying the enemy the sum of ten thousand pounds, he bribed them to depart the kingdom. This shameful expedient was attended with the success which might be expected. The Danes next year appeared off the eastern coast, in hopes of subduing a people who defended themselves by their money, which invited assailants, instead of their arms, which repelled them. But the English, sensible of their folly, had, in the interval, assembled in a great council, and had determined to collect at London a fleet able to give battle to the enemy ;[1] though that judicious measure failed of success, from the treachery of Alfric, Duke of Mercia, whose name is infamous in the annals of that age by the calamities which his repeated perfidy brought upon his country. This nobleman had, in 983, succeeded to his father, Alfere, in that extensive command ; but being deprived of it two years after, and banished the kingdom, he was obliged to employ all his intrigue, and all his power, which was too great for a subject, to be restored to his country and reinstated in his authority. Having had experience of the credit and malevolence of his enemies, he thenceforth trusted for security, not to his services or to the affections of his fellow-citizens, but to the influence which he had obtained over his vassals, and to the public calamities, which he thought must, in every revolution, render his assistance necessary. Having fixed this resolution, he determined to prevent all such successes as might establish the royal authority, or render his own situation dependent or precarious. As the English had formed the plan of surrounding and destroying the Danish fleet in harbor, he privately informed the enemy of their danger ; and when they put to sea, in consequence of this intelligence, he deserted to them, with the squadron under his command, the night before the engagement, and thereby disappointed all

[1] Chron. Sax. p. 126.

the efforts of his countrymen.[2] Ethelred, enraged at his perfidy, seized his son Alfgar, and ordered his eyes to be put out.[3] But such was the power of Alfric that he again forced himself into authority; and though he had given this specimen of his character, and received this grievous provocation, it was found necessary to intrust him anew with the government of Mercia. This conduct of the court, which in all its circumstances is so barbarous, weak, and imprudent, both merited and prognosticated the most grievous calamities.

The northern invaders, now well acquainted with the defenceless condition of England, made a powerful descent under the command of Sweyn, King of Denmark, and Olave, King of Norway; and sailing up the Humber, spread on all sides their destructive ravages. [993.] Lindesey was laid waste; Banbury was destroyed; and all the Northumbrians, though mostly of Danish descent, were constrained either to join the invaders or to suffer under their depredations. A powerful army was assembled to oppose the Danes, and a general action ensued; but the English were deserted in the battle, from the cowardice or treachery of their three leaders, all of them men of Danish race—Frena, Frithegist, and Godwin—who gave the example of a shameful flight to the troops under their command.

Encouraged by this success, and still more by the contempt which it inspired for their enemy, the pirates ventured to attack the centre of the kingdom; and, entering the Thames in ninety-four vessels, laid siege to London, and threatened it with total destruction. But the citizens, alarmed at the danger, and firmly united among themselves, made a bolder defence than the cowardice of the nobility and gentry gave the invaders reason to apprehend; and the besiegers, after suffering the greatest hardships, were finally frustrated in their attempt. In order to revenge themselves, they laid waste Essex, Sussex, and Hampshire; and having there procured horses, they were thereby enabled to spread through the more inland counties the fury of their depredations. In this extremity, Ethelred and his nobles had recourse to the former expedient; and, sending ambassadors to the two northern kings, they promised them subsistence and tribute on condition they would, for the present, put an end to their ravages and soon after depart the

[2] Chron. Sax. p. 127.   Will. Malm. p. 62.   Higden, p. 370.
[3] Chron. Sax. p. 128.   Will. Malm. p. 62.

kingdom. Sweyn and Olave agreed to the terms, and peaceably took up their quarters at Southampton, where the sum of sixteen thousand pounds was paid to them. Olave even made a journey to Andover, where Ethelred resided, and he received the rite of confirmation from the English bishops, as well as many rich presents from the king. He here promised that he would never more infest the English territories; and he faithfully fulfilled the engagement. This prince receives the appellation of St. Olave from the Church of Rome; and, notwithstanding the general presumption which lies either against the understanding or morals of every one who in those ignorant ages was dignified with that title, he seems to have been a man of merit and of virtue. Sweyn, though less scrupulous than Olave, was constrained, upon the departure of the Norwegian prince, to evacuate also the kingdom, with all his followers.

This composition brought only a short interval to the miseries of the English. The Danish pirates appeared soon after in the Severn; and, having committed spoil in Wales, as well as in Cornwall and Devonshire, they sailed round to the south coast, and, entering the Tamar, completed the devastation of these two counties. [997.] They then returned to the Bristol Channel, and, penetrating into the country by the Avon, spread themselves over all that neighborhood, and carried fire and sword even into Dorsetshire. They next changed the seat of war; and after ravaging the Isle of Wight, they entered the Thames and Medway, and laid siege to Rochester, where they defeated the Kentish men in a pitched battle. [998.] After this victory, the whole province of Kent was made a scene of slaughter, fire, and devastation. The extremity of these miseries forced the English into councils for common defence both by sea and land; but the weakness of the king, the divisions among the nobility, the treachery of some, the cowardice of others, the want of concert in all, frustrated every endeavor. Their fleets and armies either came too late to attack the enemy, or were repulsed with dishonor; and the people were thus equally ruined by resistance or by submission. The English, therefore, destitute both of prudence and unanimity in council, of courage and conduct in the field, had recourse to the same weak expedient which by experience they had already found so ineffectual. They offered the Danes to buy peace by paying them a large sum of money. These

ravagers rose continually in their demands, and now required the payment of twenty-four thousand pounds, to
which the English were so mean and imprudent as to submit.[4] The departure of the Danes procured them another
short interval of repose, which they enjoyed as if it were to
be perpetual, without making any effectual preparations
for a more vigorous resistance upon the next return of the
enemy.

Besides receiving this sum, the Danes were engaged by
another motive to depart a kingdom which appeared so little in a situation to resist their efforts. They were invited
over by their countrymen in Normandy, who at this time
were hard pressed by the arms of Robert, King of France,
and who found it difficult to defend the settlement, which,
with so much advantage to themselves and glory to their
nation, they had made in that country. It is probable, also,
that Ethelred, observing the close connections thus maintained among all the Danes, however divided in government
or situation, was desirous of forming an alliance with that
formidable people. For this purpose, being now a widower,
he made his addresses to Emma, sister to Richard II., Duke
of Normandy, [1001.] and he soon succeeded in his negotiation. The princess came over this year to England, and
was married to Ethelred.[5]

In the end of the ninth and beginning of the tenth century, when the north, not yet exhausted by that multitude
of people, or rather nations, which she had successively
emitted, sent forth a new race, not of conquerors, as before,
but of pirates and ravagers, who infested the countries possessed by her once warlike sons, lived Rollo, a petty prince
or chieftain of Denmark, whose valor and abilities soon engaged the attention of his countrymen. He was exposed in
his youth to the jealousy of the King of Denmark, who attacked his small but independent principality, and who,
being foiled in every assault, had recourse at last to perfidy
for effecting his purpose, which he had often attempted in
vain by force of arms.[6] He lulled Rollo into security by an
insidious peace, and, falling suddenly upon him, murdered
his brother and his bravest officers, and forced him to fly
for safety into Scandinavia. Here many of his ancient subjects, induced partly by affection to their prince, partly by

[4] Hoveden, p. 429. Chron. Mailr. p. 150.
[5] H. Hunting. p. 359. Higden, p. 271.
[6] Dudo, ex edit. Duchesne, pp. 70, 71. Gul. Gemet. lib. 2, cap. 2, 3.

the oppressions of the Danish monarch, ranged themselves under his standard, and offered to follow him in every enterprise. Rollo, instead of a tempting to recover his paternal dominions, where he must expect a vigorous resistance from the Danes, determined to pursue an easier but more important undertaking, and to make his fortune, in imitation of his countrymen, by pillaging the richer and more southern coasts of Europe. He collected a body of troops which, like that of all those ravagers, was composed of Norwegians, Swedes, Frisians, Danes, and adventurers of all nations, who, being accustomed to a roving, unsettled life, took delight in nothing but war and plunder. His reputation brought him associates from all quarters; and a vision, which he pretended to have appeared to him in his sleep, and which, according to his interpretation of it, prognosticated the greatest successes, proved also a powerful incentive with those ignorant and superstitious people.[7]

The first attempt made by Rollo was on England, near the end of Alfred's reign, when that great monarch, having settled Guthrum and his followers in East Anglia, and others of those freebooters in Northumberland, and having restored peace to his harassed country, had established the most excellent military as well as civil institutions among the English. The prudent Dane, finding that no advantages could be gained over such a people, governed by such a prince, soon turned his enterprises against France, which he found more exposed to his inroads;[8] and during the reigns of Eudes, a usurper, and of Charles the Simple, a weak prince, he committed the most destructive ravages both on the inland and maritime provinces of that kingdom. The French having no means of defence against a leader who united all the valor of his countrymen with the policy of more civilized nations, were obliged to submit to the expedient practised by Alfred, and to offer the invaders a settlement in some of those provinces which they had depopulated by their arms.[9]

The reason why the Danes for many years pursued measures so different from those which had been embraced by the Goths, Vandals, Franks, Burgundians, Lombards, and other northern conquerors, was the great difference in the method of attack which was practised by these several nations, and to which the nature of their respective situations

[7] Dudo, p. 71.   Gul. Gemet. in Epist. ad Gul. Conq.
[8] Gul. Gemet. lib. 2, cap. 6.   [9] Dudo, p. 82.

necessarily confined them. The latter tribes, living in an inland country, made incursions by land upon the Roman empire; and when they entered far into the frontiers, they were obliged to carry along with them their wives and families, whom they had no hopes of soon revisiting, and who could not otherwise participate in their plunder. This circumstance quickly made them think of forcing a settlement in the provinces which they had overrun; and these barbarians, spreading themselves over the country, found an interest in protecting the property and industry of the people whom they had subdued. But the Danes and Norwegians, invited by their maritime situation, and obliged to maintain themselves in their uncultivated country by fishing, had acquired some experience of navigation; and in their military excursions pursued the method practised against the Roman empire by the more early Saxons. They made descents in small bodies from their ships, or rather boats, and, ravaging the coasts, returned with their booty to their families, whom they could not conveniently carry along with them in those hazardous enterprises. But when they increased their armaments, made incursions into the inland countries, and found it safe to remain longer in the midst of the enfeebled enemy, they had been accustomed to crowd their vessels with their wives and children; and, having no longer any temptation to return to their own country, they willingly embraced an opportunity of settling in the warm climates and cultivated fields of the south.

Affairs were in this situation with Rollo and his followers, when Charles proposed to relinquish to them part of the province formerly called Neustria, and to purchase peace on these hard conditions. After all the terms were fully settled, there appeared only one circumstance shocking to the haughty Dane; he was required to do homage to Charles for this province, and, to put himself in that humiliating posture imposed on vassals by the rites of the feudal law. He long refused to submit to this indignity; but being unwilling to lose such important advantages for a mere ceremony, he made a sacrifice of his pride to his interest, and acknowledged himself, in form, the vassal of the French monarch.[10]   Charles gave him his daughter, Gisla, in marriage; and, that he might bind him faster to his interests, made him a donation of a considerable territory, besides that which he was obliged to surrender to him by his stipu-

[10] Ypod. Neust. p. 417.

lations. When some of the French nobles informed him that in return for so generous a present it was expected that he should throw himself at the king's feet and make suitable acknowledgments for his bounty, Rollo replied that he would rather decline the present; and it was with some difficulty they could persuade him to make that compliment by one of his captains. The Dane commissioned for this purpose, full of indignation at the order, and despising so unwarlike a prince, caught Charles by the foot, and, pretending to carry it to his mouth, that he might kiss it, overthrew him before all his courtiers. The French, sensible of their present weakness, found it prudent to overlook this insult.[11]

Rollo, who was now in the decline of life, and was tired of wars and depredations, applied himself, with mature counsels, to the settlement of his newly acquired territory, which was thenceforth called Normandy; and he parcelled it out among his captains and followers. He followed, in this partition, the customs of the feudal law, which was then universally established in the southern countries of Europe, and which suited the peculiar circumstances of that age. He treated the French subjects who submitted to him with mildness and justice; he reclaimed his ancient followers from their ferocious violence; he established law and order throughout his state; and, after a life spent in tumults and ravages, he died peaceably in a good old age, and left his dominions to his posterity.[12]

William I., who succeeded him, governed the duchy twenty-five years; and during that time the Normans were thoroughly intermingled with the French, had acquired their language, had imitated their manners, and had made such progress towards cultivation that on the death of William, his son Richard, though a minor,[13] inherited his dominions: a sure proof that the Normans were already somewhat advanced in civility, and that their government could now rest secure on its laws and civil institutions, and was not wholly sustained by the abilities of the sovereign. Richard, after a long reign of fifty-four years, was succeeded by his son of the same name in the year 996,[14] which was eighty-five years after the first establishment of the Normans in France. This was the duke who gave his sister Emma in

---

[11] Gul. Gemet. lib. 2, cap. 17.   [12] Gul. Gemet. cap. 19, 20, 21.
[13] Order. Vitalis, p. 459.   Gul. Gemet. lib. 4, cap. 1.
[14] Order. Vitalis, p. 459.

marriage to Ethelred, King of England, and who thereby formed connections with a country which his posterity was so soon after destined to subdue.

The Danes had been established during a longer period in England than in France; and, though the similarity of their original language to that of the Saxons invited them to a more early coalition with the natives, they had hitherto found so little example of civilized manners among the English that they retained all their ancient ferocity, and valued themselves only on their national character of military bravery. The recent as well as more ancient achievements of their countrymen tended to support this idea; and the English princes, particularly Athelstan and Edgar, sensible of that superiority, had been accustomed to keep in pay bodies of Danish troops, who were quartered about the country, and committed many violences upon the inhabitants. These mercenaries had attained to such a height of luxury, according to the old English writers,[15] that they combed their hair once a day, bathed themselves once a week, changed their clothes frequently; and by all these arts of effeminacy, as well as by their military character, had rendered themselves so agreeable to the fair sex that they debauched the wives and daughters of the English and dishonored many families. But what most provoked the inhabitants was that, instead of defending them against invaders, they were ever ready to betray them to the foreign Danes, and to associate themselves with all straggling parties of that nation. The animosity between the inhabitants of English and Danish race had from these repeated injuries risen to a great height, [1002.] when Ethelred, from a policy incident to weak princes, embraced the cruel resolution of massacring the latter throughout all his dominions.[16] Secret orders were despatched to commence the execution everywhere on the same day; and the festival of St. Brice, which fell on a Sunday, the day on which the Danes usually bathed themselves, was chosen for that purpose. It is needless to repeat the accounts transmitted concerning the barbarity of this massacre. The rage of the populace, excited by so many injuries, sanctioned by authority, and stimulated by example, distinguished not between innocence and guilt, spared neither sex nor age, and was not satiated without the tortures as well as death of the unhappy victims. Even Gunilda, sister to the king of Denmark, who

---

[15] Wallingford, p. 547.   [16] See note [D] at the end of the volume.

had married Earl Paling and had embraced Christianity, was, by the advice of Edric, Earl of Wilts, seized and condemned to death by Ethelred, after seeing her husband and children butchered before her face. This unhappy princess foretold, in the agonies of despair, that her murder would soon be avenged by the total ruin of the English nation.

Never was prophecy better fulfilled; and never did barbarous policy prove more fatal to the authors. [1003.] Sweyn and his Danes, who wanted but a pretence for invading the English, appeared off the western coast, and threatened to take full revenge for the slaughter of their countrymen. Exeter fell first into their hands, from the negligence or treachery of Earl Hugh, a Norman, who had been made governor by the interest of Queen Emma. They began to spread their devastations over the country; when the English, sensible what outrages they must now expect from their barbarous and offended enemy, assembled more early and in greater numbers than usual, and made an appearance of vigorous resistance. But all these preparations were frustrated by the treachery of Duke Alfric, who was intrusted with the command, and who, feigning sickness, refused to lead the army against the Danes, till it was dispirited, and at last dissipated, by his fatal misconduct. Alfric soon after died; and Edric, a greater traitor than he, who had married the king's daughter, and had acquired a total ascendant over him, succeeded Afric in the government of Mercia and in the command of the English armies. A great famine, proceeding partly from the bad seasons, partly from the decay of agriculture, added to all the other miseries of the inhabitants. [1007.] The country, wasted by the Danes, harassed by the fruitless expeditions of its own forces, was reduced to the utmost desolation; and at last submitted to the infamy of purchasing a precarious peace from the enemy by the payment of thirty thousand pounds.

The English endeavored to employ this interval in making preparations against the return of the Danes, which they had reason soon to expect. A law was made ordering the proprietors of eight hides of land to provide each a horseman and a complete suit of armor; and those of three hundred and ten hides to equip a ship for the defence of the coast. When this navy was assembled, which must have consisted of near eight hundred vessels,[17] all hopes of its

[17] There were 243,600 hides in England. Consequently the ships equipped must be 785. The cavalry was 30,450 men.

success were disappointed by the factions, animosities, and dissensions of the nobility. Edric had impelled his brother Brightric to prefer an accusation of treason against Wolfnoth, governor of Sussex, the father of the famous Earl Godwin; and that nobleman, well acquainted with the malevolence as well as power of his enemy, found no means of safety but in deserting with twenty ships to the Danes. Brightric pursued him with a fleet of eighty sail; but his ships being shattered in a tempest, and stranded on the coast, he was suddenly attacked by Wolfnoth, and all his vessels were burned or destroyed. The imbecility of the king was little capable of repairing this misfortune. The treachery of Edric frustrated every plan for future defence; and the English navy, disconcerted, discouraged, and divided, was at last scattered into its several harbors.

It is almost impossible, or would be tedious, to relate particularly all the miseries to which the English were thenceforth exposed. We hear of nothing but the sacking and burning of towns; the devastation of the open country; the appearance of the enemy in every quarter of the kingdom; their cruel diligence in discovering any corner which had not been ransacked by their former violence. The broken and disjointed narration of the ancient historians is here well adapted to the nature of the war, which was conducted by such sudden inroads as would have been dangerous even to a united and well-governed kingdom, but proved fatal where nothing but a general consternation and mutual diffidence and dissension prevailed. The governors of one province refused to march to the assistance of another, and were at last terrified from assembling their forces for the defence of their own province. General councils were summoned; but either no resolution was taken, or none was carried into execution. And the only expedient in which the English agreed was the base and imprudent one of buying a new peace from the Danes by the payment of forty-eight thousand pounds.

This measure did not bring them even that short interval of repose which they had expected from it. [1011.] The Danes, disregarding all engagements, continued their devastations and hostilities; levied a new contribution of eight thousand pounds upon the county of Kent alone, murdered the Archbishop of Canterbury, who had refused to countenance this exaction; and the English nobility found no other resource than that of submitting everywhere to the

Danish monarch, swearing allegiance to him, and delivering him hostages for their fidelity. [1013.] Ethelred, equally afraid of the violence of the enemy and the treachery of his own subjects, fled into Normandy, whither he had sent before him Queen Emma, and her two sons, Alfred and Edward. Richard received his unhappy guests with a generosity that does honor to his memory.

The king had not been above six weeks in Normandy, when he heard of the death of Sweyn, who expired at Gainsborough before he had time to establish himself in his newly acquired dominions. [1014.] The English prelates and nobility, taking advantage of this event, sent over a deputation to Normandy, inviting Ethelred to return to them, expressing a desire of being again governed by their native prince, and intimating their hopes that, being now tutored by experience, he would avoid all those errors which had been attended with such misfortunes to himself and to his people. But the misconduct of Ethelred was incurable; and on his resuming the government, he discovered the same incapacity, indolence, cowardice, and credulity which had so often exposed him to the insults of his enemies. His son-in-law, Edric, notwithstanding his repeated treasons, retained such influence at court as to instil into the king jealousies of Sigefert and Morcar, two of the chief nobles of Mercia. Edric allured them into his house, where he murdered them; while Ethelred participated in the infamy of the action by confiscating their estates and thrusting into a convent the widow of Sigefert. She was a woman of singular beauty and merit; and in a visit which was paid her during her confinement by Prince Edmond, the king's eldest son, she inspired him with so violent an affection that he released her from the convent, and soon after married her without the consent of his father.

Meanwhile the English found in Canute, the son and successor of Sweyn, an enemy no less terrible than the prince from whom death had so lately delivered them. He ravaged the eastern coast with merciless fury, and put ashore all the English hostages at Sandwich, after having cut off their hands and noses. He was obliged by the necessity of his affairs to make a voyage to Denmark; but returning soon after, he continued his depredations along the southern coast: he even broke into the counties of Dorset, Wilts, and Somerset, where an army was assembled against him, under the command of Prince Edmond and Duke Edric. [1015.]

The latter still continued his perfidious machinations; and, after endeavoring in vain to get the prince into his power, he found means to disperse the army; and he then openly deserted to Canute with forty vessels.

Notwithstanding this misfortune, Edmond was not disconcerted; but, assembling all the force of England, was in a condition to give battle to the enemy. The king had had such frequent experience of perfidy among his subjects that he had lost all confidence in them: he remained at London, pretending sickness, but really from apprehensions that they intended to buy their peace by delivering him into the hands of his enemies. The army called aloud for their sovereign to march at their head against the Danes; and, on his refusal to take the field, they were so discouraged that those vast preparations became ineffectual for the defence of the kingdom. Edmond, deprived of all regular supplies to maintain his soldiers, was obliged to commit equal ravages with those which were practised by the Danes; and after making some fruitless expeditions into the north, which had submitted entirely to Canute's power, he retired to London, determined there to maintain, to the last extremity, the small remains of English liberty. [1016.] He here found everything in confusion by the death of the king, who expired after an unhappy and inglorious reign of thirty-five years. He left two sons by his first marriage—Edmond, who succeeded him, and Edwy, whom Canute afterwards murdered. His two sons by the second marriage, Alfred and Edward, were immediately, upon Ethelred's death, conveyed into Normandy by Queen Emma.

This prince, who received the name of Ironside from his hardy valor, possessed courage and abilities sufficient to have prevented his country from sinking into those calamities, but not to raise it from that abyss of misery into which it had already fallen. Among the other misfortunes of the English, treachery and disaffection had crept in among the nobility and prelates; and Edmond found no better expedient for stopping the further progress of these fatal evils than to lead his army instantly into the field, and to employ them against the common enemy. After meeting with some success at Gillingham, he prepared himself to decide, in one general engagement, the fate of his crown; and at Scoerston, in the county of Gloucester, he offered battle to the enemy, who were commanded by Canute and Edric. Fortune, in the beginning of the day, declared for him; but

Edric, having cut off the head of one Osmer, whose countenance resembled that of Edmond, fixed it on a spear, carried it through the ranks in triumph, and called aloud to the English that it was time to fly; for, behold the head of their sovereign! And though Edmond, observing the consternation of the troops, took off his helmet and showed himself to them, the utmost he could gain by his activity and valor was to leave the victory undecided. Edric now took a surer method to ruin him by pretending to desert him; and as Edmond was well acquainted with his power, and probably knew no other of the chief nobility in whom he could repose more confidence, he was obliged, notwithstanding the repeated perfidy of the man, to give him a considerable command in the army. A battle soon after ensued at Assington, in Essex, where Edric, flying in the beginning of the day, occasioned the total defeat of the English, followed by a great slaughter of the nobility. The indefatigable Edmond, however, had still resources. Assembling a new army at Gloucester, he was again in a condition to dispute the field; when the Danish and English nobility, equally harassed with those convulsions, obliged their kings to come to a compromise, and to divide the kingdom between them by treaty. Canute reserved to himself the northern division, consisting of Mercia, East Anglia, and Northumberland, which he had entirely subdued; the southern parts were left to Edmond. This prince survived the treaty about a month. He was murdered at Oxford by two of his chamberlains, accomplices of Edric, who thereby made way for the succession of Canute the Dane to the crown of England.

The English, who had been unable to defend their country and maintain their independency under so active and brave a prince as Edmond, could, after his death, expect nothing but total subjection from Canute, who, active and brave himself, and at the head of a great force, was ready to take advantage of the minority of Edwin and Edward, the two sons of Edmond. [1017.] Yet this conqueror, who was commonly so little scrupulous, showed himself anxious to cover his injustice under plausible pretences. Before he seized the dominions of the English princes, he summoned a general assembly of the states, in order to fix the succession of the kingdom. He here suborned some nobles to depose that, in the treaty of Gloucester, it had been verbally agreed either to name Canute, in case of Edmond's death, successor to his dominions or tutor to his children (for historians vary in this particular); and that evidence, supported by the great power of Canute, determined the states immediately to put the Danish monarch in possession of the government. Canute, jealous of the two princes, but sensible that he should render himself extremely odious if he ordered them to be despatched in England, sent them abroad to his ally, the King of Sweden, whom he desired, as soon as they arrived at his court, to free him by their death from all further anxiety. The Swedish monarch was too generous to comply with the request; but, being afraid of drawing on himself a quarrel with Canute by protecting the young princes, he sent them to Solomon, King of Hungary, to be educated in his court. The elder, Edwin, was afterwards married to the sister of the King of Hungary; but the English prince dying without issue, Solomon gave his sister-in-law, Agatha, daughter of the Emperor Henry II., in marriage to Edward, the younger brother; and she bore him Edgar Atheling, Margaret (afterwards Queen of Scotland), and Christiana (who retired into a convent).

Canute, though he had reached the great point of his ambition in obtaining possession of the English crown, was obliged at first to make great sacrifices to it, and to gratify the chief of the nobility by bestowing on them the most extensive governments and jurisdictions. He created Thurkill Earl or Duke of East Anglia (for these titles were then nearly of the same import), Yric of Northumberland, and Edric of Mercia, reserving only to himself the administration of Wessex. But, seizing afterwards a favorable opportunity, he expelled Thurkill and Yric from their governments, and banished them the kingdom. He put to death many of the English nobility, on whose fidelity he could not rely, and whom he hated on account of their disloyalty to their native prince. And even the traitor Edric, having had the assurance to reproach him with his services, was condemned to be executed, and his body to be thrown into the Thames—a suitable reward for his multiplied acts of perfidy and rebellion.

Canute also found himself obliged, in the beginning of his reign, to load the people with heavy taxes in order to reward his Danish followers: he exacted from them at one time the sum of seventy-two thousand pounds, besides eleven thousand pounds which he levied on London alone. He was probably willing, from political motives, to mulct severely that city on account of the affection which it had borne to Edmond and the resistance which it had made to the Danish power in two obstinate sieges.[18] But these rigors were imputed to necessity; and Canute, like a wise prince, was determined that the English, now deprived of all their dangerous leaders, should be reconciled to the Danish yoke by the justice and impartiality of his administration. He sent back to Denmark as many of his followers as he could safely spare; he restored the Saxon customs in a general assembly of the states; he made no distinction between Danes and English in the distribution of justice; and he took care, by a strict execution of law, to protect the lives and properties of all his people. The Danes were gradually incorporated with his new subjects, and both were glad to obtain a little respite from those multiplied calamities from which the one no less than the other had, in their fierce contest for power, experienced such fatal consequences.

The removal of Edmond's children into so distant a country as Hungary was, next to their death, regarded by Canute as the greatest security to his government: he had no further anxiety, except with regard to Alfred and Edward, who were protected and supported by their uncle, Richard, Duke of Normandy. Richard even fitted out a great armament in order to restore the English princes to the throne of their ancestors; and, though the navy was dispersed by a storm, Canute saw the danger to which he was exposed from the enmity of so warlike a people as the Normans. In order to acquire the friendship of the Duke, he paid his addresses to Queen Emma, sister of that prince, and promised that he would leave the children whom he should have by that marriage in possession of the crown of England. Richard complied with his demand, and sent over Emma to England, where she was soon after married to Canute.[19] The English, though they disapproved of her espousing the mortal enemy of her former husband and his family, were pleased to find at court a sovereign to whom they were accustomed, and who had already formed connections with them; and thus Canute, besides securing by this marriage the alliance of Normandy, gradually acquired by the same means the confidence of his own subjects.[20]

---

[18] Will. Malm. p. 72. In one of these sieges Canute diverted the course of the Thames, and by that means brought his ships above London Bridge.
[19] Chron. Sax. p. 151. Will. Malm. p. 73.
[20] Will. Malm. p. 73. Higden, p. 275.

The Norman prince did not long survive the marriage of Emma, and he left the inheritance of the duchy to his eldest son of the same name, who, dying a year after him without children, was succeeded by his brother Robert, a man of valor and abilities.

Canute, having settled his power in England beyond all danger of a revolution, made a voyage to Denmark in order to resist the attacks of the King of Sweden, and he carried along with him a great body of the English, under the command of Earl Godwin. This nobleman had here an opportunity of performing a service by which he both reconciled the king's mind to the English nation, and, gaining to himself the friendship of his sovereign, laid the foundation of that immense fortune which he acquired to his family. He was stationed next the Swedish camp, and observing a favorable opportunity which he was obliged suddenly to seize, he attacked the enemy in the night, drove them from their trenches, threw them into disorder, pursued his advantage, and obtained a decisive victory over them. Next morning, Canute seeing the English camp entirely abandoned, imagined that those disaffected troops had deserted to the enemy: he was agreeably surprised to find that they were at that time engaged in pursuit of the discomfited Swedes. He was so pleased with this success, and with the manner of obtaining it, that he bestowed his daughter in marriage upon Godwin, and treated him ever after with entire confidence and regard.

In another voyage, which he made afterwards to Denmark, Canute attacked Norway, and, expelling the just but unwarlike Olaus, kept possession of his kingdom till the death of that prince. He had now, by his conquests and valor, attained [1028.] the utmost height of grandeur. Having leisure from wars and intrigues, he felt the unsatisfactory nature of all human enjoyments, and, equally weary of the glories and turmoils of this life, he began to cast his view towards that future existence which it is so natural for the human mind, whether satiated by prosperity or disgusted with adversity, to make the object of its attention. Unfortunately, the spirit which prevailed in that age gave a wrong direction to his devotion: instead of making compensation to those whom he had injured by his former acts of violence, he employed himself entirely in those exercises of piety which the monks represented as the most meritorious. He built churches, he endowed monasteries, he enriched the ecclesiastics, and he bestowed revenues for the support of chantries at Assington and other places, where he appointed prayers to be said for the souls of those who had there fallen in battle against him. He even undertook a pilgrimage to Rome, where he resided a considerable time. Besides obtaining from the pope some privileges for the English school erected there, he engaged all the princes through whose dominions he was obliged to pass to desist from those heavy impositions and tolls which they were accustomed to exact from the English pilgrims. By this spirit of devotion no less than by his equitable and politic administration, he gained in a good measure the affections of his subjects.

Canute, the greatest and most powerful monarch of his time, sovereign of Denmark and Norway as well as of England, could not fail of meeting with adulation from his courtiers—a tribute which is liberally paid even to the meanest and weakest princes. Some of his flatterers, breaking out one day in admiration of his grandeur, exclaimed that everything was possible for him; upon which the monarch, it is said, ordered his chair to be set on the sea-shore while the tide was rising, and as the waters approached he commanded them to retire and to obey the voice of him who was lord of the ocean. He feigned to sit some time in expectation of their submission; but when the sea still advanced towards him and began to wash him with its billows, he turned to his courtiers and remarked to them that every creature in the universe was feeble and impotent, and that power resided with one Being alone, in whose hands were all the elements of nature, who could say to the ocean, "Thus far shalt thou go, and no farther," and who could level with his nod the most towering piles of human pride and ambition.

The only memorable action which Canute performed after his return from Rome was an expedition against Malcolm, King of Scotland. [1031.] During the reign of Ethelred, a tax of a shilling a hide had been imposed on all the lands of England. It was commonly called *Danegelt*, because the revenue had been employed either in buying peace with the Danes, or in making preparations against the inroads of that hostile nation. That monarch had required that the same tax should be paid by Cumberland, which was held by the Scots; but Malcolm, a warlike prince, told him that, as he was always able to repulse the Danes by his own power, he would neither submit to buy peace of his enemies nor pay others for resisting them. Ethelred, offended at this reply, which contained a secret reproach on his own conduct, undertook an expedition against Cumberland; but though he committed ravages upon the country, he could never bring Malcolm to a temper more humble or submissive. Canute, after his accession, summoned the Scottish king to acknowledge himself a vassal for Cumberland to the crown of England; but Malcolm refused compliance, on pretence that he owed homage to those princes only who inherited that kingdom by right of blood. Canute was not of a temper to bear this insult, and the King of Scotland soon found that the sceptre was in very different hands from those of the feeble and irresolute Ethelred. Upon Canute's appearing on the frontiers with a formidable army, Malcolm agreed that his grandson and heir, Duncan, whom he put in possession of Cumberland, should make the submissions required, and that the heirs of Scotland should always acknowledge themselves vassals to England for that province.[21]

Canute passed four years in peace after this enterprise, and he died at Shaftesbury;[22] leaving three sons, Sweyn, Harold, and Hardicanute. Sweyn, whom he had by his first marriage with Alfwen, daughter of the Earl of Hampshire, was crowned in Norway; Hardicanute, whom Emma had borne him, was in possession of Denmark; Harold, who was of the same marriage with Sweyn, was at that time in England.

[1035.] Though Canute, in his treaty with Richard, Duke of Normandy, had stipulated that his children by Emma should succeed to the crown of England, he had either considered himself as released from that engagement by the death of Richard, or esteemed it dangerous to leave an unsettled and newly conquered kingdom in the hands of so young a prince as Hardicanute; he therefore appointed by his will Harold successor to the crown. This prince was, besides, present to maintain his claim; he was favored by all the Danes, and he got immediately possession of his father's treasures, which might be equally useful, whether he found it necessary to proceed by force or intrigue in insuring his succession. On the other hand, Hardicanute had the suffrages of the English, who, on account of his being born among them of Queen Emma, regarded him as their country-

[21] Will. Malm. p. 74.   [22] Chron. Sax. p. 154. Will. Malm. p. 76.

man; he was favored by the articles of treaty with the Duke of Normandy; and, above all, his party was espoused by Earl Godwin, the most powerful nobleman in the kingdom, especially in the province of Wessex, the chief seat of the ancient English. Affairs were likely to terminate in a civil war, when, by the interposition of the nobility of both parties, a compromise was made, and it was agreed that Harold should enjoy, together with London, all the provinces north of the Thames, while the possession of the south should remain to Hardicanute; and till that prince should appear and take possession of his dominions, Emma fixed her residence at Winchester, and established her authority over her son's share of the partition.

Meanwhile Robert, Duke of Normandy, died in a pilgrimage to the Holy Land; and being succeeded by a son, yet a minor, the two English princes, Alfred and Edward, who found no longer any countenance or protection in that country, gladly embraced the opportunity of paying a visit, with a numerous retinue, to their mother Emma, who seemed to be placed in a state of so much power and splendor at Winchester. But the face of affairs soon wore a melancholy aspect. Earl Godwin had been gained by the arts of Harold, who promised to espouse the daughter of that nobleman; and, while the treaty was yet a secret, these two tyrants laid a plan for the destruction of the English princes. Alfred was invited to London by Harold with many professions of friendship; but when he had reached Guilford, he was set upon by Godwin's vassals; about six hundred of his train were murdered in the most cruel manner; he himself was taken prisoner, his eyes were put out, and he was conducted to the monastery of Ely, where he died soon after.[23] Edward and Emma, apprised of the fate which was awaiting them, fled beyond sea, the former into Normandy, the latter into Flanders; while Harold, triumphing in his bloody policy, took possession, without resistance, of all the dominions assigned to his brother.

This is the only memorable action performed, during a reign of four years, by this prince, who gave so bad a specimen of his character, and whose bodily accomplishments alone are known to us by his appellation of *Harefoot*, which he acquired from his agility in running and walking. He died on the 14th of April, 1039, little regretted or esteemed by his subjects, and left the succession open to his brother, Hardicanute.

[1039.] Hardicanute, or Canute the Hardy, that is, the robust (for he too is chiefly known by his bodily accomplishments), though, by remaining so long in Denmark he had been deprived of his share in the partition of the kingdom, had not abandoned his pretensions; and he had determined, before Harold's death, to recover by arms what he had lost either by his own negligence or by the necessity of his affairs. On pretence of paying a visit to the queen dowager in Flanders, he had assembled a fleet of sixty sail, and was preparing to make a descent on England, when intelligence of his brother's death induced him to sail immediately to London, where he was received in triumph, and acknowledged king without opposition.

The first act of Hardicanute's government afforded his subjects a bad prognostic of his future conduct. He was so enraged at Harold for depriving him of his share of the kingdom, and for the cruel treatment of his brother Alfred, that, in an impotent desire of revenge against the dead, he ordered his body to be dug up, and to be thrown into the Thames; and when it was found by some fishermen and buried in London, he ordered it again to be dug up and to be thrown again into the river; but it was fished up a second time, and then interred with great secrecy. Godwin, equally servile and insolent, submitted to be his instrument in this unnatural and brutal action.

That nobleman knew that he was universally believed to have been an accomplice in the barbarity exercised on Alfred, and that he was on that account obnoxious to Hardicanute; and perhaps he hoped, by displaying this rage against Harold's memory, to justify himself from having had any participation in his counsels. But Prince Edward, being invited over by the king, immediately on his appearance preferred an accusation against Godwin for the murder of Alfred, and demanded justice for that crime. Godwin, in order to appease the king, made him a magnificent present of a galley with a gilt stern, rowed by fourscore men, who wore each of them a gold bracelet on his arm weighing sixteen ounces, and were armed and clothed in the most sumptuous manner. Hardicanute, pleased with the splendor of this spectacle, quickly forgot his brother's murder; and on

Godwin's swearing that he was innocent of the crime, he allowed him to be acquitted.

Though Hardicanute, before his accession, had been called over by the vows of the English, he soon lost the affections of the nation by his misconduct; but nothing appeared more grievous to them than his renewing the imposition of Danegelt, and obliging the nation to pay a great sum of money to the fleet which brought him from Denmark. The discontents ran high in many places: in Worces er the populace rose, and put to death two of the collectors. The king, enraged at this opposition, swore vengeance against the city, and ordered three noblemen— Godwin, Duke of Wessex; Siward, Duke of Northumberland; and Leofric, Duke of Mercia—to execute his menaces with the utmost rigor. They were obliged to set fire to the city, and deliver it up to be plundered by their soldiers; but they saved the lives of the inhabitants, whom they confined in a small island of the Severn, called Bevery, till, by their intercession, they were able to appease the king and obtain the pardon of the supplicants.

This violent government was of short duration. Hardicanute died in two years after his accession, at the nuptials of a Danish lord, which he had honored with his presence. His usual habits of intemperance were so well known that, notwithstanding his robust constitution, his sudden death gave as little surprise as it did sorrow to his subjects.

The English, on the death of Hardicanute, saw a favorable opportunity for recovering their liberty and for shaking off the Danish yoke, under which they had so long labored. [1041.] Sweyn, King of Norway, the eldest son of Canute, was absent; and as the two last kings had died without issue, none of that race presented himself, nor any whom the Danes could support, as successor to the throne. Prince Edward was fortunately at court on his brother's demise; and though the descendants of Edmond Ironside were the true heirs of the Saxon family, yet their absence in so remote a country as Hungary appeared a sufficient reason for their exclusion, to a people like the English, so little accustomed to observe a regular order in the succession of their monarchs. All delays might be dangerous; and the present occasion must hastily be embraced; while the Danes, without concert, without a leader, astonished at the present incident, and anxious only for their personal safety, durst not oppose the united voice of the nation.

But this concurrence of circumstances in favor of Edward might have failed of its effect had his succession been opposed by Godwin, whose power, alliances, and abilities gave him a great influence at all times, especially amid those sudden opportunities which always attend a revolution of government, and which, either seized or neglected, commonly prove decisive. There were opposite reasons which divided men's hopes and fears with regard to Godwin's conduct. On the one hand, the credit of that nobleman lay chiefly in Wessex, which was almost entirely inhabited by English. It was therefore presumed that he would second the wishes of that people in restoring the Saxon line and in humbling the Danes, from whom he as well as they had reason to dread, as they had already felt, the most grievous oppressions. On the other hand, there subsisted a declared animosity between Edward and Godwin, on account of Alfred's murder, of which the latter had publicly been accused by the prince, and which he might believe so deep an offence as could never, on account of any subsequent merits, be sincerely pardoned. But their common friends here interposed; and, representing the necessity of their good correspondence, obliged them to lay aside all jealousy and rancor, and concur in restoring liberty to their native country. Godwin only stipulated that Edward, as a pledge of his sincere reconciliation, should promise to marry his daughter Editha; and having fortified himself by this alliance, he summoned a general council at Gillingham, and prepared every measure for securing the succession to Edward. The English were unanimous and zealous in their resolutions; the Danes were divided and dispirited. Any small opposition which appeared in this assembly was browbeaten and suppressed; and Edward was crowned king, with every demonstration of duty and affection.

The triumph of the English, upon this signal and decisive advantage, was at first attended with some insult and violence against the Danes; but the king, by the mildness of his character, soon reconciled the latter to his administration, and the distinction between the two nations gradually disappeared. The Danes were interspersed with the English in most of the provinces. They spoke nearly the same language; they differed little in their manners and laws. Domestic dissensions in Denmark prevented, for some years, any powerful invasion from thence, which might awaken past animosities; and as the Norman Conquest, which ensued soon after, reduced both nations to equal subjection, there is no further mention in history of any difference between them. The joy, however, of their present deliverance made such impression on the minds of the English that they instituted an annual festival for celebrating that great event; and it was observed in some counties even to the time of Spellman.[24]

The popularity which Edward enjoyed on his accession was not destroyed by the first act of his administration, his resuming all the grants of his immediate predecessors—an attempt which is commonly attended with the most dangerous consequences. The poverty of the crown convinced the nation that this act of violence was become absolutely necessary; and as the loss fell chiefly on the Danes, who had obtained large grants from the late kings, their countrymen, on account of their services in subduing the kingdom, the English were rather pleased to see them reduced to their primitive poverty. The king's severity also towards his mother, the queen dowager, though exposed to some more censure, met not with very general disapprobation. He had hitherto lived on indifferent terms with that princess; he accused her of neglecting him and his brother during their adverse fortune.[25] He remarked that, as the superior qualities of Canute and his better treatment of her had made her entirely indifferent to the memory of Ethelred, she also gave the preference to her children of the second bed, and always regarded Hardicanute as her favorite. The same reasons had probably made her unpopular in England; and though her benefactions to the monks had obtained her the favor of that order, the nation was not, in general, displeased to see her stripped by Edward of immense treasures which she had amassed. He confined her during the remainder of her life in a monastery at Winchester, but carried his rigor against her no further. The stories of his accusing her of a participation in her son Alfred's murder, and of a criminal correspondence with the Bishop of Winchester, and also of her justifying herself by treading barefoot, without receiving any hurt, over nine burning ploughshares, were the inventions of the monkish historians, and were propagated and believed from the silly wonder of posterity.[26]

The English flattered themselves that by the accession of

[24] Spell. Gloss. *in verbo* Hocday. [25] Anglia Sacra, vol. i. p. 237.
[26] Higden, p. 277.

Edward they were delivered forever from the dominion of foreigners; but they soon found that this evil was not yet entirely removed. The king had been educated in Normandy, and had contracted many intimacies with the natives of that country, as well as an affection for their manners.[27] The court of England was soon filled with Normans, who, being distinguished both by the favor of Edward and by a degree of cultivation superior to that which was attained by the English in those ages, soon rendered their language, customs, and laws fashionable in the kingdom. The study of the French tongue became general among the people. The courtiers affected to imitate that nation in their dress, equipage, and entertainments; even the lawyers employed a foreign language in their deeds and papers.[28] But, above all, the Church felt the influence and dominion of those strangers; Ulf and William, two Normans, who had formerly been the king's chaplains, were created Bishops of Dorchester and London. Robert, a Norman also, was promoted to the see of Canterbury,[29] and always enjoyed the highest favor of his master, of which his abilities rendered him not unworthy. And though the king's prudence, or his want of authority, made him confer almost all the civil and military employments on the natives, the ecclesiastical preferments fell often to the share of the Normans; and as the latter possessed Edward's confidence, they had secretly a great influence on public affairs, and excited the jealousy of the English, particularly of Earl Godwin.[30]

This powerful nobleman, besides being Duke or Earl of Wessex, had the counties of Kent and Sussex annexed to his government. His eldest son, Sweyn, possessed the same authority in the counties of Oxford, Berks, Gloucester, and Hereford; and Harold, his second son, was Duke of East Anglia, and at the same time governor of Essex. The great authority of this family was supported by immense possessions and powerful alliances; and the abilities as well as ambition of Godwin himself contributed to render it still more dangerous. A prince of greater capacity and vigor than Edward would have found it difficult to support the dignity of the crown under such circumstances; and as the haughty temper of Godwin made him often forget the respect due to his prince, Edward's animosity against him was grounded

[27] Ingulph. p. 62.   [28] Ibid.
[29] Chron. Sax. p. 161.   [30] Will. Malm. p. 80.

on personal as well as political considerations, on recent as well as more ancient injuries. The king, in pursuance of his engagements, had indeed married Editha, the daughter of Godwin;[31] but this alliance became a fresh source of enmity between them. Edward's hatred of the father was transferred to that princess; and Editha, though possessed of many amiable accomplishments, could never acquire the confidence and affection of her husband. It is even pretended that, during the whole course of her life, he abstained from all commerce of love with her; and such was the absurd admiration paid to an inviolable chastity during those ages that his conduct in this particular is highly celebrated by the monkish historians, and greatly contributed to his acquiring the title of Saint and Confessor.[32]   [1048.]

The most popular pretence on which Godwin could ground his disaffection to the king and his administration was to complain of the influence of the Normans in the government; and a declared opposition had thence arisen between him and these favorites. It was not long before this animosity broke into action. Eustace, Count of Boulogne, having paid a visit to the king, passed by Dover in his return. One of his train, being refused entrance to a lodging which had been assigned him, attempted to make his way by force, and in the contest he wounded the master of the house. The inhabitants revenged this insult by the death of the stranger; the count and his train took arms, and murdered the wounded townsman; a tumult ensued; near twenty persons were killed on each side; and Eustace, being overpowered by numbers, was obliged to save his life by flight from the fury of the populace. He hurried immediately to court, and complained of the usage he had met with. The king entered zealously into the quarrel, and was highly displeased that a stranger of such distinction, whom he had invited over to his court, should, without any just cause, as he believed, have felt so sensibly the insolence and animosity of his people. He gave orders to Godwin, in whose government Dover lay, to repair immediately to the place, and to punish the inhabitants for the crime; but Godwin, who desired rather to encourage than repress the popular discontents against foreigners, refused obedience, and endeavored to throw the whole blame of the riot on the Count of Bou-

[31] Chron. Sax. p. 157.
[32] Will. Malm. p. 80. Higden, p. 277. Abbas Rieval. pp. 366, 377. Matt. West p. 221. Chron. Thom. Wykes, p. 21. Anglia Sacra, vol. i. p. 241.

logne and his retinue.[33] Edward, touched in so sensible a point, saw the necessity of exerting the royal authority; and he threatened Godwin, if he persisted in his disobedience, to make him feel the utmost effects of his resentment.

The earl, perceiving a rupture to be unavoidable, and pleased to embark in a cause where it was likely he should be supported by his countrymen, made preparations for his own defence, or rather for an attack on Edward. Under pretence, of repressing some disorders on the Welsh frontier, he secretly assembled a great army, and was approaching the king, who resided, without any military force, and without suspicion, at Gloucester.[34] Edward applied for protection to Siward, Duke of Northumberland, and Leofric, Duke of Mercia, two powerful noblemen, whose jealousy of Godwin's greatness, as well as their duty to the crown, engaged them to defend the king in this extremity. They hastened to him with such of their followers as they could assemble on a sudden; and, finding the danger much greater than they had at first apprehended, they issued orders for mustering all the forces within their respective governments, and for marching them without delay to the defence of the king's person and authority. Edward, meanwhile, endeavored to gain time by negotiation; while Godwin, who thought the king entirely in his power, and who was willing to save appearances, fell into the snare; and, not sensible that he ought to have no further reserve after he had proceeded so far, he lost the favorable opportunity of rendering himself master of the government.

The English, though they had no idea of Edward's vigor and capacity, bore him great affection, on account of his humanity, justice, and piety, as well as the long race of their native kings from whom he was descended; and they hastened from all quarters to defend him from the present danger. His army was now so considerable that he ventured to take the field, and, marching to London, he summoned a great council to judge of the rebellion of Godwin and his sons. These noblemen pretended at first that they were willing to stand their trial; but having in vain endeavored to make their adherents persist in rebellion, they offered to come to London, provided they might receive hostages for their safety. This proposal being rejected, they were obliged to disband the remains of their forces and have re-

[33] Chron. Sax. p. 163.   Will. Malm. p. 81.   Higden, p. 279.
[34] Chron. Sax. p. 163.   Will. Malm. p. 81.

course to flight. Baldwin, Earl of Flanders, gave protection to Godwin and his three sons Gurth, Sweyn, and Tosti, the latter of whom had married the daughter of that prince. Harold and Leofwin, two other of his sons, took shelter in Ireland. The estates of the father and sons were confiscated; their governments were given to others; Queen Editha was confined in a monastery at Warewel; and the greatness of this family, once so formidable, seemed now to be totally supplanted and overthrown.

But Godwin had fixed his authority on too firm a basis, and he was too strongly supported by alliances, both foreign and domestic, not to occasion further disturbances and make new efforts for his re-establishment. [1052.] The Earl of Flanders permitted him to purchase and hire ships within his harbors; and Godwin, having manned them with his followers, and with freebooters of all nations, put to sea, and attempted to make a descent at Sandwich. The king, informed of his preparations, had equipped a considerable fleet, much superior to that of the enemy; and the earl, hastily, before their appearance, made his retreat into the Flemish harbors.[35] The English court, allured by the present security, and destitute of all vigorous counsels, allowed the seamen to disband and the fleet to go to decay;[36] while Godwin, expecting this event, kept his men in readiness for action. He put to sea immediately, and sailed to the Isle of Wight, where he was joined by Harold, with a squadron which that nobleman had collected in Ireland. He was now master of the sea; and, entering every harbor in the southern coast, he seized all the ships,[37] and summoned his followers in those counties, which had so long been subject to his government, to assist him in procuring justice to himself, his family, and his country, against the tyranny of foreigners. Reinforced by great numbers from all quarters, he entered the Thames; and, appearing before London, threw everything into confusion. The king alone seemed resolute to defend himself to the last extremity; but the interposition of the English nobility, many of whom favored Godwin's pretensions, made Edward hearken to terms of accommodation; and the feigned humility of the earl, who disclaimed all intentions of offering violence to his sovereign, and desired only to justify himself by a fair and open trial, paved the way for his more easy admission. It was stipulated that he should give hostages for his good behavior, and that the primate and all the foreigners

---

[35] Sim. Dunelm. p. 186.　　　[36] Chron. Sax. p. 166.　　　[37] Ibid.

should be banished. By this treaty the present danger of a civil war was obviated, but the authority of the crown was considerably impaired, or rather entirely annihilated. Edward, sensible that he had not power sufficient to secure Godwin's hostages in England, sent them over to his kinsman, the young Duke of Normandy.

Godwin's death, which happened soon after, while he was sitting at table with the king, prevented him from farther establishing the authority which he had acquired, and from reducing Edward to still greater subjection.[38] He was succeeded in the government of Wessex, Sussex, Kent, and Essex, and in the office of steward of the household, a place of great power, by his son Harold, who was actuated by an ambition equal to that of his father, and was superior to him in address, in insinuation, and in virtue. By a modest and gentle demeanor he acquired the good-will of Edward—at least softened that hatred which the prince had so long borne his family;[39] and, gaining every day new partisans by his bounty and affability, he proceeded, in a more silent and therefore a more dangerous manner, to the increase of his authority. The king, who had not sufficient vigor directly to oppose his progress, knew of no other expedient than that hazardous one of raising him a rival in the family of Leofric, Duke of Mercia, whose son Algar was invested with the government of East Anglia, which, before the banishment of Harold, had belonged to the latter nobleman. But this policy of balancing opposite parties required a more steady hand to manage it than that of Edward, and naturally produced faction, and even civil broils, among nobles of such mighty and independent authority. Algar was soon after expelled his government by the intrigues and power of Harold ; but, being protected by Griffith, Prince of Wales, who had married his daughter, as well as by the power of his father, Leofric, he obliged Harold to submit to an accommodation, and was reinstated in the government of East Anglia. This peace was not of long duration. Harold, taking advantage of Leofric's death, which happened soon after, expelled Algar anew, and banished him the kingdom ; and though that nobleman made a fresh irruption into East Anglia with an army of Norwegians, and overran the country, his death soon freed Harold from the pretensions of so dangerous a rival. Edward, the eldest son of Algar, was indeed advanced to the government of Mercia ; but the bal-

[38] See note [E] at the end of the volume.   [39] Brompton, p. 948.

ance which the king desired to establish between those potent families was wholly lost, and the influence of Harold greatly preponderated.

The death of Siward, Duke of Northumberland, made the way still more open to the ambition of that nobleman. [1055.] Siward, besides his other merits, had acquired honor to England by his successful conduct in the only foreign enterprise undertaken during the reign of Edward. Duncan, King of Scotland, was a prince of a gentle disposition, but possessed not the genius requisite for governing a country so turbulent, and so much infested by the intrigues and animosities of the great. Macbeth, a powerful nobleman, and nearly allied to the crown, not content with curbing the king's authority, carried still further his pestilent ambition. He put his sovereign to death, chased Malcolm Kenmore, his son and heir, into England, and usurped the crown. Siward, whose daughter was married to Duncan, embraced, by Edward's orders, the protection of this distressed family. He marched an army into Scotland; and, having defeated and killed Macbeth in battle, he restored Malcolm to the throne of his ancestors.[40] This service, added to his former connections with the royal family of Scotland, brought a great accession to the authority of Siward in the north; but as he had lost his eldest son, Osberne, in the action with Macbeth, it proved in the issue fatal to his family. His second son, Walthoef, appeared, on his father's death, too young to be intrusted with the government of Northumberland; and Harold's influence obtained that dukedom for his own brother Tosti.

There are two circumstances related of Siward which discover his high sense of honor and his martial disposition. When intelligence was brought him of his son Osberne's death, he was inconsolable till he heard that the wound was received in the breast, and that he had behaved with great gallantry in the action. When he found his own death approaching, he ordered his servants to clothe him in a complete suit of armor; and, sitting erect on the couch, with a spear in his hand, declared that in that posture, the only one worthy of a warrior, he would patiently await the fatal moment.

The king, now worn out with cares and infirmities, felt himself far advanced in the decline of life; and, having no

[40] Will. Malm. p. 79. Hoveden, p. 443. Chron. Mailr. p. 158. Buchanan, p. 115, edit. 1715.

issue himself, began to think of appointing a successor to the kingdom. He sent a deputation to Hungary to invite over his nephew, Edward, son of his elder brother, and the only remaining heir of the Saxon line. That prince, whose succession to the crown would have been easy and undisputed, came to England with his children, Edgar (surnamed Atheling), Margaret, and Christina; but his death, which happened a few days after his arrival, threw the king into new difficulties. He saw that the great power and ambition of Harold had tempted him to think of obtaining possession of the throne on the first vacancy, and that Edgar, on account of his youth and inexperience, was very unfit to oppose the pretensions of so popular and enterprising a rival. The animosity which he had long borne to Earl Godwin made him averse to the succession of his son, and he could not, without extreme reluctance, think of an increase of grandeur to a family which had risen on the ruins of royal authority, and which, by the murder of Alfred, his brother, had contributed so much to the weakening of the Saxon line. In this uncertainty he secretly cast his eye towards his kinsman, William, Duke of Normandy, as the only person whose power and reputation and capacity could support any destination which he might make in his favor, to the exclusion of Harold and his family.[41]

This famous prince was natural son of Robert, Duke of Normandy, by Harlotta, daughter of a tanner in Falaise,[42] and was very early established in that grandeur from which his birth seemed to have set him at so great a distance. While he was but nine years of age, his father had resolved to undertake a pilgrimage to Jerusalem—a fashionable act of devotion, which had taken the place of pilgrimages to Rome, and which, as it was attended with more difficulty and danger, and carried those religious adventurers to the first sources of Christianity, appeared to them more meritorious. Before his departure he assembled the states of the duchy; and, informing them of his design, he engaged them to swear allegiance to his natural son, William, whom, as he had no legitimate issue, he intended, in case he should die in the pilgrimage, to leave successor to his dominions.[43] As he was a prudent prince, he could not but foresee the great inconveniences which must attend this journey, and this settlement of his succession, arising from the turbulency of the great, the claims of other branches of the ducal family

41 Ingulph. p. 68.   42 Brompton, p. 910.   43 Will. Malm. p. 95.

and the power of the French monarch. But all these considerations were surmounted by the prevailing zeal for pilgrimages;[44] and probably the more important they were, the more would Robert exult in sacrificing them to what he imagined to be his religious duty.

This prince, as he had apprehended, died in his pilgrimage; and the minority of his son was attended with all those disorders which were almost unavoidable in that situation. The licentious nobles, freed from the awe of sovereign authority, broke out into personal animosities against each other, and made the whole country a scene of war and devastation.[45] Roger, Count of Toni, and Alain, Count of Brittany, advanced claims to the dominion of the state; and Henry I., King of France, thought the opportunity favorable for reducing the power of a vassal who had orignally acquired his settlement in so violent and invidious a manner, and who had long appeared formidable to his sovereign.[46] The regency established by Robert encountered great difficulties in supporting the government under this complication of dangers; and the young prince, when he came to maturity, found himself reduced to a very low condition. But the great qualities which he soon displayed in the field and in the cabinet gave encouragement to his friends, and struck a terror into his enemies. He opposed himself on all sides against his rebellious subjects and against foreign invaders: and by his valor and conduct prevailed in every action. He obliged the French king to grant him peace on reasonable terms, he expelled all pretenders to the sovereignty; and he reduced his turbulent barons to pay submission to his authority, and to suspend their mutual animosities. The natural severity of his temper appeared in a rigorous administration of justice; and having found the happy effects of this plan of government, without which the laws in those ages became totally impotent, he regarded it as a fixed maxim that an inflexible conduct was the first duty of a sovereign.

The tranquillity which he had established in his dominions had given William leisure to pay a visit to the King of England during the time of Godwin's banishment; and he was received in a manner suitable to the great reputation which he had acquired, to the relation by which he was connected with Edward, and to the obligations which that

[44] Ypod. Neust. p. 452.
[45] Will. Malm. p. 95. Gul. Gemet. lib. 7,cap.1.   [46] Will. Malm. p. 97.

prince owed to his family.[47]   On the return of Godwin
and the expulsion of the Norman favorites, Robert, Archbishop of Canterbury, had, before his departure, persuaded
Edward to think of adopting William as his successor—a
counsel which was favored by the king's aversion to Godwin, his prepossessions for the Normans, and his esteem of
the duke.   That prelate, therefore, received a commission
to inform William of the king's intentions in his favor; and
he was the first person that opened the mind of the prince
to entertain those ambitious hopes.[48]   But Edward, irresolute and feeble in his purpose, finding that the English
would more easily acquiesce in the restoration of the Saxon
line, had in the meantime invited his brother's descendants
from Hungary, with a view of having them recognized heirs
to the crown.   The death of his nephew, and the inexperience and unpromising qualities of young Edgar, made him
resume his former intentions in favor of the Duke of Normandy; though his aversion to hazardous enterprises engaged him to postpone the execution, and even to keep his
purpose secret from all his ministers.

Harold, meanwhile, proceeded after a more open manner in increasing his popularity, in establishing his power,
and in preparing the way for his advancement on the first
vacancy—an event which, from the age and infirmities of
the king, appeared not very distant.   But there was still an
obstacle which it was requisite for him previously to overcome.   Earl Godwin, when restored to his power and fortune, had given hostages for his good behavior, and, among
the rest, one son and one grandson, whom Edward, for
greater security, as has been related, had consigned to the
custody of the Duke of Normandy.   Harold, though not
aware of the duke's being his competitor, was uneasy that
such near relations should be detained prisoners in a foreign
country; and he was afraid lest William should, in fa or of
Edgar, retain those pledges as a check on the ambition of
any other pretender.   He represented, therefore, to the king
his unfeigned submission to the royal authority, his steady
duty to his prince, and the little necessity there was, after
such a uniform trial of his obedience, to detain any longer
those hostages who had been required on the first composing of civil discords.   By these topics, enforced by his great
power, he extorted the king's consent to release them; and,

in order to effect his purpose, he immediately proceeded, with a numerous retinue, on his journey to Normandy. A tempest drove him on the territory of Guy, Count of Pon-thieu, who, being informed of his quality, immediately detained him prisoner, and demanded an exorbitant sum for his ransom. Harold found means to convey intelligence of his situation to the Duke of Normandy; and represented that while he was proceeding to *his* court, in execution of a commission from the King of England, he had met with this harsh treatment from the mercenary disposition of the Count of Ponthieu.

William was immediately sensible of the importance of the incident. He foresaw that if he could once gain Harold either by favors or menaces, his way to the throne of England would be open, and Edward would meet with no further obstacle in executing the favorable intentions which he had entertained in his behalf. He sent, therefore, a messenger to Guy, in order to demand the liberty of his prisoner; and that nobleman, not daring to refuse so great a prince, put Harold into the hands of the Norman, who conducted him to Rouen. William received him with every demonstration of respect and friendship; and, after showing himself disposed to comply with his desire in delivering up the hostages, he took an opportunity of disclosing to him the great secret of his pretensions to the crown of England, and of the will which Edward intended to make in his favor. He desired the assistance of Harold in perfecting that design; he made professions of the utmost gratitude in return for so great an obligation; he promised that the present grandeur of Harold's family, which supported itself with difficulty under the jealousy and hatred of Edward, should receive new increase from a successor who would be so greatly beholden to him for his advancement. Harold was surprised at this declaration of the duke; but, being sensible that he should never recover his own liberty, much less that of his brother and nephew, if he refused the demand, he feigned a compliance with William, renounced all hopes of the crown for himself, and professed his sincere intention of supporting the will of Edward and seconding the pretensions of the Duke of Normandy. William, to bind him faster to his interests, besides offering him one of his daughters in marriage, required him to take an oath that he would fulfil his promises; and in order to render the oath more obligatory, he employed an artifice well suited to the ignorance and superstition of the age. He secretly conveyed under the altar on which Harold agreed to swear the relics of some of the most revered martyrs; and when Harold had taken the oath, he showed him the relics, and admonished him to observe religiously an engagement which had been ratified by so tremendous a sanction.[49] The English nobleman was astonished; but, dissembling his concern, he renewed the same professions, and was dismissed with all the marks of mutual confidence by the Duke of Normandy.

When Harold found himself at liberty, his ambition suggested casuistry sufficient to justify to him the violation of an oath which had been extorted from him by fear, and which, if fulfilled, might be attended with the subjection of his native country to a foreign power. He continued still to practise every art of popularity; to increase the number of his partisans; to reconcile the minds of the English to the idea of his succession; to revive their hatred of the Normans; and, by an ostentation of his power and influence, to deter the timorous Edward from executing his intended destination in favor of William. Fortune about this time threw two incidents in his way, by which he was enabled to acquire general favor and to increase the character which he had already attained of virtue and abilities.

The Welsh, though a less formidable enemy than the Danes, had long been accustomed to infest the western borders; and after committing spoil on the Low Countries, they usually made a hasty retreat into their mountains, where they were sheltered from the pursuit of their enemies, and were ready to seize the first favorable opportunity of renewing their depredations. Griffith, the reigning prince, had greatly distinguished himself in those incursions; and his name had become so terrible to the English that Harold found he could do nothing more acceptable to the public and more honorable for himself than the suppressing of so dangerous an enemy. He formed the plan of an expedition against Wales; and, having prepared some light-armed foot to pursue the natives into their fastnesses, some cavalry to scour the open country, and a squadron of ships to attack the sea-coast, he employed at once all these forces against the Welsh, prosecuted his advantages with vigor, made no intermission in his assaults, and at last reduced the enemy to such distress that, in order to prevent

[49] Wace, pp. 459, 460. MS. penes Carte, p. 354. Will. Malm. p. 93. H. Hunting. p. 366. Hoveden, p. 449. Brompton, p. 947.

their total destruction, they made a sacrifice of their prince, whose head they cut off and sent to Harold; and they were content to receive as their sovereigns two Welsh noblemen appointed by Edward to rule over them. The other incident was no less honorable to Harold.

Tosti, brother of this nobleman, who had been created Duke of Northumberland, being of a violent, tyrannical temper, had acted with such cruelty and injustice that the inhabitants rose in rebellion, and chased him from his government. Morcar and Edwin, two brothers, who possessed great power in those parts, and who were grandsons of the great Duke Leofric, concurred in the insurrection; and the former, being elected duke, advanced with an army to oppose Harold, who was commissioned by the king to reduce and chastise the Northumbrians. Before the armies came to action, Morcar, well acquainted with the generous disposition of the English commander, endeavored to justify his own conduct. He represented to Harold that Tosti had behaved in a manner unworthy of the station to which he was advanced, and no one, not even a brother, could support such tyranny without participating, in some degree, of the infamy attending it; that the Northumbrians, accustomed to a legal administration, and regarding it as their birthright, were willing to submit to the king, but required a governor who would pay regard to their rights and privileges; that they had been taught by their ancestors that death was preferable to servitude, and had taken the field, determined to perish rather than suffer a renewal of those indignities to which they had so long been exposed; and they trusted that Harold, on reflection, would not defend in another that violent conduct from which he himself, in his own government, had always kept at so great a distance. This vigorous remonstrance was accompanied with such a detail of facts so well supported that Harold found it prudent to abandon his brother's cause; and, returning to Edward, he persuaded him to pardon the Northumbrians, and to confirm Morcar in the government. He even married the sister of that nobleman; [50] and by his interest procured Edwin, the younger brother, to be elected into the government of Mercia. Tosti, in rage, departed the kingdom, and took shelter in Flanders with Earl Baldwin, his father-in-law.

By this marriage Harold broke all measures with the

[50] Order. Vitalis, p. 492.

Duke of Normandy; and William clearly perceived that he could no longer rely on the oaths and promises which he had extorted from him. But the English nobleman was now in such a situation that he deemed it no longer necessary to dissemble. He had in his conduct towards the Northumbrians given such a specimen of his moderation as had gained him the affections of his countrymen. He saw that almost all England was engaged in his interests; while he himself possessed the government of Wessex, Morcar that of Northumberland, and Edward that of Mercia. He now openly aspired to the succession; and insisted that since it was necessary, by the confession of all, to set aside the royal family, on account of the imbecility of Edgar, the sole surviving heir, there was no one so capable of filling the throne as a nobleman of great power, of mature age, of long experience, of approved courage and abilities, who, being a native of the kingdom, would effectually secure it against the dominion and tyranny of foreigners. Edward, broken with age and infirmities, saw the difficulties too great for him to encounter; and though his inveterate prepossessions kept him from seconding the pretensions of Harold, he took but feeble and irresolute steps for securing the succession to the Duke of Normandy.[51] While he continued in this uncertainty he was surprised by sickness, which brought him to his grave on the 5th of January, 1066, in the sixty-fifth year of his age and twenty-fifth of his reign.

This prince, to whom the monks gave the title of Saint and Confessor, was the last of the Saxon line that ruled in England. Though his reign was peaceable and fortunate, he owed his prosperity less to his own abilities than to the conjunctures of the times. The Danes, employed in other enterprises, attempted not those incursions which had been so troublesome to all his predecessors and fatal to some of them. The facility of his disposition made him acquiesce under the government of Godwin and his son Harold; and the abilities as well as the power of these noblemen, while they were intrusted with authority, to preserve domestic peace and tranquillity. The most commendable circumstance of Edward's government was his attention to the administration of justice, and his compiling for that purpose a body of laws, which he collected from the laws of Ethelbert, Ina, and Alfred. This compilation, though now lost (for the laws that pass under Edward's name were composed

[51] See note [F] at the end of the volume.

afterwards),[52] was long the object of affection to the English nation.

Edward the Confessor was the first that touched for the king's evil: the opinion of his sanctity procured belief to this cure among the people. His successors regarded it as a part of their state and grandeur to uphold the same opinion. It has been continued down to our time; and the practice was first dropped by the present royal family, who observed that it would no longer give amazement even to the populace, and was attended with ridicule in the eyes of all men of understanding.

[1066.] Harold had so well prepared matters before the death of Edward that he immediatly stepped into the vacant throne; and his accession was attended with as little opposition and disturbance as if he had succeeded by the most undoubted hereditary title. The citizens of London were his zealous partisans: the bishops and clergy had adopted his cause; and all the powerful nobility, connected with him by alliance or friendship, willingly seconded his pretensions. The title of Edgar Atheling was scarcely mentioned, much less the claim of the Duke of Normandy; and Harold, assembling his partisans, received the crown from their hands, without waiting for the free deliberation of the states, or regularly submitting the question to their determination.[56] If any were averse to this measure, they were obliged to conceal their sentiments; and the new prince, taking a general silence for consent, and founding his title on the supposed suffrages of the people, which appeared unanimous, was, on the day immediately succeeding Edward's death, crowned and anointed king by Aldred, Archbishop of York. The whole nation seemed joyfully to acquiesce in his elevation.

The first symptoms of danger which the king discovered came from abroad, and from his own brother Tosti, who had submitted to a voluntary banishment in Flanders. Enraged at the successful ambition of Harold, to which he himself had fallen a victim, he filled the court of Baldwin with complaints of the injustice which he had suffered; he engaged the interests of that family against his brother; he endeavored to form intrigues with some of the discontented

---

[52] Spell. *in verbo* Belliva.
[53] Gul. Pict. p. 196. Ypod. Neust. p. 436. Order. Vitalis, p. 492. Matt. West. p. 221. Will. Malm. p. 93. Ingulph. p. 68. Brompton, p. 957. Knyghton, p. 2339. H. Hunting. p. 210. Many of the historians say that Harold was regularly elected by the states; some that Edward left him his successor by will.

nobles in England; he sent his emissaries to Norway, in order to rouse to arms the freebooters of that kingdom, and to excite their hopes of reaping advantage from the unsettled state of affairs on the usurpation of the new king; and, that he might render the combination more formidable, he made a journey to Normandy, in expectation that the duke, who had married Matilda, another daughter of Baldwin, would, in revenge of his own wrongs as well as those of Tosti, second by his counsels and forces the projected invasion of England.[54]

The Duke of Normandy, when he first received intelligence of Harold's intrigues and accession, had been moved to the highest pitch of indignation; but that he might give the better color to his pretensions, he sent an embassy to England, upbraiding that prince with his breach of faith, and summoning him to resign immediately possession of the kingdom. Harold replied to the Norman ambassadors that the oath with which he was reproached had been extorted by the well-grounded fear of violence, and could never, for that reason, be regarded as obligatory; that he had had no commission, either from the late king or the states of England, who alone could dispose of the crown, to make any tender of the succession to the Duke of Normandy; and if he, a private person, had assumed so much authority, and had even voluntarily sworn to support the duke's pretensions, the oath was unlawful, and it was his duty to seize the first opportunity of breaking it; that he had obtained the crown by the unanimous suffrages of the people; and should prove himself totally unworthy of their favor did he not strenuously maintain those national liberties with whose protection they had intrusted him; and that the duke, if he made any attempt by force of arms, should experience the power of a united nation, conducted by a prince who, sensible of the obligations imposed on him by his royal dignity, was determined that the same moment should put a period to his life and to his government.[55]

This answer was no other than William expected; and he had previously fixed his resolution of making an attempt upon England. Consulting only his courage, his resentment, and his ambition, he overlooked all the difficulties inseparable from an attack on a great kingdom by such inferior

[54] Order. Vitalis, p. 492.
[55] Will. Malm. p. 99. Higden, p. 285. Matt. West. p. 222. De Gest. Angl. incerto auctore, p. 331.

force, and he saw only the circumstances which would facilitate his enterprise. He considered that England, ever since the accession of Canute, had enjoyed profound tranquillity during a period of near fifty years; and it would require time for its soldiers, enervated by long peace, to learn discipline and its generals experience. He knew that it was entirely unprovided with fortified towns, by which it could prolong the war; but must venture its whole fortune in one decisive action against a veteran enemy, who, being once master of the field, would be in a condition to overrun the kingdom. He saw that Harold, though he had given proofs of vigor and bravery, had newly mounted a throne which he had acquired by faction, from which he had excluded a very ancient royal family, and which was likely to totter under him by its own instability, much more if shaken by any violent external impulse; and he hoped that the very circumstance of his crossing the sea, quitting his own country, and leaving himself no hopes of retreat, as it would astonish the enemy by the boldness of the enterprise, would inspirit his soldiers by despair, and rouse them to sustain the reputation of the Norman arms.

The Normans, as they had long been distinguished by valor among all the European nations, had at this time attained to the highest pitch of military glory. Besides acquiring by arms such a noble territory in France, besides defending it against continual attempts of the French monarch and all his neighbors, besides exerting many acts of vigor under their present sovereign, they had, about this very time, revived their ancient fame by the most hazardous exploits and the most wonderful successes in the other extremity of Europe. A few Norman adventurers in Italy had acquired such an ascendant, not only over the Italians and Greeks, but the Germans and Saracens, that they expelled those foreigners, procured to themselves ample establishments, and laid the foundation of the opulent kingdom of Naples and Sicily.[56] These enterprises of men who were all of them vassals in Normandy, many of them banished for faction and rebellion, excited the ambition of the haughty William, who disdained, after such examples of fortune and valor, to be deterred from making an attack on a neighboring country, where he could be supported by the whole force of his principality.

The situation also of Europe inspired William with hopes that, besides his brave Normans, he might employ against England the flower of the military force which was dispersed in all the neighboring states. France, Germany, and the Low Countries, by the progress of the feudal institutions, were divided and subdivided into many principalities and baronies; and the possessors, enjoying the civil jurisdiction within themselves, as well as the right of arms, acted, in many respects, as independent sovereigns, and maintained their properties and privileges less by the authority of laws than by their own force and valor. A military spirit had universally diffused itself throughout Europe; and the several leaders, whose minds were elevated by their princely situation, greedily embraced the most hazardous enterprises; and, being accustomed to nothing from their infancy but recitals of the success attending wars and battles, they were prompted by a natural ambition to imitate those adventures which they heard so much celebrated, and which were so much exaggerated by the credulity of the age. United, however loosely, by their duty to one superior lord, and by their connections with the great body of the community to which they belonged, they desired to spread their fame each beyond his own district; and in all assemblies, whether instituted for civil deliberations, for military expeditions, or merely for show and entertainment, to outshine each other by the reputation of strength and prowess. Hence their genius for chivalry; hence their impatience of peace and tranquillity; and hence their readiness to embark in any dangerous enterprise, how little soever interested in its failure or success.

William, by his power, his courage, and his abilities, had long maintained a pre-eminence among those haughty chieftains; and every one who desired to signalize himself by his address in military exercises, or his valor in action, had been ambitious of acquiring a reputation in the court and in the armies of Normandy. Entertained with that hospitality and courtesy which distinguished the age, they had formed attachments with the prince, and greedily attended to the prospects of the signal glory and elevation which he promised them in return for their concurrence in an expedition against England. The more grandeur there appeared in the attempt, the more it suited their romantic spirit; the fame of the intended invasion was already diffused everywhere; multitudes crowded to tender to the duke their service, with that of their vassals and retainers;[57] and William found less difficulty in completing his levies than in choosing the most veteran forces, and in rejecting the offers of those who were impatient to acquire fame under so renowned a leader.

Besides these advantages, which William owed to his personal valor and good conduct, he was indebted to fortune for procuring him some assistance, and also for removing many obstacles which it was natural for him to expect in an undertaking in which all his neighbors were so deeply interested. Conan, Count of Brittany, was his mortal enemy; in order to throw a damp upon the duke's enterprise, he chose this conjuncture for reviving his claim to Normandy itself; and he required that, in case of William's success against England, the possession of that duchy should devolve to him.[58] But Conan died suddenly after making this demand; and Hoel, his successor, instead of adopting the malignity (or, more properly speaking, the prudence) of his predecessor, zealously seconded the duke's views, and sent his eldest son, Alain Fergant, to serve under him with a body of five thousand Bretons. The Counts of Anjou and of Flanders encouraged their subjects to engage in the expedition; and even the court of France, though it might justly fear the aggrandizement of so dangerous a vassal, pursued not its interests on this occasion with sufficient vigor and resolution. Philip I., the reigning monarch, was a minor: and William, having communicated his project to the council, having desired assistance, and offered to do homage, in case of his success, for the crown of England, was indeed openly ordered to lay aside all thoughts of the enterprise; but the Earl of Flanders, his father-in-law, being at the head of the regency, favored underhand his levies, and secretly encouraged the adventurous nobility to enlist under the standard of the Duke of Normandy.

The emperor, Henry IV., besides openly giving all his vassals permission to embark in this expedition, which so much engaged the attention of Europe, promised his protection to the duchy of Normandy during the absence of the prince, and thereby enabled him to employ his whole force in the invasion of England.[59] But the most important ally whom William gained by his negotiations was the pope, who had a mighty influence over the ancient barons, no less devout in their religious principles than valorous in their military enterprises. The Roman pontiff, after an insensible

[57] Gul. Pict. p. 198.   [58] Gul. Gemet. lib. 7, cap. 33.   [59] Gul. Pict. p. 198.

progress, during several ages of darkness and ignorance, began now to lift his head openly above all the princes of Europe, to assume the office of a mediator, or even an arbiter, in the quarrels of the greatest monarchs; to interpose in all secular affairs; and to obtrude his dictates as sovereign laws on his obsequious disciples. It was a sufficient motive to Alexander II., the reigning pope, for embracing William's quarrel, that he alone had made an appeal to his tribunal, and rendered him umpire of the dispute between him and Harold; but there were other advantages which that pontiff foresaw must result from the conquest of England by the Norman arms. The kingdom, though at first converted by Romish missionaries, though it had afterwards advanced some further steps towards subjection to Rome, maintained still a considerable independence in its ecclesiastical administration; and, forming a world within itself, entirely separated from the rest of Europe, it had hitherto proved inaccessible to those exorbitant claims which supported the grandeur of the papacy. Alexander therefore hoped that the French and Norman barons, if successful in their enterprise, might import into that country a more devoted reverence to the holy see, and bring the English churches to a nearer conformity with those of the Continent. He declared immediately in favor of William's claim; pronounced Harold a perjured usurper; denounced excommunication against him and his adherents; and, the more to encourage the Duke of Normandy in his enterprise, he sent him a consecrated banner, and a ring with one of St. Peter's hairs in it.[60] Thus were all the ambition and violence of that invasion covered over safely with the broad mantle of religion.

The greatest difficulty which William had to encounter in his preparations arose from his own subjects in Normandy. The states of the duchy were assembled at Lislebonne; and supplies being demanded for the intended enterprise, which promised so much glory and advantage to their country, there appeared a reluctance in many members both to grant sums so much beyond the common measure of taxes in that age, and to set a precedent of performing their military service at a distance from their own country. The duke, finding it dangerous to solicit them in a body, conferred separately with the richest individuals in the province; and beginning with those on whose affections he most

[60] Baker, p. 22, edit. 1684.

relied, he gradually engaged all of them to advance the sums demanded. The Count of Longueville seconded him in this negotiation, as did the Count of Mortaigne, Odo (Bishop of Baieux), and especially William Fitz-Osborne (Count of Breteuil and constable of the duchy). Every person, when he himself was once engaged, endeavored to bring over others; and at last the states themselves, after stipulating that this concession should be no precedent, voted that they would assist their prince to the utmost in his intended enterprise.[61]

William had now assembled a fleet of three thousand vessels, great and small,[62] and had selected an army of sixty thousand men from among those numerous supplies which from every quarter solicited to be received into his service. The camp bore a splendid yet a martial appearance, from the discipline of the men, the beauty and vigor of the horses, the lustre of the arms, and the accoutrements of both; but, above all, from the high names of nobility who engaged under the banners of the Duke of Normandy. The most celebrated were Eustace (Count of Boulogne), Aimeri de Thouars, Hugh d'Estaples, William d'Evreux, Geoffrey de Routrou, Roger de Beaumont, William de Warenne, Roger de Montgomery, Hugh de Grantmesnil, Charles Martel, and Geoffrey Giffard.[63] To these bold chieftains William held up the spoils of England as the prize of their valor ; and, pointing to the opposite shore, called to them that *there* was the field on which they must erect trophies to their name and fix their establishments.

While he was making these mighty preparations, the duke, that he might increase the number of Harold's enemies, excited the inveterate rancor of Tosti, and encouraged him, in concert with Harold Halfagar, King of Norway, to infest the coasts of England. Tosti, having collected about sixty vessels in the ports of Flanders, put to sea; and, after committing some depredations on the south and east coasts, he sailed to Northumberland, and was there joined by Halfagar, who came over with a great armament of three hundred sail. The combined fleets entered the Humber, and disembarked the troops, who began to extend their depredations on all sides; when Morcar, Earl of Northumberland, and Edwin, Earl of Mercia, the king's brother-in-law, having hastily collected some forces, ventured

61 Camden, Introd. ad Britan. p. 212, 2d edit. Gibs.   Verstegan, p. 173.
62 Gul. Gemet. lib. 7, cap. 34.   63 Order. Vitalis, p. 501.

to give them battle. The action ended in the defeat and flight of these two noblemen.

Harold, informed of this defeat, hastened with an army to the protection of his people; and expressed the utmost ardor to show himself worthy of the crown which had been conferred upon him. This prince, though he was not sensible of the full extent of his danger, from the great combination against him, had employed every art of popularity to acquire the affections of the public; and he gave so many proofs of an equitable and prudent administration that the English found no reason to repent the choice which they had made of a sovereign. They flocked from all quarters to join his standard; and as soon as he reached the enemy at Standford, he found himself in a condition to give them battle. The action was bloody; but the victory was decisive on the side of Harold, and ended in the total rout of the Norwegians, together with the death of Tosti and Halfagar. Even the Norwegian fleet fell into the hands of Harold, who had the generosity to give Prince Olave, the son of Halfagar, his liberty, and allow him to depart with twenty vessels. But he had scarcely time to rejoice for this victory, when he received intelligence that the Duke of Normandy was landed with a great army in the south of England.

The Norman fleet and army had been assembled early in the summer at the mouth of the small river Dive, and all the troops had been instantly embarked; but the winds proved long contrary, and detained them in that harbor. The authority, however, of the duke, the good discipline maintained among the seamen and soldiers, and the great care in supplying them with provisions, had prevented any disorder; when at last the wind became favorable, and enabled them to sail along the coast till they reached St. Valori. There were, however, several vessels lost in this short passage; and as the wind again proved contrary, the army began to imagine that Heaven had declared against them, and that, notwithstanding the pope's benediction, they were destined to certain destruction. These bold warriors, who despised real dangers, were very subject to the dread of imaginary ones; and many of them began to mutiny, some of them even to desert their colors; when the duke, in order to support their drooping hopes, ordered a procession to be made with the relics of St. Valori,[64] and prayers to be said for more favorable weather. The wind instantly

64 Higden, p. 285. Order. Vit. p. 500. Matt. Paris. edit. Paris, anno 1644, p. 2.

changed; and as this incident happened on the eve of the feast of St. Michael, the tutelar saint of Normandy, the soldiers, fancying they saw the hand of Heaven in all these concurring circumstances, set out with the greatest alacrity. They met with no opposition on their passage. A great fleet which Harold had assembled, and which had cruised all summer off the Isle of Wight, had been dismissed on his receiving false intelligence that William, discouraged by contrary winds and other accidents, had laid aside his preparations. The Norman armament, proceeding in great order, arrived without any material loss at Pevensey, in Sussex; and the army quietly disembarked. The duke himself, as he leaped on shore, happened to stumble and fall, but had the presence of mind, it is said, to turn the omen to his advantage by calling aloud that he had taken possession of the country. And a soldier, running to a neighboring cottage, plucked some thatch, which, as if giving him seisin of the kingdom, he presented to his general. The joy and alacrity of William and his whole army were so great that they were nowise discouraged, even when they heard of Harold's great victory over the Norwegians; they seemed rather to wait with impatience the arrival of the enemy.

The victory of Harold, though great and honorable, had proved in the main prejudicial to his interests, and may be regarded as the immediate cause of his ruin. He lost many of his bravest officers and soldiers in the action; and he disgusted the rest by refusing to distribute the Norwegian spoils among them—a conduct which was little agreeable to his usual generosity of temper; but which his desire of sparing the people, in the war that impended over him from the Duke of Normandy, had probably occasioned. He hastened, by quick marches, to reach this new invader; but, though he was reinforced at London and other places with fresh troops, he found himself also weakened by the desertion of his old soldiers, who, from fatigue and discontent, secretly withdrew from their colors. His brother Gurth, a man of bravery and conduct, began to entertain apprehensions of the event; and remonstrated with the king that it would be better policy to prolong the war—at least, to spare his own person in the action. He urged to him that the desperate situation of the Duke of Normandy made it requisite for that prince to bring matters to a speedy decision, and put his whole fortune on the issue of a battle; but that the King of England, in his own country, beloved by his subjects, provided with every supply, had more certain and less dangerous means of insuring to himself the victory; that the Norman troops, elated, on the one hand, with the highest hopes, and seeing, on the other, no resource in case of a discomfiture, would fight to the last extremity; and, being the flower of all the warriors of the Continent, must be regarded as formidable to the English; that if their first fire, which is always the most dangerous, were allowed to languish for want of action; if they were harassed with small skirmishes, straitened in provisions, and fatigued with the bad weather and deep roads during the winter season which was approaching, they must fall an easy and a bloodless prey to their enemy; that if a general action were delayed, the English, sensible of the imminent danger to which their properties as well as liberties were exposed from those rapacious invaders, would hasten from all quarters to his assistance, and would render his army invincible; that at least, if he thought it necessary to hazard a battle, he ought not to expose his own person, but reserve, in case of disastrous accidents, some resource to the liberty and independence of the kingdom; and that, having once been so unfortunate as to be constrained to swear, and that upon the holy relics, to support the pretensions of the Duke of Normandy, it were better that the command of the army should be intrusted to another, who, not being bound by those sacred ties, might give the soldiers more assured hopes of a prosperous issue to the combat.

Harold was deaf to all these remonstrances. Elated with his past prosperity, as well as stimulated by his native courage, he resolved to give battle in person; and for that purpose he drew near to the Normans, who had removed their camp and fleet to Hastings, where they fixed their quarters. He was so confident of success that he sent a message to the duke promising him a sum of money if he would depart the kingdom without effusion of blood; but his offer was rejected with disdain; and William, not to be behind with his enemy in vaunting, sent him a message by some monks, requiring him either to resign the kingdom, or to hold it of him in fealty, or to submit their cause to the arbitration of the pope, or to fight him in single combat. Harold replied that the God of battles would soon be the arbiter of all their differences.[65]

[65] Higden, p. 286.

The English and Normans now prepared themselves for this important decision; but the aspect of things on the night before the battle was very different in the two camps. The English spent the night in riot and jollity and disorder; the Normans in silence and in prayer, and in the other functions of their religion.[66] On the morning the duke called together the most considerable of his commanders and made them a speech suitable to the occasion. He represented to them that the event which they and he had long wished for was approaching; the whole fortune of the war now depended on their swords, and would be decided in a single action; that never army had greater motives for exerting a vigorous courage, whether they considered the prize which would attend their victory, or the inevitable destruction which must ensue upon their discomfiture; that if their martial and veteran bands could once break those raw soldiers who had rashly dared to approach them, they conquered a kingdom at one blow, and were justly entitled to all its possessions as the reward of their prosperous valor; that, on the contrary, if they remitted in the least their wonted prowess, an enraged enemy hung upon their rear, the sea met them in their retreat, and an ignominious death was the certain punishment of their imprudent cowardice; that by collecting so numerous and brave a host he had insured every human means of conquest; and the commander of the enemy, by his criminal conduct, had given him just cause to hope for the favor of the Almighty, in whose hands alone lay the event of wars and battles; and that a perjured usurper, anathematized by the sovereign pontiff, and conscious of his own breach of faith, would be struck with terror on their appearance, and would prognosticate to himself that fate which his multiplied crimes had so justly merited.[67] The duke next divided his army into three lines: the first, led by Montgomery, consisted of archers and light-armed infantry; the second, commanded by Martel, was composed of his bravest battalions, heavy-armed, and ranged in close order; his cavalry, at whose head he placed himself, formed the third line, and were so disposed that they stretched beyond the infantry and flanked each wing of the army.[68] He ordered the signal of battle to be given; and the whole army, moving at once, and singing the hymn or

[66] Will. Malm. p. 101. De Gest. Angl. p. 332.
[67] H. Hunting. p. 368. Brompton, p. 959. Gul. Pict. p. 201.
[68] Gul. Pict. p. 201. Order. Vitalis, p. 501.

song of Roland, the famous peer of Charlemagne,[69] advanced in order and with alacrity towards the enemy.

Harold had seized the advantage of a rising ground, and, having likewise drawn some trenches to secure his flanks, he resolved to stand upon the defensive, and to avoid all action with the cavalry, in which he was inferior. The Kentish men were placed in the van—a post which they had always claimed as their due; the Londoners guarded the standard; and the king himself, accompanied by his two valiant brothers, Gurth and Leofwin, dismounting, placed himself at the head of his infantry, and expressed his resolution to conquer or to perish in the action. The first attack of the Normans was desperate, but was received with equal valor by the English; and after a furious combat, which remained long undecided, the former, overcome by the difficulty of the ground, and hard pressed by the enemy, began first to relax their vigor, then to retreat; and confusion was spreading among the ranks, when William, who found himself on the brink of destruction, hastened with a select band to the relief of his dismayed forces. His presence restored the action; the English were obliged to retire with loss; and the duke, ordering his second line to advance, renewed the attack with fresh forces and with redoubled courage. Finding that the enemy, aided by the advantage of ground, and animated by the example of their prince, still made a vigorous resistance, he tried a stratagem which was very delicate in its management, but which seemed advisable in his desperate situation, where, if he gained not a decisive victory, he was totally undone: he commanded his troops to make a hasty retreat, and to allure the enemy from their ground by the appearance of flight. The artifice succeeded against those inexperienced soldiers, who, heated by the action, and sanguine in their hopes, precipitately followed the Normans into the plain. William gave orders that at once the infantry should face about upon their pursuers, and the cavalry make an assault upon their wings, and both of them pursue the advantage which the surprise and terror of the enemy must give them in that critical and decisive moment. The English were repulsed with great slaughter, and driven back to the hill; where, being rallied by the bravery of Harold, they were able, notwithstanding their loss, to maintain their post and continue the combat. The duke tried

---

[69] Will. Malm. p. 101. Higden, p. 286. Matt. West. p. 223. Du Cange's Glossary, *in verbis* Cantilena Rolandi.

the same stratagem a second time with the same success; but even after this double advantage he still found a great body of the English, who, maintaining themselves in firm array, seemed determined to dispute the victory to the last extremity. He ordered his heavy-armed infantry to make an assault upon them; while his archers, placed behind, should gall the enemy, who were exposed by the situation of the ground, and who were intent on defending themselves against the swords and spears of the assailants. By this disposition he at last prevailed. Harold was slain by an arrow while he was combating with great bravery at the head of his men; his two brothers shared the same fate; and the English, discouraged by the fall of those princes, gave ground on all sides, and were pursued with great slaughter by the victorious Normans. A few troops, however, of the vanquished had still the courage to turn upon their pursuers; and, attacking them in deep and miry ground, obtained some revenge for the slaughter and dishonor of the day. But the appearance of the duke obliged them to seek their safety by flight; and darkness saved them from any farther pursuit by the enemy.

Thus was gained by William, Duke of Normandy, the great and decisive victory of Hastings, after a battle which was fought from morning till sunset, and which seemed worthy, by the heroic valor displayed by both armies and by both commanders, to decide the fate of a mighty kingdom. William had three horses killed under him; and there fell near fifteen thousand men on the side of the Normans. The loss was still more considerable on that of the vanquished, besides the death of the king and his two brothers. The dead body of Harold was brought to William, and was generously restored without ransom to his mother. The Norman army left not the field of battle without giving thanks to Heaven in the most solemn manner for their victory; and the prince, having refreshed his troops, prepared to push to the utmost his advantage against the divided, dismayed, and discomfited English.

APPENDIX I.

THE ANGLO-SAXON GOVERNMENT AND MANNERS.

FIRST SAXON GOVERNMENT.—SUCCESSION OF THE KINGS.—
THE WITENAGEMOTE.—THE ARISTOCRACY.—THE SEVERAL
ORDERS OF MEN.—COURTS OF JUSTICE.—CRIMINAL LAW.—
RULES OF PROOF.—MILITARY FORCE.—PUBLIC REVENUE.—
VALUE OF MONEY.—MANNERS.

THE government of the Germans, and that of all the
northern nations who established themselves on the ruins
of Rome, was always extremely free; and those fierce people, accustomed to independence and inured to arms, were
more guided by persuasion than authority in the submission
which they paid to their princes. The military despotism
which had taken place in the Roman empire, and which,
previously to the irruption of those conquerors, had sunk
the genius of men, and destroyed every noble principle of
science and virtue, was unable to resist the vigorous efforts
of a free people; and Europe, as from a new epoch, rekindled her ancient spirit, and shook off the base servitude
to arbitrary will and authority under which she had so long
labored. The free constitutions then established, however
impaired by the encroachments of succeeding princes, still
preserve an air of independence and legal administration
which distinguishes the European nations; and if that part
of the globe maintains sentiments of liberty, honor, equity,
and valor superior to the rest of mankind, it owes these advantages chiefly to the seeds implanted by those generous
barbarians.

The Saxons who subdued Britain, as they had enjoyed
great liberty in their own country, obstinately retained that
invaluable possession in their new settlement; and they imported into this island the same principles of independence
which they had inherited from their ancestors. The chief
tains (for such they were, more properly than kings or
princes) who commanded them in those military expedi-

tions still possessed a very limited authority; and as the Saxons exterminated, rather than subdued, the ancient inhabitants, they were indeed transplanted into a new territory, but preserved unaltered all their civil and military institutions. The language was pure Saxon; even the names of places, which often remain while the tongue entirely changes, were almost all affixed by the conquerors; the manners and customs were wholly German; and the same picture of a fierce and bold liberty which is drawn by the masterly pencil of Tacitus will suit those founders of the English government. The king, so far from being invested with arbitrary power, was only considered as the first among the citizens; his authority depended more on his personal qualities than on his station; he was even so far on a level with the people that a stated price was fixed for his head, and a legal fine was levied upon his murderer, which, though proportionate to his station and superior to that paid for the life of a subject, was a sensible mark of his subordination to the community.

It is easy to imagine that an independent people so little restrained by law and cultivated by science, would not be very strict in maintaining a regular succession of their princes. Though they paid great regard to the royal family, and ascribed to it an undisputed superiority, they either had no rule, or none that was steadily observed, in filling the vacant throne; and present convenience, in that emergency, was more attended to than general principles. We are not, however, to suppose, that the crown was considered as altogether elective, and that a regular plan was traced by the constitution for supplying, by the suffrages of the people, every vacancy made by the demise of the first magistrate. If any king left a son of an age and capacity fit for government, the young prince naturally stepped into the throne; if he was a minor, his uncle, or the next prince of the blood, was promoted to the government, and left the sceptre to his posterity. Any sovereign, by taking previous measures with the leading men, had it greatly in his power to appoint his successor. All these changes, and indeed the ordinary administration of government, required the express concurrence, or at least the tacit acquiescence, of the people; but possession, however obtained, was extremely apt to secure their obedience, and the idea of any right, which was once excluded, was but feeble and imperfect. This is so much the case in all barbarous monarchies, and occurs so often in the history of the Anglo-Saxons, that we cannot consistently entertain any other notion of their government. The idea of an hereditary succession in authority is so natural to men, and is so much fortified by the usual rule in transmitting private possessions, that it must retain a great influence on every society, which does not exclude it by the refinements of a republican constitution. But as there is a material difference between government and private possessions, and every man is not as much qualified for exercising the one as for enjoying the other, a people who are not sensible of the general advantages attending a fixed rule are apt to make great leaps in the succession, and frequently to pass over the person who, had he possessed the requisite years and abilities, would have been thought entitled to the sovereignty. Thus these monarchies are not, strictly speaking, either elective or hereditary; and, though the destination of a prince may often be followed in appointing his successor, they can as little be regarded as wholly testamentary. The states by their suffrage may sometimes establish a sovereign; but they more frequently recognize the person whom they find established. A few great men take the lead; the people, overawed and influenced, acquiesce in the government; and the reigning prince, provided he be of the royal family, passes undisputedly for the legal sovereign.

It is confessed that our knowledge of the Anglo-Saxon history and antiquity is too imperfect to afford us means of determining with certainty all the prerogatives of the crown and privileges of the people, or of giving an exact delineation of that government. It is probable, also, that the constitution might be somewhat different in the different kingdoms of the Heptarchy, and that it changed considerably during the course of six centuries, which elapsed from the first invasion of the Saxons till the Norman conquest.[1] But most of these differences and changes, with their causes and effects, are unknown to us. It only appears that at all times, and in all the kingdoms, there was a national council called a Witenagemote, or as-

---

[1] We know of one change, not inconsiderable, in the Saxon constitution. The Saxon Annals, p. 49, inform us that it was in early times the prerogative of the king to name the dukes, earls, aldermen, and sheriffs of the counties. Asser, a contemporary writer, informs us that Alfred deposed all the ignorant aldermen, and appointed men of more capacity in their place. Yet the laws of Edward the Confessor, § 35, say expressly that the heretoghs, or dukes, and the sheriffs were chosen by the freeholders in the folkmote, a county court, which was assembled once a year, and where all the freeholders swore allegiance to the king.

sem ly of the wise men (for that is the import of the term),
whose consent was requisite for enacting laws and for ratifying the chief acts of public administration. The preambles
to all the laws of Ethelbert, Ina, Alfred, Edward the Elder,
Athelstan, Edmond, Edgar, Ethelred, and Edward the Confessor—even those to the laws of Canute, though a kind of
conqueror—put this matter beyond controversy, and carry
proofs everywhere of a limited and legal government. But
who were the constituent members of this Witenagemote
has not been determined with certainty by antiquaries. It
is agreed that the bishops and abbots [2] were an essential
part; and it is also evident, from the tenor of those ancient
laws, that the Witenagemote enacted statutes which regulated the ecclesiastical as well as civil government, and that
those dangerous principles by which the Church is totally
severed from the State were hitherto unknown to the Anglo-
Saxons.[3] It also appears that the aldermen, or governors
of counties, who, after the Danish times, were often called
earls,[4] were admitted into this council, and gave their consent to the public statutes. But besides the prelates and
aldermen, there is also mention of the Wites, or wise men,
as a component part of the Witenagemote; but who *these*
were is not so clearly ascertained by the laws or the history
of that period. The matter would probably be of difficult
discussion, even were it examined impartially; but as our
modern parties have chosen to divide on this point, the
question has been disputed with the greater obstinacy, and
the arguments on both sides have become, on that account,
the more captious and deceitful. Our monarchical faction
maintain that these *Wites,* or *Sapientes,* were the judges,
or men learned in the law; the popular faction assert them
to be representatives of the boroughs, or what we now call
the Commons.

The expressions employed by all ancient historians in
mentioning the Witenagemote seem to contradict the latter
supposition. The members are almost always called the
principes, satrapœ, optimates, magnates, proceres—terms
which seem to suppose an aristocracy and to exclude the
Commons. The boroughs also, from the low state of commerce, were so small and so poor, and the inhabitants lived
in such dependence on the great men,[5] that it seemed no-

---

[2] Sometimes abbesses were admitted; at least, they often sign the king's charters or grants. Spell. Gloss. *in verbo* Parliamentum.
[3] Wilkins, passim.   [4] See note [G] at the end of the volume.
[5] Brady's Treatise of English Boroughs, pp. 3, 4, 5, etc.

wise probable they would be admitted as a part of the national councils. The Commons are well known to have had no share in the governments established by the Franks, Burgundians, and other northern nations; and we may conclude that the Saxons, who remained longer barbarous and uncivilized than those tribes, would never think of conferring such an extraordinary privilege on trade and industry. The military profession alone was honorable among all those conquerors; the warriors subsisted by their possessions in land; they became considerable by their influence over their vassals, retainers, tenants, and slaves; and it requires strong proof to convince us that they would admit any of a rank so much inferior as the burgesses to share with them in the legislative authority. Tacitus indeed affirms that among the ancient Germans the consent of all the members of the community was required in every important deliberation; but he speaks not of representatives; and this ancient practice, mentioned by the Roman historian, could only have place in small tribes, where every citizen might, without inconvenience, be assembled upon any extraordinary emergency. After principalities became extensive; after the difference of property had formed distinctions more important than those which arose from personal strength and valor, we may conclude that the national assemblies must have been more limited in their number, and composed only of the more considerable citizens.

But though we must exclude the burgesses, or Commons, from the Saxon Witenagemote, there is some necessity for supposing that this assembly consisted of other members than the prelates, abbots, aldermen, and the judges, or privy council. For as all these, excepting some of the ecclesiastics,[6] were anciently appointed by the king, had there been no other legislative authority, the royal power had been in a great measure absolute, contrary to the tenor of all the historians and to the practice of all the northern nations. We may therefore conclude that the more considerable proprietors of land were, without any election, constituent members of the national assembly; there is reason to think

---

[6] There is some reason to think that the bishops were sometimes chosen by the Witenagemote, and confirmed by the king (Eddius, cap. 2). The abbots in the monasteries of royal foundation were anciently named by the king, though Edgar gave the monks the election, and only reserved to himself the ratification. This destination was afterwards frequently violated; and the abbots as well as bishops were afterwards all appointed by the king, as we learn from Ingulf, a writer contemporary with the Conquest.

that forty hides, or between four and five thousand acres, was the estate requisite for entitling the possessor to this honorable privilege. We find a passage in an ancient author[7] by which it appears that a person of very noble birth, even one allied to the crown, was not esteemed a *princeps* (the term usually employed by ancient historians when the Witenagemote is mentioned) till he had acquired a fortune of that amount. Nor need we imagine that the public council would become disorderly or confused by admitting so great a multitude. The landed property of England was probably in few hands during the Saxon times—at least during the latter part of that period; and as men had hardly any ambition to attend those public councils, there was no danger of the assembly's becoming too numerous for the despatch of the little business which was brought before them.

It is certain that, whatever we may determine concerning the constituent members of the Witenagemote, in whom, with the king, the legislature resided, the Anglo-Saxon government, in the period preceding the Norman conquest, was become extremely aristocratical, the royal authority was very limited; the people, even if admitted to that assembly, were of little or no weight and consideration. We have hints given us by historians of the great power and riches of particular noblemen; and it could not but happen, after the abolition of the Heptarchy, when the king lived at a distance from the provinces, that those great proprietors, who resided on their estates, would much augment their authority over their vassals and retainers, and over all the inhabitants of the neighborhood. Hence the immeasurable power assumed by Harold, Godwin, Leofric, Siward, Morcar, Edwin, Edric, and Alfric, who controlled the authority of the kings, and rendered themselves quite necessary in the government. The two latter, though detested by the people on account of their joining a foreign enemy, still preserved their power and influence; and we may therefore conclude that their authority was founded, not on popularity, but on family rights and possessions. There is one Athelstan, mentioned in the reign of the king of that name, who is called Alderman of all England, and is said to be half-king; though the monarch himself was a prince of valor and abilities.[8] And we find that in the latter Saxon times,

[7] Hist. Eliensis, lib. 2, cap. 40.   [8] Hist. Rames, § 3, p. 387.

and in these alone, the great offices went from father to son, and became in a manner hereditary in the families.[9]

The circumstances attending the invasions of the Danes would also serve much to increase the power of the principal nobility. Those freebooters made unexpected inroads on all quarters; and there was a necessity that each county should resist them by its own force, and under the conduct of its own nobility and its own magistrates. For the same reason that a general war, managed by the united efforts of the whole state, commonly augments the power of the crown, those private wars and inroads turned to the advantage of the aldermen and nobles.

Among that military and turbulent people, so averse to commerce and the arts, and so little inured to industry, justice was commonly very ill administered, and great oppression and violence seemed to have prevailed. These disorders would be increased by the exorbitant power of the aristocracy; and would, in their turn, contribute to increase it. Men, not daring to rely on the guardianship of the laws, were obliged to devote themselves to the service of some chieftain, whose orders they followed, even to the disturbance of the government or the injury of their fellow-citizens, and who afforded them, in return, protection from any insult or injustice by strangers. Hence we find by the extracts which Dr. Brady has given us from Domesday that almost all the inhabitants, even of towns, had placed themselves under the clientship of some particular nobleman, whose patronage they purchased by annual payments, and whom they were obliged to consider as their sovereign, more than the king himself, or even the legislature.[10] A client, though a freeman, was supposed so much to belong to his patron that his murderer was obliged by law to pay a fine to the latter as a compensation for his loss, in like manner as he paid a fine to the master for the murder of his slave.[11] Men who were of a more considerable rank, but not powerful enough each to support himself by his own independent authority, entered into formal confederacies with each other, and composed a kind of separate community,

[9] Roger Hoveden, giving the reason why William the Conqueror made Cospatric Earl of Northumberland, says, "Nam ex materno sanguine attinebat ad eum honor ilius comitatus. Erat enim ex matre Algitha, filia Uthredi comitis." See also Sim. Dunelm. p. 205. We see in those instances the same tendency towards rendering offices hereditary, which took place, during a more early period, on the Continent, and which had already produced there its full effect.

[10] Brady's Treatise of Boroughs, pp. 3, 4, 5, etc. The case was the same with the freemen in the country. See Pref. to his Hist. pp. 8, 9, 10, etc.

[11] Leges Edw. Conf. § 8, apud Ingulph.

which rendered itself formidable to all aggressors. Dr. Hickes has preserved a curious Saxon bond of this kind, which he calls a *Sodalitium*, and which contains many particulars characteristical of the manners and customs of the times.[12] All the associates are there said to be gentlemen of Cambridgeshire, and they swear before the holy relics to observe their confederacy, and to be faithful to each other. They promise to bury any of the associates who dies, in whatever place he had appointed; to contribute to his funeral charges, and to attend at his interment; and whoever is wanting in this last duty binds himself to pay a measure of honey. When any of the associates is in danger, and calls for the assistance of his fellows, they promise, besides flying to his succor, to give information to the sheriff; and if he be negligent in protecting the person exposed to danger, they engage to levy a fine of one pound upon him: if the president of the society himself be wanting in this particular, he binds himself to pay one pound, unless he has the reasonable excuse of sickness, or of duty to his superior. When any of the associates is murdered, they are to exact eight pounds from the murderer; and if he refuse to pay it, they are to prosecute him for the sum at their joint expense. If any of the associates who happens to be poor kill a man, the society are to contribute, by a certain proportion, to pay his fine: a mark apiece if the fine be seven hundred shillings; less if the person killed be a clown or a ceorle; the half of that sum again if he be a Welshman. But where any of the associates kills a man, wilfully and without provocation, he must himself pay the fine. If any of the associates kill any of his fellows in a like criminal manner, besides paying the usual fine to the relations of the deceased, he must pay eight pounds to the society, or renounce the benefit of it; in which case they bind themselves, under the penalty of one pound, never to eat or drink with him, except in the presence of the king, bishop, or alderman. There are other regulations to protect themselves and their servants from all injuries, to revenge such as are committed, and to prevent their giving abusive language to each other: and the fine, which they engage to pay for this last offence, is a measure of honey.

It is not to be doubted but a confederacy of this kind must have been a great source of friendship and attachment when men lived in perpetual danger from enemies, robbers,

[12] Dissert. Epist. p. 21.

and oppressors, and received protection chiefly from their personal valor, and from the assistance of their friends or patrons. As animosities were then more violent, connections were also more intimate, whether voluntary or derived from blood; the most remote degree of propinquity was regarded; an indelible memory of benefits was preserved; severe vengeance was taken for injuries, both from a point of honor and as the best means of future security; and the civil union being weak, many private engagements were contracted in order to supply its place, and to procure men that safety which the laws and their own innocence were not alone able to insure to them.

On the whole, notwithstanding the seeming liberty, or rather licentiousness, of the Anglo-Saxons, the great body even of the free citizens, in those ages, really enjoyed much less true liberty than where the execution of the laws is the most severe, and where subjects are reduced to the strictest subordination and dependence on the civil magistrate. The reason is derived from the excess itself of that liberty. Men must guard themselves at any price against insults and injuries; and where they receive not protection from the laws and magistrate, they will seek it by submission to superiors, and by herding in some private confederacy which acts under the direction of a powerful leader. And thus all anarchy is the immediate cause of tyranny, if not over the state, at least over many of the individuals.

Security was provided by the Saxon laws to all members of the Witenagemote, both in going and returning, *except they were notorious thieves and robbers.*

The German Saxons, as the other nations of that continent, were divided into three ranks of men—the noble, the free, and the slaves.[13] This distinction they brought over with them into Britain.

The nobles were called thanes, and were of two kinds— the king's thanes and lesser thanes. The latter seem to have been dependent upon the former, and to have received lands for which they paid rent, services, or attendance in peace and war.[14] We know of no title which raised any one to the rank of thane, except noble birth and the possession of land. The former was always much regarded by all the German nations, even in their most barbarous state; and as the Saxon nobility, having little credit, could scarcely burden their estates with much debt, and as the Commons

[13] Nithard, Hist. lib. 4.   [14] Spell. Feuds and Tenures, p. 40.

had little trade or industry by which they could accumulate riches, these two ranks of men, even though they were not separated by positive laws, might remain long distinct, and the noble families continue many ages in opulence and splendor. There were no middle ranks of men that could gradually mix with their superiors, and insensibly procure to themselves honor and distinction. If by any extraordinary accident a mean person acquired riches, a circumstance so singular made him be known and remarked; he became the object of envy as well as of indignation to all the nobles; he would have great difficulty to defend what he had acquired; and he would find it impossible to protect himself from oppression, except by courting the patronage of some great chieftain, and paying a large price for his safety.

There are two statutes among the Saxon laws which seem calculated to confound those different ranks of men—that of Athelstan, by which a merchant, who had made three long sea-voyages on his own account, was entitled to the quality of thane;[15] and that of the same prince, by which a ceorle, or husbandman, who had been able to purchase five hides of land, and had a chapel, a kitchen, a hall, and a bell, was raised to the same distinction.[16] But the opportunities were so few by which a merchant or ceorle could thus exalt himself above his rank that the law could never overcome the reigning prejudices: the distinction between noble and base blood would still be indelible; and the well-born thanes would entertain the highest contempt for those legal and factitious ones. Though we are not informed of any of these circumstances by ancient historians, they are so much founded on the nature of things that we may admit them as a necessary and infallible consequence of the situation of the kingdom during those ages.

The cities appear by Domesday-book to have been at the Conquest little better than villages.[17] York itself, though it was always the second—at least the third[18]—city in England, and was the capital of a great province, which never was thoroughly united with the rest, contained then but one thousand four hundred and eighteen families.[19] Malmes-

[15] Wilkins, p. 71.   [16] Selden, Titles of Honor, p. 515. Wilkins, p. 70.
[17] Winchester, being the capital of the West-Saxon monarchy, was anciently a considerable city. Gul. Pict. p. 210.
[18] Norwich contained 738 houses, Exeter 315, Ispwich 538, Northampton 60, Hertford 146, Canterbury 262, Bath 64, Southampton 84, Warwick 225. See Brady on Boroughs, pp. 3, 4, 5, 6, etc. These are the most considerable he mentions. The account of them is extracted from Domesday-book.
[19] Brady's Treatise of Boroughs, p. 10. There were six wards, besides the archbishop's palace ; and five of these wards contained the number of families here mentioned, which, at the rate of five persons to a family, makes about 7000 souls. The sixth ward was laid waste.

bury tells us [20] that the great distinction between the Anglo-Saxon nobility and the French or Norman was that the latter built magnificent and stately castles, whereas the former consumed their immense fortunes in riot and hospitality and in mean houses. We may thence infer that the arts in general were much less advanced in England than in France; a greater number of idle servants and retainers lived about the great families; and as these, even in France, were powerful enough to disturb the execution of the laws, we may judge of the authority acquired by the aristocracy in England. When Earl Godwin besieged the Confessor in London, he summoned from all parts his huscarles, or houseceorles, and retainers, and thereby constrained his sovereign to accept of the conditions which he was pleased to impose upon him.

The lower rank of freemen were denominated ceorles among the Anglo-Saxons; and where they were industrious, they were chiefly employed in husbandry; whence a ceorle and a husbandman became in a manner synonymous terms. They cultivated the farms of the nobility, or thanes, for which they paid rent; and they seem to have been removable at pleasure. For there is little mention of leases among the Anglo-Saxons; the pride of the nobility, together with the general ignorance of writing, must have rendered these contracts very rare, and must have kept the husbandmen in a dependent condition. The rents of farms were then chiefly paid in kind. [21]

But the most numerous rank by far in the community seems to have been the slaves, or villeins, who were the property of their lords, and were consequently incapable themselves of possessing any property. Dr. Brady assures us, from a survey of Domesday-book,[22] that in all the counties of England the far greater part of the land was occupied by them; and that the husbandmen, and still more the socmen, who were tenants that could not be removed at pleasure, were very few in comparison. This was not the case with the German nations, as far as we can collect from the account given us by Tacitus. The perpetual wars in the Heptarchy, and the depredations of the Danes, seem to have been the cause of this great alteration with the Anglo-Saxons. Prisoners taken in battle or carried off in the frequent

[20] P. 102. See also De Gest. Angl. p. 333.
[21] Leges Inæ, § 70. These laws fixed the rents for a hide; but it is difficult to convert it into modern measures.
[22] General Preface to his Hist. pp. 7, 8, 9, etc.

inroads were then reduced to slavery, and became, by right of war,[23] entirely at the disposal of their lords. Great property in the nobles, especially if joined to an irregular administration of justice, naturally favors the power of the aristocracy, but still more so if the practice of slavery be admitted and has become very common. The nobility not only possess the influence which always attends riches, but also the power which the laws give them over their slaves and villeins. It then becomes difficult, and almost impossible, for a private man to remain altogether free and independent.

There were two kinds of slaves among the Anglo-Saxons —household slaves, after the manner of the ancients, and prædial, or rustic, after the manner of the Germans.[24] These latter resembled the serfs which are at present to be met with in Poland, Denmark, and some parts of Germany. The power of a master over his slaves was not unlimited among the Anglo-Saxons, as it was among their ancestors. If a man beat out his slave's eye or teeth, the slave recovered his liberty; [25] if he killed him, he paid a fine to the king, provided the slave died within a day after the wound or blow; otherwise it passed unpunished.[26] The selling of themselves or children to slavery was always the practice among the German nations,[27] and was continued by the Anglo-Saxons.[28]

The great lords and abbots among the Anglo-Saxons possessed a criminal jurisdiction within their territories, and could punish without appeal any thieves or robbers whom they caught there.[29] This institution must have had a very contrary effect to that which was intended, and must have procured robbers a sure protection on the lands of such noblemen as did not sincerely mean to discourage crimes and violence.

But though the general strain of the Anglo-Saxon government seems to have become aristocratical, there were still considerable remains of the ancient democracy, which were not indeed sufficient to protect the lowest of the people without the patronage of some great lord, but might give security, and even some degree of dignity, to the gentry or inferior nobility. The administration of justice, in particular, by the courts of the decennary, the hundred, and the county, was well calculated to defend general liberty

[23] Leges Edg. § 14, apud Spell. Conc. vol. i. p. 471.
[24] Spell. Gloss. *in verbo*, Servus.   [25] Leges Ælf. § 20.   [26] Leges Ælf. § 17.
[27] Tacit. de Morib. Germ.   [28] Leges Inæ, § 11.   Leges Ælf. § 12.
[29] Higden. lib. 1. cap. 50. Leges Edw. Conf. § 26. Spell. Conc. vol. i. p. 415.
Gloss. *in verb.* Haligemot *et* Infangenthefe.

and to restrain the power of the nobles. In the county courts, or shiremotes, all the freeholders were assembled twice a year, and received appeals from the inferior courts. They there decided all causes, ecclesiastical as well as civil; and the bishop, together with the alderman, or earl, presided over them.[30] The affair was determined in a summary manner, without much pleading, formality, or delay, by a majority of voices; and the bishop and alderman had no further authority than to keep order among the freeholders and interpose with their opinion.[31] Where justice was denied during three sessions by the hundred, and then by the county court, there lay an appeal to the king's court;[32] but this was not practised on slight occasions. The alderman received a third of the fines levied in those courts;[33] and as most of the punishments were then pecuniary, this perquisite formed a considerable part of the profits belonging to his office. The two-thirds also which went to the king made no contemptible part of the public revenue. Any freeholder was fined who absented himself thrice from these courts.[34]

As the extreme ignorance of the age made deeds and writing very rare, the county or hundred court was the place where the most remarkable civil transactions were finished, in order to preserve the memory of them, and prevent all future disputes. Here testaments were promulgated, slaves manumitted, bargains of sale concluded; and sometimes, for greater security, the most considerable of these deeds were inserted in the blank leaves of the parish Bible, which thus became a kind of register too sacred to be falsified. It was not unusual to add to the deed an imprecation on all such as should be guilty of that crime.[35]

Among a people who lived in so simple a manner as the Anglo-Saxons, the judicial power is always of greater importance than the legislative. There were few or no taxes imposed by the states; there were few statutes enacted; and the nation was less governed by laws than by customs, which admitted a great latitude of interpretation. Though it should therefore be allowed that the Witenagemote was altogether composed of the principal nobility, the county courts, where all the freeholders were admitted, and which regulated all the daily occurrences of life, formed a wide

[30] Leges Edg. § 5.　Wilkins, p. 78.　Leges Canut. § 17.　Wilkins, p. 136.
[31] Hickes, Dissert, Epist. pp. 2, 3, 4, 5, 6, 7, 8.
[32] Leges Edg. § 2.　Wilkins, p. 77.　Leges Canut. § 18, apud Wilkins, p. 136.
[33] Leges Edw. Conf. § 31.　　[34] Leges Ethelst. § 20.　　[35] Hickes, Dissert. Epist.

basis for the government, and were no contemptible checks on the aristocracy. But there is another power still more important than either the judicial or legislative—to wit, the power of injuring or serving by immediate force and violence, for which it is difficult to obtain redress in courts of justice. In all extensive governments, where the execution of the laws is feeble, this power naturally falls into the hands of the principal nobility; and the degree of it which prevails cannot be determined so much by the public statutes as by small incidents in history, by particular customs, and sometimes by the reason and nature of things. The Highlands of Scotland have long been entitled by law to every privilege of British subjects, but it was not till very lately that the common people could in fact enjoy these privileges.

The powers of all the members of the Anglo-Saxon government are disputed among historians and antiquaries: the extreme obscurity of the subject, even though faction had never entered into the question, would naturally have begotten those controversies. But the great influence of the lords over their slaves and tenants, the clientship of the burghers, the total want of a middling rank of men, the extent of the monarchy, the loose execution of the laws, the continued disorders and convulsions of the state—all these circumstances evince that the Anglo-Saxon government became at last extremely aristocratical; and the events during the period immediately preceding the Conquest confirm this inference or conjecture.

Both the punishments inflicted by the Anglo-Saxon courts of judicature, and the methods of proof employed in all causes, appear somewhat singular, and are very different from those which prevail at present among all civilized nations.

We must conceive that the ancient Germans were little removed from the original state of nature: the social confederacy among them was more martial than civil; they had chiefly in view the means of attack or defence against public enemies, not those of protection against their fellow-citizens; their possessions were so slender and so equal that they were not exposed to great danger; and the natural bravery of the people made every man trust to himself and to his particular friends for his defence or vengeance. This defect in the political union drew much closer the knot of particular confederacies An insult upon any man was

regarded by all his relations and associates as a common
injury; they were bound by honor as well as by a sense of
common interest to revenge his death, or any violence which
he had suffered; they retaliated on the aggressor by like
acts of violence; and if he were protected, as was natural
and usual, by his own clan, the quarrel was spread still
wider, and bred endless disorders in the nation.

The Frisians, a tribe of the Germans, had never advanced beyond this wild and imperfect state of society; and
the right of private revenge still remained among them unlimited and uncontrolled.[36] But the other German nations,
in the age of Tacitus, had made one step further towards
completing the political or civil union. Though it still continued to be an indispensable point of honor for every clan
to revenge the death or injury of a member, the magistrate
had acquired a right of interposing in the quarrel and of
accommodating the difference. He obliged the person
maimed or injured, and the relations of one killed, to accept of a present from the aggressor and his relations [37] as a
compensation for the injury,[38] and to drop all further prosecution of revenge. That the accommodation of one quarrel might not be the source of more, this present was fixed
and certain, according to the rank of the person killed or
injured, and was commonly paid in cattle, the chief property
of those rude and uncultivated nations. A present of this
kind gratified the revenge of the injured family by the loss
which the aggressor suffered; it satisfied their pride by the
submission which it expressed; it diminished their regret
for the loss or injury of a kinsman by their acquisition of a
new property; and thus general peace was for a moment restored to the society.[39]

But when the German nations had been settled some
time in the provinces of the Roman empire, they made still
another step towards a more cultivated life, and their criminal justice gradually improved and refined itself. The
magistrate, whose office it was to guard public peace and to
suppress private animosities, conceived himself to be injured
by every injury done to any of his people; and besides the
compensation to the person who suffered, or to his family,
he thought himself entitled to exact a fine called the *fridwit*

---

[36] Leges Fris. tit. 2, apud Lindenbrog. p. 491.
[37] Leges Æthelb. § 23. Leges Ælf. § 27.   [38] Called by the Saxons *mægbota*.
[39] Tacit. de Morib. Germ. The author says that the price of the composition
was fixed, which must have been by the laws and the interposition of the magistrates.

as an atonement for the breach of peace, and as a reward for the pains which he had taken in accommodating the quarrel. When this idea, which is so natural, was once suggested, it was willingly received both by sovereign and people. The numerous fines which were levied augmented the revenue of the king; and the people were sensible that he would be more vigilant in interposing with his good offices when he reaped such immediate advantage from them; and that injuries would be less frequent when, besides compensation to the person injured, they were exposed to this additional penalty.[40]

This short abstract contains the history of the criminal jurisprudence of the northern nations for several centuries. The state of England in this particular, during the period of the Anglo-Saxons, may be judged of by the collection of ancient laws published by Lambard and Wilkins. The chief purport of these laws is not to prevent or entirely suppress private quarrels, which the legislature knew to be impossible, but only to regulate and moderate them. The laws of Alfred enjoin that if any one know that his enemy or aggressor, after doing him an injury, resolves to keep within his own house *and his own lands*,[41] he shall not fight him till he require compensation for the injury. If he be strong enough to besiege him in his house, he may do it for seven days without attacking him; and if the aggressor be willing, during that time, to surrender himself and his arms, his adversary may detain him thirty days, but is afterwards obliged to restore him safe to his kindred, *and be content with the compensation*. If the criminal fly to the temple, that sanctuary must not be violated. Where the assailant has not force sufficient to besiege the criminal in his house, he must apply to the alderman for assistance; and if the alderman refuse aid, the assailant must have recourse to the king; and he is not allowed to assault the house till after this supreme magistrate has refused assistance. If any one meet with his enemy, and be ignorant that he has resolved to keep within his own lands, he must, before he attack him, require him to surrender himself prisoner, and deliver up his arms, in which case he may detain him thirty days; but

---

[40] Besides paying money to the relations of the deceased and to the king, the murderer was also obliged to pay the master of a slave or vassal a sum as a compensation for his loss. This was called the *manbote*. See Spell. Gloss. *in verb.* Fredum, Manbot.

[41] The addition of these last words in Italics appears necessary from what follows in the same law.

if he refuse to deliver up his arms, it is then lawful to fight him. A slave may fight in his master's quarrel : a father may fight in his son's with any one, except with his master.[42]

It was enacted by King Ina that no man should take revenge for an injury till he had first demanded compensation and had been refused it.[43]

King Edmond, in the preamble to his laws, mentions the general misery occasioned by the multiplicity of private feuds and battles ; and he establishes several expedients for remedying this grievance. He ordains that if any one commit murder, he may, with the assistance of his kindred, pay within a twelvemonth the fine of his crime; and if they abandon him, he shall alone sustain the deadly feud or quarrel with the kindred of the murdered person. His own kindred are free from the feud, but on condition that they neither converse with the criminal nor supply him with meat or *other necessaries:* if any of them, after renouncing him, receive him into their house, *or give him assistance,* they are finable to the king, and are involved in the feud. If the kindred of the murdered person take revenge on any but the criminal himself, *after he is abandoned by his kindred,* all their property is forfeited, and they are declared to be enemies to the king and all his friends.[44] It is also ordained that the fine for murder shall never be remitted by the king ; [45] and that no criminal shall be killed who flies to the church or any of the king's towns ; [46] and the king himself declares that his house shall give no protection to murderers till they have satisfied the Church by their penance and the kindred of the deceased by making compensation.[47] The method appointed for transacting this composition it found in the same law.[48]

These attempts of Edmond to contract and diminish the feuds were contrary to the ancient spirit of the northern barbarians, and were a step towards a more regular administration of justice. By the Salic law, any man might, by a public declaration, exempt himself from his family quarrels; but then he was considered by the law as no longer belonging to the family, and he was deprived of all right of succession as the punishment of his cowardice.[49]

The price of the king's head, or his weregild, as it was

---

[42] Leges Ælf. § 28.   Wilkins, p. 43.   [43] Leges Inæ, § 9.
[44] Leges Edm. § 1.   Wilkins, p. 73.   [45] Leges Edm. § 3.
[46] Leges Edm. § 2.   [47] Leges Edm. § 4.   [48] Leges Edm. § 7.   [49] Tit. 63.

then called, was by law thirty thousand thrimsas, near thirteen hundred pounds of present money. The price of the prince's head was fifteen thousand thrimsas; that of a bishop's or alderman's, eight thousand; a sheriff's, four thousand; a thane's or clergyman's, two thousand; a ceorle's, two hundred and sixty-six. These prices were fixed by the laws of the Angles. By the Mercian law, the price of a ceorle's head was two hundred shillings; that of a thane's six times as much; that of a king's six times more.[50] By the laws of Kent, the price of the archbishop's head was higher than that of the king's.[51] Such respect was then paid to the ecclesiastics! It must be understood that where a person was unable or unwilling to pay the fine, he was put out of the protection of law, and the kindred of the deceased had liberty to punish him as they thought proper.

Some antiquarians[52] have thought that these compensations were only given for manslaughter, not for wilful murder; but no such distinction appears in the laws; and it is contradicted by the practice of all the other barbarous nations,[53] by that of the ancient Germans,[54] and by that curious monument, above mentioned, of Saxon antiquity preserved by Hickes. There is indeed a law of Alfred's which makes wilful murder capital;[55] but this seems only to have been an attempt of that great legislator towards establishing a better police in the kingdom, and it probably remained without execution. By the laws of the same prince, a conspiracy against the life of the king might be redeemed by a fine.[56]

The price of all kinds of wounds was likewise fixed by the Saxon laws: a wound of an inch long under the hair was paid with one shilling; one of a like size in the face, two shillings; thirty shillings for the loss of an ear, and so forth.[57] There seems not to have been any difference made according to the dignity of the person. By the laws of Ethelbert, any one who committed adultery with his neighbor's wife was obliged to pay him a fine and buy him another wife.[58]

These institutions are not peculiar to the ancient Germans. They seem to be the necessary progress of criminal

---

[50] Wilkins, pp. 71, 72.   [51] Leges Ethelredi, apud Wilkins, p. 110
[52] Tyrrel, Introduction, vol. i. p. 126.   Carte, vol. i. p. 366.
[53] Lindenbrog. passim.   [54] Tacit. de Morib. Germ.
[55] Leges Ælf. § 12. Wilkins, p. 29. It is probable that by wilful murder Alfred means a treacherous murder, committed by one who has no declared feud with another.   [56] Leges Ælf. § 4. Wilkins, p. 35.
[57] Leges Ælf. § 40. See also Leges Ethelb. § 34, etc.   [58] Leges Ethelb. § 32.

jurisprudence among every free people, where the will of
the sovereign is not implicitly obeyed. We find them
among the ancient Greeks during the time of the Trojan
war. Compositions for murder are mentioned in Nestor's
speech to Achilles in the ninth Iliad, and are called *apoinai*.
The Irish, who never had any connections with the German
nations, adopted the same practice till very lately; and the
price of a man's head was called among them his *eric*, as we
learn from Sir John Davis. The same custom seems also
to have prevailed among the Jews.[59]

Theft and robbery were frequent among the Anglo-
Saxons. In order to impose some check upon these crimes,
it was ordained that no man should sell or buy anything
above twenty-pence value, except in open market;[60] and
every bargain of sale must be executed before witnesses.[61]
Gangs of robbers much disturbed the peace of the country;
and the law determined that a tribe of banditti consisting
of between seven and thirty-five persons was to be called a
turma, or troop; any greater company was denominated an
army.[62] The punishments for this crime were various, but
none of them capital.[63] If any man could track his stolen
cattle into another's ground, the latter was obliged to show
the tracks out of it, or pay their value.[64]

Rebellion, to whatever excess it was carried, was not
capital, but might be redeemed by a sum of money.[65] The
legislators, knowing it impossible to prevent all disorders,
only imposed a higher fine on breaches of the peace committed in the king's court, or before an alderman or bishop.
An alehouse too seems to have been considered as a privi-
leged place, and any quarrels that arose there were more
severely punished than elsewhere.[66]

If the manner of punishing crimes among the Anglo-
Saxons appear singular, the proofs were not less so; and
were also the natural result of the situation of those people.
Whatever we may imagine concerning the usual truth and
sincerity of men who live in a rude and barbarous state,
there is much more falsehood, and even perjury, among
them than among civilized nations. Virtue, which is nothing but a more enlarged and more cultivated reason, never

[59] Exod. cap. xxi. 29, 30.   [60] Leges Æthelst. § 12.
  [61] Leges Æthelst § 10, 12.   Leges Edg. apud Wilkins, p. 80.   Leges Ethelredi
§ 4, apud Wilkins, p. 103.   Hloth. and Eadm. § 16.   Leges Canut. § 22.
  [62] Leges Inæ, § 12.   [63] Leges Inæ, § 37.   [64] Leges Æthelst. § 2. Wilkins, p. 61.
  [65] Leges Ethelredi, apud Wilkins, p. 110.   Leges Ælf. § 4.   Wilkins. p. 35.
  [66] Leges Hloth. et Eadm. § 12, 13.   Leges Ethelredi, apud Wilkins, p. 117.

flourishes to any degree, nor is founded on steady principles of honor, except where a good education becomes general, and where men are taught the pernicious consequences of vice, treachery, and immorality. Even superstition, though more prevalent among ignorant nations, is but a poor supply for the defects in knowledge and education. Our European ancestors, who employed every moment the expedient of swearing on extraordinary crosses and relics, were less honorable in all engagements than their posterity, who, from experience, have omitted those ineffectual securities. This general proneness to perjury was much increased by the usual want of discernment in judges, who could not discuss an intricate evidence, and were obliged to number, not weigh, the testimony of the witnesses.[67] Hence the ridiculous practice of obliging men to bring compurgators, who, as they did not pretend to know anything of the fact expressed upon oath that they believed the person spoke true ; and these compurgators were in some cases multiplied to the number of three hundred.[68] The practice also of single combat was employed by most nations on the Continent as a remedy against false evidence ; [69] and though it was frequently dropped, from the opposition of the clergy, it was continually revived from experience of the falsehood attending the testimony of witnesses.[70] It became at last a species of jurisprudence ; the cases were determined by law, in which the party might challenge his adversary, or the witnesses, or the judge himself ; [71] and though these customs were absurd, they were rather an improvement on the methods of trial which had formerly been practised among those barbarous nations, and which still prevailed among the Anglo-Saxons.

When any controversy about a fact became too intricate for those ignorant judges to unravel, they had recourse to what they called the judgment of God ; that is, to fortune. Their methods of consulting this oracle were various. One of them was the decision of the *cross*. It was practised in this manner : When a person was accused of any crime, he first cleared himself by oath, and he was attended by eleven compurgators. He next took two pieces

67 Sometimes the laws fixed easy general rules for weighing the credibility of witnesses. A man whose life was estimated at 120 shillings counterbalanced six ceorles, each of whose lives was only valued at 20 shillings, and his oath was esteemed equivalent to that of all the six. See Wilkins, p. 72.
68 Praef. Nicol. ad Wilkins, p. 11.
69 Leges Burgund. cap. 45. Leges Lomb. lib. 2, tit. 55, cap. 34.
70 Leges Longob. lib. 2, tit. 55, cap. 23, apud Lindenbrog. p. 661.
71 See Desfontaines and Beaumanoir.

of wood, one of which was marked with the sign of the
cross, and, wrapping both up in wool, he placed them on
the altar, or on some celebrated relic. After solemn prayers
for the success of the experiment, a priest, or, in his stead,
some inexperienced youth, took up one of the pieces of
wood, and if he happened upon that which was marked with
the figure of the cross, the person was pronounced innocent; if otherwise, guilty.[72] This practice, as it arose from
superstition, was abolished by it in France. The emperor,
Lewis the Debonnaire, prohibited that method of trial, not
because it was uncertain, but lest that sacred figure, says
he, of the cross should be prostituted in common disputes
and controversies.[73]

The ordeal was another established method of trial
among the Anglo-Saxons. It was practised either by boil-
ing water or red-hot iron. The former was appropriated to
the common people, the latter to the nobility. The water
or iron was consecrated by many prayers, masses, fastings,
and exorcisms;[74] after which the person accused either took
up a stone sunk in the water[75] to a certain depth, or carried
the iron to a certain distance and, his hand being wrapped
up, and the covering sealed for three days, if there appeared,
on examining it, no marks of burning, he was pronounced
innocent; if otherwise, guilty.[76] The trial by cold water
was different: the person was thrown into consecrated water; if he swam, he was guilty; if he sank, innocent.[77] It
is difficult for us to conceive how any innocent person could
ever escape by the one trial, or any criminal be convicted
by the other. But there was another usage admirably calculated for allowing every criminal to escape who had confidence enough to try it. A consecrated cake, called a
corsned, was produced, which, if the person could swallow
and digest, he was pronounced innocent.[78]

The feudal law, if it had place at all among the Anglo-
Saxons, which is doubtful, was not certainly extended over
all the landed property, and was not attended with those
consequences of homage, reliefs,[79] wardship, marriage, and

---

[72] Leges Fris. tit. 14, apud Lindenbrog. p. 496.   [73] Du Cange, *in verbo* Crux.
[74] Spell. *in verbo* Ordeal. Parker, p. 155. Lindenbrog p. 1299.
[75] Leges Inæ, § 77.
[76] Sometimes the person accused walked barefoot over red-hot iron.
[77] Spell. *in verbo* Ordealium.
[78] Spell. *in verbo* Corsned. Parker, p. 156. Text. Roffens. p. 33.
[79] On the death of an alderman, a greater or lesser thane, there was a payment
made to the king of his best arms, and this was called his heriot; but this was
not of the nature of a relief. See Spell. on Tenures, p. 2. The value of this
heriot was fixed by Canute's laws, § 69.

other burdens which were inseparable from it in the kingdoms of the Continent. As the Saxons expelled, or almost entirely destroyed, the ancient Britons, they planted themselves in this island on the same footing with their ancestors in Germany, and found no occasion for the feudal institutions,[80] which were calculated to maintain a kind of standing army, always in readiness to suppress any insurrection among the conquered people. The trouble and expense of defending the state in England lay equally upon all the land; and it was usual for every five hides to equip a man for the service. The *trinoda necessitas*, as it was called, or the burden of military expeditions, of repairing highways, and of building and supporting bridges, was inseparable from landed property, even though it belonged to the Church or monasteries, unless exempted by a particular charter.[81] The ceorles, or husbandmen, were provided with arms, and were obliged to take their turn in military duty.[82] There were computed to be two hundred and forty-three thousand six hundred hides in England;[83] consequently, the ordinary military force of the kingdom consisted of forty-eight thousand seven hundred and twenty men; though, no doubt, on extraordinary occasions a greater number might be assembled. Tho king and nobility had some military tenants, who were called Sithcunmen.[84] And there were some lands annexed to the office of alderman and to other offices; but these probably were not of great extent, and were possessed only during pleasure, as in the commencement of the feudal law in other countries of Europe.

The revenue of the king seems to have consisted chiefly in his demesnes, which were large, and in the tolls and imposts which he probably levied at discretion on the boroughs and seaports that lay within his demesnes. He could not alienate any part of the crown lands, even to religious uses, without the consent of the states.[85] Danegelt was a land-tax of a shilling a hide, imposed by the states,[86] either for payment of the sums exacted by the Danes, or for putting the kingdom in a posture of defence against those invaders.[87]

[80] Bracton, De Acqu. Rer. Domin. lib. 2, cap. 16. See more fully Spell. on Feuds and Tenures, and Craigius, De Jure Feud. lib. 1, dieg. 7.
[81] Spell. Conc. vol. i. p. 256.
[82] Leges Inæ, § 51.
[83] Spell. on Feuds and Tenures, p. 17.
[84] Spell. Conc. vol. i. p. 195.
[85] Spell. Conc, vol. i. p. 340.
[86] Chron. Sax. p. 128.
[87] Leges Edw. Conf. § 12.

The Saxon pound, as likewise that which was coined for
some centuries after the Conquest, was near three times the
weight of our present money: there were forty-eight shillings in the pound, and five pence in a shilling;[88] consequently, a Saxon shilling was near a fifth heavier than ours,
and a Saxon penny near three times as heavy.[89] As to the
value of money in those times compared to commodities,
there are some, though not very certain, means of computation. A sheep, by the laws of Athelstan, was estimated
at a shilling; that is, fifteen pence of our money. The
fleece was two-fifths of the value of the whole sheep,[90] much
above its present estimation; and the reason probably was
that the Saxons, like the ancients, were little acquainted
with any clothing but what was made of wool. Silk and
cotton were quite unknown; linen was not much used. An
ox was computed at six times the value of a sheep; a cow
at four.[91] If we suppose that the cattle in that age, from
the defects in husbandry, were not so large as they are at
present in England, we may compute that money was then
near ten times of greater value. A horse was valued at
about thirty-six shillings of our money, or thirty Saxon
shillings;[92] a mare a third less; a man at three pounds.[93]
The board wages of a child the first year was eight shillings, together with a cow's pasture in summer and an ox's
in winter.[94] William of Malmesbury mentions it as a re-
markably high price that William Rufus gave fifteen marks
for a horse, or about thirty pounds of our present money.[95]
Between the years 900 and 1000, Ednoth bought a hide of
land for about a hundred and eighteen shillings of our present money.[96] This was little more than a shilling an acre,
which indeed appears to have been the usual price, as we
may learn from other accounts.[97] A palfrey was sold for
twenty shillings about the year 966.[98] The value of an ox
in King Ethelred's time was between seven and eight shillings; a cow about six shillings.[99] Gervas of Tilbury says
that, in Henry I.'s time bread which would suffice a hundred men for a day was rated at three shillings, or a shilling of that age; for it is thought that, soon after the Conquest, a pound sterling was divided into twenty shillings; a
sheep was rated at a shilling, and so of other things in pro-

88 Leges Ælf. § 40.
89 Fleetwood's Chron. Pretiosum, pp. 27, 28, etc.
90 Leges Inæ, § 69.
91 Wilkins, p. 66.   92 Wilkins, p. 126.   93 Ibid.   94 Leges Inæ, § 38.
95 P. 121.   96 Hist. Rames, p. 415.   97 Hist. Eliens. p. 473.
98 Hist. Eliens. p. 471.   99 Wilkins, p. 126.

portion. In Athelstan's time a ram was valued at a shilling, or four pence Saxon.[100] The tenants of Shireburn were obliged, at their choice, to pay either sixpence or four hens.[101] About 1232, the Abbot of St. Albans, going on a journey, hired seven handsome stout horses, and agreed, if any of them died on the road, to pay the owner thirty shillings a piece of our present money.[102] It is to be remarked that in all ancient times the raising of corn, especially wheat, being a species of manufactory, that commodity always bore a higher price, compared to cattle, than it does in our times.[103] The Saxon Chronicle tells us [104] that in the reign of Edward the Confessor there was the most terrible famine ever known ; insomuch that a quarter of wheat rose to six pennies, or fifteen shillings of our present money. Consequently it was as dear as if it now cost seven pounds ten shillings. This much exceeds the great famine in the end of Queen Elizabeth, when a quarter of wheat sold for four pounds. Money in this last period was nearly of the same value as in our time. These severe famines are a certain proof of bad husbandry.

On the whole, there are three things to be considered wherever a sum of money is mentioned in ancient times : first, the change of denomination by which a pound has been reduced to the third part of its ancient weight in silver; secondly, the change in value by the greater plenty of money, which has reduced the same weight of silver to ten times less value compared to commodities, and consequently a pound sterling to the thirtieth part of the ancient value ; thirdly, the fewer people and less industry which were then to be found in every European kingdom. This circumstance made even the thirtieth part of the sum more difficult to levy, and caused any sum to have more than thirty times greater weight and influence, both abroad and at home, than in our times; in the same manner that a sum—a hundred thousand pounds, for instance—is at present more difficult to levy in a small state such as Bavaria, and can produce greater effects on such a small community than on England. This last difference is not easy to be calculated ; but, allowing that England has now six times more industry and three times more people than it had at the Conquest, and for some reigns after that period, we are upon that supposition to conceive, taking all circumstances together, every sum of money men-

[100] Wilkins, p. 56.   [101] Monast. Anglic. vol. ii. p. 528.   [102] Matt. Paris.
[103] Fleetwood, pp. 83, 94, 96, 98.   [104] P. 157.

tioned by historians as if it were multiplied more than a hundredfold above a sum of the same denomination at present.

In the Saxon times, land was divided equally among all the male children of the deceased, according to the custom of Gavelkind. The practice of entails is to be found in those times.[105] Land was chiefly of two kinds—bockland, or land held by book or charter, which was regarded as full property, and descended to the heirs of the possessor; and folkland, or the land held by the ceorles and common people, who were removable at pleasure, and were indeed only tenants during the will of their lords.

The first attempt which we find in England to separate the ecclesiastical from the civil jurisdiction was that law of Edgar, by which all disputes among the clergy were ordered to be carried before the bishop.[106] The penances were then very severe; but as a man could buy them off with money, or might substitute others to perform them, they lay easy upon the rich.[107]

With regard to the manners of the Anglo-Saxons we can say little, but that they were in general a rude, uncultivated people, ignorant of letters, unskilled in the mechanical arts, untamed to submission under law and government, addicted to intemperance, riot, and disorder. Their best quality was their military courage, which yet was not supported by discipline or conduct. Their want of fidelity to the prince, or to any trust reposed in them, appears strongly in the history of their later period; and their want of humanity in all their history. Even the Norman historians, notwithstanding the low state of the arts in their own country, speak of them as barbarians when they mention the invasion made upon them by the Duke of Normandy.[108] The Conquest put the people in a situation of receiving slowly from abroad the rudiments of science and cultivation, and of correcting their rough and licentious manners.

[105] Leges Ælf. § 37, apud Wilkins, p. 43.
[107] Wilkins, pp. 96, 97. Spell. Conc. p. 473.
[106] Wilkins, p. 83.
[108] Gul. Pict. p. 202.

CHAPTER IV.

CONSEQUENCES OF THE BATTLE OF HASTINGS.—SUBMISSION
OF THE ENGLISH.—SETTLEMENT OF THE GOVERNMENT.
—KING'S RETURN TO NORMANDY.—DISCONTENTS OF
THE ENGLISH.—THEIR INSURRECTIONS.—RIGORS OF THE
NORMAN GOVERNMENT.—NEW INSURRECTIONS.—NEW
RIGORS OF THE GOVERNMENT.—INTRODUCTION OF THE
FEUDAL LAW.—INNOVATION IN ECCLESIASTICAL GOV-
ERNMENT.—INSURRECTION OF THE NORMAN BARONS.—
DISPUTE ABOUT INVESTITURES.—REVOLT OF PRINCE
ROBERT.—DOMESDAY - BOOK.—THE NEW FOREST.—WAR
WITH FRANCE.—DEATH AND CHARACTER OF WILLIAM
THE CONQUEROR.

[1066.] NOTHING could exceed the consternation which
seized the English when they received intelligence of the
unfortunate battle of Hastings, the death of their king, the
slaughter of their principal nobility and of their bravest
warriors, and the rout and dispersion of the remainder.
But though the loss which they had sustained in that fatal
action was considerable, it might have been repaired by a
great nation, where the people were generally armed, and
where there resided so many powerful noblemen in every
province, who could have assembled their retainers, and
have obliged the Duke of Normandy to divide his army, and
probably to waste it in a variety of actions and rencounters.
It was thus that the kingdom had formerly resisted for
many years its invaders, and had been gradually subdued
by the continued efforts of the Romans, Saxons, and Danes;
and equal difficulties might have been apprehended by
William in his bold and hazardous enterprise. But there
were several vices in the Anglo-Saxon constitution, which
rendered it difficult for the English to defend their liberties
in so critical an emergency. The people had in a great
measure lost all national pride and spirit by their recent and
long subjection to the Danes; and, as Canute had in the
course of his administration much abated the rigors of conquest, and had governed them equitably by their own laws,

they regarded with the less terror the ignominy of a foreign yoke, and deemed the inconveniences of submission less formidable than those of bloodshed, war, and resistance. Their attachment also to the ancient royal family had been much weakened by their habits of submission to the Danish princes, and by their late election of Harold, or their acquiescence in his usurpation. And as they had long been accustomed to regard Edgar Atheling, the only heir of the Saxon line, as unfit to govern them even in times of order and tranquillity, they could entertain small hopes of his being able to repair such great losses as they had sustained, or to withstand the victorious arms of the Duke of Normandy.

That they might not, however, be altogether wanting to themselves in this extreme necessity, the English took some steps towards adjusting their disjointed government, and uniting themselves against the common enemy. The two potent earls, Edwin and Morcar, who had fled to London with the remains of the broken army, took the lead on this occasion. In concert with Stigand, Archbishop of Canterbury, a man possessed of great authority and of ample revenues, they proclaimed Edgar, and endeavored to put the people in a posture of defence, and encouraged them to resist the Normans.[1] But the terror of the late defeat, and the near neighborhood of the invaders, increased the confusion inseparable from great revolutions; and every resolution proposed was hasty, fluctuating, tumultuary; disconcerted by fear or faction, ill planned, and worse executed.

William, that his enemies might have no leisure to recover from their consternation or unite their councils, immediately put himself in motion after his victory and resolved to prosecute an enterprise which nothing, but celerity and vigor could render finally successful. His first attempt was against Romney, whose inhabitants he severely punished on account of their cruel treatment of some Norman seamen and soldiers who had been carried thither by stress of weather, or by mistake in their course;[2] and, foreseeing that his conquest of England might still be attended with many difficulties and with much opposition, he deemed it necessary, before he should advance farther into the country, to make himself master of Dover, which would both secure him a retreat in case of adverse fortune, and afford

---

[1] Gul. Pict. p. 205. Order. Vitalis, p. 502. Hoveden, p. 449. Knygnton, p. 2343.   [2] Guip. Pict. 204.

him a safe landing-place for such supplies as might be requisite for pushing his advantages. The terror diffused by
his victory at Hastings was so great that the garrison of
Dover, though numerous and well provided, immediately
capitulated; and as the Normans, rushing in to take possession of the town, hastily set fire to some of the houses,
William, desirous to conciliate the minds of the English by
an appearance of lenity and justice, made compensation to
the inhabitants for their losses.[3]

The Norman army being much distressed with a dysen-
tery, was obliged to remain here eight days; but the duke,
on their recovery, advanced with quick marches towards
London, and by his approach increased the confusions
which were already so prevalent in the English councils.
The ecclesiastics in particular, whose influence was great
over the people, began to declare in his favor; and as most
of the bishops and dignified clergymen were even then
Frenchmen or Normans, the pope's bull, by which his enterprise was avowed and hallowed, was now openly insisted
on as a reason for general submission. The superior learning of those prelates, which, during the Confessor's reign,
had raised them above the ignorant Saxons, made their
opinions be received with implicit faith; and a young
prince, like Edgar, whose capacity was deemed so mean, was
but ill qualified to resist the impression which they made on
the minds of the people. A repulse which a body of Londoners received from five hundred Norman horse renewed
in the city the terror of the great defeat at Hastings; the
easy submission of all the inhabitants of Kent was an additional discouragement to them; the burning of Southwark
before their eyes made them dread a like fate to their own
city; and no man any longer entertained thoughts but of
immediate safety and of self-preservation. Even the Earls
Edwin and Morcar, in despair of making effectual resistance, retired with their troops to their own provinces; and
the people thenceforth disposed themselves unanimously to
yield to the victor. As soon as he passed the Thames at
Wallingford, and reached Berkhamstead, Stigand, the primate, made submissions to him; before he came within
sight of the city, all the chief nobility, and Edgar Atheling
himself, the new-elected king, came into his camp, and declared their intention of yielding to his authority.[4] They
requested him to mount their throne, which they now con-

sidered as vacant; and declared to him that, as they had always been ruled by regal power, they desired to follow, in this particular, the example of their ancestors, and knew of no one more worthy than himself to hold the reins of government.[5]

Though this was the great object to which the duke's enterprise tended, he feigned to deliberate on the offer; and being desirous at first of preserving the appearance of a legal administration, he wished to obtain a more explicit and formal consent of the English nation.[6] But Aimar of Aquitaine, a man equally respected for valor in the field and for prudence in council, remonstrating with him on the danger of delay in so critical a conjuncture, he laid aside all further scruples, and accepted of the crown which was tendered him. Orders were immediately issued to prepare everything for the ceremony of his coronation; but, as he was yet afraid to place entire confidence in the Londoners, who were numerous and warlike, he meanwhile commanded fortresses to be erected, in order to curb the inhabitants and to secure his person and government.[7]

Stigand was not much in the duke's favor, both because he had intruded into the see on the expulsion of Robert the Norman, and because he possessed such influence and authority over the English[8] as might be dangerous to a new-established monarch. William, therefore, pretending that the primate had obtained his pall in an irregular manner from Pope Benedict IX., who was himself a usurper, refused to be consecrated by him, and conferred this honor on Aldred, Archbishop of York. Westminster Abbey was the place appointed for that magnificent ceremony; the most considerable of the nobility, both English and Norman, attended the duke on this occasion. Aldred, in a short speech, asked the former whether they agreed to accept William as their king. The Bishop of Coutance put the same question to the latter; and both being answered with acclamations,[9] Aldred administered to the duke the usual coronation oath, by which he bound himself to protect the Church, to administer justice, and to repress violence; he then anointed him, and put the crown upon his head.[10] There appeared nothing but joy in the

[5] Gul. Pict. p. 205. Order. Vitalis, p. 503.   [6] Gul. Pict. p. 296.
[7] Ibid.   [8] Eadmer, p. 6.   [9] Order. Vitalis, p. 205.
[10] Malmesbury, p. 271, says that he also promised to govern the Normans and English by equal laws; and this addition to the usual oath seems not improbable, considering the circumstances of the times.

countenances of the spectators; but in that very moment there burst forth the strongest symptoms of the jealousy and animosity which prevailed between the nations, and which continually increased during the reign of this prince. The Norman soldiers, who were placed without, in order to guard the church, hearing the shouts within, fancied that the English were offering violence to their duke: and they immediately assaulted the populace, and set fire to the neighboring houses. The alarm was conveyed to the nobility who surrounded the prince: both English and Normans, full of apprehensions, rushed out to secure themselves from the present danger, and it was with difficulty that William himself was able to appease the tumult.[11]

[1067.] The king, thus possessed of the throne by a pretended destination of King Edward, and by an irregular election of the people, but still more by force of arms, retired from London to Berking, in Essex, and there received the submissions of all the nobility who had not attended his coronation. Edric, surnamed the Forester, grand-nephew to that Edric so noted for his repeated acts of perfidy during the reigns of Ethelred and Edmond; Earl Coxo, a man famous for bravery; even Edwin and Morcar, Earls of Mercia and Northumberland, with the other principal noblemen of England, came and swore fealty to him, were received into favor, and were confirmed in the possession of their estates and dignities.[12] Everything bore the appearance of peace and tranquillity; and William had no other occupation than to give contentment to the foreigners who had assisted him to mount the throne, and to his new subjects, who had so readily submitted to him.

He had got possession of the treasure of Harold, which was considerable; and being also supplied with rich presents from the opulent men in all parts of England, who were solicitous to gain the favor of their new sovereign, he distributed great sums among his troops, and by this liberality gave them hopes of obtaining at length those more durable establishments which they had expected from his enterprise.[13] The ecclesiastics, both at home and abroad, had much forwarded his success, and he failed not, in return, to express his gratitude and devotion in the manner which was most acceptable to them. He sent Harold's standard to the pope, accompanied with many valuable presents; all the consider-

---

[11] Gul. Pict. p. 206. Order. Vitalis, p. 503.
[12] Gul. Pict. p. 208. Order. Vitalis, p. 506.　　　[13] Gulp. Pict. p. 206.

able monasteries and churches in France, where prayers had been put up for his success, now tasted of his bounty ; [14] the English monks found him well disposed to favor their order; and he built a new convent near Hastings, which he called *Battle Abbey*, and which, on pretence of supporting monks to pray for his own soul and for that of Harold, served as a lasting memorial of his victory.[15]

He introduced into England that strict execution of justice for which his administration had been much celebrated in Normandy ; and even during this violent revolution, every disorder or oppression met with rigorous punishment.[16] His army, in particular, was governed with severe discipline ; and, notwithstanding the insolence of victory, care was taken to give as little offence as possible to the jealousy of the vanquished. The king appeared solicitous to unite, in an amicable manner, the Normans and the English, by intermarriages and alliances, and all his new subjects who approached his person were received with affability and regard. No signs of suspicion appeared, not even towards Edgar Atheling, the heir of the ancient royal family, whom William confirmed in the honors of Earl of Oxford, conferred on him by Harold, and whom he affected to treat with the highest kindness, as nephew to the Confessor, his great friend and benefactor. Though he confiscated the estates of Harold, and of those who had fought in the battle of Hastings on the side of that prince, whom he represented as a usurper, he seemed willing to admit of every plausible excuse for past opposition to his pretensions, and he received many into favor who had carried arms against him. He confirmed the liberties and immunities of London and the other cities of England, and appeared desirous of replacing everything on ancient establishments. In his whole administration he bore the semblance of the lawful prince, not of the conqueror ; and the English began to flatter themselves that they had changed, not the form of their government, but the succession only of their sovereigns, a matter which gave them small concern. The better to reconcile his new subjects to his authority, William made a progress through some parts of England ; and besides a splendid court and majestic presence, which overawed the people, already struck with his military fame, the appearance

---

[14] Gulp. Pict. p. 206.
[15] Gul. Gemet. p. 288. Chron. Sax. p. 189. Matt. West. p. 226. Matt. Paris, p. 9. Diceto, p. 482. This convent was freed by him from all episcopal jurisdiction. Monast. Ang. tom. i. pp. 311, 312.
[16] Gul. Pict. p. 208. Order. Vitalis, p. 506.

of his clemency and justice gained the approbation of the wise, attentive to the first steps of their new sovereign.

But amid this confidence and friendship which he expressed for the English, the king took care to place all real power in the hands of his Normans, and still to keep possession of the sword, to which he was sensible he owed his advancement to sovereign authority. He disarmed the city of London and other places which appeared most warlike and populous; and building citadels in that capital, as well as in Winchester, Hereford, and the cities best situated for commanding the kingdom, he quartered Norman soldiers in all of them, and left nowhere any power able to resist or oppose him. He bestowed the forfeited estates on the most eminent of his captains, and established funds for the payment of his soldiers. And thus, while his civil administration carried the face of a legal magistrate, his military institutions were those of a master and tyrant; at least, of one who reserved to himself, whenever he pleased, the power of assuming that character.

By this mixture, however, of vigor and lenity, he had so soothed the minds of the English that he thought he might safely revisit his native country, and enjoy the triumph and congratulation of his ancient subjects. He left the administration in the hands of his uterine brother, Odo, Bishop of Baieux, and of William Fitz-Osberne. That their authority might be exposed to less danger, he carried over with him all the most considerable nobility of England, who, while they served to grace his court by their presence and magnificent retinues, were in reality hostages for the fidelity of the nation. Among these were Edgar Atheling, Stigand the Primate, the Earls Edwin and Morcar, Waltheof (the son of the brave Earl Siward), with others eminent for the greatness of their fortunes and families or for their ecclesiastical and civil dignities. He was visited at the abbey of Fescamp, where he resided, during some time, by Rodulph, uncle to the King of France, and by many powerful princes and nobles, who, having contributed to his enterprise, were desirous of participating in the joy and advantages of its success. His English courtiers, willing to ingratiate themselves with their new sovereign, outvied each other in equipages and entertainments; and made a display of riches which struck the foreigners with astonishment. William of Poictiers, a Norman historian,[17] who was present,

[17] Pp. 211, 212.

speaks with admiration of the beauty of their persons, the size and workmanship of their silver plate, the costliness of their embroideries, an art in which the English then excelled; and he expresses himself in such terms as tend much to exalt our idea of the opulence and cultivation of the people.[18] But though everything bore the face of joy and festivity, and William himself treated his new courtiers with great appearance of kindness, it was impossible altogether to prevent the insolence of the Normans; and the English nobles derived little satisfaction from those entertainments, where they considered themselves as led in triumph by their ostentatious conqueror.

In England affairs took still a worse turn during the absence of the sovereign. Discontents and complaints multiplied everywhere; secret conspiracies were entered into against the government; hostilities were already begun in many places; and everything seemed to menace a revolution as rapid as that which had placed William on the throne. The historian above mentioned, who is a panegyrist of his master, throws the blame entirely on the fickle and mutinous disposition of the English, and highly celebrates the justice and lenity of Odo's and Fitz-Osberne's administration.[19] But other historians, with more probability, impute the cause chiefly to the Normans, who, despising a people that had so easily submitted to the yoke, envying their riches, and grudging the restraints imposed upon their own rapine, were desirous of provoking them to a rebellion, by which they expected to acquire new confiscations and forfeitures, and to gratify those unbounded hopes which they had formed in entering on this enterprise.[20]

It is evident that the chief reason of this alteration in the sentiments of the English must be ascribed to the departure of William, who was alone able to curb the violence of his captains and to overawe the mutinies of the people. Nothing indeed appears more strange than that this prince, in less than three months after the conquest of a great, warlike, and turbulent nation, should absent himself in order to revisit his own country, which remained in profound tranquillity, and was not menaced by any of its neighbors, and should so long leave his jealous subjects at

---

[18] As the historian chiefly insists on the silver plate, his panegyric on the English magnificence shows only how incompetent a judge he was of the matter. Silver was then of ten times the value, and was more than twenty times more rare than at present; and, consequently, of all species of luxury plate must have been the rarest. [19] P. 212. [20] Order. Vitalis, p. 507.

the mercy of an insolent and licentious army. Were we not assured of the solidity of his genius and the good sense displayed in all other circumstances of his conduct, we might ascribe this measure to a vain ostentation, which rendered him impatient to display his pomp and magnificence among his ancient subjects. It is therefore more natural to believe that in so extraordinary a step he was guided by a concealed policy; and that, though he had thought proper at first to allure the people to submission by the semblance of a legal administration, he found that he could neither satisfy his rapacious captains, nor secure his unstable government, without further exerting the rights of conquest and seizing the possessions of the English. In order to have a pretext for this violence, he endeavored, without discovering his intentions, to provoke and allure them into insurrections, which, he thought, could never prove dangerous while he detained all the principal nobility in Normandy, while a great and victorious army was quartered in England, and while he himself was so near to suppress any tumult or rebellion. But as no ancient writer has ascribed this tyrannical purpose to William, it scarcely seems allowable, from conjecture alone, to throw such an imputation upon him.

But whether we are to account for that measure from the king's vanity or from his policy, it was the immediate cause of all the calamities which the English endured during this and the subsequent reigns, and gave rise to those mutual jealousies and animosities between them and the Normans which were never appeased till a long tract of time had gradually united the two nations and made them one people. The inhabitants of Kent, who had first submitted to the conqueror, were the first that attempted to throw off the yoke; and, in confederacy with Eustace, Count of Boulogne, who had also been disgusted by the Normans, they made an attempt, though without success, on the garrison of Dover.[21] Edric the Forester, whose possessions lay on the banks of the Severn, being provoked at the depredations of some Norman captains in his neighborhood, formed an alliance with Blethyn and Rowallan, two Welsh princes; and endeavored, with their assistance, to repel force by force.[22] But though these open hostilities were not very considerable, the disaffection was general among the English, who had become sensible, though too

[21] Gul. Gemet. p. 289. Order. Vitalis, p. 508. Anglia Sacra, vol. i. p. 245.
[22] Hoveden, p. 450. Matt. West. p. 226. Sim. Dunelm. p. 197.

late, of their defenceless condition, and began already to experience those insults and injuries which a nation must always expect that allows itself to be reduced to that abject situation. A secret conspiracy was entered into to perpetrate, in one day, a general massacre of the Normans, like that which had formerly been executed upon the Danes; and the quarrel was become so general and national that the vassals of Earl Coxo, having desired him to head them in an insurrection, and finding him resolute in maintaining his fidelity to William, put him to death as a traitor to his country.

The king, informed of these dangerous discontents, hastened over to England, and, by his presence and the vigorous measures which he pursued, disconcerted all the schemes of the conspirators. Such of them as had been more violent in their mutiny betrayed their guilt by flying or concealing themselves; and the confiscation of their estates, while it increased the number of malcontents, both enabled William to gratify further the rapacity of his Norman captains, and gave them the prospect of new forfeitures and attainders. The king began to regard all his English subjects as inveterate and irreclaimable enemies; and thenceforth either embraced, or was more fully confirmed in the resolution of seizing their possessions, and of reducing them to the most abject slavery. Though the natural violence and severity of his temper made him incapable of feeling any remorse in the execution of this tyrannical purpose, he had art enough to conceal his intention, and to preserve still some appearance of justice in his oppressions. He ordered all the English who had been arbitrarily expelled by the Normans during his absence to be restored to their estates; [23] but at the same time he imposed a general tax on the people, that of Danegelt, which had been abolished by the Confessor, and which had always been extremely odious to the nation.[24]

[1068.] As the vigilance of William overawed the malcontents, their insurrections were more the result of an impatient humor in the people than of any regular conspiracy which could give them a rational hope of success against the established power of the Normans. The inhabitants of Exeter, instigated by Githa, mother to King Harold, refused

[23] Chro... Sax. p. 173. This fact is a full proof that the Normans had committed great injustice, and were the real cause of the insurrections of the English.
[24] Hoveden, p. 450. Sim. Dunelm. p. 197. Alur. Beverl. p. 127.

to admit a Norman garrison, and, betaking themselves to arms, were strengthened by the accession of the neighboring inhabitants of Devonshire and Cornwall.[25] The king hastened with his forces to chastise this revolt; and on his approach, the wiser and more considerable citizens, sensible of the unequal contest, persuaded the people to submit and to deliver hostages for their obedience. A sudden mutiny of the populace broke this agreement; and William, appearing before the walls, ordered the eyes of one of the hostages to be put out, as an earnest of that severity which the rebels must expect if they persevered in their revolt.[26] The inhabitants were anew seized with terror, and, surrendering at discretion, threw themselves at the king's feet, and supplicated his clemency and forgiveness. William was not destitute of generosity, when his temper was not hardened either by policy or passion; he was prevailed on to pardon the rebels, and he set guards on all the gates, in order to prevent the rapacity and insolence of his soldiery.[27] Githa escaped with her treasures to Flanders. The malcontents of Cornwall imitated the example of Exeter, and met with like treatment; and the king, having built a citadel in that city, which he put under the command of Baldwin, son of Earl Gilbert, returned to Winchester, and dispersed his army into their quarters. He was here joined by his wife Matilda, who had not before visited England, and whom he now ordered to be crowned by Archbishop Aldred. Soon after she brought him an accession to his family by the birth of a fourth son, whom he named Henry. His three elder sons—Robert, Richard, and William—still resided in Normandy.

But though the king appeared thus fortunate, both in public and domestic life, the discontents of his English subjects augmented daily; and the injuries committed and suffered on both sides rendered the quarrel between them and the Normans absolutely incurable. The insolence of victorious masters, dispersed throughout the kingdom, seemed intolerable to the natives; and wherever they found the Normans, separate or assembled in small bodies, they secretly set upon them, and gratified their vengeance by the slaughter of their enemies. But an insurrection in the north drew thither the general attention, and seemed to threaten more important consequences. Edwin and Morcar appeared at the head of this rebellion; and these potent noblemen,

[25] Order. Vitalis, p. 510.   [26] Ibid.   [27] Ibid.

before they took arms, stipulated for foreign succors from their nephew Blethyn, Prince of North Wales; from Malcolm, King of Scotland; and from Sweyn, King of Denmark. Besides the general discontent which had seized the English, the two earls were incited to this revolt by private injuries. William, in order to insure them to his interests, had, on his accession, promised his daughter in marriage to Edwin; but either he had never seriously intended to perform this engagement, or, having changed his plan of administration in England from clemency to rigor, he thought it was to little purpose if he gained one family while he enraged the whole nation. When Edwin, therefore, renewed his applications, he gave him an absolute denial;[28] and this disappointment, added to so many other reasons of disgust, induced that nobleman and his brother to concur with their incensed countrymen, and to make one general effort for the recovery of their ancient liberties. William knew the importance of celerity in quelling an insurrection supported by such powerful leaders, and so agreeable to the wishes of the people; and, having his troops always in readiness, he advanced by great journeys to the north. On his march he gave orders to fortify the castle of Warwick, of which he left Henry de Beaumont governor, and that of Nottingham, which he committed to the custody of William Peverell, another Norman captain.[29] He reached York before the rebels were in any condition for resistance, or were joined by any of the foreign succors which they expected, except a small reinforcement from Wales;[30] and the two earls found no means of safety but having recourse to the clemency of the victor. Archil, a potent nobleman in those parts, imitated their example, and delivered his son as a hostage for his fidelity;[31] nor were the people, thus deserted by their leaders, able to make any further resistance. But the treatment which William gave the chiefs was very different from that which fell to the share of their followers. He observed religiously the terms which he had granted to the former, and allowed them for the present to keep possession of their estates; but he extended the rigors of his confiscations over the latter, and gave away their lands to his foreign adventurers. These, planted throughout the whole country, and in possession of the military power, left Edwin and Morcar, whom he pretended to spare, destitute of all support, and ready to fall whenever he should think proper to com-

[28] Order. Vitalis, p. 511.   [29] Ibid.   Ibid.   [31] Ibid.

mand their ruin. A peace which he made with Malcolm, who did him homage for Cumberland, seemed at the same time to deprive them of all prospect of foreign assistance.[32]

The English were now sensible that their final destruction was intended; and that, instead of a sovereign whom they had hoped to gain by their submission, they had tamely surrendered themselves, without resistance, to a tyrant and a conqueror. Though the early confiscation of Harold's followers might seem iniquitous, being inflicted on men who had never sworn fealty to the Duke of Normandy, who were ignorant of his pretensions, and who only fought in defence of the government which they themselves had established in in their own country, yet were these rigors, however contrary to the ancient Saxon laws, excused on account of the urgent necessities of the prince; and those who were not involved in the present ruin hoped that they should thenceforth enjoy, without molestation, their possessions and their dignities. But the successive destruction of so many other families convinced them that the king intended to rely entirely on the support and affections of foreigners; and they foresaw new forfeitures, attainders, and acts of violence as the necessary result of this destructive plan of administration. They observed that no Englishman possessed his confidence, or was intrusted with any command or authority; and that the strangers, whom a rigorous discipline could have but ill restrained, were encouraged in their insolence and tyranny against them. The easy submission of the kingdom on its first invasion had exposed the natives to contempt; the subsequent proofs of their animosity and resentment had made them the object of hatred; and they were now deprived of every expedient by which they could hope to make themselves either regarded or beloved by their sovereign. Impressed with the sense of this dismal situation, many Englishmen fled into foreign countries, with an intention of passing their lives abroad free from oppression, or of returning on a favorable opportunity to assist their friends in the recovery of their native liberties.[33] Edgar Atheling himself, dreading the insidious caresses of William, was persuaded by Cospatric, a powerful Northumbrian, to escape with him into Scotland; and he carried thither his two sisters, Margaret and Christina. They were well received by Malcolm, who soon after espoused Margaret, the

[32] Order. Vitalis, p. 511.
[33] Order. Vitalis, p. 508.   M. West. p. 225.   M. Paris, p. 4.   Sim. Dun. p. 197.

elder sister ; and partly with a view of strengthening his kingdom by the accession of so many strangers, partly in hopes of employing them against the growing power of William, he gave great countenance to all the English exiles. Many of them settled there, and laid the foundation of families which afterwards made a figure in that country.

While the English suffered under these oppressions, even the foreigners were not much at their ease ; but finding themselves surrounded on all hands by enraged enemies, who took every advantage against them, and menaced them with still more bloody effects of the public resentment, they began to wish again for the tranquillity and security of their native country. Hugh de Grentmesnil and Humphry de Teliol, though intrusted with great commands, desired to be dismissed the service; and some others imitated their example ; a desertion which was highly resented by the king, and which he punished by the confiscation of all their possessions in England.[34] But William's bounty to his followers could not fail of alluring many new adventurers into his service; and the rage of the vanquished English served only to excite the attention of the king and those warlike chiefs. and keep them in readiness to suppress every commencement of domestic rebellion or foreign invasion.

[1069.] It was not long before they found occupation for their prowess and military conduct. Godwin, Edmond, and Magnus, three sons of Harold, had, immediately after the defeat at Hastings, sought a retreat in Ireland ; where, having met with a kind reception from Dermot and other princes of that country, they projected an invasion of England, and they hoped that all the exiles from Denmark, Scotland, and Wales, assisted by forces from these several countries, would at once commence hostilities, and rouse the indignation of the English against their haughty conquerors. They landed in Devonshire, but found Brian, son of the Count of Brittany, at the head of some foreign troops, ready to oppose them ; and, being defeated in several actions, they were obliged to retreat to their ships, and to return with great loss to Ireland.[35] The efforts of the Normans were now directed to the north, where affairs had fallen into the utmost confusion. The more impatient of the Northumbrians had attacked Robert de Comyn, who was appointed governor of Durham ; and, gaining the advantage over him

[34] Order. Vitalis, p. 512.
[35] Gul. Gemet. p. 290. Order. Vitalis, p. 513. Anglia Sacra, vol. i. p. 246.

from his negligence, they put him to death in that city, with seven hundred of his followers.[36] This success animated the inhabitants of York, who, rising in arms, slew Robert Fitz-Richard, their governor,[37] and besieged in the castle William Mallet, on whom the command now devolved. A little after, the Danish troops landed from three hundred vessels. Osberne, brother to King Sweyn, was intrusted with the command of these forces, and he was accompanied by Harold and Canute, two sons of that monarch. Edgar Atheling appeared from Scotland, and brought along with him Cospatric, Waltheof, Siward, Bearne, Merleswain, Adelin, and other leaders, who, partly from the hopes which they gave of Scottish succors, partly from their authority in those parts, easily persuaded the warlike and discontented Northumbrians to join the insurrection. Mallet, that he might better provide for the defence of the citadel of York, set fire to some houses which lay contiguous; but this expedient proved the immediate cause of his destruction. The flames, spreading into the neighboring streets, reduced the whole city to ashes : the enraged inhabitants, aided by the Danes, took advantage of the confusion to attack the castle, which they carried by assault; and the garrison, to the number of three thousand men, was put to the sword without mercy.[38]

This success proved a signal to many other parts of England, and gave the people an opportunity of showing their malevolence to the Normans. Hereward, a nobleman in East Anglia, celebrated for valor, assembled his followers, and, taking shelter in the Isle of Ely, made inroads on all the neighboring country.[39] The English in the counties of Somerset and Dorset rose in arms, and assaulted Montacute, the Norman governor; while the inhabitants of Cornwall and Devon invested Exeter, which, from the memory of William's clemency, still remained faithful to him. Edric the Forester, calling in the assistance of the Welsh, laid siege to Shrewsbury, and made head against Earl Brient and Fitz-Osberne, who commanded in those quarters.[40] The English everywhere, repenting their former easy submission, seemed determined to make by concert one great effort for

---

[36] Order. Vitalis, p. 512.   Chron. de Mailr. p. 116.   Hoveden, p. 450.   Matt. Paris. p. 5.   Sim. Dunelm. p. 198.
[37] Order. Vitalis, p. 512.   [38] Order. Vitalis, p. 513.   Hoveden, p. 451.
[39] Ingulph. p. 71.   Chron. Abb. St. Petri de Burgo, p. 47.
[40] Order. Vitalis, p. 514.

the recovery of their liberties and for the expulsion of their oppressors.

William, undismayed amid this scene of confusion, assembled his forces, and, animating them with the prospect of new confiscations and forfeitures, he marched against the rebels in the north, whom he regarded as the most formidable, and whose defeat he knew would strike a terror into all the other malcontents. Joining policy to force, he tried before his approach to weaken the enemy by detaching the Danes from them; and he engaged Osberne, by large presents, and by offering him the liberty of plundering the sea-coast, to retire, without committing further hostilities, into Denmark.[41] Cospatric, also, in despair of success, made his peace with the king, and, paying a sum of money as an atonement for his insurrection, was received into favor, and even invested with the earldom of Northumberland. Waltheof, who long defended York with great courage, was allured with this appearance of clemency; and as William knew how to esteem valor, even in an enemy, that nobleman had no reason to repent of his confidence.[42] Even Edric, compelled by necessity, submitted to the conqueror, and received forgiveness, which was soon after followed by some degree of trust and favor. Malcolm, too late to support his confederates, was constrained to retire; and all the English rebels in other parts, except Hereward, who still kept in his fastnesses, dispersed themselves, and left the Normans undisputed masters of the kingdom. Edgar Atheling, with his followers, sought again a retreat in Scotland from the pursuit of his enemies.

[1070.] But the seeming clemency of William towards the English leaders proceeded only from artifice, or from his esteem of individuals: his heart was hardened against all compassion towards the people; and he scrupled no measure, however violent or severe, which seemed requisite to support his plan of tyrannical administration. Sensible of the restless disposition of the Northumbrians, he determined to incapacitate them ever after from giving him disturbance, and he issued orders for laying entirely waste that fertile country which, for the extent of sixty miles, lies between the Humber and the Tees.[43] The houses were reduced to

41 Hoveden, p. 451. Chron. Abb. St. Petri de Burgo, p. 47. Sim. Dunelm. p. 199.   42 Will. Malm. p. 104. H. Hunting. p. 369.
43 Chron. Sax. p. 174. Ingulph. p. 79. Will. Malm. p. 103. Hoveden, p. 451. Chron. Abb. St. Petri de Burgo, p. 47. Matt. Paris, p. 5. Sim. Dunelm. p. 199. Brompton, p. 966. Knyghton, p. 2344. Anglia Sacra, vol. i. p. 702.

ashes by the merciless Normans; the cattle seized and driven away; the instruments of husbandry destroyed; and the inhabitants, compelled either to seek for a subsistence in the southern parts of Scotland, or, if they lingered in England from a reluctance to abandon their ancient habitations, they perished miserably in the woods from cold and hunger. The lives of a hundred thousand persons are computed to have been sacrificed to this stroke of barbarous policy,[44] which, by seeking a remedy for a temporary evil, thus inflicted a lasting wound on the power and populousness of the nation.

But William finding himself entirely master of a people who had given him such sensible proofs of their impotent rage and animosity, now resolved to proceed to extremities against all the natives of England, and to reduce them to a condition in which they should no longer be formidable to his government. The insurrections and conspiracies in so many parts of the kingdom had involved the bulk of the landed proprietors, more or less, in the guilt of treason; and the king took advantage of executing against them, with the utmost rigor, the laws of forfeiture and attainder. Their lives were indeed commonly spared; but their estates were confiscated, and either annexed to the royal demesnes, or conferred with the most profuse bounty on the Normans and other foreigners.[45] While the king's declared intention was to depress, or rather entirely extirpate, the English gentry,[46] it is easy to believe that scarcely the form of justice would be observed in those violent proceedings,[47] and that any suspicions served as the most undoubted proofs of guilt against a people thus devoted to destruction. It was crime sufficient in an Englishman to be opulent, or noble, or powerful; and the policy of the king, concurring with the rapacity of foreign adventurers, produced almost a total revolution in the landed property of the kingdom. Ancient and honorable families were reduced to beggary; the nobles themselves were everywhere treated with ignominy and contempt; they had the mortification of seeing their castles and manors possessed by Normans of the meanest birth and lowest stations;[48] and they found themselves carefully excluded from every road which led either to riches or preferment.[49]

44 Order. Vitalis, p. 515.   45 Will. Malm. p. 104.   46 H. Hunting. p. 370.
47 See note [H] at the end of the volume.
48 Order. Vitalis, p. 521.   Matt. West. p. 229.
49 See note [I] at the end of the volume.

As power naturally follows property, this revolution alone gave great security to the foreigners; but William, by the new institutions which he established, took also care to retain forever the military authority in those hands which had enabled him to subdue the kingdom. He introduced into England the feudal law, which he found established in France and Normandy, and which, during that age, was the foundation both of the stability and of the disorders in most of the monarchical governments of Europe. He divided all the lands of England, with very few exceptions besides the royal demesnes, into baronies, and he conferred these, with the reservation of stated services and payments, on the most considerable of his adventurers. These great barons, who held immediately of the crown, shared out a great part of their lands to other foreigners, who were denominated knights or vassals, and who paid their lord the same duty and submission, in peace and war, which he himself owed to his sovereign. The whole kingdom contained about seven hundred chief tenants and sixty thousand two hundred and fifteen knight's-fees; [50] and as none of the native English were admitted into the first rank, the few who retained their landed property were glad to be received into the second, and, under the protection of some powerful Norman, to load themselves and their posterity with this grievous burden, for estates which they had received free from their ancestors. [51] The small mixture of English which entered into this civil or military fabric (for it partook of both species) was so restrained by subordination under the foreigners that the Norman dominion seemed now to be fixed on the most durable basis, and to defy all the efforts of its enemies.

The better to unite the parts of the government, and to bind them into one system which might serve both for defence against foreigners and for the support of domestic tranquillity, William reduced the ecclesiastical revenues under the same feudal law; and though he had courted the Church on his invasion and accession, he now subjected it to services which the clergy regarded as a grievous slavery, and as totally unbefitting their profession. The bishops and abbots were obliged, when required, to furnish to the king, during war, a number of knights or military tenants propor-

[50] Order. Vitalis, p. 523. Secretum Abbatis, apud Selden, Titles of Honor, p. 573. Spell. Gloss. *in verbo* Feodum. Sir Robert Cotton.
[51] Matt. West. p. 225. Matt. Paris, p. 4. Bracton, lib. 1, cap. 11, No. 1. Fleta, lib. 1, cap. 8, n. 2.

tioned to the extent of property possessed by each see or abbey; and they were liable, in case of failure, to the same penalties which were exacted from the laity.[52] The pope and the ecclesiastics exclaimed against this tyranny, as they called it; but the king's authority was so well established over the army, who held everything from his bounty, that superstition itself, even in that age, when it was most prevalent, was constrained to bend under his superior influence.

But as the great body of the clergy were still natives, the king had much reason to dread the effects of their resentment; he therefore used the precaution of expelling the English from all the considerable dignities, and of advancing foreigners in their place. The partiality of the Confessor towards the Normans had been so great that, aided by their superior learning, it had promoted them to many of the sees in England; and even before the period of the Conquest scarcely more than six or seven of the prelates were natives of the country. But among these was Stigand, Archbishop of Canterbury; a man who, by his address and vigor, by the greatness of his family and alliances, by the extent of his possessions, as well as by the dignity of his office and his authority among the English, gave jealousy to the king.[53] Though William had, on his accession, affronted this prelate by employing the Archbishop of York to officiate at his consecration, he was careful on other occasions to load him with honors and caresses, and to avoid giving him further offence till the opportunity should offer of effecting his final destruction.[54] The suppression of the late rebellions and the total subjection of the English made him hope that an attempt against Stigand, however violent, would be covered by his great successes, and be overlooked amid the other important revolutions which affected so deeply the property and liberty of the kingdom. Yet, notwithstanding these great advantages, he did not think it safe to violate the reverence usually paid to the primate, but under cover of a new superstition, which he was the great instrument of introducing into England.

The doctrine which exalted the papacy above all human power had gradually diffused itself from the city and court of Rome, and was during that age much more prevalent in the southern than in the northern kingdoms of Europe. Pope Alexander, who had assisted William in his conquests,

[52] Matt. Paris, p. 5. Anglia Sacra, vol i. p. 248.
[53] Parker, p. 161.   [54] Parker, p. 164.

naturally expected that the French and Normans would import into England the same reverence for his sacred character with which they were impressed in their own country;
and would break the spiritual as well as civil independency
of the Saxons, who had hitherto conducted their ecclesiastical government with an acknowledgment, indeed, of primacy in the see of Rome, but without much idea of its title
to dominion or authority. As soon, therefore, as the Norman prince seemed fully established on the throne, the pope
despatched Ermenfroy, Bishop of Sion, as his legate into
England; and this prelate was the first that had ever appeared with that character in any part of the British islands.
The king, though he was probably led by principle to pay
this submission to Rome, determined, as is usual, to employ
the incident as a means of serving his political purposes,
and of degrading those English prelates who were become
obnoxious to him. The legate submitted to become the instrument of his tyranny; and thought that the more violent
the exertion of power, the more certainly did it confirm the
authority of that court from which he derived his commission. He summoned, therefore, a council of the prelates and
abbots at Winchester; and being assisted by two cardinals,
Peter and John, he cited before him Stigand, Archbishop
of Canterbury, to answer for his conduct. The primate
was accused of three crimes—the holding of the see of Winchester, together with that of Canterbury; the officiating in
the pall of Robert his predecessor; and the having received
his own pall from Benedict IX., who was afterwards deposed for simony and for intrusion into the papacy.[55] These
crimes of Stigand were mere pretences; since the first had
been a practice not unusual in England, and was never anywhere subjected to a higher penalty than a resignation
of one of the sees; the second was a pure ceremonial; and
as Benedict was the only pope who then officiated, and his
acts were never repealed, all the prelates of the Church, especially those who lay at a distance, were excusable for
making their applications to him. Stigand's ruin, however,
was resolved on, and was prosecuted with great severity.
The legate degraded him from his dignity; the king confiscated his estate and cast him into prison, where he continued in poverty and want during the remainder of his life.
Like rigor was exercised against the other English prelates:

[55] Hoveden, p. 453. Diceto, p. 482. Knyghton, p 2345. Anglia Sacra, vol. I.
pp. 5, 6. Ypod. Neust. p. 438.

Agelric, Bishop of Selesey, and Agelmare, of Elmham, were deposed by the legate and imprisoned by the king. Many considerable abbots shared the same fate; Egelwin, Bishop of Durham, fled the kingdom; Wulstan of Worcester, a man of an inoffensive character, was the only English prelate that escaped this general proscription[56] and remained in possession of his dignity. Alred, Archbishop of York, who had set the crown on William's head, had died a little before of grief and vexation, and had left his malediction to that prince on account of the breach of his coronation oath, and of the extreme tyranny with which he saw he was determined to treat his English subjects.[57]

It was a fixed maxim in this reign, as well as in some of the subsequent, that no native of the island should ever be advanced to any dignity, ecclesiastical, civil, or military.[58] The king, therefore, upon Stigand's deposition, promoted Lanfranc, a Milanese monk, celebrated for his learning and piety, to the vacant see. This prelate was rigid in defending the prerogatives of his station; and after a long process before the pope, he obliged Thomas, a Norman monk, who had been appointed to the see of York, to acknowledge the primacy of the Archbishop of Canterbury. Where ambition can be so happy as to cover its enterprises, even to the person himself, under the appearance of principle, it is the most incurable and inflexible of all human passions. Hence Lanfranc's zeal in promoting the interests of the papacy, by which he himself augmented his own authority, was indefatigable, and met with proportionable success. The devoted attachment to Rome continually increased in England; and, being favored by the sentiments of the conquerors, as well as by the monastic establishments formerly introduced by Edred and by Edgar, it soon reached the same height at which it had, during some time, stood in France and Italy.[59] It afterwards went much further, being favored by that very remote situation which had at first obstructed its progress, and being less checked by knowledge and a liberal education, which were still somewhat more common in the southern countries.

[56] Brompton relates that Wulstan was also deprived by the synod; but, refusing to deliver his pastoral staff and ring to any but the person from whom he first received them, he went immediately to King Edward's tomb and struck the staff so deeply into the stone that none but himself was able to pull it out; upon which he was allowed to keep his bishopric. This instance may serve, instead of many, as a specimen of the monkish miracles. See also the Annals of Burton, p. 284. [57] Gul. Malm. De Gest. Pont. p. 154. [58] Ingulph. pp. 70, 71. [59] Matt. West. p. 228. Lanfranc wrote in defence of the real presence against Berengarius; and in those ages of stupidity and ignorance he was greatly applauded for that performance.

The prevalence of this superstitious spirit became dangerous to some of William's successors, and incommodious to most of them; but the arbitrary sway of this king over the English, and his extensive authority over the foreigners, kept him from feeling any immediate inconveniences from it. He retained the Church in great subjection, as well as his lay subjects; and would allow none, of whatever character, to dispute his sovereign will and pleasure. He prohibited his subjects from acknowledging any one for pope whom he himself had not previously received; he required that all the ecclesiastical canons voted in any synod should first be laid before him, and be ratified by his authority; even bulls, or letters from Rome, could not legally be produced till they received the same sanction; and none of his ministers or barons, whatever offences they were guilty of, could be subjected to spiritual censures till he himself had given his consent to their excommunication.[60] These regulations were worthy of a sovereign, and kept united the civil and ecclesiastical powers, which the principles introduced by this prince himself had an immediate tendency to separate.

But the English had the cruel mortification to find that their king's authority, however acquired or however extended, was all employed in their oppression; and that the scheme of their subjection, attended with every circumstance of insult and indignity,[61] was deliberately formed by the prince and wantonly prosecuted by his followers.[62] William had even entertained the difficult project of totally abolishing the English language; and, for that purpose, he ordered that in all schools throughout the kingdom the youth should be instructed in the French tongue—a practice which was continued from custom till after the reign of Edward III., and was never indeed totally discontinued in England. The pleadings in the supreme courts of judicature were in French;[63] the deeds were often drawn in the same language; the laws were composed in that idiom;[64] no other tongue was used at court; it became the language of all fashionable company; and the English themselves, ashamed of their own country, affected to excel in that foreign dialect. From this attention of William, and from the extensive foreign dominions long annexed to the crown

[60] Eadmer, p. 6.
[61] Order. Vitalis, p. 523.   H. Hunting. p. 370.   [62] Ingulph. p. 71.
[63] 36 Edw. III. cap. 15. Selden, Spicileg. ad Eadmer, p. 189. Fortescue, De Laud. Leg. Angl. cap. 48.   [64] Chron. Rothom. A. D. 1066.

of England, proceeded that mixture of French which is at present to be found in the English tongue, and which composes the greatest and best part of our language. But amid those endeavors to depress the English nation, the king, moved by the remonstrances of some of his prelates, and by the earnest desires of the people, restored a few of the laws of King Edward; [65] which, though seemingly of no great importance towards the protection of general liberty, gave them extreme satisfaction, as a memorial of their ancient government, and an unusual mark of complaisance in their imperious conquerors.[66]

[1071.] The situation of the two great earls Morcar and Edwin became now very disagreeable. Though they had retained their allegiance during this general insurrection of their countrymen, they had not gained the king's confidence, and they found themselves exposed to the malignity of the courtiers, who envied them on account of their opulence and greatness, and at the same time involved them in that general contempt which they entertained for the English. Sensible that they had entirely lost their dignity, and could not even hope to remain long in safety, they determined, though too late, to share the same fate with their countrymen. While Edwin retired to his estate in the north, with a view of commencing an insurrection, Morcar took shelter in the Isle of Ely with the brave Hereward, who, secured by the inaccessible situation of the place, still defended himself against the Normans. But this attempt served only to accelerate the ruin of the few English who had hitherto been able to preserve their rank or fortune during the past convulsions. William employed all his endeavors to subdue the Isle of Ely; and having surrounded it with flat-bottomed boats, and made a causeway through the morasses to the extent of two miles, he obliged the rebels to surrender at discretion. Hereward alone forced his way, sword in hand, through the enemy; and still continued his hostilities by sea against the Normans, till at last William, charmed with his bravery, received him into favor, and restored him to his estate. Earl Morcar, and Egelwin, Bishop of Durham, who had joined the malcontents, were thrown into prison, and the latter soon after died in confinement. Edwin, attempting to make his escape into Scotland, was betrayed by some of his followers, and was killed by a party of Nor-

[65] Ingulph. p. 88. Brompton, p. 982. Knyghton, p. 2355. Hoveden, p. 600.
[66] See note [K] at the end of the volume.

mans, to the great affliction of the English, and even to that of William, who paid a tribute of generous tears to the memory of this gallant and beautiful youth. The King of Scotland, in hopes of profiting by these convulsions, had fallen upon the northern counties; but, on the approach of William, he retired; and when the king entered his country, he was glad to make peace, and to pay the usual homage to the English crown. To complete the king's prosperity, Edgar Atheling himself, despairing of success, and weary of a fugitive life, submitted to his enemy; and, receiving a decent pension for his subsistence, was permitted to live in England unmolested. But these acts of generosity towards the leaders were disgraced, as usual, by William's rigor against the inferior malcontents. He ordered the hands to be lopped off, and the eyes to be put out, of many of the prisoners whom he had taken in the Isle of Ely; and he dispersed them in that miserable condition throughout the country, as monuments of his severity.

[1073.] The province of Maine, in France, had, by the will of Herbert, the last count, fallen under the dominion of William some years before his conquest of England; but the inhabitants, dissatisfied with the Norman government, and instigated by Fulk, Count of Anjou, who had some pretensions to the succession, now rose in rebellion, and expelled the magistrates whom the king had placed over them. The full settlement of England afforded him leisure to punish this insult on his authority; but being unwilling to remove his Norman forces from this island, he carried over a considerable army, composed almost entirely of English; and joining them to some troops levied in Normandy, he entered the revolted province. The English appeared ambitious of distinguishing themselves on this occasion, and of retrieving that character of valor which had long been national among them, but which their late easy subjection under the Normans had somewhat degraded and obscured. Perhaps, too, they hoped that, by their zeal and activity, they might recover the confidence of their sovereign, as their ancestors had formerly, by like means, gained the affections of Canute; and might conquer his inveterate prejudices in favor of his own countrymen. The king's military conduct, seconded by these brave troops, soon overcame all opposition in Maine: the inhabitants were obliged to submit, and the Count of Anjou relinquished his pretensions.

[1074.] But during these transactions the government of

England was greatly disturbed ; and that too by those very foreigners who owed everything to the king's bounty, and who were the sole object of his friendship and regard. The Norman barons, who had engaged with their duke in the conquest of England, were men of the most independent spirit ; and though they obeyed their leader in the field, they would have regarded with disdain the richest acquisitions had they been required in return to submit, in their civil government, to the arbitrary will of one man. But the imperious character of William, encouraged by his absolute dominion over the English, and often impelled by the necessity of his affairs, had prompted him to stretch his authority over the Normans themselves beyond what the free genius of that victorious people could easily bear. The discontents were become general among those haughty nobles ; and even Roger, Earl of Hereford, son and heir of Fitz-Osberne, the king's chief favorite, was strongly infected with them. This nobleman, intending to marry his sister to Ralph de Guader, Earl of Norfolk, had thought it his duty to inform the king of his purpose, and to desire the loyal consent ; but meeting with a refusal, he proceeded nevertheless to complete the nuptials, and assembled all his friends, and those of Guader, to attend the solemnity. The two earls, disgusted by the denial of their request, and dreading William's resentment for their disobedience, here prepared measures for a revolt ; and during the gayety of the festival, while the company was heated with wine, they opened the design to their guests. They inveighed against the arbitrary conduct of the king ; his tyranny over the English, whom they affected on this occasion to commiserate ; his imperious behavior to his barons of the noblest birth ; and his apparent intention of reducing the victors and the vanquished to a like ignominious servitude. Amid their complaints, the indignity of submitting to a bastard [67] was not forgotten ; the certain prospect of success in a revolt, by the assistance of the Danes and the discontented English, was insisted on ; and the whole company, inflamed with the same sentiments, and warmed by the jollity of the entertainment, entered, by a solemn engagement, into the design of shaking off the royal authority. Even Earl Waltheof, who was present, inconsiderately expressed his approbation of the conspiracy, and promised his concurrence towards its success.

[67] William was so little ashamed of his birth that he assumed the appellation of Bastard in some of his letters and charters. Spell. Gloss. *in verbo* Bastardus. Camden *in* Richmondshire.

This nobleman, the last of the English who, for some generations, possessed any power or authority, had, after his capitulation at York, been received into favor by the Conqueror; had even married Judith, niece to that prince, and had been promoted to the earldoms of Huntingdon and Northampton.[68] Cospatric, Earl of Northumberland, having, on some new disgust from William, retired into Scotland, where he received the earldom of Dunbar from the bounty of Malcolm, Waltheof was appointed his successor in that important command, and seemed still to possess the confidence and friendship of his sovereign.[69] But as he was a man of generous principles, and loved his country, it is probable that the tyranny exercised over the English lay heavy upon his mind, and destroyed all the satisfaction which he could reap from his own grandeur and advancement. When a prospect, therefore, was opened of retrieving their liberty, he hastily embraced it; while the fumes of the liquor and the ardor of the company prevented him from reflecting on the consequences of that rash attempt. But after his cool judgment returned, he foresaw that the conspiracy of those discontented barons was not likely to prove successful against the established power of William; or, if it did, that the slavery of the English, instead of being alleviated by that event, would become more grievous under a multitude of foreign leaders, factious and ambitious, whose union and whose discord would be equally oppressive to the people. Tormented with these reflections, he opened his mind to his wife Judith, of whose fidelity he entertained no suspicion, but who, having secretly fixed her affections on another, took this opportunity of ruining her easy and credulous husband. She conveyed intelligence of the conspiracy to the king, and aggravated every circumstance which she believed would tend to incense him against Waltheof and render him absolutely implacable.[70] Meanwhile the earl, still dubious with regard to the part which he should act, discovered the secret in confession to Lanfranc, on whose probity and judgment he had a great reliance. He was persuaded by the prelate that he owed no fidelity to those rebellious barons who had by surprise gained his consent to a crime; that his first duty was to his sovereign and benefactor; his next to himself and his family; and that if he seized not the opportunity of making atonement for his guilt by revealing it, the

68 Order. Vitalis, p. 522. Hoveden, p. 454.   69 Sim. Dunelm. p. 205.
70 Order. Vitalis, p. 536.

temerity of the conspirators was so great that they would give some other persons the means of acquiring the merit of the discovery. Waltheof, convinced by these arguments, went over to Normandy; but though he was well received by the king and thanked for his fidelity, the account previously transmitted by Judith had sunk deep into William's mind, and had destroyed all the merit of her husband's repentance.

The conspirators, hearing of Waltheof's departure, immediately concluded their design to be betrayed; and they flew to arms before their schemes were ripe for execution, and before the arrival of the Danes, in whose aid they placed their chief confidence. The Earl of Hereford was checked by Walter de Lacy, a great baron in those parts, who, supported by the Bishop of Worcester and the Abbot of Evesham, raised some forces, and prevented the earl from passing the Severn, or advancing into the heart of the kingdom. The Earl of Norfolk was defeated at Fagadun, near Cambridge, by Odo, the regent, assisted by Richard de Bienfaite and William de Warenne, the two justiciaries. The prisoners taken in this action had their right foot cut off as a punishment of their treason : the earl himself escaped to Norwich, thence to Denmark, where the Danish fleet, which had made an unsuccessful attempt upon the coast of England,[71] soon after arrived, and brought him intelligence that all his confederates were suppressed, and were either killed, banished, or taken prisoners.[72] Ralph retired in despair to Brittany, where he possessed a large estate and extensive jurisdictions.

The king, who hastened over to England in order to suppress the insurrection, found that nothing remained but the punishment of the criminals, which he executed with great severity. Many of the rebels were hanged; some had their eyes put out; others their hands cut off. But William, agreeably to his usual maxims, showed more lenity to their leader, the Earl of Hereford, who was only condemned to a forfeiture of his estate, and to imprisonment during pleasure. The king seemed even disposed to remit this last part of the punishment, had not Roger, by a fresh insolence, provoked him to render his confinement perpet-

[71] Chron. Sax. p. 183. Matt. Paris, p. 7.
[72] Many of the fugitive Normans are supposed to have fled into Scotland, where they were protected, as well as the fugitive English, by Malcolm. Whence come the many French and Norman families which are found at present in that country.

ual. [1075.] But Waltheof, being an Englishman, was not treated with so much humanity; though his guilt, always much inferior to that of the other conspirators, was atoned for by an early repentance and return to his duty. William, instigated by his niece, as well as by his rapacious courtiers, who longed for so rich a forfeiture, ordered him to be tried, condemned, and executed. The English, who considered this nobleman as the last resource of their nation, grievously lamented his fate, and fancied that miracles were wrought by his relics, as a testimony of his innocence and sanctity. The infamous Judith, falling soon after under the king's displeasure, was abandoned by all the world, and passed the rest of her life in contempt, remorse, and misery.

Nothing remained to complete William's satisfaction but the punishment of Ralph de Guader; and he hastened over to Normandy in order to gratify his vengeance on that criminal. But though the contest seemed very unequal between a private nobleman and the king of England, Ralph was so well supported both by the Earl of Brittany and the King of France that William, after besieging him for some time in Dol, was obliged to abandon the enterprise, and make with those powerful princes a peace in which Ralph himself was included. England, during his absence, remained in tranquillity; and nothing remarkable occurred, except two ecclesiastical synods which were summoned—one at London, another at Winchester. In the former the precedency among the episcopal sees was settled, and the seat of some of them was removed from small villages to the most considerable town within the diocese. In the second was transacted a business of more importance.

[1076.] The industry and perseverance are surprising with which the popes had been treasuring up powers and pretensions during so many ages of ignorance; while each pontiff employed every fraud for advancing purposes of imaginary piety, and cherished all claims which might turn to the advantage of his successors, though he himself could not expect ever to reap any benefit from them. All this immense store of spiritual and civil authority was now devolved on Gregory VII. of the name of Hildebrand, the most enterprising pontiff that had ever filled that chair, and the least restrained by fear, decency, or moderation. Not content with shaking off the yoke of the emperors, who had hitherto exercised the power of appointing the pope on

every vacancy—at least, of ratifying his election—he undertook the arduous task of entirely disjoining the ecclesiastical from the civil power, and of excluding profane laymen
from the right which they had assumed of filling the vacancies of bishoprics, abbeys, and other spiritual dignities.[73]
The sovereigns who had long exercised this power, and who
had acquired it not by encroachments on the Church, but on
the people, to whom it originally belonged,[74] made great
opposition to this claim of the court of Rome; and Henry
IV., the reigning emperor, defended this prerogative of his
crown with a vigor and resolution suitable to its importance. The few offices, either civil or military, which the
feudal institutions left the sovereign the power of bestowing, made the prerogative of conferring the pastoral ring
and staff the most valuable jewel of the royal diadem, especially as the general ignorance of the age bestowed a consequence on the ecclesiastical offices even beyond the great
extent of power and property which belonged to them.
Superstition, the child of ignorance, invested the clergy
with an authority almost sacred; and as they engrossed the
little learning of the age, their interposition became requisite in all civil business, and a real usefulness in common
life was thus superadded to the spiritual sanctity of their
character.

When the usurpations, therefore, of the Church had
come to such maturity as to embolden her to attempt extorting the right of investitures from the temporal power,
Europe, especially Italy and Germany, was thrown into the
most violent convulsions, and the pope and the emperor
waged implacable war on each other. Gregory dared to
fulminate the sentence of excommunication against Henry
and his adherents, to pronounce him rightfully deposed, to
free his subjects from their oaths of allegiance; and instead
of shocking mankind by this gross encroachment on the
civil authority, he found the stupid people ready to second
his most exorbitant pretensions. Every minister, servant,
or vassal of the emperor, who received any disgust, covered
his rebellion under the pretence of principle; and even the
mother of this monarch, forgetting all the ties of nature,
was seduced to countenance the insolence of his enemies.
Princes themselves, not attentive to the pernicious consequences of those papal claims, employed them for their

[73] L'Abbé, Conc. tom. x. pp. 371, 372, com. 2.
[74] Padre Paolo, sopra benef. eccles. p. 30.

present purposes; and the controversy, spreading into every city of Italy, engendered the parties of Guelf and Ghibelline—the most durable and most inveterate factions that ever arose from the mixture of ambition and religious zeal. Besides numberless assassinations, tumults, and convulsions to which they gave rise, it is computed that the quarrel occasioned no less than sixty battles in the reign of Henry IV., and eighteen in that of his successor, Henry V., when the claims of the sovereign pontiff finally prevailed.[75]

But the bold spirit of Gregory, not dismayed with the vigorous opposition which he met with from the emperor, extended his usurpations all over Europe; and well knowing the nature of mankind, whose blind astonishment ever inclines them to yield to the most impudent pretensions, he seemed determined to set no bounds to the spiritual, or rather, temporal, monarchy which he had undertaken to erect. He pronounced the sentence of excommunication against Nicephorus, Emperor of the East. Robert Guiscard, the adventurous Norman who had acquired the dominion of Naples, was attacked by the same dangerous weapon. He degraded Boleslas, King of Poland, from the rank of king, and even deprived Poland of the title of a kingdom; he attempted to treat Philip, King of France, with the same rigor which he had employed against the emperor:[76] he pretended to the entire property and dominion of Spain, and he parcelled it out among adventurers, who undertook to conquer it from the Saracens and to hold it in vassalage under the see of Rome.[77] Even the Christian bishops, on whose aid he relied for subduing the temporal princes, saw that he was determined to reduce them to servitude; and, by assuming the whole legislative and judicial power of the Church, to centre all authority in the sovereign pontiff.[78]

William the Conqueror, the most potent, the most haughty, and the most vigorous prince in Europe, was not, amid all his splendid successes, secure from the attacks of this enterprising pontiff. Gregory wrote him a letter, requiring him to fulfil his promise in doing homage for the kingdom of England to the see of Rome, and to send him over that tribute which all his predecessors had been accustomed to pay to the vicar of Christ. By the tribute he meant Peter's pence,

[75] Padre Paolo, sopra benef. eccles. p. 113.
[76] Epist. Greg. VII. epist. 32, 35; lib. 2, epist. 5.
[77] Epist. Greg. VII. lib. 1, epist. 7   [78] Epist. Greg. VII. lib. 2, epist. 55,

which, though at first a charitable donation of the Saxon princes, was interpreted, according to the usual practice of the Romish court, to be a badge of subjection acknowledged by the kingdom. William replied that the money should be remitted as usual; but that neither had he promised to do homage to Rome, nor was it in the least his purpose to impose that servitude on his state.[79] And the better to show Gregory his independence, he ventured, notwithstanding the frequent complaints of the pope, to refuse to the English bishops the liberty of attending a general council which that pontiff had summoned against his enemies.

But though the king displayed this vigor in supporting the royal dignity, he was infected with the general superstition of the age, and he did not perceive the ambitious scope of those institutions which, under color of strictness in religion, were introduced or promoted by the court of Rome. Gregory, while he was throwing all Europe into combustion by his violence and impostures, affected an anxious care for the purity of manners; and even the chaste pleasures of the marriage-bed were inconsistent, in his opinion, with the sanctity of the sacerdotal character. He had issued a decree prohibiting the marriage of priests, excommunicating all clergymen who retained their wives, declaring such unlawful commerce to be fornication, and rendering it criminal in the laity to attend divine worship when such profane priests officiated at the altar.[80] This point was a great object in the politics of the Roman pontiffs, and it cost them infinitely more pains to establish it than the propagation of any speculative absurdity which they had ever attempted to introduce. Many synods were summoned in different parts of Europe before it was finally settled; and it was there constantly remarked that the younger clergymen complied cheerfully with the pope's decrees in this particular, and that the chief reluctance appeared in those who were more advanced in years—an event so little consonant to men's natural expectations that it could not fail to be glossed on, even in that blind and superstitious age. William allowed the pope's legate to assemble, in his absence, a synod at Winchester, in order to establish the celibacy of the clergy; but the Church of England could not yet be carried the whole length expected. The synod was

[79] Selden, Spicileg. ad Eadmer, p. 4.
[80] Hoveden, pp. 455, 457. Flor. Wigorn. p. 638. Spell. Conc. fol. 13, A. D. 1076.

content with decreeing that the bishops should not thenceforth ordain any priests or deacons without exacting from them a promise of celibacy; but they enacted that none, except those who belonged to collegiate or cathedral churches, should be obliged to separate from their wives.

The king passed some years in Normandy; but his long residence there was not entirely owing to his declared preference of that duchy : his presence was also necessary for composing those disturbances which had arisen in that favorite territory, and which had even originally proceeded from his own family. Robert, his eldest son, surnamed Gambaron, or Curthose, from his short legs, was a prince who inherited all the bravery of his family and nation; but without that policy and dissimulation by which his father was so much distinguished, and which, no less than his military valor, had contributed to his great successes. Greedy of fame, impatient of contradiction, without reserve in his friendships, declared in his enmities, this prince could endure no control even from his imperious father, and openly aspired to that independence to which his temper as well as some circumstances in his situation strongly invited him.[81] When William first received the submissions of the province of Maine, he had promised the inhabitants that Robert should be their prince; and, before he undertook the expedition against England, he had, on the application of the French court, declared him his successor in Normandy, and had obliged the barons of that duchy to do him homage as their future sovereign. By this artifice he had endeavored to appease the jealousy of his neighbors, as affording them a prospect of separating England from his dominions on the Continent; but when Robert demanded of him the execution of those engagements, he gave him an absolute refusal, and told him, according to the homely saying, that he never intended to throw off his clothes till he went to bed.[82] Robert openly declared his discontent, and was suspected of secretly instigating the King of France and the Earl of Brittany to the opposition which they made to William, and which had formerly frustrated his attempts upon the town of Dol. And, as the quarrel still augmented, Robert proceeded to entertain a strong jealousy of his two surviving brothers, William and Henry (for Richard was killed, in hunting, by a stag), who, by greater submission and com-

---

[81] Order. Vitalis, p. 545.   Hoveden, p. 457.   Flor. Wigorn. p. 639.
[82] Chron. de Mailr. p. 160.

plaisance, had acquired the affections of their father. In this disposition on both sides, the greatest trifle sufficed to produce a rupture between them.

The three princes, residing with their father in the castle of L'Aigle, in Normandy, were one day engaged in sport together; and, after some mirth and jollity, the two younger took a fancy of throwing over some water on Robert as he passed through the court on leaving their apartment[83]—a frolic which he would naturally have regarded as innocent had it not been for the suggestions of Alberic de Grentmesnil, son of that Hugh de Grentmesnil whom William had formerly deprived of his fortunes when that baron deserted him during his greatest difficulties in England. The young man, mindful of the injury, persuaded the prince that this action was meant as a public affront, which it behooved him in honor to resent; and the choleric Robert, drawing his sword, ran up-stairs, with an intention of taking revenge on his brothers.[84] The whole castle was filled with tumult, which the king himself, who hastened from his apartment, found some difficulty to appease. But he could by no means appease the resentment of his eldest son, who, complaining of his partiality, and fancying that no proper atonement had been made him for the insult, left the court that very evening, and hastened to Rouen, with an intention of seizing the citadel of that place.[85] But being disappointed in this view by the precaution and vigilance of Roger d'Ivery, the governor, he fled to Hugh de Neufchatel, a powerful Norman baron, who gave him protection in his castles; and he openly levied war against his father.[86] The popular character of the prince, and a similarity of manners, engaged all the young nobility of Normandy and Maine, as well as of Anjou and Brittany, to take part with him; and it was suspected that Matilda, his mother, whose favorite he was, supported him in his rebellion by secret remittances of money and by the encouragement which she gave his partisans.

[1079.] All the hereditary provinces of William, as well as his family, were, during several years, thrown into convulsions by this war; and he was at last obliged to have recourse to England, where that species of military government which he had established gave him greater authority than the ancient feudal institutions permitted him to exercise

[83] Order. Vitalis, p. 545.   [84] Ibid.   [85] Ibid.
[86] Ibid. Hoveden, p. 457. Sim. Dunelm. p. 210. Diceto, p. 487.

in Normandy. He called over an army of English under his ancient captains, who soon expelled Robert and his adherents from their retreats, and restored the authority of the sovereign in all his dominions. The young prince was obliged to take shelter in the castle of Gerberoy, in the Beauvoisis, which the King of France, who secretly fomented all these dissensions, had provided for him. In this fortress he was closely besieged by his father, against whom, having a strong garrison, he made an obstinate defence. There passed under the walls of this place many rencounters, which resembled more the single combats of chivalry than the military actions of armies ; but one of them was remarkable for its circumstances and its event. Robert happened to engage the king, who was concealed by his helmet ; and, both of them being valiant, a fierce combat ensued, till at last the young prince wounded his father in the arm and unhorsed him. On his calling out for assistance, his voice discovered him to his son, who, struck with remorse for his past guilt, and astonished with the apprehensions of one much greater, which he had so nearly incurred, instantly threw himself at his father's feet, craved pardon for his offences, and offered to purchase forgiveness by any atonement.[87] The resentment harbored by William was so implacable that he did not immediately correspond to this dutiful submission of his son with like tenderness ; but, giving him his malediction, departed for his own camp on Robert's horse, which that prince had assisted him to mount. He soon after raised the siege, and marched with his army to Normandy, where the interposition of the queen and other common friends brought about a reconcilement, which was probably not a little forwarded by the generosity of the son's behavior in this action, and by the returning sense of his past misconduct. The king seemed so fully appeased that he even took Robert with him into England, where he intrusted him with the command of an army, in order to repel an inroad of Malcolm, King of Scotland, and to retaliate by a like inroad into that country. The Welsh, unable to resist William's power, were, about the same time, necessitated to pay a compensation for their incursions ; and everything was reduced to full tranquillity in this island.

[1081.] The state of affairs gave William leisure to be-

[87] Will. Malm. p. 106.   H. Hunting. p. 369.   Hoveden, p. 457.   Flor. Wigorn p. 639.   Sim. Dunelm. p. 210.   Diceto, p. 287.   Knyghton, p. 2351.   Alur. Beverl. p. 135.

gin and finish an undertaking which proves his extensive genius and does honor to his memory. It was a general survey of all the lands in the kingdom, their extent in each district, their proprietors, tenures, value; the quantity of meadow, pasture, wood, and arable land which they contained; and in some counties the number of tenants, cottagers, and slaves of all denominations who lived upon them. He appointed commissioners for this purpose, who entered every particular in their register by the verdict of juries, and, after a labor of six years (for the work was so long in finishing), brought him an exact account of all the landed property of his kingdom.[88] This monument, called Domesday-book, the most valuable piece of antiquity possessed by any nation, is still preserved in the Exchequer; and though only some extracts of it have hitherto been published, it serves to illustrate to us, in many particulars, the ancient state of England. The great Alfred had finished a like survey of the kingdom in his time, which was long kept at Winchester, and which probably served as a model to William in this undertaking.[89]

The king was naturally a great economist; and though no prince had ever been more bountiful to his officers and servants, it was merely because he had rendered himself universal proprietor of England, and had a whole kingdom to bestow. He reserved an ample revenue for the crown; and in the general distribution of land among his followers, he kept possession of no less than one thousand four hundred and twenty-two manors in different parts of England,[90] which paid him rent, either in money, or in corn, cattle, and the usual produce of the soil. An ancient historian computes that his annual fixed income, besides escheats, fines, reliefs, and other casual profits to a great value, amounted to near four hundred thousand pounds a year;[91] a sum which, if all circumstances be attended to, will appear wholly incredible. A pound in that age, as we have already observed, contained three times the weight of silver that it does at present; and the same weight of silver by the most probable computation would purchase near ten times more

---

[88] Chron. Sax. p. 190.   Ingulph. p. 79.   Chron. T. Wykes, p. 23.   H. Hunting. p. 370.   Hoveden, p. 460.   Matt. West. p. 229.   Flor. Wigorn. p. 641.   Chron. Abb. St. Petri de Burgo, p. 51.   Matt. Paris, p. 8.   The more northern counties were not comprehended in this survey; I suppose because of their wild, uncultivated state.   [89] Ingulph. p. 8.

[90] West's Inquiry into the Manner of Creating Peers. p. 24.

[91] Order. Vitalis, p. 523.   He says one thousand and sixty pounds and some odd shillings and pence a day.

of the necessaries of life, though not in the same proportion of the finer manufactures. This revenue, therefore, of William would be equal to at least nine or ten millions at present; and, as that prince had neither fleet nor army to support, the former being only an occasional expense, and the latter being maintained without any charge to him by his military vassals, we must thence conclude that no emperor or prince, in any age or nation, can be compared to the Conqueror for opulence and riches. This leads us to suspect a great mistake in the computation of the historian; though, if we consider that avarice is always imputed to William as one of his vices, and that, having by the sword rendered himself master of all the lands in the kingdom, he would certainly in the partition retain a great proportion for his own share, we can scarcely be guilty of any error in asserting that perhaps no king of England was ever more opulent, was more able to support by his revenue the splendor and magnificence of a court, or could bestow more on his pleasures or in liberalities to his servants and favorites.[92]

There was one pleasure to which William, as well as all the Normans and ancient Saxons, was extremely addicted, and that was hunting; but this pleasure he indulged more at the expense of his unhappy subjects, whose interests he always disregarded, than to the loss or diminution of his own revenue. Not content with those large forests which former kings possessed in all parts of England, he resolved to make a new forest near Winchester, the usual place of his residence; and for that purpose he laid waste the country in Hampshire for an extent of thirty miles, expelled the inhabitants from their houses, seized their property, even demolished churches and convents, and made the sufferers no compensation for the injury.[93] At the same time he enacted new laws by which he prohibited all his subjects from hunting in any of his forests, and rendered the penalties more severe than ever had been inflicted for such offences. The killing of a deer or boar, or even a hare, was punished with the loss of the delinquent's eyes; and that at a time when the killing of a man could be atoned for by paying a moderate fine or composition.

The transactions recorded during the remainder of this reign may be considered more as domestic occurrences which concern the prince than as national events which re-

[92] Fortescue, De Dom. Reg. et Politic. cap. 111.
[93] Will. Malm. p. 3. H. Hunting. p. 731. Anglia Sacra, vol. i. p. 258.

gard England. Odo, Bishop of Baieux, the king's uterine brother, whom he had created Earl of Kent, and intrusted with a great share of power during his whole reign, had amassed immense riches; and agreeably to the usual progress of human wishes, he began to regard his present acquisitions but as a step to further grandeur. He had formed the chimerical project of buying the papacy; and though Gregory, the reigning pope, was not of advanced years, the prelate had confided so much in the predictions of an astrologer that he reckoned upon the pontiff's death, and upon attaining by his own intrigues and money that envied state of greatness. Resolving, therefore, to remit all his riches to Italy, he had persuaded many considerable barons, and, among the rest, Hugh, Earl of Chester, to take the same course, in hopes that, when he should mount the papal throne, he would bestow on them more considerable establishments in that country. [1082.] The king, from whom all these projects had been carefully concealed, at last got intelligence of the design, and ordered Odo to be arrested. His officers, from respect to the immunities which the ecclesiastics now assumed, scrupled to execute the command till the king himself was obliged in person to seize him; and when Odo insisted that he was a prelate, and exempt from all temporal jurisdiction, William replied that he arrested him not as Bishop of Baieux, but as Earl of Kent. He was sent prisoner to Normandy; and, notwithstanding the remonstrances and menaces of Gregory, was detained in custody during the remainder of this reign.

[1083.] Another domestic event gave the king much more concern: it was the death of Matilda, his consort, whom he tenderly loved, and for whom he had ever preserved the most sincere friendship. Three years afterwards he passed into Normandy, and carried with him Edgar Atheling, to whom he willingly granted permission to make a pilgrimage to the Holy Land. He was detained on the Continent by a misunderstanding which broke out between him and the King of France, and which was occasioned by inroads made into Normandy by some French barons on the frontiers. [1087.] It was little in the power of princes at that time to restrain their licentious nobility; but William suspected that these barons durst not have provoked his indignation had they not been assured of the countenance and protection of Philip. His displeasure was increased by the account he received of some railleries which that monarch had thrown out against him. William, who was become corpulent, had been detained in bed some time by sickness, upon which Philip expressed his surprise that his brother of England should be so long in being delivered of his big belly. The king sent him word that, as soon as he was up, he would present so many lights at Notre Dame as would perhaps give little pleasure to the King of France—alluding to the usual practice at that time of women after childbirth. Immediately on his recovery he led an army into l'Isle de France, and laid everything waste with fire and sword. He took the town of Mante, which he reduced to ashes. But the progress of these hostilities was stopped by an accident which soon after put an end to William's life. His horse starting aside of a sudden, he bruised his belly on the pommel of the saddle; and being in a bad habit of body, as well as somewhat advanced in years, he began to apprehend the consequences, and ordered himself to be carried in a litter to the monastery of St. Gervas. Finding his illness increase, and being sensible of the approach of death, he discovered at last the vanity of all human grandeur, and was struck with remorse for those horrible cruelties and acts of violence which, in the attainment and defence of it, he had committed during the course of his reign over England. He endeavored to make atonement by presents to churches and monasteries; and he issued orders that Earl Morcar, Siward, Bearne, and other English prisoners should be set at liberty. He was even prevailed on, though not without reluctance, to consent, with his dying breath, to release his brother Odo, against whom he was extremely incensed. He left Normandy and Maine to his eldest son, Robert. He wrote to Lanfranc, desiring him to crown William King of England. He bequeathed to Henry nothing but the possessions of his mother Matilda, but foretold that he would one day surpass both his brothers in power and opulence. He expired in the sixty-third year of his age, in the twenty-first year of his reign over England and in the fifty-fourth of that over Normandy.

Few princes have been more fortunate than this great monarch, or were better entitled to grandeur and prosperity, from the abilities and the vigor of mind which he displayed in all his conduct. His spirit was bold and enterprising, yet guided by prudence : his ambition, which was exorbitant, and lay little under the restraints of justice, still less under those of humanity, ever submitted to the dictates of sound policy. Born in an age when the minds of men were intractable and unacquainted with submission, he was yet able to direct them to his purposes, and, partly from the ascendant of his vehement character, partly from art and dissimulation, to establish an unlimited authority. Though not insensible to generosity, he was hardened against compassion; and he seemed equally ostentatious and equally ambitious of show and parade in his clemency and in his severity. The maxims of his administration were austere, but might have been useful had they been solely employed to preserve order in an established government; [94] they were ill calculated for softening the rigors which, under the most gentle management, are inseparable from conquest. His attempt against England was the last great enterprise of the kind which, during the course of seven hundred years, has fully succeeded in Europe; and the force of his genius broke through those limits which first the feudal institutions, then the refined policy of princes, have fixed to the several states of Christendom. Though he rendered himself infinitely odious to his English subjects, he transmitted his power to his posterity, and the throne is still filled by his descendants—a proof that the foundations which he laid were firm and solid, and that, amid all his violence, while he seemed only to gratify the present passion, he had still an eye towards futurity.

Some writers have been desirous of refusing to this prince the title of Conqueror in the sense which that title commonly bears; and, on pretence that the word is sometimes in old books applied to such as make an acquisition of territory by any means, they are willing to reject William's title by right of war to the crown of England. It is needless to enter into a controversy which, by the terms of it, must necessarily degenerate into a dispute of words. It suffices to say that the Duke of Normandy's first invasion of the island was hostile; that his subsequent administration was entirely supported by arms; that in the very frame of his laws he made a distinction between the Normans and English to the advantage of the former; [95] that he acted in everything as absolute master over the natives, whose interest and affections he totally disregarded; and that if there was an interval when he assumed the appearance of a legal sovereign, the period was very short, and was nothing but a temporary sacrifice, which he, as has been the case with

[94] Matt. West. p. 230. Anglia Sacra, vol. i. p. 258. [95] Hoveden, p. 600.

most conquerors, was obliged to make of his inclination to his present policy. Scarce any of those revolutions which both in history and in common language have always been denominated conquests appear equally violent, or were attended with so sudden an alteration both of power and property. The Roman state, which spread its dominion over Europe, left the rights of individuals in a great measure untouched; and those civilized conquerors, while they made their own country the seat of empire, found that they could draw most advantage from the subjected provinces by securing to the natives the free enjoyment of their own laws and of their private possessions. The barbarians who subdued the Roman empire, though they settled in the conquered countries, yet, being accustomed to a rude, uncultivated life, found a part only of the land sufficient to supply all their wants; and they were not tempted to seize extensive possessions, which they knew neither how to cultivate nor enjoy. But the Normans and other foreigners who followed the standard of William, while they made the vanquished kingdom the seat of government, were yet so far advanced in arts as to be acquainted with the advantages of a large property; and, having totally subdued the natives, they pushed the rights of conquest (very extensive in the eyes of avarice and ambition, however narrow in those of reason) to the utmost extremity against them. Except the former conquest of England by the Saxons themselves, who were induced, by peculiar circumstances, to proceed even to the extermination of the natives, it would be difficult to find in all history a revolution more destructive or attended with a more complete subjection of the ancient inhabitants. Contumely seems even to have been wantonly added to oppression;[96] and the natives were universally reduced to such a state of meanness and poverty that the English name became a term of reproach; and several generations elapsed before one family of Saxon pedigree was raised to any considerable honors, or could so much as attain the rank of baron of the realm.[97] These facts are so apparent from the whole tenor of the English history that none would have been tempted to deny or elude them were

[96] H. Hunting. p. 370. Brompton, p. 980.

[97] So late as the reign of King Stephen, the Earl of Albemarle, before the Battle of the Standard, addressed the officers of his army in these terms : " Proceres Angliæ clarissimi, et genere Normanni," etc. Brompton, p. 1026. See, further, Abbas Rieval. p. 339, etc. All the barons and military men of England still called themselves Normans.

they not heated by the controversies of faction; while one party was *absurdly* afraid of those *absurd* consequences which they saw the other party inclined to draw from this event. But it is evident that the present rights and privileges of the people, who are a mixture of English and Normans, can never be affected by a transaction which passed seven hundred years ago; and as all ancient authors [98] who lived nearest the time and best knew the state of the country unanimously speak of the Norman dominion as a conquest by war and arms, no reasonable man, from the fear of imaginary consequences, will ever be tempted to reject their concurring and undoubted testimony.

King William had issue, besides his three sons who survived him, five daughters—to wit (1), Cicely, a nun in the monastery of Feschamp, afterwards abbess in the Holy Trinity at Caen, where she died in 1127. (2) Constantia, married to Alan Fergent, Earl of Brittany. She died without issue. (3) Alice, contracted to Harold. (4) Adela, married to Stephen, Earl of Blois, by whom she had four sons—William, Theobald, Henry, and Stephen—of whom the elder was neglected on account of the imbecility of his understanding. (5) Agatha, who died a virgin, but was betrothed to the King of Gallicia. She died on her journey thither before she joined her bridegroom.

[98] See note [L] at the end of the volume.

CHAPTER V.

WILLIAM RUFUS.

ACCESSION OF WILLIAM RUFUS.—CONSPIRACY AGAINST THE
KING.—INVASION OF NORMANDY.—THE CRUSADES.—AC-
QUISITION OF NORMANDY.—QUARREL WITH ANSELM, THE
PRIMATE.—DEATH AND CHARACTER OF WILLIAM RUFUS.

[1087.] WILLIAM, surnamed *Rufus*, or the *Red*, from
the color of his hair, had no sooner procured his father's rec-
ommendatory letter to Lanfranc, the primate, than he hastened to take measures for securing to himself the government of England. Sensible that a deed so informal and so
little prepared, which violated Robert's right of primogeniture, might meet with great opposition, he trusted entirely
for success to his own celerity; and, having left St. Gervas
while William was breathing his last, he arrived in England
before intelligence of his father's death had reached that
kingdom.[1] Pretending orders from the king, he secured the
fortresses of Dover, Pevensey, and Hastings, whose situation
rendered them of the greatest importance; and he got possession of the royal treasure at Winchester, amounting to
the sum of sixty thousand pounds, by which he hoped to encourage and increase his partisans.[2] The primate, whose
rank and reputation in the kingdom gave him great authority, had been intrusted with the care of his education, and
had conferred on him the honor of knighthood; [3] and being
connected with him by these ties, and probably deeming his
pretensions just, declared that he would pay a willing obedience to the last will of the Conqueror, his friend and benefactor. Having assembled some bishops and some of the
principal nobility, he instantly proceeded to the ceremony
of crowning the new king; [4] and by this despatch endeavored to prevent all faction and resistance. At the same
time, Robert, who had been already acknowledged successor
to Normandy, took peaceable possession of that duchy.

[1] Will. Malm. p. 120.   Matt. Paris, p. 10.
[2] Chron. Sax. p. 192.   Brompton, p. 983.
[3] Will. Malm. p. 120.   Matt. Paris, p. 10.   Thom. Rudborne, p. 263.
[4] Hoveden, p. 461.

But though this partition appeared to have been made without any violence or opposition, there remained in England many causes of discontens, which seemed to menace that kingdom with a sudden revolution. The barons, who generally possessed large estates both in England and in Normandy, were uneasy at the separation of those territories; and foresaw that, as it would be impossible for them to preserve long their allegiance to two masters, they must necessarily resign either their ancient patrimony or their new acquisitions.[5] Robert's title to the duchy they esteemed incontestable, his claim to the kingdom plausible ; and they all desired that this prince, who alone had any pretensions to unite these states, should be put in possession of both. A comparison also of the personal qualities of the two brothers led them to give the preference to the elder. The duke was brave, open, sincere, generous : even his predominant faults, his extreme indolence and facility, were not disagreeable to those haughty barons, who affected independence, and submitted with reluctance to a vigorous administration in their sovereign. The king, though equally brave, was violent, haughty, tyrannical, and seemed disposed to govern more by the fear than by the love of his subjects. Odo, Bishop of Baieux, and Robert, Earl of Mortaigne, maternal brothers of the Conqueror, envying the great credit of Lanfranc, which was increased by his late services, enforced all these motives with their partisans, and engaged them in a formal conspiracy to dethrone the king. They communicated their design to Eustace, Count of Boulogne ; Roger, Earl of Shrewsbury and Arundel ; Robert de Belesme, his eldest son ; William, Bishop of Durham ; Robert de Moubray ; Roger Bigod ; Hugh de Grentmesnil ; and they easily procured the assent of these potent noblemen. The conspirators, retiring to their castles, hastened to put themselves in a military posture ; and, expecting to be soon supported by a powerful army from Normandy, they had already begun hostilities in many places.

The king, sensible of his perilous situation, endeavored to engage the affections of the native English. As that people were now so thoroughly subdued that they no longer aspired to the recovery of their ancient liberties, and were content with the prospect of some mitigation in the tyranny of the Norman princes, they zealously embraced William's cause upon receiving general promises of good treatment,

[5] Order. Vitalis, p. 666.

and of enjoying the license of hunting in the royal forests. The king was soon in a situation to take the field ; and as he knew the danger of delay, he suddenly marched into Kent, where his uncles had already seized the fortresses of Pevensey and Rochester. These places he successively reduced by famine; and though he was prevailed on by the Earl of Chester, William de Warenne, and Robert Fitz-Hammon, who had embraced his cause, to spare the lives of the rebels, he confiscated all their estates, and banished them the kingdom.[6] This success gave authority to his negotiations with Roger, Earl of Shrewsbury, whom he detached from the confederates; and as his powerful fleet, joined to the indolent conduct of Robert, prevented the arrival of the Norman succors, all the other rebels found no resource but in flight or submission. Some of them received a pardon ; but the greater part were attainted, and the king bestowed their estates on the Norman barons who had remained faithful to him.

[1089.] William, freed from the danger of these insurrections, took little care of fulfilling his promises to the English, who still found themselves exposed to the same oppressions which they had undergone during the reign of the Conqueror, and which were rather augmented by the violent, impetuous temper of the present monarch. The death of Lanfranc, who retained great influence over him, gave soon after a full career to his tyranny; and all orders of men found reason to complain of an arbitrary and illegal administration. Even the privileges of the Church, held sacred in those days, were a feeble rampart against his usurpations. He seized the temporalities of all the vacant bishoprics and abbeys ; he delayed the appointment of successors to those dignities, that he might the longer enjoy the profits of their revenue; he bestowed some of the Church lands in property on his captains and favorites ; and he openly set to sale such sees and abbeys as he thought proper to dispose of. Though the murmurs of the ecclesiastics, which were quickly propagated to the nation, rose high against this grievance, the terror of William's authority, confirmed by the suppression of the late insurrections, retained every one in subjection, and preserved general tranquillity in England.

[1090.] The king even thought himself enabled to disturb his brother in the possession of Normandy. The loose and negligent administration of that prince had emboldened

[6] Chron. Sax. p. 195. Order. Vitalis, p. 668.

the Norman barons to affect a great independency; and their mutual quarrels and devastations had rendered the whole territory a scene of violence and outrage. Two of them, Walter and Odo, were bribed by William to deliver the fortresses of St. Valori and Albemarle into his hands; others soon after imitated the example of revolt; while Philip, King of France, who ought to have protected his vassal in the possession of his fief, was, after making some efforts in his favor, engaged by large presents to remain neutral. The duke had also reason to apprehend danger from the intrigues of his brother Henry. This young prince, who had inherited nothing of his father's great possessions but some of his money, had furnished Robert, while he was making his preparations against England, with the sum of three thousand marks; and in return for so slender a supply had been put in possession of the Cotentin, which comprehended near a third of the duchy of Normandy. Robert afterwards, upon some suspicion, threw him into prison; but finding himself exposed to invasion from the King of England, and dreading the conjunction of the two brothers against him, he now gave Henry his liberty, and even made use of his assistance in suppressing the insurrections of his rebellious subjects. Conan, a rich burgess of Rouen, had entered into a conspiracy to deliver that city to William; but Henry, on the detection of his guilt, carried the traitor up to a high tower, and with his own hands flung him from the battlements.

The king appeared in Normandy at the head of an army; and affairs seemed to have come to extremity between the brothers, when the nobility on both sides, strongly connected by interest and alliances, interposed and mediated an accommodation. The chief advantage of this treaty accrued to William, who obtained possession of the territory of Eu, the towns of Aumale, Fescamp, and other places; but, in return, he promised that he would assist his brother in subduing Maine, which had rebelled; and that the Norman barons, attainted in Robert's cause, should be restored to their estates in England. The two brothers also stipulated that, on the demise of either without issue, the survivor should inherit all his dominions; and twelve of the most powerful barons on each side swore that they would employ their power to insure the effectual execution of the whole treaty[7]—a strong

[7] Chron. Sax. p. 197. Will. Malm. p. 121. Hoveden, p. 462. Matt. Paris, p. 11. Annal. Waverl. p. 137. W. Heming. 463. Sim. Dunelm. p. 216. Brompton, p. 986.

proof of the great independence and authority of the nobles in those ages !

Prince Henry, disgusted that so little care had been taken of his interests in this accommodation, retired to St. Michael's Mount, a strong fortress on the coast of Normandy, and infested the neighborhood with his incursions. Robert and William, with their joint forces, besieged him in this place, and had nearly reduced him by the scarcity of water; when the elder, hearing of his distress, granted him permission to supply himself, and also sent him some pipes of wine for his own table. Being reproved by William for this ill-timed generosity, he replied, "What, shall I suffer my brother to die of thirst? Where shall we find another when he is gone?" The king also, during this siege, performed an act of generosity which was less suitable to his character. Riding out one day alone to take a survey of the fortress, he was attacked by two soldiers and dismounted. One of them drew his sword in order to despatch him; when the king exclaimed, "Hold, knave! I am the King of England." The soldier suspended his blow; and, raising the king from the ground with expressions of respect, received a handsome reward, and was taken into his service. Prince Henry was soon after obliged to capitulate; and being despoiled of all his patrimony, wandered about for some time with very few attendants, and often in great poverty.

[1091.] The continued intestine discord among the barons was alone in that age destructive; the public wars were commonly short and feeble, produced little bloodshed, and were attended with no memorable event. To this Norman war, which was so soon concluded, there succeeded hostilities with Scotland, which were not of longer duration. Robert here commanded his brother's army, and obliged Malcolm to accept of peace and do homage to the crown of England. [1093.] This peace was not more durable. Malcolm, two years after, levying an army, invaded England; and after ravaging Northumberland, he laid siege to Alnwick, where a party of Earl Moubray's troops falling upon him by surprise, a sharp action ensued, in which Malcolm was slain. This incident interrupted for some years the regular succession to the Scottish crown. Though Malcolm left legitimate sons, his brother, Donald, on account of the youth of these princes, was advanced to the throne; but kept not long possession of it. Duncan, natural son of Malcolm, formed a conspiracy against him, and, being assisted by William with a small force, made himself master of the kingdom. New broils ensued with Normandy. The frank, open, remiss temper of Robert was ill fitted to withstand the interested, rapacious character of William, who, supported by greater power, was still encroaching on his brother's possessions, and instigated his turbulent barons to rebellion against him. [1094.] The king, having gone over to Normandy to support his partisans, ordered an army of twenty thousand men to be levied in England, and to be conducted to the sea-coast, as if they were instantly to be embarked. Here Ralph Flambard, the king's minister, and the chief instrument of his extortions, exacted ten shillings apiece from them in lieu of their service, and then dismissed them into their several counties. This money was so skilfully employed by William that it rendered him better service than he could have expected from the army. He engaged the French king by new presents to depart from the protection of Robert; and he daily bribed the Norman barons to desert his service, but was prevented from pushing his advantages by an incursion of the Welsh, which obliged him to return to England. He found no difficulty in repelling the enemy, but was not able to make any considerable impression on a country guarded by its mountainous situation. [1095.] A conspiracy of his own barons, which was detected at this time, appeared a more serious concern, and engrossed all his attention. Robert Moubray, Earl of Northumberland, was at the head of this combination; and he engaged in it the Count d'Eu, Richard de Tunbridge, Roger de Lacy, and many others. The purpose of the conspirators was to dethrone the king, and to advance in his stead Stephen, Count of Aumale, nephew to the Conqueror. William's despatch prevented the design from taking effect, and disconcerted the conspirators. Moubray made some resistance, but being taken prisoner, was attainted and thrown into confinement, where he died about thirty years after. [1096.] The Count d'Eu denied his concurrence in the plot; and to justify himself, fought, in the presence of the court at Windsor, a duel with Geoffrey Bainard, who accused him. But being worsted in the combat, he was condemned to be castrated, and to have his eyes put out. William de Alderi, another conspirator, was supposed to be treated with more rigor when he was sentenced to be hanged.

But the noise of these petty wars and commotions was

quite sunk in the tumult of the crusades, which now engrossed the attention of Europe, and have ever since engaged the curiosity of mankind, as the most signal and most
durable monument of human folly that has yet appeared in
any age or nation. After Mahomet had, by means of his
pretended revelations, united the dispersed Arabians under
one head, they issued forth from their deserts in great
multitudes; and being animated with zeal for their new
religion, and supported by the vigor of their new government, they made deep impression on the eastern empire,
which was far in the decline, with regard both to military
discipline and to civil policy. Jerusalem, by its situation,
became one of their most early conquests; and the
Christians had the mortification to see the holy sepulchre,
and the other places consecrated by the presence of their religious founder, fallen into the possession of infidels. But
the Arabians or Saracens were so employed in military enterprises, by which they spread their empire in a few years
from the banks of the Ganges to the Straits of Gibraltar,
that they had no leisure for theological controversy; and
though the Alcoran, the original monument of their faith,
seems to contain some violent precepts, they were much less
infected with the spirit of bigotry and persecution than the
indolent and speculative Greeks, who were continually refin-
ing on the several articles of their religious system. They
gave little disturbance to those zealous pilgrims who daily
flocked to Jerusalem; and they allowed every man, after
paying a moderate tribute, to visit the holy sepulchre, to
perform his religious duties, and to return in peace. But
the Turcomans, or Turks, a tribe of Tartars who had embraced Mahometanism, having wrested Syria from the Saracens, and having, in the year 1065, made themselves masters
of Jerusalem, rendered the pilgrimage much more difficult
and dangerous to the Christians. The barbarity of their
manners, and the confusions attending their unsettled government, exposed the pilgrims to many insults, robberies, and
extortions; and these zealots, returning from their meritorious fatigues and sufferings, filled all Christendom with indignation against the infidels, who profaned the holy city by
their presence, and derided the sacred mysteries in the very
place of their completion. Gregory VII., among the other
vast ideas which he entertained, had formed the design of
uniting all the western Christians against the Mahometans;
but the egregious and violent invasions of that pontiff on

the civil power of princes had created him so many enemies, and had rendered his schemes so suspicious, that he was not able to make great progress in this undertaking. The work was reserved for a meaner instrument, whose low condition in life exposed him to no jealousy, and whose folly was well calculated to coincide with the prevailing principles of the times.

Peter, commonly called the Hermit, a native of Amiens, in Picardy, had made the pilgrimage to Jerusalem. Being deeply affected with the dangers to which that act of piety now exposed the pilgrims, as well as with the instances of oppression under which the eastern Christians labored, he entertained the bold, and in all appearance impracticable, project of leading into Asia, from the farthest extremities of the West, armies sufficient to subdue those potent and warlike nations which now held the holy city in subjection.[8] He proposed his views to Martin II., who filled the papal chair, and who, though sensible of the advantages which the head of the Christian religion must reap from a religious war, and though he esteemed the blind zeal of Peter a proper means for effecting the purpose,[9] resolved not to interpose his authority till he saw a greater probability of success. He summoned a council at Placentia, which consisted of four thousand ecclesiastics and thirty thousand seculars, and which was so numerous that no hall could contain the multitude, and it was necessary to hold the assembly in a plain. The harangues of the pope, and of Peter himself, representing the dismal situation of their brethren in the East, and the indignity suffered by the Christian name in allowing the holy city to remain in the hands of infidels, here found the minds of men so well prepared that the whole multitude suddenly and violently declared for the war, and solemnly devoted themselves to perform this service, so meritorious, as they believed it, to God and religion.

But though Italy seemed thus to have zealously embraced the enterprise, Martin knew that, in order to insure success, it was necessary to enlist the greater and more warlike nations in the same engagement; and, having previously exhorted Peter to visit the chief cities and sovereigns of Christendom, he summoned another council at Clermont, in Auvergne.[10] The fame of this great and pious design being

8 Gul. Tyrius, lib. 1, cap. 11. Matt. Paris, p. 17.
9 Gul. Tyrius, lib. 1, cap. 13.
10 Concil. tom. x. Concil. Clarom. Matt. Paris, p. 16. Matt. West. p. 233.

now universally diffused, procured the attendance of the greatest prelates, nobles, and princes; and when the pope and the Hermit renewed their pathetic exhortations, the whole assembly, as if impelled by an immediate inspiration, not moved by their preceding impressions, exclaimed with one voice, " It is the will of God! It is the will of God!" Words deemed so memorable, and so much the result of a divine influence, that they were employed as the signal of rendezvous and battle in all the future exploits of those adventurers.[11] Men of all ranks flew to arms with the utmost ardor; and an exterior symbol too, a circumstance of chief moment, was here chosen by the devoted combatants. The sign of the cross, which had been hitherto so much revered among Christians, and which, the more it was an object of reproach among the pagan world, was the more passionately cherished by them, became the badge of union, and was affixed to the right shoulder by all who enlisted themselves in this sacred warfare.[12]

Europe was at this time sunk into profound ignorance and superstition. The ecclesiastics had acquired the greatest ascendant over the human mind; the people, who, being little restrained by honor and less by law, abandoned themselves to the worst crimes and disorders, knew of no other expiation than the observances imposed on them by their spiritual pastors; and it was easy to represent the holy war as an equivalent for all penances[13] and an atonement for every violation of justice and humanity. But, amid the abject superstition which now prevailed, the military spirit also had universally diffused itself; and, though not supported by art or discipline, was become the general passion of the nations governed by the feudal law. All the great lords possessed the right of peace and war: they were engaged in perpetual hostilities with each other. The open country was become a scene of outrage and disorder; the cities still mean and poor were neither guarded by walls nor protected by privileges, and were exposed to every insult; individuals were obliged to depend for safety on their own force, or their private alliances; and valor was the only excellence which was held in esteem, or gave one man the preeminence above another. When all the particular superstitions, therefore, were here united in one great object, the

---

[11] Hist. Bell. Sacri, tom. i. Musæi Ital.
[12] Hist. Bell. Sacri, tom. i. Musæi Ital. Order. Vitalis, p. 721.
[13] Order. Vitalis, p. 720.

ardor for military enterprises took the same direction ; and Europe, impelled by its two ruling passions, was loosened, as it were, from its foundations, and seemed to precipitate itself in one united body upon the East.

All orders of men, deeming the crusades the only road to heaven, enlisted themselves under these sacred banners, and were impatient to open the way with their sword to the holy city. Nobles, artisans, peasants, even priests,[14] enrolled their names; and to decline this meritorious service was branded with the reproach of impiety, or what perhaps was esteemed still more disgraceful, of cowardice and pusillanimity.[15] The infirm and aged contributed to the expedition by presents and money; and many of them, not satisfied with the merit of this atonement, attended it in person, and were determined, if possible, to breathe their last in sight of that city where their Saviour had died for them. Women themselves, concealing their sex under the disguise of armor, attended the camp, and commonly forgot still more the duty of their sex by prostituting themselves, without reserve, to the army.[16] The greatest criminals were forward in a service which they regarded as a propitiation for all crimes; and the most enormous disorders were, during the course of those expeditions, committed by men inured to wickedness, encouraged by example, and impelled by necessity. The multitude of the adventurers soon became so great that their more sagacious leaders, Hugh, Count of Vermandois, brother to the French king; Raymond, Count of Toulouse ; Godfrey of Bouillon, Prince of Brabant; and Stephen, Count of Blois,[17] became apprehensive lest the greatness itself of the armament should disappoint its purpose ; and they permitted an undisciplined multitude, computed at three hundred thousand men, to go before them, under the command of Peter the Hermit and Walter the Moneyless.[18] These men took the road towards Constantinople through Hungary and Bulgaria ; and, trusting that Heaven, by supernatural assistance, would supply all their necessities, they made no provision for subsistence on their march. They soon found themselves obliged to obtain by plunder what they had vainly expected from miracles; and the enraged inhabitants of the countries through which they passed, gathering together in arms, attacked the disorderly

[14] Order. Vitalis. p. 720.
[16] Vertot, Hist. de Chev. de Malte, vol. i. p. 46.
[17] Sim. Dunelm. p. 222.

[15] Will. Malm. p. 133.

Matt. Paris, p. 17.

multitude, and put them to slaughter without resistance. The more disciplined armies followed after; and, passing the straits of Constantinople, they were mustered in the plains of Asia, and amounted in the whole to the number of seven hundred thousand combatants.[19]

Amid this universal frenzy, which spread itself by contagion throughout Europe, especially in France and Germany, men were not entirely forgetful of their present interests; and both those who went on this expedition, and those who stayed behind, entertained schemes of gratifying, by its means, their avarice or their ambition. The nobles who enlisted themselves were moved, from the romantic spirit of the age, to hope for opulent establishments in the East, the chief seat of arts and commerce during those ages; and in pursuit of these chimerical projects, they sold at the lowest price their ancient castles and inheritances, which had now lost all value in their eyes. The greater princes, who remained at home, besides establishing peace in their dominions by giving occupation abroad to the inquietude and martial disposition of their subjects, took the opportunity of annexing to their crown many considerable fiefs, either by purchase or by the extinction of heirs. The pope frequently turned the zeal of the crusaders from the infidels against his own enemies, whom he represented as equally criminal with the enemies of Christ. The convents and other religious societies bought the possessions of the adventurers, and as the contributions of the faithful were commonly intrusted to their management, they often diverted to this purpose what was intended to be employed against the infidels.[20] But no one was a more immediate gainer by this epidemic fury than the King of England, who kept aloof from all connections with those fanatical and romantic warriors.

Robert, Duke of Normandy, impelled by the bravery and mistaken generosity of his spirit, had early enlisted himself in the crusade; but being always unprovided with money, he found that it would be impracticable for him to appear in a manner suitable to his rank and station, at the head of his numerous vassals and subjects, who, transported with the general rage, were determined to follow him into Asia. He resolved, therefore, to mortgage, or rather to sell, his dominions, which he had not talents to govern; and he offered them to his brother William for the very unequal sum of

[19] Matt. Paris, pp. 20, 21.   [20] Padre Paolo, Hist. delle benef. eccles. p. 128.

ten thousand marks.[21] The bargain was soon concluded: the king raised the money by violent extortions on his subjects of all ranks, even on the convents, who were obliged to melt their plate in order to furnish the quota demanded of them.[22] He was put in possession of Normandy and Maine; and Robert, providing himself with a magnificent train, set out for the Holy Land, in pursuit of glory and in full confidence of securing his eternal salvation.

The smallness of this sum, with the difficulties which William found in raising it, suffices alone to refute the account which is heedlessly adopted by historians, of the enormous revenue of the Conqueror. Is it credible that Robert would consign to the rapacious hands of his brother such considerable dominions for a sum which, according to that account, made not a week's income of his father's English revenue alone? Or that the King of England could not on demand, without oppressing his subjects, have been able to pay him the money? The Conqueror, it is agreed, was frugal as well as rapacious; yet his treasure, at his death, exceeded not sixty thousand pounds, which hardly amounted to his income for two months—another certain refutation of that exaggerated account.

The fury of the crusades, during this age, less infected England than the neighboring kingdoms; probably because the Norman conquerors, finding their settlement in that kingdom still somewhat precarious, durst not abandon their homes in quest of distant adventures. The selfish interested spirit also of the king, which kept him from kindling in the general flame, checked its progress among his subjects; and as he is accused of open profaneness,[23] and was endued with a sharp wit,[24] it is likely that he made the romantic chivalry of the crusaders the object of his perpetual raillery. As an instance of his irreligion, we are told that he once accepted of sixty marks from a Jew whose son had been converted to Christianity, and who engaged him by that present to assist him in bringing back the youth to Judaism. William employed both menaces and persuasion for that purpose; but, finding the convert obstinate in his new faith, he sent for the father and told him, that as he had not succeeded, it was not just that he should keep the present; but as he had done his utmost, it was but equitable

[21] Will. Malm. p. 123. Chron. T. Wykes, p. 24. Annal. Waverl. p. 139. W. Heming. p. 467. Flor. Wigorn. p. 648. Sim. Dunelm. p. 222. Knyghton, p. 2364. [22] Eadmer, p. 35. Will. Malm. p. 123. W. Heming. p. 467. [23] G. Newbr. p. 358. Gul. Gemet. p. 292. [24] Will. Malm. p. 122.

that he should be paid for his pains, and he would therefore retain only thirty marks of the money.[25] At another time, it is said, he sent for some learned Christian theologians and some rabbies, and bade them fairly dispute the question of their religion in his presence. He was perfectly indifferent between them; had his ears open to reason and conviction; and would embrace that doctrine which upon comparison should be found supported by the most solid arguments.[26] If this story be true, it is probable that he meant only to amuse himself by turning both into ridicule. But we must be cautious of admitting everything related by the monkish historians to the disadvantage of this prince. He had the misfortune to be engaged in quarrels with the ecclesiastics, particularly with Anselm, commonly called St. Anselm, Archbishop of Canterbury; and it is no wonder his memory should be blackened by the historians of that order.

After the death of Lanfranc, the king for several years retained in his own hands the revenues of Canterbury, as he did those of many other vacant bishoprics; but falling into a dangerous sickness, he was seized with remorse, and the clergy represented to him that he was in danger of eternal perdition if before his death he did not make atonement for those multiplied impieties and sacrileges of which he had been guilty.[27] He resolved therefore to supply instantly the vacancy of Canterbury; and for that purpose he sent for Anselm, a Piedmontese by birth, Abbot of Bec, in Normandy, who was much celebrated for his learning and piety. The abbot earnestly refused the dignity, fell on his knees, wept, and entreated the king to change his purpose;[28] and when he found the prince obstinate in forcing the pastoral staff upon him, he kept his fist so fast clenched that it required the utmost violence of the bystanders to open it, and force him to receive that ensign of spiritual dignity.[29] William soon after recovered; and his passions regaining their wonted vigor, he returned to his former violence and rapine. He detained in prison several persons whom he had ordered to be freed during the time of his penitence; he still preyed upon the ecclesiastical benefices; the sale of spiritual dignities continued as open as ever; and he kept possession of a considerable part of the revenues belonging

[25] Eadmer, p. 47.
[26] Will. Malm. p. 123.   Eadmer, p. 16.   Chron. Sax. p. 198.
[28] Eadmer, p. 17.   Diceto,   [29] Eadmer, p.

to the see of Canterbury.[30]   But he found in Anselm that persevering opposition which he had reason to expect from the ostentatious humility which that prelate had displayed in refusing his promotion.

The opposition made by Anselm was the more dangerous on account of the character of piety which he soon acquired in England by his great zeal against all abuses, particularly those in dress and ornament.   There was a mode which in that age prevailed throughout Europe, both among men and women, to give an enormous length to their shoes, to draw the toe to a sharp point, and to affix to it the figure of a bird's bill or some such ornament, which was turned upwards, and which was often sustained by gold or silver chains tied to the knee.[31]   The ecclesiastics took exception at this ornament, which they said was an attempt to belie the Scripture, where it is affirmed that no man can add a cubit to his stature ; and they declaimed against it with great vehemence, nay, assembled some synods, who absolutely condemned it.   But, such are the strange contradictions in human nature ! though the clergy, at that time, could overturn thrones, and had authority sufficient to send above a million of men on *their* errand to the deserts of Asia, they could never prevail against these long-pointed shoes ; on the contrary, that caprice, contrary to all other modes, maintained its ground during several centuries ; and if the clergy had not at last desisted from their persecution of it, it might still have been the prevailing fashion in Europe.

But Anselm was more fortunate in decrying the particular mode which was the object of his aversion, and which probably had not taken such fast hold of the affections of the people.   He preached zealously against the long hair and curled locks which were then fashionable among the courtiers ; he refused the ashes on Ash-Wednesday to those who were so accoutred ; and his authority and eloquence had such influence that the young men universally abandoned that ornament, and appeared in the cropped hair which was recommended to them by the sermons of the primate.   The noted historian of Anselm, who was also his companion and secretary, celebrates highly this effort of his zeal and piety.[32]

[30] Eadmer, pp. 19, 43.   Chron. Sax. p. 119.
[31] Order. Vitalis, p. 682.   Will. Malm. p. 123.   Knyghton, p. 2369.
[32] Eadmer, p. 23.

When William's profaneness, therefore, returned to him with his health, he was soon engaged in controversies with this austere prelate. There was at that time a schism in the Church between Urban and Clement, who both pretended to the papacy;[33] and Anselm, who, as Abbot of Bec, had already acknowledged the former, was determined, without the king's consent, to introduce his authority into England.[34] William, who, imitating his father's example, had prohibited his subjects from recognizing any pope whom he had not previously received, was enraged at this attempt; and summoned a synod at Rockingham, with an intention of deposing Anselm; but the prelate's suffragans declared that without the papal authority they knew of no expedient for inflicting that punishment on their primate.[35] The king was at last engaged by other motives to give the preference to Urban's title : Anselm received the pall from that pontiff; and matters seemed to be accommodated between the king and the primate,[36] when the quarrel broke out afresh from a new cause. William had undertaken an expedition against Wales, and required the archbishop to furnish his quota of soldiers for that service; but Anselm, who regarded the demand as an oppression on the Church, and yet durst not refuse compliance, sent them so miserably accoutred that the king was extremely displeased, and threatened him with a prosecution.[37] Anselm, on the other hand, demanded positively that all the revenues of his see should be restored to him; appealed to Rome against the king's injustice;[38] and affairs came to such extremities that the primate, finding it dangerous to remain in the kingdom, desired and obtained the king's permission to retire beyond sea. All his temporalities were seized;[39] but he was received with great respect by Urban, who considered him as a martyr in the cause of religion, and even menaced the king, on account of his proceedings against the primate and the Church, with the sentence of excommunication. Anselm assisted at the Council of Bari, where, besides fixing the controversy between the Greek and Latin churches concerning the procession of the Holy Ghost,[40] the right of election to Church preferments was declared to belong to the clergy alone, and spiritual censures were denounced against all ecclesiastics who did homage to laymen for their sees or

[33] Hoveden, p. 463.
[34] Eadmer, p. 25. Matt. Paris, p. 13. Diceto, p. 494. Spell. Conc. vol. ii. p. 16.
[35] Eadmer, p. 30.   [36] Diceto, p. 495.   [37] Eadmer, pp. 37, 43.
[38] Eadmer, p. 40.   [39] Matt. Paris, p. 13. Parker, p. 178.
[40] Eadmer, p. 49. Matt Paris, p. 13. Sim. Dunelm. p. 224.

benefices, and against all laymen who exacted it.[41] The right of homage, by the feudal customs, was that the vassal should throw himself on his knees, should put his joined hands between those of his superior, and should in that posture swear fealty to him.[42] But the council declared it execrable that pure hands, which could create God and could offer him up as a sacrifice for the salvation of mankind, should be put, after this humiliating manner, between profane hands, which, besides being inured to rapine and bloodshed, were employed day and night in impure purposes and obscene contracts.[43] Such were the reasons prevalent in that age—reasonings which, though they cannot be passed over in silence without omitting the most curious and perhaps not the least instructive part of history, can scarcely be delivered with the requisite decency and gravity.

[1097.] The cession of Normandy and Maine by Duke Robert increased the king's territories, but brought him no great increase of power, because of the unsettled state of those countries, the mutinous disposition of the barons, and the vicinity of the French king, who supported them in all their insurrections. Even Helie, Lord of La Flèche, a small town in Anjou, was able to give him inquietude; and this great monarch was obliged to make several expeditions abroad, without being able to prevail over so petty a baron, who had acquired the confidence and affections of the inhabitants of Maine. He was, however, so fortunate as at last to take him prisoner in a rencounter; but, having released him at the intercession of the French king and the Count of Anjou, he found the province of Maine still exposed to his intrigues and incursions. Helie, being introduced by the citizens into the town of Mans, besieged the garrison in the citadel. [1099.] William, who was hunting in the new forest when he received intelligence of this hostile attempt, was so provoked that he immediately turned his horse and galloped to the sea-shore at Dartmouth, declaring that he would not stop a moment till he had taken vengeance for the offence. He found the weather so cloudy and tempestuous that the mariners thought it dangerous to put to sea; but the king hurried on board, and ordered them to set sail instantly, telling them that they never yet heard of a king that was drowned.[44] By this vigor and celerity he delivered

[41] Matt. Paris, p. 14.   [42] Spellman, Du Cange, *in verbo* Hominium.
[43] W. Heming. p. 467.   Flor. Wigorn. p. 649.   Sim. Dunelm. p. 224.   Brompton, p. 994.
[44] Will. Malm. p. 124.   H. Hunting. p. 378.   Matt. Paris, p. 36.   Ypod. Neust. p. 442

the citadel of Mans from its present danger; and pursuing Helie into his own territories, [1100.] he laid siege to Majol, a small castle in those parts; but a wound which he received before this place obliged him to raise the siege, and he returned to England.

The weakness of the greatest monarchs during this age in their military expeditions against their nearest neighbors appears the more surprising when we consider the prodigious numbers which even petty princes, seconding the enthusiastic rage of the people, were able to assemble, and to conduct in dangerous enterprises to the remote provinces of Asia. William, Earl of Poictou and Duke of Guienne, inflamed with the glory, and not discouraged by the misfortunes, which had attended the former adventurers in the crusades, had put himself at the head of an immense multitude, computed by some historians to amount to sixty thousand horse and a much greater number of foot,[45] and he purposed to lead them into the Holy Land against the infidels. He wanted money to forward the preparations requisite for this expedition, and he offered to mortgage all his dominions to William, without entertaining any scruple on account of that rapacious and iniquitous hand to which he resolved to consign them.[46] The king accepted the offer, and had prepared a fleet and an army, in order to escort the money and take possession of the rich provinces of Guienne and Poictou, when an accident put an end to his life and to all his ambitious projects. He was engaged in hunting—the sole amusement, and indeed the chief occupation, of princes in those rude times, when society was little cultivated, and the arts afforded few objects worthy of attention. Walter Tyrrel, a French gentleman remarkable for his address in archery, attended him in this recreation, of which the new forest was the scene; and as William had dismounted after a chase, Tyrrel, impatient to show his dexterity, let fly an arrow at a stag which suddenly started before him. The arrow, glancing from a tree, struck the king in the breast, and instantly slew him; [47] while Tyrrel, without informing any one of the accident, put spurs to his horse, hastened to the sea-shore, embarked for France, and joined the crusade in an expedition to Jerusalem—a penance which he imposed on himself for this involuntary crime. The body of William was found in the

---

[45] Will. Malm. p. 149.   The whole is said by Order. Vitalis, p. 789, to amount to three hundred thousand men.   [46] Will. Malm. p. 127.
[47] Will. Malm. p. 126. H. Hunting. p. 378. Matt. Paris, p. 37. Petr. Blois, p. 110.

forest by the country people, and was buried without any pomp or ceremony at Winchester. His courtiers were negligent in performing the last duties to a master who was so little beloved; and every one was too much occupied in the interesting object of fixing his successor to attend the funeral of a dead sovereign.

The memory of this monarch is transmitted to us with little advantage by the churchmen, whom he had offended; and though we may suspect, in general, that their account of his vices is somewhat exaggerated, his conduct affords little reason for contradicting the character which they have assigned him, or for attributing to him any very estimable qualities. He seems to have been a violent and tyrannical prince; a perfidious, encroaching, and dangerous neighbor; an unkind and ungenerous relation. He was equally prodigal and rapacious in the management of his treasury; and if he possessed abilities, he lay so much under the government of impetuous passions that he made little use of them in his administration; and he indulged, without reserve, that domineering policy which suited his temper, and which, if supported, as it was in him, with courage and vigor, proves often more successful in disorderly times than the deepest foresight and most refined artifice.

The monuments which remain of this prince in England are the Tower, Westminster Hall, and London Bridge, which he built. The most laudible foreign enterprise which he undertook was the sending of Edgar Atheling, three years before his death, into Scotland with a small army to restore Prince Edgar, the true heir of that kingdom, son of Malcolm and of Margaret (sister of Edgar Atheling); and the enterprise proved successful. It was remarked in that age, that Richard, an elder brother of William's, perished by an accident in the new forest; Richard, his nephew, natural son of Duke Robert, lost his life in the same place, after the same manner; and all men, upon the king's fate, exclaimed that, as the Conqueror had been guilty of extreme violence in expelling all the inhabitants of that large district to make room for his game, the just vengeance of Heaven was signalized in the same place by the slaughter of his posterity. William was killed in the thirteenth year of his reign and about the fortieth of his age. As he was never married, he left no legitimate issue.

In the eleventh year of his reign, Magnus, King of Norway, made a descent on the Isle of Anglesey, but was repulsed by Hugh, Earl of Shrewsbury. This is the last attempt made by the northern nations upon England. That restless people seem about this time to have learned the practice of tillage, which thenceforth kept them at home, and freed the other nations of Europe from the devastations spread over them by those piratical invaders. This proved one great cause of the subsequent settlement and improvement of the southern nations.

CHAPTER VI.

HENRY I.

THE CRUSADES.—ACCESSION OF HENRY.—MARRIAGE OF THE
KING.—INVASION BY DUKE ROBERT.—ACCOMMODATION
WITH ROBERT.—ATTACK ON NORMANDY.—CONQUEST OF
NORMANDY.—CONTINUATION OF THE QUARREL WITH AN-
SELM, THE PRIMATE.—COMPROMISE WITH HIM.—WARS
ABROAD.—DEATH OF PRINCE WILLIAM.—KING'S SECOND
MARRIAGE.—DEATH AND CHARACTER OF HENRY.

[1100.] AFTER the adventurers in the holy war were assembled on the banks of the Bosphorus, opposite to Constantinople, they proceeded on their enterprise, but immediately
experienced those difficulties which their zeal had hitherto
concealed from them, and for which, even if they had foreseen them, it would have been almost impossible to provide
a remedy. The Greek emperor, Alexius Comnenus, who
had applied to the western Christians for succor against the
Turks, entertained hopes, and those but feeble ones, of obtaining such a moderate supply as, acting under his command,
might enable him to repulse the enemy; but he was extremely astonished to see his dominions overwhelmed, on a
sudden, by such an inundation of licentious barbarians, who,
though they pretended friendship, despised his subjects as
unwarlike and detested them as heretical. By all the arts
of policy, in which he excelled, he endeavored to divert the
torrent; but while he employed professions, caresses, civilities, and seeming services towards the leaders of the crusade, he secretly regarded those imperious allies as more
dangerous than the open enemies by whom his empire had
been formerly invaded. Having effected that difficult point
of disembarking them safely in Asia, he entered into a private correspondence with Soliman, Emperor of the Turks;
and practised every insidious art which his genius, his
power, or his situation enabled him to employ for disap-
pointing the enterprise and discouraging the Latins from
making thenceforward any such prodigious migrations. His

17

dangerous policy was seconded by the disorders inseparable from so vast a multitude, who were not united under one head, and were conducted by leaders of the most independent, intractable spirit, unacquainted with military discipline, and determined enemies to civil authority and submission. The scarcity of provisions, the excess of fatigue, the influence of unknown climates, joined to the want of concert in their operations and to the sword of a warlike enemy, destroyed the adventurers by thousands, and would have abated the ardor of men impelled to war by less powerful motives. Their zeal, however, their bravery, and their irresistible force still carried them forward and continually advanced them to the great end of their enterprise. After an obstinate siege they took Nice, the seat of the Turkish empire; they defeated Soliman in two great battles; they made themselves masters of Antioch; and entirely broke the force of the Turks, who had so long retained those countries in subjection. The Soldan of Egypt, whose alliance they had hitherto courted, recovered, on the fall of the Turkish power, his former authority in Jerusalem; and he informed them by his ambassadors that if they came disarmed to that city, they might now perform their religious vows, and that all Christian pilgrims who should thenceforth visit the holy sepulchre might expect the same good treatment which they had ever received from his predecessors. The offer was rejected; the soldan was required to yield up the city to the Christians, and on his refusal the champions of the cross advanced to the siege of Jerusalem, which they regarded as the consummation of their labors. By the detachments which they had made and the disasters which they had undergone they were diminished to the number of twenty thousand foot and fifteen hundred horse; but these were still formidable, from their valor, their experience, and the obedience which, from past calamities, they had learned to pay to their leaders. After a siege of five weeks, they took Jerusalem by assault; and, impelled by a mixture of military and religious rage, they put the numerous garrison and inhabitants to the sword without distinction. Neither arms defended the valiant nor submission the timorous; no age or sex was spared; infants on the breast were pierced by the same blow with their mothers, who implored for mercy; even a multitude to the number of ten thousand persons, who had surrendered themselves prisoners and were promised quarter, were butchered in cool blood by those ferocious conquerors.[1] The streets of Jerusalem were covered with dead bodies;[2] and the triumphant warriors, after every enemy was subdued and slaughtered, immediately turned themselves, with the sentiments of humiliation and contrition, towards the holy sepulchre. They threw aside their arms, still streaming with blood; they advanced with reclined bodies and naked feet and heads to that sacred monument; they sang anthems to their Saviour, who had there purchased their salvation by his death and agony; and their devotion, enlivened by the presence of the place where he had suffered, so overcame their fury that they dissolved in tears, and bore the appearance of every soft and tender sentiment. So inconsistent is human nature with itself, and so easily does the most effeminate superstition ally both with the most heroic courage and the fiercest barbarity!

This great event happened on the 5th of July, in the last year of the eleventh century. The Christian princes and nobles, after choosing Godfrey of Bouillon King of Jerusalem, began to settle themselves in their new conquests; while some of them returned to Europe, in order to enjoy at home that glory which their valor had acquired them in this popular and meritorious enterprise. Among these was Robert, Duke of Normandy, who, as he had relinquished the greatest dominions of any prince that attended the crusade, had all along distinguished himself by the most intrepid courage, as well as by that affable disposition and unbounded generosity which gain the hearts of soldiers and qualify a prince to shine in a military life. In passing through Italy he became acquainted with Sibylla, daughter of the Count of Conversana, a young lady of great beauty and merit, whom he espoused; indulging himself in this new passion, as well as fond of enjoying ease and pleasure, after the fatigues of so many rough campaigns, he lingered a twelvemonth in that delicious climate; and though his friends in the north looked every moment for his arrival, none of them knew when they could with certainty expect it. By this delay he lost the kingdom of England, which the great fame he had acquired during the crusades, as well as his undoubted title, both by birth and by the preceding agreement with his deceased brother, would, had he been present, have infallibly secured to him.

---

[1] Vertot, vol. i. p. 57.
[2] Matt. Paris, p. 34. Order. Vitalis, p. 756. Diceto, p. 498.

Prince Henry was hunting with Rufus in the new forest when intelligence of that monarch's death was brought him; and, being sensible of the advantage attending the conjuncture, he hurried to Winchester, in order to secure the royal treasure, which he knew to be a necessary implement for facilitating his designs on the crown. He had scarcely reached the place when William de Breteuil, keeper of the treasure, arrived, and opposed himself to Henry's pretensions. This nobleman, who had been engaged in the same party of hunting, had no sooner heard of his master's death than he hastened to take care of his charge; and he told the prince that this treasure, as well as the crown, belonged to his elder brother, who was now his sovereign; and that he himself, for his part, was determined, in spite of all other pretensions, to maintain his allegiance to him. But Henry, drawing his sword, threatened him with instant death if he dared to disobey him; and as others of the late king's retinue, who came every moment to Winchester, joined the prince's party, Breteuil was obliged to withdraw his opposition and to acquiesce in this violence.[3]

Henry, without losing a moment, hastened with the money to London; and, having assembled some noblemen and prelates, whom his address, or abilities, or presents gained to his side, he was suddenly elected, or rather saluted, king, and immediately proceeded to the exercise of royal authority. In less than three days after his brother's death, the ceremony of his coronation was performed by Maurice, Bishop of London, who was persuaded to officiate on that occasion; [4] and thus, by his courage and celerity, he intruded himself into the vacant throne. No one had sufficient spirit or sense of duty to appear in defence of the absent prince; all men were seduced or intimidated; present possession supplied the apparent defects in Henry's title, which was indeed founded on plain usurpation; and the barons, as well as the people, acquiesced in a claim which, though it could neither be justified nor comprehended, could now, they found, be opposed through the perils alone of civil war and rebellion.

But as Henry foresaw that a crown usurped against all rules of justice would sit unsteady on his head, he resolved, by fair professions at least, to gain the affections of all his subjects. Besides taking the usual coronation oath to maintain the laws and execute justice, he passed a charter which

[3] Order. Vitalis, p. 782.   [4] Chron. Sax. p. 208. Order. Vitalis, p. 783.

was calculated to remedy many of the grievous oppressions which had been complained of during the reigns of his father and brother.[5] He there promised that at the death of any bishop or abbot he never would seize the revenues of the see or abbey during the vacancy, but would leave the whole to be reaped by the successor; and that he would never let to farm any ecclesiastical benefice, nor dispose of it for money. After this concession to the Church, whose favor was of so great importance, he proceeded to enumerate the civil grievances which he purposed to redress. He promised that upon the death of any earl, baron, or military tenant, his heir should be admitted to the possession of his estate on paying a just and lawful relief, without being exposed to such violent exactions as had been usual during the late reigns; he remitted the wardship of minors, and allowed guardians to be appointed who should be answerable for the trust; he promised not to dispose of any heiress in marriage but by the advice of all the barons; and if any baron intended to give his daughter, sister, niece, or kinswoman in marriage, it should only be necessary for him to consult the king, who promised to take no money for his consent, nor ever to refuse permission, unless the person to whom it was purposed to marry her should happen to be his enemy; he granted his barons and military tenants the power of bequeathing, by will, their money or personal estates; and if they neglected to make a will, he promised that their heirs should succeed to them; he renounced the right of imposing moneyage, and of levying taxes at pleasure on the farms which the barons retained in their own hands;[6] he made some general professions of moderating fines; he offered a pardon for all offences; and he remitted all debts due to the crown; he required that the vassals of the barons should enjoy the same privileges which he granted to his own barons; and he promised a general confirmation and observance of the laws of King Edward. This is the substance of the chief articles contained in that famous charter.[7]

To give greater authenticity to these concessions, Henry lodged a copy of his charter in some abbey of each county, as if desirous that it should be exposed to the view of all his subjects, and remain a perpetual rule for the limitation and direction of his government; yet it is certain that, after

[5] Chron. Sax. p. 208. Sim. Dunelm. p. 225.   [6] See Appendix II.
[7] Matt. Paris, p. 38.   Hoveden, p. 468.   Brompton, p. 1021. Hagulstadt, p. 310.

the present purpose was served, he never once thought during his reign of observing one single article of it; and the whole fell so much into neglect and oblivion that in the following century, when the barons, who had heard an obscure tradition of it desired to make it the model of the great charter which they exacted from King John, they could with difficulty find a copy of it in the kingdom. But as to the grievances here meant to be redressed, they were still continued in their full extent; and the royal authority, in all those particulars, lay under no manner of restriction. Reliefs of heirs, so capital an article, were never effectually fixed till the time of Magna Charta; [8] and it is evident that the general promise here given of accepting a just and lawful relief ought to have been reduced to more precision, in in order to give security to the subject. The oppression of wardship and marriage was perpetuated even till the reign of Charles II. And it appears from Glanville,[9] the famous justiciary of Henry II., that in his time, where any man died intestate, an accident which must have been very frequent when the art of writing was so little known, the king, or the lord of the fief, pretended to seize all the movables, and to exclude every heir, even the children of the deceased : a sure mark of a tyrannical and arbitrary government.

The Normans, indeed, who domineered in England were during this age so licentious a people that they may be pronounced incapable of any true or regular liberty, which requires such improvement in knowledge and morals as can only be the result of reflection and experience, and must grow to perfection during several ages of settled and established government. A people so insensible to the rights of their sovereign as to disjoint, without necessity, the hereditary succession, and permit a younger brother to intrude himself into the place of the elder, whom they esteemed, and who was guilty of no crime but being absent, could not expect that that prince would pay any greater regard to their privileges, or allow his engagements to fetter his power, and debar him from any considerable interest or convenience. They had, indeed, arms in their hands, which prevented the establishment of a total despotism, and left their posterity

---

[8] Glanv. lib. 2, cap. 36. What is called a relief in the Conqueror's laws, preserved by Ingulf, seems to have been the heriot; since reliefs, as well as the other burdens of the feudal law, were unknown in the age of the Confessor, whose laws these originally were.

[9] Lib. 7, cap. 16. This practice was contrary to the laws of King Edward, ratified by the Conqueror, as we learn from Ingulf, p. 91. But laws had at that time very little influence; power and violence governed everything.

sufficient power, whenever they should attain a sufficient degree of reason, to assume true liberty; but their turbulent disposition frequently prompted them to make such use of their arms that they were more fitted to obstruct the execution of justice than to stop the career of violence and oppression. The prince, finding that greater opposition was often made to him when he enforced the laws than when he violated them, was apt to render his own will and pleasure the sole rule of government; and, on every emergency, to consider more the power of the persons whom he might offend than the rights of those whom he might injure. The very form of this charter of Henry proves that the Norman barons (for they, rather than the people of England, were chiefly concerned in it) were totally ignorant of the nature of limited monarchy, and were ill qualified to conduct, in conjunction with their sovereign, the machine of government. It is an act of his sole power, is the result of his free grace, contains some articles which bind others as well as himself, and is therefore unfit to be the deed of any one who possesses not the whole legislative power, and who may not at pleasure revoke all his concessions.

Henry, further to increase his popularity, degraded and committed to prison Ralph Flambard, Bishop of Durham, who had been the chief instrument of oppression under his brother; [10] but this act was followed by another, which was a direct violation of his own charter, and was a bad prognostic of his sincere intentions to observe it: he kept the see of Durham vacant for five years, and during that time retained possession of all its revenues. Sensible of the great authority which Anselm had acquired by his character of piety and by the persecutions which he had undergone from William, he sent repeated messages to him at Lyons, where he resided, and invited him to return and take possession of his dignities.[11] On the arrival of the prelate, he proposed to him the renewal of that homage which he had done his brother, and which he had never been refused by any English bishop; but Anselm had acquired other sentiments by his journey to Rome, and gave the king an absolute refusal. He objected to the decrees of the Council of Bari, at which he himself had assisted, and he

[10] Chron. Sax. p. 208. Will. Malm. p. 156. Matt. Paris, p. 39. Alur. Beverl. p. 144.
[11] Chron. Sax. 208. Order. Vitalis, p. 783. Matt. Paris, p. 39. T. Rudborne, p. 273.

declared that, so far from doing homage for his spiritual
dignity, he would not so much as communicate with any
ecclesiastic who paid that submission, or who accepted of
investitures from laymen. Henry, who expected, in his
present delicate situation, to reap great advantages from
the authority and popularity of Anselm, durst not insist on
his demand; [12] he only desired that the controversy might
be suspended, and that messengers might be sent to Rome,
in order to accommodate matters with the pope, and obtain
his confirmation of the laws and customs of England.

There immediately occurred an important affair, in
which the king was obliged to have recourse to the authority of Anselm. Matilda, daughter of Malcolm III., King of
Scotland, and niece of Edgar Atheling, had, on her father's
death, and the subsequent revolutions in the Scottish government, been brought to England, and educated under her
aunt Christina in the nunnery of Rumsey. This princess
Henry purposed to marry; but as she had worn the veil,
though never taken the vows, doubts might arise concerning the lawfulness of the act; and it behooved him to be
very careful not to shock, in any particular, the religious
prejudices of his subjects. The affair was examined by
Anselm in a council of the prelates and nobles, which was
summoned at Lambeth; Matilda there proved that she had
put on the veil, not with the view of entering into a religious life, but merely in consequence of a custom familiar
to the English ladies, who protected their chastity from the
brutal violence of the Normans by taking shelter under that
habit,[13] which, amid the horrible licentiousness of the times,
was yet generally revered. The council, sensible that even
a princess had otherwise no security for her honor, admitted
this reason as valid : they pronounced that Matilda was still
free to marry; [14] and her espousals with Henry were celebrated by Anselm with great pomp and solemnity.[15] No act
of the king's reign rendered him equally popular with his
English subjects, and tended more to establish him on the
throne. Though Matilda, during the life of her uncle and
brothers, was not heir of the Saxon line, she was become
very dear to the English on account of her connections with
it; and that people, who, before the Conquest, had fallen
into a kind of indifference towards their ancient royal family, had felt so severely the tyranny of the Normans that
they reflected with extreme regret on their former liberty,

[12] Will. Malm. p. 225.   [13] Eadmer, p. 57.   [14] Ibid.   [15] Hoveden, p. 468.

and hoped for a more equal and mild administration, when the blood of their native princes should be mingled with that of their new sovereigns.[16]

But the policy and prudence of Henry, which, if time had been allowed for these virtues to produce their full effect, would have secured him possession of the crown, ran great hazard of being frustrated by the sudden appearance of Robert, who returned to Normandy about a month after the death of his brother William. [1101.] He took possession, without opposition, of that duchy; and immediately made preparations for recovering England, of which, during his absence, he had, by Henry's intrigues, been so unjustly defrauded. The great fame which he had acquired in the East forwarded his pretensions; and the Norman barons, sensible of the consequences, expressed the same discontent at the separation of the duchy and kingdom which had appeared on the accession of William. Robert de Bellesme (Earl of Shrewsbury and Arundel), William de la Warenne (Earl of Surrey), Arnulf de Montgomery, Walter Giffard, Robert de Pontefract, Robert de Mallet, Yvo de Grentmesnil, and many others of the principal nobility,[17] invited Robert to make an attempt upon England, and promised, on his landing, to join him with all their forces. Even the seamen were affected with the general popularity of his name, and they carried over to him the greater part of a fleet which had been equipped to oppose his passage. Henry, in this extremity, began to be apprehensive for his life, as well as for his crown, and had recourse to the superstition of the people, in order to oppose their sentiment of justice. He paid diligent court to Anselm, whose sanctity and wisdom he pretended to revere. He consulted him in all difficult emergencies; seemed to be governed by him in every measure; promised a strict regard to ecclesiastical privileges; professed a great attachment to Rome, and a resolution of persevering in an implicit obedience to the decrees of councils and to the will of the sovereign pontiff. By these caresses and declarations he entirely gained the confidence of the primate, whose influence over the people and authority with the barons were of the utmost service to him in his present situation. Anselm scrupled not to assure the nobles of the king's sincerity in those professions which he made of avoiding the tyrannical and oppressive government of his father and brother. He even rode through the

[16] Matt. Paris, p. 40.   [17] Order. Vitalis, p. 785.

ranks of the army, recommended to the soldiers the defence
of their prince, represented the duty of keeping their oaths
of allegiance, and prognosticated to them the greatest happiness from the government of so wise and just a sovereign.
By this expedient, joined to the influence of the Earls of
Warwick and Mellent, of Roger Bigod, Richard de Red-
vers, and Robert Fitz-Hamon, powerful barons, who still
adhered to the present government, the army was retained
in the king's interest, and marched, with seeming union and
firmness, to oppose Robert, who had landed with his forces
at Portsmouth.

The two armies lay in sight of each other for some days
without coming to action; and both princes, being apprehensive of the event, which would probably be decisive,
hearkened the more willingly to the counsels of Anselm and
the other great men who mediated an accommodation between them. After employing some negotiation, it was
agreed that Robert should resign his pretensions to England,
and receive in lieu of them an annual pension of three thousand marks; that if either of the princes died without issue
the other should succeed to his dominions; that the adherents
of each should be pardoned and restored to all their possessions either in Normandy or England; and that neither
Robert nor Henry should thenceforth encourage, receive, or
protect the enemies of the other.[18]

[1102.] This treaty, though calculated so much for
Henry's advantage, he was the first to violate. He restored,
indeed, the estates of all Robert's adherents, but was secretly
determined that noblemen so powerful and so ill-affected,
who had both inclination and ability to disturb his government, should not long remain unmolested in their present
opulence and grandeur. He began with the Earl of Shrewsbury, who was watched for some time by spies, and then indicted on a charge consisting of forty-five articles. This
turbulent nobleman, knowing his own guilt as well as the
prejudices of his judges and the power of his prosecutor, had
recourse to arms for defence; but, being soon suppressed by
the activity and address of Henry, he was banished the kingdom and his great estate was confiscated. His ruin involved
that of his two brothers, Arnulf de Montgomery and Roger,
Earl of Lancaster. Soon after followed the prosecution and
condemnation of Robert de Pontefract and Robert de Mallet, who had distinguished themselves among Robert's ad-

[18] Chron. Sax. p. 209.   Will. Malm. p. 156.

herents. [1103.] William de Warenne was the next victim : even William, Earl of Cornwall, son of the Earl of Mortaigne, the king's uncle, having given matter of suspicion against him, lost all the vast acquisitions of his family in England. Though the usual violence and tyranny of the Norman barons afforded a plausible pretence for those prosecutions, and it is probable that none of the sentences pronounced against these noblemen was wholly iniquitous, men easily saw or conjectured that the chief part of their guilt was not the injustice or illegality of their conduct. Robert, enraged at the fate of his friends, imprudently ventured to come into England, and he remonstrated with his brother in severe terms against this breach of treaty; but met with so bad a reception that he began to apprehend danger to his own liberty, and was glad to purchase an escape by resigning his pension.

The indiscretion of Robert soon exposed him to more fatal injuries. This prince, whose bravery and candor procured him respect while at a distance, had no sooner attained the possession of power and enjoyment of peace than all the vigor of his mind relaxed, and he fell into contempt among those who approached his person or were subjected to his authority. Alternately abandoned to dissolute pleasures and to womanish superstition, he was so remiss, both in the care of his treasure and the exercise of his government, that his servants pillaged his money with impunity, stole from him his very clothes, and proceeded thence to practise every species of extortion on his defenceless subjects. The barons, whom a severe administration alone could have restrained, gave reins to their unbounded rapine upon their vassals and inveterate animosities against each other; and all Normandy, during the reign of this benign prince, was become a scene of violence and depredation. The Normans, at last observing the regular government which Henry, notwithstanding his usurped title, had been able to establish in England, applied to him that he might use his authority for the suppression of these disorders, and they thereby afforded him a pretence for interposing in the affairs of Normandy. Instead of employing his mediation to render his brother's government respectable, or to redress the grievances of the Normans, he was only attentive to support his own partisans, and to increase their number by every art of bribery, intrigue, and insinuation. Having found, in a visit which he made to that duchy, that the nobility were more disposed to pay submission to him than to their legal sovereign, he collected by arbitrary extortions on England a great army and treasure, and returned next year to Normandy in a situation to obtain, either by violence or corruption, the dominion of that province. [1105.] He took Baieux by storm after an obstinate siege. He made himself master of Caen by the voluntary submission of the inhabitants; but, being repulsed at Falaise, and obliged by the winter to raise the siege, he returned into England after giving assurance to his adherents that he would persevere in supporting and protecting them.

[1106.] Next year he opened the campaign with the siege of Tenchebray; and it became evident from his preparations and progress that he intended to usurp the entire possession of Normandy. Robert was at last roused from his lethargy; and being supported by the Earl of Mortaigne and Robert de Bellesme, the king's inveterate enemies, he raised a considerable army, and approached his brother's camp with a view of finishing, in one decisive battle, the quarrel between them. He was now entered on that scene of action in which alone he was qualified to excel; and he so animated his troops by his example that they threw the English into disorder, and had nearly obtained the victory,[19] when the flight of Bellesme spread a panic among the Normans and occasioned their total defeat. Henry, besides doing great execution on the enemy, made near ten thousand prisoners, among whom was Duke Robert himself, and all the most considerable barons who adhered to his interests.[20] This victory was followed by the final reduction of Normandy. Rouen immediately submitted to the conqueror. Falaise, after some negotiations, opened its gates; and by this acquisition, besides rendering himself master of an important fortress, he got into his hands Prince William, the only son of Robert. He assembled the states of Normandy, and having received the homage of all the vassals of the duchy, having settled the government, revoked his brother's donations, and dismantled the castles lately built, he returned into England, and carried along with him the duke as prisoner. The unfortunate prince was detained in custody during the remainder of his life, which was no less than twenty-eight years, and he died in the castle of Cardiff, in Glamorganshire, happy if, without losing his liberty, he could have re-

---

[19] H. Hunting. p. 379.   Matt. Paris, p. 43.   Brompton, p. 1002.
[20] Eadmer, p. 90.   Chron. Sax. p. 214.   Order. Vitalis, p. 821.

linquished that power which he was not qualified either to hold or exercise. Prince William was committed to the care of Helie de St. Saen, who had married Robert's natural daughter, and who, being a man of probity and honor beyond what was usual in those ages, executed the trust with great affection and fidelity. Edgar Atheling, who had followed Robert in the expedition to Jerusalem, and who had lived with him ever since in Normandy, was another illustrious prisoner taken in the battle of Tenchebray.[21] Henry gave him his liberty, and settled a small pension on him, with which he retired; and he lived to a good old age in England totally neglected and forgotten. This prince was distinguished by personal bravery; but nothing can be a stronger proof of his mean talents in every other respect than that, notwithstanding he possessed the affections of the English and enjoyed the only legal title to the throne, he was allowed, during the reigns of so many violent and jealous usurpers, to live unmolested and to go to his grave in peace.

[1107.] A little after Henry had completed the conquest of Normandy and settled the government of that province, he finished a controversy, which had been long pending between him and the pope, with regard to the investitures in ecclesiastical benefices; and, though he was here obliged to relinquish some of the ancient rights of the crown, he extricated himself from the difficulty on easier terms than most princes who, in that age, were so unhappy as to be engaged in disputes with the apostolic see. The king's situation, in the beginning of his reign, obliged him to pay great court to Anselm. The advantages which he had reaped from the zealous friendship of that prelate had made him sensible how prone the minds of his people were to superstition, and what an ascendant the ecclesiastics had been able to assume over them. He had seen, on the accession of his brother Rufus, that, though the rights of primogeniture were then violated, and the inclinations of almost all the barons thwarted, yet the authority of Lanfranc, the primate, had prevailed over all other considerations. His own case, which was still more unfavorable, afforded an instance in which the clergy had more evidently shown their influence and authority. These recent examples, while they made him cautious not to offend that powerful body, convinced him at the same time that it was extremely his interest to retain the former prerogative of the crown in filling offices of such vast importance, and to check the ecclesiastics in that independence to which they visibly aspired. The choice, which his brother, in a fit of penitence, had made of Anselm was so far unfortunate to the king's pretensions that this prelate was celebrated for his piety and zeal and austerity of manners; and, though his monkish devotion and narrow principles prognosticated no great knowledge of the world or depth of policy, he was, on that very account, a more dangerous instrument in the hands of politicians, and retained a greater ascendant over the bigoted populace. The prudence and temper of the king appeared in nothing more conspicuous than in the management of this delicate affair, where he was always sensible that it had become necessary for him to risk his whole crown in order to preserve the most invaluable jewel of it.[22]

Anselm had no sooner returned from banishment than his refusal to do homage to the king raised a dispute which Henry evaded at that critical juncture by promising to send a messenger, in order to compound the matter with Pascal II., who then filled the papal throne. The messenger, as was probably foreseen, returned with an absolute refusal of the king's demands,[23] and that fortified by many reasons which were well qualified to operate on the understandings of men in those ages. Pascal quoted the Scriptures to prove that Christ was the door; and he thence inferred that all ecclesiastics must enter into the Church through Christ alone, not through the civil magistrate, or any profane layman.[24] "It is monstrous," added the pontiff, "that a son should pretend to beget his father, or a man to create his God. Priests are called gods in Scripture, as being the vicars of God; and will you, by your abominable pretensions to grant them their investiture, assume the right of creating them?"[25]

But how convincing soever these arguments, they could not persuade Henry to resign so important a prerogative; and perhaps, as he was possessed of great reflection and learning, he thought that the absurdity of a man's creating his God, even allowing priests to be gods, was not urged

[22] Eadmer, p. 56.   [23] Will. Malm. p. 225.
[24] Eadmer, p. 60. This topic is further enforced in pp. 73, 74. See also Will. Malm. p. 163.
[25] Eadmer, p. 61. I must suspect that this text of Scripture is a forgery of his holiness; for I have not been able to find it. Yet it passed current in those ages, and was often quoted by the clergy as the foundation of their power. See Epist. St. Thom. p. 169.

with the best grace by the Roman pontiff. But as he desired still to avoid, at least to delay, the coming to any dangerous extremity with the Church, he persuaded Anselm that he should be able, by further negotiation, to obtain some composition with Pascal; and for that purpose he despatched three bishops to Rome, while Anselm sent two messengers of his own to be more fully assured of the pope's intentions.[26] Pascal wrote back letters equally positive and arrogant, both to the king and primate; urging to the former that, by assuming the right of investitures, he committed a kind of spiritual adultery with the Church, who was the spouse of Christ, and who must not admit of such a commerce with any other person;[27] and insisting with the latter that the pretension of kings to confer benefices was the source of all simony—a topic which had but too much foundation in those ages.[28]

Henry had now no other expedient than to suppress the letter addressed to himself, and to persuade the three bishops to prevaricate, and assert, upon their episcopal faith, that Pascal had assured them in private of his good intentions towards Henry, and of his resolution not to resent any future exertion of his prerogative in granting investitures; though he himself scrupled to give this assurance under his hand, lest other princes should copy the example and assume a like privilege.[29] Anselm's two messengers, who were monks, affirmed to him that it was impossible this story could have any foundation; but their word was not deemed equal to that of three bishops; and the king, as if he had finally gained his cause, proceeded to fill the sees of Hereford and Salisbury, and to invest the new bishops in the usual manner.[30] But Anselm, who, as he had good reason, gave no credit to the asseveration of the king's messengers, refused not only to consecrate them, but even to communicate with them; and the bishops themselves, finding how odious they were become, returned to Henry the ensigns of their dignity. The quarrel every day increased between the king and the primate: the former, notwithstanding the prudence and moderation of his temper, threw out menaces against such as should pretend to oppose him in exerting the ancient prerogatives of his crown; and Anselm, sensible of his own dangerous situation, desired leave to make a journey to

[26] Eadmer, p. 62. Will. Malm. p. 225. [27] Eadmer, p. 63.
[28] Eadmer, pp. 64, 66. [29] Eadmer, p. 65. Will. Malm. p. 225.
[30] Eadmer, p. 66. Will. Malm. p. 225. Hoveden, p. 469. Sim. Dunelm. p. 228.

Rome, in order to lay the case before the sovereign pontiff. Henry, well pleased to rid himself, without violence, of so inflexible an antagonist, readily granted him permission. The prelate was attended to the shore by infinite multitudes, not only of monks and clergymen, but people of all ranks, who scrupled not in this manner to declare for their primate against their sovereign, and who regarded his departure as the final abolition of religion and true piety in the kingdom.[31] The king, however, seized all the revenues of his see; and sent William de Warelwast to negotiate with Pascal, and to find some means of accommodation in this delicate affair.

The English minister told Pascal that his master would rather lose his crown than part with the right of granting investitures. "And I," replied Pascal, "would rather lose my head than allow him to retain it."[34] Henry secretly prohibited Anselm from returning, unless he resolved to conform himself to the laws and usages of the kingdom; and the primate took up his residence at Lyons, in expectation that the king would at last be obliged to yield the point which was the present object of controversy between them. Soon after he was permitted to return to his monastery at Bec, in Normandy; and Henry, besides restoring to him the revenues of his see, treated him with the greatest respect, and held several conferences with him, in order to soften his opposition and bend him to submission.[33] The people of England, who thought all differences now accommodated, were inclined to blame their primate for absenting himself so long from his charge; and he daily received letters from his partisans, representing the necessity of his speedy return. The total extinction, they told him, of religion and Christianity was likely to ensue from the want of his fatherly care: the most shocking customs prevail in England; and the dread of his severity being now removed, sodomy, and the practice of wearing long hair, gain ground among all ranks of men, and these enormities openly appear everywhere without sense of shame or fear of punishment.[34]

The policy of the court of Rome has commonly been much admired, and men, judging by success, have bestowed the highest eulogies on that prudence by which a power from such slender beginnings could advance, without force of arms, to establish a universal and almost absolute monarchy in Europe. But the wisdom of so long a succession

[31] Eadmer, p. 71.   [32] Eadmer, p. 73.   Will. Malm. p. 226.   Matt. Paris, p. 40.
[33] Hoveden, p. 471.   [34] Eadmer, p. 81.

of men who filled the papal throne, and who were of such different ages, tempers, and interests, is not intelligible, and could never have place in nature. The instrument, indeed, with which they wrought—the ignorance and superstition of the people—is so gross an engine, of such universal prevalence, and so little liable to accident or disorder, that it may be successful even in the most unskilful hands; and scarce any indiscretion can frustrate its operations. While the court of Rome was openly abandoned to the most flagrant disorders, even while it was torn with schisms and factions, the power of the Church daily made a sensible progress in Europe; and the temerity of Gregory and caution of Pascal were equally fortunate in promoting it. The clergy, feeling the necessity which they lay under of being protected against the violence of princes or rigor of the laws, were well pleased to adhere to a foreign head, who, being removed from the fear of the civil authority, could freely employ the power of the whole Church in defending her ancient or usurped properties and privileges when invaded in any particular country; the monks, desirous of an independence of their diocesans, professed a still more devoted attachment to the triple crown; and the stupid people possessed no science or reason which they could oppose to the most exorbitant pretensions. Nonsense passed for demonstration; the most criminal means were sanctified by the piety of the end; treaties were not supposed to be binding where the interests of God were concerned; the ancient laws and customs of states had no authority against a divine right; impudent forgeries were received as authentic monuments of antiquity; and the champions of Holy Church, if successful, were celebrated as heroes; if unfortunate, were worshipped as martyrs; and all events thus turned out equally to the advantage of clerical usurpations. Pascal himself, the reigning pope, was, in the course of this very controversy concerning investitures, involved in circumstances, and necessitated to follow a conduct, which would have drawn disgrace and ruin on any temporal prince that had been so unfortunate as to fall into a like situation. His person was seized by the Emperor Henry V., and he was obliged by a formal treaty to resign to that monarch the right of granting investitures, for which they had so long contended.[35] In order to add greater solemnity to this agreement, the emperor and pope communicated together

[35] Will. Malm. p. 167.

18

on the same host, one half of which was given to the prince, the other taken by the pontiff. The most tremendous imprecations were publicly denounced on either of them who should violate the treaty; yet no sooner did Pascal recover his liberty than he revoked all his concessions, and pronounced the sentence of excommunication against the emperor, who, in the end, was obliged to submit to the terms required of him, and to yield up all his pretensions, which he never could resume.[36]

The King of England had very nearly fallen into the same dangerous situation. Pascal had already excommunicated the Earl of Mellent, and the other ministers of Henry who were instrumental in supporting his pretensions.[37] He daily menaced the king himself with a like sentence; and he suspended the blow only to give him leisure to prevent it by a timely submission. The malcontents waited impatiently for the opportunity of disturbing his government by conspiracies and insurrections.[38] The king's best friends were anxious at the prospect of an incident which would set their religious and civil duties at variance; and the Countess of Blois, his sister, a princess of piety, who had great influence over him, was affrighted with the danger of her brother's eternal damnation.[39] Henry, on the other hand, seemed determined to run all hazards rather than resign a prerogative of such importance, which had been enjoyed by all his predecessors; and it seemed probable, from his great prudence and abilities, that he might be able to sustain his rights and finally prevail in the contest. While Pascal and Henry thus stood mutually in awe of each other, it was the more easy to bring about an accommodation between them, and to find a medium in which they might agree.

Before bishops took possession of their dignities, they had formerly been accustomed to pass through two ceremonies: they received from the hands of the sovereign a ring and crosier as symbols of their office, and this was called their *investiture;* they also made those submissions to the prince which were required of vassals by the rights of the feudal law, and which received the name of *homage.* And as the king might refuse both to grant the *investiture* and to receive the *homage,* though the chapter had, by some canons of the Middle Age, been endowed with the right of election,

[36] Padre Paolo, sopra benef. eccles. p. 112. Will. Malm. p. 170. Chron. Abb. St. Petri de Burgo, p. 63. Sim. Dunelm. p. 233. [37] Eadmer, p. 79. [38] Eadmer, p. 80. [39] Eadmer, p. 79.

the sovereign had in reality the sole power of appointing prelates. Urban II. had equally deprived laymen of the rights of granting investiture and of receiving homage ;[40] the emperors never were able, by all their wars and negotiations, to make any distinction be admitted between them. The interposition of profane laymen, in any particular, was still represented as impious and abominable ; and the Church openly aspired to a total independence on the State. But Henry had put England as well as Normandy in such a situation as gave greater weight to his negotiations ; and Pascal was for the present satisfied with his resigning the right of granting investitures, by which the spiritual dignity was supposed to be conferred, and he allowed the bishops to do homage for their temporal properties and privileges.[41] The pontiff was well pleased to have made this acquisition, which, he hoped, would in time involve the whole ; and the king, anxious to procure an escape from a very dangerous situation, was content to retain some, though a more precarious authority, in the election of prelates.

After the principal controversy was accommodated, it was not difficult to adjust the other differences. The pope allowed Anselm to communicate with the prelates who had already received investitures from the crown ; and he only required of them some submissions for their past misconduct.[42] He also granted Anselm a plenary power of remedying every other disorder, which, he said, might arise from the barbarousness of the country.[43] Such was the idea which the pope then entertained of the English ; and nothing can be a stronger proof of the miserable ignorance in which that people were then plunged than that a man who sat on the papal throne, and who subsisted by absurdities and nonsense, should think himself entitled to treat them as barbarians.

During the course of these controversies, a synod was held at Westminster, where the king, intent only on the main dispute, allowed some canons of less importance to be enacted, which tended to promote the usurpations of the clergy. The celibacy of priests was enjoined, a point which it was still found very difficult to carry into execution ; and even laymen were not allowed to marry within the seventh degree of affinity.[44] By this contrivance the pope augmented

[40] Eadmer, p. 91. Will. Malm. p. 163. Sim. Dunelm. p. 230.
[41] Eadmer, p. 91. Will. Malm. pp. 164, 227. Hoveden, p. 471. Matt. Paris, p. 43. T. Rudborne, p. 274. Brompton, p. 1000. Wilkins, p. 303. Chron. Dunst. p. 21.   [42] Eadmer, p. 87.   [43] Eadmer, p. 91.
[44] Eadmer, pp. 67, 68. Spell. Conc. vol. ii. p. 22.

the profits which he reaped from granting dispensations, and likewise those from divorces. For as the art of writing was then rare, and parish registers were not regularly kept, it was not easy to ascertain the degrees of affinity even among people of rank; and any man who had money sufficient to pay for it might obtain a divorce, on pretence that his wife was more nearly related to him than was permitted by the canons. The synod also passed a vote prohibiting the laity from wearing long hair.[45] The aversion of the clergy to this mode was not confined to England. When the king went to Normandy, before he had conquered that province, the Bishop of Seez, in a formal harangue, earnestly exhorted him to redress the manifold disorders under which the government labored, and to oblige the people to poll their hair in a decent form. Henry, though he would not resign his prerogatives to the Church, willingly parted with his hair : he cut it in the form which they required of him, and obliged all the courtiers to imitate his example.[46]

The acquisition of Normandy was a great point of Henry's ambition, being the ancient patrimony of his family, and the only territory which, while in his possession, gave him any weight or consideration on the Continent; but the injustice of his usurpation was the source of great inquietude, involved him in frequent wars, and obliged him to impose on his English subjects those many heavy and arbitrary taxes of which all the historians of that age unanimously complain.[47] His nephew, William, was but six years of age when he committed him to the care of Helie de St. Saen ; and it is probable that his reason for intrusting that important charge to a man of so unblemished a character was to prevent all malignant suspicions in case any accident should befall the life of the young prince. [1110.] He soon repented of his choice; for when he desired to recover possession of William's person, Helie withdrew his pupil, and carried him to the court of Fulk, Count of Anjou, who gave him protection.[48] In proportion as the prince grew up to man's estate, he discovered virtues becoming his birth ; and, wandering through different courts of Europe, he excited the friendly compassion of many princes, and raised a general indignation against his uncle, who had so unjustly bereaved him of his inheritance.

45 Eadmer, p. 68.   46 Order Vitalis, p. 816.
    47 Eadmer, p. 83.   Chron. Sax. pp. 211, 212, 213, 219, 220, 228.   H. Hunting. p.
380. Hoveden, p. 470.   Annal. Waverl. p. 143.   48 Order. Vitalis, p. 837.

Lewis the Gross, son of Philip, was at this time King of France, a brave and generous prince, who, having been obliged during the lifetime of his father to fly into England in order to escape the persecutions of his stepmother, Bertrude, had been protected by Henry, and had thence conceived a personal friendship for him. But these ties were soon dissolved after the accession of Lewis, who found his interests to be in so many particulars opposite to those of the English monarch, and who became sensible of the danger attending the annexation of Normandy to England. He joined, therefore, the Counts of Anjou and Flanders in giving disquiet to Henry's government; and this monarch, in order to defend his foreign dominions, found himself obliged to go over to Normandy, where he resided two years. The war which ensued among those princes was attended with no memorable event, and produced only slight skirmishes on the frontiers, agreeably to the weak condition of the sovereigns in that age, whenever their subjects were not roused by some great and urgent occasion. Henry, by contracting his eldest son, William, to the daughter of Fulk, detached that prince from the alliance, and obliged the others to come to an accommodation with him. This peace was not of long duration. His nephew, William, retired to the court of Baldwin, Earl of Flanders, who espoused his cause; and the King of France having soon after, for other reasons, joined the party, a new war was kindled in Normandy, which produced no event more memorable than had attended the former. At last the death of Baldwin, [1113.] who was slain in an action near Eu, gave some respite to Henry, and enabled him to carry on war with more advantage against his enemies.

Lewis, finding himself unable to wrest Normandy from the king by force of arms, had recourse to the dangerous expedient of applying to the spiritual power, and of affording the ecclesiastics a pretence to interpose in the temporal concerns of princes. He carried young William to a general council, which was assembled at Rheims by Pope Calixtus II., presented the Norman prince to them, complained of the manifest usurpation and injustice of Henry, craved the assistance of the Church for reinstating the true heir in his dominions, and represented the enormity of detaining in captivity so brave a prince as Robert, one of the most eminent champions of the cross, and who, by that very quality, was placed under the immediate protection of the holy see. Henry knew how to defend the rights of his crown with vigor, and yet with dexterity. He had sent over the English bishops to this synod, but at the same time had warned them that if any further claims were started by the pope or the ecclesiastics, he was determined to adhere to the laws and customs of England, and maintain the prerogatives transmitted to him by his predecessors. "Go," said he to them, "salute the pope in my name; hear his apostolical precepts; but take care to bring none of his new inventions into my kingdom." Finding, however, that it would be easier for him to elude than oppose the efforts of Calixtus, he gave his ambassadors orders to gain the pope and his favorites by liberal presents and promises. [1119.] The complaints of the Norman prince were thenceforth heard with great coldness by the council; and Calixtus confessed, after a conference which he had the same summer with Henry, and when that prince probably renewed his presents, that, of all men he had ever yet been acquainted with, he was beyond comparison the most eloquent and persuasive.

The warlike measures of Lewis proved as ineffectual as his intrigues. He had laid a scheme for surprising Noyon; but Henry, having received intelligence of the design, marched to the relief of the place, and suddenly attacked the French at Brenneville as they were advancing towards it. A sharp conflict ensued, where Prince William behaved with great bravery, and the king himself was in the most imminent danger. He was wounded in the head by Crispin, a gallant Norman officer who had followed the fortunes of William; [49] but, being rather animated than terrified by the blow, he immediately beat his antagonist to the ground, and so encouraged his troops by the example that they put the French to total rout, and had very nearly taken their king prisoner. The dignity of the persons engaged in this skirmish rendered it the most memorable action of the war, for in other respects it was not of great importance. There were nine hundred horsemen, who fought on both sides; yet were there only two persons slain. The rest were defended by that heavy armor worn by the cavalry in those times.[50] An accommodation soon after ensued between the kings of France and England, and the interests of young William were entirely neglected in it.

[49] H. Hunting. p. 381. Matt. Paris, p. 47. Diceto, p. 503.
[50] Order. Vitalis, p. 854.

[1120.] But this public prosperity of Henry was much overbalanced by a domestic calamity which befell him. His only son, William, had now reached his eighteenth year; and the king, from the facility with which he himself had usurped the crown, dreading that a like revolution might subvert his family, had taken care to have him recognized successor by the states of the kingdom, and had carried him over to Normandy, that he might receive the homage of the barons of that duchy. The king, on his return, set sail from Barfleur, and was soon carried by a fair wind out of sight of land. The prince was detained by some accident; and his sailors, as well as their captain, Thomas Fitz-Stephens, having spent the interval in drinking, were so flustered that, being in a hurry to follow the king, they heedlessly carried the ship on a rock, where she immediately foundered. William was put into the long-boat, and had got clear of the ship, when, hearing the cries of his natural sister, the Countess of Perche, he ordered the seamen to row back in hopes of saving her; but the numbers who then crowded in soon sank the boat; and the prince, with all his retinue, perished. Above a hundred and forty young noblemen, of the principal families of England and Normandy, were lost on this occasion. A butcher of Rouen was the only person on board who escaped.[51] He clung to the mast, and was taken up next morning by fishermen. Fitz-Stephens also took hold of the mast, but, being informed by the butcher that Prince William had perished, he said that he would not survive the disaster; and he threw himself headlong into the sea.[52] Henry entertained hopes for three days that his son had put into some distant port of England; but when certain intelligence of the calamity was brought him, he fainted away; and it was remarked that he never after was seen to smile, nor ever recovered his wonted cheerfulness.[53]

The death of William may be regarded in one respect as a misfortune to the English, because it was the immediate source of those civil wars which, after the demise of the king, caused such confusion in the kingdom; but it is remarkable that the young prince had entertained a violent aversion to the natives, and had been heard to threaten that when he should be king he would make them draw the plough, and would turn them into beasts of burden. These

[51] Sim. Dunelm. p. 242.   Alur. Beverl. p. 148.
[52] Order. Vitalis. p. 868.   [53] Hoveden, p 476   Order. Vitalis. p .869.

prepossessions he inherited from his father, who, though he was wont, when it might serve his purpose, to value himself on his birth as a native of England,[54] showed, in the course of his government, an extreme prejudice against that people. All hopes of preferment, to ecclesiastical as well as civil dignities, were denied them during this whole reign; and any foreigner, however ignorant or worthless, was sure to have the preference in every competition.[55] As the English had given no disturbance to the government during the course of fifty years, this inveterate antipathy in a prince of so much temper as well as penetration forms a presumption that the English of that age were still a rude and barbarous people even compared to the Normans, and impresses us with no very favorable idea of the Anglo-Saxon manners.

Prince William left no children; and the king had not now any legitimate issue, except one daughter, Matilda, whom, in 1110, he had betrothed, though only eight years of age,[56] to the Emperor Henry V., and whom he had then sent over to be educated in Germany.[57] But as her absence from the kingdom and her marriage into a foreign family might endanger the succession, Henry, who was now a widower, was induced to marry in hopes of having male heirs; [1121.] and he made his addresses to Adelais, daughter of Godfrey, Duke of Lovaine, and niece of Pope Calixtus, a young princess of an amiable person.[58] But Adelais brought him no children; and the prince who was most likely to dispute the succession, and even the immediate possession of the crown, recovered hopes of subverting his rival, who had successively seized all his patrimonial dominions. William, the son of Duke Robert, was still protected in the French court; and as Henry's connections with the Count of Anjou were broken off by the death of his son, Fulk joined the party of the unfortunate prince, gave him his daughter in marriage, and aided him in raising disturbances in Normandy. But Henry found the means of drawing off the Count of Anjou by forming anew with him a nearer connection than the former, and one more material to the interests of that count's family. [1227.] The emperor, his son-in-law, dying without issue, he bestowed his daughter on Geoffrey, the eldest son of Fulk, and endeavored to insure her succession by having her recognized heir to all his domin-

[54] Gul. Neub. lib. 1, cap. 3.   [55] Eadmer, p. 110.
[56] Chron. Sax. p. 215.   Will. Malm. p. 166.   Order. Vitalis, p. 83.
[57] See note [M.] at the end of the volume.
[58] Chron. Sax. p. 223.   Will. Malm. p. 165.

ions, and obliging the barons, both of Normandy and England, to swear fealty to her. [1128.] He hoped that the choice of this husband would be more agreeable to all his subjects than that of the emperor, as securing them from the danger of falling under the dominion of a great and distant potentate, who might bring them into subjection and reduce their country to the rank of a province; but the barons were displeased that a step so material to national interests had been taken without consulting them;[59] and Henry had too sensibly experienced the turbulence of their disposition not to dread the effects of their resentment. It seemed probable that his nephew's party might gain force from the increase of the malcontents. An accession of power which that prince acquired a little after tended to render his pretensions still more dangerous. Charles, Earl of Flanders, being assassinated during the celebration of divine service, King Lewis immediately put the young prince in possession of that country, to which he had pretensions in the right of his grandmother Matilda, wife to the Conqueror. But William survived a very little time this piece of good fortune, which seemed to open the way to still further prosperity. He was killed in a skirmish with the Landgrave of Alsace, his competitor for Flanders; and his death put an end, for the present, to the jealousy and inquietude of Henry.

The chief merit of this monarch's government consists in the profound tranquillity which he established and maintained throughout all his dominions during the greater part of his reign. The mutinous barons were retained in subjection; and his neighbors, in every attempt which they made upon him, found him so well prepared that they were discouraged from continuing or renewing their enterprises. In order to repress the incursions of the Welsh, he brought over some Flemings, in the year 1111, and settled them in Pembrokeshire, where they long maintained a different language, and customs, and manners from their neighbors. Though his government seems to have been arbitrary in England, it was judicious and prudent, and was as little oppressive as the necessity of his affairs would permit. He wanted not attention to the redress of grievances; and historians mention in particular the levying of purveyance, which he endeavored to moderate and restrain. The tenants in the

[59] Will. Malm. p. 175. The Annals of Waverley, p. 150, say that the king asked and obtained the consent of all the barons.

king's demesne lands were at that time obliged to supply, *gratis*, the court with provisions, and to furnish carriages on the same hard terms, when the king made a progress, as he did frequently, into any of the counties. These exactions were so grievous, and levied in so licentious a manner, that the farmers, when they heard of the approach of the court, often deserted their houses as if an enemy had invaded the country,[60] and sheltered their persons and families in the woods from the insults of the king's retinue. Henry prohibited those enormities, and punished the persons guilty of them by cutting off their hands, legs, or other members.[61] But the prerogative was perpetual; the remedy applied by Henry was temporary; and the violence itself of this remedy, so far from giving security to the people, was only a proof of the ferocity of the government, and threatened a quick return of like abuses.

One great and difficult object of the king's prudence was the guarding against the encroachments of the court of Rome, and protecting the liberties of the Church of England. The pope, in the year 1101, had sent Guy, Archbishop of Vienne, as legate into Britain; and though he was the first that for many years had appeared there in that character, and his commission gave general surprise,[62] the king, who was then in the commencement of his reign, and was involved in many difficulties, was obliged to submit to this encroachment on his authority. But in the year 1116, Anselm, Abbot of St. Sabas, who was coming over with a like legatine commission, was prohibited from entering the kingdom;[63] and Pope Calixtus, who, in his turn, was then laboring under many difficulties by reason of the pretensions of Gregory, an anti-pope, was obliged to promise that he never would for the future, except when solicited by the king himself, send any legate into England.[64] Notwithstanding this engagement, the pope, as soon as he had suppressed his antagonist, granted the Cardinal de Crema a legatine commission over that kingdom; and the king, who, by reason of his nephew's intrigues and invasions, found himself at that time in a dangerous situation, was obliged to submit to the exercise of this commission.[65] A synod was called by the legate at London, where, among other canons, a vote passed enacting severe penalties on the marriages of the clergy.[66] The cardinal, in a public harangue, declared

[60] Eadmer, p. 94. Chron. Sax. p. 212.
[62] Eadmer, p. 58. [63] Hoveden, p. 474.
[65] Chron. Sax. p. 229.
[61] Eadmer, p. 94.
[64] Eadmer, pp. 125, 137, 138.
[66] Spell. Conc. vol. ii. p. 34.

it to be an unpardonable enormity that a priest should dare to consecrate and touch the body of Christ immediately after he had risen from the side of a strumpet, for that was the decent appellation which he gave to the wives of the clergy. But it happened that, the very next night, the officers of justice, breaking into a disorderly house, found the cardinal in bed with a courtesan [67]—an incident which threw such ridicule upon him that he immediately stole out of the kingdom. The synod broke up, and the canons against the marriage of clergymen were worse executed than ever.[68]

Henry, in order to prevent this alternate revolution of concessions and encroachments, sent William, then Archbishop of Canterbury, to remonstrate with the court of Rome against those abuses, and to assert the liberties of the English Church. It was a usual maxim with every pope, when he found that he could not prevail in any pretension, to grant princes or states a power which they had always exercised, to resume, at a proper juncture, the claim which seemed to be resigned, and to pretend that the civil magistrate had possessed the authority only from a special indulgence of the Roman pontiff. After this manner, the pope, finding that the French nation would not admit his claim of granting investitures, had passed a bull giving the king that authority; and he now practised a like invention to elude the complaints of the King of England. He made the Archbishop of Canterbury his legate, renewed his commission from time to time, and still pretended that the rights which that prelate had ever exercised as metropolitan were entirely derived from the indulgence of the apostolic see. The English princes, and Henry in particular, who were glad to avoid any immediate contest of so dangerous a nature, commonly acquiesced by their silence in these pretensions of the court of Rome.[69]

[1131.] As everything in England remained in tranquillity, Henry took the opportunity of paying a visit to Normandy, to which he was invited as well by his affection for that country as by his tenderness for his daughter, the Empress Matilda, who was always his favorite. Some time after, that princess was delivered of a son, [1132.] who received the name of Henry; and the king, further to insure

---

[67] Hoveden, p. 478. Matt. Paris, p. 48. Matt. West. ad. ann. 1125. H. Hunting. p. 382. It is remarkable that this last writer, who was a clergyman as well as the others, makes an apology for using such freedom with the fathers of the Church; but says that the fact was notorious, and ought not to be concealed.
[68] Chron. Sax. p. 234.   [69] See note [N] at the end of the volume.

her succession, made all the nobility of England and Normandy renew the oath of fealty which they had already sworn to her.[70] The joy of this event and the satisfaction which he reaped from his daughter's company, who bore successively two other sons, [1135.] made his residence in Normandy very agreeable to him;[71] and he seemed determined to pass the remainder of his days in that country, when an incursion of the Welsh obliged him to think of returning into England. He was preparing for the journey, but was seized with a sudden illness at St. Dennis le Forment, from eating too plentifully of lampreys, a food which always agreed better with his palate than his constitution.[72] He died in the sixty-seventh year of his age and the thirty-fifth of his reign, leaving by will his daughter, Matilda, heir of all his dominions without making any mention of her husband, Geoffrey, who had given him several causes of displeasure.[73]

This prince was one of the most accomplished that have filled the English throne, and possessed all the great qualities both of body and mind, natural and acquired, which could fit him for the high station to which he attained. His person was manly, his countenance engaging, his eyes clear, serene, and penetrating. The affability of his address encouraged those who might be overawed by the sense of his dignity or of his wisdom; and though he often indulged his facetious humor, he knew how to temper it with discretion, and ever kept at a distance from all indecent familiarities with his courtiers. His superior eloquence and judgment would have given him an ascendant even had he been born in a private station; and his personal bravery would have procured him respect, though it had been less supported by art than policy. By his great progress in literature he acquired the name of *Beauclerc*, or the Scholar; but his application to those sedentary pursuits abated nothing of the activity and vigilance of his government; and though the learning of that age was better fitted to corrupt than improve the understanding, his natural good sense preserved itself untainted both from the pedantry and superstition which were then so prevalent among men of letters. His temper was susceptible of the sentiments as well of friendship as of resentment;[74] and his ambition, though high, might be deemed moderate and reasonable had not his con-

70 Will. Malm. p. 177.   71 H. Hunting. p. 385.   72 Ibid. Matt. Paris, p. 50.
73 Will. Malm. p 178.   74 Order. Vitalis, p. 805.

duct towards his brother and nephew showed that he was too much disposed to sacrifice to it all the maxims of justice and equity. But the total incapacity of Robert for government afforded his younger brother a reason or pretence for seizing the sceptre both of England and Normandy; and when violence and usurpation are once begun, necessity obliges a prince to continue in the same criminal course, and engages him in measures which his better judgment and sounder principles would otherwise have induced him to reject with warmth and indignation.

King Henry was much addicted to women; and historians mention no less than seven illegitimate sons and six daughters born to him.[75] Hunting was also one of his favorite amusements; and he exercised great rigor against those who encroached on the royal forests, which were augmented during his reign,[76] though their number and extent were already too great. To kill a stag was as criminal as to murder a man. He made all the dogs be mutilated which were kept on the borders of his forests; and he sometimes deprived his subjects of the liberty of hunting on their own lands, or even cutting their own woods. In other respects, he executed justice, and that with rigor—the best maxim which a prince in that age could follow. Stealing was first made capital in this reign;[77] false coining, which was then a very common crime, and by which the money had been extremely debased, was severly punished by Henry.[78] Near fifty criminals of this kind were at one time hanged or mutilated; and though these punishments seem to have been exercised in a manner somewhat arbitrary, they were grateful to the people, more attentive to present advantages than jealous of general laws. There is a code which passes under the name of Henry I., but the best antiquaries have agreed to think it spurious. It is, however, a very ancient compilation, and may be useful to instruct us in the manners and customs of the times. We learn from it that a great distinction was then made between the English and Normans, much to the advantage of the latter.[79] The deadly feuds, and the liberty of private revenge, which had been avowed by the Saxon laws, were still continued, and were not yet wholly illegal.[80]

[75] Gul. Gemet. lib. 8, cap. 29.   [76] Will. Malm. p. 179.
[77] Sim. Dunelm. p. 231. Brompton, p. 1000. Flor. Wigorn. p. 653. Hoveden, p. 471.
[78] Sim. Dunelm. p. 231. Brompton, p. 1000. Hoveden, p. 471. Annal. Waverl. p. 149.
[79] Leges Hen. I. § 18, 75.   [80] Leges Hen. I. § 82.

Among the laws granted on the king's accession, it is remarkable that the reunion of the civil and ecclesiastical courts, as in the Saxon times, was enacted.[81] But this law, like the articles of his charter, remained without effect, probably from the opposition of Archbishop Anselm.

Henry, on his accession, granted a charter to London, which seems to have been the first step towards rendering that city a corporation. By this charter, the city was empowered to keep the farm of Middlesex at three hundred pounds a year, to elect its own sheriff and justiciary, and to hold pleas of the crown; and it was exempted from scot, Danegelt, trials by combat, and lodging the king's retinue. These, with a confirmation of the privileges of their court of hustings, ward-motes, and common halls, and their liberty of hunting in Middlesex and Surrey, are the chief articles of this charter.[82]

It is said [83] that this prince, from indulgence to his tenants, changed the rents of his demesnes, which were formerly paid in kind, into money, which was more easily remitted to the exchequer. But the great scarcity of coin would render that commutation difficult to be executed, while at the same time provisions could not be sent to a distant quarter of the kingdom. This affords a probable reason why the ancient kings of England so frequently changed their place of abode : they carried their court from one place to another, that they might consume upon the spot the revenue of their several demesnes.

[81] Spell. p. 305. Blackstone, vol. iii. p. 63. Coke, 2 Inst. 70.
[82] Lambardi Archaionomia, ex edit. Twisden. Wilkins, p. 235.
[83] Dial. de Scaccario, lib. i. cap. 7.

CHAPTER VII.

STEPHEN.

ACCESSION OF STEPHEN.—WAR WITH SCOTLAND.—INSUR-
RECTION IN FAVOR OF MATILDA.—STEPHEN TAKEN PRIS-
ONER. — MATILDA CROWNED. — STEPHEN RELEASED. —
RESTORED TO THE CROWN.—CONTINUATION OF THE CIVIL
WARS.—COMPROMISE BETWEEN THE KING AND PRINCE
HENRY.—DEATH OF THE KING.

[1135.] In the progress and settlement of the feudal law,
the male succession to fiefs had taken place some time before the female was admitted; and estates, being considered
as military benefices, not as property, were transmitted to
such only as could serve in the armies and perform in person the conditions upon which they were originally granted.
But when the continuance of rights, during some generations, in the same family, had, in a great measure, obliterated the primitive idea, the females were gradually admitted
to the possession of feudal property; and the same revolution of principles which procured them the inheritance of
private estates naturally introduced their succession to government and authority. The failure, therefore, of male heirs
to the kingdom of England and duchy of Normandy seemed
to leave the succession open, without a rival, to the Empress
Matilda; and as Henry had made all his vassals, in both
states, swear fealty to her, he presumed that they would not
easily be induced to depart at once from her hereditary right
and from their own reiterated oaths and engagements. But
the irregular manner in which he himself had acquired the
crown might have instructed him that neither his Norman
nor English subjects were as yet capable of adhering to a
strict rule of government; and as every precedent of this
kind seems to give authority to new usurpations, he had
reason to dread, even from his own family, some invasion
of his daughter's title, which he had taken such pains to
establish.

Adela, daughter of William the Conqueror, had been

married to Stephen, Count of Blois, and had brought him several sons, among whom Stephen and Henry, the two youngest, had been invited over to England by the late king, and had received great honors, riches, and preferment, from the zealous friendship which that prince bore to every one that had been so fortunate as to acquire his favor and good opinion. Henry, who had betaken himself to the ecclesiastical profession, was created Abbot of Glastonbury and Bishop of Winchester; and though these dignities were considerable, Stephen had, from his uncle's liberality, attained establishments still more solid and durable.[1] The king had married him to Matilda, who was daughter and heir of Eustace, Count of Boulogne, and who brought him, besides that feudal sovereignty in France, an immense property in England, which, in the distribution of lands, had been conferred by the Conqueror on the family of Boulogne. Stephen also by this marriage acquired a new connection with the royal family of England; as Mary, his wife's mother was sister to David, the reigning King of Scotland, and to Matilda, the first wife of Henry, and mother of the empress. The king, still imagining that he strengthened the interests of his family by the aggrandizement of Stephen, took pleasure in enriching him by the grant of new possessions; and he conferred on him the great estate forfeited by Robert Mallet in England, and that forfeited by the Earl of Mortaigne in Normandy. Stephen, in return, professed great attachment to his uncle; and appeared so zealous for the succession of Matilda that when the barons swore fealty to that princess, he contended with Robert, Earl of Gloucester, the king's natural son, who should first be admitted to give her this testimony of devoted zeal and fidelity.[2] Meanwhile he continued to cultivate, by every art of popularity, the friendship of the English nation; and many virtues with which he seemed to be endowed favored the success of his intentions. By his bravery, activity, and vigor he acquired the esteem of the barons; by his generosity, and by an affable and familiar address unusual in that age among men of his high quality, he obtained the affections of the people, particularly of the Londoners.[3] And though he dared not to take any steps towards his further grandeur, lest he should expose himself to the jealousy of so penetrating a prince as Henry, he still hoped that, by accumulating riches and power

[1] Gul. Neub. p. 360.   Brompton, p. 1023.
[3] Will. Malm. p. 179.   Gest. Steph. p. 928.
[2] Will. Malm. p. 192.

and by acquiring popularity, he might in time be able to open his way to the throne.

No sooner had Henry breathed his last than Stephen, insensible to all the ties of gratitude and fidelity, and blind to danger, gave full reins to his criminal ambition, and trusted that, even without any previous intrigue, the celerity of his enterprise and the boldness of his attempt might overcome the weak attachment which the English and Normans in that age bore to the laws and to the rights of their sovereign. He hastened over to England ; and though the citizens of Dover and those of Canterbury, apprised of his purpose, shut their gates against him, he stopped not till he arrived at London, where some of the lower rank, instigated by his emissaries, as well as moved by his general popularity, immediately saluted him king. His next point was to acquire the good-will of the clergy ; and by performing the ceremony of his coronation, to put himself in possession of the throne, from which he was confident it would not be easy afterwards to expel him. His brother, the Bishop of Winchester, was useful to him in these capital articles. Having gained Roger, Bishop of Salisbury, who, though he owed a great fortune and advancement to the favor of the late king, preserved no sense of gratitude to that prince's family, he applied, in conjunction with that prelate, to William, Archbishop of Canterbury, and required him, in virtue of his office, to give the royal unction to Stephen. The primate, who, as all the others, had shown fealty to Matilda, refused to perform this ceremony ; but his opposition was overcome by an expedient equally dishonorable with the other steps by which this revolution was effected. Hugh Bigod, steward of the household, made oath before the primate that the late king, on his death-bed, had shown a dissatisfaction with his daughter Matilda, and had expressed his intention of leaving the Count of Boulogne heir to all his dominions.[4] William, either believing, or feigning to believe, Bigod's testimony, anointed Stephen and put the crown upon his head ; and from this religious ceremony that prince, without any shadow either of hereditary title or consent of the nobility or people, was allowed to proceed to the exercise of sovereign authority. Very few barons attended his coronation ;[5] but none opposed his usurpation, however unjust or flagrant. The sentiment of religion, which, if corrupted into supersti-

---

[4] Matt. Paris, p. 51. Diceto, p. 505. Chron. Dunst. p. 23.
[5] Brompton, p. 1023.

tion, has often little efficacy in fortifying the duties of civil society, was not affected by the multiplied oaths taken in favor of Matilda, and only rendered the people obedient to a prince who was countenanced by the clergy, and who had received from the primate the right of royal unction and consecration.[6]

Stephen, that he might further secure his tottering throne, passed a charter, in which he made liberal promises to all orders of men : to the clergy, that he would speedily fill all vacant benefices, and would never levy the rents of any of them during the vacancy; to the nobility, that he would reduce the royal forests to their ancient boundaries, and correct all encroachments; and to the people, that he would remit the tax of Danegelt, and restore the laws of King Edward.[7] The late king had a great treasure at Winchester, amounting to a hundred thousand pounds; and Stephen, by seizing this money, immediately turned against Henry's family the precaution which that prince had employed for their grandeur and security—an event which naturally attends the policy of amassing treasures. By means of this money, the usurper insured the compliance, though not the attachment, of the principal clergy and nobility; but, not trusting to this frail security, he invited over from the Continent, particularly from Brittany and Flanders, great numbers of those bravoes, or disorderly soldiers, with whom every country in Europe, by reason of the general ill police and turbulent government, extremely abounded.[8] These mercenary troops guarded his throne by the terrors of the sword; and Stephen, that he might also overawe all malcontents by new and additional terrors of religion, procured a bull from Rome, which ratified his title, and which the pope, seeing this prince in possession of the throne, and pleased with an appeal to his authority in secular controversies, very readily granted him.[9]

Matilda and her husband, Geoffrey, were as unfortunate in Normandy as they had been in England. The Norman nobility, [1136.] moved by an hereditary animosity against the Angevins, first applied to Theobald, Count of Blois, Stephen's elder brother, for protection and assistance; but hearing afterwards that Stephen had got possession of the

[6] Such stress was formerly laid on the rite of coronation that the monkish writers never give any prince the title of king till he is crowned, though he had for some time been in possession of the crown and exercised all the powers of sovereignty. [7] Will. Malm. p. 179. Hoveden, p. 482.
[8] Will. Malm. p. 179. [9] Hagulstadt, pp. 259, 313.

English crown, and having many of them the same reasons as formerly for desiring a continuance of their union with that kingdom, they transferred their allegiance to Stephen, and put him in possession of their government. Lewis the younger, the reigning King of France, accepted the homage of Eustace, Stephen's eldest son, for the duchy; and the more to corroborate his connections with that family, he betrothed his sister, Constantia, to the young prince. The Count of Blois resigned all his pretensions, and received, in lieu of them, an annual pension of two thousand marks; and Geoffrey himself was obliged to conclude a truce for two years with Stephen, on condition of the king's paying him, during that time, a pension of five thousand.[10] Stephen, who had taken a journey to Normandy, finished all these transactions in person, and soon after returned to England.

Robert, Earl of Gloucester, natural son of the late king, was a man of honor and abilities, and as he was much attached to the interests of his sister, Matilda, and zealous for the lineal succession, it was chiefly from his intrigues and resistance that the king had reason to dread a new revolution of government. This nobleman, who was in Normandy when he received intelligence of Stephen's accession, found himself much embarrassed concerning the measures which he should pursue in that difficult emergency. To swear allegiance to the usurper appeared to him dishonorable, and a breach of his oath to Matilda; to refuse giving this pledge of his fidelity was to banish himself from England, and be totally incapacitated from serving the royal family or contributing to their restoration.[11] He offered Stephen to do him homage and to take the oath of fealty, but with an express condition that the king should maintain all his stipulations, and should never invade any of Robert's rights or dignities; and Stephen, though sensible that this reserve, so unusual in itself, and so unbefitting the duty of a subject, was meant only to afford Robert a pretence for a revolt on the first favorable opportunity, was obliged, by the numerous friends and retainers of that nobleman, to receive him on those terms.[12] The clergy, who could scarcely at this time be deemed subjects to the crown, imitated that dangerous example; they annexed to their oaths of allegiance this condition, that they were only bound so long as the king defended the ecclesiastical liberties, and supported the

---

[10] Matt. Paris, p. 52.   [11] Will. Malm. p. 179.   [12] Ibid. Matt. Paris, p. 51.

discipline of the Church.[13] The barons, in return for their
submission, exacted terms still more destructive of public
peace as well as of royal authority; many of them required
the right of fortifying their castles, and of putting themselves in a posture of defence; and the king found himself
totally unable to refuse his consent to this exorbitant demand.[14]   All England was immediately filled with those
fortresses which the nobleman garrisoned either with their
vassals or with licentious soldiers, who flocked to them from
all quarters. Unbounded rapine was exercised upon the
people for the maintenance of these troops; and private
animosities, which had with difficulty been restrained by
law, now breaking out without control, rendered England
a scene of uninterrupted violence and devastation. Wars
between the nobles were carried on with the utmost fury in
every quarter; the barons even assumed the right of coining money, and of exercising, without appeal, every act of
jurisdiction;[15] and the inferior gentry as well as the people,
finding no defence from the laws during this total dissolution of sovereign authority, were obliged, for their immediate safety, to pay court to some neighboring chieftain, and
to purchase his protection both by submitting to his exactions and by assisting him in his rapine upon others. The
erection of one castle proved the immediate cause of building many others; and even those who obtained not the
king's permission thought that they were entitled, by the
great principle of self-preservation, to put themselves on an
equal footing with their neighbors, who commonly were
also their enemies and rivals. The aristocratical power,
which is usually so oppressive in the feudal governments,
had now risen to its utmost height during the reign of a
prince who, though endowed with vigor and abilities, had
usurped the throne without the pretence of a title, and who
was necessitated to tolerate in others the same violence to
which he himself had been beholden for his sovereignty.

But Stephen was not of a disposition to submit long to
these usurpations without making some effort for the recovery of royal authority. Finding that the legal prerogatives of the crown were resisted and abridged, he was also
tempted to make his power the sole measure of his conduct,
and to violate all those concessions which he himself had
made on his accession,[16] as well as the ancient privileges of

[13] Will. Malm. p. 179.   [14] Will. Malm. p. 180.
[15] Trivet, p. 19. Gul. Neub. p. 372. Chron. Heming. p. 487. Brompton, p.
1035.   [16] Will. Malm. p. 180. Matt. Paris, p. 51.

his subjects. The mercenary soldiers, who chiefly supported his authority, having exhausted the royal treasure, subsisted by depredations; and every place was filled with the best-grounded complaints against the government. [1137.] The Earl of Gloucester, having now settled with his friends the plan of an insurrection, retired beyond sea, sent the king a defiance, solemnly renounced his allegiance, and upbraided him with the breach of those conditions which had been annexed to the oath of fealty sworn by that nobleman.[17] David, King of Scotland, appeared at the head of an army in defence of his niece's title. [1138.] and, penetrating into Yorkshire, committed the most barbarous devastations on that country. The fury of his massacres and ravages enraged the northern nobility, who might otherwise have been inclined to join him; and William, Earl of Albemarle, Robert de Ferrers, William Piercy, Robert de Brus, Roger Moubray, Ilbert Lacey, Walter l'Espec, powerful barons in those parts, assembled an army with which they encamped at North-Allerton, and awaited the arrival of the enemy. A great battle was here fought, called the Battle of the Standard, from a high crucifix, erected by the English on a wagon, and carried along with the army as a military ensign. The King of Scots was defeated, and he himself, as well as his son Henry, narrowly escaped falling into the hands of the English. This success overawed the malcontents in England, and might have given some stability to Stephen's throne had he not been so elated with prosperity as to engage in a controversy with the clergy, who were at that time an overmatch for any monarch.

Though the great power of the Church in ancient times weakened the authority of the crown and interrupted the course of the laws, it may be doubted whether in ages of such violence and outrage it was not rather advantageous that some limits were set to the power of the sword, both in the hands of the prince and nobles, and that men were taught to pay regard to some principles and privileges. The chief misfortune was that the prelates on some occasions acted entirely as barons, employed military power against their sovereign or their neighbors, and thereby often increased those disorders which it was their duty to repress. The Bishop of Salisbury, in imitation of the nobility, had built two strong castles—one at Sherborne, another at Devizes—and had laid the foundations of a third at Malmesbury;

[17] Will. Malm. p. 180.

his nephew, Alexander, Bishop of Lincoln, had erected a
fortress at Newark; and Stephen, who was now sensible
from experience of the mischiefs attending these multiplied
citadels, resolved to begin with destroying those of the
clergy, who, by their function, seemed less entitled than the
barons to such military securities.[18]   [1139.]   Making pretence of a fray which had arisen in court between the retinue of the Bishop of Salisbury and that of the Earl of
Brittany, he seized both that prelate and the Bishop of Lincoln, threw them into prison, and obliged them by menaces
to deliver up those places of strength which they had lately
erected.[19]

Henry, Bishop of Winchester, the king's brother, being
armed with a legatine commission, now conceived himself to
be an ecclesiastical sovereign no less powerful than the civil,
and, forgetting the ties of blood which connected him with
the king, he resolved to vindicate the clerical privileges
which, he pretended, were here openly violated. He assembled a synod at Westminster, and there complained of
the impiety of Stephen's measures, who had employed violence against the dignitaries of the Church, and had not
awaited the sentence of a spiritual court, by which alone, he
affirmed, they could lawfully be tried and condemned, if
their conduct had anywise merited censure or punishment.[20]
The synod ventured to send a summons to the king, charging him to appear before them and to justify his measures;[21]
and Stephen, instead of resenting this indignity, sent Aubrey
de Vere to plead his cause before that assembly. De Vere
accused the two prelates of treason and sedition; but the
synod refused to try the cause, or examine their conduct,
till those castles of which they had been dispossessed were
previously restored to them.[22]   The Bishop of Salisbury declared that he would appeal to the pope; and had not Stephen and his partisans employed menaces, and even shown a
disposition of executing violence by the hands of the soldiery, affairs had instantly come to extremity between the
crown and the mitre.[23]

While this quarrel, joined to so many other grievances,
increased the discontents among the people, the empress,
invited by the opportunity and secretly encouraged by the
legate himself, landed in England, with Robert, Earl of

[18] Gul. Neub. p. 362.   [19] Chron. Sax. p. 238. Will. Malm. p. 181.
[20] Will. Malm. p. 182.   [21] Ibid. Matt. Paris, p. 53.
[22] Will. Malm. p. 183.   [23] Ibid.

Gloucester, and a retinue of a hundred and forty knights. She fixed her residence at Arundel Castle, whose gates were opened to her by Adelais, the queen dowager, now married to William d'Albini, Earl of Sussex; and she excited, by messengers, her partisans to take arms in every county of England. Adelais, who had expected that her daughter-in-law would have invaded the kingdom with a much greater force, became apprehensive of danger; and Matilda, to ease her of her fears, removed first to Bristol, which belonged to her brother Robert, thence to Gloucester, where she remained under the protection of Milo, a gallant nobleman in those parts, who had embraced her cause. Soon after Geoffrey Talbot, William Mohun, Ralph Lovel, William Fitz-John, William Fitz-Alan, Paganell, and many other barons, declared for her; and her party, which was generally favored in the kingdom, seemed every day to gain ground upon that of her antagonist.

Were we to relate all the military events transmitted to us by contemporary and authentic historians, it would be easy to swell our accounts of this reign into a large volume; but those incidents, so little memorable in themselves, and so confused both in time and place, could afford neither instruction nor entertainment to the reader. It suffices to say that the war was spread into every quarter, and that those turbulent barons who had already shaken off, in a great measure, the restraint of government, having now obtained the pretence of a public cause, carried on their devastations with redoubled fury, exercised implacable vengeance on each other, and set no bounds to their oppressions over the people. The castles of the nobility were become receptacles of licensed robbers, who, sallying forth day and night, committed spoil on the open country, on the villages, and even on the cities; put the captives to torture, in order to make them reveal their treasures; sold their persons to slavery; and set fire to their houses after they had pillaged them of everything valuable. The fierceness of their disposition, leading them to commit wanton destruction, frustrated their rapacity of its purpose; and the property and persons even of the ecclesiastics, generally so much revered, were at last, from necessity, exposed to the same outrage which had laid waste the rest of the kingdom. The land was left untilled; the instruments of husbandry were destroyed or abandoned; and a grievous famine, the natural result of those disorders, affected equally both parties, and

reduced the spoilers as well as the defenceless people to the
most extreme want and indigence.[24]

[1140.] After several fruitless negotiations and treaties
of peace, which never interrupted these destructive hostilities, there happened at last an event which seemed to
promise some end of the public calamities. Ralph, Earl of
Chester, and his half-brother, William de Roumara, partisans of Matilda, had surprised the castle of Lincoln ; but
the citizens, who were better affected to Stephen, having
invited him to their aid, that prince laid close siege to the
castle, in hopes of soon rendering himself master of the
place either by assault or by famine. The Earl of Gloucester
hastened with an army to the relief of his friends ; and
Stephen, informed of his approach, took the field with the
resolution of giving him battle. [1141.] After a violent
shock, the two wings of the royalists were put to flight ;
and Stephen himself, surrounded by the enemy, was at
last, after exerting great efforts of valor, borne down by
numbers and taken prisoner. He was conducted to Gloucester ; and, though at first treated with humanity, was
soon after, on some suspicion, thrown into prison and
loaded with irons.

Stephen's party was entirely broken by the captivity of
their leader, and the barons came in daily from all quarters
and did homage to Matilda. The princess, however, amid
all her prosperity, knew that she was not secure of success
unless she could gain the confidence of the clergy ; and as
the conduct of the legate had been of late very ambiguous,
and shown his intentions to have rather aimed at humbling
his brother than totally ruining him, she employed every
endeavor to fix him in her interests. She held a conference
with him in an open plain near Winchester, where she
promised upon oath that if he would acknowledge her for
sovereign, would recognize her title as the sole descendant
of the late king, and would again submit to the allegiance
which he, as well as the rest of the kingdom, had sworn to
her, he should in return be entire master of the administration, and, in particular, should, at his pleasure, dispose of
all vacant bishoprics and abbeys. Earl Robert (her brother),
Brian Fitz-Count, Milo of Gloucester, and other great men,
became guarantees for her observing these engagements ;[25]
and the prelate was at last induced to promise her allegiance,

[24] Chron. Sax. p. 238.   Will. Malm. p. 185.   Gest. Steph. p. 961.
[25] Will. Malm. p. 187.

but that still burdened with the express condition that she should, on her part, fulfil her promises. He then conducted her to Winchester, led her in procession to the cathedral, and with great solemnity, in the presence of many bishops and abbots, denounced curses against all those who cursed her, poured out blessings on those who blessed her, granted absolution to such as were obedient to her, and excommunicated such as were rebellious.[26] Theobald, Archbishop of Canterbury, soon after came also to court, and swore allegiance to the empress.[27]

Matilda, that she might further insure the attachment of the clergy, was willing to receive the crown from their hands; and instead of assembling the states of the kingdom, the measure which the constitution, had it been either fixed or regarded, seemed necessarily to require, she was content that the legate should assemble an ecclesiastical synod, and that her title to the throne should there be acknowledged. The legate, addressing himself to the assembly, told them that in the absence of the empress, Stephen, his brother, had been permitted to reign, and, previously to his ascending the throne, had seduced them by many fair promises of honoring and exalting the Church, of maintaining the laws, and of reforming all abuses ; that it grieved him to observe how much that prince had, in every particular, been wanting to his engagements; public peace was interrupted, crimes were daily committed with impunity, bishops were thrown into prison and forced to surrender their possessions, abbeys were put to sale, churches were pillaged, and the most enormous disorders prevailed in the administration ; that he himself, in order to procure a redress of these grievances, had formerly summoned the king before a council of bishops ; but, instead of inducing him to amend his conduct, had rather offended him by that expedient ; that, how much soever misguided, that prince was still his brother, and the object of his affections; but his interests, however, must be regarded as subordinate to those of their heavenly Father, who had now rejected him, and thrown him into the hands of his enemies ; that it principally belonged to the clergy to elect and ordain kings; he had summoned them together for that purpose, and having invoked the divine assistance, he now pronounced Matilda, the only descendant of Henry, their late sovereign, Queen of England. The whole as-

[26] Chron. Sax. p. 242. Contin. Flor. Wigorn. p. 676.   [27] Will. Malm. p. 187.

sembly, by their acclamations or silence, gave, or seemed to give, their assent to this declaration.[28]

The only laymen summoned to this council, which decided the fate of the crown, were the Londoners; and even these were required not to give their opinion, but to submit to the decrees of the synod. The deputies of London, however, were not so passive. They insisted that their king should be delivered from prison, but were told by the legate that it became not the Londoners, who were regarded as noblemen in England, to take part with those barons who had basely forsaken their lord in battle, and who had treated the holy Church with contumely.[29] It is with reason that the citizens of London assumed so much authority, if it be true what is related by Fitz-Stephen, a contemporary author, that that city could at this time bring into the field no less than eighty thousand combatants.[30]

London, notwithstanding its great power and its attachment to Stephen, was at length obliged to submit to Matilda; and her authority, by the prudent conduct of Earl Robert, seemed to be established over the whole kingdom; but affairs remained not long in this situation. That princess, besides the disadvantages of her sex, which weakened her influence over a turbulent and martial people, was of a passionate, imperious spirit, and knew not how to temper with affability the harshness of a refusal. Stephen's queen, seconded by many of the nobility, petitioned for the liberty of her husband; and offered that, on this condition, he should renounce the crown and retire into a convent. The legate desired that Prince Eustace, his nephew, might inherit Boulogne and the other patrimonial estates of his father.[31] The Londoners applied for the establishment of King Edward's laws instead of those of King Henry, which, they said, were grievous and oppressive.[32] All these petitions were rejected in the most haughty and peremptory manner.

[28] Will. Malm. p. 188. This author, a judicious man, was present, and says that he was very attentive to what passed. This speech, therefore, may be regarded as entirely genuine. [29] Will. Malm. p. 188.
[30] P. 4. Were this account to be depended on, London must at that time have contained near four hundred thousand inhabitants, which is above double the number it contained at the death of Queen Elizabeth. But these loose calculations, or rather guesses, deserve very little credit. Peter Blois, a contemporary writer, and a man of sense, says there were then only forty thousand inhabitants in London, which is much more likely. See Epist. 151. What Fitz-Stephen says of the prodigious riches, splendor, and commerce of London proves only the great poverty of the other towns of the kingdom, and, indeed, of all the northern parts of Europe.
[31] Brompton, p. 1031. [32] Contin. Flor. Wigorn. p. 677. Gervase, p. 1355.

The legate, who had probably never been sincere in his compliance with Matilda's government, availed himself of the ill-humor excited by this imperious conduct, and secretly instigated the Londoners to a revolt. A conspiracy was entered into to seize the person of the empress, and she saved herself from the danger by a precipitate retreat. She fled to Oxford. Soon after she went to Winchester, whither the legate, desirous to save appearances, and watching the opportunity to ruin her cause, had retired. But having assembled all his retainers, he openly joined his force to that of the Londoners, and to Stephen's mercenary troops, who had not yet evacuated the kingdom, and he besieged Matilda in Winchester. The princess, being hard pressed by famine, made her escape; but in the flight Earl Robert, her brother, fell into the hands of the enemy. This nobleman, though a subject, was as much the life and soul of his own party as Stephen was of the other; and the empress, sensible of his merit and importance, consented to exchange the prisoners on equal terms. The civil war was again kindled with greater fury than ever.

[1142.] Earl Robert, finding the successes on both sides nearly balanced, went over to Normandy, which, during Stephen's captivity, had submitted to the Earl of Anjou; and he persuaded Geoffrey to allow his eldest son, Henry, a young prince of great hopes, to take a journey into England, and appear at the head of his partisans. This expedient, however, produced nothing decisive. [1143.] Stephen took Oxford after a long siege; he was defeated by Earl Robert at Wilton; and the empress, though of a masculine spirit, yet being harassed with a variety of good and bad fortune, and alarmed with continual dangers to her person and family, at last retired into Normandy, whither she had sent her son some time before. [1146.] The death of her brother, which happened nearly about the same time, would have proved fatal to her interests had not some incidents occurred which checked the course of Stephen's prosperity. This prince, finding that the castles built by the noblemen of his own party encouraged the spirit of independence, and were little less dangerous than those which remained in the hands of the enemy, endeavored to extort from them a surrender of those fortresses; and he alienated the affections of many of them by this equitable demand. The artillery also of the Church, which his brother had brought over to his side, had, after some interval, joined the other party.

Eugenius III. had mounted the papal throne; the Bishop of Winchester was deprived of the legatine commission, which was conferred on Theobald, Archbishop of Canterbury, the enemy and rival of the former legate. That pontiff also, having summoned a general council at Rheims, in Champagne, instead of allowing the Church of England, as had been usual, to elect its own deputies, nominated five English bishops to represent that Church, and required their attendance in the council. Stephen, who, notwithstanding his present difficulties, was jealous of the rights of his crown, refused them permission to attend,[33] and the pope, sensible of his advantage in contending with a prince who reigned by a disputed title, took revenge by laying all Stephen's party under an interdict.[34] [1147.] The discontents of the royalists at being thrown into this situation were augmented by a comparison with Matilda's party, who enjoyed all the benefits of the sacred ordinances; and Stephen was at last obliged, by making proper submissions to the see of Rome, to remove the reproach from his party.[35]

[1148.] The weakness of both sides, rather than any decrease of mutual animosity, having produced a tacit cessation of arms in England, many of the nobility, Roger de Moubray, William de Warenne, and others, finding no opportunity to exert their military ardor at home, enlisted themselves in a new crusade, which, with surprising success, after former disappointments and misfortunes, was now preached by St. Bernard.[36] But an event soon after happened which threatened a revival of hostilities in England. Prince Henry, who had reached his sixteenth year, was desirous of receiving the honor of knighthood—a ceremony which every gentleman in that age passed through before he was admitted to the use of arms, and which was even deemed requisite for the greatest princes. He intended to receive his admission from his great-uncle, David, King of Scotland; and for that purpose he passed through England with a great retinue, and was attended by the most considerable of his partisans. He remained some time with the King of Scotland; made incursions into England; and by his dexterity and vigor in all manly exercises, by his valor in war, and his prudent conduct in every occurrence, he roused the hopes of his party, and gave symptoms of those great qualities which he afterwards displayed when

[33] Epist. St. Thom. p. 225.   [34] Chron. W. Thorn. p. 1807.
[35] Epist. St. Thom. p. 226.   [36] Hagulstadt, pp. 275, 276.

he mounted the throne of England. [1150.] Soon after his return to Normandy, he was, by Matilda's consent, invested in that duchy; and upon the death of his father, Geoffrey, which happened in the subsequent year, he took possession both of Anjou and Maine, and concluded a marriage, which brought him a great accession of power, and rendered him extremely formidable to his rival. Eleanor, the daughter and heir of William, Duke of Guienne and Earl of Poictou, had been married sixteen years to Lewis VII., King of France, and had attended him in a crusade which that monarch conducted against the infidels; [1152.] but having there lost the affections of her husband, and even fallen under some suspicion of gallantry with a handsome Saracen, Lewis, more delicate than politic, procured a divorce from her, and restored her those rich provinces which by her marriage she had annexed to the crown of France. Young Henry, neither discouraged by the inequality of years, nor by the reports of Eleanor's gallantries, made successful courtship to that princess, and, espousing her six weeks after her divorce, got possession of all her dominions as her dowry. The lustre which he received from this acquisition, and the prospect of his rising fortune, had such an effect in England that when Stephen, desirous to insure the crown to his son Eustace, required the Archbishop of Canterbury to anoint that prince as his successor, the primate refused compliance, and made his escape beyond sea to avoid the violence and resentment of Stephen.

Henry, informed of these dispositions in the people, made an invasion on England. Having gained some advantage over Stephen at Malmesbury, and having taken that place, he proceeded thence to throw succors into Wallingford, which the king had advanced with a superior army to besiege. [1153.] A decisive action was every day expected, when the great men of both sides, terrified at the prospect of further bloodshed and confusion, interposed with their good offices, and set on foot a negotiation between the rival princes. The death of Eustace during the course of the treaty facilitated its conclusion; an accommodation was settled by which it was agreed that Stephen should possess the crown during his lifetime; that justice should be administered in his name, even in the provinces which had submitted to Henry; and that this latter prince should, on Stephen's demise, succeed to the kingdom, and William, Stephen's son, to Boulogne and his patrimonial es-

tate. After all the barons had sworn to the observance of
this treaty, and done homage to Henry as to the heir of the
crown, that prince evacuated the kingdom ; and the death
of Stephen, [1154.] which happened the next year, after
a short illness, prevented all those quarrels and jealousies
which were likely to have ensued in so delicate a situation.

England suffered great miseries during the reign of this
prince ; but his personal character, allowing for the temerity and injustice of his usurpation, appears not liable to any
great exception ; and he seems to have been well qualified,
had he succeeded by a just title, to have promoted the happiness and prosperity of his subjects.[37] He was possessed
of industry, activity, and courage to a great degree; though
not endowed with a sound judgment, he was not deficient
in abilities ; he had the talent of gaining men's affections ;
and, notwithstanding his precarious situation, he never indulged himself in the exercise of any cruelty or revenge.[38]
His advancement to the throne procured him neither tranquillity nor happiness ; and though the situation of England prevented the neighboring states from taking any
durable advantage of her confusions, her intestine disorders
were to the last degree ruinous and destructive. The court
of Rome was also permitted during those civil wars to make
further advances in her usurpation ; and appeals to the
pope. which had always been strictly prohibited by the
English laws, became now common in every ecclesiastical
controversy.[39]

[37] Will. Malm. p. 180.   [38] Matt. Paris, p. 51.   Hagulstadt, p. 312.
[39] H. Hunting. p. 395.

CHAPTER VIII.

HENRY II.

STATE OF EUROPE—OF FRANCE.—FIRST ACTS OF HENRY'S GOVERNMENT. — DISPUTES BETWEEN THE CIVIL AND ECCLESIASTICAL POWERS.—THOMAS À BECKET, ARCHBISHOP OF CANTERBURY.—QUARREL BETWEEN THE KING AND BECKET.—CONSTITUTIONS OF CLARENDON.—BANISHMENT OF BECKET.—COMPROMISE WITH HIM.—HIS RETURN FROM BANISHMENT.—HIS MURDER.—GRIEF AND SUBMISSION OF THE KING.

[1154.] THE extensive confederacies by which the European potentates are now at once united and set in opposition to each other, and which, though they are apt to diffuse the least spark of dissension throughout the whole, are at least attended with this advantage, that they prevent any violent revolutions or conquests in particular states, were totally unknown in ancient ages; and the theory of foreign politics in each kingdom formed a speculation much less complicated and involved than at present. Commerce had not yet bound together the most distant nations in so close a chain; wars, finished in one campaign, and often in one battle, were little affected by the movements of remote states; the imperfect communication among the kingdoms, and their ignorance of each other's situation, made it impracticable for a great number of them to combine in one project or effort; and, above all, the turbulent spirit and independent situation of the barons or great vassals in each state gave so much occupation to the sovereign that he was obliged to confine his attention chiefly to his own state and his own system of government, and was more indifferent about what passed among his neighbors. Religion alone, not politics, carried abroad the views of princes; while it either fixed their thoughts on the Holy Land, whose conquest and defence were deemed a point of common honor and interest, or engaged them in intrigues with the Roman pontiff, to whom they had yielded the direction of ecclesiastical affairs, and who was every day assuming more authority than they were willing to allow him.

Before the conquest of England by the Duke of Normandy, this island was as much separated from the rest of the world in politics as in situation; and except from the inroads of the Danish pirates, the English, happily confined at home, had neither enemies nor allies on the Continent. The foreign dominions of William connected them with the king and great vassals of France; and while the opposite pretensions of the pope and emperor in Italy produced a continual intercourse between Germany and that country, the two great monarchs of France and England formed, in another part of Europe, a separate system, and carried on their wars and negotiations without meeting either with opposition or support from the others.

On the decline of the Carlovingian race, the nobles in every province of France, taking advantage of the weakness of the sovereign, and obliged to provide, each for his own defence, against the ravages of the Norman freebooters, had assumed, both in civil and military affairs, an authority almost independent, and had reduced within very narrow limits the prerogative of their princes. The accession of Hugh Capet, by annexing a great fief to the crown, had brought some addition to the royal dignity; but this fief, though considerable for a subject, appeared a narrow basis of power for a prince who was placed at the head of so great a community. The royal demesnes consisted only of Paris, Orleans, Estampes, Compiègne, and a few places scattered over the northern provinces. In the rest of the kingdom, the prince's authority was rather nominal than real. The vassals were accustomed—nay, entitled—to make war, without his permission, on each other; they were even entitled, if they conceived themselves injured, to turn their arms against their sovereign; they exercised all civil jurisdiction, without appeal, over their tenants and inferior vassals. Their common jealousy of the crown easily united them against any attempt on their exorbitant privileges; and as some of them had attained the power and authority of great princes, even the smallest baron was sure of immediate and effectual protection. Besides six ecclesiastical peerages, which, with the other immunities of the Church, cramped extremely the general execution of justice, there were six lay peerages—Burgundy, Normandy, Guienne, Flanders, Toulouse, and Champagne—which formed very extensive and puissant sovereignties.

And though the combination of all these princes and barons could, on urgent occasions, muster a mighty power, yet it was very difficult to set that great machine in movement; it was almost impossible to preserve harmony in its parts; a sense of common interest alone could, for a time, unite them under their sovereign against a common enemy; but if the king attempted to turn the force of the community against any mutinous vassal, the same sense of common interest made the others oppose themselves to the success of his pretensions. Lewis the Gross, the last sovereign, marched at one time to his frontiers against the Germans at the head of an army of two hundred thousand men; but a petty lord of Corbeil, of Puiset, of Couci, was able at another period to set that prince at defiance, and to maintain open war against him.

The authority of the English monarch was much more extensive within his kingdom, and the disproportion much greater between him and the most powerful of his vassals. His demesnes and revenue were large compared to the greatness of his state. He was accustomed to levy arbitrary exactions on his subjects; his courts of judicature extended their jurisdiction into every part of the kingdom; he could crush by his power, or by a judicial sentence, well or ill founded, any obnoxious baron; and though the feudal institutions which prevailed in his kingdom had the same tendency as in other states to exalt the aristocracy and depress the monarchy, it required, in England, according to its present constitution, a great combination of the vassals to oppose their sovereign lord, and there had not hitherto arisen any baron so powerful as of himself to levy war against the prince and to afford protection to the inferior barons.

While such were the different situations of France and England, and the latter enjoyed so many advantages above the former, the accession of Henry II., a prince of great abilities, possessed of so many rich provinces on the Continent, might appear an event dangerous, if not fatal, to the French monarchy, and sufficient to break entirely the balance between the states. He was master, in the right of his father, of Anjou and Touraine; in that of his mother, of Normandy and Maine; in that of his wife, of Guienne, Poictou, Saintonge, Auvergne, Périgord, Angoumois, the Limousin. He soon after annexed Brittany to his other states, and was already possessed of the superiority over that province which, on the first cession of Normandy to Rollo, the

Dane, had been granted by Charles the Simple in vassalage to that formidable ravager. These provinces composed above a third of the whole French monarchy, and were much superior in extent and opulence to those territories which were subjected to the immediate jurisdiction and government of the king. The vassal was here more powerful than his liege lord; the situation which had enabled Hugh Capet to depose the Carlovingian princes seemed to be renewed, and that with much greater advantages on the side of the vassal; and when England was added to so many provinces, the French king had reason to apprehend from this conjuncture some great disaster to himself and to his family; but in reality it was this circumstance, which appeared so formidable, that saved the Capetian race, and, by its consequences, exalted them to that pitch of grandeur which they at present enjoy.

The limited authority of the prince in the feudal constitutions prevented the King of England from employing with advantage the force of so many states which were subjected to his government; and these different members, disjoined in situation, and disagreeing in laws, language, and manners, were never thoroughly cemented into one monarchy. He soon became, both from his distant place of residence and from the incompatibility of interests, a kind of foreigner to his French dominions; and his subjects on the Continent considered their allegiance as more naturally due to their superior lord, who lived in their neighborhood, and who was acknowledged to be the supreme head of their nation. He was always at hand to invade them; their immediate lord was often at too great a distance to protect them; and any disorder in any part of his dispersed dominions gave advantages against him. The other powerful vassals of the French crown were rather pleased to see the expulsion of the English, and were not affected with that jealousy which would have arisen from the oppression of a co-vassal who was of the same rank with themselves. By this means, the King of France found it more easy to conquer those numerous provinces from England than to subdue a Duke of Normandy or Guienne, a Count of Anjou, Maine, or Poictou. And after reducing such extensive territories, which immediately incorporated with the body of the monarchy, he found greater facility in uniting to the crown the other great fiefs which still remained separate and independent.

But as these important consequences could not be foreseen by human wisdom, the King of France remarked with terror the rising grandeur of the house of Anjou, or Plantagenet; and, in order to retard its progress, he had ever maintained a strict union with Stephen, and had endeavored to support the tottering fortunes of that bold usurper. But after this prince's death it was too late to think of opposing the succession of Henry, or preventing the performance of those stipulations which, with the unanimous consent of the nation, he had made with his predecessor. The English, harassed with civil wars, and disgusted with the bloodshed and depredations which, during the course of so many years, had attended them, were little disposed to violate their oaths by excluding the lawful heir from the succession of their monarchy.[1] Many of the most considerable fortresses were in the hands of his partisans; the whole nation had had occasion to see the noble qualities with which he was endowed,[2] and to compare them with the mean talents of William, the son of Stephen; and as they were acquainted with his great power, and were rather pleased to see the accession of so many foreign dominions to the crown of England, they never entertained the least thoughts of resisting them. Henry himself, sensible of the advantages attending his present situation, was in no hurry to arrive in England; and being engaged in the siege of a castle on the frontiers of Normandy when he received intelligence of Stephen's death, he made it a point of honor not to depart from his enterprise till he had brought it to an issue. He then set out on his journey, and was received in England with the acclamations of all orders of men, who swore with pleasure the oath of fealty and allegiance to him.

[1155.] The first acts of Henry's government corresponded to the high idea entertained of his abilities, and prognosticated the re-establishment of justice and tranquillity, of which the kingdom had so long been bereaved. He immediately dismissed all those mercenary soldiers who had committed great disorders in the nation; and he sent them abroad together with William of Ypres, their leader, the friend and confidant of Stephen.[3] He revoked all the grants made by his predecessor,[4] even those which necessity had extorted from the Empress Matilda; and that princess, who had resigned her rights in favor of Henry, made no opposition to a measure so necessary for supporting the dignity

---

[1] Matt. Paris, p. 65.　　　　　　　　　　[2] Gul. Neub. p. 381.
[3] Fitz-Steph. p. 13. Matt. Paris, p. 65. Gul. Neub. p. 381. Chron. T. Wykes, p. 30.　　　　　　　　　　　　　[4] Gul. Neub. p. 382.

of the crown, he repaired the coin, which had been extremely
debased during the reign of his predecessor; and he took proper
measures against the return of a like abuse.[5] He was rigorous
in the execution of justice and in the suppression of robbery
and violence; and that he might restore authority to the laws,
he caused all the new-erected castles to be demolished, which
had proved so many sanctuaries to freebooters and rebels.[6]
The Earl of Albemarle, Hugh Mortimer, and Roger the son
of Milo of Gloucester, were inclined to make some resistance
to this salutary measure; but the approach of the king with
his forces soon obliged them to submit.

[1156.] Everything being restored to full tranquillity in
England, Henry went abroad in order to oppose the attempts
of his brother Geoffrey, who, during his absence, had made an
incursion into Anjou and Maine, had advanced some pretensions to those provinces, and had got possession of a
considerable part of them.[7] On the king's appearance, the
people returned to their allegiance; and Geoffrey, resigning
his claim for an annual pension of a thousand pounds,
departed and took possession of the county of Nantz, which
the inhabitants, who had expelled Count Hoel, their prince,
had put into his hands. [1157.] Henry returned to England the following year; the incursions of the Welsh then
provoked him to make an invasion upon them; where the
natural fastnesses of the country occasioned him great
difficulties, and even brought him into danger. His van-
guard, being engaged in a narrow pass, was put to rout.
Henry de Essex, the hereditary standard-bearer, seized with
a panic, threw down the standard, took to flight, and
exclaimed that the king was slain; and had not the prince
immediately appeared in person and led on his troops with
great gallantry, the consequences might have proved fatal
to the whole army.[8] For this misbehavior, Essex was afterwards accused of felony by Robert de Montfort, was vanquished in single combat, his estate was confiscated, and he
himself was thrust into a convent.[9] The submissions of the
Welsh procured them an accommodation with England.

[1158.] The martial disposition of the princes in that
age engaged them to head their own armies in every enterprise, even the most frivolous; and their feeble authority

  [5] Hoveden, p. 491.
  [6] Hoveden, p. 491.   Fitz-Steph. p. 13.   Matt. Paris. p. 65.   Gul. Neub. p. 381.
  Brompton, p. 1043.   [7] See note [O] at the end of the volume.
  [8] Gul. Neub. p. 383.   Chron. W. Heming. p. 492.
  [9] Matt. Paris, p. 70.   Gul. Neub. p. 383.

made it commonly impracticable for them to delegate, on occasion, the command to their generals. Geoffrey, the king's brother, died soon after he had acquired possession of Nantz; though he had no other title to that country than the voluntary submission or election of the inhabitants two years before, Henry laid claim to the territory as devolved to him by hereditary right, and he went over to support his pretensions by force of arms. Conan, Duke or Earl of Brittany (for these titles are given indifferently by historians to those princes), pretended that Nantz had lately separated by rebellion from his principality, to which of right it belonged; and immediately on Geoffrey's death he took possession of the disputed territory. Lest Lewis, the French king, should interpose in the controversy, Henry paid him a visit, and so allured him by caresses and civilities that an alliance was contracted between them; and they agreed that young Henry, heir to the English monarchy, should be affianced to Margaret of France, though the former was only five years of age and the latter was still in her cradle. Henry, now secure of meeting with no interruption on this side, advanced with his army into Brittany; and Conan, in despair of being able to make resistance, delivered up the county of Nantz to him. The able conduct of the king procured him further and more important advantages from this incident. Conan, harassed with the turbulent disposition of his subjects, was desirous of procuring to himself the support of so great a monarch; and he betrothed his daughter and only child, yet an infant, to Geoffrey, the king's third son, who was of the same tender years. The Duke of Brittany died about seven years after; and Henry being *mesne* lord, and also natural guardian to his son and daughter-in-law, put himself in possession of that principality, and annexed it for the present to his other great dominions.

[1159.] The king had a prospect of making still further acquisitions, and the activity of his temper suffered no opportunity of that kind to escape him. Philippa, Duchess of Guienne, mother of Queen Eleanor, was the only issue of William IV., Count of Toulouse, and would have inherited his dominions had not that prince, desirous of preserving the succession in the male line, conveyed the principality to his brother, Raymond de St. Gilles, by a contract of sale, which was in that age regarded as fictitious and illusory. By this means the title to the county of Toulouse came to be disputed between the male and female heirs, and the one or the other, as opportunities favored them, had obtained possession. Raymond, grandson of Raymond de St. Gilles, was the reigning sovereign; and on Henry's reviving his wife's claim this prince had recourse for protection to the King of France, who was so much concerned in policy to prevent the further aggrandizement of the English monarch. Lewis himself, when married to Eleanor, had asserted the justice of her claim, and had demanded possession of Toulouse; [10] but, his sentiments changing with his interest, he now determined to defend, by his power and authority, the title of Raymond. Henry found that it would be requisite to support his pretensions against potent antagonists, and that nothing but a formidable army could maintain a claim which he had in vain asserted by arguments and manifestoes.

An army, composed of feudal vassals, was commonly very intractable and undisciplined, both because of the independent spirit of the persons who served in it, and because the commands were not given, either by the choice of the sovereign or from the military capacity and experience of the officers. Each baron conducted his own vassals; his rank was greater or less, proportioned to the extent of his property; even the supreme command under the prince was often attached to birth; and as the military vassals were obliged to serve only forty days at their own charge (though, if the expedition were distant, they were put to great expense), the prince reaped little benefit from their attendance. Henry, sensible of these inconveniences, levied upon his vassals in Normandy, and other provinces which were remote from Toulouse, a sum of money in lieu of their service; and this commutation, by reason of the great distance, was still more advantageous to his English vassals. He imposed, therefore, a scutage of one hundred and eighty thousand pounds on the knight's-fees, a commutation to which, though it was unusual, and the first, perhaps, to be met with in history,[11] the military tenants willingly submitted; and with this money he levied an army which was more under his command, and whose services was more durable and constant. [1160.] Assisted by Berenger, Count of Barcelona, and Trincaval, Count of Nismes, whom he had gained to his party, he invaded the county of Toulouse, and after taking Verdun, Castelnau, and other places, he besieged the capital of the province, and was likely to prevail in the enterprise,

[10] Gul. Neub. p. 387.   Chron. W. Heming. p. 494.
[11] Madox, p. 435.   Gervase, p. 1381.   See note [P] at the end of the volume.

when Lewis, advancing before the arrival of his main body, threw himself into the place with a small reinforcement. Henry was urged by some of his ministers to prosecute the siege, to take Lewis prisoner, and to impose his own terms in the pacification; but he either thought it so much his interest to maintain the feudal principles by which his foreign dominions were secured, or bore so much respect to his superior lord, that he declared he would not attack a place defended by him in person, and he immediately raised the siege.[12] He marched into Normandy, to protect that province against an incursion which the Count de Dreux, instigated by King Lewis, his brother, had made upon it. War was now openly carried on between the two monarchs, but produced no memorable event; it soon ended in a cessation of arms, and that followed by a peace, which was not, however, attended with any confidence or good correspondence between those rival princes. The fortress of Gisors, being part of the dowry stipulated to Margaret of France, had been consigned by agreement to the Knights Templars, on condition that it should be delivered into Henry's hands after the celebration of the nuptials. The king, that he might have a pretence for immediately demanding the place, ordered the marriage to be solemnized between the prince and princess, though both infants;[13] and he engaged the Grand Master of the Templars—by large presents, as was generally suspected—to put him in possession of Gisors.[14] [1161.] Lewis, resenting this fraudulent conduct, banished the Templars, and would have made war upon the King of England had it not been for the mediation and authority of Pope Alexander III., who had been chased from Rome by the anti-pope, Victor IV., and resided at that time in France. That we may form an idea of the authority possessed by the Roman pontiff during those ages, it may be proper to observe that the two kings had, the year before, met the pope at the castle of Torci, on the Loire; and they gave him such marks of respect that both dismounted to receive him, and, holding each of them one of the reins of his bridle, walked on foot by his side and conducted him in that submissive manner into the castle.[15] "A spectacle," cries Baronius, in an

---

[12] Fitz-Steph. p. 22. Diceto, p. 531.
[13] Hoveden, p. 492. Gul. Neub. p. 400. Diceto, p. 532. Brompton, p. 1450.
[14] Since the first publication of this history, Lord Lyttelton has published a copy of the treaty between Henry and Lewis, by which it appears, if there was no secret article, that Henry was not guilty of any fraud in this transaction.
[15] Trivet, p. 48.

ecstasy, " to God, angels, and men ; and such as had never before been exhibited to the world ! "

[1162.] Henry, soon after he had accommodated his differences with Lewis by the pope's mediation, returned to England, where he commenced an enterprise which, though required by sound policy, and even conducted in the main with prudence, bred him great disquietude, involved him in danger, and was not concluded without some loss and dishonor.

The usurpations of the clergy, which had at first been gradual, were now become so rapid, and had mounted to such a height, that the contest between the *regale* and *pontificale* was really arrived at a crisis in England ; and it became necessary to determine whether the king or the priests, particularly the Archbishop of Canterbury, should be sovereign of the kingdom.[16] The aspiring spirit of Henry, which gave inquietude to all his neighbors, was not likely long to pay a tame submission to the encroachments of subjects ; and as nothing opens the eyes of men so readily as their interests, he was in no danger of falling, in this respect, into that abject superstition which retained his people in subjection. From the commencement of his reign, in the government of his foreign dominions as well as of England, he had shown a fixed purpose to repress clerical usurpations and to maintain those prerogatives which had been transmitted to him by his predecessors. During the schism of the papacy between Alexander and Victor, he had determined, for some time, to remain neuter ; and when informed that the Archbishop of Rouen and the Bishop of Mans had, from their own authority, acknowledged Alexander as legitimate pope, he was so enraged that, though he spared the archbishop on account of his great age, he immediately issued orders for overthrowing the houses of the Bishop of Mans and Archdeacon of Rouen ;[17] and it was not till he had deliberately examined the matter by those views which usually enter into the councils of princes that he allowed that pontiff to exercise authority over any of his dominions. In England, the mild character and advanced years of Theobald, Archbishop of Canterbury, together with his merits in refusing to put the crown on the head of Eustace, son of Stephen, prevented Henry, during the lifetime of that primate, from taking any measures against the multiplied encroachments of the clergy ; but after his death, the king resolved to exert himself with

---

[16] Fitz-Steph. p. 27.   [17] See note [Q] at the end of the volume.

more activity, and that he might be secure against any opposition, he advanced to that dignity Becket, his chancellor, on whose compliance he thought he could entirely depend.

Thomas à Becket, the first man of English descent who, since the Norman conquest, had, during the course of a whole century, risen to any considerable station, was born of reputable parents in the city of London, and being endowed both with industry and capacity, he early insinuated himself into the favor of Archbishop Theobald, and obtained from that prelate some preferments and offices. By their means he was enabled to travel for improvement to Italy, where he studied the civil and canon law at Bologna; and on his return he appeared to have made such proficiency in knowledge that he was promoted by his patron to the Archdeaconry of Canterbury, an office of considerable trust and profit. He was afterwards employed with success by Theobald in transacting business at Rome, and on Henry's accession he was recommended to that monarch as worthy of further preferment. Henry, who knew that Becket had been instrumental in supporting that resolution of the archbishop which had tended so much to facilitate his own advancement to the throne, was already prepossessed in his favor, and finding, on further acquaintance, that his spirit and abilities entitled him to any trust, he soon promoted him to the dignity of chancellor, one of the first civil offices in the kingdom. The chancellor, in that age, besides the custody of the great seal, had possession of all vacant prelacies and abbeys; he was the guardian of all such minors and pupils as were the king's tenants; all baronies which escheated to the crown were under his administration; he was entitled to a place in council, even though he were not particularly summoned; and as he exercised also the office of secretary of state, and it belonged to him to countersign all commissions, writs, and letters patent, he was a kind of prime minister, and was concerned in the despatch of every business of importance.[18] Besides exercising this high office, Becket, by the favor of the king or archbishop, was made Provost of Beverley, Dean of Hastings, and Constable of the Tower; he was put in possession of the honors of Eye and Berkham, large baronies that had escheated to the crown; and, to complete his grandeur, he was intrusted with the education of Prince Henry, the king's eldest son, and heir of the monarchy.[19] The pomp of his retinue, the sumptuousness of his

[18] Fitz-Steph. p. 13.　　　[19] Fitz-Steph. p. 15. Hist. Quad. pp. 9, 14.

furniture, the luxury of his table, the munificence of his presents corresponded to these great preferments, or rather exceeded anything that England had ever before seen in any subject. His historian and secretary, Fitz-Stephen,[20] mentions, among other particulars, that his apartments were every day in winter covered with clean straw or hay, and in summer with green rushes or boughs, lest the gentlemen who paid court to him, and who could not, by reason of their great number, find a place at table, should soil their fine clothes by sitting on a dirty floor.[21] A great number of knights were retained in his service; the greatest barons were proud of being received at his table; his house was a place of education for the sons of the chief nobility; and the king himself frequently vouchsafed to partake of his entertainments. As his way of life was splendid and opulent, his amusements and occupations were gay, and partook of the cavalier spirit, which, as he had only taken deacon's orders, he did not think unbefitting his character. He employed himself at leisure hours in hunting, hawking, gaming, and horsemanship; he exposed his person in several military actions; [22] he carried over, at his own charge, seven hundred knights to attend the king in his wars at Toulouse; in the subsequent wars on the frontiers of Normandy he maintained during forty days, twelve hundred knights and four thousand of their train; [23] and in an embassy to France, with which he was entrusted, he astonished that court with the number and magnificence of his retinue.

Henry, besides committing all his more important business to Becket's management, honored him with his friendship and intimacy; and whenever he was disposed to relax himself by sports of any kind, he admitted his chancellor to the party.[24] An instance of their familiarity is mentioned by Fitz-Stephen, which, as it shows the manners of the age, it may not be improper to relate. One day, as the king and the chancellor were riding together in the streets of London, they observed a beggar, who was shivering with cold. Would it not be very praiseworthy, said the king, to give that poor man a warm coat in this severe season? It would,

---

[20] P. 15.
[21] John Baldwin held the manor of Oterarsfee, in Aylesbury, of the king, in soccage, by the service of finding litter for the king's bed—viz., in summer, grass or herbs and two gray geese; and in winter, straw and three eels—thrice in the year, if the king should come thrice in the year to Aylesbury. Madox, Bar, Anglica, p. 247.
[22] Fitz-Steph. p. 23. Hist. Quad. p. 9.   [23] Fitz-Steph. pp. 19, 20, 22, 23.
[24] Fitz-Steph. p. 16. Hist. Quad. p. 8.

surely, replied the chancellor; and you do well, sir, in thinking of such good actions. Then he shall have one presently, cried the king; and, seizing the skirt of the chancellor's coat, which was scarlet and lined with ermine, began to pull it violently. The chancellor defended himself for some time; and they had both of them liked to have tumbled off their horses in the street, when Becket, after a vehement struggle, let go his coat, which the king bestowed on the beggar, who, being ignorant of the quality of the persons, was not a little surprised at the present.[25]

Becket, who, by his complaisance and good-humor, had rendered himself agreeable, and by his industry and abilities useful to his master, appeared to him the fittest person for supplying the vacancy made by the death of Theobald. As he was well acquainted with the king's intentions [26] of retrenching, or rather confining within the ancient bounds all ecclesiastical privileges, and always showed a ready disposition to comply with them,[27] Henry, who never expected any resistance from that quarter, immediately issued orders for electing him Archbishop of Canterbury. But this resolution, which was taken contrary to the opinion of Matilda and many of the ministers,[28] drew after it very unhappy consequences; and never prince of so great penetration appeared, in the issue, to have so little understood the genius and character of his minister.

No sooner was Becket installed in this high dignity, which rendered him for life the second person in the kingdom, with some pretensions of aspiring to be the first, than he totally altered his demeanor and conduct, and endeavored to acquire the character of sanctity, of which his former busy and ostentatious course of life might, in the eyes of the people, have naturally bereaved him. Without consulting the king, he immediately returned into his hands the commission of chancellor; pretending that he must thenceforth detach himself from secular affairs, and be solely employed in the exercise of his spiritual functions; but in reality that he might break off all connections with Henry, and apprise him that Becket, as Primate of England, was now become entirely a new personage. He maintained in his retinue and attendants alone his ancient pomp and lustre, which was useful to strike the vulgar; in his own person he affected the greatest austerity and most rigid mortification, which he was sensible

---

[25] Fitz-Steph. p. 16.
[27] Fitz-Steph. p. 23. Epist. St. Thom. p. 232.
[26] Fitz-Steph. p. 17.
[28] Epist. St. Thom. p. 167.

would have an equal or a greater tendency to the same end. He wore sackcloth next his skin, which, by his affected care to conceal it, was necessarily the more remarked by all the world; he changed it so seldom that it was filled with dirt and vermin; his usual diet was bread; his drink water, which he even rendered further unpalatable by the mixture of unsavory herbs; he tore his back with the frequent discipline which he inflicted on it; he daily on his knees washed, in imitation of Christ, the feet of thirteen beggars, whom he afterwards dismissed with presents; [29] he gained the affections of the monks by his frequent charities to the convents and hospitals; every one who made profession of sanctity was admitted to his conversation, and returned full of panegyrics on the humility as well as on the piety and mortification of the holy primate; he seemed to be perpetually employed in reciting prayers and pious lectures, or in perusing religious discourses; his aspect wore the appearance of seriousness and mental recollection and secret devotion; and all men of penetration plainly saw that he was meditating some great design, and that the ambition and ostentation of his character had turned itself towards a new and more dangerous object.

[1163.] Becket waited not till Henry should commence those projects against the ecclesiastical power which, he knew, had been formed by that prince: he was himself the aggressor, and endeavored to overawe the king by the intrepidity and boldness of his enterprises. He summoned the Earl of Clare to surrender the barony of Tunbridge, which, ever since the Conquest, had remained in the family of that nobleman, but which, as it had formerly belonged to the see of Canterbury, Becket pretended his predecessors were prohibited by the canons to alienate. The Earl of Clare, besides the lustre which he derived from the greatness of his own birth and the extent of his possessions, was allied to all the principal families in the kingdom; his sister, who was a celebrated beauty, had further extended his credit among the nobility, and was even supposed to have gained the king's affections; and Becket could not better discover than by attacking so powerful an interest his resolution of maintaining with vigor the rights, real or pretended, of his see.[30]

William de Eynsford, a military tenant of the crown, was patron of a living which belonged to a manor that held

[29] Fitz-Steph. p. 25. Hist. Quad. p 19.   [30] Fitz-Steph. p. 28. Gervase, p. 1384.

of the Archbishop of Canterbury ; but Becket, without regard to William's right, presented, on a new and illegal pretext, one Laurence to that living, who was violently expelled by Eynsford. The primate, making himself, as was usual in spiritual courts, both judge and party, issued, in a summary manner, the sentence of excommunication against Eynsford, who complained to the king that he who held *in capite* of the crown should, contrary to the practice established by the Conqueror, and maintained ever since by his successors, be subjected to that terrible sentence, without the previous consent of the sovereign.[31] Henry, who had now broken off all personal intercourse with Becket, sent him, by a messenger, his orders to absolve Eynsford, but received for answer that it belonged not to the king to inform him whom he should absolve and whom excommunicate ;[32] and it was not till after many remonstrances and menaces that Becket, though with the worst grace imaginable, was induced to comply with the royal mandate.

Henry, though he found himself thus grievously mistaken in the character of the person whom he had promoted to the primacy, determined not to desist from his former intention of retrenching clerical usurpations. He was entirely master of his extensive dominions : the prudence and vigor of his administration, attended with perpetual success, had raised his character above that of any of his predecessors :[33] the papacy seemed to be weakened by a schism which divided all Europe, and he rightly judged that, if the present favorable opportunity were neglected, the crown must, from the prevalent superstition of the people, be in danger of falling into an entire subordination under the mitre.

The union of the civil and ecclesiastical power serves extremely, in every civilized government, to the maintenance of peace and order ; and prevents those mutual encroachments which, as there can be no ultimate judge between them, are often attended with the most dangerous consequences. Whether the supreme magistrate, who unites these powers, receives the appellation of prince or prelate, is not material : the superior weight which temporal interests commonly bear in the apprehensions of men above spiritual, renders the civil part of his character most prevalent ; and in time prevents those gross impostures and bigoted

[31] Matt. Paris, p. 7. Diceto, p. 536. [32] Fitz-Steph. p. 23.
[33] Epist. St. Thom. p. 130.

persecutions which, in all false religions, are the chief foundation of clerical authority. But during the progress of ecclesiastical usurpations, the state, by the resistance of the civil magistrate, is naturally thrown into convulsions; and it behooves the prince, both for his own interest and for that of the public, to provide, in time, sufficient barriers against so dangerous and insidious a rival. This precaution had hitherto been much neglected in England, as well as in other Catholic countries; and affairs at last seemed to have come to a dangerous crisis. A sovereign of the greatest abilities was now on the throne; a prelate of the most inflexible and intrepid character was possessed of the primacy; the contending powers appeared to be armed with their full force, and it was natural to expect some extraordinary event to result from their conflict.

Among their other inventions to obtain money, the clergy had inculcated the necessity of penance as an atonement for sin; and having again introduced the practice of paying them large sums as a commutation, or species of atonement, for the remission of those penances, the sins of the people, by these means, had become a revenue to the priests; and the king computed that by this invention alone they levied more money upon his subjects than flowed, by all the funds and taxes, into the royal exchequer.[34] That he might ease the people of so heavy and arbitrary an imposition, Henry required that a civil officer of his appointment should be present in all ecclesiastical courts, and should, for the future, give his consent to every composition which was made with sinners for their spiritual offences.

The ecclesiastics, in that age, had renounced all immediate subordination to the magistrate; they openly pretended to an exemption, in criminal accusations, from a trial before courts of justice; and were gradually introducing a like exemption in civil causes; spiritual penalties alone could be inflicted on their offences; and as the clergy had extremely multiplied in England, and many of them were consequently of very low characters, crimes of the deepest dye, murders, robberies, adulteries, rapes, were daily committed with impunity by the ecclesiastics. It had been found, for instance, on inquiry, that no less than a hundred murders had, since the king's accession, been perpetrated by men of that profession, who had never been

[34] Fitz-Steph. p. 32.

called to account for these offences;[35] and holy orders were become a full protection for all enormities. A clerk in Worcestershire, having debauched a gentleman's daughter, had at this time proceeded to murder the father; and the general indignation against this crime moved the king to attempt the remedy of an abuse which was become so palpable, and to require that the clerk should be delivered up and receive condign punishment from the magistrate.[36] Becket insisted on the privileges of the Church; confined the criminal in the bishop's prison, lest he should be seized by the king's officers; maintained that no greater punishment could be inflicted on him than degradation; and when the king demanded that immediately after he was degraded he should be tried by the civil power, the primate asserted that it was iniquitous to try a man twice upon the same accusation and for the same offence.[37]

Henry, laying hold of so plausible a pretence, resolved to push the clergy with regard to all their privileges, which they had raised to an enormous height, and to determine at once those controversies which daily multiplied between the civil and the ecclesiastical jurisdictions. He summoned an assembly of all the prelates of England, and he put to them this concise and decisive question, whether or not they were willing to submit to the ancient laws and customs of the kingdom? The bishops unanimously replied that they were willing, *saving their own order*[38]—a device by which they thought to elude the present urgency of the king's demand, yet reserve to themselves on a favorable opportunity the power of resuming all their pretensions. The king was sensible of the artifice, and was provoked to the highest indignation. He left the assembly with visible marks of his displeasure; he required the primate instantly to surrender the honors and castles of Eye and Berkham; the bishops were terrified, and expected still further effects of his resentment. Becket alone was inflexible; and nothing but the interposition of the pope's legate and almoner, Philip, who dreaded a breach with so powerful a prince at so unseasonable a juncture, could have prevailed on him to retract the saving clause and give a general and absolute promise of observing the ancient customs.[39]

[35] Gul. Neub. p. 394.　　　　[36] Fitz-Steph. p. 33.　Hist. Quad. p. 32.
[37] Fitz-Steph. p. 29.　Hist. Quad. pp. 33, 45.　Hoveden, p. 492.　Matt. Paris, p. 72.　Diceto, pp. 536, 537.　Brompton, p. 1058.　Gervase, p. 1394.　Epist. St. Thom. pp. 208. 209.
[38] Fitz-Steph. p. 31.　Hist. Quad. p. 34.　Hoveden, p. 492.
[39] Hist. Quad. p. 37.　Hoveden, p. 493.　Gervase, p. 1385.

But Henry was not content with a declaration in these general terms; he resolved, ere it was too late, to define expressly those customs with which he required compliance, and to put a stop to clerical usurpations before they were fully consolidated, and could plead antiquity, as they already did a sacred authority, in their favor. The claims of the Church were open and visible. After a gradual and insensible progress during many centuries the mask had at last been taken off, and several ecclesiastical councils by their canons, which were pretended to be irrevocable and infallible, had positively defined those privileges and immunities which gave such general offence and appeared so dangerous to the civil magistrate. Henry, therefore, deemed it necessary to define with the same precision the limits of the civil power; to oppose his legal customs to their divine ordinances; to determine the exact boundaries of the rival jurisdictions; and for this purpose he summoned a general council of the nobility and prelates at Clarendon, to whom he submitted this great and important question.

[1164.] The barons were all gained to the king's party either by the reasons which he urged or by his superior authority; the bishops were overawed by the general combination against them; and the following laws, commonly called the *Constitutions of Clarendon,* were voted without opposition by this assembly.[40] It was enacted that all suits concerning the advowson and presentation of churches should be determined in the civil courts; that the churches belonging to the king's see should not be granted in perpetuity without his consent; that clerks accused of any crime should be tried in the civil courts; that no person, particularly no clergyman of any rank, should depart the kingdom without the king's license; that excommunicated persons should not be bound to give security for continuing in their present place of abode; that laics should not be accused in spiritual courts except by legal and reputable promoters and witnesses; that no chief tenant of the crown should be excommunicated, nor his lands be put under an interdict, except with the king's consent; that all appeals in spiritual causes should be carried from the archdeacon to the bishop, from the bishop to the primate, from him to the king, and should be carried no further without the king's consent; that if any lawsuit arose between a layman and a clergyman concerning a tenant, and it be disputed whether

---

[40] Fitz-Steph. p. 33.

the land be a lay or an ecclesiastical fee, it should first be determined by the verdict of twelve lawful men to what class it belonged; and if it be found to be a lay fee, the cause should finally be determined in the civil courts; that no inhabitant in demesne should be excommunicated for non-appearance in a spiritual court, till the chief officer of the place where he resides be consulted, that he may compel him by the civil authority to give satisfaction to the Church; that the archbishops, bishops, and other spiritual dignitaries should be regarded as barons of the realm; should possess the privileges and be subjected to the burdens belonging to that rank; and should be bound to attend the king in his great councils, and assist at all trials till the sentence, either of death or loss of members, be given against the criminal; that the revenue of vacant sees should belong to the king; the chapter, or such of them as he pleases to summon, should sit in the king's chapel till they made the new election with his consent, and that the bishop elect should do homage to the crown; that if any baron or tenant *in capite* should refuse to submit to the spiritual courts, the king should employ his authority in obliging him to make such submissions; if any of them throw off his allegiance to the king, the prelates should assist the king with their censures in reducing him; that goods forfeited to the king should not be protected in churches or church-yards; that the clergy should no longer pretend to the right of enforcing payment of debts contracted by oath or promise, but should leave these lawsuits, equally with others, to the determination of the civil courts; and that the sons of villeins should not be ordained clerks without the consent of their lord.[41]

These articles, to the number of sixteen, were calculated to prevent the chief abuses which had prevailed in ecclesiastical affairs, and to put an effectual stop to the usurpations of the Church, which, gradually stealing on, had threatened the total destruction of the civil power. Henry, therefore, by reducing those ancient customs of the realm to writing, and by collecting them in a body, endeavored to prevent all future dispute with regard to them; and by passing so many ecclesiastical ordinances in a national and civil assembly, he fully established the superiority of the legislature above all papal decrees or spiritual canons, and gained a signal victory over the ecclesiastics. But as he knew that the

[41] Hist. Quad. p. 163. Matt Paris, pp. 70, 71. Spell. Conc. vol. p. 63. Gervase, pp. 1386, 1387. Wilkins, p. 321.

bishops, though overawed by the present combination of the crown and the barons, would take the first favorable opportunity of denying the authority which had enacted these constitutions, he resolved that they should all set their seal to them, and give a promise to observe them. None of the prelates dared to oppose his will, except Becket, who, though urged by the Earls of Cornwall and Leicester, the barons of principal authority of the kingdom, obstinately withheld his assent. At last Richard de Hastings, Grand Prior of the Templars in England, threw himself on his knees before him, and with many tears entreated him, if he paid any regard either to his own safety or that of the Church, not to provoke by a fruitless opposition the indignation of a great monarch, who was resolutely bent on his purpose, and who was determined to take full revenge on every one that should dare to oppose him.[42] Becket, finding himself deserted by all the world, even by his own brethren, was at last obliged to comply ; and he promised, *legally, with good faith, and without fraud or reserve*,[43] to observe the constitutions ; and he took an oath to that purpose.[44] The king, thinking that he had now finally prevailed in this great enterprise, sent the constitutions to Pope Alexander, who then resided in France ; and he required that pontiff's ratification of them ; but Alexander, who, though he had owed the most important obligations to the king, plainly saw that these laws were calculated to establish the independency of England of the papacy, and of the royal power of the clergy, condemned them in the strongest terms, abrogated, annulled, and rejected them. There were only six articles (the least important) which, for the sake of peace, he was willing to ratify.

Becket, when he observed that he might hope for support in an opposition, expressed the deepest sorrow for his compliance ; and endeavored to engage all the other bishops in a confederacy to adhere to their common rights, and to the ecclesiastical privileges, in which he represented the interest and honor of God to be so deeply concerned. He redoubled his austerities, in order to punish himself for his criminal assent to the constitutions of Clarendon. He proportioned his discipline to the enormity of his supposed offence, and he refused to exercise any part of his archiepis-

---

[42] Hist. Quad. p. 38. Hoveden, p. 493.
[43] Fitz-Steph. p. 35. Epist. St. Thom. p. 25.
[44] Fitz-Steph. p. 45. Hist. Quad. p. 39. Gervase, p. 1386.

copal function till he should receive absolution from the pope, which was readily granted him. Henry, informed of his present dispositions, resolved to take vengeance for this refractory behavior, and he attempted to crush him by means of that very power which Becket made such merit in supporting. He applied to the pope that he should grant the commission of legate in his dominions to the Archbishop of York ; but Alexander, as politic as he, though he granted the commission, annexed a clause that it should not empower the legate to execute any act in prejudice of the Archbishop of Canterbury ; [45] and the king, finding how fruitless such an authority would prove, sent back the commission by the same messenger that brought it. [46]

The primate, however, who found himself still exposed to the king's indignation, endeavored twice to escape secretly from the kingdom, but was as often detained by contrary winds ; and Henry hastened to make him feel the effects of an obstinacy which he deemed so criminal. He instigated John, mareschal of the exchequer, to sue Becket in the archiepiscopal court for some lands, part of the manor of Pageham, and to appeal thence to the king's court for justice. [47] On the day appointed for trying the cause, the primate sent four knights to represent certain irregularities in John's appeal; and at the same time to excuse himself, on account of sickness, for not appearing personally that day in the court. This slight offence (if it even deserve the name) was represented as a grievous contempt; the four knights were menaced, and with difficulty escaped being sent to prison as offering falsehoods to the court. [48] And Henry, being determined to prosecute Becket to the utmost, summoned at Northampton a great council, which he proposed to make the instrument of his vengeance against the inflexible prelate.

The king had raised Becket from a low station to the highest offices, had honored him with his countenance and friendship, had trusted to his assistance in forwarding his favorite project against the clergy; and when he found him become of a sudden his most rigid opponent, while every one besides complied with his will, rage at the disappointment, and indignation against such signal ingratitude, transported him beyond all bounds of moderation ; and there

[45] Epist. St. Thom. pp. 13, 14.   [46] Hoveden, p. 493, Gervase, p. 1388.
[47] Hoveden, p. 494. Matt. Paris, p. 72. Diceto, p. 537.
[48] See note [R] at the end of the volume.

seems to have entered more of passion than of justice, or
even of policy, in this violent prosecution.[49] The barons,
notwithstanding, in the great council voted whatever sentence he was pleased to dictate to them; and the bishops
themselves, who undoubtedly bore a secret favor to Becket,
and regarded him as the champion of their privileges, concurred with the rest in the design of oppressing their primate. In vain did Becket urge that his court was proceeding with the utmost regularity and justice in trying the
mareschal's cause; which, however, he said would appear,
from the sheriff's testimony, to be entirely unjust and iniquitous; that he himself had discovered no contempt of the
king's court, but, on the contrary, by sending four knights
to excuse his absence, he had virtually acknowledged its
authority; that he also, in consequence of the king's summons, personally appeared at present in the great council,
ready to justify his cause against the mareschal, and to submit his conduct to their inquiry and jurisdiction; that even
should it be found that he had been guilty of non-appearance, the laws had affixed a very slight penalty to that
offence; and that, as he was an inhabitant of Kent, where
his archiepiscopal palace was seated, he was by law entitled
to some greater indulgence than usual in the rate of his
fine.[50] Notwithstanding these pleas, he was condemned as
guilty of a contempt of the king's court, and as wanting in
the fealty which he had sworn to his sovereign. All his
goods and chattels were confiscated;[51] and that this triumph
over the Church might be carried to the utmost, Henry,
Bishop of Winchester, the prelate who had been so powerful in the former reign, was, in spite of his remonstrances,
obliged by order of the court to pronounce the sentence
against him.[52] The primate submitted to the decree; and
all the prelates, except Folliot, Bishop of London, who paid
court to the king by this singularity, became sureties for
him.[53] It is remarkable that several Norman barons voted
in this council; and we may conclude, with some probability,
that a like practice had prevailed in many of the great councils summoned since the Conquest. For the contemporary
historian who has given us a full account of these transactions does not mention this circumstance as anywise singular;[54] and Becket, in all his subsequent remonstrances with

[49] Gul. Neub. p. 394.   [50] Fitz-Steph. pp. 37, 42.
[51] Hist. Quad. p. 47.   Hoveden, p. 494.   Gervase, p. 1389.
[52] Fitz-Steph. p. 37.   [53] Ibid.   [54] Fitz-Steph. p. 36.

regard to the severe treatment which he had met with, never founds any objection on an irregularity which to us appears very palpable and flagrant. So little precision was there at that time in the government and constitution!

The king was not content with this sentence, however violent and oppressive. Next day he demanded of Becket the sum of three hundred pounds, which the primate had levied upon the honors of Eye and Berkham while in his possession. Becket, after premising that he was not obliged to answer to this suit because it was not contained in his summons, after remarking that he had expended more than that sum in the repairs of those castles and of the royal palace at London, expressed, however, his resolution that money should not be any ground of quarrel between him and his sovereign. He agreed to pay the sum, and immediately gave sureties for it.[55] In the subsequent meeting the king demanded five hundred marks, which, he affirmed, he had lent Becket during the war at Toulouse;[56] and another sum to the same amount for which that prince had been surety for him to a Jew. Immediately after these two claims he preferred a third of still greater importance. He required him to give in the accounts of his administration while chancellor, and to pay the balance due from the revenues of all the prelacies, abbeys, and baronies which had, during that time, been subjected to his management.[57] Becket observed that, as this demand was totally unexpected, he had not come prepared to answer it; but he required a delay, and promised in that case to give satisfaction. The king insisted upon sureties, and Becket desired leave to consult his suffragans in a case of such importance.[58]

It is apparent, from the known character of Henry and from the usual vigilance of his government, that when he promoted Becket to the see of Canterbury he was, on good grounds, well pleased with his administration in the former high office with which he had intrusted him; and that, even if that prelate had dissipated money beyond the income of his place, the king was satisfied that his expenses were not blamable, and had in the main been calculated for his service.[59] Two years had since elapsed. No demand had during that time been made upon him. It was not till the quarrel arose concerning ecclesiastical privileges that the

[55] Fitz-Steph. p. 38. [56] Hist. Quad. p. 47. [57] Hoveden, p. 494. Diceto, p. 537.
[58] Fitz-Steph. p. 38. [59] Hoveden, p. 495.

claim was started, and the primate was of a sudden required to produce accounts of such intricacy and extent before a tribunal which had shown a determined resolution to ruin and oppress him. To find sureties that he should answer so boundless and uncertain a claim, which in the king's estimation amounted to forty-four thousand marks,[60] was impracticable; and Becket's suffragans were extremely at a loss what counsel to give him in such a critical emergency. By the advice of the Bishop of Winchester, he offered two thousand marks as a general satisfaction for all demands; but this offer was rejected by the king.[61] Some prelates exhorted him to resign his see, on condition of receiving an acquittal; others were of opinion that he ought to submit himself entirely to the king's mercy;[62] but the primate, thus pushed to the utmost, had too much courage to sink under oppression. He determined to brave all his enemies, to trust to the sacredness of his character for protection, to involve his cause with that of God and religion, and to stand the utmost efforts of royal indignation.

After a few days spent in deliberation, Becket went to church and said mass, where he had previously ordered that the Introit to the communion-service should begin with these words, *Princes sat, and spake against me*—the passage appointed for the martyrdom of St. Stephen, whom the primate thereby tacitly pretended to resemble in his sufferings for the sake of righteousness. He went thence to court, arrayed in his sacred vestments. As soon as he arrived within the palace-gate, he took the cross into his own hands, bore it aloft as his protection, and marched in that posture into the royal apartments.[63] The king, who was in an inner room, was astonished at this parade, by which the primate seemed to menace him and his court with the sentence of excommunication, and he sent some of the prelates to remonstrate with him on account of such audacious behavior. These prelates complained to Becket that by subscribing himself to the constitutions of Clarendon he had seduced them to imitate his example; and that now, when it was too late, he pretended to shake off all subordination to the civil power, and appeared desirous of involving them in the guilt which must attend any violation of those laws established by their consent and ratified by their

---

[60] Epist. St. Thom. p. 315.　　　　[61] Fitz-Steph. p. 38.

[62] Fitz-Steph. p. 39.　Gervase, p. 1390.

[63] Fitz-Steph. p. 40.　Hist. Quad. p. 53.　Hoveden, p. 404.　Gul. Neub. p. 394. Epist. St. Thom. p. 43.

subscriptions.[64] Becket replied that he had indeed subscribed the constitutions of Clarendon, *legally, with good faith, and without fraud or reserve;* but in these words was virtually implied a salvo for the rights of their order, which, being connected with the cause of God and his Church, could never be relinquished by their oaths and engagements; that if he and they had erred in resigning the ecclesiastical privileges, the best atonement they could now make was to retract their consent, which, in such a case, could never be obligatory, and to follow the pope's authority, who had solemnly annulled the constitutions of Clarendon, and had absolved them from all oaths which they had taken to observe them; that a determined resolution was evidently embraced to oppress the Church. The storm had first broken upon him; for a slight offence, and which, too, was falsely imputed to him, he had been tyrannically condemned to a grievous penalty; a new and unheard-of claim was since started, in which he could expect no justice; and he plainly saw that he was the destined victim, who, by his ruin, must prepare the way for the abrogation of all spiritual immunities; that he strictly inhibited them who were his suffragans from assisting at any such trial, or giving their sanction to any sentence against him; he put himself and his see under the protection of the supreme pontiff; and appealed to him against any penalty which his iniquitous judges might think proper to inflict upon him; and that, however terrible the indignation of so great a monarch as Henry, his sword could only kill the body; while that of the Church, intrusted into the hands of the primate, could kill the soul, and throw the disobedient into infinite and eternal perdition.[65]

Appeals to the pope, even in ecclesiastical causes, had been abolished by the constitutions of Clarendon, and were become criminal by law; but an appeal in a civil cause, such as the king's demand upon Becket, was a practice altogether new and unprecedented; it tended directly to the subversion of the government, and could receive no color of excuse, except from the determined resolution, which was but too apparent in Henry and the great council, to effectuate, without justice, but under color of law, the total ruin of the inflexible primate. The king, having now obtained a pretext so much more plausible for his violence, would prob-

[64] Fitz-Steph. p. 53.
[65] Fitz-Steph. pp. 42, 44, 45, 46. Hist. Quad. p. 57. Hoveden, p. 495. Matt. Paris, p. 72. Epist. St. Thom. pp. 45, 195.

ably have pushed the affair to the utmost extremity against him, but Becket gave him no leisure to conduct the prosecution. He refused so much as to hear the sentence which the barons, sitting apart from the bishops, and joined to some sheriffs and barons of the second rank,[66] had given upon the king's claim. He departed from the palace; asked Henry's immediate permission to leave Northampton; and upon meeting with a refusal, he withdrew secretly, wandered about in disguise for some time, and at last took shipping and arrived safely at Gravelines.

The violent and unjust prosecution of Becket had a natural tendency to turn the public favor on his side, and to make men overlook his former ingratitude towards the king, and his departure from all oaths and engagements, as well as the enormity of those ecclesiastical privileges of which he affected to be the champion. There were many other reasons which procured him countenance and protection in foreign countries. Philip, Earl of Flanders,[67] and Lewis, King of France,[68] jealous of the rising greatness of Henry, were well pleased to give him disturbance in his government; and, forgetting that this was the common cause of princes, they affected to pity extremely the condition of the exiled primate; and the latter even honored him with a visit at Soissons, in which city he had invited him to fix his residence.[69] The pope, whose interests were more immediately concerned in supporting him, gave a cold reception to a magnificent embassy which Henry sent to accuse him; while Becket himself, who had come to Sens in order to justify his cause before the sovereign pontiff, was received with the greatest marks of distinction. The king, in revenge, sequestered the revenues of Canterbury; and, by a conduct which might be esteemed arbitrary had there been at that time any regular check on royal authority, he banished all the primate's relations and domestics, to the number of four hundred, whom he obliged to swear, before their departure, that they would instantly join their patron. But this policy, by which Henry endeavored to reduce Becket sooner to necessity, lost its effect. The pope, when they arrived beyond sea, absolved them from their oath, and dis-

---

[66] Fitz-Steph. p. 46. This historian is supposed to mean the more considerable vassals of the chief barons : these had no title to sit in the great council, and the giving them a place there was a palpable irregularity, which, however, is not insisted on in any of Becket's remonstrances. A further proof how little fixed the constitution was at that time.

[67] Epist. St. Thom. p. 35.   [68] Epist. St. Thom. pp. 36, 37.   [69] Hist. Quad. p. 76.

tributed them among the convents in France and Flanders : a residence was assigned to Becket himself in the convent of Pontigny, where he lived for some years in great magnificence, partly from a pension granted him on the revenues of that abbey, partly from remittances made him by the French monarch.

[1165.] The more to ingratiate himself with the pope, Becket resigned into his hands the see of Canterbury, to which he affirmed he had been uncanonically elected by the authority of the royal mandate ; and Alexander, in his turn, besides investing him anew with that dignity, pretended to abrogate, by a bull, the sentence which the great council of England had passed against him. Henry, after attempting in vain to procure a conference with the pope, who departed soon after for Rome, whither the prosperous state of his affairs now invited him, made provisions against the consequences of that breach which impended between his kingdom and the apostolic see. He issued orders to his justiciaries inhibiting, under severe penalties, all appeals to the pope or archbishop ; forbidding any one to receive any mandates from them, or apply in any case to their authority ; declaring it treasonable to bring from either of them an interdict upon the kingdom, and punishable in secular clergymen by the loss of their eyes and by castration, in regulars by amputation of their feet, and in laics with death ; and menacing with sequestration and banishment the persons themselves, as well as their kindred, who should pay obedience to any such interdict ; and he further obliged all his subjects to swear to the observance of those orders.[70] These were edicts of the utmost importance, affected the lives and properties of all the subjects, and even changed, for the time, the national religion by breaking off all communication with Rome ; yet were they enacted by the sole authority of the king, and were derived entirely from his will and pleasure.

The spiritual powers, which, in the primitive Church, were in a great measure dependent on the civil, had, by a gradual progress, reached an equality and independence ; and though the limits of the two jurisdictions were difficult to ascertain or define, it was not impossible but, by moderation on both sides, government might still have been conducted in that imperfect and irregular manner which attends all human institutions. But as the ignorance of the

[70] Hist. Quad. pp. 88, 167. Hoveden, p. 496. Matt. Paris, p. 73.

age encouraged the ecclesiastics daily to extend their privileges, and even to advance maxims totally incompatible with civil government,[71] Henry had thought it high time to put an end to their pretensions, and formally, in a public council, to fix those powers which belonged to the magistrate, and which he was for the future determined to maintain. In this attempt he was led to re-establish customs which, though ancient, were beginning to be abolished by a contrary practice, and which were still more strongly opposed by the prevailing opinions and sentiments of the age. Principle, therefore, stood on the one side, power on the other; and if the English had been actuated by conscience more than by present interest, the controversy must soon, by the general defection of Henry's subjects, have been decided against him. Becket, in order to forward this event, filled all places with exclamations against the violence which he had suffered. He compared himself to Christ, who had been condemned by a lay tribunal,[72] and who was crucified anew in the present oppressions under which his Church labored; he took it for granted, as a point incontestable, that his cause was the cause of God;[73] he assumed the character of champion for the patrimony of the Divinity; he pretended to be the spiritual father of the king and all the people of England;[74] he even told Henry that kings reigned solely by the authority of the Church;[75] and though he had thus torn off the veil more openly on the one side than that prince had on the other, he seemed still, from the general favor borne him by the ecclesiastics, to have all the advantage in the argument. The king, that he might employ the weapons of temporal power remaining in his hands, suspended the payment of Peter's pence; he made advances towards an alliance with the Emperor Frederic Barbarossa, who was at that time engaged in violent wars with Pope Alexander; he discovered some intentions of acknowledging Pascal III., the present anti-pope, who was protected by that emperor; and by these expedients he endeavored to terrify the enterprising though prudent pontiff from proceeding to extremities against him.

But the violence of Becket, still more than the nature of

---

[71] "Quis dubitet," says Becket to the king, "sacerdotes Christi regum et principum omniumque fidelium patres et magistros censeri." Epist. St. Thom. pp. 97, 148.

[72] Epist. St. Thom. pp. 63, 105, 194.   [73] Epist. St. Thom. pp. 29, 30, 31, 226.

[74] Fitz-Steph. p. 46.   Epist. St. Thom. pp. 52, 148.

[75] Brady's Append. No. 36.   Epist. St, Thom. pp. 94, 95, 97, 99, 197.   Hoveden, p. 497.

the controversy, kept affairs from remaining long in suspense between the parties. [1166.] That prelate, instigated by revenge and animated by the present glory attending his situation, pushed matters to a decision, and issued a censure excommunicating the king's chief ministers by name, and comprehending in general all those who favored or obeyed the constitutions of Clarendon. These constitutions he abrogated and annulled; he absolved all men from the oaths which they had taken to observe them; and he suspended the spiritual thunder over Henry himself, only that the prince might avoid the blow by a timely repentance.[76]

The situation of Henry was so unhappy that he could employ no expedient for saving his ministers from this terrible censure but by appealing to the pope himself, and having recourse to a tribunal whose authority he had himself attempted to abridge in this very article of appeals, and which, he knew, was so deeply engaged on the side of his adversary. But even this expedient was not likely to be long effectual. Becket had obtained from the pope a legatine commission over England; and, in virtue of that authority, which admitted of no appeal, he summoned the Bishops of London, Salisbury, and others to attend him, and ordered, under pain of excommunication, the ecclesiastics sequestered on his account to be restored in two months to all their benefices. But John of Oxford, the king's agent with the pope, had the address to procure orders for suspending this sentence; and he gave the pontiff such hopes of a speedy reconcilement between the king and Becket that two legates, William of Pavia and Otho, were sent to Normandy, where the king then resided, and they endeavored to find expedients for that purpose. But the pretensions of the parties were as yet too opposite to admit of an accommodation. The king required that all the constitutions of Clarendon should be ratified; Becket, that previously to any agreement he and his adherents should be restored to their possessions; and as the legates had no power to pronounce a definitive sentence on either side, the negotiation soon after came to nothing. The Cardinal of Pavia also, being much attached to Henry, took care to protract the negotiation—to mitigate the pope by the accounts which he sent of that prince's conduct, and to procure him every possible indulgence from the see of Rome.

[76] Fitz-Steph. p. 56. Hist. Quad. p. 93. Matt. Paris, p. 74. Beaulieu, Vie de St. Thom. p. 213. Epist. St. Thom. pp. 149, 229. Hoveden, p. 499.

About this time the king had also the address to obtain a
dispensation for the marriage of his third son, Geoffrey, with
the heiress of Brittany—a concession which, considering
Henry's demerits towards the Church, gave great scandal
both to Becket and to his zealous patron, the King of
France.

[1167.] The intricacies of the feudal law had in that
age rendered the boundaries of power between the prince
and his vassals, and between one prince and another, as uncertain as those between the crown and the mitre; and all
wars took their origin from disputes which, had there been
any tribunal possessed of power to enforce their decrees,
ought to have been decided only before a court of judicature.
Henry, in prosecution of some controversies in which he was
involved with the Count of Auvergne, a vassal of the duchy
of Guienne, had invaded the territories of that nobleman,
who had recourse to the King of France, his superior lord,
for protection, and thereby kindled a war between the two
monarchs. But this war was, as usual, no less feeble in its
operations than it was frivolous in its cause and object;
and, after occasioning some mutual depredations,[77] and some
insurrections among the barons of Poictou and Guienne,
was terminated by a peace. The terms of this peace were
rather disadvantageous to Henry, and prove that that prince
had, by reason of his contest with the Church, lost the
superiority which he had hitherto maintained over the
crown of France—an additional motive to him for accommodating those differences.

The pope and the king began at last to perceive that, in
the present situation of affairs, neither of them could expect
a final and decisive victory over the other, and that they
had more to fear than to hope from the duration of the controversy. Though the vigor of Henry's government had
confirmed his authority in all his dominions, his throne
might be shaken by a sentence of excommunication ; and if
England itself could, by its situation, be more easily guarded
against the contagion of superstitious prejudices, his French
provinces at least, whose communication was open with the
neighboring states, would be much exposed on that account
to some great revolution or convulsion.[78] He could not
therefore reasonably imagine that the pope, while he retained
such a check upon him, would formally recognize the con-

[77] Hoveden, p. 517. Matt. Paris, p. 75. Diceto, p. 547. Gervase, pp. 1402,
1403. Robert de Monte.   [78] Epist. St. Thom. p. 230.

stitutions of Clarendon, which both put an end to papal pretensions in England, and would give an example to other states of asserting a like independency.[79] [1168.] Pope Alexander, on the other hand, being still engaged in dangerous wars with the Emperor Frederic, might justly apprehend that Henry, rather than relinquish claims of such importance, would join the party of his enemy; and as the trials hitherto made of the spiritual weapons by Becket had not succeeded to his expectation, and everything had remained quiet in all the king's dominions, nothing seemed impossible to the capacity and vigilance of so great a monarch. The disposition of minds on both sides, resulting from these circumstances, produced frequent attempts towards an accommodation; but as both parties knew that the essential articles of the dispute could not then be terminated, they entertained a perpetual jealousy of each other, and were anxious not to lose the least advantage in the negotiation. The nuncios, Gratian and Vivian, having received a commission to endeavor a reconciliation, met with the king in Normandy; and, after all differences seemed to be adjusted, Henry offered to sign the treaty, with a salvo to his royal dignity, which gave such umbrage to Becket that the negotiation, in the end, became fruitless, and the excommunications were renewed against the king's ministers. Another negotiation was conducted at Montmirail, in presence of the King of France and the French prelates, where Becket also offered to make his submissions with a salvo to the honor of God and the liberties of the Church, which, for the like reason, was extremely offensive to the king, and rendered the treaty abortive. [1169.] A third conference, under the same mediation, was broken off by Becket's insisting on a like reserve in his submission; and even a fourth treaty, when all the terms were adjusted, and when the primate expected to be introduced to the king, and to receive the kiss of peace which it was usual for princes to grant in those times, and which was regarded as a sure pledge of forgiveness, Henry refused him that honor, under pretence that, during his anger, he had made a rash vow to that purpose. This formality served, among such jealous spirits, to prevent the conclusion of the treaty; and though the difficulty was attempted to be overcome by a dispensation which the pope granted to Henry from his vow, that

[79] Epist. St. Thom. p. 276.

prince could not be prevailed on to depart from the resolution which he had taken.

In one of these conferences, at which the French king was present, Henry said to that monarch, " There have been many kings of England, some of greater, some of less authority than myself; there have also been many Archbishops of Canterbury, holy and good men, and entitled to every kind of respect; let Becket but act towards me with the same submission which the greatest of his predecessors have paid to the least of mine, and there shall be no controversy between us." Lewis was so struck with this state of the case, and with an offer which Henry made to submit his cause to the French clergy, that he could not forbear condemning the primate and withdrawing his friendship from him during some time; but the bigotry of that prince, and their common animosity against Henry, soon produced a renewal of their former good correspondence.

[1170.] All difficulties were at last adjusted between the parties; and the king allowed Becket to return on conditions which may be esteemed both honorable and advantageous to that prelate. He was not required to give up any rights of the Church, or resign any of those pretensions which had been the original ground of the controversy. It was agreed that all these questions should be buried in oblivion, but that Becket and his adherents should, without making further submission, be restored to all their livings, and that even the possessors of such benefices as depended on the see of Canterbury, and had been filled during the primate's absence, should be expelled, and Becket have liberty to supply the vacancies.[80] In return for concessions which intrenched so deeply on the honor and dignity of the crown, Henry reaped only the advantage of seeing his ministers absolved from the sentence of excommunication pronounced against them, and of preventing the interdict, which, if these hard conditions had not been complied with, was ready to be laid on all his dominions.[81] It was easy to see how much he dreaded that event, when a prince of so high a spirit could submit to terms so dishonorable in order to prevent it. So anxious was Henry to accommodate all differences, and to reconcile himself fully with Becket, that he took the most extraordinary steps to flatter his vanity, and even on

[80] Fitz-Steph. pp. 68, 69. Hoveden, p. 520.
[81] Hist. Quad. p. 104. Brompton, p. 1062. Gervase, p. 1408. Epist. St. Thom. pp. 704, 705, 706, 707, 792, 793, 794. Benedict. Abbas. p. 70.

one occasion humiliated himself so far as to hold the stirrup of that haughty prelate while he mounted.[82]

But the king attained not even that temporary tranquillity which he had hoped to reap from these expedients. During the heat of his quarrel with Becket, while he was every day expecting an interdict to be laid on his kingdom and a sentence of excommunication to be fulminated against his person, he had thought it prudent to have his son, Prince Henry, associated with him in the royalty, and to make him be crowned king by the hands of Roger, Archbishop of York. By this precaution he both insured the succession of that prince—which, considering the many past irregularities in that point, could not but be esteemed somewhat precarious—and he preserved at least his family on the throne, if the sentence of excommunication should have the effect which he dreaded, and should make his subjects renounce their allegiance to him. Though this design was conducted with expedition and secrecy, Becket, before it was carried into execution, had got intelligence of it; and being desirous of obstructing all Henry's measures, as well as anxious to prevent this affront to himself, who pretended to the sole right, as Archbishop of Canterbury, to officiate in the coronation, he had inhibited all the prelates of England from assisting at this ceremony, had procured from the pope a mandate to the same purpose,[83] and had incited the King of France to protest against the coronation of young Henry, unless the princess, daughter of that monarch, should at the same time receive the royal unction. There prevailed in that age an opinion, which was akin to its other superstitions, that the royal unction was essential to the exercise of royal power;[84] it was therefore natural both for the King of France, careful of his daughter's establishment, and for Becket, jealous of his own dignity, to demand, in the treaty with Henry, some satisfaction in this essential point. Henry, after apologizing to Lewis for the omission with regard to Margaret, and excusing it on account of the secrecy and despatch requisite for conducting that measure, promised that the ceremony should be renewed in the persons both of the prince and princess; and he assured Becket that, besides receiving the acknowledgments of Roger and the other bishops for the seeming affront put

[82] Epist. 45, lib. 5.
[83] Hist. Quad. p. 103. Epist. St. Thom. p. 682. Gervase, p. 1412.
[84] Epist. St. Thom. p. 708.

on the see of Canterbury, the primate should, as a further satisfaction, recover his rights by officiating in this coronation. But the violent spirit of Becket, elated by the power of the Church, and by the victory which he had already obtained over his sovereign, was not content with this voluntary compensation, but resolved to make the injury which he pretended to have suffered a handle for taking revenge on all his enemies. On his arrival in England, he met the Archbishop of York and the Bishops of London and Salisbury, who were on their journey to the king in Normandy; he notified to the archbishop the sentence of suspension, and to the two bishops that of excommunication, which, at his solicitation, the pope had pronounced against them. Reginald de Warenne and Gervase de Cornhill, two of the king's ministers who were employed on their duty in Kent, asked him, on hearing of this bold attempt, whether he meant to bring fire and sword into the kingdom. But the primate, heedless of the reproof, proceeded, in the most ostentatious manner, to take possession of his diocese. In Rochester and all the towns through which he passed he was received with the shouts and acclamations of the populace. As he approached Southwark, the clergy, the laity, men of all ranks and ages, came forth to meet him, and celebrated with hymns of joy his triumphant entrance. And though he was obliged, by order of the young prince, who resided at Woodstoke, to return to his diocese, he found that he was not mistaken when he reckoned upon the highest veneration of the public towards his person and his dignity. He proceeded, therefore, with the more courage to dart his spiritual thunders; he issued the sentence of excommunication against Robert de Brock and Nigel de Sackville, with many others who either had assisted at the coronation of the prince or been active in the late persecution of the exiled clergy. This violent measure, by which he in effect denounced war against the king himself, is commonly ascribed to the vindictive disposition and imperious character of Becket; but as this prelate was also a man of acknowledged abilities, we are not, in his passions alone, to look for the cause of his conduct, when he proceeded to these extremities against his enemies. His sagacity had led him to discover all Henry's intentions; and he proposed, by this bold and unexpected assault, to prevent the execution of them.

The king, from his experience of the dispositions of his

people, was become sensible that his enterprise had been too bold in establishing the constitutions of Clarendon, in defining all the branches of royal power, and in endeavoring to extort from the Church of England, as well as from the pope, an express avowal of these disputed prerogatives. Conscious also of his own violence in attempting to break or subdue the inflexible primate, he was not displeased to undo that measure which had given his enemies such advantage against him; and he was contented that the controversy should terminate in that ambiguous manner, which was the utmost that princes in those ages could hope to attain in their disputes with the see of Rome. Though he dropped for the present the prosecution of Becket, he still reserved to himself the right of maintaining that the constitutions of Clarendon, the original ground of the quarrel, were both the ancient customs and the present law of the realm; and though he knew that the papal clergy asserted them to be impious in themselves as well as abrogated by the sentence of the sovereign pontiff, he intended, in spite of their clamors, steadily to put those laws in execution,[85] and to trust to his own abilities and to the course of events for success in that perilous enterprise. He hoped that Becket's experience of a six years' exile would, after his pride was fully gratified by his restoration, be sufficient to teach him more reserve in his opposition; or, if any controversy arose, he expected thenceforth to engage in a more favorable cause, and to maintain with advantage, while the primate was now in his power,[86] the ancient and undoubted customs of the kingdom against the usurpations of the clergy. But Becket determined not to betray the ecclesiastical privileges by his connivance,[87] and, apprehensive lest a prince of such profound policy, if allowed to proceed in his own way, might probably in the end prevail, resolved to take all the advantage which his present victory gave him, and to disconcert the cautious measures of the king by the vehemence and vigor of his own conduct.[88] Assured of support from Rome, he was little intimidated by dangers which his courage taught him to despise, and which, even if attended with the most fatal consequences, would serve only to gratify his ambition and thirst of glory.[89]

When the suspended and excommunicated prelates ar-

[85] Epist. St. Thom. pp. 837, 839.   [86] Fitz-Steph. p. 65.
[87] Epist. St. Thom. p. 345.   [88] Fitz-Steph. p. 74.
[89] Epist. St. Thom. pp. 818 848.

rived at Baieux, where the king then resided, and complained to him of the violent proceedings of Becket, he instantly perceived the consequences, was sensible that his whole plan of operations was overthrown, foresaw that the dangerous contest between the civil and spiritual powers—a contest which he himself had first roused, but which he had endeavored, by all his late negotiations and concessions, to appease—must come to an immediate and decisive issue, and he was thence thrown into the most violent commotion. The Archbishop of York remarked to him that so long as Becket lived he could never expect to enjoy peace or tranquillity : the king himself, being vehemently agitated, burst forth into an exclamation against his servants, whose want of zeal, he said, had so long left him exposed to the enterprises of that ungrateful and imperious prelate.[90] Four gentlemen of his household—Reginald Fitz-Urse, William de Traci, Hugh de Moreville, and Richard Brito—taking these passionate expressions to be a hint for Becket's death, immediately communicated their thoughts to each other; and, swearing to avenge their prince's quarrel, secretly withdrew from court.[91] Some menacing expressions which they had dropped gave a suspicion of their design, and the king despatched a messenger after them, charging them to attempt nothing against the person of the primate ;[92] but these orders arrived too late to prevent their fatal purpose. The four assassins, although they took different roads to England, arrived nearly about the same time at Saltwoode, near Canterbury; and being there joined by some assistants, they proceeded in great haste to the archiepiscopal palace. They found the primate, who trusted entirely to the sacredness of his character, very slenderly attended ; and though they threw out many menaces and reproaches against him, he was so incapable of fear that, without using any precautions against their violence, he immediately went to St. Benedict's Church to hear vespers. They followed him thither, attacked him before the altar, and, having cloven his head with many blows, retired without meeting any opposition. This was the tragical end of Thomas à Becket, a prelate of the most lofty, intrepid, and inflexible spirit, who was able to cover to the world, and probably to himself, the enterprises of pride and ambition under the disguise of sanctity and of

[90] Gervase, p. 1414. Parker, p. 207.
[91] Matt. Paris, p. 86. Brompton, p. 1065. Benedict. Appas, p. 10.
[92] Hist. Quad. p. 144. Trivet, p. 55.

of zeal for the interests of religion; an extraordinary personage, surely, had he been allowed to remain in his first station, and had directed the vehemence of his character to the support of law and justice, instead of being engaged, by the prejudices of the times, to sacrifice all private duties and public connections to ties which he imagined or represented as superior to every civil and political consideration. But no man who enters into the genius of that age can reasonably doubt of this prelate's sincerity. The spirit of superstition was so prevalent that it infallibly caught every careless reasoner, much more every one whose interest and honor and ambition were engaged to support it. All the wretched literature of the times was enlisted on that side; some faint glimmerings of common-sense might sometimes pierce through the thick cloud of ignorance, or, what was worse, the illusions of perverted science, which had blotted out the sun and enveloped the face of nature. But those who preserved themselves untainted by the general contagion proceeded on no principles which they could pretend to justify; they were more indebted to their total want of instruction than to their knowledge, if they still retained some share of understanding. Folly was possessed of all the schools as well as all the churches; and her votaries assumed the garb of philosophers, together with the ensigns of spiritual dignities. Throughout the large collection of letters which bears the name of St. Thomas, we find, in all the retainers of that aspiring prelate, no less than in himself, a most entire and absolute conviction of the reason and piety of their own party and a disdain of their antagonists; nor is there less cant and grimace in their style when they address each other than when they compose manifestoes for the perusal of the public. The spirit of revenge, violence, and ambition which accompanied their conduct, instead of forming a presumption of hypocrisy, are the surest pledges of their sincere attachment to a cause which so much flattered these domineering passions.

Henry, on the first report of Becket's violent measures, had proposed to have him arrested, and had already taken some steps towards the execution of that design; but the intelligence of his murder threw the prince into great consternation, and he was immediately sensible of the dangerous consequences which he had reason to apprehend from so unexpected an event. An archbishop of reputed sanctity assassinated before the altar, in the exercise of his functions,

and on account of his zeal in maintaining ecclesiastical privileges, must attain the highest honors of martyrdom, while
his murderer would be ranked among the most bloody tyrants that ever were exposed to the hatred and detestation
of mankind. Interdicts and excommunications, weapons in
themselves so terrible, would, he foresaw, be armed with
double force when employed in a cause so much calculated
to work on the human passions, and so peculiarly adapted to
the eloquence of popular preachers and declaimers. In vain
would he plead his own innocence, and even his total ignorance of the fact; he was sufficiently guilty, if the Church
thought proper to esteem him such: and his concurrence in
Becket's martyrdom, becoming a religious opinion, would be
received with all the implicit credit which belonged to the
most established articles of faith. These considerations gave
the king the most unaffected concern; and as it was extremely
his interest to clear himself from all suspicion, he took no
care to conceal the depth of his affliction.[93] He shut himself up from the light of day, and from all commerce with
his servants: he even refused, during three days, all food
and sustenance.[94] The courtiers, apprehending dangerous
effects from his despair, were at last obliged to break in upon
his solitude; and they employed every topic of consolation,
induced him to accept of nourishment, and occupied his
leisure in taking precautions against the consequences which
he so justly apprehended from the murder of the primate.

[1171.] The point of chief importance to Henry was to
convince the pope of his innocence; or, rather, to persuade
him that he would reap greater advantages from the submissions of England than from proceeding to extremities
against that kingdom. The Archbishop of Rouen, the
Bishops of Worcester and Evreux, with five persons of inferior quality, were immediately despatched to Rome,[95] and
orders were given them to perform their journey with the utmost expedition. Though the name and authority of the court
of Rome were so terrible in the remote countries of Europe,
which were sunk in profound ignorance, and were entirely
unacquainted with its character and conduct, the pope was
so little revered at home that his inveterate enemies surrounded the gates of Rome itself, and even controlled his government in that city; and the ambassadors who from a distant extremity of Europe carried to him the humble, or rather

[93] Ypod. Neust. p. 447. Matt. Paris, p. 87. Diceto, p. 556. Gervase, p. 1419.
[94] Hist. Quad. p. 143.　　　　　　　[95] Hoveden, p. 526. Matt. Paris, p. 87.

abject, submissions of the greatest potentate of the age, found the utmost difficulty to make their way to him and to throw themselves at his feet. It was at length agreed that Richard Barre, one of their number, should leave the rest behind, and run all the hazards of the passage,[96] in order to prevent the fatal consequences which might ensue from any delay in giving satisfaction to his holiness. He found, on his arrival, that Alexander was already wrought up to the greatest rage against the king; that Becket's partisans were daily stimulating him to revenge; that the King of France had exhorted him to fulminate the most dreadful sentence against England; and that the very mention of Henry's name before the sacred college was received with every expression of horror and execration. The Thursday before Easter was now approaching, when it is customary for the pope to denounce annual curses against all his enemies; and it was expected that Henry should, with all the preparations peculiar to the discharge of that sacred artillery, be solemnly comprehended in the number. But Barre found means to appease the pontiff, and to deter him from a measure which, if it failed of success, could not afterwards be easily recalled: the anathemas were only levelled in general against all the actors, accomplices, and abettors of Becket's murder. The Abbot of Valasse and the Archdeacons of Salisbury and Lisieux, with others of Henry's ministers who soon after arrived, besides asserting their prince's innocence, made oath before the whole consistory that he would stand to the pope's judgment in the affair, and make every submission that should be required of him. The terrible blow was thus artfully eluded. The Cardinals Albert and Theodin were appointed legates to examine the cause, and were ordered to proceed to Normandy for that purpose; and though Henry's foreign dominions were already laid under an interdict by the Archbishop of Sens, Becket's great partisan and the pope's legate in France, the general expectation that the monarch would easily exculpate himself from any concurrence in the guilt kept every one in suspense, and prevented all the bad consequences which might be dreaded from that sentence.

The clergy, meanwhile, though their rage was happily diverted from falling on the king, were not idle in magnifying the sanctity of Becket, in extolling the merits of his martyrdom, and in exalting him above all that devoted tribe

[96] Hoveden, p. 26. Epist. St. Thom. p. 868.

who in several ages had, by their blood, cemented the fabric of the temple. Other saints had only borne testimony by their sufferings to the general doctrines of Christianity, but Becket had sacrificed his life to the power and privileges of the clergy; and this peculiar merit challenged, and not in vain, a suitable acknowledgment to his memory. Endless were the panegyrics on his virtues; and the miracles wrought by his relics were more numerous, more nonsensical, and more impudently attested than those which ever filled the legend of any confessor or martyr. Two years after his death he was canonized by Pope Alexander; a solemn jubilee was established for celebrating his merits; his body was removed to a magnificent shrine, enriched with presents from all parts of Christendom ; pilgrimages were performed to obtain his intercession with Heaven ; and it was computed that in one year above a hundred thousand pilgrims arrived in Canterbury and paid their devotions at his tomb. It is indeed a mortifying reflection to those who are actuated by the love of fame, so justly denominated the last infirmity of noble minds, that the wisest legislator and most exalted genius that ever reformed or enlightened the world can never expect such tributes of praise as are lavished on the memory of pretended saints, whose whole conduct was probably to the last degree odious or contemptible, and whose industry was entirely directed to the pursuit of objects pernicious to mankind. It is only a conqueror, a personage no less entitled to our hatred, who can pretend to the attainment of equal renown and glory.

It may not be amiss to remark, before we conclude the subject of Thomas à Becket, that the king, during his controversy with that prelate, was on every occasion more anxious than usual to express his zeal for religion, and to avoid all appearance of a profane negligence on that head. He gave his consent to the imposing of a tax on all his dominions for the delivery of the Holy Land, now threatened by the famous Saladin ; this tax amounted to twopence a pound for one year, and a penny a pound for the four subsequent.[97] Almost all the princes of Europe laid a like imposition on their subjects, which received the name of Saladin's tax. During this period there came over from Germany about thirty heretics of both sexes, under the direction of one Gerard : simple, ignorant people, who could give no account of their faith, but declared themselves ready to suffer for the

[97] Chron. Gervase, p. 1399.   Matt. Paris, p. 74.

tenets of their master. They made only one convert in England a woman as ignorant as themselves; yet they gave such umbrage to the clergy that they were delivered over to the secular arm, and were punished by being burned on the forehead and then whipped through the streets. They seemed to exult in their sufferings, and, as they went along, sang the beatitude, " Blessed are ye when men hate you and persecute you." [98] After they were whipped they were thrust out, almost naked, in the midst of winter, and per·ished through cold and hunger; no one daring, or being willing, to give them the least relief. We are ignorant of the particular tenets of these people; for it would be imprudent to rely on the representations left of them by the clergy, who affirmed that they denied the efficacy of the sacraments and the unity of the church. It is probable that their departure from the standard of orthodoxy was still more subtle and minute. They seem to have been the first that ever suffered for heresy in England.

As soon as Henry found that he was in no immediate danger from the thunders of the Vatican, he undertook an expedition against Ireland; a design which he had long projected, and by which he hoped to recover his credit, somewhat impaired by his late transactions with the hierarchy.

[98] Gul. Neub. p. 391. Matt. Paris, p. 74. Heming. p. 494.

CHAPTER IX.

STATE OF IRELAND.—CONQUEST OF THAT ISLAND.—THE KING'S ACCOMMODATION WITH THE COURT OF ROME.— REVOLT OF YOUNG HENRY AND HIS BROTHERS.—WARS AND INSURRECTIONS.—WAR WITH SCOTLAND.—PENANCE OF HENRY FOR BECKET'S MURDER.—WILLIAM, KING OF SCOTLAND, DEFEATED AND TAKEN PRISONER.—THE KING'S ACCOMMODATION WITH HIS SONS.—THE KING'S EQUITABLE ADMINISTRATION.—CRUSADES.—REVOLT OF PRINCE RICHARD.—DEATH AND CHARACTER OF HENRY. —MISCELLANEOUS TRANSACTIONS OF HIS REIGN.

[1172.] As Britain was first peopled from Gaul, so was Ireland probably from Britain; and the inhabitants of all these countries seem to have been so many tribes of the Celtæ, who derive their origin from an antiquity that lies far beyond the records of any history or tradition. The Irish, from the beginning of time, had been buried in the most profound barbarism and ignorance; and as they were never conquered or even invaded by the Romans, from whom all the western world derived its civility, they continued still in the most rude state of society, and were distinguished by those vices alone to which human nature, not tamed by education or restrained by laws, is forever subject. The small principalities into which they were divided exercised perpetual rapine and violence against each other; the uncertain succession of their princes was a continual source of domestic convulsions; the usual title of each petty sovereign was the murder of his predecessor; courage and force, though exercised in the commission of crimes, were more honored than any pacific virtues; and the most simple arts of life, even tillage and agriculture, were almost wholly unknown among them. They had felt the invasions of the Danes and the other northern tribes; but these inroads, which had spread barbarism in other parts of Europe, tended rather to improve the Irish; and the only towns which were to be found in the island had been planted along the coast by the freebooters of Norway and Denmark. The other inhabitants exercised pasturage in the open country; sought protection from any danger in their forests and morasses; and, being divided by the fiercest animosities against each other, were still more intent on the means of mutual injury than on the expedients for common, or even for private, interest.

Besides many small tribes, there were in the age of Henry II. five principal sovereignties in the island—Munster, Leinster, Meath, Ulster, and Connaught; and as it had been usual for the one or the other of these to take the lead in their wars, there was commonly some prince who seemed, for the time, to act as monarch of Ireland. Roderic O'Connor, King of Connaught, was then advanced to this dignity; [1] but his government, ill obeyed even within his own territory, could not unite the people in any measures either for the establishment of order or for defence against foreigners. The ambition of Henry had, very early in his reign, been moved by the prospect of these advantages to attempt the subjecting of Ireland; and a pretence was only wanting to invade a people who, being always confined to their own island, had never given any reason of complaint to any of their neighbors. For this purpose he had recourse to Rome, which assumed a right to dispose of kingdoms and empires; and, not foreseeing the dangerous disputes which he was one day to maintain with that see, he helped, for present, or rather for an imaginary, convenience to give sanction to claims which were now become dangerous to all sovereigns. Adrian III., who then filled the papal chair, was by birth an Englishman, and, being on that account the more disposed to oblige Henry, he was easily persuaded to act as master of the world, and to make, without any hazard or expense, the acquisition of a great island to his spiritual jurisdiction. The Irish had, by precedent missions from the Britons, been imperfectly converted to Christianity; and, what the pope regarded as the surest mark of their imperfect conversion, they followed the doctrines of their first teachers, and had never acknowledged any subjection to the see of Rome. Adrian, therefore, in the year 1156, issued a bull in favor of Henry, in which, after premising that this prince had ever shown an anxious care to enlarge the Church of God on earth and to increase the number of his saints and elect in heaven, he represents his design of subduing Ireland as derived from the same pious motives; he considers his care of previously applying for the apostolic sanction as a

[1] Hoveden, p. 527.

sure earnest of success and victory; and, having established it as a point incontestable, that all Christian kingdoms belong to the patrimony of St. Peter, he acknowledges it to be his own duty to sow among them the seeds of the gospel, which might in the last day fructify to their eternal salvation. He exhorts the king to invade Ireland, in order to extirpate the vice and wickedness of the natives, and oblige them to pay yearly from every house a penny to the see of Rome; he gives him entire right and authority over the island, commands all the inhabitants to obey him as their sovereign, and invests with full power all such godly instruments as he should think proper to employ in an enterprise thus calculated for the glory of God and the salvation of the souls of men.[2] Henry, though armed with this authority, did not immediately put his design in execution, but, being detained by more interesting business on the Continent, waited for a favorable opportunity of invading Ireland.

Dermot Macmorrogh, King of Leinster, had, by his licentious tyranny, rendered himself odious to his subjects, who seized with alacrity the first occasion that offered of throwing off the yoke, which was become grievous and oppressive to them. This prince had formed a design on Dovergilda, wife of Ororic, Prince of Breffny, and, taking advantage of her husband's absence (who, being obliged to visit a distant part of his territory, had left his wife secure, as he thought, in an island surrounded by a bog), he suddenly invaded the place and carried off the princess.[3] This exploit, though usual among the Irish, and rather deemed a proof of gallantry and spirit,[4] provoked the resentment of the husband, who, having collected forces, and being strengthened by the alliance of Roderic, King of Connaught, invaded the dominions of Dermot, and expelled him his kingdom. The exiled prince had recourse to Henry, who was at this time in Guienne, craved his assistance in restoring him to his sovereignty, and offered, on that event, to hold his kingdom in vassalage under the crown of England. Henry, whose views were already turned towards making acquisitions in Ireland, readily accepted the offer; but being at that time embarrassed by the rebellions of his French subjects, as well as by his disputes with the see of Rome, he declined for the present embarking in the enterprise, and gave Dermot no further assistance than letters patent, by which he em-

[2] Matt. Paris, p. 67.   Girald. Cambr.   Spell. Conc. vol. ii. p. 51.   Rymer, vol. i. p. 15.   [3] Girald. Cambr. p. 760.   [4] Spencer, vol. vi.

powered all his subjects to aid the Irish prince in the recovery of his dominions.[5] Dermot, supported by this authority, came to Bristol, and after endeavoring, though for some time in vain, to engage adventurers in the enterprise, he at last formed a treaty with Richard, surnamed Strongbow, Earl of Strigul. This nobleman, who was of the illustrious house of Clare, had impaired his fortune by expensive pleasures, and being ready for any desperate undertaking, he promised assistance to Dermot, on condition that he should espouse Eva, daughter of that prince, and be declared heir to all his dominions.[6] While Richard was assembling his succors, Dermot went into Wales, and meeting with Robert Fitz-Stephens, Constable of Abertivi, and Maurice Fitz-Gerald, he also engaged them in his service and obtained their promise of invading Ireland. Being now assured of succor, he returned privately to his own state, and lurking in the monastery of Fernes, which he had founded (for this ruffian was also a founder of monasteries), he prepared everything for the reception of his English allies.[7]

The troops of Fitz-Stephens were first ready. That gentleman landed in Ireland with thirty knights, sixty esquires, and three hundred archers; but this small body being brave men, not unacquainted with discipline, and completely armed—a thing almost unknown in Ireland—struck a great terror into the barbarous inhabitants, and seemed to menace them with some signal revolution. The conjunction of Maurice de Pendergast, who, about the same time, brought over ten knights and sixty archers, enabled Fitz-Stephens to attempt the siege of Wexford, a town inhabited by the Danes; and after gaining an advantage, he made himself master of the place.[8] Soon after, Fitz-Gerald arrived with ten knights, thirty esquires, and a hundred archers;[9] and being joined by the former adventurers, composed a force which nothing in Ireland was able to withstand. Roderic, the chief monarch of the island, was foiled in different actions; the Prince of Ossory was obliged to submit and give hostages for his peaceable behavior; and Dermot, not content with being restored to his kingdom of Leinster, projected the dethroning of Roderic, and aspired to the sole dominion over the Irish.

In prosecution of these views he sent over a messenger to the Earl of Strigul, challenging the performance of his

5 Girald. Cambr. p. 760.   6 Girald. Cambr. p. 761.   7 Ibid.
3 Girald. Cambr. pp. 761, 762.   9 Girald. Cambr. p. 766.

promise, and displaying the mighty advantages which might now be reaped by a reinforcement of warlike troops from England. Richard, not satisfied with the general allowance given by Henry to all his subjects, went to that prince, then in Normandy, and, having obtained a cold or ambiguous permission, prepared himself for the execution of his designs. He first sent over Raymond, one of his retinue, with ten knights and seventy archers, who, landing near Waterford, defeated a body of three thousand Irish that had ventured to attack him ; [10] and as Richard himself, who brought over two hundred horse and a body of archers, joined, a few days after, the victorious English, they made themselves masters of Waterford, and proceeded to Dublin, which was taken by assault. Roderic, in revenge, cut off the head of Dermot's natural son, who had been left as a hostage in his hands; and Richard, marrying Eva, became soon after, by the death of Dermot, master of the kingdom of Leinster, and prepared to extend his authority over all Ireland. Roderic and the other Irish princes were alarmed at the danger, and, combining together, besieged Dublin with an army of thirty thousand men ; but Earl Richard, making a sudden sally at the head of ninety knights, with their followers, put this numerous army to rout, chased them off the field, and pursued them with great slaughter. None in Ireland now dared to oppose themselves to the English.[11]

Henry, jealous of the progress made by his own subjects, sent orders to recall all the English, and he made preparations to attack Ireland in person ; [12] but Richard and the other adventurers found means to appease him by making him the most humble submissions, and offering to hold all their acquisitions in vassalage to his crown.[13] That monarch landed in Ireland at the head of five hundred knights besides other soldiers. He found the Irish so dispirited by their late misfortunes that, in a progress which he made through the island, he had no other occupation than to receive the homage of his new subjects. He left most of the Irish chieftains or princes in possession of their ancient territories ; bestowed some lands on the English adventurers ; gave Earl Richard the commission of Seneschal of Ireland ; and after a stay of a few months, returned in triumph to England. By these trivial exploits, scarcely worth relating except for the importance of the consequences, was Ireland subdued and annexed to the English crown.

[10] Girald. Cambr. p. 767.　　[11] Girald. Cambr. p. 773.
[12] Girald. Cambr. p. 770.　　[13] Girald. Cambr. p. 775.

The low state of commerce and industry during those ages made it impracticable for princes to support regular armies, which might retain a conquered country in subjection; and the extreme barbarism and poverty of Ireland could still less afford means of bearing the expense. The only expedient by which a durable conquest could then be made or maintained was by pouring in a multitude of new inhabitants, dividing among them the lands of the vanquished, establishing them in all offices of trust and authority, and thereby transforming the ancient inhabitants into a new people. By this policy, the northern invaders of old, and of late the Duke of Normandy, had been able to fix their dominions, and to erect kingdoms which remained stable on their foundations, and were transmitted to the posterity of the first conquerors. But the state of Ireland rendered that island so little inviting to the English that only a few of desperate fortunes could be persuaded, from time to time, to transport themselves thither; [14] and instead of reclaiming the natives from their uncultivated manners, they were gradually assimilated to the ancient inhabitants, and degenerated from the customs of their own nation. It was also found requisite to bestow great military and arbitrary powers on the leaders, who commanded a handful of men amid such hostile multitudes; and law and equity, in a little time, became as much unknown in the English settlements as they had ever been among the Irish tribes. Palatinates were erected in favor of the new adventurers; independent authority conferred. The natives, never fully subdued, still retained their animosity against the conquerors; their hatred was retaliated by like injuries; and from these causes the Irish, during the course of four centuries, remained still savage and untractable. It was not till the latter end of Elizabeth's reign that the island was fully subdued, nor till that of her successor that it gave hopes of becoming a useful conquest to the English nation.

Besides that the easy and peaceable submission of the Irish left Henry no further occupation in that island, he was recalled from it by another incident, which was of the last importance to his interest and safety. The two legates, Albert and Theodin, to whom was committed the trial of his conduct in the murder of Archbishop Becket, were arrived in Normandy; and, being impatient of delay, sent him frequent letters full of menaces if he protracted any longer

[14] Brompton, p. 1069. Gul. Neub. p. 403.

making his appearance before them.[15] He hastened therefore to Normandy, and had a conference with them at
Savigny, where their demands were so exorbitant that he
broke off the negotiation, threatened to return to Ireland,
and bade them do their worst against him. They perceived
that the season was now past for taking advantage of that
tragical incident; which, had it been hotly pursued by interdicts and excommunications, was capable of throwing the
whole kingdom into combustion. But the time which Henry
had happily gained had contributed to appease the minds
of men. The event could not now have the same influence
as when it was recent; and, as the clergy every day looked
for an accommodation with the king, they had not opposed
the pretensions of his partisans, who had been very industrious in representing to the people his entire innocence in
the murder of the primate, and his ignorance of the designs
formed by the assassins. The legates, therefore, found themselves obliged to lower their terms, and Henry was so fortunate as to conclude an accommodation with them. He declared upon oath, before the relics of the saints, that, so far
from commanding or desiring the death of the archbishop,
he was extremely grieved when he received intelligence of
it; but as the passion which he had expressed on account of
that prelate's conduct had probably been the occasion of his
murder, he stipulated the following conditions as an atonement for the offence. He promised that he should pardon
all such as had been banished for adhering to Becket, and
should restore them to their livings; that the see of Canterbury should be reinstated in all its ancient possessions;
that he should pay the Templars a sum of money for the
subsistence of two hundred knights during a year in the
Holy Land; that he should himself take the cross at the
Christmas following, and, if the pope required it, serve three
years against the infidels either in Spain or Palestine; that
he should not insist on the observance of such customs, derogatory to ecclesiastical privileges, as had been introduced
in his own time; and that he should not obstruct appeals to
the pope in ecclesiastical causes, but should content himself
with exacting sufficient security from such clergymen as left
his dominions to prosecute an appeal that they should attempt nothing against the rights of his crown.[16] Upon sign-

 [15] Girald. Cambr. p. 718.
 [16] Matt. Paris, p. 88. Benedict. Abb. p. 34. Hoveden, p. 529. Diceto, p. 560.
Chron. Gerv. p. 1422.

ing these concessions, Henry received absolution from the legates, and was confirmed in the grant of Ireland made by Pope Adrian; [17] and nothing proves more strongly the great abilities of this monarch than his extricating himself on such easy terms from so difficult a situation. He had always insisted that the laws established at Clarendon contained not any new claims, but the ancient customs of the kingdom, and he was still at liberty, notwithstanding the articles of this agreement, to maintain his pretensions. Appeals to the pope were indeed permitted by that treaty; but as the king was also permitted to exact reasonable securities from the parties, and might stretch his demands on this head as far as he pleased, he had it virtually in his power to prevent the pope from reaping any advantage by this seeming concession. And, on the whole, the constitutions of Clarendon remained still the law of the realm, though the pope and his legates seem so little to have conceived the king's power to lie under any legal limitations that they were satisfied with his departing, by treaty, from one of the most momentous articles of these constitutions without requiring any repeal by the states of the kingdom.

Henry, freed from this dangerous controversy with the ecclesiastics and with the see of Rome, seemed now to have reached the pinnacle of human grandeur and felicity, and to be equally happy in his domestic situation and in his political government. A numerous progeny of sons and daughters gave both lustre and authority to his crown, prevented the dangers of a disputed succession, and repressed all pretensions of the ambitious barons. The king's precaution, also, in establishing the several branches of his family seemed well calculated to prevent all jealousy among the brothers, and to perpetuate the greatness of his family. He had appointed Henry, his eldest son, to be his successor in the kingdom of England, the duchy of Normandy, and the counties of Anjou, Maine, and Touraine—territories which lay contiguous, and which by that means might easily lend to each other mutual assistance both against intestine commotions and foreign invasions. Richard, his second son, was invested in the duchy of Guienne and county of Poictou ; Geoffrey, his third son, inherited, in right of his wife, the duchy of Brittany ; and the new conquest of Ireland was destined for the appanage of John, his fourth son. He had also negotiated, in favor of this last prince, a marriage with Adelais,

[17] Brompton, p. 1071. Liber. Nig. Scac. p. 47.

the only daughter of Humbert, Count of Savoy and Mau-
rienne, and was to receive as her dowry considerable demesnes in Piedmont, Savoy, Bresse, and Dauphiny.[18] But
this exaltation of his family excited the jealousy of all his
neighbors, who made those very sons whose fortunes he had
so anxiously established the means of embittering his future
life and disturbing his government.

Young Henry, who was rising to man's estate, began to
display his character and aspire to independence. Brave,
ambitious, liberal, munificent, affable, he discovered qualities which give great lustre to youth, prognosticate a shining fortune, but unless tempered in mature age with discretion, are the forerunners of the greatest calamities.[19] It is
said that at the time when this prince received the royal
unction, his father, in order to give greater dignity to the
ceremony, officiated at table as one of the retinue, and observed to his son that never king was more royally served.
"It is nothing extraordinary," said young Henry to one of
his courtiers, "if the son of a count should serve the son of a
king." This saying, which might pass only for an innocent
pleasantry, or even for an oblique compliment to his father,
was, however, regarded as a symptom of his aspiring temper,
and his conduct soon after justified the conjecture.

Henry, agreeably to the promise which he had given
both to the pope and French king, permitted his son to be
crowned anew by the hands of the Archbishop of Rouen, and
associated the Princess Margaret, spouse to young Henry,
in the ceremony.[20] [1173.] He afterwards allowed him to
pay a visit to his father-in-law at Paris, who took the opportunity of instilling into the young prince those ambitious
sentiments to which he was naturally but too much inclined.[21] Though it had been the constant practice of
France, ever since the accession of the Capetian line, to
crown the son during the lifetime of the father, without
conferring on him any present participation of royalty,
Lewis persuaded his son-in-law that by this ceremony,
which in those ages was deemed so important, he had acquired a title to sovereignty, and that the king could not,
without injustice, exclude him from immediate possession

---

[18] Ypod. Neust. p. 448.   Benedict. Abb. p. 38.   Hoveden, p. 532.   Diceto, p.
562.   Brompton, p. 1081.   Rymer, vol. i. p. 33.   [19] Chron. Gerv. p. 1463.
[20] Hoveden, p. 529.   Diceto, p. 560.   Brompton, p. 1080.   Chron. Gerv. p. 1421.
Trivet, p. 58.   It appears from Madox's History of the Exchequer that silk gar-
ments were then known in England, and that the coronation robes of the young
king and queen cost eighty-seven pounds ten shillings and four pence, money of
that age.   [22] Girald. Cambr. p. 782.

of the whole, or at least a part, of his dominions. In consequence of these extravagant ideas, young Henry, on his return, desired the king to resign to him either the crown of England or the duchy of Normandy; discovered great discontent on the refusal; spoke in the most undutiful terms of his father; and soon after, in concert with Lewis, made his escape to Paris, where he was protected and supported by that monarch.

While Henry was alarmed at this incident and had the prospect of dangerous intrigues, or even of a war, which, whether successful or not, must be extremely calamitous and disagreeable to him, he received intelligence of new misfortunes, which must have affected him in the most sensible manner. Queen Eleanor, who had disgusted her first husband by her gallantries, was no less offensive to her second by her jealousy; and after this manner carried to extremity, in the different periods of her life, every circumstance of female weakness. She communicated her discontents against Henry to her two younger sons, Geoffrey and Richard; persuaded them that they were also entitled to present possession of the territories assigned to them; engaged them to fly secretly to the court of France; and was meditating, herself, an escape to the same court, and had even put on man's apparel for that purpose, when she was seized by orders from her husband, and thrown into confinement. Thus Europe saw with astonishment the best and most indulgent of parents at war with his whole family. Three boys, scarcely arrived at the age of puberty, required a great monarch, in the full vigor of his age and height of his reputation, to dethrone himself in their favor; and several princes not ashamed to support them in these unnatural and absurd pretensions.

Henry, reduced to this perilous and disagreeable situation, had recourse to the court of Rome. Though sensible of the danger attending the interposition of ecclesiastical authority in temporal disputes, he applied to the pope as his superior lord to excommunicate his enemies, and by these censures to reduce to obedience his undutiful children, whom he found such reluctance to punish by the sword of the magistrate.[22] Alexander, well pleased to exert his power in so justifiable a cause, issued the bulls required of him;

[22] Epist. Petri Bles. epist. 136, in Biblioth. Patr. vol. xxiv. p. 1048. His words are : " Vestræ jurisdictionis est regnum Angliæ, et quantum ad feudatorii juris obligationem, vobis duntaxat obnoxius teneor." The same strange paper is in Rymer, vol. i. p. 35, and Trivet, vol. i. p. 62.

but it was soon found that these spiritual weapons had not the same force as when employed in a spiritual controversy, and that the clergy were very negligent in supporting a sentence which was nowise calculated to promote the immediate interests of their order. The king, after taking in vain this humiliating step, was obliged to have recourse to arms, and to enlist such auxiliaries as are the usual resource of tyrants, and have seldom been employed by so wise and just a monarch.

The loose government which prevailed in all the states of Europe, the many private wars carried on among the neighboring nobles, and the impossibility of enforcing any general execution of the laws, had encouraged a tribe of banditti to disturb everywhere the public peace, to infest the highways, to pillage the open country, and to brave all the efforts of the civil magistrate, and even the excommunications of the Church which were fulminated against them.[23] Troops of them were sometimes enlisted in the service of one prince or baron, sometimes in that of another: they often acted in an independent manner, under leaders of their own. The peaceable and industrious inhabitants, reduced to poverty by their ravages, were frequently obliged, for subsistence, to betake themselves to a like disorderly course of life; and a continual intestine war, pernicious to industry as well as to the execution of justice, was thus carried on in the bowels of every kingdom.[24] Those desperate ruffians received the name sometimes of Brabançons, sometime of Routiers or Cottereaux, but for what reason is not agreed by historians; and they formed a kind of society or government among themselves which set at defiance the rest of mankind. The greatest monarchs were not ashamed, on occasion, to have recourse to their assistance; and as their habits of war and depredation had given them experience, hardiness, and courage, they generally composed the most formidable part of those armies which decided the political quarrels of princes. Several of them were enlisted among the forces levied by Henry's enemies;[25] but the great treasures amassed by that prince enabled him to engage more numerous troops of them in his service; and the situation of his affairs rendered even such banditti the only forces on whose fidelity he could repose any confidence. His licentious barons, disgusted with a vigilant government, were more desirous of being ruled by young princes, igno-

[23] Gul. Neub. p. 413.   [24] Chron. Gerv. p. 1461.   [25] Petr. Bles. epist. 47.

rant of public affairs, remiss in their conduct, and profuse in their grants; [26] and as the king had insured to his sons the succession to every particular province of his dominions, the nobles dreaded no danger in adhering to those who, they knew, must some time become their sovereigns. Prompted by these motives, many of the Norman nobility had deserted to his son Henry. The Breton and Gascon barons seemed equally disposed to embrace the quarrel of Geoffrey and Richard. Disaffection had crept in among the English, and the Earls of Leicester and Chester in particular had openly declared against the king. Twenty thousand Brabançons, therefore, joined to some troops which he brought over from Ireland, and a few barons of approved fidelity, formed the sole force with which he intended to resist his enemies.

Lewis, in order to bind the confederates in a closer union, summoned at Paris an assembly of the chief vassals of the crown, received their approbation of his measures, and engaged them by oath to adhere to the cause of young Henry. This prince, in return, bound himself by a like tie never to desert his French allies; and, having made a new great seal, he lavishly distributed among them many considerable parts of those territories which he proposed to conquer from his father. The Counts of Flanders, Boulogne, Blois, and Eu, partly moved by the general jealousy arising from Henry's power and ambition, partly allured by the prospect of reaping advantage from the inconsiderate temper and the necessities of the young prince, declared openly in favor of the latter. William, King of Scotland, had also entered into this great confederacy; and a plan was concerted for a general invasion on different parts of the king's extensive and factious dominions.

Hostilities were first commenced by the Counts of Flanders and Boulogne on the frontiers of Normandy. Those princes laid siege to Aumale, which was delivered into their hands by the treachery of the count of that name. This nobleman surrendered himself prisoner, and, on pretence of thereby paying his ransom, opened the gates of all his other fortresses. The two counts next besieged and made themselves masters of Drincourt; but the count of Boulogne was here mortally wounded in the assault, and this incident put some stop to the progress of the Flemish arms.

[26] Diceto, p. 570.

In another quarter the King of France, being strongly assisted by his vassals, assembled a great army of seven thousand knights and their followers on horseback, and a proportionable number of infantry. Carrying young Henry along with him, he laid siege to Verneuil, which was vigorously defended by Hugh de Lacy and Hugh de Beauchamp, the governors. After he had lain a month before the place, the garrison, being straitened for provisions, were obliged to capitulate; and they engaged, if not relieved within three days, to surrender the town and to retire into the citadel. On the last of these days Henry appeared with his army upon the heights above Verneuil. Lewis, dreading an attack, sent the Archbishop of Sens and the Count of Blois to the English camp, and desired that next day should be appointed for a conference, in order to establish a general peace and terminate the difference between Henry and his sons. The king, who passionately desired this accommodation, and suspected no fraud, gave his consent; but Lewis, that morning, obliging the garrison to surrender, according to the capitulation, set fire to the place and began to retire with his army. Henry, provoked at this artifice, attacked the rear with vigor, put them to rout, did some execution, and took several prisoners. The French army, as their time of service was now expired, immediately dispersed themselves into their several provinces, and left Henry free to prosecute his advantages against his other enemies.

The nobles of Brittany, instigated by the Earl of Chester and Ralph de Fougères, were all in arms; but their progress was checked by a body of Brabançons, which the king, after Lewis's retreat, had sent against them. The two armies came to an action near Dol, where the rebels were defeated, fifteen hundred killed on the spot, and the leaders, the Earls of Chester and Fougères, obliged to take shelter in the town of Dol. Henry hastened to form the siege of that place, and carried on the attack with such ardor that he obliged the governor and garrison to surrender themselves prisoners. By these vigorous measures and happy successes the insurrections were entirely quelled in Brittany; and the king, thus fortunate in all quarters, willingly agreed to a conference with Lewis, in hopes that his enemies, finding all their mighty efforts entirely frustrated, would terminate hostilities on some moderate and reasonable conditions.

The two monarchs met between Trie and Gisors; and

Henry had here the mortification to see his three sons in the retinue of his mortal enemy. As Lewis had no other pretence for war than supporting the claims of the young princes, the king made them such offers as children might be ashamed to insist on, and could be extorted from him by nothing but his parental affection or by the present necessity of his affairs.[27] He insisted only on retaining the sovereign authority in all his dominions, but offered young Henry half the revenues of England, with some places of surety in that kingdom; or if he rather chose to reside in Normandy, half the revenues of that duchy, with all those of Anjou. He made a like offer to Richard in Guienne; he promised to resign Brittany to Geoffrey; and if these concessions were not deemed sufficient, he agreed to add to them whatever the pope's legates, who were present, should require of him.[28] The Earl of Leicester was also present at the negotiation; and either from the impetuosity of his temper or from a view of abruptly breaking off a conference which must cover the allies with confusion, he gave vent to the most violent reproaches against Henry, and he even put his hand to his sword, as if he meant to attempt some violence against him. This furious action threw the whole company into confusion, and put an end to the treaty.[29]

The chief hopes of Henry's enemies seemed now to depend on the state of affairs in England, where his authority was exposed to the most eminent danger. One article of Prince Henry's agreement with his foreign confederates was that he should resign Kent, with Dover and all its other fortresses, into the hands of the Earl of Flanders;[30] yet so little national or public spirit prevailed among the independent English nobility, so wholly bent were they on the aggrandizement each of himself and his own family, that, notwithstanding this pernicious concession, which must have produced the ruin of the kingdom, the greater part of them had conspired to make an insurrection and to support the prince's pretensions. The king's principal resources lay in the church and the bishops, with whom he was now in perfect agreement; whether that the decency of their character made them ashamed of supporting so unnatural a rebellion, or that they were entirely satisfied with Henry's atonement for the murder of Becket and for his

[27] Hoveden, p. 538.　　　[28] Hoveden, p. 536.　Brompton, p. 1088.
[29] Hoveden, p. 536.
[30] Hoveden, p. 533.　Brompton, p. 1084.　Gul. Neub. p. 508.

former invasion of ecclesiastical immunities. That prince, however, had resigned none of the essential rights of his crown in the accommodation; he maintained still the same prudent jealousy of the court of Rome; admitted no legate into England without his swearing to attempt nothing against the royal prerogatives; and he had even obliged the monks of Canterbury, who pretended to a free election on the vacancy made by the death of Becket, to choose Roger, prior of Dover, in the place of that turbulent prelate.[31]

The King of Scotland made an irruption into Northumberland, and committed great devastation; but, being opposed by Richard de Lucy, whom Henry had left guardian of the realm, he retreated into his own country, and agreed to a cessation of arms. This truce enabled the guardian to march southward with his army, in order to oppose an invasion which the Earl of Leicester, at the head of a great body of Flemings, had made upon Suffolk. The Flemings had been joined by Hugh Bigod, who made them masters of his castle of Framlingham, and, marching into the heart of the kingdom, where they hoped to be supported by Leicester's vassals, they were met by Lucy, who, assisted by Humphrey Bohun, the constable, and the Earls of Arundel, Gloucester, and Cornwall, had advanced to Farnham, with a less numerous but braver army to oppose them. The Flemings, who were mostly weavers and artificers (for manufactures were now beginning to be established in Flanders) were broken in an instant, ten thousand of them were put to the sword, the Earl of Leicester was taken prisoner, and the remains of the invaders were glad to compound for a safe retreat into their own country.

[1174.] This great defeat did not dishearten the malcontents, who, being supported by the alliance of so many foreign princes and encouraged by the king's own sons, determined to persevere in their enterprise. The Earl of Ferrars, Roger de Moubray, Architel de Mallory, Richard de Moreville, Hamo de Mascie, together with many friends of the Earls of Leicester and Chester, rose in arms; the fidelity of the Earls of Clare and Gloucester was suspected; and the guardian, though vigorously supported by Geoffrey, Bishop of Lincoln, the king's natural son by the fair Rosamond, found it difficult to defend himself in all quarters from so many open and concealed enemies. The more to augment the confusion, the King of Scotland, on the expira-

[31] Hoveden, p. 537.

tion of the truce, broke into the northern provinces with a great army [32] of eighty thousand men, which, though undisciplined and disorderly, and better fitted for committing devastation than for executing any military enterprise, was become dangerous from the present factious and turbulent spirit of the kingdom. Henry, who had baffled all his enemies in France, and had put his frontiers in a posture of defence, now found England the seat of danger; and he determined by his presence to overawe the malcontents, or by his conduct and courage to subdue them. He landed at Southampton; and knowing the influence of superstition over the minds of the people, he hastened to Canterbury, in order to make atonement to the ashes of Thomas à Becket and tender his submissions to a dead enemy. As soon as he came within sight of the church of Canterbury, he dismounted, walked barefoot towards it, prostrated himself before the shrine of the saint, remained in fasting and prayer during a whole day, and watched all night the holy relics. Not content with this hypocritical devotion towards a man whose violence and ingratitude had so long disquieted his government and had been the object of his most inveterate animosity, he submitted to a penance still more singular and humiliating. He assembled a chapter of the monks, disrobed himself before them, put a scourge of discipline into the hands of each, and presented his bare shoulders to the lashes which these ecclesiastics successively inflicted upon him. Next day he received absolution; and, departing for London, got soon after the agreeable intelligence of a great victory which his generals had obtained over the Scots, and which, being gained, as was reported, on the very day of his absolution, was regarded as the earnest of his final reconciliation with Heaven and with Thomas à Becket.

William, King of Scots, though repulsed before the castle of Prudhow and other fortified places, had committed the most horrible depredations upon the northern provinces; but on the approach of Ralph de Glanville, the famous justiciary, seconded by Bernard de Baliol, Robert de Stuteville, Odonel de Umfreville, William de Vesci, and other northern barons, together with the gallant Bishop of Lincoln, he thought proper to retreat nearer his own country, and he fixed his camp at Alnwick. He had here weakened his army extremely by sending out numerous detachments

[32] Heming. p. 501.

in order to extend his ravages; and he lay absolutely safe, as he imagined, from any attack of the enemy. But Glanville, informed of his situation, made a hasty and fatiguing march to Newcastle; and, allowing his soldiers only a small interval for refreshment, he immediately set out towards evening for Alnwick. He marched that night above thirty miles; arrived in the morning, under cover of a mist, near the Scottish camp; and, regardless of the numbers of the enemy, he began the attack with his small but determined body of cavalry. William was living in such supine security that he took the English at first for a body of his own ravagers, who were returning to the camp; but the sight of their banners convincing him of his mistake, he entered on the action with no greater body than a hundred horse, in confidence that the numerous army which surrounded him would soon hasten to his relief. He was dismounted on the first shock and taken prisoner; while his troops, hearing of this disaster, fled on all sides with the utmost precipitation. The dispersed ravagers made the best of their way to their own country; and discord arising among them, they proceeded even to mutual hostilities, and suffered more from each other's swords than from that of the enemy.

This great and important victory proved at last decisive in favor of Henry, and entirely broke the spirit of the English rebels. The Bishop of Durham, who was preparing to revolt, made his submissions; Hugh Bigod, though he had received a strong reinforcement of Flemings, was obliged to surrender all his castles and throw himself on the king's mercy. No better resource was left to the Earl of Ferrars and Roger de Moubray. The inferior rebels imitating the example, all England was restored to tranquillity in a few weeks; and as the king appeared to lie under the immediate protection of Heaven, it was deemed impious any longer to resist him. The clergy exalted anew the merits and powerful intercession of Becket; and Henry, instead of opposing this superstition, plumed himself on the new friendship of the saint, and propagated an opinion which was so favorable to his interests.[33]

Prince Henry, who was ready to embark at Gravelines, with the Earl of Flanders and a great army, hearing that his partisans in England were suppressed, abandoned all thoughts of the enterprise, and joined the camp of Lewis who, during the absence of the king, had made an irruption into Normandy, and had laid siege to Rouen.[34] The place was defended with great vigor by the inhabitants;[35] and Lewis, despairing of success by open force, tried to gain the town by a stratagem which, in that superstitious age, was deemed not very honorable. He proclaimed in his own camp a cessation of arms, on pretence of celebrating the festival of St. Laurence; and when the citizens, supposing themselves in safety, were so imprudent as to remit their guard, he proposed to take advantage of their security. Happily, some priests had, from mere curiosity, mounted a steeple where the alarm-bell hung; and, observing the French camp in motion, they immediately rang the bell, and gave warning to the inhabitants, who ran to their several stations. The French, who, on hearing the alarm, hurried to the assault, had already mounted the walls in several places, but, being repulsed by the enraged citizens, were obliged t oretreat with considerable loss.[36] Next day, Henry, who had hastened to the defence of his Norman dominions, passed over the bridge in triumph, and entered Rouen in sight of the French army. The city was now in absolute safety; and the king, in order to brave the French monarch, commanded the gates, which had been walled up, to be opened; and he prepared to push his advantages against the enemy. Lewis saved himself from this perilous situation by a new piece of deceit, not so justifiable. He proposed a conference for adjusting the terms of a general peace, which he knew would be greedily embraced by Henry; and while the king of England trusted to the execution of his promise, he made a retreat with his army into France.

There was, however, a necessity on both sides for an accommodation. Henry could no longer bear to see his three sons in the hands of his enemy; and Lewis dreaded lest this great monarch, victorious in all quarters, crowned with glory, and absolute master of his dominions, might take revenge for the many dangers and disquietudes, which the arms, and still more the intrigues, of France had, in his disputes both with Becket and his sons, found means to raise him. After making a cessation of arms, a conference was agreed on near Tours, where Henry granted his sons much less advantageous terms than he had formerly offered,

34 Brompton, p. 1096. 35 Diceto, p. 578.
36 Brompton, p. 1096. Gul. Neub. p. 411, Heming. p. 503.

and he received their submissions. The most material of his concessions were some pensions which he stipulated to pay them, and some castles which he granted them for the place of their residence, together with an indemnity for all their adherents, who were restored to their estates and honors.[37]

Of all those who had embraced the cause of the young princes, William, King of Scotland, was the only considerable loser by that invidious and unjust enterprise. Henry delivered from confinement, without exacting any ransom, about nine hundred knights whom he had taken prisoners; but it cost William the ancient independency of his crown as the price of his liberty. He stipulated to do homage to Henry for Scotland and all his other possessions; he engaged that all the barons and nobility of his kingdom should also do homage; that the bishops should take an oath of fealty; that both should swear to adhere to the King of England against their native prince if the latter should break his engagements; and that the fortresses of Edinburgh, Stirling, Berwick, Roxburgh, and Jedburgh should be delivered into Henry's hands till the performance of articles.[38] [1175.] This severe and humiliating treaty was executed in its full rigor. William, being released, brought up all his barons, prelates, and abbots; and they did homage to Henry in the cathedral of York, and acknowledged him and his successors for their superior lord.[39] The English monarch stretched still further the rigor of the conditions which he exacted. He engaged the King and States of Scotland to make a perpetual cession of the fortresses of Berwick and Roxburgh, and to allow the castle of Edinburgh to remain in his hands for a limited time. This was the first great ascendant which England obtained over Scotland, and indeed the first important transaction which had passed between the kingdoms. Few princes have been so fortunate as to gain considerable advantages over their weaker neighbors with less violence and injustice than were practised by Henry against the King of Scots, whom he had taken prisoner in battle, and who had wantonly engaged in a war in which all the neighbors of that prince, and even his

---

[37] Rymer, vol. i. p. 35. Benedict. Abb. p. 88. Hoveden, p. 540. Diceto, p. 583. Brompton, p. 1098. Heming. p. 505. Chron. Dunst. p. 36.
[38] Matt. Paris, p. 91. Chron. Dunst. p. 36. Hoveden, p. 545. Matt. West. p. 251. Diceto, p. 584. Brompton, p. 1103. Rymer, vol. i. p. 39. Liber Nig. Scac. p. 36.   [39] Benedict. Abb. p. 113.

own family, were, without provocation, combined against him.[40]

Henry having thus, contrary to expectation, extricated himself with honor from a situation in which his throne was exposed to great danger, was employed for several years in the administration of justice, in the execution of the laws, and in guarding against those inconveniences which either the past convulsions of his state or the political institutions of that age unavoidably occasioned. The provisions which he made show such largeness of thought as qualified him for being a legislator; and they were commonly calculated as well for the future as the present happiness of his kingdom.

[1176.] He enacted severe penalties against robbery, murder, false coining, arson, and ordained that these crimes should be punished by the amputation of the right hand and right foot.[41] The pecuniary commutation for crimes, which has a false appearance of lenity, had been gradually disused, and seems to have been entirely abolished by the rigor of these statutes. The superstitious trial by water ordeal, though condemned by the Church,[42] still subsisted; but Henry ordained that any man accused of murder, or any heinous felony, by the oath of the legal knights of the county, should, even though acquitted by the ordeal, be obliged to abjure the realm.[43]

All advances towards reason and good sense are slow and gradual. Henry, though sensible of the great absurdity attending the trial by duel or battle, did not venture to abolish it; he only admitted either of the parties to challenge a trial by an assize or jury of twelve freeholders.[44] This latter method of trial seems to have been very ancient in England, and was fixed by the laws of King Alfred; but the barbarous and violent genius of the age had of late given more credit to the trial by battle, which had become the general method of deciding all important controversies. It was never abolished by law in England, and there is an instance of it so late as the reign of Elizabeth; but the institution revived by this king, being found more reasonable and more suitable to a civilized people, gradually prevailed over it.

---

[40] Some Scotch historians pretend that William paid, besides, 100,000 pounds of ransom, which is quite incredible. The ransom of Richard I., who, besides England, possessed so many rich territories in France, was only 150,000 marks, and yet was levied with great difficulty. Indeed, two thirds of it only could be paid before his deliverance.

[41] Benedict. Abb. p. 132. Hoveden, p. 549.

[42] Seld. Spicileg. ad Eadmer, p. 204.   [43] Benedict. Abb. p. 132.

[44] Glanv. lib. 2, cap. 7.

The partition of England into four divisions, and the appointment of itinerant justices to go the circuit in each division and to decide the causes in the counties, was another important ordinance of this prince, which had a direct tendency to curb the oppressive barons and to protect the inferior gentry and common people in their property.[45] Those justices were either prelates or considerable noblemen, who, besides carrying the authority of the king's commission, were able, by the dignity of their own character, to give weight and credit to the laws.

That there might be fewer obstacles to the execution of justice, the king was vigilant in demolishing all the new-erected castles of the nobility, in England as well as in his foreign dominions; and he permitted no fortress to remain in the custody of those whom he found reason to suspect.[46]

But lest the kingdom should be weakened by this demolition of the fortresses, the king fixed an assize of arms, by which all his subjects were obliged to put themselves in a situation for defending themselves and the realm. Every man possessed of a knight's-fee was ordained to have for each fee a coat of mail, a helmet, a shield, and a lance; every free layman possessed of goods to the value of sixteen marks was to be armed in like manner; every one that possessed ten marks was obliged to have an iron gorget, a cap of iron, and a lance; all burgesses were to have a cap of iron, a lance, and a wambais (that is, a coat quilted with wool, tow, or such like materials).[47] It appears that archery, for which the English were afterwards so renowned, had not at this time become very common among them. The spear was the chief weapon employed in battle.

The clergy and the laity were during that age in a strange situation with regard to each other, and such as may seem totally incompatible with a civilized, and, indeed, with any species of government. If a clergyman were guilty of murder, he could be punished with degradation only; if he were murdered, the murderer was exposed to nothing but excommunication and ecclesiastical censures, and the crime was atoned for by penances and submission.[48] Hence the assassins of Thomas à Becket himself, though guilty of the most atrocious wickedness, and the most repugnant to the sentiments of that age, lived securely in their

[45] Hoveden, p. 590.   [46] Benedict. Abb. p. 202. Diceto, p. 585.
[47] Benedict. Abb. p. 305. Annal. Waverl. p. 161.
[48] Petr. Bles. epist. 73, apud Bibl. Patr. vol. xxiv. p. 992.

own houses without being called to account by Henry himself, who was so much concerned, both in honor and interest, to punish that crime, and who professed, or affected on all occasions, the most extreme abhorrence of it. It was not till they found their presence shunned by every one as excommunicated persons that they were induced to take a journey to Rome, to throw themselves at the feet of the pontiff, and to submit to the penances imposed upon them, after which they continued to possess, without molestation, their honors and fortunes, and seemed even to have recovered the countenance and good opinion of the public. But as the king, by the constitutions of Clarendon, which he endeavored still to maintain,[49] had subjected the clergy to a trial by the civil magistrate, it seemed but just to give them the protection of that power to which they owed obedience. It was enacted that the murderers of clergymen should be tried before the justiciary, in the presence of the bishop or his official, and, besides the usual punishment for murder, should be subjected to a forfeiture of their estates and a confiscation of their goods and chattels.[50]

The king passed an equitable law—that the goods of a vassal should not be seized for the debt of his lord unless the vassal be surety for the debt; and that the rents of vassals should be paid to the creditors of the lord, not to the lord himself. It is remarkable that this law was enacted by the king in a council which he held at Verneuil, and which consisted of some prelates and barons of England, as well as some of Normandy, Poictou, Anjou, Maine, Touraine, and Brittany; and the statute took place in all these last-mentioned territories,[51] though totally unconnected with each other[52]—a certain proof how irregular the ancient feudal government was, and how near the sovereigns, in some instances, approached to despotism, though in others they seemed scarcely to possess any authority. If a prince, much dreaded and revered like Henry, obtained but the appearance of general consent to an ordinance which was equitable and just, it became immediately an established law, and all his subjects acquiesced in it. If the prince was hated or despised; if the nobles who supported him had

[49] Chron. Gerv. p. 1433. [50] Diceto, p. 592. Chron. Gerv. p. 1433.
[51] Benedict. Abb. p. 248. It was usual for the kings of England, after the conquest of Ireland, to summon barons and members of that country to the English Parliament. Mollineux's Case of Ireland, pp. 64, 65, 66.
[52] Spellman even doubts whether the law were not also extended to England. If it were not, it could only be because Henry did not choose it; for his authority was greater in that kingdom than in his transmarine dominions.

small influence; if the humors of the times disposed the people to question the justice of his ordinance, the fullest and most authentic assembly had no authority. Thus all was confusion and disorder; no regular idea of a constitution; force and violence decided everything.

The success which had attended Henry in his wars did not much encourage his neighbors to form any attempt against him; and his transactions with them, during several years, contain little memorable. Scotland remained in that state of feudal subjection to which he had reduced it, and gave him no further inquietude. He sent over his fourth son, John, into Ireland, with a view of making a more complete conquest of the island; but the petulance and incapacity of this prince, by which he enraged the Irish chieftains, obliged the king soon after to recall him.[53] The King of France had fallen into an abject superstition; and was induced, by a devotion more sincere than that of Henry, to make a pilgrimage to the tomb of Becket, in order to obtain his intercession for the cure of Philip, his eldest son. He probably thought himself well entitled to the favor of that saint on account of their ancient intimacy, and hoped that Becket, whom he had protected while on earth, would not now, when he was so highly exalted in heaven, forget his old friend and benefactor. The monks, sensible that their saint's honor was concerned in the case, failed not to publish that Lewis's prayers were answered, and that the young prince was restored to health by Becket's intercession. That king himself was soon after struck with an apoplexy which deprived him of his understanding. Philip, though a youth of fifteen, took on him the administration, till his father's death, which happened soon after, opened his way to the throne; and he proved the ablest and greatest monarch that had governed that kingdom since the age of Charlemagne. The superior years, however, and experience of Henry, while they moderated his ambition, gave him such an ascendant over this prince that no dangerous rivalship, for a long time, arose between them. [1180.] The English monarch, instead of taking advantage of his own situation, rather employed his good offices in composing the quarrels which arose in the royal family of France; and he was successful in mediating a reconciliation between Philip and his mother and uncles. These services were but ill requited by Philip, who, when he came to man's estate, fomented all the

<hr />

[53] Benedict. Abb. p. 437, etc.

domestic discords in the royal family of England, and encouraged Henry's sons in their ungrateful and undutiful behavior towards him.

Prince Henry, equally impatient of obtaining power and incapable of using it, renewed to the king the demand of his resigning Normandy; and on meeting with a refusal, he fled with his consort to the court of France; but not finding Philip at that time disposed to enter into war for his sake, he accepted of his father's offers of reconciliation, and made him submissions. It was a cruel circumstance in the king's fortune that he could hope for no tranquillity from the criminal enterprises of his sons but by their mutual discord and animosities, which disturbed his family and threw his state into convulsions. Richard, whom he had made master of Guienne, and who had displayed his valor and military genius by suppressing the revolts of his mutinous barons, refused to obey Henry's orders, in doing homage to his elder brother for that duchy, and he defended himself against young Henry and Geoffrey, who, uniting their arms, carried war into his territories.[54] The king with some difficulty composed this difference, but immediately found his eldest son engaged in conspiracies, and ready to take arms against himself. [1183.] While the young prince was conducting these criminal intrigues, he was seized with a fever at Martel, a castle near Turenne, to which he had retired in discontent; and seeing the approaches of death, he was at last struck with remorse for his undutiful behavior towards his father. He sent a message to the king, who was not far distant; expressed his contrition for his faults; and entreated the favor of a visit, that he might at least die with the satisfaction of having obtained his forgiveness. Henry, who had so often experienced the prince's ingratitude and violence, apprehended that his sickness was entirely feigned, and he durst not intrust himself into his son's hands; but when he soon after received intelligence of young Henry's death, and the proofs of his sincere repentance, this good prince was affected with the deepest sorrow; he thrice fainted away; he accused his own hardheartedness in refusing the dying request of his son; and he lamented that he had deprived that prince of the last opportunity of making atonement for his offences, and of pouring out his soul in the bosom of his reconciled father.[55] This prince died in the twenty-eighth year of his age.

[54] Ypod. Neust. p. 451. Benedict. Abb. p. 383. Diceto, p. 617.
[55] Benedict. Abb. p. 393. Hoveden. p. 621. Trivet. vol. i. p. 84.

The behavior of his surviving children did not tend to give the king any consolation for the loss. As Prince Henry had left no posterity, Richard was become heir to all his dominions; and the king intended that John, his third surviving son and favorite, should inherit Guienne as his appanage; but Richard refused his consent, fled into that duchy, and even made preparations for carrying on war, as well against his father as against his brother Geoffrey, who was now put in possession of Brittany. Henry sent for Eleanor, his queen, the heiress of Guienne, and required Richard to deliver up to her the dominion of these territories, which that prince, either dreading an insurrection of the Gascons in her favor, or retaining some sense of duty towards her, readily performed, and he peaceably returned to his father's court. No sooner was this quarrel accommodated than Geoffrey, the most vicious, perhaps, of all Henry's unhappy family, broke out into violence; demanded Anjou to be annexed to his dominions of Brittany; and, on meeting with a refusal, fled to the court of France, and levied forces against his father.[56] [1185.] Henry was freed from this danger by his son's death, who was killed in a tournament at Paris.[57] The widow of Geoffrey, soon after his decease, was delivered of a son, who received the name of Arthur, and was invested in the duchy of Brittany, under the guardianship of his grandfather, who, as Duke of Normandy, was also superior lord of that territory. Philip, as lord paramount, disputed some time his title to this wardship; but was obliged to yield to the inclinations of the Bretons, who preferred the government of Henry.

But the rivalship between these potent princes, and all their inferior interests, seemed now to have given place to the general passion for the relief of the Holy Land and the expulsion of the Saracens. Those infidels, though obliged to yield to the immense inundation of Christians in the first crusade, had recovered courage after the torrent was past, and attacking on all quarters the settlements of the Europeans, had reduced these adventurers to great difficulties, and obliged them to apply again for succors from the West. A second crusade, under the Emperor Conrad and Lewis VII., king of France, in which there perished above two hundred thousand men, brought them but a temporary relief; and those princes, after losing such immense armies, and seeing the flower of their nobility fall by their side, re-

[56] Gul. Neub. p. 422.   [57] Benedict. Abb. p. 451. Chron. Gerv. p. 1480.

turned with little honor into Europe. But these repeated misfortunes, which drained the western world of its people and treasure, were not yet sufficient to cure men of their passion for those spiritual adventures, and a new incident rekindled with fresh fury the zeal of the ecclesiastics and military adventurers among the Latin Christians. Saladin, a prince of great generosity, bravery, and conduct, having fixed himself on the throne of Egypt, began to extend his conquests over the East; and finding the settlement of the Christians in Palestine an invincible obstacle to the progress of his arms, he bent the whole force of his policy and valor to subdue that small and barren but important territory. Taking advantage of dissensions which prevailed among the champions of the cross, and having secretly gained the Count of Tripoli, who commanded their armies, he invaded the frontiers with a mighty power, and, aided by the treachery of that count, gained over them at Tiberiade a complete victory, which utterly annihilated the force of the already languishing kingdom of Jerusalem. The holy city itself fell into his hands, after a feeble resistance; the kingdom of Antioch was almost entirely subdued; and, except some maritime towns, nothing considerable remained of those boasted conquests which, near a century before, it had cost the efforts of all Europe to acquire.[58]

The western Christians were astonished on receiving this dismal intelligence. [1187.] Pope Urban III., it is pretended, died of grief, and his successor, Gregory VIII., employed the whole time of his short pontificate in rousing to arms all the Christians who acknowledged his authority. The general cry was that they were unworthy of enjoying any inheritance in heaven who did not vindicate from the dominion of the infidels the inheritance of God on earth, and deliver from slavery that country which had been consecrated by the footsteps of their Redeemer. [1188.] William, Archbishop of Tyre, having procured a conference between Henry and Philip near Gisors, enforced all these topics; gave a pathetic description of the miserable state of the eastern Christians, and employed every argument to excite the ruling passions of the age, superstition and jealousy of military honor. [59] The two monarchs immediately took the cross; many of their most considerable vassals imitated the example;[60] and as the Emperor Frederick I. entered

---

[58] Matt. Paris, p. 100.
[59] Benedict. Abb. p. 531.   [60] Gul. Neub. p. 435. Heming. p. 512.

24

into the same confederacy, some well-grounded hopes of success were entertained, and men flattered themselves that an enterprise which had failed under the conduct of many independent leaders, or of imprudent princes, might at last, by the efforts of such potent and able monarchs, be brought to a happy issue.

The kings of France and England imposed a tax, amounting to the tenth of all movable goods on such as remained at home; [61] but as they exempted from this burden most of the regular clergy, the secular aspired to the same immunity; pretended that their duty obliged them to assist the crusade with their prayers alone; and it was with some difficulty they were constrained to desist from an opposition, which in them who had been the chief promoters of those pious enterprises appeared with the worst grace imaginable.[62] This backwardness of the clergy is perhaps a symptom that the enthusiastic ardor which had at first seized the people for crusades was now, by time and ill success, considerably abated; and that the frenzy was chiefly supported by the military genius and love of glory in the monarchs.

But before this great machine could be put in motion, there were still many obstacles to surmount. Philip, jealous of Henry's power, entered into a private confederacy with young Richard; and, working on his ambitious and impatient temper, persuaded him, instead of supporting and aggrandizing that monarchy which he was one day to inherit, to seek present power and independence by disturbing and dismembering it. [1189.] In order to give a pretence for hostilities between the two kings, Richard broke into the territories of Raymond, Count of Toulouse, who immediately carried complaints of this violence before the King of France as his superior lord. Philip remonstrated with Henry; but received for answer that Richard had confessed to the Archbishop of Dublin that his enterprise against Raymond had been undertaken by the approbation of Philip himself, and was conducted by his authority. The King of France, who might have been covered with shame and confusion by this detection, still prosecuted his design and invaded the provinces of Berri and Auvergne under color of revenging the quarrel of the Count of Toulouse.[63] Henry retaliated by making inroads upon the frontiers of France, and burning Dreux. As this war, which destroyed all hopes of success in the projected crusade, gave great

[61] Benedict. Abb. p. 498.   [62] Petr. Bles. epist. 112.   [63] Benedict. Abb. p. 508.

scandal, the two kings held a conference at the accustomed place between Gisors and Trie, in order to find means of accommodating their differences. They separated on worse terms than before; and Philip, to show his disgust, ordered a great elm, under which the conferences had been usually held, to be cut down,[64] as if he had renounced all desire of accommodation, and was determined to carry the war to extremities against the King of England. But his own vassals refused to serve under him in so invidious a cause,[65] and he was obliged to come anew to a conference with Henry, and to offer terms of peace. These terms were such as entirely opened the eyes of the King of England, and fully convinced him of the perfidy of his son, and his secret alliance with Philip, of which he had before only entertained some suspicion. The King of France required that Richard should be crowned King of England in the lifetime of his father, should be invested in all his transmarine dominions, and should immediately espouse Alice, Philip's sister, to whom he had formerly been affianced, and who had already been conducted into England.[66] Henry had experienced such fatal effects, both from the crowning of his eldest son and from that prince's alliance with the royal family of France, that he rejected these terms, and Richard, in consequence of his secret agreement with Philip, immediately revolted from him,[67] did homage to the King of France for all the dominions which Henry held of that crown, and received the investitures as if he had already been the lawful possessor. Several historians assert that Henry himself had become enamoured of young Alice, and mention this as an additional reason for his refusing these conditions, but he had so many other just and equitable motives for his conduct that it is superfluous to assign a cause which the great prudence and advanced age of that monarch rendered somewhat improbable.

Cardinal Albano, the pope's legate, displeased with these increasing obstacles to the crusade, excommunicated Richard, as the chief spring of discord; but the sentence of excommunication, which, when it was properly prepared, and was zealously supported by the clergy, had often great influence in that age, proved entirely ineffectual in the present case. The chief barons of Poictou, Guienne, Normandy, and Anjou,

[64] Benedict. Abb. pp. 517, 532.
[65] Benedict. Abb. p. 519.   [66] Benedict. Abb. p. 521.   Hoveden, p. 652.
[67] Brompton, p. 1149.   Gul. Neub. p. 437.

being attached to the young prince, and finding that he had
now received the investiture from their superior lord, declared for him, and made inroads into the territories of
such as still adhered to the king. Henry, disquieted by the
daily revolts of his mutinous subjects, and dreading still
worse effects from their turbulent disposition, had again recourse to papal authority; and engaged the Cardinal Anagni,
who had succeeded Albano in the legateship, to threaten
Philip with laying an interdict on all his dominions. But
Philip, who was a prince of great vigor and capacity, despised the menace, and told Anagni that it belonged not to
the pope to interpose in the temporal disputes of princes,
much less in those between him and his rebellious vassal.
He even proceeded so far as to reproach him with partiality,
and with receiving bribes from the King of England; [68]
while Richard, still more outrageous, offered to draw his
sword against the legate, and was hindered by the interposition alone of the company from committing violence
upon him. [69]

The King of England was now obliged to defend his dominions by arms, and to engage in a war with France, and
with his eldest son, a prince of great valor, on such disadvantageous terms. Ferté-Bernard fell first into the hands of the
enemy; Mans was next taken by assault; and Henry, who had
thrown himself into that place, escaped with some difficulty; [70] Amboise, Chaumont, and Château de Loire opened
their gates on the appearance of Philip and Richard; Tours
was menaced; and the king, who had retired to Saumur, and
had daily instances of the cowardice or infidelity of his governors, expected the most dismal issue to all his enterprises.
While he was in this state of despondency, the Duke of
Burgundy, the Earl of Flanders, and the Archbishop of
Rheims interposed with their good offices; and the intelligence which he received of the taking of Tours, and which
made him fully sensible of the desperate situation of his
affairs, so subdued his spirit that he submitted to all the
rigorous terms which were imposed upon him. He agreed
that Richard should marry the Princess Alice; that that
prince should receive the homage and oath of fealty of all
his subjects both in England and his transmarine dominions;
that he himself should pay twenty thousand marks to the

[68] Matt. Paris, p. 104.   Benedict. Abb. p. 542.   Hoveden, p. 652.
[69] Matt. Paris, p. 104.
[70] Matt. Paris, p. 105.   Benedict. Abb. p. 543.   Hoveden, p. 653.

King of France as a compensation for the charges of the war ; that his own barons should engage to make him observe this treaty by force, and, in case of his violating it, should promise to join Philip and Richard against him ; and that all his vassals who had entered into confederacy with Richard should receive an indemnity for the offence.[71]

But the mortification which Henry, who had been accustomed to give the law in most treaties, received from these disadvantageous terms was the least that he met with on this occasion. When he demanded a list of those barons to whom he was bound to grant a pardon for their connections with Richard, he was astonished to find at the head of them the name of his second son, John,[72] who had always been his favorite, whose interests he had ever anxiously at heart, and who had even, on account of his ascendant over him, often excited the jealousy of Richard.[73] The unhappy father, already overloaded with cares and sorrows, finding this last disappointment in his domestic tenderness, broke out into expressions of the utmost despair, cursed the day in which he received his miserable being, and bestowed on his ungrateful and undutiful children a malediction which he never could be prevailed on to retract.[74] The more his heart was disposed to friendship and affection, the more he resented the barbarous return which his four sons had successively made to his parental care ; and this finishing blow, by depriving him of every comfort in life, quite broke his spirit and threw him into a lingering fever, of which he expired at the castle of Chinon, near Saumur. [July 6.] His natural son Geoffrey, who alone had behaved dutifully towards him, attended his corpse to the nunnery of Fontevrault, where it lay in state in the abbey church. Next day Richard, who came to visit the dead body of his father, and who, notwithstanding his criminal conduct, was not wholly destitute of generosity, was struck with horror and remorse at the sight ; and as the attendants observed that at that very instant blood gushed from the mouth and nostrils of the corpse,[75] he exclaimed, agreeably to a vulgar superstition, that he was his father's murderer ; and he expressed a deep sense, though too late, of that undutiful behavior which had brought his parent to an untimely grave.[76]

Thus died, in the fifty-eighth year of his age and thirty-

[71] Matt. Paris, p. 106.   Benedict. Abb. p. 545.   Hoveden, p. 653.
[72] Hoveden, p. 654.   [73] Benedict. Abb. p. 541.
[74] Hoveden, p. 654.   [75] Benedict. Abb. p. 547.   Brompton, p. 1151.
[76] Matt. Paris, p. 107.

fifth of his reign, the greatest prince of his time for wisdom, virtue, and abilities, and the most powerful in extent of dominion of all those that had ever filled the throne of England. His character, in private as well as in public life, is almost without a blemish ; and he seems to have possessed every accomplishment, both of body and mind, which makes a man either estimable or amiable. He was of a middle stature, strong and well-proportioned ; his countenance was lively and engaging ; his conversation affable and entertaining ; his elocution easy, persuasive, and ever at command. He loved peace, but possessed both bravery and conduct in war ; was provident without timidity ; severe in the execution of justice without rigor ; and temperate without austerity. He preserved health, and kept himself from corpulency, to which he was somewhat inclined, by an abstemious diet and by frequent exercise, particularly hunting. When he could enjoy leisure, he recreated himself either in learned conversation or in reading ; and he cultivated his natural talents by study, above any prince of his time. His affections as well as his enmities were warm and durable ; and his long experience of the ingratitude and infidelity of men never destroyed the natural sensibility of his temper, which disposed him to friendship and society. His character has been transmitted to us by several writers who were his contemporaries ; [77] and it extremely resembles, in its most remarkable features, that of his maternal grandfather, Henry I. ; excepting only that ambition, which was a ruling passion in both, found not in the first Henry such unexceptionable means of exerting itself, and pushed that prince into measures which were both criminal in themselves and were the cause of further crimes, from which his grandson's conduct was happily exempted.

This prince, like most of his predecessors of the Norman line, except Stephen, passed more of his time on the Continent than in this island : he was surrounded with the English gentry and nobility when abroad ; the French gentry and nobility attended him when he resided in England. Both nations acted in the government as if they were the same people ; and, on many occasions, the legislatures seem not to have been distinguished. As the king and all the English barons were of French extraction, the manners of that people acquired the ascendant, and were regarded as

[77] Petr. Bles. epist. 46, 47, in Biblioth. Patr. vol. xxiv. pp. 985, 986, etc. Girald. Cambr. p. 783, etc.

the models of imitation. All foreign improvements, therefore, such as they were, in literature and politeness, in laws and arts, seem now to have been, in a good measure, transplanted into England; and that kingdom was become little inferior in all the fashionable accomplishments to any of its neighbors on the Continent. The more homely but more sensible manners and principles of the Saxons were exchanged for the affectations of chivalry and the subtleties of school philosophy. The feudal ideas of civil government, the Romish sentiments in religion, had taken entire possession of the people : by the former, the sense of submission towards princes was somewhat diminished in the barons ; by the latter the devoted attachment to papal authority was much augmented among the clergy. The Norman and other foreign families established in England had now struck deep root ; and, being entirely incorporated with the people, whom at first they oppressed and despised, they no longer thought that they needed the protection of the crown for the enjoyment of their possessions, or considered their tenure as precarious. They aspired to the same liberty and independence which they saw enjoyed by their brethren on the Continent, and desired to restrain those exorbitant prerogatives and arbitrary practices which the necessities of war and the violence of conquest had at first obliged them to indulge in their monarch. The memory, also, of a more equal government under the Saxon princes, which remained with the English, diffused still farther the spirit of liberty, and made the barons both desirous of more independence to themselves and willing to indulge it to the people. And it was not long ere this secret revolution in the sentiments of men produced, first violent convulsions in the state, then an evident alteration in the maxims of government.

The history of all the preceding kings of England since the Conquest gives evident proofs of the disorders attending the feudal institutions—the licentiousness of the barons, their spirit of rebellion against the prince and laws, and of animosity against each other. The conduct of the barons in the transmarine dominions of those monarchs afforded perhaps still more flagrant instances of these convulsions ; and the history of France during several ages consists almost entirely of narrations of this nature. The cities, during the continuance of this violent government, could neither be very numerous nor populous ; and there occur instances which seem to evince that though these are always the first seat of law and liberty, their police was in general loose and irregular, and exposed to the same disorders with those by which the country was generally infested. It was a custom in London for great numbers, to the amount of a hundred or more, the sons and relations of considerable citizens, to form themselves into a licentious confederacy, to break into rich houses and plunder them, to rob and murder the passengers, and to commit with impunity all sorts of disorder. By these crimes, it had become so dangerous to walk the streets by night that the citizens durst no more venture abroad after sunset than if they had been exposed to the incursions of a public enemy. The brother of the Earl of Ferrars had been murdered by some of those nocturnal rioters; and the death of so eminent a person, which was much more regarded than that of many thousands of an inferior station, so provoked the king that he swore vengeance against the criminals, and became thenceforth more rigorous in the execution of the laws.[78]

There is another instance given by historians which proves to what a height such riots had proceeded, and how open these criminals were in committing their robberies. A band of them had attacked the house of a rich citizen with an intention of plundering it, had broken through a stone wall with hammers and wedges; and had already entered the house sword in hand; when the citizen, armed cap-a-pie and supported by his faithful servants, appeared in the passage to oppose them: he cut off the right hand of the first robber that entered, and made such stout resistance that his neighbors had leisure to assemble and come to his relief. The man who lost his hand was taken; and was tempted by the promise of pardon to reveal his confederates; among whom was one John Senex, esteemed among the richest and best-born citizens of London. He was convicted by the ordeal; and though he offered five hundred marks for his life, the king refused the money, and ordered him to be hanged.[79] It appears from a statute of Edward I. that these disorders were not remedied even in that reign. It was then made penal to go out at night after the hour of the curfew, to carry a weapon, or to walk without a light or lantern.[80] It is said in the preamble to this law that, both by night and by day, there were continual frays in the streets of London.

---

[78] Benedict. Abb. p. 196.   [79] Benedict. Abb. pp. 197, 198.
[80] Observations on the Ancient Statutes, p. 216.

Henry's care in administering justice had gained him so great a reputation that even foreign and distant princes made him arbiter, and submitted their differences to his judgment. Sanchez, King of Navarre, having some controversies with Alphonso, King of Castile, was contented, though Alphonso had married the daughter of Henry, to choose this prince for a referee; and they agreed each of them to consign three castles into neutral hands, as a pledge of their not departing from his award. Henry made the cause be examined before his great council, and gave a sentence, which was submitted to by both parties. These two Spanish kings sent each a stout champion to the court of England, in order to defend his cause by arms, in case the way of duel had been chosen by Henry.[81]

Henry so far abolished the barbarous and absurd practice of confiscating ships which had been wrecked on the coast that he ordained if one man or animal were alive in the ship, that the vessel and goods should be restored to the owners.[82]

The reign of Henry was remarkable also for an innovation which was afterwards carried farther by his successors, and was attended with the most important consequences. This prince was disgusted with the species of military force which was established by the feudal institutions, and which, though it was extremely burdensome to the subject, yet rendered very little service to the sovereign. The barons, or military tenants, came late into the field; they were obliged to serve only forty days, they were unskilful and disorderly in all their operations; and they were apt to carry into the camp the same refractory and independent spirit to which they were accustomed in their civil government. Henry, therefore, introduced the practice of making a commutation of their military service for money; and he levied scutages from his baronies and knight's-fees, instead of requiring the personal attendance of his vassals. There is mention made in the History of the Exchequer of these scutages in his second, fifth, and eighteenth year,[83] and other writers give us an account of three more of them.[84] When the prince had thus obtained money, he made a contract with some of those adventurers in which Europe at that time abounded. They found him soldiers of the same character

[81] Rymer, vol. iv. p. 43. Benedict. Abb. p. 172.   Diceto, p. 597.   Brompton, p. 1120. [82] Rymer, vol. i. p. 36.
[83] Madox, pp. 435, 436, 437, 438.   [84] Tyrrel, vol. ii. p. 466, from the records.

with themselves, who were bound to serve for a stipulated time. The armies were less numerous, but more useful, than when composed of all the military vassals of the crown. The feudal institutions began to relax; the kings became rapacious for money, on which all their power depended; the barons, seeing no end of exactions, sought to defend their property; and as the same causes had nearly the same effects in the different countries of Europe, the several crowns either lost or acquired authority, according to their different success in the contest.

This prince was also the first that levied a tax on the movables or personal estates of his subjects, nobles as well as commons. Their zeal for the holy wars made them submit to this innovation; and, a precedent being once obtained, this taxation became in following reigns the usual method of supplying the necessities of the crown. The tax of Danegelt, so generally odious to the nation, was remitted in this reign.

It was a usual practice of the kings of England to repeat the ceremony of their coronation thrice every year, on assembling the states at the three great festivals. Henry, after the first years of his reign, never renewed this ceremony, which was found to be very expensive and very useless. None of his successors revived it. It is considered as a great act of grace in this prince that he mitigated the rigor of the forest laws, and punished any transgressions of them, not capitally, but by fines, imprisonments, and other more moderate penalties.

Since we are here collecting some detached incidents, which show the genius of the age, and which could not so well enter into the body of our history, it may not be improper to mention the quarrel between Roger, Archbishop of York, and Richard, Archbishop of Canterbury. We may judge of the violence of military men and laymen, when ecclesiastics could proceed to such extremities. Cardinal Haguezun being sent, in 1176, as legate into Britain, summoned an assembly of the clergy at London; and, as both the archbishops pretended to sit on his right hand, this question of precedency begat a controversy between them. The monks and retainers of Archbishop Richard fell upon Roger, in the presence of the cardinal and of the synod, threw him to the ground, trampled him underfoot, and so bruised him with blows that he was taken up half dead, and his life was with difficulty saved from their violence. The

Archbishop of Canterbury was obliged to pay a large sum of money to the legate, in order to suppress all complaints with regard to this enormity.[85]

We are told by Giraldus Cambrensis that the monks and prior of St. Swithun threw themselves one day prostrate on the ground and in the mire before Henry, complaining, with many tears and much doleful lamentation, that the Bishop of Winchester, who was also their abbot, had cut off three dishes from their table. "How many has he left you?" said the king. "Ten only," replied the disconsolate monks. "I myself," exclaimed the king, "never have more than three; and I enjoin your bishop to reduce you to the same number." [86]

This king left only two legitimate sons—Richard, who succeeded him, and John, who inherited no territory, though his father had often intended to leave him a part of his extensive dominions. He was thence commonly denominated *Lackland*. Henry left three legitimate daughters—Maud, born in 1156, and married to Henry, Duke of Saxony; Eleanor, born in 1162, and married to Alphonso, King of Castile; Joan, born in 1165, and married to William, King of Sicily.[87]

Henry is said by ancient historians to have been of a very amorous disposition. They mention two of his natural sons by Rosamond, daughter of Lord Clifford; namely, Richard Longespée, or Longsword (so called from the sword he usually wore), who was afterwards married to Ela, the daughter and heir of the Earl of Salisbury; and Geoffrey, first Bishop of Lincoln, then Archbishop of York. All the other circumstances of the story commonly told of that lady seem to be fabulous.

---

[85] Benedict. Abb. pp. 138, 139.   Brompton, p. 1109.   Chron. Gerb. p. 1433. Gul. Neub. p. 413.

[86] Girald. Cambr. cap. 5, in Anglia Sacra, vol. ii.   [87] Diceto, p. 616.

CHAPTER X.

RICHARD I.

THE KING'S PREPARATIONS FOR THE CRUSADE.—SETS OUT
ON THE CRUSADE.—TRANSACTIONS IN SICILY.—KING'S
ARRIVAL IN PALESTINE.—STATE OF PALESTINE.—DISOR-
DERS IN ENGLAND.—THE KING'S HEROIC ACTIONS IN PAL-
ESTINE.—HIS RETURN FROM PALESTINE.—CAPTIVITY IN
GERMANY.—WAR WITH FRANCE.—THE KING'S DELIVERY.
—RETURN TO ENGLAND.—WAR WITH FRANCE.—DEATH
AND CHARACTER OF THE KING.—MISCELLANEOUS TRANS-
ACTIONS OF THIS REIGN.

[1189.] THE compunction of Richard for his undutiful
behavior towards his father was durable, and influenced
him in the choice of his ministers and servants after his
accession. Those who had seconded and favored his rebellion, instead of meeting with that trust and honor which
they expected, were surprised to find that they lay under
disgrace with the new king, and were on all occasions hated
and despised by him. The faithful ministers of Henry who
had vigorously opposed all the enterprises of his sons
were received with open arms, and were continued in those
offices which they had honorably discharged to their former
master.[1] This prudent conduct might be the result of
reflection; but in a prince like Richard, so much guided by
passion and so little by policy, it was commonly ascribed to
a principle still more virtuous and more honorable.

Richard, that he might make atonement to one parent
for his breach of duty to the other, immediately sent orders
for releasing the queen dowager from the confinement in
which she had long been detained; and he intrusted her
with the government of England till his arrival in that
kingdom. His bounty to his brother John was rather profuse and imprudent. Besides bestowing on him the county
of Mortaigne, in Normandy, granting him a pension of four
thousand marks a year, and marrying him to Avisa, the

[1] Hoveden, p. 655. Benedict. Abb. p. 547. Matt. Paris, p. 107.

daughter of the Earl of Gloucester, by whom he inherited all the possessions of that opulent family, he increased his appanage which the late king had destined him by other extensive grants and concessions. He conferred on him the whole estate of William Peverell, which had escheated to the crown; he put him in possession of eight castles, with all the forests and honors annexed to them; he delivered over to him no less than six earldoms—Cornwall, Devon, Somerset, Nottingham, Dorset, Lancaster, and Derby; and endeavoring by favors to fix that vicious prince in his duty, he put it too much in his power, whenever he pleased, to depart from it.

The king, impelled more by the love of military glory than by superstition, acted from the beginning of his reign as if the sole purpose of his government had been the relief of the Holy Land and the recovery of Jerusalem from the Saracens. This zeal against infidels, being communicated to his subjects, broke out in London on the day of his coronation, and made them find a crusade less dangerous and attended with more immediate profit. The prejudices of the age had made the lending of money on interest pass by the invidious name of usury; yet the necessity of the practice had still continued it, and the greater part of that kind of dealing fell everywhere into the hands of the Jews, who, being already infamous on account of their religion, had no honor to lose, and were apt to exercise a profession odious in itself by every kind of rigor, and even sometimes by rapine and extortion. The industry and frugality of this people had put them in possession of all the ready money, which the idleness and profusion common to the English, with other European nations, enabled them to lend at exorbitant and unequal interest. The monkish writers represent it as a great stain on the wise and equitable government of Henry that he had carefully protected this infidel race from all injuries and insults; but the zeal of Richard afforded the populace a pretence for venting their animosity against them. The king had issued an edict prohibiting their appearance at his coronation; but some of them, bringing him large presents from their nation, presumed, in confidence of that merit, to approach the hall in which he dined. Being discovered, they were exposed to the insults of the bystanders. They took to flight; the people pursued them. The rumor was spread that the king had issued orders to massacre all the Jews. A command so agreeable was executed in an instant on such as fell into the hands of the populace. Those who had kept at home were exposed to equal danger. The people, moved by rapacity and zeal, broke into their houses, which they plundered, after having murdered the owners; where the Jews barricaded their doors and defended themselves with vigor, the rabble set fire to the houses, and made way through the flames to exercise their pillage and violence. The usual licentiousness of London, which the sovereign power with difficulty restrained, broke out with fury, and continued these outrages. The houses of the richest citizens, though Christians, were next attacked and plundered, and weariness and satiety at last put an end to the disorder; yet, when the king empowered Glanville, the judiciary, to inquire into the authors of these crimes, the guilt was found to involve so many of the most considerable citizens that it was deemed more prudent to drop the prosecution, and very few suffered the punishment due to this enormity. But the disorder stopped not at London. The inhabitants of the other cities of England, hearing of this slaughter of the Jews, imitated the example. In York, five hundred of that nation, who had retired into the castle for safety and found themselves unable to defend the place, murdered their own wives and children, threw the dead bodies over the walls upon the populace, and then setting fire to the houses, perished in the flames. The gentry of the neighborhood, who were all indebted to the Jews, ran to the cathedral, where their bonds were kept, and made a solemn bonfire of the papers before the altar. The compiler of the Annals of Waverley, in relating these events, blesses the Almighty for thus delivering over this impious race to destruction.[2]

The ancient situation of England, when the people possessed little riches and the public no credit, made it impossible for sovereigns to bear the expense of a steady or durable war, even on their frontiers; much less could they find regular means for the support of distant expeditions like those into Palestine, which were more the result of popular frenzy than of sober reason or deliberate policy. Richard, therefore, knew that he must carry with him all the treasure necessary for his enterprise, and that both the remoteness of his own country and its poverty made it unable to furnish him with those continued supplies which the exigencies of so perilous a war must

[2] Gale's Collect. vol. iii. p. 165.

necessarily require. His father had left him a treasure of above a hundred thousand marks; and the king, negligent of every consideration but his present object, endeavored to augment this sum by all expedients, how pernicious soever to the public or dangerous to royal authority. He put to sale the revenues and manors of the crown; the offices of the greatest trust and power, even those of forester and sheriff, which anciently were so important,[3] became venal; the dignity of chief justiciary, in whose hands was lodged the whole execution of the laws, was sold to Hugh de Puzas, Bishop of Durham, for a thousand marks; the same prelate bought the earldom of Northumberland for life;[4] many of the champions of the cross who had repented of the vow purchased the liberty of violating it; and Richard, who stood less in need of men than of money, dispensed, on these conditions, with their attendance. Elated with the hopes of fame, which in that age attended no wars but those against the infidels, he was blind to every other consideration; and when some of his wiser ministers objected to this dissipation of the revenue and power of the crown, he replied that he would sell London itself, could he find a purchaser.[5] Nothing, indeed, could be a stronger proof how negligent he was of all future interests, in comparison of the crusade, than his selling, for so small a sum as ten thousand marks, the vassalage of Scotland, together with the fortresses of Roxburgh and Berwick (the greatest acquisition that had been made by his father during the course of his victorious reign), and his accepting the homage of William in the usual terms merely for the territories which that prince held in England.[6] The English of all ranks and stations were oppressed by numerous exactions; menaces were employed both against the innocent and the guilty, in order to extort money from them; and where a pretence was wanting against the rich, the king obliged them, by the fear of his displeasure, to lend him sums which, he knew, it would never be in his power to repay.

But Richard, though he sacrificed every interest and consideration to the success of the pious enterprise, carried so little the appearance of sanctity in his conduct that Fulk, curate of Neuilly, a zealous preacher of the crusade, who

---

[3] The sheriff had anciently both the administration of justice and the management of the king's revenue committed to him in the county. See Hale of Sheriff's Accounts.
[4] Matt. Paris. p. 109.   [5] W. Heming. p. 519. Knyghton, p. 2402.
[6] Hoveden, p. 662.   Rymer, vol. i. p. 64.   Matt. West. p. 257.

from that merit had acquired the privilege of speaking the boldest truths, advised him to rid himself of his notorious vices, particularly his pride, avarice, and voluptuousness, which he called the king's three favorite daughters. "You counsel well," replied Richard, "and I hereby dispose of the first to the Templars, of the second to the Benedictines, and of the third to my prelates."

Richard, jealous of attempts which might be made on England during his absence, laid Prince John, as well as his natural brother, Geoffrey, Archbishop of York, under engagements, confirmed by their oaths, that neither of them should enter the kingdom till his return ; though he thought proper, before his departure, to withdraw his prohibition. The administration was left in the hands of Hugh, Bishop of Durham, and of Longchamp, Bishop of Ely, whom he appointed justiciaries and guardians of the realm. The latter was a Frenchman of mean birth, and of a violent character, who, by art and address, had insinuated himself into favor, whom Richard had created chancellor, and whom he had engaged the pope also to invest with the legatine authority that, by centring every kind of power in his person, he might the better insure the public tranquillity. All the military and turbulent spirits flocked about the person of the king, and were impatient to distinguish themselves against the infidels in Asia, whither his inclinations, his engagements, led him, and whither he was impelled by messages from the King of France, ready to embark in this enterprise.

The Emperor Frederick, a prince of great spirit and conduct, had already taken the road to Palestine at the head of one hundred and fifty thousand men, collected from Germany and all the northern states. Having surmounted every obstacle thrown in his way by the artifices of the Greeks and the power of the infidels, he had penetrated to the borders of Syria, when, bathing in the cold river Cydnus during the greatest heat of the summer season, he was seized with a mortal distemper, which put an end to his life and his rash enterprise.[7] His army, under the command of his son, Conrad, reached Palestine, but was so diminished by fatigue, famine, maladies, and the sword that it scarcely amounted to eight thousand men, and was unable to make any progress against the great power, valor, and conduct of Saladin. These reiterated calamities attending the cru-

[7] Benedict. Abb. p. 556.

sades had taught the kings of France and England the necessity of trying another road to the Holy Land, and they determined to conduct their armies thither by sea, to carry provisions along with them, and, by means of their naval power, to maintain an open communication with their own states and with the western parts of Europe. The place of rendezvous was appointed in the plains of Vezelay, on the borders of Burgundy.[8] [1190.] Philip and Richard, on their arrival there, found their combined army amount to one hundred thousand men[9]—a mighty force, animated with glory and religion, conducted by two warlike monarchs, provided with everything which their several dominions could supply, and not to be overcome but by their own misconduct or by the unsurmountable obstacles of nature.

The French prince and the English here reiterated their promises of cordial friendship, pledged their faith not to invade each other's dominions during the crusade, mutually exchanged the oaths of all their barons and prelates to the same effect, and subjected themselves to the penalty of interdicts and excommunications if they should ever violate this public and solemn engagement. They then separated. Philip took the road to Genoa, Richard that to Marseilles, with a view of meeting their fleets, which were severally appointed to rendezvous in these harbors. They put to sea; and, nearly about the same time, were obliged by stress of weather to take shelter in Messina, where they were detained during the whole winter. This incident laid the foundation of animosities which proved fatal to their enterprise.

Richard and Philip were, by the situation and extent of their dominions, rivals in power; by their age and inclinations, competitors for glory; and these causes of emulation, which, had the princes been employed in the field against the common enemy, might have stimulated them to martial enterprises, soon excited, during the present leisure and repose, quarrels between monarchs of such a fiery character. Equally haughty, ambitious, intrepid, and inflexible, they were irritated with the least appearance of injury, and were incapable, by mutual condescensions, to efface those causes of complaint which unavoidably arose between them. Richard, candid, sincere, undesigning, impolitic, violent, laid himself open on every occasion to the designs of his antag-

[8] Hoveden, p. 660. [9] Vinisauf. p. 305.

onist, who, provident, interested, intriguing, failed not to take all advantages against him; and thus, both the circumstances of their disposition in which they were similar, and those in which they differed, rendered it impossible for them to persevere in that harmony which was so necessary to the success of their undertaking.

The last king of Sicily and Naples was William II., who had married Joan, sister to Richard, and who, dying without issue, had bequeathed his dominions to his paternal aunt, Constantia, the only legitimate descendant surviving of Roger, the first sovereign of those states who had been honored with the royal title. This princess had, in expectation of that rich inheritance, been married to Henry VI., the reigning emperor;[10] but Tancred, her natural brother, had fixed such an interest among the barons that, taking advantage of Henry's absence, he had acquired possession of the throne, and maintained his claim by force of arms against all the efforts of the Germans.[11] The approach of the crusaders naturally gave him apprehensions for his unstable government; and he was uncertain whether he had most reason to dread the presence of the French or of the English monarch. Philip was engaged in a strict alliance with the emperor, his competitor. Richard was disgusted by his rigors towards the queen dowager, whom the Sicilian prince had confined in Palermo, because she had opposed with all her interest his succession to the crown. Tancred, therefore, sensible of the present necessity, resolved to pay court to both these formidable princes; and he was not unsuccessful in his endeavors. He persuaded Philip that it was highly improper for him to interrupt his enterprise against the infidels by any attempt against a Christian state. He restored Queen Joan to her liberty, and even found means to make an alliance with Richard, who stipulated by treaty to marry his nephew, Arthur, the young Duke of Brittany, to one of the daughters of Tancred.[12] But before these terms of friendship were settled, Richard, jealous both of Tancred and of the inhabitants of Messina, had taken up his quarters in the suburbs, and had possessed himself of a small fort which commanded the harbor; and he kept himself extremely on his guard against their enterprises. The citizens took umbrage. Mutual insults and attacks passed between them and the English.

[10] Benedict. Abb. p. 580.   [11] Hoveden, p. 663.
[12] Hoveden, pp. 676, 677. Benedict. Abb. p. 615.

Philip, wno had quartered his troops in the town, endeavored to accommodate the quarrel, and held a conference with Richard for that purpose. While the two kings, meeting in the open fields, were engaged in discourse on this subject, a body of those Sicilians seemed to be drawing towards them, and Richard pushed forward in order to inquire into the reason of this extraordinary movement.[13] The English, insolent from their power, and inflamed with former animosities, wanted but a pretence for attacking the Messinese. They soon chased them off the field, drove them into the town, and entered with them at the gates. The king employed his authority to restrain them from pillaging and massacring the defenceless inhabitants; but he gave orders, in token of his victory, that the standard of England should be erected on the walls. Philip, who considered that place as his quarters, exclaimed against the insult, and ordered some of his troops to pull down the standard. But Richard informed him by a messenger that, though he himself would willingly remove that ground of offence, he would not permit it to be done by others; and if the French king attempted such an insult upon him, he should not succeed but by the utmost effusion of blood. Philip, content with this species of haughty submission, recalled his orders.[14] The difference was seemingly accommodated, but still left the remains of rancor and jealousy in the breasts of the two monarchs.

[1191.] Tancred, who for his own security desired to inflame their mutual hatred, employed an artifice which might have been attended with consequences still more fatal. He showed Richard a letter, signed by the French king, and delivered to him, as he pretended, by the Duke of Burgundy, in which that monarch desired Tancred to fall upon the quarters of the English, and promised to assist him in putting them to the sword as common enemies. The unwary Richard gave credit to the information, but was too candid not to betray his discontent to Philip, who absolutely denied the letter and charged the Sicilian prince with forgery and falsehood. Richard either was, or pretended to be, entirely satisfied.[15]

Lest these jealousies and complaints should multiply between them, it was proposed that they should, by a solemn treaty, obviate all future differences, and adjust every point

[13] Benedict. Abb. p. 608.   [14] Hoveden. p. 674.
[15] Hoveden, p. 688.   Benedict. Abb. pp. 642, 643.   Brompton, p. 1195.

that could possibly hereafter become a controversy between them. But this expedient started a new dispute, which might have proved more dangerous than any of the foregoing, and which deeply concerned the honor of Philip's family. When Richard, in every treaty with the late king, insisted so strenuously on being allowed to marry Alice of France, he had only sought a pretence for quarrelling, and never meant to take to his bed a princess suspected of a criminal amour with his own father. After he became master, he no longer spoke of that alliance; he even took measures for espousing Berengaria, daughter of Sanchez, King of Navarre, with whom he had become enamored during his abode in Guienne.[16] Queen Eleanor was daily expected with that princess at Messina;[17] and when Philip renewed to him his applications for espousing his sister Alice, Richard was obliged to give him an absolute refusal. It is pretended by Hoveden and other historians[18] that he was able to produce such convincing proofs of Alice's infidelity, and even of her having borne a child to Henry, that her brother desisted from his applications, and chose to wrap up the dishonor of his family in silence and oblivion. It is certain, from the treaty itself, which remains,[19] that, whatever were his motives, he permitted Richard to give his hand to Berengaria; and, having settled all other controversies with that prince, he immediately set sail for the Holy Land. Richard awaited some time the arrival of his mother and bride; and when they joined him, he separated his fleet into two squadrons, and set forward on his enterprise. Queen Eleanor returned to England, but Berengaria and the queen dowager of Sicily, his sister, attended him on the expedition.[20]

The English fleet, on leaving the port of Messina, met with a furious tempest; and the squadron on which the two princesses were embarked was driven on the coast of Cyprus, and some of the vessels were wrecked near Limisso, in that island. Isaac, Prince of Cyprus, who assumed the magnificent title of emperor, pillaged the ships that were stranded, threw the seamen and passengers into prison, and even refused to the princesses liberty, in their dangerous situation, of entering the harbor of Limisso. But Richard, who arrived soon after, took ample vengeance on him

---

[16] Vinisauf, p. 316.
[17] Matt. Paris, p. 112. Trivet, p. 102. W. Heming. p. 519.
[18] Hoveden, p. 688.
[19] Rymer, vol i. p. 69. Chron. de Dunst. p. 44.   [20] Benedict. Abb. p. 644.

for the injury. He disembarked his troops, defeated the
tyrant, who opposed his landing, entered Limisso by storm,
gained next day a second victory, obliged Isaac to surrender
at discretion, and established governors over the island.
The Greek prince, being thrown into prison and loaded with
irons, complained of the little regard with which he was
treated, upon which Richard ordered silver fetters to be
made for him; and this emperor, pleased with the distinction, expressed a sense of the generosity of his conqueror.[21]
The king here espoused Berengaria, who, immediately embarking, carried along with her to Palestine the daughter of
the Cypriot prince, a dangerous rival, who was believed to
have seduced the affections of her husband. Such were
the libertine character and conduct of the heroes engaged
in this pious enterprise.

The English army arrived in time to partake in the glory
of the siege of Acre, or Ptolemais, which had been attacked
for above two years by the united force of all the Christians
in Palestine, and had been defended by the utmost efforts
of Saladin and the Saracens. The remains of the German
army, conducted by the Emperor Frederick, and the separate
bodies of adventurers who continually poured in from the
West, had enabled the King of Jerusalem to form this important enterprise.[22] But Saladin, having thrown a strong
garrison into the place under the command of Caracos, his
own master in the art of war, and molesting the besiegers with
continual attacks and sallies, had protracted the success of
the enterprise, and wasted the force of his enemies. The
arrival of Philip and Richard inspired new life into the
Christians; and these princes, acting by concert, and sharing the honor and danger of every action, gave hopes of a
final victory over the infidels. They agreed on this plan of
operations : when the French monarch attacked the town,
the English guarded the trenches; next day, when the English prince conducted the assault, the French succeeded him
in providing for the safety of the assailants. The emulation
between those rival kings and rival nations produced extraordinary acts of valor; Richard in particular, animated
with a more precipitate courage than Philip, and more
agreeable to the romantic spirit of that age, drew to himself
the general attention, and acquired a great and splendid
reputation. But this harmony was of short duration; and

21 Benedict. Abb. p. 650. Annal. Waverl. p. 164. Vinisauf, p. 328. W. Heming. p. 523.   22 Vinisauf, pp. 269, 271, 279.

occasions of discord soon arose between these jealous and haughty princes.

The family of Bouillon, which had first been placed on the throne of Jerusalem, ending in a female, Fulk, Count of Anjou, grandfather to Henry II. of England, married the heiress of that kingdom, and transmitted his title to the younger branches of his family. The Angevin race, ending also in a female, Guy de Lusignan, by espousing Sibylla, the heiress, had succeeded to the title; and though he lost his kingdom by the invasion of Saladin, he was still acknowledged by all the Christians for King of Jerusalem.[23] But as Sibylia died without issue, during the siege of Acre, Isabella, her younger sister, put in her claim to that titular kingdom, and required Lusignan to resign his pretensions to her husband, Conrad, Marquis of Montferrat. Lusignan, maintaining that the royal title was unalienable and indefeasible, had recourse to the protection of Richard, attended on him before he left Cyprus, and engaged him to embrace his cause.[24] There needed no other reason for throwing Philip into the party of Conrad; and the opposite views of these great monarchs brought faction and dissension into the Christian army and retarded all its operations. The Templars, the Genoese, and the Germans declared for Philip and Conrad; the Flemings, the Pisans, the Knights of the Hospital of St. John, adhered to Richard and Lusignan. But notwithstanding these disputes, as the length of the siege had reduced the Saracen garrison to the last extremity, they surrendered themselves prisoners; stipulated, in return for their lives, other advantages to the Christians, such as the restoring of the Christian prisoners and the delivery of the wood of the true cross;[25] and this great enterprise, which had long engaged the attention of all Europe and Asia, was at last, after the loss of three hundred thousand men, brought to a happy period.

But Philip, instead of pursuing the hopes of further conquest and of redeeming the holy city from slavery, being disgusted with the ascendant assumed and acquired by Richard, and having views of many advantages which he might reap by his presence in Europe, declared his resolution of re-

---

[23] Vinisauf, p. 281.
[24] Trivet, p. 134. Vinisauf. p. 342. W. Heming. p. 524.
[25] This true cross was lost in the battle of Tiberiade, to which it had been carried by the crusaders for their protection. Rigord, an author of that age, says that after this dismal event all the children who were born throughout all Christendom had only twenty or twenty-two teeth, instead of thirty or thirty-two, which was their former complement (p. 14).

turning to France; and he pleaded his bad state of health as an excuse for his desertion of the common cause. He left, however, to Richard ten thousand of his troops, under the command of the Duke of Burgundy; and he renewed his oath never to commence hostilities against that prince's dominions during his absence. But he had no sooner reached Italy than he applied, it is pretended, to Pope Celestine III. for a dispensation from his vow; and when denied that request, he still proceeded, though after a covert manner, in a project which the present situation of England rendered inviting, and which gratified, in an eminent degree, both his resentment and his ambition.

Immediately after Richard had left England and begun his march to the Holy Land, the two prelates whom he had appointed guardians of the realm broke out into animosities against each other, and threw the kingdom into combustion. Longchamp, presumptuous in his nature, elated by the favor which he enjoyed with his master, and armed with the legatine commission, could not submit to an equality with the Bishop of Durham; he even went so far as to arrest his colleague, and to extort from him a resignation of the earldom of Northumberland, and of his other dignities, as the price of his liberty.[26] The king, informed of these dissensions, ordered, by letters from Marseilles, that the bishop should be reinstated in his offices; but Longchamp had still the boldness to refuse compliance, on pretence that he himself was better acquainted with the king's secret intentions.[27] He proceeded to govern the kingdom by his sole authority; to treat all the nobility with arrogance, and to display his power and riches with an invidious ostentation. He never travelled without a strong guard of fifteen hundred foreign soldiers, collected from that licentious tribe with which the age was generally infested. Nobles and knights were proud of being admitted into his train; his retinue wore the aspect of royal magnificence; and when in his progress through the kingdom he lodged in any monastery, his attendants, it is said, were sufficient to devour in one night the revenue of several years.[28] The king, who was detained in Europe longer than the haughty prelate expected, hearing of this ostentation, which exceeded even what the habits of that age indulged in ecclesiastics, being also informed of the insolent, tyrannical conduct of his minister, thought proper

26 Hoveden, p. 665. Knyghton, p. 2403.   27 W. Heming. p. 528.
28 Hoveden, p. 680. Benedict. Abb. pp. 626, 700. Brompton, p. 1193.

to restrain his power. He sent new orders, appointing Walter (Archbishop of Rouen), William Mareschal (Earl of
Strigul), Geoffrey Fitz-Peter, William Briewere, and Hugh
Bardolf counsellors to Longchamp, and commanding him to
take no measure of importance without their concurrence
and approbation. But such general terror had this man
impressed by his violent conduct that even the Archbishop
of Rouen and the Earl of Strigul durst not produce this
mandate of the king's; and Longchamp still maintained an
uncontrolled authority over the nation. But when he proceeded so far as to throw into prison Geoffrey, Archbishop
of York, who had opposed his measures, this breach of
ecclesiastical privileges excited such a universal ferment that
Prince John, disgusted with the small share he possessed in
the government, and personally disobliged by Longchamp,
ventured to summon at Reading a general council of the
nobility and prelates, and cite him to appear before them.
Longchamp thought it dangerous to intrust his person in
their hands, and he shut himself up in the Tower of London;
but being soon obliged to surrender that fortress, he fled
beyond sea, concealed under a female habit, and was
deprived of his offices of chancellor and chief justiciary;
the last of which was conferred on the Archbishop of Rouen,
a prelate of prudence and moderation. The commission of
legate, however, which had been renewed to Longchamp by
Pope Celestine, still gave him, notwithstanding his absence,
great authority in the kingdom, enabled him to disturb the
government, and forwarded the views of Philip, who watched
every opportunity of annoying Richard's dominions. [1192.]
That monarch first attempted to carry open war into Normandy; but as the French nobility refused to follow him in
an invasion of a state which they had sworn to protect, and
as the pope, who was the general guardian of all princes
that had taken the cross, threatened him with ecclesiastical
censures, he desisted from his enterprise, and employed
against England the expedient of secret policy and intrigue.
He debauched Prince John from his allegiance, promised
him his sister Alice in marriage, offered to give him
possession of all Richard's transmarine dominions; and had
not the authority of Queen Eleanor and the menaces of the
English council prevailed over the inclinations of that turbulent prince, he was ready to have crossed the seas and to
have put in execution his criminal enterprises.

The jealousy of Philip was every moment excited by

the glory which the great actions of Richard were gaining him in the East, and which, being compared to his own desertion of that popular cause, threw a double lustre on his rival. His envy, therefore, prompted him to obscure that fame which he had not equalled ; and he embraced every pretence of throwing the most violent and most improbable calumnies on the King of England. There was a petty prince in Asia, commonly called " The Old Man of the Mountain," who had acquired such an ascendant over his fanatical subjects that they paid the most implicit deference to his commands; esteemed assassination meritorious when sanctified by his mandate ; courted danger, and even certain death, in the execution of his orders ; and fancied that when they sacrificed their lives for his sake, the highest joys of paradise were the infallible reward of their devoted obedience.[29] It was the custom of this prince, when he imagined himself injured, to despatch secretly some of his subjects against the aggressor, to charge them with the execution of his revenge, to instruct them in every art of disguising their purpose ; and no precaution was sufficient to guard any man, however powerful, against the attempts of these subtle and determined ruffians. The greatest monarchs stood in awe of this Prince of the Assassins (for that was the name of his people; whence the word has passed into most European languages), and it was the highest indiscretion in Conrad, Marquis of Montferrat, to offend and affront him. The inhabitants of Tyre, who were governed by that nobleman, had put to death some of this dangerous people ; the prince demanded satisfaction ; for, as he piqued himself on never beginning any offence,[30] he had his regular and established formalities in requiring atonement. Conrad treated his messengers with disdain ; the prince issued the fatal order ; two of his subjects, who had insinuated themselves in disguise among Conrad's guards, openly, in the streets of Sidon, wounded him mortally; and when they were seized and put to the most cruel tortures, they triumphed amid their agonies, and rejoiced that they had been destined by Heaven to suffer in so just and meritorious a cause.

Every one in Palestine knew from what hand the blow came. Richard was entirely free from suspicion. Though that monarch had formerly maintained the cause of Lusignan against Conrad, he had become sensible of the bad effects at-

[29] W. Heming. p. 532. Brompton, p. 1243.   [30] Rymer, vol. i. p. 71.

tending those dissensions, and had voluntarily conferred on the former the kingdom of Cyprus, on condition that he should resign to his rival all pretensions to the crown of Jerusalem.[31] Conrad himself, with his dying breath, had recommended his widow to the protection of Richard.[32] The Prince of the Assassins avowed the action in a formal narrative which he sent to Europe ; [33] yet, on this foundation, the King of France thought fit to build the most egregious calumnies, and to impute to Richard the murder of the Marquis of Montferrat, whose elevation he had once openly opposed. He filled all Europe with exclamations against the crime ; appointed a guard for his own person, in order to defend himself against a like attempt ; [34] and endeavored, by these shallow artifices, to cover the infamy of attacking the dominions of a prince whom he himself had deserted, and who was engaged with so much glory in a war universally acknowledged to be the common cause of Christendom.

But Richard's heroic actions in Palestine were the best apology for his conduct. The Christian adventurers under his command determined, on opening the campaign, to attempt the siege of Ascalon, in order to prepare the way for that of Jerusalem ; and they marched along the sea-coast with that intention. Saladin purposed to intercept their passage ; and he placed himself on the road with an army amounting to three hundred thousand combatants. On this occasion was fought one of the greatest battles of that age, and the most celebrated for the military genius of the commanders, for the number and valor of the troops, and for the great variety of events which attended it. Both the right wing of the Christians, commanded by D'Avesnes, and the left, conducted by the Duke of Burgundy, were, in the beginning of the day, broken and defeated ; when Richard, who led on the main body, restored the battle, attacked the enemy with intrepidity and presence of mind, performed the part both of a consummate general and gallant soldier, and not only gave his two wings leisure to recover from their confusion, but obtained a complete victory over the Saracens, of whom forty thousand are said to have perished in the field.[35] Ascalon soon after fell into the hands of the Christians. Other sieges were carried on with equal success : Richard was even able to advance within sight of Jerusalem,

31 Vinisauf, p. 391.   32 Brompton, p. 1243.
33 Rymer, vol. i. p. 71.   Trivet, p. 124.   W. Heming. p. 544.   Diceto, p. 680.
34 W. Heming. p. 532.   Brompton, p. 1245.
35 Hoveden, p. 698. Benedict. Abb. p. 677. Diceto, p. 662. Brompton, p. 1214.

the object of his enterprise, when he had the mortification to find that he must abandon all hopes of immediate success, and must put a stop to his career of victory. The crusaders, animated with an enthusiastic ardor for the holy wars, broke at first through all regards to safety or interest in the prosecution of their purpose; and, trusting to the immediate assistance of Heaven, set nothing before their eyes but fame and victory in this world and a crown of glory in the next. But long absence from home, fatigue, disease, want, and the variety of incidents which naturally attend war, had gradually abated that fury which nothing was able directly to withstand; and every one, except the King of England, expressed a desire of speedily returning into Europe. The Germans and the Italians declared their resolution of desisting from the enterprise; the French were still more obstinate in this purpose; the Duke of Burgundy, in order to pay court to Philip, took all opportunities of mortifying and opposing Richard; [36] and there appeared an absolute necessity of abandoning for the present all hopes of further conquest, and of securing the acquisitions of the Christians by an accommodation with Saladin. Richard, therefore, concluded a truce with that monarch, and stipulated that Acre, Joppa, and other seaport towns of Palestine should remain in the hands of the Christians, and that every one of that religion should have liberty to perform his pilgrimage to Jerusalem unmolested. This truce was concluded for three years, three months, three weeks, three days, and three hours—a magical number, which had probably been devised by the Europeans, and which was suggested by a superstition well suited to the object of the war.

The liberty in which Saladin indulged the Christians, to perform their pilgrimages to Jerusalem, was an easy sacrifice on his part; and the furious wars which he waged in defence of the barren territory of Judea were not with him, as with the European adventurers, the result of superstition, but of policy. The advantage, indeed, of science, moderation, humanity, was at that time entirely on the side of the Saracens; and this gallant emperor in particular displayed, during the course of the war, a spirit and generosity which even his bigoted enemies were obliged to acknowledge and admire. Richard, equally martial and brave, carried with him more of the barbarian character, and was guilty of acts of ferocity which threw a stain on his celebrated victories.

[36] Vinisauf, p. 380.

When Saladin refused to ratify the capitulation of Acre, the King of England ordered all his prisoners, to the number of five thousand, to be butchered; and the Saracens found themselves obliged to retaliate upon the Christians by a like cruelty.[37] Saladin died at Damascus soon after concluding this truce with the princes of the crusade. It is memorable that, before he expired, he ordered his winding-sheet to be carried as a standard through every street of the city; while a crier went before, and proclaimed with a loud voice, " This is all that remains to the mighty Saladin, the conqueror of the East." By his last will he ordered charities to be distributed to the poor without distinction of Jew, Christian, or Mahometan.

There remained, after the truce, no business of importance to detain Richard in Palestine; and the intelligence which he received concerning the intrigues of his brother John and those of the King of France made him sensible that his presence was necessary in Europe. As he dared not to pass through France, he sailed to the Adriatic; and being shipwrecked near Aquileia, he put on the disguise of a pilgrim, with a purpose of taking his journey secretly through Germany. Pursued by the Governor of Istria, he was forced out of the direct road to England, and was obliged to pass by Vienna, where his expenses and liberalities betrayed the monarch in the habit of the pilgrim, and he was arrested by orders of Leopold, Duke of Austria. This prince had served under Richard at the siege of Acre; but, being disgusted by some insult of that haughty monarch, he was so ungenerous as to seize the present opportunity of gratifying at once his avarice and revenge, and he threw the king into prison. [1193.] The emperor, Henry VI., who also considered Richard as an enemy on account of the alliance contracted by him with Tancred, King of Sicily, despatched messengers to the Duke of Austria, required the royal captive to be delivered to him, and stipulated a large sum of money as a reward for this service. Thus, the King of England, who had filled the whole world with his renown, found himself, during the most critical state of his affairs, confined in a dungeon and loaded with irons, in the heart of Germany,[38] and entirely at the mercy of his enemies, the basest and most sordid of mankind

The English council was astonished on receiving this fa-

[37] Hoveden, p. 697. Benedict. Abb. p. 673. Matt. Paris, p. 115. Vinisauf, p. 346. W. Heming. p. 531.   [38] Chron. T. Wykes, p. 35.

tal intelligence, and foresaw all the dangerous consequences which might naturally arise from that event. The queen dowager wrote reiterated letters to Pope Celestine, exclaiming against the injury which her son had sustained ; representing the impiety of detaining in prison the most illustrious prince that had yet carried the banners of Christ into the Holy Land ; claiming the protection of the apostolic see, which was due even to the meanest of those adventurers ; and upbraiding the pope that in a cause where justice, religion, and the dignity of the church were so much concerned—a cause which it might well befit his holiness himself to support by taking in person a journey to Germany— the spiritual thunders should so long be suspended over those sacrilegious offenders.[39] The zeal of Celestine corresponded not to the impatience of the queen-mother ; and the regency of England were for a long time left to struggle alone with all their domestic and foreign enemies.

The King of France, quickly informed of Richard's confinement by a message from the emperor,[40] prepared himself to take advantage of the incident ; and he employed every means of force and intrigue, of war and negotiation, against the dominions and the person of his unfortunate rival. He revived the calumny of Richard's assassinating the Marquis of Montferrat ; and by that absurd pretence he induced his barons to violate their oaths, by which they had engaged that, during the crusade, they never would, on any account, attack the dominions of the King of England. He made the emperor the largest offers if he would deliver into his hands the royal prisoner, or at least detain him in perpetual captivity ; he even formed an alliance by marriage with the King of Denmark, desired that the ancient Danish claim to the crown of England should be transferred to him, and solicited a supply of shipping to maintain it. But the most successful of Philip's negotiations was with Prince John, who, forgetting every tie to his brother, his sovereign, and his benefactor, thought of nothing but how to make his own advantage of the public calamities. That traitor, on the first invitation from the court of France, suddenly went abroad, had a conference with Philip, and made a treaty of which the object was the perpetual ruin of his unhappy brother. He stipulated to deliver into Philip's hands a great part of Normandy ;[41] he received in return the investiture

39 Rymer, vol. i. pp. 72, 73, 74, 75, 76, etc.   40 Rymer, vol. i. p. 70.
41 Rymer, vol. i. p. 85.

of all Richard's transmarine dominions; and it is reported by several historians that he even did homage to the French king for the crown of England.

In consequence of this treaty, Philip invaded Normandy; and, by the treachery of John's emissaries, made himself master, without opposition, of many fortresses—Neufchatel, Neaufle, Gisors, Pacey, Ivrée. He subdued the counties of Eu and Aumale; and, advancing to form the siege of Rouen, he threatened to put all the inhabitants to the sword if they dared to make resistance. Happily Robert, Earl of Leicester, appeared in that critical moment—a gallant nobleman, who had acquired great honor during the crusade, and who, being more fortunate than his master in finding his passage homewards, took on him the command in Rouen, and exerted himself, by his exhortations and example, to infuse courage into the dismayed Normans. Philip was repulsed in every attack; the time of service from his vassals expired; and he consented to a truce with the English regency, received in return the promise of twenty thousand marks, and had four castles put into his hands as security for the payment.[42]

Prince John, who, with a view of increasing the general confusion, went over to England, was still less successful in his enterprises. He was only able to make himself master of the castles of Windsor and Wallingford; but when he arrived in London, and claimed the kingdom as heir to his brother, of whose death he pretended to have received certain intelligence, he was rejected by all the barons, and measures were taken to oppose and subdue him.[43] The justiciaries, supported by the general affection of the people, provided so well for the defence of the kingdom that John was obliged, after some fruitless efforts, to conclude a truce with them; and before its expiration he thought it prudent to return to France, where he openly avowed his alliance with Philip.[44]

Meanwhile the high spirit of Richard suffered in Germany every kind of insult and indignity. The French ambassadors, in their master's name, renounced him as a vassal to the crown of France, and declared all his fiefs to be forfeited to his liege lord. The emperor, that he might render him more impatient for the recovery of his liberty and make him submit to the payment of a larger ransom, treated him with the greatest severity, and reduced him to a condition

---

[42] Hoveden, pp. 730, 731. Rymer, vol. i. p. 81.   [43] Hoveden, p. 724.
[44] W. Heming, p. 536.

worse than that of the meanest malefactor. He was even
produced before the diet of the empire at Worms, and accused by Henry of many crimes and misdemeanors—of making an alliance with Tancred, the ursurper of Sicily ; of
turning the arms of the crusade against a Christian prince,
and subduing Cyprus ; of affronting the Duke of Austria before Acre ; of obstructing the progress of the Christian arms
by his quarrels with the King of France ; of assassinating
Conrad, Marquis of Montferrat ; and of concluding a truce
with Saladin, and leaving Jerusalem in the hands of the Saracen emperor.[45]   Richard, whose spirit was not broken by his
misfortunes, and whose genius was rather roused by these
frivolous or scandalous imputations, after premising that his
dignity exempted him from answering before any jurisdiction except that of Heaven, yet condescended, for the sake
of his reputation, to justify his conduct before that great
assembly.   He observed that he had no hand in Tancred's
elevation, and only concluded a treaty with a prince whom he
found in possession of the throne ; that the king, or rather
tyrant, of Cyprus had provoked his indignation by the most
ungenerous and unjust proceedings ; and though he chastised
this aggressor, he had not retarded a moment the progress
of his chief enterprise ; that if he had at any time been wanting in civility to the Duke of Austria, he had already been
sufficiently punished for that sally of passion ; and it better
became men embarked together in so holy a cause to forgive
each other's infirmities than to pursue a slight offence with
such unrelenting vengeance ; that it had sufficiently appeared
by the event whether the King of France or he were most
zealous for the conquest of the Holy Land, and were most
likely to sacrifice private passions and animosities to that
great object ; that if the whole tenor of his life had not
shown him incapable of a base assassination, and justified
him from that imputation in the eyes of his very enemies, it
was in vain for him at present to make his apology or plead
the many irrefragable arguments which he could produce
in his own favor ; and that, however he might regret the necessity, he was so far from being ashamed of his truce with
Saladin that he rather gloried in that event ; and thought
it extremely honorable that, though abandoned by all the
world, supported only by his own courage and by the small
remains of his national troops, he could yet obtain such conditions from the most powerful and most warlike emperor

[45] Matt. Paris, p. 122.   W. Heming. p. 536.

that the East had ever yet produced. Richard, after thus deigning to apologize for his conduct, burst out into indignation at the cruel treatment which he had met with; that he, the champion of the cross, still wearing that honorable badge, should, after expending the blood and treasure of his subjects in the common cause of Christendom, be intercepted by Christian princes in his return to his own country, be thrown into a dungeon, be loaded with irons, be obliged to plead his cause, as if he were a subject and a malefactor; and, what he still more regretted, be thereby prevented from making preparations for a new crusade, which he had projected after the expiration of the truce, and from redeeming the sepulchre of Christ, which had so long been profaned by the dominion of infidels. The spirit and eloquence of Richard made such impression on the German princes that they exclaimed loudly against the conduct of the emperor; the pope threatened him with excommunication; and Henry, who had hearkened to the proposals of the King of France and Prince John, found that it would be impracticable for him to execute his and their base purposes, or to detain the King of England any longer in captivity. He therefore concluded with him a treaty for his ransom, and agreed to restore him to his freedom for the sum of a hundred and fifty thousand marks, about three hundred thousand pounds of our present money; of which a hundred thousand marks were to be paid before he received his liberty, and sixty-seven hostages delivered for the remainder.[46] The emperor, as if to gloss over the infamy of this transaction, made at the same time a present to Richard of the kingdom of Arles, comprehending Provence, Dauphiny, Narbonne, and other states, over which the empire had some antiquated claims—a present which the king very wisely neglected.

The captivity of the superior lord was one of the cases provided for by the feudal tenures; and all the vassals were in that event obliged to give an aid for his ransom. Twenty shillings were therefore levied on each knight's-fee in England; but as this money came in slowly and was not sufficient for the intended purpose, the voluntary zeal of the people readily supplied the deficiency. The churches and monasteries melted down their plate, to the amount of thirty thousand marks; the bishops, abbots, and nobles paid a fourth of their yearly rent; the parochial clergy contributed a tenth of their tithes; and the requisite sum being thus

[46] Rymer, vol. i. p. 84.

collected, Queen Eleanor, and Walter, Archbishop of Rouen, set out with it for Germany; paid the money to the emperor and the Duke of Austria at Mentz; delivered them hostages for the remainder, and freed Richard from captivity. [1194.] His escape was very critical. Henry had been detected in the assassination of the Bishop of Liege, and in an attempt of a like nature on the Duke of Louvaine; and, finding himself extremely obnoxious to the German princes on account of these odious practices, he had determined to seek support from an alliance with the King of France; to detain Richard, the enemy of that prince, in perpetual captivity; to keep in his hands the money which he had already received for his ransom; and to extort fresh sums from Philip and Prince John, who were very liberal in their offers to him. He therefore gave orders that Richard should be pursued and arrested; but the king, making all imaginable haste, had already embarked at the mouth of the Scheldt, and was out of sight of land when the messengers of the emperor reached Antwerp.

The joy of the English was extreme on the appearance of their monarch, who had suffered so many calamities, who had acquired so much glory, and who had spread the reputation of their name into the farthest East, whither their fame had never before been able to extend. He gave them, soon after his arrival, an opportunity of publicly displaying their exultation by ordering himself to be crowned anew at Winchester; as if he intended by that ceremony to reinstate himself in his throne and to wipe off the ignominy of his captivity. Their satisfaction was not damped even when he declared his purpose of resuming all those exorbitant grants which he had been necessitated to make before his departure for the Holy Land. The barons, also, in a great council confiscated, on account of his treason, all Prince John's possessions in England; and they assisted the king in reducing the fortresses which still remained in the hands of his brother's adherents.[47] Richard, having settled everything in England, passed over with an army into Normandy; being impatient to make war on Philip, and to revenge himself for the many injuries which he had received from that monarch.[48] As soon as Philip heard of the king's deliverance from captivity, he wrote to his confederate John in these terms: "Take care of yourself; the devil is broken loose." [49]

[47] Hoveden, p. 737. Annal. Waverl. p. 165. W. Heming. p. 540.
[48] Hoveden, p. 740.   [49] Hoveden, p. 739.

When we consider such powerful and martial monarchs inflamed with personal animosity against each other, enraged by mutual injuries, excited by rivalship, impelled by opposite interests, and instigated by the pride and violence of their own temper, our curiosity is naturally raised, and we expect an obstinate and furious war, distinguished by the greatest events, and concluded by some remarkable catastrophe. Yet are the incidents which attend those hostilities so frivolous that scarce any historian can entertain such a passion for military descriptions as to venture on a detail of them—a certain proof of the extreme weakness of princes in those ages, and of the little authority they possessed over their refractory vassals! The whole amount of the exploits on both sides is the taking of a castle, the surprise of a straggling party, a rencounter of horse, which resembles more a rout than a battle. Richard obliged Philip to raise the siege of Verneuil; he took Loches, a small town in Anjou; he made himself master of Beaumont and some other places of little consequence; and after these trivial exploits, the two kings began already to hold conferences for an accommodation. Philip insisted that, if a general peace were concluded, the barons on each side should for the future be prohibited from carrying on private wars against each other; but Richard replied that this was a right claimed by his vassals, and he could not debar them from it. After this fruitless negotiation there ensued an action between the French and English cavalry at Fretteval, in which the former were routed, and the King of France's cartulary and records, which commonly at that time attended his person, were taken. But this victory leading to no important advantages, a truce for a year was at last, from mutual weakness, concluded between the two monarchs.

During this war Prince John deserted from Philip, threw himself at his brother's feet, craved pardon for his offences, and by the intercession of Queen Eleanor was received into favor. "I forgive him," said the king, "and hope I shall as easily forget his injuries as he will my pardon." John was incapable even of returning to his duty without committing a baseness. Before he left Philip's party, he invited to dinner all the officers of the garrison which that prince had placed in the citadel of Evreux. He massacred them during the entertainment; fell, with the assistance of the townsmen, on the garrison, whom he put to the sword, and then delivered up the place to his brother.

The King of France was the great object of Richard's resentment and animosity. The conduct of John, as well as that of the emperor and Duke of Austria, had been so base and was exposed to such general odium and reproach that the king deemed himself sufficiently revenged for their injuries; and he seems never to have entertained any project of vengeance against any of them. The Duke of Austria about this time, having crushed his leg by the fall of his horse at a tournament, was thrown into a fever; and, being struck, on the approaches of death, with remorse for his injustice to Richard, he ordered by will all the English hostages in his hands to be set at liberty, and the remainder of the debt due to him to be remitted. His son, who seemed inclined to disobey these orders, was constrained by his ecclesiastics to execute them.[50] [1195.] The emperor also made advances for Richard's friendship, and offered to give him a discharge of all the debt not yet paid to him, provided he would enter into an offensive alliance against the King of France—a proposal which was very acceptable to Richard, and was greedily embraced by him. The treaty with the emperor took no effect, but it served to rekindle the war between France and England before the expiration of the truce. This war was not distinguished by any more remarkable instances than the foregoing. After mutually ravaging the open country and taking a few insignificant castles, the two kings concluded a peace at Louviers, and made an exchange of some territories with each other.[51] [1196.] Their inability to wage war occasioned the peace; their mutual antipathy engaged them again in war before two months expired. Richard imagined that he had now found an opportunity of gaining great advantages over his rival by forming an alliance with the counts of Flanders, Toulouse, Boulogne, Champagne, and other considerable vassals of the crown of France.[52] But he soon experienced the insincerity of those princes, and was not able to make any impression on that kingdom while governed by a monarch of so much vigor and activity as Philip. The most remarkable incident of this war was the taking prisoner in battle the Bishop of Beauvais, a martial prelate, who was of the family of Dreux, and a near relation of the French king's. Richard, who hated that bishop, threw him into prison and loaded him with irons; and when the pope de-

---

[50] Rymer, vol. i. pp. 88, 102.   [51] Rymer, vol. i. p. 91.
[52] W. Heming, p. 549. Brompton, p. 1273. Rymer, vol. i. p. 94.

manded his liberty and claimed him as his son, the king
sent to his holiness the coat of mail which the prelate had
worn in battle and which was all besmeared with blood;
and he replied to him in the terms employed by Jacob's
sons to that patriarch, " This have we found: know now
whether it be thy son's coat or no." [53]   This new war
between England and France, though carried on with such
animosity that both kings frequently put out the eyes of
their prisoners, was soon finished by a truce of five years;
and immediately after signing this treaty the kings were
ready on some new offence to break out again into hostilities; when the mediation of the Cardinal of St. Mary,
the pope's legate, accommodated the difference. [54]   This
prelate even engaged the princes to commence a treaty for
a more durable peace; but the death of Richard put an end
to the negotiation.

Vidomar, Viscount of Limoges, a vassal of the king's,
had found a treasure, of which he sent part to that prince
as a present. [1199.] Richard, as superior lord, claimed
the whole; and at the head of some Brabançons besieged
the viscount in the castle of Chalons, near Limoges, in order
to make him comply with his demand. [55]   The garrison
offered to surrender; but the king replied that since he had
taken the pains to come thither and besiege the place in
person, he would take it by force, and would hang every
one of them.   The same day Richard, accompanied by
Marcadée, leader of his Brabançons, approached the castle
in order to survey it; when one Bertrand de Gourdon, an
archer, took aim at him, and pierced his shoulder with an
arrow.   The king, however, gave orders for the assault,
took the place, and hanged all the garrison, except Gourdon,
who had wounded him, and whom he reserved for a more
deliberate and more cruel execution. [56]

The wound was not in itself dangerous; but the unskil-
fulness of the surgeon made it mortal.   He so rankled
Richard's shoulder in pulling out the arrow that a gangrene
ensued; and that prince was now sensible that his life was
drawing towards a period.   He sent for Gourdon, and asked
him, " Wretch, what have I ever done to you to oblige you
to seek my life?"   " What have you done to me?" replied
coolly the prisoner.   " You killed with your own hands my
father and my two brothers; and you intended to have

---

[53] Genesis, chap. xxxvii. ver. 32.   Matt. Paris, p. 128.   Brompton, p. 1273.
[54] Rymer, vol. i. pp. 109, 110.   [55] Hoveden, p. 791.   Knyghton, p. 2413.
[56] Ibid.

hanged myself. I am now in your power, and you may take revenge by inflicting on me the most severe torments; but I shall endure them all with pleasure, provided I can think that I have been so happy as to rid the world of such a nuisance." [57] Richard, struck with the reasonableness of this reply, and humbled by the near approach of death, ordered Gourdon to be set at liberty, and a sum of money to be given him; but Marcadée, unknown to him, seized the unhappy man, flayed him alive, and then hanged him. Richard died in the tenth year of his reign and the forty-second of his age, and he left no issue behind him.

The most shining parts of this prince's character are his military talents. No man, even in that romantic age, carried personal courage and intrepidity to a greater height; and this quality gained him the appellation of the Lion-hearted (*Cœur de Lion*). He passionately loved glory, chiefly military glory; and as his conduct in the field was not inferior to his valor, he seems to have possessed every talent necessary for acquiring it. His resentments also were high, his pride unconquerable; and his subjects as well as his neighbors had therefore reason to apprehend from the continuance of his reign a perpetual scene of blood and violence. Of an impetuous and vehement spirit, he was distinguished by all the good as well as the bad qualities incident to that character. He was open, frank, generous, sincere, and brave; he was revengeful, domineering, ambitious, haughty, and cruel; and was thus better calculated to dazzle men by the splendor of his enterprises than either to promote their happiness or his own grandeur by a sound and well-regulated policy. As military talents made great impression on the people, he seems to have been much beloved by his English subjects; and he is remarked to have been the first prince of the Norman line that bore any sincere regard to them. He passed, however, only four months of his reign in that kingdom. The crusade employed him near three years; he was detained about fourteen months in captivity; the rest of his reign was spent either in war or preparations for war against France; and he was so pleased with the fame which he had acquired in the East that he determined, notwithstanding his past misfortunes, to have further exhausted his kingdom, and to have exposed himself to new hazards, by conducting another expedition against the infidels.

[57] Hoveden, p. 791. Brompton, p. 1277. Knyghton, p. 2413.

Though the English pleased themselves with the glory which the king's martial genius procured them, his reign was very oppressive and somewhat arbitrary by the high taxes which he levied on them, and often without consent of the states or great council. In the ninth year of his reign, he levied five shillings on each hide of land; and, because the clergy refused to contribute their share, he put them out of the protection of law, and ordered the civil courts to give them no sentence for any debts which they might claim.[58] Twice in his reign he ordered all his charters to be sealed anew, and the parties to pay fees for the renewal.[59] It is said that Hubert, his justiciary, sent him over to France, in the space of two years, no less a sum than one million one hundred thousand marks, besides bearing all the charges of the government in England. But this account is quite incredible, unless we suppose that Richard made a thorough dilapidation of the demesnes of the crown, which it is not likely he could do with any advantage after his former resumption of all grants. A king who possessed such a revenue could never have endured fourteen months' captivity for not paying a hundred and fifty thousand marks to the emperor, and be obliged at last to leave hostages for a third of the sum. The prices of commodities in this reign are also a certain proof that no such enormous sum could be levied on the people. A hide of land, or about a hundred and twenty acres, was commonly let at twenty shillings a year, money of that time. As there were two hundred and forty-three thousand six hundred hides in England, it is easy to compute the amount of all the landed rents of the kingdom. The general and stated price of an ox was four shillings; of a laboring horse the same; of a sow, one shilling; of a sheep with fine wool, tenpence; with coarse wool, sixpence.[60] These commodities seem not to have advanced in their prices since the Conquest,[61] and to have still been ten times cheaper than at present.

Richard renewed the severe laws against transgressors in his forests, whom he punished by castration and putting out their eyes, as in the reign of his great-grandfather. He established by law one weight and measure throughout his kingdom [62]—a useful institution which the mercenary dispo-

[58] Hoveden, p. 743.   Tyrrel, vol. ii. p. 563.
[59] Prynne's Chronol. Vindic. vol. i. p. 1133.
[60] Hoveden, p. 745.   [61] See note [S] at the end of the volume.
[62] Matt. Paris, pp. 109, 134.   Trivet, p. 127.   Annal. Waverl. p. 165.   Hoveden, p. 774.

sition and necessities of his successor engaged him to dispense with for money.

The disorders in London, derived from its bad police, had risen to a great height during this reign; and in the year 1196 there seemed to be formed so regular a conspiracy among the numerous malefactors as threatened the city with destruction. There was one William Fitz-Osbert, commonly called *Longbeard*, a lawyer, who had rendered himself extremely popular among the lower rank of citizens; and, by defending them on all occasions, had acquired the appellation of the advocate or savior of the poor. He exerted his authority by injuring and insulting the more substantial citizens, with whom he lived in a state of hostility, and who were every moment exposed to the most outrageous violences from him and his licentious emissaries. Murders were daily committed in the streets; houses were broken open and pillaged in daylight; and it is pretended that no less than fifty-two thousand persons had entered into an association by which they bound themselves to obey all the orders of this dangerous ruffian. Archbishop Hubert, who was then chief justiciary, summoned him before the council to answer for his conduct; but he came so well attended that no one durst accuse him, or give evidence against him; and the primate, finding the impotence of law, contented himself with exacting from the citizens hostages for their good behavior. He kept, however, a watchful eye on Fitz-Osbert, and seizing a favorable opportunity, attempted to commit him to custody; but the criminal, murdering one of the public officers, escaped with his concubine to the church of St. Mary le Bow, where he defended himself by force of arms. He was at last forced from his retreat, condemned, and executed, amid the regrets of the populace, who were so devoted to his memory that they stole his gibbet, paid the same veneration to it as to the cross, and were equally zealous in propagating and attesting reports of the miracles wrought by it.[63] But though the sectaries of this superstition were punished by the justiciary,[64] it received so little encouragement from the established clergy, whose property was endangered by such seditious practices, that it suddenly sank and vanished.

It was during the crusades that the custom of using coats of arms was first introduced into Europe. The

---

[63] Hoveden, p. 765.   Diceto, p. 691.   Gul. Neub. pp. 492, 493.
[64] Gervase. p. 1551.

knights, cased up in armor, had no way to make themselves be known and distinguished in battle but by the devices on their shields; and these were gradually adopted by their posterity and families, who were proud of the pious and military enterprises of their ancestors.

King Richard was a passionate lover of poetry. There even remain some poetical works of his composition; and he bears a rank among the Provençal poets, or *Trobadores*, who were the first of the modern Europeans that distinguished themselves by attempts of that nature.

CHAPTER XI.

JOHN.

ACCESSION OF THE KING.—HIS MARRIAGE.—WAR WITH
FRANCE.—MURDER OF ARTHUR, DUKE OF BRITTANY.—
THE KING EXPELLED THE FRENCH PROVINCES.—THE
KING'S QUARREL WITH THE COURT OF ROME.—CARDINAL
LANGTON APPOINTED ARCHBISHOP OF CANTERBURY.—
INTERDICT OF THE KINGDOM.—EXCOMMUNICATION OF
THE KING.—THE KING'S SUBMISSION TO THE POPE.—DIS-
CONTENTS OF THE BARONS.—INSURRECTION OF THE
BARONS.—MAGNA CHARTA.—RENEWAL OF THE CIVIL
WARS.—PRINCE LEWIS CALLED OVER.—DEATH AND CHAR-
ACTER OF THE KING.

[1199.] THE noble and free genius of the ancients,
which made the government of a single person be always
regarded as a species of tyranny and usurpation, and kept
them from forming any conception of a legal and regular
monarchy, had rendered them entirely ignorant both of the
rights of *primogeniture* and a *representation* in succession,
inventions so necessary for preserving order in the lines of
princes, for obviating the evils of civil discord and of usurpation, and for begetting moderation in that species of government by giving security to the ruling sovereign. These
innovations arose from the feudal law; which, first introducing the right of primogeniture, made such a distinction
between the families of the elder and younger brothers that
the son of the former was thought entitled to succeed to his
grandfather, preferably to his uncles, though nearer allied
to the deceased monarch. But though this progress of
ideas was natural, it was gradual. In the age of which we
treat, the practice of representation was indeed introduced,
but not thoroughly established, and the minds of men fluc-
tuated between opposite principles. Richard, when he entered on the holy war, declared his nephew, Arthur, Duke of
Brittany, his successor; and by a formal deed he set aside in
his favor the title of his brother John, who was younger than

Geoffrey, the father of that prince.[1] But John so little acquiesced in that destination that when he gained the
ascendant in the English ministry by expelling Longchamp,
the chancellor and great justiciary, he engaged all the English barons to swear that they would maintain his right of
succession; and Richard, on his return, took no steps towards restoring or securing the order which he had at first
established. He was even careful, by his last will, to declare his brother John heir to all his dominions;[2] whether
that he now thought Arthur, who was only twelve years of
age, incapable of asserting his claim against John's faction,
or was influenced by Eleanor, the queen-mother, who hated
Constantia, mother of the young duke, and who dreaded the
credit which that princess would naturally acquire if her
son should mount the throne. The authority of a testament
was great in that age, even where the succession of a kingdom was concerned; and John had reason to hope that this
title, joined to his plausible right in other respects, would
insure him the succession. But the idea of representation
seems to have made at this time greater progress in France
than in England. The barons of the transmarine provinces,
Anjou, Maine, and Touraine, immediately declared in favor
of Arthur's title, and applied for assistance to the French
monarch as their superior lord. Philip, who desired only
an occasion to embarrass John and dismember his dominions, embraced the cause of the young Duke of Brittany,
took him under his protection, and sent him to Paris to be
educated, along with his own son Lewis.[3] In this emergence, John hastened to establish his authority in the chief
members of the monarchy; and, after sending Eleanor into
Poictou and Guienne, where her right was incontestable,
and was readily acknowledged, he hurried to Rouen, and
having secured the duchy of Normandy, he passed over,
without loss of time, to England. Hubert, Archbishop of
Canterbury; William Mareschal, Earl of Strigul, who also
passes by the name of Earl of Pembroke; and Geoffrey Fitz-
Peter, the justiciary—the three most favored ministers of
the late king--—were already engaged on his side;[4] and the
submission or acquiescence of all the other barons put him,
without opposition, in possession of the throne.

The king soon returned to France, in order to conduct

---

[1] Hoveden, p. 677. Matt. Paris, p. 112. Chron. Dunst. p. 43. Rymer, vol. i.
pp. 66, 68. Benedict. Abb. p. 619.   [2] Hoveden, p. 791. Trivet, p. 138.
[3] Hoveden, p. 792. Matt. Paris, p. 137. Matt. West. p. 263. Knygh
2414.   [4] Hoveden, p. 793. Matt. Paris, p. 137.

the war against Philip and to recover the revolted provinces from his nephew Arthur. The alliances which Richard had formed with the Earl of Flanders [5] and other potent French princes, though they had not been very effectual, still subsisted, and enabled John to defend himself against all the efforts of his enemy. In an action between the French and Flemings, the elect Bishop of Cambray was taken prisoner by the former; and when the Cardinal of Capua claimed his liberty, Philip, instead of complying, reproached him with the weak efforts which he had employed in favor of the Bishop of Beauvais, who was in a like condition. The legate, to show his impartiality, laid, at the same time, the kingdom of France and the duchy of Normandy under an interdict, and the two kings found themselves obliged to make an exchange of these military prelates.

[1200.] Nothing enabled the king to bring this war to a happy issue so much as the selfish, intriguing character of Philip, who acted in the provinces that had declared for Arthur without any regard to the interests of that prince. Constantia, seized with a violent jealousy that he intended to usurp the entire dominion of them,[6] found means to carry off her son secretly from Paris. She put him into the hands of his uncle, restored the provinces which had adhered to the young prince, and made him do homage for the duchy of Brittany, which was regarded as a rerefief of Normandy. From this incident, Philip saw that he could not hope to make any progress against John, and, being threatened with an interdict on account of his irregular divorce from Ingelburga, the Danish princess whom he had espoused, he became desirous of concluding a peace with England. After some fruitless conferences, the terms were at last adjusted, and the two monarchs seemed in this treaty to have an intention, besides ending the present quarrel, of preventing all future causes of discord, and of obviating every controversy which could hereafter arise between them. They adjusted the limits of all their territories, mutually secured the interests of their vassals; and, to render the union more durable, John gave his niece, Blanche of Castile, in marriage to Prince Lewis, Philip's eldest son, and with her the baronies of Issoudun and Graçai, and other fiefs in Berri. Nine barons of the King of England, and as many of the King of France, were guarantees of this treaty; and all of them

5 Rymer, vol. i. p. 114. Hoveden, p. 794. M. Paris, p. 138.   6 Hoveden, p. 795.

swore that if their sovereign violated any article of it, they would declare themselves against him and embrace the cause of the injured monarch.[7]

John, now secure, as he imagined, on the side of France, indulged his passion for Isabella, the daughter and heir of Aymar Taillefer, Count of Angoulême, a lady with whom he had become much enamored. His queen, the heiress of the family of Gloucester, was still alive. Isabella was married to the Count de la Marche, and was already consigned to the care of that nobleman; though, by reason of her tender years, the marriage had not been consummated. The passion of John made him overlook all these obstacles: he persuaded the Count of Angoulême to carry off his daughter from her husband; and having, on some pretence or other, procured a divorce from his own wife, he espoused Isabella; regardless both of the menaces of the pope, who exclaimed against these irregular proceedings, and of the resentment of the injured count, who soon found means of punishing his powerful and insolent rival.

[1201.] John had not the art of attaching his barons either by affection or by fear. The Count de la Marche, and his brother, the Count d'Eu, taking advantage of the general discontent against him, excited commotions in Poictou and Normandy, and obliged the king to have recourse to arms in order to suppress the insurrection of his vassals. He summoned together the barons of England, and required them to pass the sea under his standard and to quell the rebels. He found that he possessed as little authority in that kingdom as in his transmarine provinces. The English barons unanimously replied that they would not attend him on this expedition, unless he would promise to restore and preserve their privileges[8]—the first symptom of a regular association and plan of liberty among those noblemen. But affairs were not yet fully ripe for the revolution projected. John, by menacing the barons, broke the concert, and both engaged many of them to follow him into Normandy, and obliged the rest who stayed behind to pay him a scutage of two marks on each knight's-fee as the price of their exemption from the service.

The force which John carried abroad with him, and that which joined him in Normandy, rendered him much superior to his malcontent barons; and so much the more as Philip did not publicly give them any countenance, and seemed as yet determined to persevere steadily in the alliance which he had contracted with England. But the king, elated with his superiority, advanced claims which gave a universal alarm to his vassals, and diffused still wider the general discontent. As the jurisprudence of those times required that the causes in the lord's court should chiefly be decided by duel, he carried along with him certain bravoes, whom he retained as champions, and whom he destined to fight with his barons, in order to determine any controversy which he might raise against them.[9] The Count de la Marche and other noblemen regarded this proceeding as an affront as well as an injury, and declared that they would never draw their swords against men of such inferior quality. The king menaced them with vengeance, but he had not vigor to employ against them the force in his hands, or to prosecute the injustice by crushing entirely the nobles who opposed it.

This government, equally feeble and violent, gave the injured barons courage as well as inclination to carry further their opposition. They appealed to the King of France, complained of the denial of justice in John's court, demanded redress from him as their superior lord, and entreated him to employ his authority and prevent their final ruin and oppression. [1202.] Philip perceived his advantage, opened his mind to great projects, interposed in behalf of the French barons, and began to talk in a high and menacing style to the King of England. John, who could not disavow Philip's authority, replied that it belonged to himself first to grant them a trial by their peers in his own court; it was not till he failed in this duty that he was answerable to his peers in the supreme court of the French king;[10] and he promised, by a fair and equitable judicature, to give satisfaction to his barons. When the nobles, in consequence of this engagement, demanded a safe-conduct, that they might attend his court, he at first refused it; upon the renewal of Philip's menaces, he promised to grant their demand; he violated this promise. Fresh menaces extorted from him a promise to surrender to Philip the fortresses of Tillières and Boutavant as a security for performance; he again violated his engagement. His enemies, sensible both of his weakness and want of faith, combined still closer in the resolution of pushing him to extremities; and a new

9 Annal. Burton, p. 262.   10 Philipp. lib. vi.

and powerful ally soon appeared to encourage them in their invasion of this odious and despicable government.

[1203.] The young Duke of Brittany, who was now rising to man's estate, sensible of the dangerous character of his uncle, determined to seek both his security and elevation by a union with Philip and the malcontent barons. He joined the French army, which had begun hostilities against the King of England; he was received with great marks of distinction by Philip; was knighted by him; espoused his daughter Mary; and was invested not only in the duchy of Brittany, but in the counties of Anjou and Maine, which he had formerly resigned to his uncle.[11] Every attempt succeeded with the allies. Tillières and Boutavant were taken by Philip, after making a feeble defence. Mortimer and Lyons fell into his hands almost without resistance. That prince next invested Gournai, and, opening the sluices of a lake which lay in the neighborhood, poured such a torrent of water into the place that the garrison deserted it; and the French monarch, without striking a blow, made himself master of that important fortress. The progress of the French arms was rapid, and promised more considerable success than usually in that age attended military enterprises. In answer to every advance which the king made towards peace, Philip still insisted that he should resign all his transmarine dominions to his nephew, and rest contented with the kingdom of England; when an event happened which seemed to turn the scales in favor of John, and to give him a decisive superiority over his enemies.

Young Arthur, fond of military renown, had broken into Poictou at the head of a small army; and, passing near Mirebeau, he heard that his grandmother, Queen Eleanor, who had always opposed his interests, was lodged in that place, and was protected by a weak garrison and ruinous fortifications.[12] He immediately determined to lay siege to the fortress, and make himself master of her person; but John, roused from his indolence by so pressing an occasion, collected an army of English and Brabançons, and advanced from Normandy with hasty marches to the relief of the queen-mother. He fell on Arthur's camp before that prince was aware of the danger; dispersed his army; took him prisoner, together with the Count de la Marche, Geoffrey de Lusignan, and the most considerable of the revolted

---

[11] Trivet, p. 142.   [12] Annal. Waverl. p. 167. Matt. West. p. 264.

barons; and returned in triumph to Normandy.[13] Philip, who was lying before Arques, in that duchy, raised the siege, and retired upon his approach.[14] The greater part of the prisoners were sent over to England; but Arthur was shut up in the castle of Falaise.

The king had here a conference with his nephew, represented to him the folly of his pretensions, and required him to renounce the French alliance which had encouraged him to live in a state of enmity with all his family. But the brave though imprudent youth, rendered more haughty from misfortunes, maintained the justice of his cause; asserted his claim not only to the French provinces, but to the crown of England; and, in his turn, required the king to restore the son of his elder brother to the possession of his inheritance.[15] John, sensible from these symptoms of spirit that the young prince, though now a prisoner, might hereafter prove a dangerous enemy, determined to prevent all future peril by despatching his nephew; and Arthur was never more heard of. The circumstances which attended this deed of darkness were, no doubt, carefully concealed by the actors, and are variously related by historians; but the most probable account is as follows: The king, it is said, first proposed to William de la Bray, one of his servants, to despatch Arthur; but William replied that he was a gentleman, not a hangman, and he positively refused compliance. Another instrument of murder was found, and was despatched with proper orders to Falaise; but Hubert de Bourg, chamberlain to the king, and constable of the castle, feigning that he himself would execute the king's mandate, sent back the assassin, spread the report that the young prince was dead, and publicly performed all the ceremonies of his interment; but finding that the Bretons vowed revenge for the murder, and that all the revolted barons persevered more obstinately in their rebellion, he thought it prudent to reveal the secret, and to inform the world that the Duke of Brittany was still alive and in his custody. This discovery proved fatal to the young prince; John first removed him to the castle of Rouen; and coming in a boat, during the night-time, to that place, commanded Arthur to be brought forth to him. The young prince, aware of his danger, and now more subdued by the continuance of his misfortunes and by the approach of death,

13 Ann. Marg. p. 213. Matt. West. p. 264.   14 Matt. West. p. 264.
15 Ibid.

threw himself on his knees before his uncle, and begged for mercy; but the barbarous tyrant, making no reply, stabbed him with his own hands; and fastening a stone to the dead body, threw it into the Seine.

All men were struck with horror at this inhuman deed; and from that moment the king, detested by his subjects, retained a very precarious authority over both the people and the barons in his dominions. The Bretons, enraged at this disappointment in their fond hopes, waged implacable war against him; and fixing the succession of their government, put themselves in a posture to revenge the murder of their sovereign. John had got into his power his niece, Eleanor, sister to Arthur, commonly called *the damsel of Brittany*, and, carrying her over to England, detained her ever after in captivity;[16] but the Bretons, in despair of recovering this princess, chose Alice for their sovereign, a younger daughter of Constantia by her second marriage with Guy de Thouars; and they intrusted the government of the duchy to that nobleman. The states of Brittany, meanwhile, carried their complaints before Philip, as their liege lord, and demanded justice for the violence committed by John on the person of Arthur, so near a relation, who, notwithstanding the homage which he did to Normandy, was always regarded as one of the chief vasals of the crown. Philip received their application with pleasure; summoned John to stand a trial before him, and on his non-appearance passed sentence, with the concurrence of the peers, upon that prince; declared him guilty of felony and parricide, and adjudged him to forfeit to his superior lord all his seignories and fiefs in France.[17]

The King of France, whose ambitious and active spirit had been hitherto confined, either by the sound policy of Henry or the martial genius of Richard, seeing now the opportunity favorable against this base and odious prince, embraced the project of expelling the English, or rather the English king, from France, and of annexing to the crown so many considerable fiefs, which, during several ages, had been dismembered from it. Many of the other great vassals, whose jealousy might have interposed, and have obstructed the execution of this project, were not at present in a situation to oppose it; and the rest either looked on with indifference, or gave their assistance to this dangerous ag-

16 Trivet, p. 145.　T. Wykes, p. 36.　Ypod. Neust. p. 459.
17 W. Heming. p. 455.　Matt. West. p. 264.　Knyghton, p. 2420.

grandizement of their superior lord. The Earls of Flanders and Blois were engaged in the holy war; the Count of Champagne was an infant, and under the guardianship of Philip; the duchy of Brittany, enraged at the murder of their prince, vigorously promoted all his measures; and the general defection of John's vassals made every enterprise easy and successful against him. Philip, after taking several castles and fortresses beyond the Loire, which he either garrisoned or dismantled, received the submission of the Count of Alençon, who deserted John, and delivered up all the places under his command to the French : upon which Philip broke up his camp, in order to give the troops some repose after the fatigues of the campaign. John, suddenly recollecting some forces, laid siege to Alençon; and Philip, whose dispersed army could not be brought together in time to succor it, saw himself exposed to the disgrace of suffering the oppression of his friend and confederate. But his active and fertile genius found an expedient against this evil. There was held at that very time a tournament at Moret, in the Gatinois, whither all the chief nobility of France and the neighboring countries had resorted in order to signalize their prowess and address. Philip presented himself before them, craved their assistance in his distress, and pointed out the plains of Alençon as the most honorable field in which they could display their generosity and martial spirit. Those valorous knights vowed that they would take vengeance on the base parricide, the stain of arms and of chivalry; and, putting themselves with all their retinue under the command of Philip, instantly marched to raise the siege of Alençon. John, hearing of their approach, fled from before the place, and in the hurry abandoned all his tents, machines, and baggage to the enemy.

This feeble effort was the last exploit of that slothful and cowardly prince for the defence of his dominions. He thenceforth remained in total inactivity at Rouen, passing all his time with his young wife in pastimes and amusements, as if his state had been in the most profound tranquillity, or his affairs in the most prosperous condition. If he ever mentioned war, it was only to give himself vaunting airs, which, in the eyes of all men, rendered him still more despicable and ridiculous. "Let the French go on," said he, "I will retake in a day what it has cost them years to acquire." [18] His stupidity and indolence appeared so ex-

[18] Matt. Paris, p. 146. Matt. West. p. 266.

traordinary that the people endeavored to account for the infatuation by sorcery, and believed that he was thrown into this lethargy by some magic or witchcraft. The English barons, finding that their time was wasted to no purpose, and that they must suffer the disgrace of seeing, without resistance, the progress of the French arms, withdrew from their colors, and secretly returned to their own country.[19] No one thought of defending a man who seemed to have deserted himself; and his subjects regarded his fate with the same indifference to which in this pressing exigency they saw him totally abandoned.

John, while he neglected all domestic resources, had the meanness to betake himself to a foreign power, whose protection he claimed. He applied to the pope, Innocent III., and entreated him to interpose his authority between him and the French monarch. Innocent, pleased with any occasion of exerting his superiority, sent Philip orders to stop the progress of his arms, and to make peace with the King of England. But the French barons received the message with indignation, disclaimed the temporal authority assumed by the pontiff, and vowed that they would, to the uttermost, assist their prince against all his enemies. Philip, seconding their ardor, proceeded, instead of obeying the pope's envoys, to lay siege to Château Gaillard, the most considerable fortress which remained to guard the frontiers of Normandy.

[1204.] Château Gaillard was situated partly on an island in the river Seine, partly on a rock opposite to it, and was secured by every advantage which either art or nature could bestow upon it. The late king, having cast his eye on this favorable situation, had spared no labor or expense in fortifying it; and it was defended by Roger de Laci, Constable of Chester, a determined officer, at the head of a numerous garrison. Philip, who despaired of taking the place by force, purposed to reduce it by famine; and that he might cut off its communication with the neighboring country, he threw a bridge across the Seine, while he himself with his army blockaded it by land. The Earl of Pembroke, the man of greatest vigor and capacity in the English court, formed a plan for breaking through the French intrenchments and throwing relief into the place. He carried with him an army of four thousand infantry and three thousand cavalry, and suddenly attacked, with great suc-

[19] Matt. Paris, p. 146.   Matt. West. p. 264.

cess, Philip s camp in the night-time; having left orders that a fleet of seventy flat-bottomed vessels should sail up the Seine, and fall at the same instant on the bridge. But the wind and the current of the river, by retarding the vessels, disconcerted this plan of operations; and it was morning before the fleet appeared, when Pembroke, though successful in the beginning of the action, was already repulsed with considerable loss, and the King of France had leisure to defend himself against these new assailants, who also met with a repulse. After this misfortune, John made no further efforts for the relief of Château Gaillard; and Philip had all the leisure requisite for conducting and finishing the siege. Roger de Laci defended himself for a twelvemonth with great obstinacy; and having bravely repelled every attack, and patiently borne all the hardships of famine, he was at last overpowered by a sudden assault in the night-time, and made prisoner of war, with his garrison.[20] Philip, who knew how to respect valor even in an enemy, treated him with civility, and gave him the whole city of Paris for the place of his confinement.

When this bulwark of Normandy was once subdued, all the province lay open to the inroads of Philip, and the King of England despaired of being any longer able to defend it. He secretly prepared vessels for a scandalous flight; and, that the Normans might no longer doubt of his resolution to abandon them, he ordered the fortifications of Pont de l'Arche, Molineaux, and Montfort l'Amauri to be demolished. Not daring to repose confidence in any of his barons, whom he believed to be universally engaged in a conspiracy against him, he intrusted the government of the province to Archas Martin and Lupicaire, two mercenary Brabançons, whom he had retained in his service. Philip, now secure of his prey, pushed his conquest with vigor and success against the dismayed Normans. Falaise was first besieged, and Lupicaire, who commanded in this impregnable fortress, after surrendering the place, enlisted himself with his troops in the service of Philip, and carried on hostilities against his ancient master. Caen, Coutance, Seez, Evreux, Baieux, soon fell into the hands of the French monarch, and all the Lower Normandy was reduced under his dominion. To forward his enterprises on the other division of the province, Guy de Thouars, at the head of the Bretons, broke into the territory, and took Mount St. Michael, Avranches, and all the

[20] Trivet, p. 144. Gul. Britto, lib. 7. Annal. Waverl. p. 168.

other fortresses in that neighborhood. The Normans, who abhorred the French yoke, and who would have defended themselves to the last extremity if their prince had appeared to conduct them, found no resource but in submission; and every city opened its gates as soon as Philip appeared before it. [1205.] Rouen alone, Arques, and Verneuil, determined to maintain their liberties, and formed a confederacy for mutual defence. Philip began with the siege of Rouen : the inhabitants were so inflamed with hatred to France that on the appearance of his army they fell on all the natives of that country whom they found within their walls, and put them to death. But after the French king had begun his operations with success, and had taken some of their outworks, the citizens, seeing no resource, offered to capitulate, and demanded only thirty days to advertise their prince of their danger and to require succors against the enemy. Upon the expiration of the term, as no supply had arrived, they opened their gates to Philip; [21] and the whole province soon after imitated the example and submitted to the victor. Thus was this important territory reunited to the crown of France, about three centuries after the cession of it by Charles the Simple to Rollo, the first duke; and the Normans, sensible that this conquest was probably final, demanded the privilege of being governed by French laws, which Philip, making a few alterations on the ancient Norman customs, readily granted them. But the French monarch had too much ambition and genius to stop in his present career of success. He carried his victorious army into the western provinces, soon reduced Anjou, Maine, Touraine, and part of Poictou; [22] and in this manner the French crown, during the reign of one able and active prince, received such an accession of power and grandeur as in the ordinary course of things it would have required several ages to attain.

John, on his arrival in England, that he might cover the disgrace of his own conduct, exclaimed loudly against his barons, who, he pretended, had deserted his standard in Normandy; and he arbitrarily extorted from them a seventh of all their movables as a punishment for the offence. [23] Soon after he forced them to grant him a scutage of two marks and a half on each knight's-fee for an expedition into Normandy; but he did not attempt to execute the service for

[21] Trivet, p. 147.   Ypod. Neust. p. 459.   Trivet, p. 149.
[23] Matt. Paris, 146.   Matt. West. p. 265.

which he pretended to exact it. Next year he summoned all the barons of his realm to attend him on this foreign expedition, and collected ships from all the seaports ; but meeting with opposition from some of his ministers, and abandoning his design, he dismissed both fleet and army and then renewed his exclamations against the barons for deserting him. He next put to sea with a small army, and his subjects believed that he was resolved to expose himself to the utmost hazard for the defence and recovery of his dominions; but they were surprised, after a few days, to see him return again into harbor without attempting anything. [1206.] In the subsequent season, he had the courage to carry his hostile measures a step further. Guy de Thouars, who governed Brittany, jealous of the rapid progress made by his ally, the French king, promised to join the King of England with all his forces ; and John ventured abroad with a considerable army, and landed at Rochelle. He marched to Angers, which he took and reduced to ashes. But the approach of Philip with an army threw him into a panic ; and he immediately made proposals for peace, and fixed a place of interview with his enemy ; but instead of keeping his engagement, he stole off with his army, embarked at Rochelle, and returned, loaded with new shame and disgrace, into England The mediation of the pope procured him at last a truce for two years with the French monarch ; [24] almost all the transmarine provinces were ravished from him ; and his English barons, though harassed with arbitrary taxes and fruitless expeditions, saw themselves and their country baffled and affronted in every enterprise.

In an age when personal valor was regarded as the chief accomplishment, such conduct as that of John, always disgraceful, must be exposed to peculiar contempt ; and he must thenceforth have expected to rule his turbulent vassals with a very doubtful authority. But the government exercised by the Norman princes had wound up the royal power to so high a pitch, and so much beyond the usual tenor of the feudal constitutions, that it still behooved him to be debased by new affronts and disgraces ere his barons could entertain the view of conspiring against him in order to retrench his prerogatives. The Church, which at that time declined not a contest with the most powerful and vigorous monarchs, took first advantage of John's imbecility, and,

[24] Rymer, vol. i. p. 141.

with the most aggravating circumstances of insolence and scorn, fixed her yoke upon him.

The papal chair was then filled by Innocent III., who, having attained that dignity at the age of thirty-seven years, and being endowed with a lofty and enterprising genius, gave full scope to his ambition, and attempted, perhaps more openly than any of his predecessors, to convert that superiority which was yielded him by all the European princes into a real dominion over them. [1207.] The hierarchy, protected by the Roman pontiff, had already carried to an enormous height its usurpations upon the civil power ; but in order to extend them further, and render them useful to the court of Rome, it was necessary to reduce the ecclesiastics themselves under an absolute monarchy, and to make them entirely dependent on their spiritual leader. For this purpose Innocent first attempted to impose taxes at pleasure upon the clergy ; and in the first year of this century, taking advantage of the popular frenzy for crusades, he sent collectors over all Europe, who levied, by his authority, the fortieth of all ecclesiastical revenues for the relief of the Holy Land, and received the voluntary contributions of the laity to a like amount.[25] The same year Hubert, Archbishop of Canterbury, attempted another innovation favorable to ecclesiastical and papal power. In the king's absence he summoned, by his legatine authority, a synod of all the English clergy, contrary to the inhibition of Geoffrey Fitz-Peter, the chief justiciary ; and no proper censure was ever passed on this encroachment, the first of the kind, upon the royal power. But a favorable incident soon after happened, which enabled so aspiring a pontiff as Innocent to extend still further his usurpations on so contemptible a prince as John.

Hubert the primate died in 1205 ; and as the monks or canons of Christ-church, Canterbury, possessed a right of voting in the election of their archbishop, some of the juniors of the order, who lay in wait for that event, met clandestinely the very night of Hubert's death, and, without any congé d'élire from the king, chose Reginald, their sub-prior, for the successor ; installed him in the archiepiscopal throne before midnight ; and, having enjoined him the strictest secrecy, sent him immediately to Rome, in order to solicit the confirmation of his election.[26] The vanity of Reginald prevailed over his prudence ; and he no sooner arrived in

Flanders than he revealed to every one the purpose of his journey, which was immediately known in England.[27] The King was enraged at the novelty and temerity of the attempt in filling so important an office without his knowledge or consent. The suffragan bishops of Canterbury, who were accustomed to concur in the choice of their primate, were no less displeased at the exclusion given them in this election. The senior monks of Christ-church were injured by the irregular proceedings of their juniors. The juniors themselves, ashamed of their conduct, and disgusted with the levity of Reginald, who had broken his engagements with them, were willing to set aside his election;[28] and all men concurred in the design of remedying the false measures which had been taken. But as John knew that this affair would be canvassed before a superior tribunal, where the interposition of royal authority in bestowing ecclesiastical benefices were very invidious—where even the cause of suffragan bishops were not so favorable as that of monks—he determined to make the new election entirely unexceptionable; he submitted the affair wholly to the canons of Christ-church, and, departing from the right claimed by his predecessors, ventured no further than to inform them privately that they would do him an acceptable service if they chose John de Gray, Bishop of Norwich, for their primate.[29] The election of that prelate was accordingly made without a contradictory vote; and the king, to obviate all contests, endeavored to persuade the suffragan bishops not to insist on their claim of concurring in the election; but those prelates, persevering in their pretensions, sent an agent to maintain their cause before Innocent; while the king and the convent of Christ-church despatched twelve monks of that order to support, before the same tribunal, the election of the Bishop of Norwich.

Thus there lay three different claims before the pope, whom all parties allowed to be the supreme arbiter in the contest. The claim of the suffragans, being so opposite to the usual maxims of the papal court, was soon set aside. The election of Reginald was so obviously fraudulent and irregular that there was no possibility of defending it; but Innocent maintained that, though this election was null and invalid, it ought previously to have been declared such by the sovereign pontiff, before the monks could proceed to a

---

[27] Matt. Paris, p. 148.   Matt. West. p. 266.   [28] Matt. West. p. 266.
[29] Matt. Paris, p. 149.   Matt. West. p. 266.

new election; and that the choice of the Bishop of Norwich was, of course, as uncanonical as that of his competitor.[30] Advantage was therefore taken of this subtlety for introducing a precedent by which the see of Canterbury, the most important dignity in the Church after the papal throne, should ever after be at the disposal of the court of Rome.

While the pope maintained so many fierce contests in order to wrest from princes the right of granting investitures, and to exclude laymen from all authority in conferring ecclesiastical benefices, he was supported by the united influence of the clergy, who, aspiring to independence, fought with all the ardor of ambition and of all the zeal of superstition under his sacred banners. But no sooner was this point, after a great effusion of blood and the convulsions of many states, established in some tolerable degree than the victorious leader, as is usual, turned his arms against his own community, and aspired to centre all power in his person. By the invention of reserves, provisions, commendams, and other devices, the pope gradually assumed the right of filling vacant benefices; and the plenitude of his apostolic power, which was not subject to any limitations, supplied all defects of title in the person on whom he bestowed preferment. The canons which regulated elections were purposely rendered intricate and involved. Frequent disputes arose among candidates. Appeals were every day carried to Rome. The apostolic see, besides reaping pecuniary advantages from these contests, often exercised the power of setting aside both the litigants, and, on pretence of appeasing faction, nominated a third person, who might be more acceptable to the contending parties.

The present controversy about the election to the see of Canterbury afforded Innocent an opportunity of claiming this right; and he failed not to perceive and avail himself of the advantage. He sent for the twelve monks deputed by the convent to maintain the cause of the Bishop of Norwich; and commanded them, under the penalty of excommunication, to choose for their primate Cardinal Langton, an Englishman by birth, but educated in France, and connected, by his interest and attachments, with the see of Rome.[31] In vain did the monks represent that they had received from their convent no authority for this purpose;

[30] Matt. Paris, p. 155.   Chron. de Mailr. p. 182.
[31] Matt. Paris, p. 155.   Annal. Waverl. p. 169.   W. Heming. p. 553.   Knyghton, p. 2415.

that an election, without a previous writ from the king, would be deemed highly irregular; and that they were merely agents for another person, whose right they had no power or pretence to abandon. None of them had the courage to persevere in this opposition, except one, Elias de Brantefield. All the rest, overcome by the menaces and authority of the pope, complied with his orders and made the election required of them.

Innocent, sensible that this flagrant usurpation would be highly resented by the court of England, wrote John a mollifying letter; sent him four golden rings set with precious stones; and endeavored to enhance the value of the present by informing him of the many mysteries implied in it. He begged him to consider seriously the *form* of the rings, their *number*, their *matter*, and their *color*. Their form, he said, being round, shadowed out eternity, which had neither beginning nor end; and he ought thence to learn his duty of aspiring from earthly objects to heavenly, from things temporal to things eternal. The number four, being a square, denoted steadiness of mind, not to be subverted either by adversity or prosperity, fixed forever on the firm basis of the four cardinal virtues. Gold, which is the matter, being the most precious of metals, signified wisdom, which is the most valuable of all accomplishments, and justly preferred by Solomon to riches, power, and all exterior attainments. The blue color of the sapphire represented faith; the verdure of the emerald, hope; the redness of the ruby, charity; and the splendor of the topaz, good works.[32] By these conceits Innocent endeavored to repay John for one of the most important prerogatives of his crown, which he had ravished from him—conceits probably admired by Innocent himself; for it is easily possible for a man, especially in a barbarous age, to unite strong talents for business with an absurd taste for literature and the arts.

John was inflamed with the utmost rage when he heard of this attempt of the court of Rome;[33] and he immediately vented his passion on the monks of Christ-church, whom he found inclined to support the election made by their fellows at Rome. He sent Fulke de Cantelupe and Henry de Cornhulle, two knights of his retinue, men of violent tempers and rude manners, to expel them the convent and take possession of their revenues. These knights entered the monastery with drawn swords, commanded the prior and the monks to depart the kingdom, and menaced them that in case of disobedience they would instantly burn them with the convent.[34] Innocent, prognosticating from the violence and imprudence of these measures that John would finally sink in the contest, persevered the more vigorously in his pretensions, and exhorted the king not to oppose God and the Church any longer, nor to prosecute that cause for which the holy martyr St. Thomas had sacrificed his life, and which had exalted him equal to the highest saints in heaven.[35] A clear hint to John to profit by the example of his father, and to remember the prejudices and established principles of his subjects, who bore a profound veneration to that martyr, and regarded his merits as the subjects of their chief glory and exultation.

Innocent, finding that John was not sufficiently tamed to submission, sent three prelates—the Bishops of London, Ely, and Worcester—to intimate that if he persevered in his disobedience, the sovereign pontiff would be obliged to lay the kingdom under an interdict.[36] All the other prelates threw themselves on their knees before him, and entreated him, with tears in their eyes, to prevent the scandal of this sentence by making a speedy submission to his spiritual father, by receiving from his hands the new-elected primate, and by restoring the monks of Christ-church to all their rights and possessions. He burst out into the most indecent invectives against the prelates; swore by God's teeth (his usual oath) that if the pope presumed to lay his kingdom under an interdict, he would send to him all the bishops and clergy of England, and would confiscate all their estates; and threatened that if thenceforth he caught any Romans in his dominions, he would put out their eyes and cut off their noses, in order to set a mark upon them which might distinguish them from all other nations.[37] Amid all this idle violence, John stood on such bad terms with his nobility that he never dared to assemble the states of the kingdom, who, in so just a cause, would probably have adhered to any other monarch, and have defended with vigor the liberties of the nation against these palpable usurpations of the court of Rome. Innocent, therefore, perceiving the king's weakness, fulminated at last the sentence of interdict, which he had for some time held suspended over him.[38]

The sentence of interdict was at that time the great in-

[34] Matt. Paris, p. 156.   Trivet, p. 151.   Annal. Waverl. p. 169.
[35] Matt. Paris, p. 157.   [36] Matt. Paris, p. 157.   [37] Ibid.
[38] Matt. Paris, p. 157.   Trivet, p. 152.   Annal. Waverl. p. 170.   Matt. West. p. 268.

strument of vengeance and policy employed by the court of Rome ; was denounced against sovereigns for the lightest offences ; and made the guilt of one person involve the ruin of millions, even in their spiritual and eternal welfare. The execution of it was calculated to strike the senses in the highest degree, and to operate with irresistible force on the superstitious minds of the people. The nation was of a sudden deprived of all exterior exercise of its religion ; the altars were despoiled of their ornaments ; the crosses, the relics, the images, the statues of the saints, were laid on the ground ; and, as if the air itself were profaned and might pollute them by its contact, the priests carefully covered them up, even from their own approach and veneration. The use of bells entirely ceased in all the churches ; the bells themselves were removed from the steeples, and laid on the ground with the other sacred utensils. Mass was celebrated with shut doors, and none but the priests were admitted to that holy institution. The laity partook of no religious rite, except baptism to new-born infants and the communion to the dying. The dead were not interred in consecrated ground : they were thrown into ditches or buried in common fields, and their obsequies were not attended with prayers or any hallowed ceremony. Marriage was celebrated in the churchyard ; [39] and, that every action in life might bear the marks of this dreadful situation, the people were prohibited the use of meat, as in Lent or times of the highest penance ; were debarred from all pleasures and entertainments ; and were forbidden even to salute each other, or so much as to shave their beards and give any decent attention to their person and apparel. Every circumstance carried symptoms of the deepest distress and of the most immediate apprehension of divine vengeance and indignation.

The king, that he might oppose *his* temporal to *their* spiritual terrors, immediately, from his own authority, confiscated the estates of all the clergy who obeyed the interdict ; [40] banished the prelates ; confined the monks in their convents, and gave them only such a small allowance from their own estates as would suffice to provide them with food and raiment. He treated with the utmost rigor all Langton's adherents, and every one that showed any disposition to obey the commands of Rome ; and in order to distress the clergy in the tenderest point, and at the same

[39] Chron. Dunst. vol. i. p. 51.　　　　　[40] Annal. Waverl. p. 170.

time expose them to reproach and ridicule, he threw into prison all their concubines, and required high fines as the price of their liberty.[41]

After the canons which established the celibacy of the clergy were, by the zealous endeavors of Archbishop Anselm, more rigorously executed in England, the ecclesiastics gave almost universally and avowedly into the use of concubinage; and the court of Rome, which had no interest in prohibiting this practice, made very slight opposition to it. The custom was become so prevalent that in some cantons of Switzerland, before the Reformation, the laws not only permitted, but, to avoid scandal, enjoined, the use of concubines to the younger clergy; [42] and it was usual everywhere for priests to apply to the ordinary and obtain from him a formal liberty for this indulgence. The bishop commonly took care to prevent the practice from degenerating into licentiousness : he confined the priest to the use of one woman, required him to be constant to her bed, obliged him to provide for her subsistence and that of her children ; and, though the offspring was in the eye of the law deemed illegitimate, this commerce was really a kind of inferior marriage, such as is still practised in Germany among the nobles, and may be regarded by the candid as an appeal from the tyranny of civil and ecclesiastical institutions to the more virtuous and more unerring laws of nature.

The quarrel between the king and the see of Rome continued for some years ; and though many of the clergy, from the fear of punishment, obeyed the orders of John and celebrated divine service, they complied with the utmost reluctance, and were regarded both by themselves and the people as men who betrayed their principles and sacrificed their conscience to temporal regards and interests. During this violent situation, the king, in order to give a lustre to his government, attempted military expeditions against Scotland, against Ireland, against the Welsh ; [43] and he commonly prevailed, more from the weakness of his enemies than from his own vigor or abilities. Meanwhile, the danger to which his government stood continually exposed from the discontents of the ecclesiastics increased his natural propension to tyranny ; and he seems to have even wantonly disgusted all orders of men, especially his nobles, from whom

41 Matt. Paris, p. 158. Annal. Waverl. p. 170.
42 Padre Paolo, Hist. Conc. Trid. lib. 1.
43 W. Heming. p. 556. Ypod. Neust. p. 460. Knyghton, p. 2420.

alone he could reasonably expect support and assistance. He dishonored their families by his licentious amours; he published edicts prohibiting them from hunting feathered game, and thereby restrained them from their favorite occupation and amusement;[44] he ordered all the hedges and fences near his forests to be levelled, that his deer might have more ready access into the fields for pasture; and he continually loaded the nation with arbitrary impositions. [1208.] Conscious of the general hatred which he had incurred, he required his nobility to give him hostages for security of their allegiance; and they were obliged to put into his hands their sons, nephews, or near relations. When his messengers came with like orders to the castle of William de Braouse, a baron of great note, the lady of that nobleman replied that she would never intrust her son into the hands of one who had murdered his own nephew while in his custody. Her husband reproved her for the severity of this speech; but, sensible of his danger, he immediately fled with his wife and son into Ireland, where he endeavored to conceal himself. The king discovered the unhappy family in their retreat; seized the wife and son, whom he starved to death in prison; and the baron himself narrowly escaped by flying into France.

[1209.] The court of Rome had artfully contrived a gradation of sentences by which it kept offenders in awe, still affording them an opportunity of preventing the next anathema by submission; and, in case of their obstinacy, was able to refresh the horror of the people against them by new denunciations of the wrath and vengeance of Heaven. As the sentence of interdict had not produced the desired effect on John, and as his people, though extremely discontented, had hitherto been restrained from rising in open rebellion against him, he was soon to look for the sentence of excommunication; and he had reason to apprehend that, notwithstanding all his precautions, the most dangerous consequences might ensue from it. He was witness of the other scenes which at that very time were acting in Europe, and which displayed the unbounded and uncontrolled power of the papacy. Innocent, far from being dismayed at his contests with the King of England, had excommunicated the Emperor Otho, John's nephew,[45] and soon brought that powerful and haughty prince to submit to his authority.

44 Matt. West. p. 268.
45 Matt. Paris, p. 160. Trivet, p. 154. Matt. West. p. 269.

He published a crusade against the Albigenses, a species of enthusiasts in the south of France, whom he denominated heretics, because, like other enthusiasts, they neglected the rites of the Church and opposed the power and influence of the clergy. The people from all parts of Europe, moved by their superstition and their passion for wars and adventures, flocked to his standard. Simon de Montfort, the general of the crusade, acquired to himself a sovereignty in these provinces; the Count of Toulouse, who protected, or perhaps only tolerated, the Albigenses, was stripped of his dominions; and these sectaries themselves, though the most innocent and inoffensive of mankind, were exterminated with all the circumstances of extreme violence and barbarity. Here were therefore both an army and a general, dangerous from their zeal and valor, who might be directed to act against John; and Innocent, after keeping the thunder long suspended, gave at last authority to the Bishops of London, Ely, and Worcester to fulminate the sentence of excommunication against him.[46] These prelates obeyed; though their brethren were deterred from publishing, as the pope required of them, the sentence in the several churches of their dioceses.

No sooner was the excommunication known than the effects of it appeared. Geoffrey, Archdeacon of Norwich, who was intrusted with a considerable office in the court of exchequer, being informed of it while sitting on the bench, observed to his colleagues the danger of serving under an excommunicated king, and he immediately left his chair and departed the court. John gave orders to seize him, to throw him into prison, to cover his head with a great leaden cope, and by this and other severe usage he soon put an end to his life;[47] nor was there anything wanting to Geoffrey, except the dignity and rank of Becket, to exalt him to an equal station in heaven with that great and celebrated martyr. Hugh de Wells, the chancellor, being elected by the king's appointment Bishop of Lincoln, upon a vacancy in that see, desired leave to go abroad, in order to receive consecration from the Archbishop of Rouen; but he no sooner reached France than he hastened to Pontigny, where Langton then resided, and paid submissions to him as his primate. The bishops, finding themselves exposed either to the jealousy of the king or hatred of the people, gradually stole out of the kingdom; and, at last, there remained only three prelates to perform the functions of the episcopal office.[48] Many of the nobility, terrified by John's tyranny, and obnoxious to him on different accounts, imitated the example of the bishops; and most of the others who remained were, with reason, suspected of having secretly entered into a confederacy against him.[49] John was alarmed at his dangerous situation—a situation which prudence, vigor, and popularity might formerly have prevented, but which no virtues or abilities were now sufficient to retrieve. He desired a conference with Langton at Dover; offered to acknowledge him as primate, to submit to the pope, to restore the exiled clergy, even to pay them a limited sum as a compensation for the rents of their confiscated estates. But Langton, perceiving his advantage, was not satisfied with these concessions; he demanded that full restitution and reparation should be made to all the clergy—a condition so exorbitant that the king, who probably had not the power of fulfilling it, and who foresaw that this estimation of damages might amount to an immense sum, finally broke off the conference.[50]

[1212.] The next gradation of papal sentences was to absolve John's subjects from their oaths of fidelity and allegiance, and to declare every one excommunicated who had any commerce with him in public or in private, at his table, in his council, or even in private conversation;[51] and this sentence was accordingly, with all imaginable solemnity, pronounced against him. But as John still persevered in his contumacy, there remained nothing but the sentence of deposition, which, though intimately connected with the former, had been distinguished from it by the artifice of the court of Rome; and Innocent determined to dart this last thunderbolt against the refractory monarch. But as a sentence of this kind required an armed force to execute it, the pontiff, casting his eyes around, fixed at last on Philip, King of France, as the person into whose powerful hand he could most properly intrust that weapon, the ultimate resource of his ghostly authority. And he offered the monarch, besides the remission of all his sins and endless spiritual benefits, the property and possession of the kingdom of England as the reward of his labor.[52]

[1213.] It was the common concern of all princes to oppose these exorbitant pretensions of the Roman pontiff, by

48 Annal. Waverl. p 170   Ann. Marg. p. 14.
49 Matt. Paris, p. 162.   Matt. West. pp. 270, 271.   50 Annal. Waverl. p. 171.
51 Matt. Paris, p. 161.   Matt. West. p. 270.
52 Matt. Paris, p. 162.   Matt. West. p. 271.

which they themselves were rendered vassals, and vassals totally dependent, of the papal crown; yet even Philip, the most able monarch of the age, was seduced by present interest, and by the prospect of so tempting a prize, to accept this liberal offer of the pontiff, and thereby to ratify that authority which, if he ever opposed its boundless usurpations, might next day tumble him from the throne. He levied a great army; summoned all the vassals of the crown to attend him at Rouen; collected a fleet of seventeen hundred vessels, great and small, in the seaports of Normandy and Picardy; and, partly from the zealous spirit of the age, partly from the personal regard universally paid him, prepared a force which seemed equal to the greatness of his enterprise. The king, on the other hand, issued out writs requiring the attendance of all his military tenants at Dover, and even of all able-bodied men, to defend the kingdom in this dangerous extremity. A great number appeared; and he selected an army of sixty thousand men—a power invincible had they been united in affection to their prince, and animated with a becoming zeal for the defence of their native country.[53] But the people were swayed by superstition, and regarded their king with horror, as anathematized by papal censures. The barons, besides lying under the same prejudices, were all disgusted by his tyranny, and were, many of them, suspected of holding a secret correspondence with the enemy; and the incapacity and cowardice of the king himself, ill fitted to contend with those mighty difficulties, made men prognosticate the most fatal effects from the French invasion.

Pandolf, whom the pope had chosen for his legate and appointed to head this important expedition, had, before he left Rome, applied for a secret conference with his master, and had asked him whether, if the King of England, in this desperate situation, were willing to submit to the apostolic see, the Church should, without the consent of Philip, grant him any terms of accommodation?[54] Innocent, expecting from his agreement with a prince so abject both in character and fortune more advantages than from his alliance with a great and victorious monarch, who, after such mighty acquisitions, might become too haughty to be bound by spiritual chains, explained to Pandolf the conditions on which he was willing to be reconciled to the King of England. The legate, therefore, as soon as he arrived in the north of

[53] Matt. Paris, p. 163.   Matt. West. p. 271.   [54] Matt. Par. 162.

France, sent over two Knights Templars to desire an interview with John at Dover, which was readily granted. He there represented to him, in such strong and probably in such true colors, his lost condition, the disaffection of his subjects, the secret combination of his vassals against him, the mighty armament of France, that John yielded at discretion,[55] and subscribed to all the conditions which Pandolf was pleased to impose upon him. He promised, among other articles, that he would submit himself entirely to the judgment of the pope; that he would acknowledge Langton for primate; that he would restore all the exiled clergy and laity, who had been banished on account of the contest; that he would make them full restitution of their goods, and compensation for all damages, and instantly consign eight thousand pounds in part of payment; and that every one outlawed or imprisoned for his adherence to the pope should immediately be received into grace and favor.[56] Four barons swore along with the king to the observance of this ignominious treaty.[57]

But the ignominy of the king was not yet carried to its full height. Pandolf required him, as the first trial of obedience, to resign his kingdom to the Church; and he persuaded him that he could nowise so effectually disappoint the French invasion as by thus putting himself under the immediate protection of the apostolic see. John, lying under the agonies of present terror, made no scruple of submitting to this condition. He passed a charter, in which he said that, not constrained by fear, but of his own free-will, and by the common advice and consent of his barons, he had, for remission of his own sins and those of his family, resigned England and Ireland to God, to St. Peter and St. Paul, and to Pope Innocent and his successors in the apostolic chair. He agreed to hold these dominions as feudatory of the Church of Rome by the annual payment of a thousand marks—seven hundred for England, three hundred for Ireland—and he stipulated if he or his successors should ever presume to revoke or infringe this charter, they should instantly, except upon admonition they repented of their offence, forfeit all right to their dominions.[58]

In consequence of this agreement, John did homage to Pandolf, as the pope's legate, with all the submissive

[55] Matt. West. p. 271.
[56] Rymer, vol. i. p. 166. Matt. Paris, p. 163. Annal. Burt. p. 268.
[57] Rymer, vol. i. p. 170. Matt. Paris, p. 163.
[58] Rymer, vol. i. p. 176. Matt. Paris, p. 165.

rites which the feudal law required of vassals before their liege lord and superior. He came disarmed into the legate's presence, who was seated on a throne; he flung himself on his knees before him; he lifted up his joined hands and put them within those of Pandolf; he swore fealty to the pope; and he paid part of the tribute which he owed for his kingdom as the patrimony of St. Peter. The legate, elated by this supreme triumph of sacerdotal power, could not forbear discovering extravagant symptoms of joy and exultation. He trampled on the money which was laid at his feet as an earnest of the subjection of the kingdom—an insolence of which, however offensive to all the English, no one present, except the Archbishop of Dublin, dared to take any notice. But though Pandolf had brought the king to submit to these base conditions, he still refused to free him from the excommunication and interdict till an estimation should be taken of the losses of the ecclesiastics, and full compensation and restitution should be made them.

John, reduced to this abject situation under a foreign power, still showed the same disposition to tyrannize over his subjects which had been the chief cause of all his misfortunes. One Peter of Pomfret, a hermit, had foretold that the king, this very year, should lose his crown; and for that rash prophecy he had been thrown into prison in Corfe Castle. John now determined to bring him to punishment as an impostor; and, though the man pleaded that his prophecy was fulfilled, and that the king had lost the royal and independent crown which he formerly wore, the defence was supposed to aggravate his guilt. He was dragged at horses' tails to the town of Warham, and there hanged on a gibbet with his son.[59]

When Pandolf, after receiving the homage of John, returned to France, he congratulated Philip on the success of his pious enterprise; and informed him that John, moved by the terror of the French arms, had now come to a just sense of his guilt; had returned to obedience under the apostolic see, and even consented to do homage to the pope for his dominions; and, having thus made his kingdom a part of St. Peter's patrimony, had rendered it impossible for any Christian prince, without the most manifest and most flagrant impiety, to attack him.[60] Philip was enraged on receiving this intelligence. He exclaimed that, having, at the pope's instigation, undertaken an expedition which had

⁵⁹ Matt. Paris, p. 165. Chron. Dunst. vol. i. p. 56.   ⁶⁰ Trivet, p. 160.

cost him above sixty thousand pounds sterling, he was frustrated of his purpose at the time when its success was become infallible. He complained that all the expense had fallen upon him; all the advantages had accrued to Innocent. He threatened to be no longer the dupe of these hypocritical pretences; and, assembling his vassals, he laid before them the ill-treatment which he had received, exposed the interested and fraudulent conduct of the pope, and required their assistance to execute his enterprise against England, in which he told them that, notwithstanding the inhibitions and menaces of the legate, he was determined to persevere. The French barons were, in that age, little less ignorant and superstitious than the English; yet, so much does the influence of those religious principles depend on the present dispositions of men, they all vowed to follow their prince on his intended expedition, and were resolute not to be disappointed of that glory and those riches which they had long expected from this enterprise. The Earl of Flanders alone, who had previously formed a secret treaty with John, declaring against the injustice and impiety of the undertaking, retired with his forces; [61] and Philip, that he might not leave so dangerous an enemy behind him, first turned his arms against the dominions of that prince. Meanwhile, the English fleet was assembled under the Earl of Salisbury, the king's natural brother; and, though inferior in number, received orders to attack the French in their harbors. Salisbury performed this service with so much success that he took three hundred ships, destroyed a hundred more, [62] and Philip, finding it impossible to prevent the rest from falling into the hands of the enemy, set fire to them himself, and thereby rendered it impossible for him to proceed any further in his enterprise.

John, exulting in his present security, insensible to his past disgrace, was so elated with this success that he thought of no less than invading France in his turn, and recovering all those provinces which the prosperous arms of Philip had formerly ravished from him. He proposed this expedition to the barons who were already assembled for the defence of the kingdom. But the English nobles both hated and despised their prince. They prognosticated no success to any enterprise conducted by such a leader; and, pretending that their time of service was elapsed and all their provi-

[61] Matt. Paris, p. 166.
[62] Ibid. Chron. Dunst. vol. i. p. 59. Trivet, p. 157.

sions exhausted, they refused to second his undertaking.[63] The king, however, resolute in his purpose, embarked with a few followers, and sailed to Jersey, in the foolish expectation that the barons would at last be ashamed to stay behind.[64] But finding himself disappointed, he returned to England, and, raising some troops, threatened to take vengeance on all his nobles for their desertion and disobedience. The Archbishop of Canterbury, who was in a confederacy with the barons, here interposed ; strictly inhibited the king from thinking of such an attempt; and threatened him with a renewal of the sentence of excommunication if he pretended to levy war upon any of his subjects before the kingdom were freed from the sentence of interdict.[65]

The Church had recalled the several anathemas pronounced against John by the same gradual progress with which she had at first issued them.   By receiving his homage and admitting him to the rank of a vassal, his deposition had been virtually annulled, and his subjects were again bound by their oaths of allegiance.   The exiled prelates had then returned, in great triumph, with Langton at their head ; and the king, hearing of their approach, went forth to meet them, and, throwing himself on the ground before them, he entreated them, with tears, to have compassion on him and the kingdom of England.[66]   The primate, seeing these marks of sincere penitence, led him to the chapter-house of Winchester, and there administered an oath to him, by which he again swore fealty and obedience to Pope Innocent and his successors ; promised to love, maintain, and defend Holy Church and the clergy ; engaged that he would re-establish the good laws of his predecessors, particularly those of St. Edward, and would abolish the wicked ones; and expressed his resolution of maintaining justice and right in all his dominions.[67]   The primate next gave him absolution in the requisite forms, and admitted him to dine with him, to the great joy of all the people.   The sentence of interdict, however, was still upheld against the kingdom. A new legate, Nicholas, Bishop of Frescati, came into England in the room of Pandolf, and he declared it to be the pope's intention never to loosen that sentence till full restitution were made to the clergy of everything taken from them, and ample reparation for all damages which they had

[63] Matt. Paris, p. 166.
[64] Ibid.
[65] Matt. Paris, p. 167.
[66] Matt. Paris p. 166.   Annal. Waverl. p. 178.
[67] Matt. Paris, p. 166.

sustained. He only permitted mass to be said with a low voice in the churches till those losses and damages could be estimated to the satisfaction of the parties. Certain barons were appointed to take an account of the claims, and John was astonished at the greatness of the sums to which the clergy made their losses to amount. No less than twenty thousand marks were demanded by the monks of Canterbury alone; twenty-three thousand for the see of Lincoln; and the king, finding these pretensions to be exorbitant and endless, offered the clergy the sum of a hundred thousand marks for a final acquittal. The clergy rejected the offer with disdain; but the pope, willing to favor his new vassal, whom he found zealous in his declarations of fealty and regular in paying the stipulated tribute to Rome, directed his legate to accept of forty thousand. The issue of the whole was that the bishops and considerable abbots got reparation beyond what they had any title to demand; the inferior clergy were obliged to sit down contented with their losses; and the king, after the interdict was taken off, renewed, in the most solemn manner, and by a new charter, sealed with gold, his professions of homage and obedience to the see of Rome.

[1214.] When this vexatious affair was at last brought to a conclusion, the king, as if he had nothing further to attend to but triumphs and victories, went over to Poictou, which still acknowledged his authority,[68] and he carried war into Philip's dominions. He besieged a castle near Angiers; but the approach of Prince Lewis, Philip's son, obliged him to raise the siege with such precipitation that he left his tents, machines, and baggage behind him, and he returned to England with disgrace. About the same time he heard of the great and decisive victory gained by the King of France at Bovines over the Emperor Otho, who had entered France at the head of a hundred and fifty thousand Germans—a victory which established forever the glory of Philip, and gave full security to all his dominions. John could, therefore, think henceforth of nothing further than of ruling peaceably his own kingdom; and his close connections with the pope, which he was determined at any price to maintain, insured him, as he imagined, the certain attainment of that object. But the last and most grievous scene of this prince's misfortunes still awaited him, and he was destined to pass through a series of more humiliating

68 Queen Eleanor died in 1203 or 1204.

circumstances than had ever yet fallen to the lot of any other monarch.

The introduction of the feudal law into England by William the Conqueror had much infringed the liberties, however imperfect, enjoyed by the Anglo-Saxons in their ancient government, and had reduced the whole people to a state of vassalage under the king or barons, and even the greater part of them to a state of real slavery. The necessity also of intrusting great power in the hands of a prince who was to maintain military dominion over a vanquished nation had engaged the Norman barons to submit to a more severe and absolute prerogative than that to which men of their rank in other feudal governments were commonly subjected. The power of the crown, once raised to a high pitch, was not easily reduced; and the nation, during the course of a hundred and fifty years, was governed by an authority unknown, in the same degree, to all the kingdoms founded by the northern conquerors. Henry I., that he might allure the people to give an exclusion to his elder brother Robert, had granted them a charter favorable in many particulars to their liberties. Stephen had renewed the grant; Henry II. had confirmed it; but the concessions of all these princes had still remained without effect, and the same unlimited, at least irregular authority, continued to be exercised both by them and their successors. The only happiness was that arms were never yet ravished from the hands of the barons and people. The nation by a great confederacy might still vindicate its liberties, and nothing was more likely than the character, conduct, and fortunes of the reigning prince to produce such a general combination against him. Equally odious and contemptible both in public and private life, he affronted the barons by his insolence, dishonored their families by his gallantries, enraged them by his tyranny, and gave discontent to all ranks of men by his endless exactions and impositions.[69] The effect of these lawless practices had already appeared in the general demand made by the barons of a restoration of their privileges; and after he had reconciled himself to the pope by abandoning the independence of the kingdom, he appeared to all his subjects in so mean a light that they universally thought they might with safety and honor insist upon their pretensions.

[69] Chron. Mailr. p. 188. T. Wykes, p. 36. Annal. Waverl. p. 181. W. Heming. p. 557.

But nothing forwarded this confederacy so much as the concurrence of Langton, Archbishop of Canterbury—a man whose memory, though he was obtruded on the nation by a palpable encroachment of the see of Rome, ought always to be respected by the English. This prelate, whether he was moved by the generosity of his nature and his affection to public good, or had entertained an animosity against John on account of the long opposition made by that prince to his election, or thought that an acquisition of liberty to the people would serve to increase and secure the privileges of the Church, had formed the plan of reforming the government, and had prepared the way for that great innovation by inserting those singular clauses above mentioned in the oath which he administered to the king before he would absolve him from the sentence of excommunication. Soon after, in a private meeting of some principal barons at London, he showed them a copy of Henry I.'s charter, which, he said, he had happily found in a monastery; and he exhorted them to insist on the renewal and observance of it. The barons swore that they would sooner lose their lives than depart from so reasonable a demand.[70] The confederacy began now to spread wider, and to comprehend almost all the barons in England; and a new and more numerous meeting was summoned by Langton at St. Edmondsbury, under color of devotion. He again produced to the assembly the old charter of Henry; renewed his exhortations of unanimity and vigor in the prosecution of their purpose; and represented in the strongest colors the tyranny to which they had so long been subjected, and from which it now behooved them to free themselves and their posterity.[71] The barons, inflamed by his eloquence, incited by the sense of their own wrongs, and encouraged by the appearance of their power and numbers, solemnly took an oath, before the high altar, to adhere to each other, to insist on their demands, and to make endless war on the king till he should submit to grant them.[72] They agreed that, after the festival of Christmas, they would prefer in a body their common petition; and in the meantime they separated, after mutually engaging that they would put themselves in a posture of defence, would enlist men and purchase arms, and would supply their castles with the necessary provisions.

[1215.] The barons appeared in London on the day ap-

[70] Matt. Paris, p. 167.   [71] Matt. Paris, p. 173.   [72] Matt. Paris, p. 176.

pointed, and demanded of the king that, in consequence of his own oath before the primate, as well as in deference to their just rights, he should grant them a renewal of Henry's charter and a confirmation of the laws of St. Edward. The king, alarmed with their zeal and unanimity, as well as with their power, required a delay; promised that, at the festival of Easter, he would give them a positive answer to their petition; and offered them the Archbishop of Canterbury, the Bishop of Ely, and the Earl of Pembroke, the mareschal, as sureties for his fulfilling this engagement.[73] The barons accepted of the terms, and peaceably returned to their castles.

During this interval, John, in order to break or subdue the league of his barons, endeavored to avail himself of the ecclesiastical power, of whose influence he had, from his own recent misfortunes, had such fatal experience. He granted to the clergy a charter, relinquishing forever that important prerogative for which his father and all his ancestors had zealously contended; yielding to them the free election on all vacancies ; reserving only the power to issue a *congé d'élire*, and to subjoin a confirmation of the election; and declaring that, if either of these were withheld, the choice should nevertheless be deemed just and valid.[74] He made a vow to lead an army into Palestine against the infidels, and he took on him the cross, in hopes that he should receive from the Church that protection which she tendered to every one that had entered into this sacred and meritorious engagement.[75] And he sent to Rome his agent, William de Mauclerc, in order to appeal to the pope against the violence of his barons, and procure him a favorable sentence from that powerful tribunal.[76] The barons also were not negligent on their part in endeavoring to engage the pope in their interests; they despatched Eustace de Vescie to Rome; laid their case before Innocent as their feudal lord: and petitioned him to interpose his authority with the king, and oblige him to restore and confirm all their just and undoubted privileges.[77]

Innocent beheld with regret the disturbances which had arisen in England, and was much inclined to favor John in his pretensions. He had no hopes of retaining and extending his newly acquired superiority over that kingdom but

[73] Matt. Paris, p. 176. Matt. West. p. 273. [74] Rymer, vol. i. p. 197.
[75] Rymer, vol. i. p. 200. Trivet, p. 162. T. Wykes, p. 37. Matt. West. p. 273.
[76] Rymer, vol. i. p. 184. [77] Ibid.

by supporting so base and degenerate a prince, who was willing to sacrifice every consideration to his present safety ; and he foresaw that, if the administration should fall into the hands of those gallant and high-spirited barons, they would vindicate the honor, liberty, and independence of the nation with the same ardor which they now exerted in defence of their own. He wrote letters therefore to the prelates, to the nobility, and to the king himself. He exhorted the first to employ their good offices in conciliating peace between the contending parties, and putting an end to civil discord ; to the second he expressed his disapprobation of their conduct in employing force to extort concessions from their reluctant sovereign ; the last he advised to treat his nobles with grace and indulgence, and to grant them such of their demands as should appear just and reasonable.[78]

The barons easily saw, from the tenor of these letters, that they must reckon on having the pope as well as the king for their adversary ; but they had already advanced too far to recede from their pretensions, and their passions were so deeply engaged that it exceeded even the power of superstition itself any longer to control them. They also foresaw that the thunders of Rome, when not seconded by the efforts of the English ecclesiastics, would be of small avail against them ; and they perceived that the most considerable of the prelates, as well as all the inferior clergy, professed the highest approbation of their cause. Besides that these men were seized with the national passion for laws and liberty, blessings of which they themselves expected to partake, there concurred very powerful causes to loosen their devoted attachment to the apostolic see. It appeared from the late usurpations of the Roman pontiff that he pretended to reap alone all the advantages accruing from that victory which, under his banners, though at their own peril, they had everywhere obtained over the civil magistrate. The pope assumed a despotic power over all the churches ; their particular customs, privileges, and immunities were treated with disdain ; even the canons of general councils were set aside by his dispensing power ; the whole administration of the Church was centred in the court of Rome ; all preferments ran of course in the same channel ; and the provincial clergy saw, at least felt, that there was a necessity for limiting these pretensions. The legate, Nicholas, in filling those numerous vacancies which had fallen in England during an interdict of six years, had proceeded in the most arbitrary manner; and had paid no regard, in conferring dignities, to personal merit, to rank, to the inclination of the electors, or to the customs of the country. The English Church was universally disgusted; and Langton himself, though he owed his elevation to an encroachment of the Romish see, was no sooner established in his high office than he became jealous of the privileges annexed to it, and formed attachments with the country subjected to his jurisdiction. These causes, though they opened slowly the eyes of men, failed not to produce their effect; they set bounds to the usurpations of the papacy; the tide first stopped, and then turned against the sovereign pontiff; and it is otherwise inconceivable how that age, so prone to superstition and so sunk in ignorance, or rather so devoted to a spurious erudition, could have escaped falling into an absolute and total slavery under the court of Rome.

About the time that the pope's letters arrived in England, the malcontent barons, on the approach of the festival of Easter, when they were to expect the king's answer to their petition, met by agreement at Stamford; and they assembled a force, consisting of above two thousand knights, besides their retainers and inferior persons without number. Elated with their power, they advanced in a body to Brackley, within fifteen miles of Oxford, the place where the court then resided; and they there received a message from the king, by the Archbishop of Canterbury and the Earl of Pembroke, desiring to know what those liberties were which they so zealously challenged from their sovereign. They delivered to these messengers a schedule containing the chief articles of their demands, which was no sooner shown to the king than he burst into a furious passion, and asked why the barons did not also demand of him his kingdom, swearing that he would never grant them such liberties as must reduce himself to slavery.[79]

No sooner were the confederated nobles informed of John's reply than they chose Robert Fitz-Walter their general, whom they called *the mareschal of the army of God and of Holy Church;* and they proceeded, without further ceremony, to levy war upon the king. They besieged the castle of Northampton during fifteen days, though without success;[80] the gates of Bedford Castle were willingly opened to them by William Beauchamp, its owner. They

<hr/>

[79] Matt. Paris, p. 176.   [80] Matt. Paris, p. 177.   Chron. Dunst. vol. i. p. 71.

advanced to Ware in their way to London, where they held a correspondence with the principal citizens; they were received without opposition into that capital; and, finding now the great superiority of their force, they issued proclamations requiring the other barons to join them, and menacing them, in case of refusal or delay, with committing devastation on their houses and estates.[81] In order to show what might be expected from their prosperous arms, they made incursions from London, and laid waste the king's parks and palaces; and all the barons, who had hitherto carried the semblance of supporting the royal party, were glad of this pretence for openly joining a cause which they always had secretly favored. The king was left at Odiham, in Hampshire, with a poor retinue of only seven knights; and after trying several expedients to elude the blow, after offering to refer all differences to the pope alone, or to eight barons—four to be chosen by himself, and four by the confederates[82]—he found himself at last obliged to submit at discretion.

A conference between the king and the barons was appointed at Runnymede, between Windsor and Staines, a place which has ever since been extremely celebrated on account of this great event. The two parties encamped apart like open enemies; and, after a debate of a few days, the king, with a facility somewhat suspicious, signed and sealed the charter which was required of him. This famous deed, commonly called the GREAT CHARTER, either granted or secured very important liberties and privileges to every order of men in the kingdom—to the clergy, to the barons, and to the people.

The freedom of elections was secured to the clergy; the former charter of the king was confirmed, by which the necessity of a royal *congé d'élire* and confirmation was superseded; all check upon appeals to Rome was removed, by the allowance granted every man to depart the kingdom at pleasure; and the fines to be imposed on the clergy for any offence were ordained to be proportional to their lay estates, not to their ecclesiastical benefices.

The privileges granted to the barons were either abatements in the rigor of the feudal law, or determinations in points which had been left by that law, or had become, by practice, arbitrary and ambiguous. The reliefs of heirs succeeding to a military fee were ascertained—an earl's and

[81] Matt. Paris, p. 177.   [82] Rymer, vol. i. p. 200.

baron's at a hundred marks, a knight's at a hundred shillings. It was ordained by the charter that if the heir be a minor, he shall immediately, upon his majority, enter upon his estate, without paying any relief. The king shall not sell his wardship; he shall levy only reasonable profits upon the estate, without committing waste or hurting the property; he shall uphold the castles, houses, mills, parks, and ponds; and if he commit the guardianship of the estate to the sheriff, or any other, he shall previously oblige them to find surety to the same purpose. During the minority of a baron, while his lands are in wardship, and are not in his own possession, no debt which he owes to the Jews shall bear any interest. Heirs shall be married without disparagement; and before the marriage be contracted, the nearest relations of the person shall be informed of it. A widow, without paying any relief, shall enter upon her dower, the third part of her husband's rents; she shall not be compelled to marry, so long as she chooses to continue single; she shall only give security never to marry without her lord's consent. The king shall not claim the wardship of any minor who holds lands by military tenure of a baron, on pretence that he also holds lands of the crown by soccage or any other tenure. Scutages shall be estimated at the same rate as in the time of Henry I.; and no scutage or aid, except in the three general feudal cases—the king's captivity, the knighting of his eldest son, and the marrying of his eldest daughter—shall be imposed but by the great council of the kingdom; the prelates, earls, and great barons shall be called to this great council, each by a particular writ; the lesser barons by a general summons of the sheriff. The king shall not seize any baron's land for a debt to the crown, if the baron possesses as many goods and chattels as are sufficient to discharge the debt. No man shall be obliged to perform more service for his fee than he is bound to by his tenure. No governor or constable of a castle shall oblige any knight to give money for castle-guard, if the knight be willing to perform the service in person or by another ablebodied man; and if the knight be in the field himself by the king's command, he shall be exempted from all other service of this nature. No vassal shall be allowed to sell so much of his land as to incapacitate himself from performing his service to his lord.

These were the principal articles calculated for the interest of the barons; and had the charter contained nothing further, national happiness and liberty had been very little promoted by it, as it would only have tended to increase the power and independence of an order of men who were already too powerful, and whose yoke might have become more heavy on the people than even that of an absolute monarch. But the barons, who alone drew and imposed on the prince this memorable charter, were necessitated to insert in it other clauses of a more extensive and more beneficent nature. They could not expect the concurrence of the people without comprehending, together with their own, the interests of inferior ranks of men ; and all provisions which the barons, for their own sake, were obliged to make, in order to insure the free and equitable administration of justice, tended directly to the benefit of the whole community. The following were the principal clauses of this nature :

It was ordained that all the privileges and immunities above mentioned, granted to the barons against the king, should be extended by the barons to their inferior vassals. The king bound himself not to grant any writ empowering a baron to levy aids from his vassals, except in the three feudal cases. One weight and one measure shall be established throughout the kingdom. Merchants shall be allowed to transact all business without being exposed to any arbitrary tolls and impositions. They and all freemen shall be allowed to go out of the kingdom and return to it at pleasure. London and all cities and burghs shall preserve their ancient liberties, immunities, and free customs. Aids shall not be required of them but by the consent of the great council. No towns or individuals shall be obliged to make or support bridges but by ancient custom. The goods of every freeman shall be disposed of according to his will ; if he die intestate, his heirs shall succeed to them. No officer of the crown shall take any horses, carts, or wood without the consent of the owner. The king's courts of justice shall be stationary, and shall no longer follow his person ; they shall be open to every one, and justice shall no longer be sold, refused, or delayed by them. Circuits shall be regularly held every year. The inferior tribunals of justice, the county court, sheriff's turn, and court-leet shall meet at their appointed time and place. The sheriffs shall be incapacitated to hold pleas of the crown, and shall not put any person upon his trial from rumor or suspicion alone, but upon the evidence of lawful witnesses. No freeman shall be

taken or imprisoned, or dispossessed of his free tenement
and liberties, or outlawed, or banished, or anywise hurt or
injured, unless by the legal judgment of his peers or by the
law of the land and all who suffered otherwise, in this or
the two former reigns, shall be restored to their rights and
possessions. Every freeman shall be fined in proportion to
his fault ; and no fine shall be levied on him to his utter
ruin. Even a villein or rustic shall not, by any fine, be bereaved of his carts, ploughs, and implements of husbandry.
This was the only article calculated for the interests of this
body of men, probably at that time the most numerous in
the kingdom.

It must be confessed that the former articles of the great
charter contain such mitigations and explanations of the
feudal law as are reasonable and equitable, and that the
latter involve all the chief outlines of a legal government,
and provide for the equal distribution of justice and free
enjoyment of property—the great objects for which political
society was at first founded by men, which the people have
a perpetual and unalienable right to recall, and which no
time, nor precedent, nor statute, nor positive institution,
ought to deter them from keeping ever uppermost in their
thoughts and attention. Though the provisions made by
this charter might, conformably to the genius of the age, be
esteemed too concise, and too bare of circumstances to maintain the execution of its articles in opposition to the
chicanery of lawyers supported by the violence of power,
time gradually ascertained the sense of all the ambiguous
expressions; and those generous barons who first extorted
this concession still held their swords in their hands, and
could turn them against those who dared, on any pretence,
to depart from the original spirit and meaning of the grant.
We may now, from the tenor of this charter, conjecture
what those laws were of King Edward which the English
nation, during so many generations, still desired, with such
an obstinate perseverance, to have recalled and established.
They were chiefly these latter articles of *Magna Charta ;*
and the barons, who at the beginning of these commotions
demanded the revival of the Saxon laws, undoubtedly
thought that they had sufficiently satisfied the people by
procuring them this concession, which comprehended the
principal objects to which they had so long aspired. But
what we are most to admire is the prudence and moderation
of those haughty nobles themselves, who were enraged by

injuries, inflamed by opposition, and elated by a total victory over their sovereign. They were content, even in this plenitude of power, to depart from some articles of Henry I.'s charter which they made the foundation of their demands, particularly from the abolition of wardships—a matter of the greatest importance—and they seem to have been sufficiently careful not to diminish too far the power and revenue of the crown. If they appear, therefore, to have carried other demands to too great a height, it can be ascribed only to the faithless and tyrannical character of the king himself, of which they had long had experience, and which, they foresaw, would, if they provided no further security, lead him soon to infringe their new liberties and revoke his own concessions. This alone gave birth to those other articles, seemingly exorbitant, which were added as a rampart for the safeguard of the great charter.

The barons obliged the king to agree that London should remain in their hands, and the Tower be consigned to the custody of the primate till the fifteenth of August ensuing, or till the execution of the several articles of the great charter.[83] The better to insure the same end, he allowed them to choose five-and-twenty members from their own body as conservators of the public liberties; and no bounds were set to the authority of these men either in extent or duration. If any complaint were made of a violation of the charter, whether attempted by the king, justiciaries, sheriffs, or foresters, any four of these barons might admonish the king to redress the grievance. If satisfaction were not obtained, they could assemble the whole council of twenty-five, who, in conjunction with the great council, were empowered to compel him to observe the charter, and, in case of resistance, might levy war against him, attack his castles, and employ every kind of violence, except against his royal person and that of his queen and children. All men throughout the kingdom were bound, under the penalty of confiscation, to swear obedience to the twenty-five barons; and the freeholders of each county were to choose twelve knights, who were to make report of such evil customs as required redress, conformably to the tenor of the great charter.[84] The names of those conservators were, the Earls of Clare, Albemarle, Gloucester, Winchester, Hereford; Roger Bigod, Earl of

[83] Rymer, vol. i. p. 201. Chron. Dunst. vol. i. p. 73.
[84] This seems a very strong proof that the House of Commons was not then in being, otherwise the knights and burgesses from the several counties could have given in to the Lords a list of grievances without so unusual an election.

Norfolk; Robert de Vere, Earl of Oxford; William Mareschal the younger; Robert Fitz-Walter; Gilbert de Clare; Eustace de Vescie; Gilbert Delaval; William de Moubray; Geoffrey de Say; Roger de Mombezon; William de Huntingfield; Robert de Ros; the Constable of Chester; William d Aubenie; Richard de Perci; William Malet; John Fitz-Robert; William de Lanvalay; Hugh de Bigod; and Roger de Montfichet.[85]   These men were, by this convention, really invested with the sovereignty of the kingdom; they were rendered co-ordinate with the king, or rather superior to him, in the exercise of the executive power; and as there was no circumstance of government which, either directly or indirectly, might not bear a relation to the security or observance of the great charter, there could scarcely occur any incident in which they might not lawfully interpose their authority.

John seemed to submit passively to all these regulations, however injurious to majesty. He sent writs to all the sheriffs, ordering them to constrain every one to swear obedience to the twenty-five barons;[86] he dismissed all his foreign forces; he pretended that his government was thenceforth to run in a new tenor, and be more indulgent to the liberty and independence of his people. But he only dissembled, till he should find a favorable opportunity for annulling all his concessions. The injuries and indignities which he had formerly suffered from the pope and the King of France, as they came from equals or superiors, seemed to make but small impression on him; but the sense of this perpetual and total subjection under his own rebellious vassals sank deep in his mind, and he was determined, at all hazards, to throw off so ignominious a slavery.[87] He grew sullen, silent, and reserved; he shunned the society of his courtiers and nobles; he retired into the Isle of Wight, as if desirous of hiding his shame and confusion, but in this retreat he meditated the most fatal vengeance against all his enemies.[88] He secretly sent abroad his emissaries to enlist foreign soldiers, and to invite the rapacious Brabançons into his service by the prospect of sharing the spoils of England and reaping the forfeitures of so many opulent barons, who had incurred the guilt of rebellion by rising in arms against him;[89] and he despatched a messenger to Rome, in order to lay before

---

[85] Matt. Paris, p. 181.   [86] Matt. Paris, p. 182.
[87] Matt. Paris, p. 183.   [88] Ibid.
[89] Matt. Paris, p. 183. Chron. Dunst. vol. i. p. 72. Chron. Mailr. p. 188.

the pope the great charter which he had been compelled to
sign, and to complain before that tribunal of the violence
which had been imposed upon him.[90]

Innocent, considering himself as feudal lord of the kingdom, was incensed at the temerity of the barons, who,
though they pretended to appeal to his authority, had dared,
without waiting for his consent, to impose such terms on a
prince who, by resigning to the Roman pontiff his crown
and independence, had placed himself immediately under
the papal protection. He issued, therefore, a bull, in which,
from the plenitude of his apostolic power, and from the
authority which God had committed to him to build and
destroy kingdoms, to plant and overthrow, he annulled and
abrogated the whole charter, as unjust in itself, as obtained
by compulsion, and as derogatory to the dignity of the
apostolic see. He prohibited the barons from exacting the
observance of it; he even prohibited the king himself from
paying any regard to it; he absolved him and his subjects
from all oaths which they had been constrained to take to
that purpose; and he pronounced a general sentence of
excommunication against every one who should persevere
in maintaining such treasonable and iniquitous pretensions.[91]

The king, as his foreign forces arrived along with this
bull, now ventured to take off the mask, and, under sanction
of the pope's decree, recalled all the liberties which he had
granted to his subjects, and which he had solemnly sworn
to observe. But the spiritual weapon was found upon trial
to carry less force with it than he had reason, from his own
experience, to apprehend. The primate refused to obey the
pope in publishing the sentence of excommunication against
the barons; and though he was cited to Rome that he might
attend a general council there assembled, and was suspended
on account of his disobedience to the pope and his secret
correspondence with the king's enemies,[92] though a new and
particular sentence of excommunication was pronounced by
name against the principal barons,[93] John still found that
his nobility and people, and even his clergy, adhered to the
defence of their liberties and to their combination against
him. The sword of his foreign mercenaries was all he had
to trust to for restoring his authority.

The barons, after obtaining the great charter, seem to

[90] Matt. Paris, p. 183. Chron. Dunst. vol. i. p. 73.
[91] Rymer, vol. i. pp. 203, 204, 205, 208. Matt. Paris, pp. 184, 185, 187.
[92] Matt. Paris, p. 189.   [93] Rymer, vol. i. p. 211. Matt. Paris, p. 192.

have been lulled into a fatal security, and to have taken no rational measures, in case of the introduction of a foreign force, for reassembling their armies. The king was, from the first, master of the field, and immediately laid siege to the castle of Rochester, which was obstinately defended by William d'Aubenie, at the head of a hundred and forty knights with their retainers, but was at last reduced by famine. John, irritated with the resistance, intended to have hanged the governor and all the garrison; but on the representation of William de Mauleon, who suggested to him the danger of reprisals, he was content to sacrifice in this barbarous manner the inferior prisoners only.[94] The captivity of William d'Aubenie, the best officer among the confederated barons, was an irreparable loss to their cause; and no regular opposition was thenceforth made to the progress of the royal arms. The ravenous and barbarous mercenaries, incited by a cruel and enraged prince, were let loose against the estates, tenants, manors, houses, parks of the barons, and spread devastation over the face of the kingdom. Nothing was to be seen but the flames of villages and castles reduced to ashes, the consternation and misery of the inhabitants, tortures exercised by the soldiery to make them reveal their concealed treasures, and reprisals no less barbarous committed by the barons and their partisans on the royal demesnes and on the estates of such as still adhered to the crown. The king, marching through the whole extent of England, from Dover to Berwick, laid the provinces waste on each side of him, and considered every estate which was not his immediate property as entirely hostile, and the object of military execution. The nobility of the north, in particular, who had shown the greatest violence in the recovery of their liberties, and who, acting in a separate body, had expressed their discontent even at the concessions made by the great charter, as they could expect no mercy, fled before him with their wives and families, and purchased the friendship of Alexander, the young King of Scots, by doing homage to him.

The barons, reduced to this desperate extremity, and menaced with the total loss of their liberties, their properties, and their lives, employed a remedy no less desperate; and, making applications to the court of France, they offered to acknowledge Lewis, the eldest son of Philip, for their sovereign, on condition that he would afford them protection from the violence of their enraged prince. Though the sense of the common rights of mankind—the only rights that are entirely indefeasible—might have justified them in the deposition of their king, they declined insisting, before Philip, on a pretension which is commonly so disagreeable to sovereigns, and which sounds harshly in the royal ears. They affirmed that John was incapable of succeeding to the crown by reason of the attainder passed upon him during his brother's reign, though that attainder had been reversed, and Richard had even, by his last will, declared him his successor. They pretended that he was already legally deposed by sentence of the peers of France on account of the murder of his nephew; though that sentence could not possibly regard anything but his transmarine dominions, which alone he held in vassalage to that crown. On more plausible grounds they affirmed that he had already deposed himself by doing homage to the pope, changing the nature of his sovereignty, and resigning an independent crown for a fee under a foreign power. And as Blanche of Castile, the wife of Lewis, was descended by her mother from Henry II., they maintained, though many other princes stood before her in the order of succession, that they had not shaken off the royal family in choosing her husband for their sovereign.

Philip was strongly tempted to lay hold on the rich prize which was offered to him. The legate menaced him with interdicts and excommunications if he invaded the patrimony of St. Peter, or attacked a prince who was under the immediate protection of the holy see;[95] but as Philip was assured of the obedience of his own vassals, his principles were changed with the times, and he now undervalued as much all papal censures as he formerly pretended to pay respect to them. His chief scruple was with regard to the fidelity which he might expect from the English barons in their new engagements, and the danger of intrusting his son and heir into the hands of men who might, on any caprice or necessity, make peace with their native sovereign by sacrificing a pledge of so much value. He therefore exacted from the barons twenty-five hostages of the most noble birth in the kingdom;[96] and having obtained this security, he sent over first a small army to the relief of the confederates; then more numerous forces, which arrived with Lewis himself at their head.

[95] Matt. Paris, p. 194.   Matt. West. p. 275.
[96] Matt. Paris, p. 193.   Chron. Dunst. vol. i. p. 74.

The first effect of the young prince's appearance in England was the desertion of John's foreign troops, who, being mostly levied in Flanders and other provinces of France, refused to serve against the heir of their monarchy.[97] The Gascons and Poictevins alone, who were still John's subjects, adhered to his cause; but they were too weak to maintain that superiority in the field which they had hitherto supported against the confederated barons. Many considerable noblemen deserted John's party—the Earls of Salisbury, Arundel, Warrenne, Oxford, Albemarle, and William Mareschal the younger; his castles fell daily into the hands of the enemy; Dover was the only place which, from the valor and fidelity of Hubert de Burgh, the governor, made resistance to the progress of Lewis;[98] and the barons had the melancholy prospect of finally succeeding in their purpose, and of escaping the tyranny of their own king, by imposing on themselves and the nation a foreign yoke. But this union was of short duration between the French and English nobles; and the imprudence of Lewis, who on every occasion showed too visible a preference to the former, increased that jealousy which it was so natural for the latter to entertain in their present situation.[99] The Viscount of Melun, too, it is said, one of his courtiers, fell sick at London, and, finding the approaches of death, he sent for some of his friends among the English barons, and, warning them of their danger, revealed Lewis's secret intentions of exterminating them and their families as traitors to their prince, and of bestowing their estates and dignities on his native subjects, in whose fidelity he could more reasonably place confidence.[100] This story, whether true or false, was universally reported and believed, and, concurring with other circumstances which rendered it credible, did great prejudice to the cause of Lewis. The Earl of Salisbury and other noblemen deserted again to John's party;[101] and, as men easily change sides in a civil war, especially where their power is founded on an hereditary and independent authority, and is not derived from the opinion and favor of the people, the French prince had reason to dread a sudden reverse of fortune. The king was assembling a considerable army, with a view of fighting one great battle for his crown; but passing from Lynn to Lincolnshire, his road lay along the

[97] Matt. Paris, p. 195.
[98] Matt. Paris, p. 198.   Chron. Dunst. vol. i. pp. 75, 76.
[99] W. Heming. p. 559.   [100] Matt. Paris, p. 199.   Matt. West. p. 277.
[101] Chron. Dunst. vol. i. p. 78.

sea-shore, which was overflowed at high water ; and, not choosing the proper time for his journey, he lost in the inundation all his carriages, treasure, baggage, and regalia. The affliction for this disaster, and vexation from the distracted state of his affairs, increased the sickness under which he then labored ; and though he reached the castle of Newark, he was obliged to halt there, and his distemper soon after put an end to his life, in the forty-ninth year of his age and eighteenth of his reign, and freed the nation from the dangers to which it was equally exposed by his success or by his misfortunes.

The character of this prince is nothing but a complication of vices equally mean and odious, ruinous to himself and destructive to his people. Cowardice, inactivity, folly, levity, licentiousness, ingratitude, treachery, tyranny, and cruelty —all these qualities appear too evidently in the several incidents of his life to give us room to suspect that the disagreeable picture has been anywise overcharged by the prejudices of the ancient historians. It is hard to say whether his conduct to his father, his brother, his nephew, or his subjects was most culpable, or whether his crimes in these respects were not even exceeded by the baseness which appeared in his transactions with the King of France, the pope, and the barons. His European dominions, when they devolved to him by the death of his brother, were more extensive than have ever, since his time, been ruled by an English monarch ; but he first lost, by his misconduct, the flourishing provinces in France, the ancient patrimony of his family. He subjected his kingdom to a shameful vassalage under the see of Rome. He saw the prerogatives of his crown diminished by law, and still more reduced by faction ; and he died at last when in danger of being totally expelled by a foreign power, and of either ending his life miserably in prison or seeking shelter, as a fugitive, from the pursuit of his enemies.

The prejudices against this prince were so violent that he was believed to have sent an embassy to the Miramoulin, or Emperor of Morocco, and to have offered to change his religion and become Mahometan in order to purchase the protection of that monarch. But though this story is told us on plausible authority, by Matthew Paris,[102] it is in itself utterly improbable, except that there is nothing so incred-

[102] P. 169.

ible but may be believed to proceed from the folly and wickedness of John.

The monks throw great reproaches on this prince for his impiety and even infidelity; and as an instance of it, they tell us that having one day caught a very fat stag, he exclaimed, "How plump and well fed is this animal! and yet I dare swear he never heard mass." [103] This sally of wit upon the usual corpulency of the priests, more than all his enormous crimes and iniquities, made him pass with them for an atheist.

John left two legitimate sons behind him—Henry, born on the first of October, 1207, and now nine years of age; and Richard, born on the sixth of January, 1209; and three daughters—Jane, afterwards married to Alexander, King of Scots; Eleanor, married first to William Mareschal the younger, Earl of Pembroke, and then to Simon de Montfort, Earl of Leicester; and Isabella, married to the Emperor Frederick II. All these children were born to him by Isabella of Angoulême, his second wife. His illegitimate children were numerous, but none of them were anywise distinguished.

It was this king who, in the ninth year of his reign, first gave by charter to the city of London the right of electing, annually, a mayor out of its own body, an office which was till now held for life. He gave the city also power to elect and remove its sheriffs at pleasure, and its common-councilmen annually. London Bridge was finished in this reign. The former bridge was of wood. Maud, the empress, was the first that built a stone bridge in England.

[103] Matt. Paris, p. 170.

APPENDIX II.

THE FEUDAL AND ANGLO-NORMAN GOVERNMENT AND MANNERS.

ORIGIN OF THE FEUDAL LAW.—ITS PROGRESS.—FEUDAL GOVERNMENT OF ENGLAND.—THE FEUDAL PARLIAMENT.—THE COMMONS.—JUDICIAL POWER.—REVENUE OF THE CROWN.—COMMERCE.—THE CHURCH.—CIVIL LAWS. —MANNERS.

THE feudal law is the chief foundation both of the political government and of the jurisprudence established by the Normans in England. Our subject therefore requires that we should form a just idea of this law in order to explain the state as well of that kingdom as of all other kingdoms of Europe, which, during those ages, were governed by similar institutions. And, though I am sensible that I must here repeat many observations and reflections which have been communicated by others,[1] yet, as every book—agreeably to the observation of a great historian [2]—should be as complete as possible within itself, and should never refer for anything material to other books, it will be necessary in this place, to deliver a short plan of that prodigious fabric which for several centuries preserved such a mixture of liberty and oppression, order and anarchy, stability and revolution, as was never experienced in any other age or any other part of the world.

After the northern nations had subdued the provinces of the Roman empire, they were obliged to establish a system of government which might secure their conquests, as well against the revolt of their numerous subjects who remained in the provinces as from the inroads of other tribes who might be tempted to ravish from them their new acquisitions. The great change of circumstances made them here depart from those institutions which prevailed among them while they remained in the forests of Germany; yet it was

---

[1] L'Esprit des Loix. Dr. Robertson's History of Scotland.
[2] Padre Paolo, Hist. Conc. Trid.

still natural for them to retain, in their present settlement, as much of their ancient customs as was compatible with their new situation.

The German governments, being more a confederacy of independent warriors than a civil subjection, derived their principal force from many inferior and voluntary associations which individuals formed under a particular head or chieftain, and which it became the highest point of honor to maintain with inviolable fidelity. The glory of the chief consisted in the number, the bravery, and the zealous attachment of his retainers. The duty of the retainers required that they should accompany their chief in all wars and dangers, that they should fight and perish by his side, and that they should esteem his renown or his favor a sufficient recompense for all their services.[3] The prince himself was nothing but a great chieftain, who was chosen from among the rest on account of his superior valor or nobility, and who derived his power from the voluntary association or attachment of the other chieftains.

When a tribe, governed by these ideas and actuated by these principles, subdued a large territory, they found that, though it was necessary to keep themselves in military posture, they could neither remain united in a body nor take up their quarters in several garrisons, and that their manners and institutions debarred them from using these expedients—the obvious ones which, in a like situation, would have been employed by a more civilized nation. Their ignorance in the art of finances, and, perhaps, the devastations inseparable from such violent conquests, rendered it impracticable for them to levy taxes sufficient for the pay of numerous armies; and their repugnance to subordination, with their attachment to rural pleasures, made the life of the camp or garrison, if perpetuated during peaceful times, extremely odious and disgustful to them. They seized, therefore, such a portion of the conquered lands as appeared necessary; they assigned a share for supporting the dignity of their prince and government; they distributed other parts, under the title of fiefs, to the chiefs. These made a new partition among their retainers. The express condition of all these grants was that they might be resumed at pleasure, and that the possessor, so long as he enjoyed them, should still remain in readiness to take the field for the defence of the nation. And, though the conquerors immedi-

[3] Tacit. De Mor. Germ.

ately separated, in order to enjoy their new acquisitions, their martial disposition made them readily fulfil the terms of their engagement—they assembled on the first alarm. Their habitual attachment to the chieftain made them willingly submit to his command; and thus a regular military force, though concealed, was always ready to defend on any emergency the interest and honor of the community.

We are not to imagine that all the conquered lands were seized by the northern conquerors, or that the whole of the land thus seized was subjected to those military services. This supposition is confuted by the history of all the nations on the Continent. Even the idea given us of the German manners by the Roman historian may convince us that that bold people would never have been content with so precarious a subsistence, or have fought to procure establishments which were only to continue during the good pleasure of their sovereign. Though the northern chieftains accepted of lands which, being considered as a kind of military pay, might be resumed at the will of the king or general, they also took possession of estates which, being hereditary and independent, enabled them to maintain their native liberty, and support, without court favor, the honor of their rank and family.

But there is a great difference in the consequences between the distribution of a pecuniary subsistence and the assignment of lands burdened with the condition of military service. The delivery of the former at the weekly, monthly, or annual terms of payment still recalls the idea of a voluntary gratuity from the prince, and reminds the soldier of the precarious tenure by which he holds his commission. But the attachment naturally formed with a fixed portion of land gradually begets the idea of something like property, and makes the possessor forget his dependent situation and the condition which was first annexed to the grant. It seemed equitable that one who had cultivated and sowed a field should reap the harvest; hence fiefs, which were at first entirely precarious, were soon made annual. A man who had employed his money in building, planting, or other improvements, expected to reap the fruits of his labor or expense; hence they were next granted during a term of years. It would be thought hard to expel a man from his possessions who had always done his duty and performed the conditions on which he originally received them; hence the chieftains, in a subsequent period, thought themselves entitled to demand the enjoyment of their feudal lands during life. It was found that a man would more willingly expose himself in battle if assured that his family should inherit his possessions, and should not be left by his death in want and poverty; hence fiefs were made hereditary in families, and descended during one age to the son, then to the grandson, next to the brothers, and afterwards to more distant relations.[4] The idea of property stole in gradually upon that of military pay, and each century made some sensible addition to the stability of fiefs and tenures.

In all these successive acquisitions, the chief was supported by his vassals, who, having originally a strong connection with him, augmented by the constant intercourse of good offices and by the friendship arising from vicinity and dependence, were inclined to follow their leader against all his enemies, and voluntarily, in his private quarrels, paid him the same obedience to which, by their tenure, they were bound in foreign wars. While he daily advanced new pretensions to secure the possession of his superior fief, they expected to find the same advantage in acquiring stability to their subordinate ones; and they zealously opposed the intrusion of a new lord who would be inclined—as he was fully entitled—to bestow the possession of their lands on his own favorites and retainers. Thus the authority of the sovereign gradually decayed; and each noble, fortified in his own territory by the attachment of his vassals, became too powerful to be expelled by an order from the throne, and he secured by law what he had at first acquired by usurpation.

During this precarious state of the supreme power, a difference would immediately be experienced between those portions of territory which were subjected to the feudal tenures and those which were possessed by an allodial or free title. Though the latter possessions had at first been esteemed much preferable, they were soon found, by the progressive changes introduced into public and private law, to be of an inferior condition to the former. The possessors of a feudal territory, united by a regular subordination under one chief and by the mutual attachment of the vassals, had the same advantages over the proprietors of the other that a disciplined army enjoys over a dispersed multitude, and were enabled to commit with impunity all injuries on their defenceless neighbors. Every one, therefore, hastened to seek that protection which he found so necessary;

----

4 Lib. Feud. lib. 1, tit. 1.

and each allodial proprietor, resigning his possessions into the hands of the king, or of some nobleman respected for power or valor, received them back with the condition of feudal services [5] which, though a burden somewhat grievous, brought him ample compensation by connecting him with the neighboring proprietors and placing him under the guardianship of a potent chieftain. The decay of the political government thus necessarily occasioned the extension of the feudal. The kingdoms of Europe were universally divided into baronies, and these into inferior fiefs; and the attachment of vassals to their chief, which was at first an essential part of the German manners, was still supported by the same causes from which it at first arose—the necessity of mutual protection, and the continued intercourse between the head and the members of benefits and services.

But there was another circumstance which corroborated these feudal dependencies, and tended to connect the vassals with their superior lord by an indissoluble bond of union. The northern conquerors, as well as the more early Greeks and Romans, embraced a policy which is unavoidable to all nations that have made slender advances in refinement—they everywhere united the civil jurisdiction with the military power. Law, in its commencement, was not an intricate science, and was more governed by maxims of equity —which seem obvious to common-sense—than by numerous and subtle principles applied to a variety of cases by profound reasonings from analogy. An officer, though he had passed his life in the field, was able to determine all legal controversies which could occur within the district committed to his charge; and his decisions were the most likely to meet with a prompt and ready obedience from men who respected his person and were accustomed to act under his command. The profit arising from punishments, which were then chiefly pecuniary, was another reason for his desiring to retain the judicial power; and when his fief became hereditary, this authority, which was essential to it, was also transmitted to his posterity. The counts and other magistrates, whose power was merely official, were tempted, in imitation of the feudal lords, whom they resembled in so many particulars, to render their dignity perpetual and hereditary; and in the decline of the regal power, they found no difficulty in making good their pretensions. After this manner, the vast fabric of feudal subordination became quite

[5] Marculf. Form. 47, apud Lindenbrog. p. 1238.

solid and comprehensive ; it formed everywhere an essential part of the political constitution ; and the Norman and
other barons who followed the fortunes of William were so
accustomed to it that they could scarcely form an idea of any
other species of civil government.[6]

The Saxons who conquered England, as they exterminated the ancient inhabitants, and thought themselves secured by the sea against new invaders, found it less requisite
to maintain themselves in a military posture. The quantity
of land which they annexed to offices seems to have been of
small value, and for that reason continued the longer in its
original situation, and was always possessed, during pleasure, by those who were intrusted with the command. These
conditions were too precarious to satisfy the Norman barons,
who enjoyed more independent possessions and jurisdictions
in their own country ; and William was obliged, in the new
distribution of land, to copy the tenures which were now
become universal on the Continent. England of a sudden
became a feudal kingdom,[7] and received all the advantages,
and was exposed to all the inconveniences, incident to that
species of civil polity.

According to the principles of the feudal law, the king
was the supreme lord of the landed property. All possessors who enjoyed the fruits or revenue of any part of it held
those privileges either mediately or immediately of him ;
and their property was conceived to be in some degree conditional.[8] The land was still apprehended to be a species
of *benefice*, which was the original conception of a feudal
property ; and the vassal owed in return for it stated services to his baron, as the baron himself did for his land to
the crown. The vassal was obliged to defend his baron in
war ; and the baron, at the head of his vassals, was bound
to fight in defence of the king and kingdom. But besides
these military services, which were casual, there were others
imposed of a civil nature, which were more constant and
durable.

The northern nations had no idea that any man trained
up to honor and inured to arms was ever to be governed
without his own consent by the absolute will of another ; or
that the administration of justice was ever to be exercised

---

[6] The ideas of the feudal government were so rooted that even lawyers, in those
ages, could not form a notion of any other constitution. "Regnum" (says Bracton, lib. 2, cap. 34) "quod ex comitatibus et baronibus dicitur esse constitutem."
[7] Coke, Comm. on Lit. pp. 1, 2, ad sect. 1.
[8] Somner of Gavelk. p. 109. Smith de Rep. lib. 3. cap. 10.

by the private opinion of any one magistrate without the
concurrence of some other persons, whose interest might induce them to check his arbitrary and iniquitous decisions.
The king, therefore, when he found it necessary to demand
any service of his barons or chief tenants beyond what was
due by their tenures, was obliged to assemble them in order
to obtain their *consent ;* and when it was necessary to determine any controversy which might arise among the barons themselves, the question must be discussed in their
presence and be decided according to their opinion or *advice.*
In these two circumstances of consent and advice consisted
chiefly the civil services of the ancient barons ; and these
implied all the considerable incidents of government. In
one view, the barons regarded this attendance as their principal *privilege ;* in another, as a grievous *burden.* That no
momentous affairs could be transacted without their consent
and advice was in *general* esteemed the great security of
their possessions and dignities ; but as they reaped no immediate profit from their attendance at court, and were exposed to great inconvenience and charge by an absence from
their own estates, every one was glad to exempt himself
from each *particular* exertion of this power, and was pleased
both that the call for that duty should seldom return upon
him, and that others should undergo the burden in his stead.
The king, on the other hand, was usually anxious, for several
reasons, that the assembly of the barons should be full at
every stated or casual meeting. The attendance was the
chief badge of their subordination to his crown, and drew
from them that independence which they were apt to affect
in their own castles and manors ; and where the meeting
was thin or ill attended, its determinations had less authority,
and commanded not so ready an obedience from the whole
community.

The case was the same with the barons in their courts
as with the king in the supreme council of the nation. It
was requisite to assemble the vassals, in order to determine
by their vote any question which regarded the barony ; and
they sat along with the chief in all trials, whether civil or
criminal, which occurred within the limits of their jurisdiction. They were bound to pay suit and service at the
court of their baron ; and as their tenure was military, and
consequently honorable, they were admitted into his society
and partook of his friendship. Thus, a kingdom was considered only as a great barony, and a barony as a small

kingdom. The barons were peers to each other in the national council, and, in some degree, companions to the king. The vassals were peers to each other in the court of barony and companions to their baron.[9]

But though this resemblance so far took place, the vassals, by the natural course of things, universally in the feudal constitutions fell into a greater subordination under the baron than the baron himself under his sovereign; and these governments had a necessary and infallible tendency to augment the power of the nobles. The great chief residing in his country-seat, which he was commonly allowed to fortify, lost, in a great measure, his connection or acquaintance with the prince; and added every day new force to his authority over the vassals of the barony. They received from him education in all military exercises; his hospitality invited them to live and enjoy society in his hall; their leisure, which was great, made them perpetual retainers on his person and partakers of his country sports and amusements; they had no means of gratifying their ambition but by making a figure in his train. His favor and countenance was their greatest honor; his displeasure exposed them to contempt and ignominy; and they felt every moment the necessity of his protection, both in the controversies which occurred with other vassals, and, what was more material, in the daily inroads and injuries which were committed by the neighboring barons. During the time of general war, the sovereign, who marched at the head of his armies and was the great protector of the state, always acquired some accession to his authority, which he lost during the intervals of peace and tranquillity: but the loose police incident to the feudal constitutions maintained a perpetual though secret hostility between the several members of the state; and the vassals found no means of securing themselves against the injuries to which they were continually exposed but by closely adhering to their chief and falling into a submissive dependence upon him.

If the feudal government was so little favorable to the true liberty even of the military vassal, it was still more destructive of the independence and security of the other members of the state, or what, in a proper sense, we call the people. A great part of them were *serfs*, and lived in a state of absolute slavery or villeinage; the other inhabitants

---

[9] Du Cange, Glos. *in verb.* Par   Cujac. Commun. in Lib. Feud. lib. 1, tit. p. 18. Spell. Gloss. *in verb.*

of the country paid their rents in services which were in a great measure arbitrary; and they could expect no redress of injuries in a court of barony from men who thought they had a right to oppress and tyrannize over them. The towns were situated either within the demesnes of the king or the lands of the great barons, and were almost entirely subjected to the absolute will of their master. The languishing state of commerce kept the inhabitants poor and contemptible, and the political institutions were calculated to render that poverty perpetual. The barons and gentry, living in rustic plenty and hospitality, gave no encouragement to the arts, and had no demand for any of the more elaborate manufactures. Every profession was held in contempt but that of arms; and if any merchant or manufacturer rose by industry and frugality to a degree of opulence, he found himself but the more exposed to injuries from the envy and avidity of the military nobles.

These concurring causes gave the feudal governments so strong a bias towards aristocracy that the royal authority was extremely eclipsed in all the European states; and, instead of dreading the growth of monarchical power, we might rather expect that the community would everywhere crumble into so many independent baronies, and lose the political union by which they were cemented. In elective monarchies, the event was commonly answerable to this expectation; and the barons, gaining ground on every vacancy of the throne, raised themselves almost to a state of sovereignty, and sacrificed to their power both the rights of the crown and the liberties of the people. But hereditary monarchies had a principle of authority which was not so easily subverted; and there were several causes which still maintained a degree of influence in the hands of the sovereign.

The greatest baron could never lose view entirely of those principles of the feudal constitution which bound him, as a vassal, to submission and fealty towards his prince; because he was every moment obliged to have recourse to those principles in exacting fealty and submission from his own vassals. The lesser barons, finding that the annihilation of royal authority left them exposed without protection to the insults and injuries of more potent neighbors, naturally adhered to the crown, and promoted the execution of general and equal laws. The people had still a stronger interest to desire the grandeur of the sovereign; and the king, being the legal magistrate, who suffered by every internal convulsion or oppression, and who regarded the great nobles as his immediate rivals, assumed the salutary office of general guardian or protector of the Commons. Besides the prerogatives with which the law invested him, his large demesnes and numerous retainers rendered him, in one sense, the greatest baron in his kingdom; and where he was possessed of personal vigor and abilities (for his situation required these advantages), he was commonly able to preserve his authority, and maintain his station as head of the community and the chief fountain of law and justice.

The first kings of the Norman race were favored by another circumstance which preserved them from the encroachments of their barons. They were generals of a conquering army, which was obliged to continue in a military posture, and to maintain great subordination under their leader, in order to secure themselves from the revolt of the numerous natives, whom they had bereaved of all their properties and privileges. But though this circumstance supported the authority of William and his immediate successors, and rendered them extremely absolute, it was lost as soon as the Norman barons began to incorporate with the nation, to acquire a security in their possessions, and to fix their influence over their vassals, tenants, and slaves; and the immense fortunes which the Conqueror had bestowed on his chief captains served to support their independence, and make them formidable to their sovereign.

He gave, for instance, to Hugh d'Abrincis, his sister's son, the whole county of Chester, which he erected into a palatinate, and rendered by his grant almost independent of the crown.[10] Robert, Earl of Mortaigne, had 973 manors and lordships; Allan, Earl of Brittany and Richmond, 442; Odo, Bishop of Baieux, 439;[11] Geoffrey, Bishop of Coutance, 280;[12] Walter Giffard, Earl of Buckingham, 107; William, Earl Warrenne, 298, besides 28 towns or hamlets in Yorkshire; Todenei, 81; Roger Bigod, 123; Robert, Earl of Eu, 119; Roger Mortimer, 132, besides several hamlets; Robert de Stafford, 130; Walter d'Eurus, Earl of Salisbury, 46; Geoffrey de Mandeville, 118; Richard de Clare, 171; Hugh de Beauchamp, 47; Baldwin de Ridvers, 164; Henry de Ferrars, 222; William de Percy, 119;[13] Norman d'Arcy,

---

[10] Camd. in Chesh. Spell. Gloss. *in verb.* Comes Palatinus.
[11] Brady's Hist. pp. 198, 200.　　　　[12] Order. Vitalis.
[13] Dugdale's Baronage, from Domesday Book, vol. i. pp. 60, 74; vol. iii. 112, 132, 136, 138, 156, 174, 200, 207, 223, 254, 257, 269.

33.[14] Sir Henry Spellman computes that, in the large county of Norfolk, there were not, in the Conqueror's time, above sixty-six proprietors of land.[15] Men possessed of such princely revenues and jurisdictions could not long be retained in the rank of subjects. The great Earl Warrenne, in a subsequent reign, when he was questioned concerning his right to the lands which he possessed, drew his sword, which he produced as his title; adding that William the Bastard did not conquer the kingdom himself, but that the barons, and his ancestor among the rest, were joint adventurers in the enterprise.[16]

The supreme legislative power of England was lodged in the king and great council, or what was afterwards called the Parliament. It is not doubted but the archbishops, bishops, and most considerable abbots were constituent members of this council. They sat by a double title—by prescription, as having always possessed that privilege, through the whole Saxon period, from the first establishment of Christianity; and by their right of baronage, as holding of the king *in capite* by military service. These two titles of the prelates were never accurately distinguished. When the usurpations of the Church had risen to such a height as to make the bishops affect a separate dominion and regard their seat in Parliament as a degradation of their episcopal dignity, the king insisted that they were barons, and on that account obliged by the general principles of the feudal law to attend on him in his great councils.[17] Yet there still remained some practices which supposed their title to be derived merely from ancient possession. When a bishop was elected, he sat in Parliament before the king had made him restitution of his temporalities; and during the vacancy of a see, the guardian of the spiritualities was summoned to attend along with the bishops.

The barons' were another constituent part of the great council of the nation. These held immediately of the crown by a military tenure; they were the most honorable members of the state, and had a *right* to be consulted in all public deliberations; they were the immediate vassals of the crown, and owed as a *service* their attendance in the court of their supreme lord. A resolution taken without their con-

[14] Dugdale's Baronage, p. 369. It is remarkable that this family of d'Arcy seems to be the only male descendant of any of the Conqueror's barons now remaining among the Peers. Lord Holdernesse is the heir of that family.
[15] Spell. Gloss. *in verbo* Domesday.
[16] Dugdale's Baronage, vol. i. p. 79. Ibid. Origines Juridicales, p. 13.
[17] Spell. Gloss. *in verbo* Baro.

sent was likely to be but ill executed; and no determination of any cause or controversy among them had any validity where the vote and advice of the body did not concur. The dignity of earl or count was official and territorial as well as hereditary; and as all the earls were also barons, they were considered as military vassals of the crown, were admitted in that capacity into the general council, and formed the most honorable and powerful branch of it.

But there was another class of the immediate military tenants of the crown, no less, or probably more, numerous than the barons—the tenants *in capite* by knights' service; and these, however inferior in power or property, held by a tenure which was equally honorable with that of the others. A barony was commonly composed of several knight's-fees, and, though the number seems not to have been exactly defined, seldom consisted of less than fifty hides of land; [18] but where a man held of the king only one or two knight's-fees, he was still an immediate vassal of the crown, and as such had a title to have a seat in the general councils. But as this attendance was usually esteemed a burden, and one too great for a man of slender fortune to bear constantly, it is probable that, though he had a title, if he pleased, to be admitted, he was not obliged by any penalty, like the barons, to pay a regular attendance. All the immediate military tenants of the crown amounted not fully to 700 when Domesday-book was framed; and as the members were well pleased, on any pretext, to excuse themselves from attendance, the assembly was never likely to become too numerous for the despatch of public business.

So far the nature of a general council, or ancient Parliament, is determined, without any doubt or controversy. The only question seems to be with regard to the Commons, or the representatives of counties and boroughs, whether they were also, in more early times, constituent parts of Parliament? This question was once disputed in England with great acrimony; but such is the force of time and evidence that they can sometimes prevail even over faction; and the question seems by general consent, and even by their own, to be at last determined against the ruling party. It is agreed that the Commons were no part of the great council

---

[18] Four hides made one knight's-fee; the relief of a barony was twelve times greater than that of a knight's-fee; whence we may conjecture its usual value. Spell. Gloss. *in verbo* Feodum. There were 243,600 hides in England, and 60,215 knight's-fees; whence it is evident that there were a little more than four hides in each knight's-fee.

till some ages after the Conquest; and that the military tenants alone of the crown composed that supreme and legislative assembly.

The vassals of a baron were, by their tenure, immediately dependent on him, owed attendance at his court, and paid all their duty to the king, through that dependence which their lord was obliged by *his* tenure to acknowledge to his sovereign and superior. Their land, comprehended in the barony, was represented in Parliament by the baron himself, who was supposed, according to the fictions of the feudal law, to possess the direct property of it; and it would have been deemed incongruous to give it any other representation. They stood in the same capacity to him that he and the other barons did to the king. The former were peers of the barony; the latter were peers of the realm. The vassals possessed a subordinate rank within their district; the baron enjoyed a superior dignity in the great assembly: they were in some degree his companions at home; he the king's companion at court. And nothing can be more evidently repugnant to all feudal ideas, and to that gradual subordination which was essential to those ancient institutions, than to imagine that the king would apply either for the advice or consent of men who were of a rank so much inferior, and whose duty was immediately paid to the *mesne* lord that was interposed between them and the throne.[19]

If it be unreasonable to think that the vassals of a barony, though their tenure was military and noble and honorable, were ever summoned to give their opinion in national councils, much less can it be supposed that the tradesmen or inhabitants of boroughs, whose condition was so much inferior, would be admitted to that privilege. It appears from Domesday that the greatest boroughs were, at the time of the Conquest, scarcely more than country villages; and that the inhabitants lived in entire dependence on the king or great lords, and were of a station little better than servile.[20] They were not then so much as incorporated; they formed no community; were not regarded as a body politic; and being really nothing but a number of low dependent tradesmen, living, without any particular civil tie, in neighborhood together, they were incapable of being represented in the states of the kingdom. Even in

---

[19] Spell. Gloss. *in verbo* Baro.
[20] *Liber homo* anciently signified a gentleman; for scarce any one besides was entirely free. Spell. Gloss. *in verbo.*

France, a country which made more early advances in arts and civility than England, the first corporation is sixty years posterior to the Conquest under the Duke of Normandy; and the erecting of these communities was an invention of Lewis the Gross, in order to free the people from slavery under the lords, and to give them protection, by means of certain privileges and a separate jurisdiction.[21] An ancient French writer calls them a new and wicked device to procure liberty to slaves, and encourage them in shaking off the dominion of their masters.[22] The famous charter, as it is called, of the Conqueror to the city of London, though granted at a time when he assumed the appearance of gentleness and lenity, is nothing but a letter of protection, and a declaration that the citizens should not be treated as slaves.[23] By the English feudal law, the superior lord was prohibited from marrying his female ward to a burgess or a villein;[24] so near were these two ranks esteemed to each other, and so much inferior to the nobility and gentry. Besides possessing the advantages of birth, riches, civil powers, and privileges, the nobles and gentlemen alone were armed; a circumstance which give them a mighty superiority, in an age when nothing but the military profession was honorable, and when the loose execution of laws gave so much encouragement to open violence, and rendered it so decisive in all disputes and controversies.[25]

The great similarity among the feudal governments of Europe is well known to every man that has any acquaintance with ancient history; and the antiquaries of all foreign countries, where the question was never embarrassed by party disputes, have allowed that the Commons came very late to be admitted to a share in the legislative power. In Normandy particularly, whose constitution was most likely to be William's model in raising his new fabric of English government, the states were entirely composed of the clergy and nobility; and the first incorporated boroughs or communities of that duchy were Rouen and Falaise, which enjoyed their privileges by a grant of Philip Augustus in the year 1207.[26] All the ancient English historians, when they mention the great council of the nation, call it an assembly of the baronage, nobility, or great men; and none of their expressions, though several hundred passages might be pro-

---

[21] Du Cange, Gloss. *in verb.* Commune, Communitas.
[22] Guibertus, de vita sua, lib. 2, cap. 7.   [23] Stat. of Merton, 1235, cap. 6.
[24] Hollinshed, vol. iii. p. 15.   [25] Madox, Baron. Angl. p. 19.
[26] Norman. Duchesnii, p. 1066.   Du Cange, Gloss. *in verbo* Commune.

duced, can, without the utmost violence, be tortured to a meaning which will admit the Commons to be constituent members of that body.[27] If, in the long period of two hundred years which elapsed between the Conquest and the latter end of Henry III., and which abounded in factions, revolutions, and convulsions of all kinds, the House of Commons never performed one single legislative act so considerable as to be once mentioned by any of the numerous historians of that age, they must have been totally insignificant; and, in that case, what reason can be assigned for their ever being assembled? Can it be supposed that men of so little weight or importance possessed a negative voice against the king and the barons? Every page of the subsequent histories discovers their existence; though these histories are not written with greater accuracy than the preceding ones, and indeed scarcely equal them in that particular. The *Magna Charta* of King John provides that no scutage or aid should be imposed, either on the land or towns, but by consent of the great council; and for more security, it enumerates the persons entitled to a seat in that assembly, the prelates and immediate tenants of the crown, without any mention of the Commons—an authority so full, certain, and explicit that nothing but the zeal of party could ever have procured credit to any contrary hypothesis.

It was probably the example of the French barons which first emboldened the English to require greater independence from their sovereign; it is also probable that the boroughs and corporations of England were established in imitation of those of France. It may therefore be proposed, as no unlikely conjecture, that both the chief privileges of the Peers in England and the liberty of the Commons were originally the growth of that foreign country.

In ancient times, men were little solicitous to obtain a place in the legislative assemblies, and rather regarded their attendance as a burden which was not compensated by any

[27] Sometimes the historians mention the people, *populus*, as part of the Parliament; but they always mean the laity, in opposition to the clergy. Sometimes the word *communitas* is found; but it always means *communitas baronagii*. These points are clearly proved by Dr. Brady. There is also mention sometimes made of a crowd or multitude that thronged into the great council on particular interesting occasions; but as deputies from boroughs are never once spoken of, the proof that they had not then any existence becomes the more certain and undeniable. These never could make a crowd, as they must have had a regular place assigned them if they had made a regular part of the legislative body. There were only one hundred and thirty boroughs who received writs of summons from Edward I. It is expressly said in Gesta Reg. Steph. p. 932, that it was usual for the populus, *vulgus*, to crowd into the great councils, where they were plainly mere spectators, and could only gratify their curiosity.

return of profit or honor proportionate to the trouble and expense. The only reason for instituting those public councils was, on the part of the subject, that they desired some security from the attempts of arbitrary power; and, on the part of the sovereign, that he despaired of governing men of such independent spirits without their own consent and concurrence. But the Commons, or the inhabitants of boroughs, had not as yet reached such a degree of consideration as to desire *security* against their prince, or to imagine that, even if they were assembled in a representative body, they had power or rank sufficient to enforce it. The only protection which they aspired to was against the immediate violence and injustice of their fellow-citizens; and this advantage each of them looked for from the courts of justice, or from the authority of some great lord to whom, by law or his own choice, he was attached. On the other hand, the sovereign was sufficiently assured of obedience in the whole community if he procured the concurrence of the nobles; nor had he reason to apprehend that any order of the state could resist his and their united authority. The military sub-vassals could entertain no idea of opposing both their prince and their superiors; the burgesses and tradesmen could much less aspire to such a thought; and thus, even if history were silent on the head, we have reason to conclude, from the known situation of society during those ages, that the Commons were never admitted as members of the legislative body.

The *executive* power of the Anglo-Norman government was lodged in the king. Besides the stated meetings of the national council at the three great festivals of Christmas, Easter, and Whitsuntide,[28] he was accustomed, on any sudden exigence, to summon them together. He could at his pleasure command the attendance of his barons and their vassals, in which consisted the military force of the kingdom; and could employ them during forty days either in resisting a foreign enemy or reducing his rebellious subjects. And, what was of great importance, the whole *judicial* power was ultimately in his hands, and was exercised by officers and ministers of his appointment.

The general plan of the Anglo-Norman government was, that the court of barony was appointed to decide such controversies as arose between the several vassals or subjects of the same barony: the hundred court and county court,

28 Dugd. Orig. Jurid. p. 15.   Spell. Gloss. *in verbo* Parliamentum.

which were still continued as during the Saxon times,[29] to judge between the subjects of different baronies;[30] and the *curia regis*, or king's court, to give sentence among the barons themselves.[31] But this plan, though simple, was attended with some circumstances which, being derived from a very extensive authority assumed by the Conqueror, contributed to increase the royal prerogative; and, as long as the state was not disturbed by arms, reduced every order of the community to some degree of dependence and subordination.

The king himself often sat in his court, which always attended his person.[32] He there heard causes and pronounced judgment;[33] and though he was assisted by the advice of the other members, it is not to be imagined that a decision could easily be obtained contrary to his inclination or opinion. In his absence the chief justiciary presided, who was the first magistrate in the state, and a kind of viceroy on whom depended all the civil affairs of the kingdom.[34] The other chief officers of the crown—the constable, mareschal, seneschal, chamberlain, treasurer, and chancellor[35]—were members, together with such feudal barons as thought proper to attend, and the barons of the exchequer (who at first were also feudal barons) appointed by the king.[36] This court, which was sometimes called the king's court, sometimes the court of exchequer, judged in all causes, civil and criminal, and comprehended the whole business which is now shared out among four courts—the chancery, the king's bench, the common-pleas, and the exchequer.[37]

Such an accumulation of powers was itself a great source

[29] Anglia Sacra, vol. i. p. 334, etc. Dugd. Orig. Jurid. pp. 27, 29. Madox, Hist. Exch. pp. 75, 76. Spell. Gloss. *in verbo* Hundred.
[30] None of the feudal governments in Europe had such institutions as the county courts, which the great authority of the Conqueror still retained from the Saxon customs. All the freeholders of the county, even the greatest barons, were obliged to attend the sheriffs in these courts, and to assist them in the administration of justice. By these means they received frequent and sensible admonitions of their dependence on the king or supreme magistrate; they formed a kind of community with their fellow barons and freeholders; they were often drawn from their individual and independent state, peculiar to the feudal system, and were made members of a political body; and, perhaps, this institution of county courts in England has had greater effects on the government than has yet been distinctly pointed out by historians or traced by antiquaries. The barons were never able to free themselves from this attendance on the sheriffs and itinerant justices till the reign of Henry III.
[31] Brady, Pref. p. 143.
[32] Madox, Hist. Exch. p. 103.
[33] Bracton, lib. 3, cap. 9, § 1; cap. 10, § 1.
[34] Spell. Gloss. *in verbo* Justiciarii.
[35] Madox, Hist. Exch. pp. 27, 29, 33, 38, 41, 54. The Normans introduced the practice of sealing charters, and the chancellor's office was to keep the great seal. Ingulph. Dugd. pp. 33, 34.
[36] Madox, Hist. Exch. pp. 134, 135. Gerv. Dorob. p. 1387.
[37] Madox, Hist. Exch. pp. 56, 70.

of authority, and rendered the jurisdiction of the court formidable to all the subjects; but the turn which judicial trials took soon after the Conquest served still more to increase its authority and to augment the royal prerogatives. William, among the other violent changes which he attempted and effected, had introduced the Norman law into England,[38] had ordered all the pleadings to be in that tongue, and had interwoven with the English jurisprudence all the maxims and principles which the Normans, more advanced in cultivation, and naturally litigious, were accustomed to observe in the distribution of justice. Law now became a science, which at first fell entirely into the hands of the Normans, and which, even after it was communicated to the English, required so much study and application that the laity, in those ignorant ages, were incapable of attaining it, and it was a mystery almost solely confined to the clergy, and chiefly to the monks.[39] The great officers of the crown, and the feudal barons, who were military men, found themselves unfit to penetrate into those obscurities; and though they were entitled to a seat in the supreme judicature, the business of the court was wholly managed by the chief justiciary and the law barons, who were men appointed by the king, and entirely at his disposal.[40] This natural course of things was forwarded by the multiplicity of business which flowed into that court, and which daily augmented by the appeals from all the subordinate judicatures of the kingdom.

In the Saxon times, no appeal was received in the king's court, except upon the denial or delay of justice by the inferior courts; and the same practice was still observed in most of the feudal kingdoms of Europe. But the great power of the Conqueror established, at first in England, an authority which the monarchs in France were not able to attain till the reign of St. Lewis, who lived near two centuries after. He empowered his court to receive appeals both from the courts of barony and the county courts, and by that means brought the administration of justice ultimately into the hands of the sovereign.[41] And lest the expense or trouble of a journey to courts should discourage suitors, and make them acquiesce in the decision of the

[38] Dial. de Scac. p. 30, apud Madox, Hist. Exch.
[39] Will. Malm. lib. 4, p. 123.   [40] Dugd. Orig. Jurid. p. 25.
[41] Madox, Hist. Exch. p. 65. Glanv. lib. 12, cap. 1, 7. Leges Hen. I. § 31, apud Wilkins, p. 248. Fitz-Steph. p. 36. Coke's Comment. on the Statute of Marlbridge, cap. 20.

inferior judicatures, itinerant judges were afterwards established, who made their circuits throughout the kingdom and tried all causes that were brought before them.[42] By this expedient the courts of barony were kept in awe; and if they still preserved some influence, it was only from the apprehensions which the vassals might entertain of disobliging their superior, by appealing from his jurisdiction. But the county courts were much discredited; and as the freeholders were found ignorant of the intricate principles and forms of the new law, the lawyers gradually brought all business before the king's judges, and abandoned the ancient simple and popular judicature. After this manner the formalities of justice, which, though they appear tedious and cumbersome, are found requisite to the support of liberty in all monarchical governments, proved at first, by a combination of causes, very advantageous to royal authority in England.

The power of the Norman kings was also much supported by a great revenue; and by a revenue that was fixed, perpetual, and independent of the subject. The people, without betaking themselves to arms, had no check upon the king, and no regular security for the due administration of justice. In those days of violence many instances of oppression passed unheeded, and soon after were openly pleaded as precedents which it was unlawful to dispute or control. Princes and ministers were too ignorant to be themselves sensible of the advantages attending an equitable administration, and there was no established council or assembly which could protect the people, and, by withdrawing supplies, regularly and peaceably admonish the king of his duty and insure the execution of the laws.

The first branch of the king's stated revenue was the royal demesnes or crown-lands, which were very extensive, and comprehended, besides a great number of manors, most of the chief cities of the kingdom. It was established by law that the king could alienate no part of his demesne, and that he himself, or his successor, could at any time resume such donations.[43] But this law was never regularly observed, which happily rendered in time the crown some-

<hr/>

[42] Madox, Hist. Exch. pp. 83, 84, 100. Gerv. Dorob. p. 1410. What made the Anglo-Norman barons more readily submit to appeals from their court to the king's court of exchequer was their being accustomed to like appeals in Normandy to the ducal court of exchequer. See Gilbert's History of the Exchequer, pp. 1, 2; though the author thinks it doubtful whether the Norman court was not rather copied from the English, p. 6.

[43] Fleta, lib. 1, cap 8, § 17; lib. 3, cap. 6, § 3. Bracton, lib. 2, cap. 5.

what more dependent. The rent of the crown-lands, considered merely as so much riches, was a source of power; the influence of the king over his tenants and the inhabitants of his towns increased this power; but the other numerous branches of his revenue, besides supplying his treasury, gave, by their very nature, a great latitude to arbitrary authority, and were a support of the prerogative, as will appear from an enumeration of them.

The king was never content with the stated rents, but levied heavy talliages at pleasure on the inhabitants both of town and country who lived within his demesne. All bargains of sale, in order to prevent theft, being prohibited, except in boroughs and public markets,[44] he pretended to exact tolls on all goods which were there sold.[45] He seized two hogsheads, one before and one behind the mast, from every vessel that imported wine. All goods paid to his customs a proportionate part of their value;[46] passage over bridges and on rivers was loaded with tolls at pleasure;[47] and though the boroughs by degrees bought the liberty of farming those impositions, yet the revenue profited by these bargains; new sums were often exacted for the renewal and confirmation of their charters,[48] and the people were thus held in perpetual dependence.

Such was the situation of the inhabitants within the royal demesnes. But the possessors of land, or the military tenants, though they were better protected both by law and by the great privilege of carrying arms, were, from the nature of their tenures, much exposed to the inroads of power, and possessed not what we should esteem in our age a very durable security. The Conqueror ordained that the barons should be obliged to pay nothing beyond their stated services,[49] except a reasonable aid to ransom his person if he were taken in war, to make his eldest son a knight, and to marry his eldest daughter. What should on these occasions be deemed a reasonable aid was not determined; and the demands of the crown were so far discretionary.

The king could require in war the personal attendance of his vassals—that is, of almost all the landed proprietors; and if they declined the service, they were obliged to pay him a composition in money, which was called a scutage.

[44] Leges Will. I. cap. 61.   [45] Madox, p. 530.
[46] Madox, p. 529. This author says a fifteenth. But it is not easy to reconcile this account to other authorities.
[47] Madox, p. 529.   [48] Madox, Hist. Exch. pp. 275, 276, 277, etc.
[49] Leges Will. Conq. § 55.

The sum was, during some reigns, precarious and uncertain ; it was sometimes levied without allowing the vassals the liberty of personal service ;[50] and it was a usual artifice of the king to pretend an expedition that he might be entitled to levy the scutage from his military tenants. Danegelt was another species of land-tax levied by the early Norman kings arbitrarily, and contrary to the laws of the Conqueror.[51] Moneyage was also a general land-tax of the same nature, levied by the first two Norman kings, and abolished by the charter of Henry I.[52] It was a shilling, paid every three years by each hearth, to induce the king not to use his prerogative in debasing the coin. Indeed, it appears from that charter that, though the Conqueror had granted his military tenants an immunity from all taxes and talliages, he and his son William had never thought themselves bound to observe that rule, but had levied impositions at pleasure on all the landed estates of the kingdom. The utmost that Henry grants is, that the land cultivated by the military tenant himself shall not be so burdened ; and he reserves the power of taxing the farmers ; and as it is known that Henry's charter was never observed in any one article, we may be assured that this prince and his successors retracted even this small indulgence, and levied arbitrary impositions on all the lands of all their subjects. These taxes were sometimes very heavy, since Malmesbury tells us that in the reign of William Rufus the farmers, on account of them, abandoned tillage, and a famine ensued.[53]

The escheats were a great branch both of power and of revenue, especially during the first reigns after the Conquest. In default of posterity from the first baron, his land reverted to the crown, and continually augmented the king's possessions. The prince had indeed by law a power of alienating these escheats ; but by this means he had an opportunity of establishing the fortunes of his friends and servants, and thereby enlarging his authority. Sometimes he retained them in his own hands; and they were gradually confounded with the royal demesnes, and became difficult to be distinguished from them. This confusion is probably the reason why the king acquired the right of alienating his demesnes.

But besides escheats from default of heirs, those which

[50] Gervase de Tilbury, p. 25.   [51] Madox, Hist. Exch. p. 475.
[52] Matt. Paris, p. 38.
[53] So also Chron. Abb. St. Petri de Burgo, p. 55.   Knyghton, p. 2366.

ensued from crimes, or breach of duty towards the superior lord, were frequent in ancient times. If the vassal, being thrice summoned to attend his superior's court and do fealty, neglected or refused obedience, he forfeited all title to his land.[54] If he denied his tenure or refused his service, he was exposed to the same penalty.[55] If he sold his estate without license from his lord,[56] or if he sold it upon any other tenure or title than that by which he himself held it,[57] he lost all right to it. The adhering to his lord's enemies,[58] deserting him in war,[59] betraying his secrets,[60] debauching his wife or his near relations,[61] or even using indecent freedoms with them,[62] might be punished by forfeiture. The higher crimes—rapes, robbery, murder, arson, etc.—were called felony; and being interpreted want of fidelity to his lord, made him lose his fief.[63] Even where the felon was vassal to a baron, though his immediate lord enjoyed the forfeiture, the king might retain possession of his estate during a twelvemonth, and had the right of spoiling and destroying it, unless the baron paid him a reasonable composition.[64] We have not here enumerated all the species of felonies or of crimes by which forfeiture was incurred; we have said enough to prove that the possession of feudal property was anciently somewhat precarious, and that the primary idea was never lost, of its being a kind of *fee* or *benefice*.

When a baron died, the king immediately took possession of the estate, and the heir, before he recovered his right, was obliged to make application to the crown, and desire that he might be admitted to do homage for his land and pay a composition to the king. This composition was not at first fixed by law, at least by practice. The king was often exorbitant in his demands, and kept possession of the land till they were complied with.

If the heir were a minor, the king retained the whole profit of the estate till his majority, and might grant what sum he thought proper for the education and maintenance of the young baron. This practice was also founded on the notion that a fief was a benefice, and that while the heir could not perform his military services, the revenue devolved to the superior, who employed another in his stead. It is

[54] Hottom. De Feud. Disp. cap. 38, col. 886.
[55] Lib. Feud. lib. 3, tit. 1; lib. 4, tit. 1, 39.   [56] Id. lib. 1, tit. 21.
[57] Id. lib. 4, tit. 44.   [58] Id. lib. 3, tit. 1.   [59] Id. lib. 4, tit. 14, 21.
[60] Id. lib. 4, tit. 14.   [61] Id. lib. 1, tit. 14, 21.   [62] Id. lib. 1, tit. 1.
[63] Spell. Gloss. *in verbo* Felonia.
[64] Spell. Gloss. *in verbo* Felonia. Glanville, lib. 7, cap. 17.

obvious that a great proportion of the landed property must, by means of this device, be continually in the hands of the prince, and that all the noble families were thereby held in perpetual dependence. When the king granted the ward-ship of a rich heir to any one, he had the opportunity of en-riching a favorite or minister; if he sold it, he thereby levied a considerable sum of money. Simon de Montfort paid Henry III. ten thousand marks (an immense sum in those days) for the wardship of Gilbert d'Umfreville.[65] Geoffrey de Mandeville paid to the same prince the sum of twenty thousand marks that he might marry Isabel, Countess of Gloucester, and possess all her lands and knight's-fees. This sum would be equivalent to three hundred thousand (per-haps four hundred thousand) pounds in our time.[66]

If the heir were a female, the king was entitled to offer her any husband of her rank he thought proper; and if she refused him, she forfeited her land. Even a male heir could not marry without the royal consent, and it was usual for men to pay large sums for the liberty of making their own choice in marriage.[67] No man could dispose of his land, either by sale or will, without the consent of his superior. The possessor was never considered as full proprietor; he was still a kind of beneficiary, and could not oblige his superior to accept of any vassal that was not agreeable to him.

Fines, amerciaments, and oblatas, as they were called, were another considerable branch of the royal power and revenue. The ancient records of the exchequer, which are still preserved, give surprising accounts of the numerous fines and amerciaments levied in those days,[68] and of the strange inventions fallen upon to exact money from the sub-ject. It appears that the ancient kings of England put them-selves entirely on the footing of the barbarous Eastern princes, whom no man must approach without a present, who sell all their good offices, and who intrude themselves into every business that they may have a pretence for extorting money. Even justice was avowedly bought and sold. The king's court itself, though the supreme judicature of the kingdom, was open to none that brought not presents to the king. The bribes given for the expedition, delay,[69] suspension, and doubtless for the perversion, of justice were entered in the public registers of the royal revenue, and remain as monu-

[65] Madox, Hist. Exch. p. 223.   [66] Id. p. 322.
[67] Madox, Hist. Exch. p. 320.   [68] Id. p. 272.   [69] Id. pp. 274, 309.

ments of the perpetual iniquity and tyranny of the times. The barons of the exchequer, for instance—the first nobility of the kingdom—were not ashamed to insert, as an article in their records, that the county of Norfolk paid a sum that they might be fairly dealt with ;[70] the borough of Yarmouth, that the king's charters, which they have for their liberties, might not be violated;[71] Richard, son of Gilbert, for the king's helping him to recover his debts from the Jews;[72] Serlo, son of Terlavaston, that he might be permitted to make his defence in case he were accused of a certain homicide ;[73] Walter de Burton, for free law if accused of wounding another ;[74] Robert d'Essart, for having an inquest to find whether Roger the Butcher and Wace and Humphrey accused him of robbery and theft out of envy and ill-will or not ;[75] William Buhurst, for having an inquest to find whether he were accused of the death of one Godwin out of ill-will or for just cause.[76] I have selected these few instances from a great number of a like kind which Madox had selected from a still greater number preserved in the ancient rolls of the exchequer.[77]

Sometimes the party litigant offered the king a certain portion—a half, a third, a fourth—payable out of the debts which he, as the executor of justice, should assist him in recovering.[78] Theophania de Westland agreed to pay the half of two hundred and twelve marks that she might recover that sum against James de Fughleston ;[79] Solomon the Jew engaged to pay one mark out of every seven that he should recover against Hugh de la Hose ;[80] Nicholas Morrel promised to pay sixty pounds that the Earl of Flanders might be distrained to pay him three hundred and forty-three pounds which the earl had taken from him, and these sixty pounds were to be paid out of the first money that Nicholas should recover from the earl.[81]

As the king assumed the entire power over trade, he was to be paid for a permission to exercise commerce or industry of any kind.[82] Hugh Oisel paid four hundred marks for liberty to trade in England ;[83] Nigel de Havene gave fifty marks for the partnership in merchandise which he had with Gervase de Hanton ;[84] the men of Worcester paid one hundred shillings that they might have the liberty of selling and

---

[70] Madox, Hist. Exch. p. 295. [71] Ibid.
[72] Madox, Hist. Exch. p. 296. He paid two hundred marks. a great sum in those days. [73] Id. 296. [74] Ibid. [75] Id. p. 298.
[76] Id. p. 302. [77] Id. ch. 12. [78] Id. p. 311. [79] Ibid.
[80] Id. pp. 79, 312. [81] 312. [82] Id. p. 323. [83] Ibid.
[84] Ibid.

buying dyed cloth as formerly;[85] several other towns paid for a like liberty.[86] The commerce, indeed, of the kingdom was so much under the control of the king that he erected guilds, corporations, and monopolies wherever he pleased, and levied sums for these exclusive privileges.[87]

There were no profits so small as to be below the king's attention. Henry, son of Arthur, gave ten dogs to have a recognition against the Countess of Copland for one knight's-fee;[88] Roger, son of Nicholas, gave twenty lampreys and twenty shads for an inquest to find whether Gilbert, son of Alured, gave to Roger two hundred muttons to obtain his confirmation for certain lands, or whether Roger took them from him by violence;[89] Geoffrey Fitz-Pierre, the chief justiciary, gave two good Norway hawks that Walter le Madine might have leave to export a hundred weight of cheese out of the king's dominions.[90]

It is really amusing to remark the strange business in which the king sometimes interfered, and never without a present. The wife of Hugh de Neville gave the king two hundred hens that she might lie with her husband one night,[91] and she brought with her two sureties who answered each for a hundred hens. It is probable that her husband was a prisoner, which debarred her from having access to him. The Abbot of Rucford paid ten marks for leave to erect houses and place men upon his land near Welhang, in order to secure his wood there from being stolen;[92] Hugh, Archdeacon of Wells, gave one tun of wine for leave to carry six hundred sums of corn whither he would;[93] Peter de Peraris gave twenty marks for leave to salt fishes as Peter Chevalier used to do.[94]

It was usual to pay high fines in order to gain the king's good-will or mitigate his anger. In the reign of Henry II. Gilbert, the son of Fergus, fines in nine hundred and nineteen pounds nine shillings to obtain that prince's favor; William de Chataignes, a thousand marks that he would remit his displeasure. In the reign of Henry III., the city of London fines in no less a sum than twenty thousand pounds on the same account.[95]

The king's protection and good offices of every kind were bought and sold. Robert Grislet paid twenty marks of silver that the king would help him against the Earl of Mor-

85 Madox, Hist. Exch. 324.   86 Ibid.   87 Id. p. pp. 232, 233, etc.
88 Id. p. 298.   89 Id. p. 305.   90 Id. p. 325.   91 Id. p. 320.
92 Id. p. 326.   93 Id. p. 320.   94 Id. p. 326.   95 Id. pp. 327, 329.

taigne in a certain plea; [96] Robert de Cundet gave thirty
marks of silver that the king would bring him to an accord
with the Bishop of Lincoln; [97] Ralph de Breckham gave a
hawk that the king would protect him, [98] and this is a very
frequent reason for payments; John, son of Ordgar, gave a
Norway hawk to have the king's request to the King of
Norway to let him have his brother Godard's chattels; [99]
Richard de Neville gave twenty palfreys to obtain the king's
request to Isolda Bisset that she should take him for a husband; [100] Roger Fitz-Walter gave three good palfreys to
have the king's letter to Roger Bertram's mother that she
should marry him; [101] Eling, the dean, paid one hundred
marks that his whore and his children might be let out upon
bail; [102] the Bishop of Winchester gave one tun of good
wine for his not putting the king in mind to give a girdle to
the Countess of Albemarle; [103] Robert de Veaux gave five
of the best palfreys that the king would hold his tongue
about Henry Pinel's wife. [104] There are in the records of
exchequer many other singular instances of a like nature. [105]
It will, however, be just to remark that the same ridiculous
practices and dangerous abuses prevailed in Normandy, and
probably in all the other states of Europe. [106] England was
not, in this respect, more barbarous than its neighbors.

These iniquitous practices of the Norman kings were so
well known that on the death of Hugh Bigod, in the reign

[96] Madox, Hist. Exch. p. 329.   [97] Id. p. 330.
[98] Id. p. 332.   [99] Ibid.   [100] Id. p. 333.   [101] Ibid.
[102] Id. p. 342.   " Pro habenda amica sua et filiis," etc.   [103] Id. p. 352.
[104] Ibid.   " Ut rex taceret de uxore Henrici Pinel."
[105] We shall gratify the reader's curiosity by subjoining a few more instances
from Madox, p. 332. Hugh Oisel was to give the king two robes of a good green
color to have the king's letters patent to the merchants of Flanders, with a request to render him one thousand marks which he lost in Flanders ; the Abbot of
Hyde paid thirty marks to have the king's letters of request to the Archbishop of
Canterbury to remove certain monks that were against the abbot ; Roger de Tri-
hanton paid twenty marks and a palfrey to have the king's request to Richard
d'Umfreville to give him his sister to wife, and to the sister that she would accept
him for a husband ; William de Cheveringworth paid five marks to have the king's
letter to the Abbot of Perfore to let him enjoy peaceably his tithes as formerly ;
Matthew de Hereford, clerk, paid ten marks for a letter of request to the Bishop
of Llandaff to let him enjoy peaceably his church of Schenfrith ; Andrew Neulun
gave three Flemish caps for the king's request to the Prior of Chikesand for performance of an agreement made between them ; Henry de Fontibus gave a Lom-
bardy horse of value to have the king's request to Henry Fitz-Hervey that he
would grant him his daughter to wife ; Roger, son of Nicholas, promised all the
lampreys he could get to have the king's request to Earl William Marshall that
he would grant him the manor of Langeford, at Firm ; the burgesses of Gloucester promised three hundred lampreys that they might not be distrained to find
the prisoners of Poictou with necessaries unless they pleased. Id. p. 352. Jordan, son of Reginald, paid twenty marks to have the king's request to William
Paniel that he would grant him the land of Mill Nierenuit and the custody of his
heirs ; and if Jordan obtained the same he was to pay the twenty marks, otherwise not. Id. p. 333.   [106] Madox, Hist. Exch. p. 359.

of Henry II., the best and most just of these princes, the eldest son and the widow of this nobleman came to court, and strove, by offering large presents to the king, each of them to acquire possession of that rich inheritance. The king was so equitable as to order the cause to be tried by the great council; but, in the meantime, he seized all the money and treasure of the deceased.[107] Peter of Blois, a judicious and even an elegant writer for that age, gives a pathetic description of the venality of justice and the oppressions of the poor under the reign of Henry; and he scruples not to complain to the king himself of these abuses.[108] We may judge what the case would be under the government of worse princes. The articles of inquiry concerning the conduct of sheriffs which Henry promulgated in 1170 show the great power as well as the licentiousness of these officers.[109]

Amerciaments, or fines for crimes and trespasses, were another considerable branch of the royal revenue.[110] Most crimes were atoned for by money. The fines imposed were not limited by any rule or statute, and frequently occasioned the total ruin of the person, even for the slightest trespasses. The forest laws particularly were a great source of oppression. The king possessed sixty-eight forests, thirteen chases, and seven hundred and eighty-one parks in different parts of England;[111] and, considering the extreme passion of the English and Normans for hunting, these were so many snares laid for the people by which they were allured into trespasses and brought within the reach of arbitrary and rigorous laws which the king had thought proper to enact by his own authority.

But the most barefaced acts of tyranny and oppression were practised against the Jews, who were entirely out of the protection of law, were extremly odious from the bigotry of the people, and were abandoned to the immeasurable rapacity of the king and his ministers. Besides many other indignities to which they were continually exposed, it appears that they were once all thrown into prison and the sum of sixty-six thousand marks exacted for their liberty.[112] At another time Isaac the Jew paid alone five thousand one hundred marks;[113] Brun, three thousand marks;[114] Jurnet,

[107] Benedict, Abb. pp. 180, 181.
[108] Pet. Bles. epist. 95, apud Biblioth. Patr. vol. xxiv. p. 2014.
[109] Hoveden, Chron. Gerv. p. 1410.
[110] Madox, ch. 14.
[111] Spell. Gloss. *in verbo* Foresta.
[112] Madox, Hist. Exch. p. 151. This happened in the reign of King John.
[113] Id. p. 151.
[114] Id. p. 153.

two thousand; Bennet, five hundred. At another Licorica, widow of David, the Jew of Oxford, was required to pay six thousand marks, and she was delivered over to six of the richest and discreetest Jews in England who were to answer for the sum.[115] Henry III. borrowed five thousand marks from the Earl of Cornwall, and for his repayment consigned over to him all the Jews in England.[116] The revenue arising from exactions upon this nation was so considerable that there was a particular court of exchequer set apart for managing it.[117]

We may judge concerning the low state of commerce among the English when the Jews, notwithstanding these oppressions, could still find their account in trading among them and lending them money. And, as the improvements of agriculture were also much checked by the immense possessions of the nobility, by the disorders of the times, and by the precarious state of feudal property, it appears that industry of no kind could then have place in the kingdom.[118]

It is asserted by Sir Henry Spellman [119] as an undoubted truth that, during the reigns of the First Norman princes, every edict of the king issued with the consent of his privy council had the full force of law. But the barons, surely, were not so passive as to intrust a power entirely arbitrary and despotic into the hands of the sovereign. It only appears that the constitution had not fixed any precise boundaries to the royal power; that the right of issuing proclamations on any emergency, and of exacting obedience to them—a right which was always supposed inherent in the crown—is very difficult to be distinguished from a legislative authority; that the extreme imperfection of the ancient laws, and the sudden exigencies which often occurred in such turbulent governments, obliged the prince to exert frequently the latent powers of his prerogative; that he naturally proceeded from the acquiescence of the people to assume, in many particulars of moment, an authority from which he had excluded himself by express statutes, charters, or concessions, and which was, in the main, repugnant to

---

[115] Madox, Hist. Exch. p. 168.   [116] Id. p. 156.   [117] Id. ch. 7.
[118] We learn from the extracts given us of Domesday by Brady, in his Treatise of Boroughs, that almost all the boroughs of England had suffered in the shock of the Conquest, and had extremely decayed between the death of the Confessor and the time when Domesday was framed.
[119] Gloss. *in verb.* Judicium Dei. The author of the Miroir des Justices complains that ordinances are only made by the king and his clerks, and by aliens and others who dare not contradict the king, but study to please him. Whence he concludes laws are oftener dictated by will than founded on right.

the general genius of the constitution; and that the lives, the personal liberty, and the properties of all his subjects were less secured by law against the exertion of his arbitrary authority than by the independent power and private connections of each individual. It appears from the great charter itself that not only John, a tyrannical prince, and Richard, a violent one, but their father, Henry, under whose reign the prevalence of gross abuses is the least to be suspected, were accustomed from their sole authority, without process of law, to imprison, banish, and attaint the freemen of their kingdom.

A great baron in ancient times considered himself as a kind of sovereign within his territory, and was attended by courtiers and dependants more zealously attached to him than the ministers of state and the great officers were commonly to *their* sovereign. He often maintained in his court the parade of royalty by establishing a justiciary, constable, mareschal, chamberlain, seneschal, and chancellor, and assigning to each of these officers a separate province and command. He was usually very assiduous in exercising his jurisdiction, and took such delight in that image of sovereignty that it was found necessary to restrain his activity, and prohibit him by law from holding courts too frequently.[120] It is not to be doubted but the example set him by the prince of a mercenary and sordid extortion would be faithfully copied, and that all his good and bad offices, his justice and injustice, were equally put to sale. He had the power, with the king's consent, to exact talliages even from the free citizens who lived within his barony; and as his necessities made him rapacious, his authority was usually found to be more oppressive and tyrannical than that of the sovereign.[121] He was ever engaged in hereditary or personal animosities or confederacies with his neighbors, and often gave protection to all desperate adventurers and criminals who could be useful in serving his violent purposes. He was able alone, in times of tranquillity, to obstruct the execution of justice within his territories, and by combining with a few malcontent barons of high rank and power he could throw the state into convulsions. And, on the whole, though the royal authority was confined within bounds, and often within very narrow ones, yet the check was irregular, and frequently the source of great disorders; nor was it derived from the liberty of the people, but from the military

[120] Dugd. Orig. Jurid. p. 26.   [121] Madox, Hist. Exch. p. 520.

power of many petty tyrants, who were equally dangerous to the prince and oppressive to the subject.

The power of the Church was another rampart against royal authority; but this defence was also the cause of many mischiefs and inconveniences. The dignified clergy, perhaps, were not so prone to immediate violence as the barons; but as they pretended to a total independence of the state, and could always cover themselves with the appearances of religion, they proved, in one respect, an obstruction to the settlement of the kingdom and to the regular execution of the laws. The policy of the Conqueror was in this particular liable to some exception. He augmented the superstitious veneration for Rome to which that age was so much inclined, and he broke these bands of connection which, in the Saxon times, had preserved a union between the lay and the clerical orders. He prohibited the bishops from sitting in the county courts; he allowed ecclesiastical causes to be tried in spiritual courts only; [122] and he so much exalted the power of the clergy that of sixty thousand two hundred and fifteen knight's-fees, into which he divided England, he placed no less than twenty-eight thousand and fifteen under the Church. [123]

The right of primogeniture was introduced with the feudal law—an institution which is hurtful, by producing and maintaining an unequal division of private property; but is advantageous in another respect, by accustoming the people to a preference in favor of the eldest son, and thereby preventing a partition or disputed succession in the monarchy. The Normans introduced the use of surnames, which tend to preserve the knowledge of families and pedigrees. They abolished none of the old absurd methods of trial by the cross or ordeal, and they added a new absurdity, the trial by single combat, [124] which became a regular part of jurisprudence, and was conducted with all the order, method, devotion, and solemnity imaginable. [125] The ideas of chivalry also seem to have been imported by the Normans. No traces of those fantastic notions are to be found among the plain and rustic Saxons.

The feudal institutions, by raising the military tenants

---

[122] Char. Will. apud Wilkins, p. 230. Spell. Conc. vol. ii. p. 14.

[123] Spell. Gloss. *in verb.* Manus Mortua. We are not to imagine, as some have done, that the Church possessed lands in this proportion, but only that they and their vassals enjoyed such a proportionable part of the landed property.

[124] Leges Will. cap. 68.

[125] Spell. Gloss. *in verb.* Campus. The last instance of these duels was in the 15th of Elizabeth. So long did that absurdity remain.

to a kind of sovereign dignity, by rendering personal strength and valor requisite, and by making every knight and baron his own protector and avenger, begat that martial pride and sense of honor which, being cultivated and embellished by the poets and romance-writers of the age, ended in chivalry. The virtuous knight fought not only in his own quarrel, but in that of the innocent, of the helpless, and, above all, of the fair, whom he supposed to be forever under the guardianship of his valiant arm. The uncourteous knight who, from his castle, exercised robbery on travellers and committed violence on virgins, was the object of his perpetual indignation; and he put him to death without scruple, or trial, or appeal, wherever he met with him. The great independence of men made personal honor and fidelity the chief tie among them, and rendered it the capital virtue of every true knight or genuine professor of chivalry. The solemnities of single combat, as established by law, banished the notion of everything unfair or unequal in rencounters, and maintained an appearance of courtesy between the combatants till the moment of their engagement. The credulity of the age grafted on this stock the notion of giants, enchanters, dragons, spells,[126] and a thousand wonders which still multiplied during the time of the crusades, when men, returning from so great a distance, used the liberty of imposing every fiction on their believing audience. These ideas of chivalry infected the writings, conversation, and behavior of men during some ages; and even after they were in a great measure banished by the revival of learning, they left modern *gallantry* and the *point of honor*, which still maintain their influence, and are the genuine offspring of those ancient affectations.

The concession of the great charter, or rather its full establishment (for there was a considerable interval of time between the one and the other), gave rise by degrees to a new species of government, and introduced some order and justice into the administration. The ensuing scenes of our history are, therefore, somewhat different from the preceding. Yet the great charter contained no establishment of new courts, magistrates, or senates, nor abolition of the old. It introduced no new distribution of the powers of the commonwealth, and no innovation in the political or pub-

[126] In all legal single combats, it was part of the champion's oath that he carried not about him any herb, spell, or enchantment, by which he might procure victory. Dugd. Orig. Jurid. p. 82.

lic law of the kingdom. It only guarded, and that merely by verbal clauses, against such tyrannical practices as are incompatible with civilized government, and, if they become very frequent, are incompatible with all government. The barbarous license of the kings, and perhaps of the nobles, was thenceforth somewhat more restrained. Men acquired some more security for their properties and their liberties; and government approached a little nearer to that end for which it was originally instituted—the distribution of justice and the equal protection of the citizens. Acts of violence and iniquity in the crown, which before were only deemed injurious to individuals, and were hazardous chiefly in proportion to the number, power, and dignity of the persons affected by them, were now regarded in some degree as public injuries, and as infringements of a charter calculated for general security. And thus the establishment of the great charter, without seeming anywise to innovate in the distribution of political power, became a kind of epoch in the constitution.

CHAPTER XII.

HENRY III.

SETTLEMENT OF THE GOVERNMENT. — GENERAL PACIFI-
CATION. — DEATH OF THE PROTECTOR. — SOME COM-
MOTIONS. — HUBERT DE BURGH DISPLACED. — THE BISHOP
OF WINCHESTER MINISTER. — KING'S PARTIALITY TO
FOREIGNERS. — GRIEVANCES. — ECCLESIASTICAL GRIEV-
ANCES. — EARL OF CORNWALL ELECTED KING OF THE
ROMANS. — DISCONTENT OF THE BARONS. — SIMON DE
MONTFORT, EARL OF LEICESTER. — PROVISIONS OF OX-
FORD. — USURPATION OF THE BARONS. — PRINCE EDWARD.
— CIVIL WARS OF THE BARONS. — REFERENCE TO THE
KING OF FRANCE. — RENEWAL OF THE CIVIL WARS. —
BATTLE OF LEWES. — HOUSE OF COMMONS. — BATTLE OF
EVESHAM AND DEATH OF LEICESTER. — SETTLEMENT OF
THE GOVERNMENT. — DEATH AND CHARACTER OF THE
KING. — MISCELLANEOUS TRANSACTIONS OF THIS REIGN.

[1216.] MOST sciences, in proportion as they increase
and improve, invent methods by which they facilitate
their reasonings; and, employing general theorems, are enabled to comprehend in a few propositions a great number
of inferences and conclusions. History also, being a collection of facts which are multiplying without end, is obliged
to adopt such arts of abridgment to retain the more material
events, and to drop all the minute circumstances which are
only interesting during the time or to the persons engaged
in the transactions. This truth is nowhere more evident
than with regard to the reign upon which we are going to
enter. What mortal could have the patience to write or
read a long detail of such frivolous events as those with
which it is filled, or attend to a tedious narrative which
would follow through a series of fifty-six years the caprices
and weakness of so mean a prince as Henry? The chief
reason why Protestant writers have been so anxious to
spread out the incidents of this reign is in order to expose

the rapacity, ambition, and artifices of the court of Rome; and to prove that the great dignitaries of the Catholic Church, while they pretended to have nothing in view but the salvation of souls, had bent all their attention to the acquisition of riches, and were restrained by no sense of justice or of honor in the pursuit of that great object.[1] But this conclusion would readily be allowed them, though it were not illustrated by such a detail of uninteresting incidents, and follows, indeed, by an evident necessity, from the very situation in which that Church was placed with regard to the rest of Europe. For, besides that ecclesiastical power, as it can always cover its operations under a cloak of sanctity, and attacks men on the side where they dare not employ their reason, lies less under control than civil government—besides this general cause, I say, the pope and his courtiers were foreigners to most of the churches which they governed. They could not possibly have any other object than to pillage the provinces for present gain; and, as they lived at a distance, they would be little awed by shame or remorse in employing every lucrative expedient which was suggested to them. England being one of the most remote provinces attached to the Romish hierarchy, as well as the most prone to superstition, felt severely during this reign, while its patience was not yet fully exhausted, the influence of these causes; and we shall often have occasion to touch cursorily upon such incidents. But we shall not attempt to comprehend every transaction transmitted to us; and, till the end of the reign, when the events become more memorable, we shall not always observe an exact chronological order in our narration.

The Earl of Pembroke, who, at the time of John's death, was Mareschal of England, was by his office at the head of the armies, and, consequently, during a state of civil wars and convulsions, at the head of the government; and it happened fortunately for the young monarch and for the nation that the power could not have been entrusted into more able and more faithful hands. This nobleman, who had maintained his loyalty unshaken to John during the lowest fortune of that monarch, determined to support the authority of the infant prince; nor was he dismayed at the number and violence of his enemies. Sensible that Henry, agreeably to the prejudices of the times, would not be deemed a sovereign till crowned and anointed by a church-

[1] Matt. Paris, p. 623.

man, he immediately carried the young prince to Gloucester,
where the ceremony of coronation was performed in the
presence of Gualo, the legate, and of a few noblemen
by the Bishops of Winchester and Bath.[2] As the concurrence of the papal authority was requisite to support the
tottering throne, Henry was obliged to swear fealty to the
pope, and renew that homage to which his father had
already subjected the kingdom;[3] and in order to enlarge
the authority of Pembroke, and to give him a more regular
and legal title to it, a general council of the barons was
soon after summoned at Bristol, where that nobleman was
chosen protector of the realm.

Pembroke, that he might reconcile all men to the government of his pupil, made him grant a new charter of liberties, which, though mostly copied from the former concessions extorted from John, contains some alterations which
may be deemed remarkable.[4] The full privilege of elections in the clergy, granted by the late king, was not confirmed, nor the liberty of going out of the kingdom without the royal consent. Whence we may conclude that
Pembroke and the barons, jealous of the ecclesiastical
power, both were desirous of renewing the king's claim to
issue a *congé d'élire* to the monks and chapters, and thought
it requisite to put some check to the frequent appeals to
Rome. But what may chiefly surprise us is, that the obligation to which John had subjected himself of obtaining the
consent of the great council before he levied any aids or
scutages upon the nation was omitted; and this article was
even declared hard and severe, and was expressly left to
future deliberation. But we must consider that, though
this limitation may perhaps appear to us the most momentous in the whole charter of John, it was not regarded in
that light by the ancient barons, who were more jealous in
guarding against particular acts of violence in the crown
than against such general impositions, which, unless they
were evidently reasonable and necessary, could scarcely,
without general consent, be levied upon men who had arms
in their hands, and who could repel any act of oppression
by which they were all immediately affected. We accordingly find that Henry, in the course of his reign, while he
gave frequent occasions for complaint with regard to his
violations of the great charter, never attempted by his mere

---

[2] Matt. Paris, p. 200.   Hist. Croyl. cont. p. 474.   W. Heming. p. 562.   Trivet,
p. 168.   [3] Matt. Paris, p. 200.   [4] Rymer, vol. i. p. 215.

will to levy any aids or scutages, though he was often reduced to great necessities, and was refused supply by his
people. So much easier was it for him to transgress the
law when individuals alone were affected than even to exert
his acknowledged prerogatives where the interest of the
whole body was concerned.

This charter was again confirmed by the king in the ensuing year, with the addition of some articles to prevent
the oppressions by sheriffs, and also with an additional
charter of forests—a circumstance of great moment in those
ages, when hunting was so much the occupation of the nobility, and when the king comprehended so considerable a
part of the kingdom within his forests, which he governed
by peculiar and arbitrary laws. All the forests which had
been enclosed since the reign of Henry II. were disaffor-
ested, and new perambulations were appointed for that purpose. Offences in the forests were declared to be no longer
capital, but punishable by fine, imprisonment, and more
gentle penalties; and all the proprietors of land recovered
the power of cutting and using their own wood at their
pleasure.

Thus these famous charters were brought nearly to the
shape in which they have ever since stood; and they were,
during many generations, the peculiar favorites of the English nation, and esteemed the most sacred rampart to national liberty and independence. As they secured the rights
of all orders of men, they were anxiously defended by all,
and became the basis, in a manner, of the English monarchy, and a kind of original contract, which both limited
the authority of the king and insured the conditional allegiance of his subjects. Though often violated, they were
still claimed by the nobility and people; and, as no precedents were supposed valid that infringed them, they rather
acquired than lost authority from the frequent attempts
made against them in several ages by regal and arbitrary
power.

While Pembroke, by renewing and confirming the great
charter, gave so much satisfaction and security to the nation in general, he also applied himself successfully to individuals. He wrote letters in the king's name to all the malcontent barons, in which he represented to them that, whatever jealousy and animosity they might have entertained
against the late king, a young prince, the lineal heir of their
ancient monarchs, had now succeeded to the throne without

succeeding either to the resentments or principles of his predecessor; that the desperate expedient which they had employed of calling in a foreign potentate had, happily for them as well as for the nation, failed of entire success; and it was still in their power by a speedy return to their duty to restore the independence of the kingdom, and to secure that liberty for which they so zealously contended; that as all past offences of the barons were now buried in oblivion, they ought, on their part, to forget their complaints against their late sovereign, who, if he had been anywise blamable in his conduct, had left to his son the salutary warning to avoid the paths which had led to such fatal extremities; and that, having now obtained a charter for their liberties, it was their interest to show by their conduct that this acquisition was not incompatible with their allegiance, and that the rights of king and people, so far from being hostile and opposite, might mutually support and sustain each other.[5]

These considerations, enforced by the character of honor and constancy which Pembroke had ever maintained, had a mighty influence on the barons; and most of them began secretly to negotiate with him, and many of them openly returned to their duty. The diffidence which Lewis discovered of their fidelity forwarded this general propension towards the king; and when the French prince refused the government of the castle of Hertford to Robert Fitz-Walter, who had been so active against the late king, and who claimed that fortress as his property, they plainly saw that the English were excluded from every trust, and that foreigners had engrossed all the confidence and affection of their new sovereign.[6] The excommunication, too, denounced by the legate against all the adherents of Lewis failed not, in the turn which men's dispositions had taken, to produce a mighty effect upon them; and they were easily persuaded to consider a cause as impious for which they had already entertained an unsurmountable aversion.[7] Though Lewis made a journey to France, and brought over succors from that kingdom,[8] he found on his return, that his party was still more weakened by the desertion of his English confederates, and that the death of John had, contrary to his expectations, given an incurable wound to his cause. The

5 Rymer, vol. i. p. 215.   Brady's App. No. 143.
6 Matt. Paris, pp. 200, 202.   7 Matt. Paris, p. 200.   Matt. West. p. 277.
8 Chron. Dunst. vol. i. p. 79.   Matt. West. p. 277.

Earls of Salisbury, Arundel, and Warrenne, together with William Mareschal, eldest son of the protector, had embraced Henry's party, and every English nobleman was plainly watching for an opportunity of returning to his allegiance. Pembroke was so much strengthened by these accessions that he ventured to invest Mountsorel; though, upon the approach of the Count de Perche with the French army, he desisted from his enterprise and raised the siege.[9] The count, elated with this success, marched to Lincoln; and, being admitted into the town, he began to attack the castle, which he soon reduced to extremity. The protector summoned all his forces from every quarter, in order to relieve a place of such importance, and he appeared so much superior to the French that they shut themselves up within the city, and resolved to act upon the defensive.[10] But the garrison of the castle having received a strong reinforcement, made a vigorous sally upon the besiegers; while the English army by concert assaulted them in the same instant from without, mounted the walls by escalade, and, bearing down all resistance, entered the city sword in hand. Lincoln was delivered over to be pillaged; the French army was totally routed. The Count de Perche, with only two persons more, was killed; but many of the chief commanders, and about four hundred knights, were made prisoners by the English.[11] So little blood was shed in this important action, which decided the fate of one of the most powerful kingdoms in Europe, and such wretched soldiers were those ancient barons, who yet were unacquainted with everything but arms!

Prince Lewis was informed of this fatal event while employed in the siege of Dover, which was still valiantly defended against him by Hubert de Burgh. He immediately retreated to London, the centre and life of his party; and he there received intelligence of a new disaster, which put an end to all his hopes. A French fleet bringing over a strong reinforcement had appeared on the coast of Kent, where they were attacked by the English under the command of Philip d'Albiney, and were routed with considerable loss. D'Albiney employed a stratagem against them which is said to have contributed to the victory. Having gained the wind of the French, he came down upon them with violence; and throwing in their faces a great quantity of quicklime, which he

9 Matt. Paris, p. 203.   10 Chron. Dunst. vol. i. p. 81.
11 Matt. Paris, pp. 204, 205. Chron. de Mailr. p. 195.

purposely carried on board, he so blinded them that they were disabled from defending themselves.[12]

After this second misfortune of the French, the English barons hastened everywhere to make peace with the protector, and, by an early submission, to prevent those attainders to which they were exposed on account of their rebellion. Lewis, whose cause was now totally desperate, began to be anxious for the safety of his person, and was glad, on any honorable conditions, to make his escape from a country where he found everything was now become hostile to him. He concluded a peace with Pembroke, promised to evacuate the kingdom, and only stipulated in return an indemnity to his adherents, and a restitution of their honors and fortunes, together with the free and equal enjoyment of those liberties which had been granted to the rest of the nation.[13] Thus was happily ended a civil war, which seemed to be founded on the most incurable hatred and jealousy, and had threatened the kingdom with the most fatal consequences.

The precautions which the King of France used in the conduct of this whole affair are remarkable. He pretended that his son had accepted of the offer from the English barons without his advice and contrary to his inclination; the armies sent to England were levied in Lewis's name. When that prince came over to France for aid, his father publicly refused to grant him any assistance, and would not so much as admit him to his presence. Even after Henry's party acquired the ascendant, and Lewis was in danger of falling into the hands of his enemies, it was Blanche of Castile, his wife, not the king his father, who raised armies and equipped fleets for his succor.[14] All these artifices were employed, not to satisfy the pope, for he had too much penetration to be so easily imposed upon; nor yet to deceive the people, for they were too gross even for that purpose. They only served for a coloring to Philip's cause; and in public affairs men are often better pleased that the truth, though known to everybody, should be wrapped up under a decent cover than if it were exposed in open daylight to the eyes of all the world.

After the expulsion of the French, the prudence and

---

[12] Matt. Paris, p. 206. Annal. Waverl. p. 183. W. Heming. p. 563. Trivet, p. 169. Matt. West. p. 277. Knyghton, p. 2428.
[13] Rymer, vol. i. p. 221. Matt. Paris, p. 207. Chron. Dunst. vol. i. p. 83. Matt. West. p. 278. Knyghton, p. 2429.
[14] Matt. Paris, p. 256. Chron. Dunst. vol. i. p. 82.

equity of the protector's subsequent conduct contributed to cure entirely those wounds which had been made by intestine discord. He received the rebellious barons into favor, observed strictly the terms of peace which he had granted them, restored them to their possessions, and endeavored by an equal behavior to bury all past animosities in perpetual oblivion. The clergy alone, who had adhered to Lewis, were sufferers in this revolution. As they had rebelled against their spiritual sovereign by disregarding the interdict and excommunication, it was not in Pembroke's power to make any stipulations in their favor; and Gualo, the legate, prepared to take vengeance on them for their disobedience.[15] Many of them were deposed; many suspended, some banished, and all who escaped punishment made atonement for their offence by paying large sums to the legate, who amassed an immense treasure by this expedient.

The Earl of Pembroke did not long survive the pacification which had been chiefly owing to his wisdom and valor;[16] and he was succeeded in the government by Peter de Roches, Bishop of Winchester, and Hubert de Burgh, the justiciary. The councils of the latter were chiefly followed; and had he possessed equal authority in the kingdom with Pembroke, he seemed to be every way worthy of filling the place of that virtuous nobleman. But the licentious and powerful barons, who had once broken the reins of subjection to their prince, and had obtained by violence an enlargement of their liberties and independence, could ill be restrained by laws under a minority; and the people, no less than the king, suffered from their outrages and disorders. They retained by force the royal castles which they had seized during the past convulsions, or which had been committed to their custody by the protector;[17] they usurped the king's demesnes;[18] they opposed their vassals; they infested their weaker neighbors; they invited all disorderly people to enter in their retinue, and to live upon their lands; and they gave them protection in all their robberies and extortions.

No one was more infamous for these violent and illegal practices than the Earl of Albemarle, who, though he had early returned to his duty and had been serviceable in expelling the French, augmented to the utmost the general disorder and committed outrages in all the counties of the

15 Brady's App. No. 144.   Chron. Dunst, vol. i. p. 83.
16 Matt. Paris, p. 210.   17 Trivet, p. 174.   18 Rymer, vol. i. p. 276.

north. In order to reduce him to obedience, Hubert seized an opportunity of getting possession of Rockingham Castle, which Albemarle had garrisoned with his licentious retinue; but this nobleman, instead of submitting, entered into a secret confederacy with Fawkes de Breauté, Peter de Mauleon, and other barons, and both fortified the castle of Biham for his defence and made himself master, by surprise, of that of Fotheringay. Pandolf, who was restored to his legateship, was active in suppressing this rebellion; and with the concurrence of eleven bishops, he pronounced the sentence of excommunication against Albemarle and his adherents.[19] An army was levied; a scutage of ten shillings a knight's-fee was imposed on all the military tenants; Albemarle's associates gradually deserted him, and he himself was obliged at last to sue for mercy. He received a pardon, and was restored to his whole estate.

This impolitic lenity, too frequent in those times, was probably the result of a secret combination among the barons, who never could endure to see the total ruin of one of their own order; but it encouraged Fawkes de Breauté, a man whom King John had raised from a low origin, to persevere in the course of violence to which he had owed his fortune, and to set at naught all law and justice. When thirty-five verdicts were at one time found against him, on account of his violent expulsion of so many freeholders from their possessions, he came to the court of justice with an armed force, seized the judge who had pronounced the verdicts, and imprisoned him in Bedford Castle. He then levied open war against the king; but being subdued and taken prisoner, his life was granted him; but his estate was confiscated, and he was banished the kingdom.[20]

[1222.] Justice was executed with greater severity against disorders less premeditated, which broke out in London. A frivolous emulation in a match of wrestling, between the Londoners, on the one hand, and the inhabitants of Westminster and those of the neighboring villages on the other, occasioned this commotion. The former rose in a body and pulled down some houses belonging to the Abbot of Westminster; but this riot, which, considering the tumultuous disposition familiar in that capital, would have been little regarded, seemed to become more serious by the symp-

[19] Chron. Dunst. vol. i. p. 102.
[20] Rymer, vol. i. p. 198. Matt. Paris, pp. 221, 224. Annal. Waverl. p. 188. Chron. Dunst. vol. i. pp. 141, 146. Matt. West. p. 283.

toms which then appeared of the former attachment of citizens to the French interest. The populace, in the tumult, made use of the cry of war commonly employed by the French troops : " Mountjoy, Mountjoy, God help us and our Lord Lewis ! " The justiciary made inquiry into the disorder, and finding one Constantine Fitz-Arnulf to have been the ringleader, an insolent man who justified his crime in Hubert's presence, he proceeded against him by martial law, and ordered him immediately to be hanged, without trial or form of process. He also cut off the feet of some of Constantine's accomplices.[21]

This act of power was complained of as an infringement of the great charter; yet the justiciary, in a Parliament summoned at Oxford (for the great councils about this time began to receive that appellation), made no scruple to grant, in the king's name, a renewal and confirmation of that charter. When the assembly made application to the crown for this favor, as a law in those times seemed to lose its validity if not frequently renewed, William de Briewere, one of the council of regency, was so bold as to say openly that those liberties were extorted by force, and ought not to be observed; but he was reprimanded by the Archbishop of Canterbury, and was not countenanced by the king or his chief ministers.[22] A new confirmation was demanded and granted two years after ; and an aid, amounting to a fifteenth of all movables, was given by the Parliament in return for this indulgence. This king issued writs anew to the sheriffs, enjoining the observance of the charter; but he inserted a remarkable clause in the writs, that those who paid not the fifteenth should not for the future be entitled to the benefit of those liberties.[23]

The low state into which the crown was fallen made it requisite for a good minister to be attentive to the preservation of the royal prerogatives as well as to the security of public liberty. Hubert applied to the pope, who had always great authority in the kingdom, and was now considered as its superior lord, and desired him to issue a bull declaring the king to be of full age, and entitled to exercise in person all the acts of royalty.[24] In consequence of this declaration, the justiciary resigned into Henry's hands the two important fortresses of the Tower and Dover Castle, which

[21] Matt. Paris, pp. 217, 218, 259. Annal. Waverl. p. 187. Chron. Dunst. vol. i. p. 129.
[22] Matt. West. p. 282.
[23] Clause 9, H. 3, m. 9, and m. 6, d.
[24] Matt. Paris, p. 220.

had been intrusted to his custody; and he required the
other barons to imitate his example. They refused compliance. The Earls of Chester and Albemarle, John Constable of Chester, John de Lacy, Brian de l'Isle, and William
de Cantel, with some others, even formed a conspiracy to
surprise London, and met in arms at Waltham with that
intention; but, finding the king prepared for defence, they
desisted from their enterprise. When summoned to court
in order to answer for their conduct, they scrupled not to
appear and to confess the design; but they told the king
that they had no bad intentions against his person, but only
against Hubert de Burgh, whom they were determined to
remove from his office.[25] They appeared too formidable to
be chastised; and they were so little discouraged by the
failure of their first enterprise that they again met in arms
at Leicester, in order to seize the king, who then resided at
Northampton; but Henry, informed of their purpose, took
care to be so well armed and attended that the barons found
it dangerous to make the attempt; and they sat down and
kept Christmas in his neighborhood.[26] The archbishop and
the prelates, finding everything tending towards a civil war,
interposed with their authority, and threatened the barons
with the sentence of excommunication if they persisted in
detaining the king's castles. This menace at last prevailed;
most of the fortresses were surrendered; though the barons
complained that Hubert's castles were soon after restored to
him, while the king still kept theirs in his own custody.
There are said to have been eleven hundred and fifteen
castles at that time in England.[27]

It must be acknowledged that the influence of the prelates and the clergy was often of great service to the public.
Though the religion of that age can merit no better name
than that of superstition, it served to unite together a body
of men who had great sway over the people, and who kept
the community from falling to pieces by the factions and
independent power of the nobles; and, what was of great
importance, it threw a mighty authority into the hands of
men who, by their profession, were averse to arms and violence, who tempered by their mediation the general disposition towards military enterprises, and who still maintained, even amid the shock of arms, those secret links without which it is impossible for human society to subsist.

[25] Chron. Dunst. vol. i. p. 137.
[26] Matt. Paris, p. 221. Chron. Dunst. vol. i. p. 138.
[27] Coke's Comment. on Magna Charta, ch. 17.

Notwithstanding these intestine commotions in England and the precarious authority of the crown, Henry was obliged to carry on war in France; and he employed to that purpose the fifteenth which had been granted him by Parliament. Lewis VIII., who had succeeded his father Philip, instead of complying with Henry's claim, who demanded the restitution of Normandy and the other provinces wrested from England, made an irruption into Poictou, took Rochelle,[28] after a long siege, and seemed determined to expel the English from the few provinces which still remained to them. Henry sent over his uncle, the Earl of Salisbury, together with his brother, Prince Richard, to whom he had granted the earldom of Cornwall, which had escheated to the crown. Salisbury stopped the progress of Lewis's arms, and retained the Poictevin and Gascon vassals in their allegiance; but no military action of any moment was performed on either side. The Earl of Cornwall, after two years' stay in Guienne, returned to England.

This prince was nowise turbulent or factious in his disposition; his ruling passion was to amass money, in which he succeeded so well as to become the richest subject in Christendom. [1227.] Yet his attention to gain threw him sometimes into acts of violence, and gave disturbance to the government. There was a manor which had formerly belonged to the earldom of Cornwall, but had been granted to Waleran de Ties before Richard had been invested with that dignity, and while the earldom remained in the crown. Richard claimed this manor, and expelled the proprietor by force. Waleran complained; the king ordered his brother to do justice to the man and restore him to his rights; the earl said that he would not submit to these orders till the cause should be decided against him by the judgment of his peers. Henry replied that it was first necessary to reinstate Waleran in possession before the cause could be tried; and he reiterated his orders to the earl.[29] We may judge of the state of the government when this affair had nearly produced a civil war. The Earl of Cornwall, finding Henry peremptory in his commands, associated himself with the young Earl of Pembroke, who had married his sister, and who was displeased on account of the king's requiring him to deliver up some royal castles which were in his custody. These two malcontents took into the confederacy the Earls of Chester, Warrenne, Glou-

28 Rymer, vol. i. p. 269. Trivet, p. 179. 29 Matt. Paris, p. 233.

cester, Hereford, Warwick, and Ferrars, who were all disgusted on a like account.[30]   They assembled an army, which
the king had not the power or courage to resist; and he was
obliged to give his brother satisfaction by grants of much
greater importance than the manor which had been the first
ground of the quarrel.[31]

The character of the king, as he grew to man's estate,
became every day better known ; and he was found in every
respect unqualified for maintaining a proper sway among
those turbulent barons whom the feudal constitution subjected to his authority.   Gentle, humane, and merciful even
to a fault, he seems to have been steady in no other circumstance of his character, but to have received every impression from those who surrounded him, and whom he
loved for the time, with the most imprudent and most un-
reserved affection.   Without activity or vigor, he was unfit
to conduct war; without policy or art, he was ill fitted to
maintain peace.   His resentments, though hasty and violent, were not dreaded, while he was found to drop them
with such facility; his friendships were little valued, because they were neither derived from choice nor maintained
with constancy.   A proper pageant of state in a regular
monarchy, where his ministers could have conducted all
affairs in his name and by his authority, but too feeble in
those disorderly times to sway a sceptre, whose weight depended entirely on the firmness and dexterity of the hand
which held it.

The ablest and most virtuous minister that Henry ever
possessed was Hubert de Burgh [32]—a man who had been
steady to the crown in the most difficult and dangerous
times, and who yet showed no disposition, in the height of
his power, to enslave or oppress the people.   The only ex-
ceptional part of his conduct is that which is mentioned
by Matthew Paris [33] (if the fact be really true), and proceeded from Hubert's advice—namely, the recalling publicly
and the annulling of the charter of forests, a concession so
reasonable in itself, and so passionately claimed both by the
nobility and people.   But it must be confessed that this
measure is so unlikely, both from the circumstances of the
times and character of the minister, that there is reason to
doubt of its reality, especially as it is mentioned by no other

---

[30] Matt. Paris, p. 233.   [31] Ibid.   [32] Ypod. Neust. p. 464.
[33] P. 232.   Matt. West. p. 216, ascribes this council to Peter, Bishop of Winchester.

historian. Hubert, while he enjoyed his authority, had an entire ascendant over Henry, and was loaded with honors and favors beyond any other subject. Besides acquiring the property of many castles and manors, he married the eldest sister of the King of Scots, was created Earl of Kent, and, by an unusual concession, was made chief justiciary of England for life. [1231.] Yet Henry, in a sudden caprice, threw off this faithful minister, and exposed him to the violent persecutions of his enemies. Among other frivolous crimes objected to him, he was accused of gaining the king's affections by enchantment, and of purloining from the royal treasury a gem which had the virtue to render the wearer invulnerable, and of sending this valuable curiosity to the Prince of Wales.[34] The nobility, who hated Hubert on account of his zeal in resuming the rights and possessions of the crown, no sooner saw the opportunity favorable than they inflamed the king's animosity against him, and pushed him to seek the total ruin of his minister. Hubert took sanctuary in a church ; the king ordered him to be dragged from thence ; he recalled those orders ; he afterwards renewed them ; he was obliged by the clergy to restore him to the sanctuary ; he constrained him soon after to surrender himself prisoner, and he confined him in the castle of Devizes. Hubert made his escape, was expelled the kingdom, was again received into favor, recovered a great share of the king's confidence, but never showed any inclination to reinstate himself in power and authority.[35]

The man who succeeded him in the government of the king and kingdom was Peter, Bishop of Winchester, a Poictevin by birth, who had been raised by the late king, and who was no less distinguished by his arbitrary principles and violent conduct than by his courage and abilities. This prelate had been left by King John justiciary and regent of the kingdom during an expedition which that prince made into France ; and his illegal administration was one chief cause of that great combination among the barons which finally extorted from the crown the charter of liberties, and laid the foundations of the English constitution. Henry, though incapable, from his character, of pursuing the same violent maxims which had governed his father, had imbibed the same arbitrary principles ; and, in prosecution of

[34] Matt. Paris, p. 259.
[35] Matt. Paris, pp. 259, 260, 261, 266. Chron. T. Wykes, pp. 41, 42. Chron. Dunst. vol. i. pp. 220, 221. Matt. West. pp. 291, 301.

Peter's advice, he invited over a great number of Poictevins and other foreigners, who, he believed, could more safely be trusted than the English, and who seemed useful to counterbalance the great and independent power of the nobility.[36] Every office and command was bestowed on these strangers: they exhausted the revenues of the crown, already too much impoverished;[37] they invaded the rights of the people; and their insolence, still more provoking than their power, drew on them the hatred and envy of all orders of men in the kingdom.[38]

[1233.] The barons formed a combination against this odious ministry, and withdrew from Parliament, on pretence of the danger to which they were exposed from the machinations of the Poictevins. When again summoned to attend, they gave for answer that the king should dismiss his foreigners, otherwise they would drive both him and them out of the kingdom, and put the crown on another head more worthy to wear it;[39] such was the style they used to their sovereign! They at last came to Parliament, but so well attended that they seemed in a condition to prescribe laws to the king and ministry. Peter des Roches, however, had in the interval found means of sowing dissension among them, and of bringing over to his party the Earl of Cornwall, as well as the Earls of Lincoln and Chester. The confederates were disconcerted in their measures; Richard, Earl Mareschal, who had succeeded to that dignity on the death of his brother William, was chased into Wales; he thence withdrew into Ireland, where he was treacherously murdered by the contrivance of the Bishop of Winchester.[40] The estates of the more obnoxious barons were confiscated, without legal sentence or trial by their peers,[41] and were bestowed with a profuse liberality on the Poictevins. Peter even carried his insolence so far as to declare publicly that the barons of England must not pretend to put themselves on the same footing with those of France, or assume the same liberties and privileges: the monarch in the former country had a more absolute power than in the latter. It had been more justifiable for him to have said that men so unwilling to submit to the authority of laws could with the worst grace claim any shelter or protection from them.

When the king at any time was checked in his illegal

[36] Matt. Paris, p. 263.
[37] Chron. Dunst. vol. i. p. 151.
[38] Matt. Paris, p. 268.
[39] Matt. Paris, p. 265.
[40] Chron. Dunst. vol. i. p. 219.
[41] Matt. Paris, p. 265.

practices, and when the authority of the great charter was objected to him, he was wont to reply, " Why should I observe this charter which is neglected by all my grandees, both prelates and nobility ? " It was very reasonably said to him, " You ought, sir, to set them the example." [42]

So violent a ministry as that of the Bishop of Winchester could not be of long duration ; but its fall proceeded at last from the influence of the Church, not from the efforts of the nobles. Edmond, the primate, came to court attended by many of the other prelates, and represented to the king the pernicious measures embraced by Peter des Roches, the discontents of his people, the ruin of his affairs, and, after requiring the dismission of the minister and his associates, threatened him with excommunication in case of his refusal. Henry, who knew that an excommunication so agreeable to the sense of the people could not fail of producing the most dangerous effects, was obliged to submit. Foreigners were banished; the natives were restored to their place in council ; [43] the primate, who was a man of prudence, and who took care to execute the laws and observe the charter of liberties, bore the chief sway in the government.

[1236.] But the English in vain flattered themselves that they should be long free from the dominion of foreigners. The king, having married Eleanor, daughter of the Count of Provence, [44] was surrounded by a great number of strangers from that country, whom he caressed with the fondest affection and enriched by an imprudent generosity. [45] The Bishop of Valence, a prelate of the house of Savoy and maternal uncle to the queen, was his chief minister, and employed every art to amass wealth for himself and his relations. Peter of Savoy, a brother of the same family, was invested in the honor of Richmond, and received the rich wardship of Earl Warrenne ; Boniface of Savoy was promoted to the see of Canterbury. Many young ladies were invited over from Provence and married to the chief noblemen in England, who were the king's wards. [46] And as the source of Henry's bounty began to fail, his Savoyard ministry applied to Rome and obtained a bull permitting him to resume all past grants ; absolving him from the oath which he had taken to maintain them; even enjoining him to make such a resumption, and representing those grants as invalid

42 Matt. Paris, p. 609.   43 Matt. Paris, pp. 271, 272.
44 Rymer, vol. i. p. 448.   Matt. Paris, p. 286.
45 Matt. Paris, pp. 236, 301, 305, 316, 541.   Matt. West. pp. 302, 304.
46 Matt. Paris, p. 484.   Matt. West. p. 338.

on account of the prejudice which ensued from them to the Roman pontiff, in whom the superiority of the kingdom was vested.[47] The opposition made to the intended resumption prevented it from taking place; but the nation saw the indignities to which the king was willing to submit in order to gratify the avidity of his foreign favorites. About the same time, he published in England the sentence of excommunication pronounced against the Emperor Frederick, his brother-in-law,[48] and said, in excuse, that, being the pope's vassal, he was obliged by his allegiance to obey all the commands of his holiness. In this weak reign, when any neighboring potentate insulted the king's dominions, instead of taking revenge for the injury, he complained to the pope as his superior lord, and begged him to give protection to his vassal.[49]

The resentment of the English barons rose high at the preference given to foreigners; but no remonstrance or complaint could ever prevail on the king to abandon them, or even to moderate his attachment towards them. After the Provençals and Savoyards might have been supposed pretty well satiated with the dignities and riches which they had acquired, a new set of hungry foreigners were invited over, and shared among them those favors which the king ought in policy to have conferred on the English nobility, by whom his government could have been supported and defended. His mother, Isabella, who had been unjustly taken by the late king from the Count de la Marche, to whom she was betrothed, was no sooner mistress of herself, by the death of her husband, than she married that nobleman; [50] and she had borne him four sons—Guy, William, Geoffrey, and Aymer—whom she sent over to England in order to pay a visit to their brother. [1247.] The good-natured and affectionate disposition of Henry was moved at the sight of such near relations, and he considered neither his own circumstances nor the inclinations of his people in the honors and riches which he conferred upon them.[51] Complaints rose as high against the credit of the Gascon as ever they had done against that of the Poictevin and of the Savoyard favorites; and to a nation prejudiced against them, all their measures appeared exceptionable and criminal. Violations of the great charter were frequently mentioned, and it is

[47] Matt. Paris, pp. 295, 301.   [48] Rymer, vol. i. p. 383.
[49] Chron. Dunst. vol. i. p. 150.   [50] Trivet, p. 174.
[51] Matt. Paris, p. 491.   Matt. West. p. 338.   Knyghton, p. 2436.

indeed more than probable that foreigners, ignorant of the laws and relying on the boundless affections of a weak prince, would, in an age when a regular administration was not anywhere known, pay more attention to their present interest than to the liberties of the people. It is reported that the Poictevins and other strangers, when the laws were at any time appealed to in opposition to their oppressions, scrupled not to reply, "What did the English laws signify to them? they minded them not." And as words are often more offensive than actions, this open contempt of the English tended much to aggravate the general discontent, and made every act of violence committed by the foreigners appear not only an injury, but an affront to them.[52]

I reckon not among the violations of the great charter some arbitrary exertions of prerogative to which Henry's necessities pushed him, and which, without producing any discontent, were uniformly continued by all his successors till the last century. As the Parliament often refused him supplies, and that in a manner somewhat rude and indecent,[53] he obliged his opulent subjects, particularly the citizens of London, to grant him loans of money; and it is natural to imagine that the same want of economy which reduced him to the necessity of borrowing would prevent him from being very punctual in the repayment.[54] He demanded benevolences, or pretended voluntary contributions, from his nobility and prelates.[55] He was the first King of England since the Conquest that could fairly be said to lie under the restraint of law, and he was also the first that practised the dispensing power and employed the clause of *non obstante* in his grants and patents. When objections were made to this novelty, he replied that the pope exercised that authority, and why might not he imitate the example? But the abuse which the pope made of his dispensing power in violating the canons of general councils, in invading the privileges and customs of all particular churches, and in usurping on the rights of patrons, was more likely to excite the jealousy of the people than to reconcile them to a similar practice in their civil government. Roger de Thurkesby, one of the king's justices, was so displeased with the precedent that he exclaimed, " Alas ! what times we are falling into ! Behold, the civil court is corrupted in imitation of

---

[52] Matt. Paris, pp. 566, 666.   Annal. Waverl. p. 214.   Chron. Dunst. vol. i. p. 335.
[53] Matt. Paris, p. 301.   [54] Matt. Paris, p. 406.   [55] Matt. Paris, p 507.

the ecclesiastical, and the river is poisoned from that fountain."

The king's partiality and profuse bounty to his foreign relations, and to their friends and favorites, would have appeared more tolerable to the English had anything been done meanwhile for the honor of the nation, or had Henry's enterprises in foreign countries been attended with any success or glory to himself or to the public; at least such military talents in the king would have served to keep his barons in awe and have given weight and authority to his government. But, though he declared war against Lewis IX. in 1242, and made an expedition into Guienne, upon the invitation of his father-in-law, the Count de la Marche, who promised to join him with all his forces, he was unsuccessful in his attempts against that great monarch, was worsted at Taillebourg, was deserted by his allies, lost what remained to him of Poictou, and was obliged to return, with loss of honor, into England.[56] The Gascon nobility were attached to the English government because the distance of their sovereign allowed them to remain in a state of almost total independence; and they claimed, some time after, Henry's protection against an invasion which the King of Castile made upon that territory. [1253.] Henry returned into Guienne and was more successful in this expedition; but he thereby involved himself and his nobility in an enormous debt, which both increased their discontents and exposed him to greater danger from their enterprises.[57]

Want of economy and an ill-judged liberality were Henry's great defects; and his debts, even before this expedition, had become so troublesome that he sold all his plate and jewels in order to discharge them. When this expedient was first proposed to him, he asked where he should find purchasers. It was replied, the citizens of London. "On my word," said he, "if the treasury of Augustus were brought to sale, the citizens are able to be the purchasers. These clowns, who assume to themselves the name of barons, abound in everything, while we are reduced to necessities."[58] And he was thenceforth observed to be more forward and greedy in his exactions upon the citizens.[59]

But the grievances which the English during this reign had reason to complain of in the civil government seem to

---

[56] Matt. Paris, pp. 393, 394, 398, 399, 405. W. Heming, p. 574. Chron. Dunst. vol. i. p. 153. [58] Matt. Paris, p. 614. [58] Matt. Paris, p. 501. [59] Matt. Paris, pp. 501, 507, 518, 578, 606, 625, 648.

have been still less burdensome than those which they suffered from the usurpations and exactions of the court of Rome. On the death of Langton (in 1228), the monks of Christ-church elected Walter de Hemesham, one of their own body, for his successor ; but, as Henry refused to confirm the election, the pope at his desire annulled it,[60] and immediately appointed Richard, Chancellor of Lincoln, for. archbishop without waiting for a new election. On the death of Richard (in 1231), the monks elected Ralph de Neville Bishop of Chichester ; and, though Henry was much pleased with the election, the pope, who thought that prelate too much attached to the crown, assumed the power of annulling his election.[61] He rejected two clergymen more whom the monks had successively chosen ; and he at last told them that if they would elect Edmond, treasurer of the church of Salisbury, he would confirm their choice, and his nomination was complied with. The pope had the prudence to appoint both times very worthy primates ; but men could not forbear observing his intention of thus drawing gradually to himself the right of bestowing that important dignity.

The avarice, however, more than the ambition, of the see of Rome seems to have been in this age the ground of general complaint. The papal ministers finding a vast stock of power amassed by their predecessors, were desirous of turning it to immediate profit, which they enjoyed at home, rather than of enlarging their authority in distant countries where they never intended to reside. Everything was become venal in the Roman tribunals : simony was openly practised ; no favors, and even no justice, could be obtained without a bribe ; the highest bidder was sure to have the preference, without regard either to the merits of the person or of the cause ; and, besides the usual perversions of right in the decision of controversies, the pope openly assumed an absolute and uncontrolled authority of setting aside, by the plenitude of his apostolic power, all particular rules, and all privileges of patrons, churches, and convents. On pretence of remedying these abuses, Pope Honorius, in 1226, complaining of the poverty of his see as the source of all grievances, demanded from every cathedral two of the best prebends, and from every convent two monks' portions, to be set apart as a perpetual and settled revenue of the papal crown ; but all men being sensible that the revenue

[60] Matt. Paris, p. 224.   [61] Matt. Paris, p. 254.

would continue forever; the abuses immediately return, his demand was unanimously rejected. About three years after, the pope demanded and obtained the tenth of all ecclesiastical revenues, which he levied in a very oppressive manner, requiring payment before the clergy had drawn their rents or tithes, and sending about usurers who advanced them the money at exorbitant interest. In the year 1240, Otho, the legate, having in vain attempted the clergy in a body, obtained separately, by intrigues and menaces, large sums from the prelates and convents, and on his departure is said to have carried more money out of the kingdom than he left in it. This experiment was renewed four years after with success by Martin the nuncio, who brought from Rome powers of suspending and excommunicating all clergymen that refused to comply with his demands. The king, who relied on the pope for the support of his tottering authority, never failed to countenance those exactions.

Meanwhile, all the chief benefices of the kingdom were conferred on Italians; great numbers of that nation were sent over at one time to be provided for; non-residence and pluralities were carried to an enormous height; Mansel, the king's chaplain, is computed to have held at once seven hundred ecclesiastical livings; and the abuses became so evident as to be palpable to the blindness of superstition itself. The people, entering into associations, rose against the Italian clergy; pillaged their barns, wasted their lands, insulted the persons of such of them as they found in the kingdom; [62] and when the justices made inquiry into the authors of this disorder, the guilt was found to involve so many, and those of such high rank, that it passed unpunished. At last, when Innocent IV., in 1245, called a general council at Lyons, in order to excommunicate the Emperor Frederick, the king and nobility sent over agents to complain before the council of the rapacity of the Romish Church. They represented, among many other grievances, that the benefices of the Italian clergy in England had been estimated, and were found to amount to sixty thousand marks [63] a year, a sum which exceeded the annual revenue of the crown itself.[64] They obtained only an evasive an-

[62] Rymer, vol. i. p. 323. Matt. Paris, pp. 255, 257.

[63] Innocent's bull in Rymer, vol. i. p. 471, says only fifty thousand marks a year.

[64] Matt. Paris, p. 451. The customs were part of Henry's revenue, and amounted to six thousand pounds a year. They were at first small sums paid by the merchants for the use of the king's warehouses, measures, weights, etc. See Gilbert's History of the Exchequer, p. 214.

swer from the pope; but as mention had been made before the council of the feudal subjection of England to the see of Rome, the English agents, at whose head was Roger Bigod, Earl of Norfolk, exclaimed against the pretension, and insisted that King John had no right, without the consent of his barons, to subject the kingdom to so ignominious a servitude.[65] The popes, indeed, afraid of carrying matters too far against England, seem thenceforth to have little insisted on that pretension.

This check, received at the Council of Lyons, was not able to stop the court of Rome in its rapacity. Innocent exacted the revenues of all vacant benefices; the twentieth of all ecclesiastical revenues without exception; the third of such as exceeded a hundred marks a year, and the half of such as were possessed by non-residents.[66] He claimed the goods of all intestate clergymen;[67] he pretended a title to inherit all money gotten by usury; he levied benevolences upon the people; and when the king, contrary to his usual practice, prohibited these exactions, he threatened to pronounce against him the same censures which he had emitted against the Emperor Frederick.[63]

[1255.] But the most oppressive expedient employed by the pope was the embarking of Henry in a project for the conquest of Naples or Sicily on this side the Fare, as it was called—an enterprise which threw much dishonor on the king, and involved him during some years in great trouble and expense. The Romish Church, taking advantage of favorable incidents, had reduced the kingdom of Sicily to the same state of feudal vassalage which she pretended to extend over England, and which, by reason of the distance as well as high spirit of this latter kingdom, she was not able to maintain. After the death of the Emperor Frederick II., the succession of Sicily devolved to Conradin, grandson of that monarch; and Mainfroy, his natural son, under pretence of governing the kingdom during the minority of the prince, had formed a scheme of establishing his own authority. Pope Innocent, who had carried on violent war against the Emperor Frederick, and had endeavored to dispossess him of his Italian dominions, still continued hostilities against his grandson; but, being disappointed in all his schemes by the activity and artifices of Mainfroy, he found that his own force alone was not suffi-

[65] Matt. Paris, p. 460.   [66] Matt. Paris, p. 480.   Annal. Burt. pp. 305, 373.
[67] Matt. Paris, p. 474.   [68] Matt. Paris, p. 476.

cient to bring to a happy issue so great an enterprise. He pretended to dispose of the Sicilian crown, both as superior lord of that particular kingdom, and as vicar of Christ, to whom all kingdoms of the earth were subjected; and he made a tender of it to Richard, Earl of Cornwall, whose immense riches, he flattered himself, would be able to support the military operations against Mainfroy. As Richard had the prudence to refuse the present,[69] he applied to the king, whose levity and thoughtless disposition gave Innocent more hopes of success; and he offered him the crown of Sicily for his second son, Edmond.[70] Henry, allured by so magnificent a present, without reflecting on the consequences, without consulting either with his brother or the Parliament, accepted of the insidious proposal, and gave the pope unlimited credit to expend whatever sums he thought necessary for completing the conquest of Sicily. Innocent, who was engaged by his own interests to wage war with Mainfroy, was glad to carry on his enterprises at the expense of his ally. Alexander IV., who succeeded him in the papal throne, continued the same policy, and Henry was surprised to find himself on a sudden involved in an immense debt which he had never been consulted in contracting. The sum already amounted to one hundred and thirty-five thousand five hundred and forty-one marks, besides interest;[71] and he had the prospect, if he answered this demand, of being soon loaded with more exorbitant expenses; if he refused it, of both incurring the pope's displeasure and losing the crown of Sicily, which he hoped soon to have the glory of fixing on the head of his son.

He applied to the Parliament for supplies; and that he might be sure not to meet with opposition, he sent no writs to the more refractory barons; but even those who were summoned, sensible of the ridiculous cheat imposed by the pope, determined not to lavish their money on such chimerical projects, and, making a pretext of the absence of their brethren, they refused to take the king's demands into consideration.[72] In this extremity the clergy were his only resource; and as both their temporal and spiritual sovereign concurred in loading them, they were ill able to defend themselves against this united authority.

The pope published a crusade for the conquest of Sicily,

[69] Matt. Paris, p. 650.
[70] Rymer, vol. i. pp. 502, 512, 530. Matt. Paris, pp. 599, 613.
[71] Rymer, vol. i. p. 587. Chron. Dunst. vol. i. p. 319.
[72] Matt. Paris, p. 416.

and required every one who had taken the cross against the infidels, or had vowed to advance money for that service, to support the war against Mainfroy—a more terrible enemy, as he pretended, to the Christian faith than any Saracen.[73] He levied a tenth on all ecclesiastical benefices in England for three years, and gave orders to excommunicate all bishops who made not punctual payment. He granted to the king the goods of intestate clergymen, the revenues of vacant benefices, the revenues of all non-residents.[74] But these taxations, being levied by some rule, were deemed less grievous than another imposition which arose from the suggestion of the Bishop of Hereford, and which might have opened the door to endless and intolerable abuses.

This prelate, who resided at the court of Rome, by a deputation from the English Church, drew bills of different values, but amounting on the whole to one hundred and fifty thousand five hundred and forty marks, on all the bishops and abbots of the kingdom; and granted these bills to Italian merchants, who, it was pretended, had advanced money for the service of the war against Mainfroy.[75] As there was no likelihood of the English prelates submitting, without compulsion, to such an extraordinary demand, Rustand, the legate, was charged with the commission of employing authority to that purpose; and he summoned an assembly of the bishops and abbots, whom he acquainted with the pleasure of the pope and of the king. Great were the surprise and indignation of the assembly. The Bishop of Worcester exclaimed that he would lose his life rather than comply; the Bishop of London said that the pope and king were more powerful than he; but if his mitre were taken off his head, he would clap on a helmet in its place.[76] The legate was no less violent on the other hand; and he told the assembly in plain terms that all ecclesiastical benefices were the property of the pope, and he might dispose of them, either in whole or in part, as he saw proper.[77] In the end the bishops and abbots, being threatened with excommunication, which made all the revenues fall into the king's hands, were obliged to submit to the exaction; and the only mitigation which the legate allowed them was that the tenths already granted should be accepted as a partial payment of the bills. But the money was still insufficient for

[73] Rymer, vol. i. pp. 547, 548, etc.   [74] Rymer, vol. i. pp. 597, 598.
[75] Matt. Paris, pp. 612, 628. Chron. T. Wykes, p. 54.
[76] Matt. Paris, p. 614.   [77] Matt. Paris, p. 619.

the pope's purpose; the conquest of Sicily was as remote as ever; the demands which came from Rome were endless. Pope Alexander became so urgent a creditor that he sent over a legate to England, threatening the kingdom with an interdict and the king with excommunication if the arrears, which he pretended to be due to him, were not instantly remitted.[78] And at last Henry, sensible of the cheat, began to think of breaking off the agreement, and of resigning into the pope's hands that crown which it was not intended by Alexander that he or his family should ever enjoy.[79]

The Earl of Cornwall had now reason to value himself on his foresight in refusing the fraudulent bargain with Rome, and in preferring the solid honors of an opulent and powerful prince of the blood of England to the empty and precarious glory of a foreign dignity. But he had not always firmness sufficient to adhere to this resolution; his vanity and ambition prevailed at last over his prudence and his avarice, and he was engaged in an enterprise no less extensive and vexatious than that of his brother, and not attended with much greater probability of success. The immense opulence of Richard having made the German princes cast their eye on him as a candidate for the empire, he was tempted to expend vast sums of money on his election; and he succeeded so far as to be chosen King of the Romans, which seemed to render his succession infallible to the imperial throne. He went over to Germany, and carried out of the kingdom no less a sum than seven hundred thousand marks, if we may credit the account given by some ancient authors,[80] which is probably much exaggerated.[81] His money, while it lasted, procured him friends and partisans; but it was soon drained from him by the avidity of the German princes. And, having no personal or family connections in that country, and no solid foundation of power, he found at last that he had lavished away the frugality of a whole life

[78] Rymer, vol. i. p. 624. Matt. Paris, p. 648·   [79] Rymer, vol. i. p. 630.
[80] Matt. Paris, p. 638. The same author, a few pages before, makes Richard's treasures amount to little more than half the sum, p. 634. The king's dissipations and expenses, throughout his whole reign, according to the same author, had amounted only to about nine hundred and forty thousand marks, p. 638.
[81] The sums mentioned by ancient authors, who were almost all 'monks, are often improbable, and never consistent. But we know, from an infallible authority—the public remonstrance to the Council of Lyons—that the king's revenues were below sixty thousand marks a year. His brother, therefore, could never have been master of seven hundred thousand marks, especially as he did not sell his estates in England, as we learn from the same author. And we hear afterwards of his ordering all his woods to be cut, in order to satisfy the rapacity of the German princes. His son succeeded to the earldom of Cornwall and his other revenues.

in order to procure a splendid title; and that his absence from England, joined to the weakness of his brother's government, gave reins to the factious and turbulent dispositions of the English barons, and involved his own country and family in great calamities.

The successful revolt of the nobility from King John, and their imposing on him and his successors limitations of their royal power, had made them feel their own weight and importance, had set a dangerous precedent of resistance, and, being followed by a long minority, had impoverished as well as weakened that crown which they were at last induced, from the fear of worse consequences, to replace on the head of young Henry. In the king's situation, either great abilities and vigor were requisite to overawe the barons, or great caution and reserve to give them no pretence for complaints; and it must be confessed that this prince was possessed of neither of these talents. He had not prudence to choose right measures; he wanted even that constancy which sometimes gives weight to wrong ones; he was entirely devoted to his favorites, who were always foreigners; he lavished on them, without discretion, his diminished revenue; and, finding that his barons indulged their disposition towards tyranny, and observed not to their own vassals the same rules which they had imposed on the crown, he was apt, in his administration, to neglect all the salutary articles of the great charter, which he remarked to be so little regarded by his nobility. This conduct had extremely lessened his authority in the kingdom; had multiplied complaints against him; and had frequently exposed him to affronts, and even to dangerous attempts upon his prerogative. In the year 1244, when he desired a supply from Parliament, the barons, complaining of the frequent breaches of the great charter, and of the many fruitless applications which they had formerly made for the redress of this and other grievances, demanded in return that he should give them the nomination of the great justiciary and of the chancellor, to whose hands chiefly the administration of justice was committed; and, if we may credit the historian,[82] they had formed the plan of other limitations as well as of associations to maintain them, which would have reduced the king to be an absolute cipher, and have held the crown in perpetual pupilage and dependence. The king, to satisfy them, would agree to nothing but a renewal of the

[82] Matt. Paris, p. 432.

charter, and a general permission to excommunicate all the violators of it; and he received no supply, except a scutage of twenty shillings on each knight's-fee, for the marriage of his eldest daughter to the King of Scotland—a burden which was expressly annexed to their feudal tenures.

Four years after, in a full Parliament, when Henry demanded a new supply, he was openly reproached with a breach of his word and the frequent violations of the charter. He was asked whether he did not blush to desire any aid from his people, whom he professedly hated and despised, to whom, on all occasions, he preferred aliens and foreigners, and who groaned under the oppressions which he either permitted or exercised over them. He was told that, besides disparaging his nobility by forcing them to contract unequal and mean marriages with strangers, no rank of men was so low as to escape vexations from him or his ministers; that even the victuals consumed in his household, the clothes which himself and his servants wore, still more the wine which they used, were all taken by violence from the lawful owners, and no compensation was ever made them for the injury; that foreign merchants, to the great prejudice and infamy of the kingdom, shunned the English harbors as if they were possessed by pirates, and the commerce with all nations was thus cut off by these acts of violence; that loss was added to loss, and injury to injury, while the merchants, who had been despoiled of their goods, were also obliged to carry them at their own charge to whatever place the king was pleased to appoint them; that even the poor fishermen on the coast could not escape his oppressions and those of his courtiers; and, finding that they had not full liberty to dispose of their commodities in the English market, were frequently constrained to carry them to foreign ports, and to hazard all the perils of the ocean rather than those which awaited them from his oppressive emissaries; and that his very religion was a ground of complaint to his subjects, while they observed that the waxen tapers and splendid silks employed in so many useless processions were the spoils which he had forcibly ravished from the true owners.[83] Throughout this remonstrance, in which the complaints, derived from an abuse of the ancient right of purveyance, may be supposed to be somewhat exaggerated, there appears a strange mixture of regal tyranny in the practices which gave rise to it, and of aristocratical liberty or rather licentious-

[83] Matt. Paris, p. 498. See, further, p. 578. Matt. West. p. 348

ness in the expressions employed by the Parliament. But a mixture of this kind is observable in all the ancient feudal governments, and both of them proved equally hurtful to the people.

As the king, in answer to their remonstrance, gave the Parliament only good words and fair promises, attended with the most humble submissions, which they had often found deceitful, he obtained at that time no supply; and therefore, in the year 1253, when he found himself again under the necessity of applying to Parliament, he had provided a new pretence, which he deemed infallible, and, taking the vow of a crusade, he demanded their assistance in that pious enterprise.[84] The Parliament, however, for some time hesitated to comply; and the ecclesiastical order sent a deputation, consisting of four prelates—the primate, and the Bishops of Winchester, Salisbury, and Carlisle—in order to remonstrate with him on his frequent violations of their privileges, the oppressions with which he had loaded them and all his subjects,[85] and the uncanonical and forced elections which were made to vacant dignities. "It is true," replied the king, "I have been somewhat faulty in this particular: I obtruded you, my Lord of Canterbury, upon your see; I was obliged to employ both entreaties and menaces, my Lord of Winchester, to have you elected; my proceedings, I confess, were very irregular, my Lords of Salisbury and Carlisle, when I raised you from the lowest stations to your present dignities. I am determined henceforth to correct these abuses; and it will also become you, in order to make a thorough reformation, to resign your present benefices, and try to enter again in a more regular and canonical manner."[86] The bishops, surprised at these unexpected sarcasms, replied that the question was not at present how to correct past errors, but to avoid them for the future. The king promised redress both of ecclesiastical and civil grievances, and the Parliament in return agreed to grant him a supply, a tenth of the ecclesiastical benefices, and a scutage of three marks on each knight's-fee; but as they had experienced his frequent breach of promise, they required that he should ratify the great charter in a manner still more authentic and more solemn than any which he had hitherto employed. All the prelates and abbots were assembled; they held burning tapers in their hands; the great

[84] Matt. Paris, pp. 518, 558, 568. Chron. Dunst. vol. i. p. 293.
[85] Matt. Paris, p. 568.   [86] Matt. Paris, p. 579.

charter was read before them; they denounced the sentence of excommunication against every one who should thenceforth violate that fundamental law; they threw their tapers on the ground, and exclaimed, "May the soul of every one who incurs this sentence to stink and corrupt in hell!" The king bore a part in this ceremony, and subjoined, "So help me God, I will keep all these articles inviolate, as I am a man, as I am a Christian, as I am a knight, and as I am a king crowned and anointed." [87] Yet was the tremendous ceremony no sooner finished than his favorites, abusing his weakness, made him return to the same arbitrary and irregular administration; and the reasonable expectations of his people were thus perpetually eluded and disappointed. [88]

[1258.] All these imprudent and illegal measures afforded a pretence to Simon de Montfort, Earl of Leicester, to attempt an innovation in the government, and to wrest the sceptre from the feeble and irresolute hand which held it. This nobleman was a younger son of that Simon de Montfort who had conducted with such valor and renown the crusade against the Albigenses, and who, though he tarnished his famous exploits by cruelty and ambition, had left a name very precious to all the bigots of that age, particularly to the ecclesiastics. A large inheritance in England fell by succession to this family; but as the elder brother enjoyed still more opulent possessions in France, and could not perform fealty to two masters, he transferred his right to Simon, his younger brother, who came over to England, did homage for his lands, and was raised to the dignity of Earl of Leicester. In the year 1238, he espoused Eleanor, dowager of William, Earl of Pembroke, and sister to the king; [89] but the marriage of this princess with a subject and a foreigner, though contracted with Henry's consent, was loudly complained of by the Earl of Cornwall and all the barons of England; and Leicester was supported against their violence by the king's favor and authority alone. [90] But he had no sooner established himself in his possessions and dignities than he acquired, by insinuation and address, a strong interest with the nation, and gained equally the affections of all orders of men. He lost, however, the friendship of Henry, from the usual levity and fickleness of that prince; he was banished the court; he was recalled; he was intrusted with the command of Guienne, [91] where he did good service

[87] Matt. Paris, p. 580.   Annal. Burt. p. 323.   Annal. Waverl. p. 210.   W. Heming p. 571.   Matt. West. p. 353.   [88] Matt. Paris, pp. 597, 608.
[89] Matt. Paris, p. 314.   [90] Matt. Paris, p. 315.   [91] Rymer, vol. i. pp. 459, 513.

and acquired honor; he was again disgraced by the king, and his banishment from court seemed now final and irrevocable. Henry called him traitor to his face; Leicester gave him the lie, and told him that if he were not his sovereign, he would soon make him repent of that insult. Yet was this quarrel accommodated, either from the good nature or timidity of the king; and Leicester was again admitted into some degree of favor and authority. But as this nobleman was become too great to preserve an entire complaisance to Henry's humors, and to act in subserviency to his other minions, he found more advantage in cultivating his interest with the public, and in inflaming the general discontents which prevailed against the administration. He filled every place with complaints against the infringement of the great charter, the acts of violence committed on the people, the combination between the pope and the king in their tyranny and extortions, Henry's neglect of his native subjects and barons; and though he himself a foreigner, he was more loud than any in representing the indignity of submitting to the dominion of foreigners. By his hypocritical pretensions to devotion, he gained the favor of the zealots and clergy; by his seeming concern for public good, he acquired the affections of the public; and, besides the private friendships which he had cultivated with the barons, his animosity against the favorites created a union of interests between him and that powerful order.

A recent quarrel which broke out between Leicester and William de Valence, Henry's half-brother and chief favorite, brought matters to extremity,[92] and determined the former to give full scope to his bold and unbounded ambition, which the laws and the king's authority had hitherto with difficulty restrained. He secretly called a meeting of the most considerable barons, particularly Humphrey de Bohun, high constable; Roger Bigod, earl mareschal; and the Earls of Warwick and Gloucester—men who, by their family and possessions, stood in the first rank of the English nobility. He represented to this company the necessity of reforming the state and of putting the execution of the laws into other hands than those which had hitherto appeared, from repeated experience, so unfit for the charge with which they were intrusted. He exaggerated the oppressions exercised against the lower orders of the state, the violations of the barons' privileges, the continued depredations made on the clergy; and, in order to aggravate the enormity of his conduct, he appealed to the great charter, which Henry had so often ratified, and which was calculated to prevent forever the return of those intolerable grievances. He magnified the generosity of their ancestors, who, at a great expense of blood, had extorted that famous concession from the crown; but lamented their own degeneracy, who allowed so important an advantage, once obtained, to be wrested from them by a weak prince and by insolent strangers. And he insisted that the king's word, after so many submissions and fruitless promises on his part, could no longer be relied on; and that nothing but his absolute inability to violate national privileges could henceforth insure the regular observance of them.

These topics, which were founded in truth and suited so well to the sentiments of the company, had the desired effect; and the barons embraced a resolution of redressing the public grievances by taking into their own hands the administration of government. Henry having summoned a Parliament, in expectation of receiving supplies for his Sicilian project, the barons appeared in the hall clad in complete armor, and with their sword by their sides; the king, on his entry, struck with the unusual appearance, asked them what was their purpose, and whether they intended to make him their prisoner.[93] Roger Bigod replied, in the name of the rest, that he was not their prisoner, but their sovereign; that they even intended to grant him large supplies, in order to fix his son on the throne of Sicily; that they only expected some return for this expense and service; and that as he had frequently made submissions to the Parliament, had acknowledged his past errors, and had still allowed himself to be carried into the same path, which gave them such just reasons of complaint, he must now yield to more strict regulations, and confer authority on those who were able and willing to redress the national grievances. Henry, partly allured by the hopes of supply, partly intimidated by the union and martial appearance of the barons, agreed to their demand, and promised to summon another Parliament at Oxford, in order to digest the new plan of government, and to elect the persons who were to be instrusted with the chief authority.

This Parliament, which the royalists, and even the nation, from experience of the confusions that attended its measures, afterwards denominated the *mad Parliament*, met on

[93] Annal. Theokesbury.

the day appointed; and as all the barons brought along with them their military vassals, and appeared with an armed force, the king, who had taken no precautions against them, was in reality a prisoner in their hands, and was obliged to submit to all the terms which they were pleased to impose upon him. Twelve barons were selected from among the king's ministers; twelve more were chosen by Parliament; to these twenty-four unlimited authority was granted to reform the state; and the king himself took an oath that he would maintain whatever ordinances they should think proper to enact for that purpose.[94] Leicester was at the head of the supreme council, to which the legislative power was thus in reality transferred; and all their measures were taken by his secret influence and direction. Their first step bore a specious appearance, and seemed well calculated for the end which they professed to be the object of all these innovations. They ordered that four knights should be chosen by each county; that they should make inquiry into the grievances of which their neighborhood had reason to complain, and should attend the ensuing Parliament, in order to give information to that assembly of the state of their particular counties[95]—a nearer approach to our present constitution than had been made by the barons in the reign of King John, when the knights were only appointed to meet in their several counties, and there to draw up a detail of their grievances. Meanwhile the twenty-four barons proceeded to enact some regulations as a redress of such grievances as were supposed to be sufficiently notorious. They ordered that three sessions of Parliament should be regularly held every year in the months of February, June, and October; that a new sheriff should be annually elected by the votes of the freeholders in each county;[96] that the sheriffs should have no power of fining the barons who did not attend their courts, or the circuits of the justiciaries; that no heirs should be committed to the wardship of foreigners, and no castles intrusted to their custody; and that no new warrens or forests should be created, nor the revenues of any counties or hundreds be let to farm. Such were the regulations which the twenty-four barons established at Oxford for the redress of public grievances.

But the Earl of Leicester and his associates, having ad-

---

[94] Rymer, vol. i. p. 655. Chron. Dunst. vol. i. p. 334. Knyghton, p. 2445.
[95] Matt. Paris, p. 657. Addit. p. 140. Annal. Burt. p. 412.
[96] Chron. Dunst. vol. i. p. 336.

vanced so far to satisfy the nation, instead of continuing in this popular course, or granting the king that supply which they had promised him, immediately provided for the extension and continuance of their own authority. They roused anew the popular clamor which had long prevailed against foreigners; and they fell with the utmost violence on the king's half-brothers, who were supposed to be the authors of all national grievances, and whom Henry had no longer any power to protect. The four brothers, sensible of their danger, took to flight, with an intention of making their escape out of the kingdom; they were eagerly pursued by the barons. Aymer, one of the brothers, who had been elected to the see of Winchester, took shelter in his episcopal palace, and carried the others along with him. They were surrounded in that place, and threatened to be dragged out by force, and to be punished for their crimes and misdemeanors; and the king, pleading the sacredness of an ecclesiastical sanctuary, was glad to extricate them from this danger by banishing them the kingdom. In this act of violence, as well as in the former usurpations of the barons, the queen and her uncles were thought to have secretly concurred, being jealous of the credit acquired by the brothers, which they found had eclipsed and annihilated their own.

But the subsequent proceedings of the twenty-four barons were sufficient to open the eyes of the nation, and to prove their intention of reducing forever both the king and the people under the arbitrary power of a very narrow aristocracy, which must at last have terminated either in anarchy or in a violent usurpation and tyranny. They pretended that they had not yet digested all the regulations necessary for the reformation of the state and for the redress of grievances; and they must still retain their power till that great purpose were thoroughly effected. In other words, that they must be perpetual governors, and must continue to reform till they were pleased to abdicate their authority. They formed an association among themselves, and swore that they would stand by each other with their lives and fortunes; they displaced all the chief officers of the crown—the justiciary, the chancellor, the treasurer—and advanced either themselves or their own creatures in their place; even the officers of the king's household were disposed of at their pleasure; the government of all the castles was put into hands in whom they found reason to confide; and the whole power of the state being thus transferred to them, they ventured to impose an oath, to which all the subjects were obliged to swear, under the penalty of being declared public enemies, that they would obey and execute all the regulations, both known and unknown, of the twenty-four barons; and all this for the greater glory of God, the honor of the Church, the service of the king, and the advantage of the kingdom.[97]   No one dared to withstand this tyrannical authority.   Prince Edward himself, the king's eldest son, a youth of eighteen, who began to give indications of that great and manly spirit which appeared throughout the whole course of his life, was, after making some opposition, constrained to take that oath which really deposed his father and his family from sovereign authority.[98]   Earl Warrenne was the last person in the kingdom that could be brought to give the confederated barons this mark of submission.

But the twenty-four barons, not content with the usurpation of the royal power, introduced an innovation in the constitution of Parliament, which was of the utmost importance.   They ordained that this assembly should choose a committee of twelve persons, who should, in the intervals of the sessions, possess the authority of the whole Parliament, and should attend, on a summons, the person of the king in all his motions.   But so powerful were these barons that this regulation was also submitted to: the whole government was overthrown, or fixed on new foundations; and the monarchy was totally subverted, without its being possible for the king to strike a single stroke in defence of the constitution against the newly-elected oligarchy.

The report that the King of the Romans intended to pay a visit to England gave alarm to the ruling barons, who dreaded lest the extensive influence and established authority of that prince would be employed to restore the prerogatives of his family, and overturn their plan of government.[99]   [1259.]   They sent over the Bishop of Worcester, who met him at St. Omars; asked him, in the name of the barons, the reason of his journey, and how long he intended to stay in England, and insisted that, before he entered the kingdom, he would swear to observe the regulations established at Oxford.   On Richard's refusal to take this oath, they prepared to resist him as a public enemy; they fitted out a fleet, assembled an army, and, exciting the inveterate prejudices of the people against foreigners, from whom they had suffered so many oppressions, spread the report that Richard, attended by a number of strangers, meant to restore by force the authority of his exiled brothers, and to violate all the securities provided for public liberty. The King of the Romans was at last obliged to submit to the terms required of him.[100]

But the barons, in proportion to their continuance in power, began gradually to lose that popularity which had assisted them in obtaining it; and men repined that regulations, which were occasionally established for the reformation of the state, were likely to become perpetual, and to subvert entirely the ancient constitution. They were apprehensive lest the power of the nobles, always oppressive, should now exert itself without control, by removing the counterpoise of the crown; and their fears were increased by some new edicts of the barons, which were plainly calculated to procure to themselves an impunity in all their violences. They appointed that the circuits of the itinerant justices, the sole check on their arbitrary conduct, should be held only once in seven years; and men easily saw that a remedy, which returned after such long intervals against an oppressive power, which was perpetual, would prove totally insignificant and useless.[101] The cry became loud in the nation that the barons should finish their intended regulations. The knights of the shires, who seem now to have been pretty regularly assembled, and sometimes in a separate house, made remonstrances against the slowness of their proceedings. They represented that, though the king had performed all the conditions required of him, the barons had hitherto done nothing for the public good, and had only been careful to promote their own private advantage, and to make inroads on the royal authority; and they even appealed to Prince Edward, and claimed his interposition for the interests of the nation and the reformation of the government.[102] The prince replied that though it was from constraint, and contrary to his private sentiments, he had sworn to maintain the provisions of Oxford, he was determined to observe his oath. But he sent a message to the barons, requiring them to bring their undertaking to a speedy conclusion, and fulfil their engagements to the public; otherwise he menaced them, that, at the expense of his life, he would oblige them to do their duty, and would

---

[100] Matt Paris, pp. 661, 662. Chron. T. Wykes. p. 53.
[101] Matt. Paris. p. 667. Trivet, p. 209. [102] Annal. Burt. p. 427.

shed the last drop of his blood in promoting the interests and satisfying the just wishes of the nation.[103]

The barons, urged by so pressing a necessity, published at last a new code of ordinances for the reformation of the state;[104] but the expectations of the people were extremely disappointed when they found that these consisted only of some trivial alterations in the municipal law, and still more when the barons pretended that the task was not yet finished, and that they must further prolong their authority, in order to bring the work of reformation to the desired period. The current of popularity was now much turned to the side of the crown; and the barons had little to rely on for their support, besides the private influence and power of their families, which, though exorbitant, was likely to prove inferior to the combination of king and people. Even this basis of power was daily weakened by their intestine jealousies and animosities; their ancient and inveterate quarrels broke out when they came to share the spoils of the crown; and the rivalship between the Earls of Leicester and Gloucester, the chief leaders among them, began to disjoint the whole confederacy. The latter, more moderate in his pretensions, was desirous of stopping or retarding the career of the barons' usurpations; but the former, enraged at the opposition which he met with in his own party, pretended to throw up all concern in English affairs, and he retired into France.[105]

The kingdom of France, the only state with which England had any considerable intercourse, was at this time governed by Lewis IX., a prince of the most singular character that is to be met with in all the records of history. This monarch united to the mean and abject superstition of a monk all the courage and magnanimity of the greatest hero; and, what may be deemed more extraordinary, the justice and integrity of a disinterested patriot, the mildness and humanity of an accomplished philosopher. So far from taking advantage of the divisions among the English, or attempting to expel those dangerous rivals from the provinces which they still possessed in France, he had entertained many scruples with regard to the sentence of attainder pronounced against the king's father, had even expressed some intention of restoring the other provinces, and was only prevented from taking that imprudent resolution by the united remonstrances of his own barons, who represented the ex-

---

[103] Ibid.   [104] Annal. Burt. pp. 428, 439.   [105] Chron. Dunst. vol. i. p. 348.

treme danger of such a measure,[106] and, what had a greater influence on Lewis, the justice of punishing, by a legal sentence, the barbarity and felony of John. Whenever this prince interposed in English affairs, it was always with an intention of composing the differences between the king and his nobility; he recommended to both parties every peaceable and reconciling measure; and he used all his authority with the Earl of Leicester, his native subject, to bend him to compliance with Henry. He made a treaty with England, at a time when the distractions of that kingdom were at the greatest height, and when the king's authority was totally annihilated; and the terms which he granted might, even in a more prosperous state of their affairs, be deemed reasonable and advantageous to the English. He yielded up some territories which had been conquered from Poictou and Guienne; he insured the peaceable possession of the latter province to Henry; he agreed to pay that prince a large sum of money; and he only required that the king should, in return, make a final cession of Normandy and the other provinces, which he could never entertain any hopes of recovering by force of arms.[107] This cession was ratified by Henry, by his two sons, and two daughters, and by the King of the Romans and his three sons. Leicester alone, either moved by a vain arrogance or desirous to ingratiate himself with the English populace, protested against the deed, and insisted on the right, however distant, which might accrue to his consort.[108] Lewis saw, in his obstinacy, the unbounded ambition of the man; and as the barons insisted that the money due by treaty should be at their disposal, not at Henry's, he also saw, and probably with regret, the low condition to which this monarch, who had more erred from weakness than from any bad intention, was reduced by the turbulence of his own subjects.

[1261.] But the situation of Henry soon after wore a more favorable aspect. The twenty-four barons had now enjoyed the sovereign power near three years, and had visibly employed it, not for the reformation of the state—which was their first pretence—but for the aggrandizement of themselves and of their families. The breach of trust was apparent to all the world; every order of men felt it and murmured against it; the dissensions among the barons them-

---

[106] Matt. Paris, p. 604.
[107] Rymer, vol. i. p. 675. Matt. Paris, p. 566. Chron. T. Wykes, p. 53. Trivet, p. 208. Matt. West. p. 371. [108] Chron. T. Wykes, p. 53.

selves, which increased the evil, made also the remedy more
obvious and easy; and the secret desertion, in particular, of
the Earl of Gloucester to the crown seemed to promise Henry
certain success in any attempt to resume his authority. Yet
durst he not take that step, so reconcilable both to justice
and policy, without making a previous application to Rome,
and desiring an absolution from his oaths and engagements.[109]

The pope was at this time much dissatisfied with the
conduct of the barons, who, in order to gain the favor of the
people and clergy of England, had expelled all the Italian
ecclesiastics, had confiscated their benefices, and seemed determined to maintain the liberties and privileges of the English Church, in which the rights of patronage belonging to
their own families were included. The extreme animosity
of the English clergy against the Italians was also a source
of his disgust to this order, and an attempt which had been
made by them for further liberty and greater independence
on the civil power was therefore less acceptable to the court
of Rome.[110]   About the same time that the barons at Oxford
had annihilated the prerogatives of the monarchy, the clergy
met in a synod at Merton and passed several ordinances,
which were no less calculated to promote their own grandeur, at the expense of the crown.   They decreed that it
was unlawful to try ecclesiastics by secular judges; that the
clergy were not to regard any prohibitions from civil courts;
that lay patrons had no right to confer spiritual benefices;
that the magistrate was obliged, without further inquiry, to
imprison all excommunicated persons; and that ancient
usage, without any particular grant or charter, was a sufficient authority for any clerical possessions or privileges.[111]
About a century before, these claims would have been supported by the court of Rome beyond the most fundamental
articles of faith.   They were the chief points maintained by
the great martyr Becket, and his resolution in defending
them had exalted him to the high station which he held in
the catalogue of Romish saints.   But principles were changed
with the times; the pope was become somewhat jealous of
the great independence of the English clergy which made
them stand less in need of his protection, and even emboldened them to resist his authority and to complain of the
preference given to the Italian courtiers, whose interests, it
is natural to imagine, were the chief object of his concern.

[109] Annal. Burt. p. 389.   [110] Rymer, vol. i. p. 755.   [111] Annal. Burt. p. 389.

He was ready, therefore, on the king's application, to annul these new constitutions of the Church of England ; [112] and, at the same time, he absolved the king and all his subjects from the oath which they had taken to observe the provisions of Oxford.[113]

Prince Edward, whose liberal mind—though in such early youth—had taught him the great prejudice which his father had incurred by his levity, inconstancy, and frequent breach of promise, refused for a long time to take advantage of this absolution, and declared that the provisions of Oxford, how unreasonable soever in themselves and how much soever abused by the barons, ought still to be adhered to by those who had sworn to observe them.[114] He himself had been constrained by violence to take that oath, yet he was determined to keep it. By this scrupulous fidelity the prince acquired the confidence of all parties, and was afterwards enabled to recover fully the royal authority and to perform such great actions both during his own reign and that of his father.

The situation of England during this period, as well as that of most European kingdoms, was somewhat peculiar. There was no regular military force maintained in the nation. The sword, however, was not, properly speaking, in the hands of the people ; the barons were alone intrusted with the defence of the community. And after any effort which they made, either against their own prince or against foreigners, as the military retainers departed home, the armies were disbanded and could not speedily be reassembled at pleasure. It was easy, therefore, for a few barons, by a combination, to get the start of the other party, to collect suddenly their troops, and to appear unexpectedly in the field with an army which their antagonists, though equal or even superior in power and interest, would not dare to encounter. Hence the sudden revolutions which often took place in those governments ; hence the frequent victories obtained without a blow by one faction over the other ; and hence it happened that the seeming prevalence of a party was seldom a prognostic of its long continuance in power and authority.

[1262.] The king, as soon as he received the pope's absolution from his oath, accompanied with menaces of ex-

[112] Rymer, vol. i. p. 755.
[113] Rymer, vol. i. p. 722. Matt. Paris, p. 666. W. Heming. p. 580. Ypod. Neust. p. 468. Knyghton, p. 2446. [114] Matt. Paris, p. 667.

communication against all opponents, trusting to the countenance of the Church, to the support promised him by many considerable barons, and to the returning favor of the people, immediately took off the mask After justifying his conduct by a proclamation, in which he set forth the private ambition and the breach of trust conspicuous in Leicester and his associates, he declared that he had resumed the government, and was determined thenceforth to exert the royal authority for the protection of his subjects. He removed Hugh le Despenser and Nicholas de Ely, the justiciary and chancellor appointed by the barons, and put Philip Basset and Walter de Merton in their place ; he substituted new sheriffs in all the counties, men of character and honor; he placed new governors in most of the castles ; he changed all the officers of his household ; he summoned a Parliament in which the resumption of his authority was ratified with only five dissenting voices ; and the barons, after making one fruitless effort to take the king by surprise at Winchester, were obliged to acquiesce in those new regulations.[115]

The king, in order to cut off every objection to his conduct, offered to refer all the differences between him and the Earl of Leicester to Margaret, Queen of France.[116] The celebrated integrity of Lewis gave a mighty influence to any decision which issued from his court ; and Henry probably hoped that the gallantry, on which all barons as true knights valued themselves, would make them ashamed not to submit to the award of that princess. Lewis merited the confidence reposed in him. By an admirable conduct, probably as politic as just, he continually interposed his good offices to allay the civil discords of the English ; he forwarded all healing measures which might give security to both parties ; and he still endeavored, though in vain, to soothe by persuasion the fierce ambition of the Earl of Leicester, and to convince him how much it was his duty to submit peaceably to the authority of his sovereign.

That bold and artful conspirator was nowise discouraged by the bad success of his past enterprises. [1263.] The death of Richard, Earl of Gloucester, who was the chief rival in power, and who, before his decease, had joined the royal party, seemed to open a new field to his violence and to expose the throne to fresh insults and injuries. It was in vain that the king professed his intentions of observing strictly the great charter—even of maintaining all the regu-

lations made by the reforming barons at Oxford or afterwards, except those which entirely annihilated the royal
authority. These powerful chieftains, now obnoxious to
the court, could not peaceably resign the hopes of entire independence and uncontrolled power with which they had
flattered themselves and which they had so long enjoyed.
Many of them engaged in Leicester's views : and among
the rest Gilbert, the young Earl of Gloucester, who brought
him a mighty accession of power from the extensive authority possessed by that opulent family. Even Henry, son of
the King of the Romans, commonly called Henry d'Allmaine—though a prince of the blood—joined the party of
the barons against the king—the head of his own family.
Leicester himself, who still resided in France, secretly
formed the links of this great conspiracy, and planned the
whole scheme of operations.

The Princes of Wales, notwithstanding the great power
of the monarchs, both of the Saxon and Norman line, still
preserved authority in their own country. Though they
had often been constrained to pay tribute to the crown of
England, they were with difficulty retained in subordination, or even in peace ; and almost through every reign
since the Conquest they had infested the English frontiers
with such petty incursions and sudden inroads as seldom
merit to have place in a general history. The English, still
content with repelling their invasions and chasing them
back into their mountains, had never pursued the advantages obtained over them, nor been able, even under their
greatest and most active princes, to fix a total or so much
as a feudal subjection on the country. This advantage was
reserved to the present king—the weakest and most indolent. In the year 1237, Llewellyn, Prince of Wales, declining in years and broken with infirmities, but still more
harassed with the rebellion and undutiful behavior of his
youngest son, Griffin, had recourse to the protection of
Henry ; and consenting to subject his principality (which
had so long maintained, or soon recovered, its independence)
to vassalage under the crown of England, had purchased
security and tranquillity on these dishonorable terms. His
eldest son and heir, David, renewed the homage to England ;
and having taken his brother prisoner, delivered him into
Henry's hands, who committed him to custody in the Tower,
That prince, endeavoring to make his escape, lost his life in
the attempt ; and the Prince of Wales, freed from the ap-

prehensions of so dangerous a rival, paid thenceforth less regard to the English monarch, and even renewed those incursions by which the Welsh, during so many ages, had been accustomed to infest the English borders. Llewellyn, however, the son of Griffin, who succeeded to his uncle, had been obliged to renew the homage, which was now claimed by England as an established right; but he was well pleased to inflame those civil discords on which he rested his present security and founded his hopes of future independence. He entered into a confederacy with the Earl of Leicester; and, collecting all the force of his principality, invaded England with an army of thirty thousand men. He ravaged the lands of Roger de Mortimer, and of all the barons who adhered to the crown;[117] he marched into Cheshire and committed like depredations on Prince Edward's territories. Every place where his disorderly troops appeared was laid waste with fire and sword; and though Mortimer, a gallant and expert soldier, made stout resistance, it was found necessary that the prince himself should head the army against this invader. Edward repulsed Prince Llewellyn and obliged him to take shelter in the mountains of North Wales; but he was prevented from making further progress against the enemy by the disorders which soon after broke out in England.

The Welsh invasion was the appointed signal for the malcontent barons to rise in arms; and Leicester, coming over secretly from France, collected all the forces of his party and commenced an open rebellion. He seized the person of the Bishop of Hereford, a prelate obnoxious to all the inferior clergy on account of his devoted attachment to the court of Rome;[118] Simon, Bishop of Norwich, and John Mansel, because they had published the pope's bull absolving the king and kingdom from their oaths to observe the provisions of Oxford, were made prisoners, and exposed to the rage of the party. The king's demesnes were ravaged with unbounded fury;[119] and as it was Leicester's interest to allure to his side, by the hopes of plunder, all the disorderly ruffians in England, he gave them a general license to pillage the barons of the opposite party, and even all neutral persons. But one of the principal resources of his faction was the populace of the cities, particularly of London; and as he had, by his hypocritical pretensions to sanc-

117 Chron. Dunst. vol. i. p. 354.   118 Trivet, p. 211. Matt. West. pp. 382, 392.
119 Trivet, p. 211. Matt. West. p. 382.

tity and his zeal against Rome, engaged the monks and lower ecclesiastics in his party, his dominion over the inferior ranks of men became uncontrollable. Thomas Fitz-Richard, Mayor of London, a furious and licentious man, gave the countenance of authority to these disorders in the capital; and, having declared war against the substantial citizens, he loosened all the bands of government by which that turbulent city was commonly but ill restrained. On the approach of Easter, the zeal of superstition, the appetite for plunder, or, what is often as prevalent with the populace as either of these motives, the pleasure of committing havoc and destruction, prompted them to attack the unhappy Jews, who were first pillaged without resistance, then massacred to the number of five hundred persons.[120] The Lombard bankers were next exposed to the rage of the people; and though, by taking sanctuary in the churches, they escaped with their lives, all their money and goods became a prey to the licentious multitude. Even the houses of the rich citizens, though English, were attacked by night; and way was made by sword and by fire to the pillage of their goods, and often to the destruction of their persons. The queen, who, though defended by the Tower, was terrified by the neighborhood of such dangerous commotions, resolved to go by water to the castle of Windsor; but as she approached the bridge, the populace assembled against her. The cry ran, "Drown the witch!" and, besides abusing her with the most opprobrious language and pelting her with rotten eggs and dirt, they had prepared large stones to sink her barge when she should attempt to shoot the bridge, and she was so frightened that she returned to the Tower.[121]

The violence and fury of Leicester's faction had risen to such a height in all parts of England that the king, unable to resist their power, was obliged to set on foot a treaty of peace, and to make an accommodation with the barons on the most disadvantageous terms.[122] He agreed to confirm anew the provisions of Oxford, even those which entirely annihilated the royal authority; and the barons were again reinstated in the sovereignty of the kingdom. They restored Hugh le Despenser to the office of chief justiciary; they appointed their own creatures sheriffs in every county in England; they took possession of all the royal castles and fortresses; they even named all the officers of the king's

[120] Chron. T. Wykes, p. 59.   [121] Chron. T. Wykes, p. 57.
[122] Chron. Dunst. vol. i. p. 358.   Trivet, p. 211.

household; and they summoned a Parliament to meet at Westminster in order to settle more fully their plan of government. They here produced a new list of twenty-four barons, to whom they proposed that the administration should be entirely committed; and they insisted that the authority of this junto should continue, not only during the reign of the king, but also during that of Prince Edward.

This prince, the life and soul of the royal party, had unhappily, before the king's accommodation with the barons, been taken prisoner by Leicester in a parley at Windsor;[123] and that misfortune, more than any other incident, had determined Henry to submit to the ignominious conditions imposed upon him. But Edward, having recovered his liberty by the treaty, employed his activity in defending the prerogatives of his family; and he gained a great party even among those who had at first adhered to the cause of the barons. His cousin Henry d'Allmaine, Roger Bigod (earl marshal), Earl Warrenne, Humphrey Bohun (Earl of Hereford), John Lord Basset, Ralph Basset, Hammond l'Estrange, Roger Mortimer, Henry de Piercy, Robert de Brus, Roger de Leybourne, with almost all the lords marchers, as they were called, on the borders of Wales and of Scotland, the most warlike parts of the kingdom, declared in favor of the royal cause; and hostilities, which were scarcely well composed, were again renewed in every part of England. But the near balance of the parties, joined to the universal clamor of the people, obliged the king and barons to open anew the negotiations for peace; and it was agreed by both sides to submit their differences to the arbitration of the King of France.[124]

This virtuous prince, the only man who, in like circumstances, could safely have been intrusted with such an authority by a neighboring nation, had never ceased to interpose his good offices between the English factions, and had even, during the short interval of peace, invited over to Paris, both the king and the Earl of Leicester, in order to accommodate the differences between them; but found that the fears and animosities on both sides, as well as the ambition of Leicester, were so violent as to render all his endeavors ineffectual. But when this solemn appeal, ratified by the oaths and subscriptions of the leaders in both factions, was

    [123] Matt. Paris, p. 669. Trivet, p. 213.
    [124] Matt. Paris, p. 668. Chron. T. Wykes, p. 58. W. Heming, p. 580. Chron. Dunst. vol. i. p. 363.

made to his judgment, he was not discouraged from pursuing his honorable purpose. [1264.] He summoned the states of France at Amiens; and there, in the presence of that assembly as well as in that of the King of England and Peter de Montfort, Leicester's son, he brought this great cause to a trial and examination. It appeared to him that the provisions of Oxford, even had they not been extorted by force, had they not been so exorbitant in their nature and subversive of the ancient constitution, were expressly established as a temporary expedient, and could not, without breach of trust, be rendered perpetual by the barons. He therefore annulled these provisions; restored to the king the possession of his castles and the power of nomination to the great offices; allowed him to retain what foreigners he pleased in his kingdom, and even to confer on them places of trust and dignity; and, in a word, re-established the royal power in the same condition on which it stood before the meeting of the Parliament at Oxford. But while he thus suppressed dangerous innovations, and preserved unimpaired the prerogatives of the English crown, he was not negligent of the rights of the people; and, besides ordering that a general amnesty should be granted for all past offences, he declared that his award was not anywise meant to derogate from the privileges and liberties which the nation enjoyed by any former concessions or charters of the crown.[125]

This equitable sentence was no sooner known in England than Leicester and his confederates determined to reject it, and to have recourse to arms in order to procure to themselves more safe and advantageous conditions.[126] Without regard to his oaths and subscriptions, that enterprising conspirator directed his two sons, Richard and Peter de Montfort, in conjunction with Robert de Ferrars, Earl of Derby, to attack the city of Worcester; while Henry and Simon de Montfort, two others of his sons, assisted by the Prince of Wales, were ordered to lay waste the estate of Roger de Mortimer. He himself resided at London; and employing as his instrument Fitz-Richard, the seditious mayor, who had violently and illegally prolonged his authority, he wrought up that city to the highest ferment and agitation. The populace formed themselves into bands and companies; chose leaders; practised all military

[125] Rymer, vol. i. pp. 776, 777, etc. Chron. T. Wykes, p. 58. Knyghton, 2446.   [126] Chron. Dunst. vol. i. p. 363.

exercises; committed violence on the royalists; and, to give them greater countenance in their disorders, an association was entered into between the city and eighteen great barons never to make peace with the king but by common consent and approbation. At the head of those who swore to maintain this association were the Earls of Leicester, Gloucester, and Derby, with Le Despenser, the chief justiciary—men who had all previously sworn to submit to the award of the French monarch. Their only pretence for this breach of faith was that the latter part of Lewis's sentence was, as they affirmed, a contradiction to the former. He ratified the charter of liberties, yet annulled the provisions of Oxford, which were only calculated, as they maintained, to preserve that charter; and without which, in their estimation, they had no security for its observance.

The king and prince, finding a civil war inevitable, prepared themselves for defence; and summoning the military vassals from all quarters, and being reinforced by Baliol (Lord of Galloway), Brus (Lord of Annandale), Henry Piercy, John Comyn,[127] and other barons of the north, they composed an army, formidable as well from its numbers as its military prowess and experience. The first enterprise of the royalists was the attack of Northampton, which was defended by Simon de Montfort, with many of the principal barons of that party; and a breach being made in the walls by Philip Basset, the place was carried by assault, and both the governor and the garrison were made prisoners. The royalists marched thence to Leicester and Nottingham, both which places having opened their gates to them, Prince Edward proceeded with a detachment into the county of Derby, in order to ravage with fire and sword the lands of the earl of that name, and take revenge on him for his disloyalty. Like maxims of war prevailed with both parties throughout England; and the kingdom was thus exposed in a moment to greater devastation, from the animosities of the rival barons, than it would have suffered from many years of foreign or even domestic hostilities conducted by more humane and more generous principles.

The Earl of Leicester, master of London and of the counties in the southeast of England, formed the siege of Rochester, which alone declared for the king in those parts, and which, besides Earl Warrenne, the governor, was garrisoned by many noble and powerful barons of the royal party. The king and prince hastened from Nottingham, where they were then quartered, to the relief of the place; and on their approach Leicester raised the siege, and retreated to London, which, being the centre of his power; he was afraid might, in his absence, fall into the king's hands, either by force or by a correspondence with the principal citizens, who were all secretly inclined to the royal cause. Reinforced by a great body of Londoners, and having summoned his partisans from all quarters, he thought himself strong enough to hazard a general battle with the royalists, and to determine the fate of the nation in one great engagement, which, if it proved successful, must be decisive against the king, who had no retreat for his broken troops in those parts; while Leicester himself, in case of any sinister accident, could easily take shelter in the city. To give the better coloring to his cause, he previously sent a message with conditions of peace to Henry, submissive in the language, but exorbitant in the demands; [128] and when the messenger returned with the lie and defiance from the king, the prince, and the King of the Romans, he sent a new message, renouncing, in the name of himself and of the associated barons, all fealty and allegiance to Henry. He then marched out of the city, with his army divided into four bodies—the first commanded by his two sons, Henry and Guy de Montfort, together with Humphrey de Bohun, Earl of Hereford, who had deserted to the barons; the second led by the Earl of Gloucester, with William de Montchesney and John Fitz-John; the third composed of Londoners, under the command of Nicholas de Segrave; the fourth headed by himself in person. The Bishop of Chichester gave a general absolution to the army, accompanied with assurances that, if any of them fell in the ensuing action, they would infallibly be received into heaven as the reward of their suffering in so meritorious a cause.

Leicester, who possessed great talents for war, conducted his march with such skill and secrecy that he had well-nigh surprised the royalists in their quarters at Lewes, in Sussex; but the vigilance and activity of Prince Edward soon repaired this negligence, and he led out the king's army to the field in three bodies. He himself conducted the van, attended by Earl Warrenne and William de Valence; the main body was commanded by the King of the Romans and

128 Matt. Paris. p 669. W. Heming. p. 583.

his son Henry; the king himself was placed in the rear at the head of his principal nobility. Prince Edward rushed upon the Londoners, who had demanded the post of honor in leading the rebel army, but who, from their ignorance of discipline and want of experience, were ill fitted to resist the gentry and military men, of whom the prince's body was composed. They were broken in an instant, were chased off the field; and Edward, transported by his martial ardor and eager to revenge the insolence of the Londoners against his mother,[129] put them to the sword for the length of four miles, without giving them any quarter, and without reflecting on the fate which in the meantime attended the rest of the army. The Earl of Leicester, seeing the royalists thrown into confusion by their eagerness in the pursuit, led on his remaining troops against the bodies commanded by the two royal brothers. He defeated, with great slaughter, the forces headed by the King of the Romans, and that prince was obliged to yield himself prisoner to the Earl of Gloucester. He penetrated to the body where the king himself was placed, threw it into disorder, pursued his advantage, chased it into the town of Lewes, and obliged Henry to surrender himself prisoner.[130]

Prince Edward, returning to the field of battle from his precipitate pursuit of the Londoners, was astonished to find it covered with the dead bodies of their friends, and still more to hear that his father and uncle were defeated and taken prisoners, and that Arundel, Comyn, Brus, Hammond L'Estrange, Roger Leybourne, and many considerable barons of his party, were in the hands of the victorious enemy. Earl Warrenne, Hugh Bigod, and William de Valence, struck with despair at this event, immediately took to flight, hurried to Pevensey, and made their escape beyond sea;[131] but the prince, intrepid amid the greatest disasters, exhorted his troops to revenge the death of their friends, to relieve the royal captives, and to snatch an easy conquest from an enemy disordered by their own victory.[132] He found his followers intimidated by their situation; while Leicester, afraid of a sudden and violent blow from the prince, amused him by a feigned negotiation, till he was able to recall his troops from the pursuit, and to bring them into order.[133] There now appeared no further resource to the royal party, surrounded

[129] Matt. Paris, p. 670. Chron. T. Wykes, p. 62. W. Heming. p. 583. Matt. West. p. 387. Ypod. Neust. p. 469. Knyghton, p. 2450.
[130] Matt. Paris, p. 670. Matt. West. p. 387.   [131] Chron. T. Wykes, p. 63.
[132] W. Heming. p. 584.   [133] Ibid.

by the armies and garrisons of the enemy, destitute of forage and provisions, and deprived of their sovereign as well as of their principal leaders, who could alone inspirit them to an obstinate resistance. The prince, therefore, was obliged to submit to Leicester's terms, which were short and severe, agreeably to the suddenness and necessity of the situation. He stipulated that he and Henry d'Allmaine should surrender themselves prisoners as pledges in lieu of the two kings; that all other prisoners on both sides should be released;[134] and that, in order to settle fully the terms of agreement, application should be made to the King of France that he should name six Frenchmen—three prelates and three noblemen; these six to choose two others of their own country; and these two to choose one Englishman, who, in conjunction with themselves, were to be invested by both parties with full powers to make what regulations they thought proper for the settlement of the kingdom. The prince and young Henry accordingly delivered themselves into Leicester's hands, who sent them under a guard to Dover Castle. Such are the terms of agreement commonly called the *mise* of Lewes, from an obsolete French term of that meaning; for it appears that all the gentry and nobility of England, who valued themselves on their Norman extraction, and who disdained the language of their native country, made familiar use of the French tongue till this period, and for some time after.

Leicester had no sooner obtained this great advantage, and gotten the whole royal family in his power, than he openly violated every article of the treaty, and acted as sole master, and even tyrant, of the kingdom. He still detained the king in effect a prisoner, and made use of that prince's authority to purposes the most prejudicial to his interests and the most oppressive of his people.[135] He everywhere disarmed the royalists, and kept all his own partisans in a military posture;[136] he observed the same partial conduct in the deliverance of the captives, and even threw many of the royalists into prison, besides those who were taken in the battle of Lewes; he carried the king from place to place, and obliged all the royal castles, on pretence of Henry's commands, to receive a governor and garrison of his own appointment; all the officers of the crown and of the household were named by him; and the whole authority, as well

[134] Matt. Paris, p. 671. Knyghton, p. 2451. [135] Rymer, vol. i. pp. 790, 791, etc.
[136] Rymer, p. 795. Brady's App. No. 211, 212. Chron. T. Wykes, p. 63.

as arms of the state, was lodged in his hands. He instituted in the counties a new kind of magistracy, endowed with new and arbitrary powers, that of conservators of the peace; [137] his avarice appeared barefaced, and might induce us to question the greatness of his ambition, at least the largeness of his mind, if we had not reason to think that he intended to employ his acquisitions as the instruments for attaining further power and grandeur. He seized the estates of no less than eighteen barons as his share of the spoil gained in the battle of Lewes; he engrossed to himself the ransom of all the prisoners, and told his barons, with a wanton insolence, that it was sufficient for them that he had saved them, by that victory, from the forfeitures and attainders which hung over them; [138] he even treated the Earl of Gloucester in the same injurious manner, and applied to his own use the ransom of the King of the Romans, who, in the field of battle, had yielded himself prisoner to that nobleman. Henry, his eldest son, made a monopoly of all the wool in the kingdom, the only valuable commodity for foreign markets which it at that time produced. [139] The inhabitants of the Cinque Ports, during the present dissolution of government, betook themselves to the most licentious piracy, preyed on the ships of all nations, threw the mariners into the sea, and by these practices soon banished all merchants from the English coasts and harbors. Every foreign commodity rose to an exorbitant price, and woollen cloth, which the English had not then the art of dyeing, was worn by them white, and without receiving the last hand of the manufacturer. In answer to the complaints which arose on this occasion, Leicester replied that the kingdom could well enough subsist within itself, and needed no intercourse with foreigners; and it was found that he even combined with the pirates of the Cinque Ports, and received as his share the third of their prizes. [140]

No further mention was made of the reference to the King of France, so essential an article in the agreement of Lewes; and Leicester summoned a Parliament, composed altogether of his own partisans, in order to rivet, by their authority, that power which he had acquired by so much violence, and which he used with so much tyranny and injustice. An ordinance was there passed, to which the king's consent had been previously extorted, that every act of royal power should be exercised by a council of nine per-

[137] Rymer, vol. i. p. 792.
[138] Knyghton, p. 2451.   [139] Chron. T. Wykes, p. 65.   [140] Ibid.

sons, who were to be chosen and removed by the majority of three—Leicester himself, the Earl of Gloucester, and the Bishop of Chichester.[141] By this intricate plan of government, the sceptre was really put into Leicester's hands, as he had the entire direction of the Bishop of Chichester, and thereby commanded all the resolutions of the council of three, who could appoint or discard at pleasure every member of the supreme council.

But it was impossible that things could long remain in this strange situation. It behooved Leicester either to descend with some peril into the rank of a subject, or to mount up with no less into that of a sovereign; and his ambition, unrestrained either by fear or by principle, gave too much reason to suspect him of the latter intention. Meanwhile he was exposed to anxiety from every quarter, and felt that the smallest incident was capable of overturning that immense and ill-cemented fabric which he had reared. The queen, whom her husband had left abroad, had collected in foreign parts an army of desperate adventurers, and had assembled a great number of ships, with a view of invading the kingdom, and of bringing relief to her unfortunate family. Lewis, detesting Leicester's usurpations and perjuries, and disgusted at the English barons, who had refused to submit to his award, secretly favored all her enterprises, and was generally believed to be making preparations for the same purpose. An English army, by the pretended authority of the captive king, was assembled on the sea-coast to oppose this projected invasion;[142] but Leicester owed his safety more to cross winds, which long detained, and at last dispersed and ruined, the queen's fleet, than to any resistance which, in their present situation, could have been expected from the English.

Leicester found himself better able to resist the spiritual thunders which were levelled against him. The pope, still adhering to the king's cause against the barons, despatched Cardinal Guido as his legate into England, with orders to excommunicate, by name, the three earls, Leicester, Gloucester, and Norfolk, and all others, in general, who concurred in the oppression and captivity of their sovereign.[143] Leicester menaced the legate with death if he set foot within the kingdom; but Guido, meeting in France the Bishops of

141 Rymer, vol. i. p. 793. Brady's App. No. 213.
142 Brady's App. No. 216, 217. Chron. Dunst. vol. i. p. 373. Matt. West. p. 385.   143 Rymer, vol. i. p. 798. Chron. Dunst. vol. i. p. 373.

Winchester, London and Worcester, who had been sent thither on a negotiation, commanded them, under the penalty of ecclesiastical censures, to carry his bull into England and to publish it against the barons. When the prelates arrived off the coast, they were boarded by the piratical mariners of the Cinque Ports, to whom probably they gave a hint of the cargo which they brought along with them. The bull was torn and thrown into the sea, which furnished the artful prelates with a plausible excuse for not obeying the orders of the legate. Leicester appealed from Guido to the pope in person; but before the ambassadors appointed to defend his cause could reach Rome, the pope was dead; and they found the legate himself, from whom they had appealed, seated on the papal throne, by the name of Urban IV. That daring leader was nowise dismayed with this incident; and as he found that a great part of his popularity in England was founded on his opposition to the court of Rome, which was now become odious, he persisted with the more obstinacy in the prosecution of his measures.

[1265.] That he might both increase and turn to advantage his popularity, Leicester summoned a new Parliament in London, where he knew his power was uncontrollable; and he fixed this assembly on a more democratical basis than any which had ever been summoned since the foundation of the monarchy. Besides the barons of his own party, and several ecclesiastics who were not immediate tenants of the crown, he ordered returns to be made of two knights from each shire, and, what is more remarkable, of deputies from the boroughs—an order of men which in former ages had always been regarded as too mean to enjoy a place in the national councils.[144] This period is commonly esteemed the epoch of the House of Commons in England; and it is certainly the first time that historians speak of any representatives sent to Parliament by the boroughs. In all the general accounts given in preceding times of those assemblies, the prelates and barons only are mentioned as the constituent members; and even in the most particular narratives delivered of parliamentary transactions, as in the trial of Thomas à Becket, where the events of each day, and almost of each hour, are carefully recorded by contemporary authors,[145] there is not, throughout the whole, the least appearance of a House of Commons. But though that House derived its existence from so precarious and even so in-

---

[144] Rymer, vol. i. p. 802.   [145] Fitz-Steph. Hist. Quadrip. Hoveden, etc.

vidious an origin as Leicester's usurpation, it soon proved, when summoned by the legal princes, one of the most useful, and in process of time one of the most powerful, members of the national constitution ; and gradually rescued the kingdom from aristocratical as well as from legal tyranny. But Leicester's policy, if we must ascribe to him so great a blessing, only forwarded by some years an institution for which the general state of things had already prepared the nation ; and it is otherwise inconceivable that a plan set by so inauspicious a hand could have attained to so vigorous a growth, and have flourished in the midst of such tempests and convulsions. The feudal system, with which the liberty, much more the power, of the Commons was totally incompatible, began gradually to decline, and both the king and the commonalty, who felt its inconveniences, contributed to favor this new power, which was more submissive than the barons to the regular authority of the crown, and at the same time afforded protection to the inferior orders of the state.

Leicester, having thus assembled a Parliament of his own model, and trusting to the attachment of the populace of London, seized the opportunity of crushing his rivals among the powerful barons. Robert de Ferrars, Earl of Derby, was accused in the king's name, seized, and committed to custody without being brought to any legal trial.[146] John Gifford, menaced with the same fate, fled from London, and took shelter in the borders of Wales. Even the Earl of Gloucester, whose power and influence had so much contributed to the success of the barons, but who of late was extremely disgusted with Leicester's arbitrary conduct, found himself in danger from the prevailing authority of his ancient confederate, and he retired from Parliament.[147] This known dissension gave courage to all Leicester's enemies and to the king's friends, who were now sure of protection from so potent a leader. Though Roger Mortimer, Hamond l'Estrange, and other powerful marchers of Wales had been obliged to leave the kingdom, their authority still remained over the territories subjected to their jurisdiction ; and there were many others who were disposed to give disturbance to the new government. The animosities inseparable from the feudal aristocracy broke out with fresh violence, and threatened the kingdom with new convulsions and disorders.

[146] Chron. T. Wykes, p. 66. Annal. Waverl. p. 216.
[147] Matt. Paris, p. 671. Annal. Waverl. p. 216.

The Earl of Leicester, surrounded with these difficulties, embraced a measure from which he hoped to reap some present advantages, but which proved in the end the source of all his future calamities. The active and intrepid Prince Edward had languished in prison ever since the fatal battle of Lewes; and as he was extremely popular in the kingdom, there arose a general desire of seeing him again restored to liberty.[148] Leicester, finding that he could with difficulty oppose the concurring wishes of the nation, stipulated with the prince that, in return, he should order his adherents to deliver up to the barons all their castles, particularly those on the borders of Wales; and should swear neither to depart the kingdom during three years, nor introduce into it any foreign orces.[149] The king took an oath to the same effect, and he also passed a charter in which he confirmed the agreement, or *mise*, of Lewes, and even permitted his subjects to rise in arms against him if he should ever attempt to infringe it.[150] So little care did Leicester take, though he constantly made use of the authority of this captive prince, to preserve to him any appearance of royalty or kingly prerogatives!

In consequence of this treaty, Prince Edward was brought into Westminster Hall, and was declared free by the barons; but instead of really recovering his liberty, as he had vainly expected, he found that the whole transaction was a fraud on the part of Leicester; that he himself still continued a prisoner at large, and was guarded by the emissaries of that nobleman; and that, while the faction reaped all the benefit from the performance of his part of the treaty, care was taken that he should enjoy no advantage by it. As Gloucester, on his rupture with the barons, had retired for safety to his estates on the borders of Wales, Leicester followed him with an army to Hereford,[151] continued still to menace and negotiate, and, that he might add authority to his cause, he carried both the king and prince along with him. The Earl of Gloucester here concerted with young Edward the manner of that prince's escape. He found means to convey to him a horse of extraordinary swiftness, and appointed Roger Mortimer, who had returned into the kingdom, to be ready at hand with a small party to receive the prince and

[148] Knyghton, p. 2451.   [149] Annal. Waverl. p. 216.
[150] Blackstone's Mag. Charta.   Chron. Dunst. vol. i. p. 378.
[151] Chron. T. Wykes, p. 67.   Annal. Waverl. p. 218.   W. Heming. p. 585.
Chron. Dunst. vol. i. pp. 383, 384.

to guard him to a place of safety. Edward pretended to take the air with some of Leicester's retinue, who were his guards; and, making matches between their horses, after he thought he had tired and blown them sufficiently, he suddenly mounted Gloucester's horse, and called to his attendants that he had long enough enjoyed the pleasure of their company, and now bade them adieu. They followed them for some time, without being able to overtake him; and the appearance of Mortimer with his company put an end to their pursuit.

The royalists, secretly prepared for this event, immediately flew to arms; and the joy of this gallant prince's deliverance, the oppressions under which the nation labored, the expectation of a new scene of affairs, and the countenance of the Earl of Gloucester procured Edward an army which Leicester was utterly unable to withstand. This nobleman found himself in a remote quarter of the kingdom, surrounded by his enemies, barred from all communication with his friends by the Severn, whose bridges Edward had broken down, and obliged to fight the cause of his party under these multiplied disadvantages. In this extremity he wrote to his son, Simon de Montfort, to hasten from London with an army for his relief; and Simon had advanced to Kenilworth with that view, where, fancying that all Edward's force and attention were directed against his father, he lay secure and unguarded. But the prince, making a sudden and forced march, surprised him in his camp, dispersed his army, and took the Earl of Oxford and many other noblemen prisoners, almost without resistance. Leicester, ignorant of his son's fate, passed the Severn in boats during Edward's absence, and lay at Evesham, in expectation of being every hour joined by his friends from London; when the prince, who availed himself of every favorable moment, appeared in the field before him. Edward made a body of his troops advance from the road which led to Kenilworth, and ordered them to carry the banners taken from Simon's army; while he himself, making a circuit with the rest of his forces, purposed to attack the ememy on the other quarter. Leicester was long deceived by this stratagem, and took one division of Edward's army for his friends; but at last perceiving his mistake, and observing the great superiority and excellent disposition of the royalists, he exclaimed that they had learned from him the art of war, adding, "The Lord have mercy on our souls, for I see our bodies are the prince's!" The battle immediately began, though on very unequal terms. Leicester's army, by living on the mountains of Wales without bread, which was not then much used among the inhabitants, had been extremely weakened by sickness and desertion, and was soon broken by the victorious royalists; while his Welsh allies, accustomed only to a desultory kind of war, immediately took to flight, and were pursued with great slaughter. Leicester himself, asking for quarter, was slain in the heat of the action, with his eldest son Henry, Hugh le Despenser, and about one hundred and sixty knights, and many other gentlemen of his party. The old king had been purposely placed by the rebels in the front of the battle; and being clad in armor, and thereby not known by his friends, he received a wound, and was in danger of his life; but crying out, " I am Henry of Winchester, your king," he was saved, and put in a place of safety by his son, who flew to his rescue.

The violence, ingratitude, tyranny, rapacity, and treachery of the Earl of Leicester give a very bad idea of his moral character, and make us regard his death as the most fortunate event which, in this conjuncture, could have happened to the English nation; yet must we allow the man to have possessed great abilities, and the appearance of great virtues, who, though a stranger, could at a time when strangers were the most odious and the most universally decried, have acquired so extensive an interest in the kingdom, and have so nearly paved his way to the throne itself. His military capacity and his political craft were equally eminent: he possessed the talents both of governing men and conducting business; and though his ambition was boundless, it seems neither to have exceeded his courage nor his genius; and he had the happiness of making the low populace, as well as the haughty barons, co-operate towards the success of his selfish and dangerous purposes. A prince of greater abilities and vigor than Henry might have directed the talents of this nobleman either to the exaltation of his throne or to the good of his people; but the advantages given to Leicester by the weak and variable administration of the king brought on the ruin of royal authority, and produced great confusions in the kingdom, which, however, in the end, preserved and extremely improved national liberty and the constitution. His popularity, even after his death, continued so great that though he was excommunicated by

Rome, the people believed him to be a saint; and many miracles were said to be wrought upon his tomb.[152]

The victory of Evesham, with the death of Leicester, proved decisive in favor of the royalists, and made an equal, though an opposite, impression on friends and enemies in every part of England. The King of the Romans recovered his liberty : the other prisoners of the royal party were not only freed, but courted by their keepers. Fitz-Richard, the seditious Mayor of London, who had marked out forty of the most wealthy citizens for slaughter, immediately stopped his hand on receiving intelligence of this great event ; and almost all the castles garrisoned by the barons hastened to make their submissions, and to open their gates to the king, The isle of Axholme alone, and that of Ely, trusting to the strength of their situation, ventured to make resistance, but were at last reduced, as well as the castle of Dover, by the valor and activity of Prince Edward.[153] Adam de Gourdon, a courageous baron, maintained himself during some time in the forests of Hampshire, committed depredations in the neighborhood, and obliged the prince to lead a body of troops into that country against him. [1266.] Edward attacked the camp of the rebels ; and, being transported by the ardor of battle, leaped over the trench with a few followers, and encountered Gourdon in single combat. The victory was long disputed between these valiant combatants, but ended at last in the prince's favor, who wounded his antagonist, threw him from his horse, and took him prisoner. He not only gave him his life, but introduced him that very night to the queen at Guildford, procured him his pardon, restored him to his estate, received him into favor, and was ever after faithfully served by him.[154]

A total victory of the sovereign over so extensive a rebellion commonly produces a revolution of government, and strengthens as well as enlarges, for some time, the prerogatives of the crown : yet no sacrifices of national liberty were made on this occasion ; the great charter remained still inviolate ; and the king, sensible that his own barons, by whose assistance alone he had prevailed, were no less jealous of their independence than the other party, seems thenceforth to have more carefully abstained from all these exertions of power which had afforded so plausible a pretence to the rebels. The clemency of this victory is also

---

[152] Chron. de Mailr. p. 232.
[153] Matt. Paris, p. 676. W. Heming. p. 588.   [154] Matt. Paris, p. 675.

remarkable: no blood was shed on the scaffold; no attainders, except of the Montfort family, were carried into
execution; and though a Parliament, assembled at Winchester, attainted all those who had borne arms against the
king, easy compositions were made with them for their
lands,[155] and the highest sum levied on the most obnoxious
offenders exceeded not five years' rent of their estate.
Even the Earl of Derby, who again rebelled, after having
been pardoned and restored to his fortune, was obliged to
pay only seven years' rent, and was a second time restored.
The mild disposition of the king and the prudence of the
prince tempered the insolence of victory, and gradually restored order to the several members of the state, disjointed
by so long a continuance of cival wars and commotions.

The city of London, which had carried furthest the rage
and animosity against the king, and which seemed determined to stand upon its defence after almost all the kingdom had submitted, was, after some interval, restored to
most of its liberties and privileges; and Fitz-Richard, the
mayor, who had been guilty of so much illegal violence, was
only punished by fine and imprisonment. The Countess of
Leicester, the king's sister, who had been extremely forward
in all attacks on the royal family, was dismissed the kingdom with her two sons, Simon and Guy, who proved very
ungrateful for this lenity. Five years afterwards, they
assassinated, at Viterbo, in Italy, their cousin Henry d'Allmaine, who at that very time was endeavoring to make their
peace with the king; and by taking sanctuary in the church
of the Franciscans, they escaped the punishment due to so
great an enormity.[156]

[1267.] The merits of the Earl of Gloucester, after he
returned to his allegiance, had been so great in restoring
the prince to his liberty, and assisting him in his victories
against the rebellious barons, that it was almost impossible
to content him in his demands; and his youth and temerity,
as well as his great power, tempted him, on some new disgust, to raise again the flames of rebellion in the kingdom.
The mutinous populace of London, at his instigation, took
up arms; and the prince was obliged to levy an army of thirty
thousand men in order to suppress them. Even this second
rebellion did not provoke the king to any act of cruelty;

[155] Matt. Paris, p. 675.
[156] Rymer, vol. i. p. 879; vol. ii. pp. 4, 5. Chron. T. Wykes, p. 94. W. Heming.
p. 589. Trivet, p. 240.

and the Earl of Gloucester himself escaped with total impunity. He was only obliged to enter into a bond of twenty thousand marks, that he should never again be guilty of rebellion : a strange method of enforcing the laws, and a proof of the dangerous independence of the barons in those ages! These potent nobles were, from the danger of the precedent, averse to the execution of the laws of forfeiture and felony against any of their fellows; though they could not, with a good grace, refuse to concur in obliging them to fulfil any voluntary contract and engagement into which they had entered.

[1270.] The prince, finding the state of the kingdom tolerably composed, was seduced, by his avidity for glory and by the prejudices of the age, as well as by the earnest solicitations of the King of France, to undertake an expedition against the infidels in the Holy Land; [157] and he endeavored previously to settle the state in such a manner as to dread no bad effects from his absence. As the formidable power and turbulent disposition of the Earl of Gloucester gave him apprehensions, he insisted on carrying him along with him, in consequence of a vow which that nobleman had made to undertake the same voyage: in the meantime he obliged him to resign some of his castles, and to enter into a new bond not to disturb the peace of the kingdom.[158] He sailed from England with an army, and arrived in Lewis's camp before Tunis, in Africa, where he found that monarch already dead from the intemperance of the climate and the fatigues of his enterprise. The great, if not only, weakness of this prince in his government was the imprudent passion for crusades; but it was his zeal chiefly that procured him from the clergy the title of St. Lewis, by which he is known in the French history ; and if that appellation had not been so extremely prostituted as to become rather a term of reproach, he seems by his uniform probity and goodness, as well as his piety, to have fully merited the title. He was succeeded by his son Philip, denominated the Hardy—a prince of some merit, though much inferior to that of his father.

[1271.] Prince Edward, not discouraged by this event, continued his voyage to the Holy Land, where he signalized himself by acts of valor; revived the glory of the English name in those parts; and struck such terror into the Saracens that they employed an assassin to murder him, who

[157] Matt. Paris, p. 677.   [158] Chron. T. Wykes, p. 90.

wounded him in the arm, but perished in the attempt.[159]
Meanwhile, his absence from England was attended with
many of those pernicious consequences which had been
dreaded from it. The laws were not executed; the barons
oppressed the common people with impunity; [160] they gave
shelter on their estates to bands of robbers, whom they employed in committing ravages on the estates of their enemies :
the populace of London returned to their usual licentiousness; and the old king, unequal to the burden of public
affairs, called aloud for his gallant son to return,[161] and to
assist him in swaying that sceptre which was ready to drop
from his feeble and irresolute hands. [1272.] At last,
overcome by the cares of government and the infirmities of
age, he visibly declined, and he expired at St. Edmondsbury, in the sixty-fourth year of his age and fifty-sixth of his
reign—the longest reign that is to be met with in the English annals. His brother, the King of the Romans (for he
never attained the title of emperor), died about seven months
before him.

The most obvious circumstance of Henry's character is
his incapacity for government, which rendered him as much
a prisoner in the hands of his own ministers and favorites,
and as little at his own disposal, as when detained a captive
in the hands of his enemies. From this source, rather than
from insincerity or treachery, arose his negligence in observing his promises ; and he was too easily induced, for the
sake of present convenience, to sacrifice the lasting advantages arising from the trust and confidence of his people.
Hence, too, were derived his profusion to favorites, his attachment to strangers, the variableness of his conduct, his
hasty resentments, and his sudden forgiveness and return of
affection. Instead of reducing the dangerous power of his
nobles by obliging them to observe the laws towards their inferiors and setting them the salutary example in his own government, he was seduced to imitate their conduct, and to make
his arbitrary will, or rather that of his ministers, the rule of
his actions. Instead of accommodating himself by a strict
frugality to the embarrassed situation in which his revenue
had been left by the military expeditions of his uncle, the dissipations of his father, and the usurpations of the barons, he
was tempted to levy money by irregular exactions, which,
without enriching himself, impoverished, at least disgusted,

159 Matt. Paris, pp 678, 679.   W. Heming. p. 520.
160 Chron. Dunst. vol. i. p. 404.   161 Rymer, vol. i. p. 869.   Matt. Paris, p. 678.

his people. Of all men, nature seemed least to have fitted him for being a tyrant; yet there are instances of oppression in his reign which, though derived from the precedents left him by his predecessors, had been carefully guarded against by the great charter, and are inconsistent with all rules of good government. And, on the whole, we may say that greater abilities, with his good dispositions, would have prevented him from falling into his faults; or, with worse dispositions, would have enabled him to maintain and defend them.

This prince was noted for his piety and devotion, and his regular attendance on public worship; and a saying of his on that head is much celebrated by ancient writers. He was engaged in a dispute with Lewis IX. of France concerning the preference between sermons and masses. He maintained the superiority of the latter, and affirmed that he would rather have one hour's conversation with a friend than hear twenty of the most elaborate discourses pronounced in his praise.[162]

Henry left two sons—Edward, his successor, and Edmond, Earl of Lancaster; and two daughters—Margaret, Queen of Scotland, and Beatrix, Duchess of Brittany. He had five other children, who died in their infancy.

The following are the most remarkable laws enacted during this reign. There had been great disputes between the civil and ecclesiastical courts concerning bastardy. The common law had deemed all those to be bastards who were born before wedlock. By the canon law they were legitimate, and when any dispute of inheritance arose, it had formerly been usual for the civil courts to issue writs to the spiritual, directing them to inquire into the legitimacy of the person. The bishop always returned an answer agreeable to the canon law, though contrary to the municipal law of the kingdom. For this reason the civil courts had changed the terms of their writ, and, instead of requiring the spiritual courts to make inquisition concerning the legitimacy of the person, they only proposed the simple question of fact, whether he were born before or after wedlock? The prelates complained of this practice to the Parliament assembled at Merton in the twentieth of this king, and desired that the municipal law might be rendered conformable to the canon; but received from all the nobility the memora-

[162] Walsing. Edw. I. p. 43.

ble reply, "Nolumus leges Angliæ mutare"—We will not change the laws of England.[163]

After the civil wars, the Parliament, summoned at Marlebridge, gave their approbation to most of the ordinances which had been established by the reforming barons, and which, though advantageous to the security of the people, had not received the sanction of a legal authority. Among other laws, it was there enacted that all appeals of the courts of inferior lords should be carried directly to the king's courts without passing through the courts of the lords immediately superior.[164] It was ordained that money should bear no interest during the minority of the debtors.[165] This law was reasonable, as the estates of minors were always in the hands of their lords, and the debtors could not pay interest where they had no revenue. The charter of King John had granted this indulgence. It was omitted in that of Henry III., for what reason is not known; but it was renewed by this statute of Marlebridge. Most of the other articles of the statute are calculated to restrain the oppressions of the sheriffs, and the violence and iniquities committed in distraining cattle and other goods. Cattle and the instruments of husbandry formed at that time the chief riches of the people.

In the thirty-fifth year of this king an assize was fixed of bread, the price of which was settled, according to the different prices of corn, from one shilling a quarter to seven shillings and sixpence,[166] money of that age. These great variations are alone a proof of bad tillage.[167] Yet did the prices often rise much higher than any taken notice of by the statute. The Chronicle of Dunstable tells us that, in this reign, wheat was once sold for a mark, nay, for a pound, a quarter; that is, three pounds of our present money.[168] The same law affords us a proof of the little communication between the parts of the kingdom, from the very different prices which the same commodity bore at the same time. A brewer, says the statute, may sell two gallons of ale for a penny in cities, and three or four gallons for the same price in the country. At present, such commodities, by the great consumption of the people and the great stocks of the brew-

---

[163] Statute of Merton, ch. 9.   [164] Statute of Marleb. ch. 20.
[165] Statute of Marleb. ch. 16.   [166] Statutes at Large, p. 6.
[167] We learn from Cicero's Orations against Verres, lib. 3, cap. 84, 92, that the price of corn in Sicily was during the prætorship of Sacerdos, five denarii a modius; during that of Verres, which immediately succeeded, only two sesterces; that is, ten times lower—a presumption, or rather a proof, of the very bad state of tillage in ancient times.   [168] See also Knyghton, p. 2444.

ers, are rather cheapest in cities. The Chronicle above mentioned observes that wheat one year was sold in many places for eight shillings a quarter, but never rose in Dunstable above a crown.

Though commerce was still very low, it seems rather to have increased since the Conquest—at least if we may judge of the increase of money by the price of corn. The medium between the highest and lowest prices of wheat, assigned by the statute, is four shillings and threepence a quarter; that is, twelve shillings and ninepence of our present money. This is near half of the middling price in our time. Yet the middling price of cattle, so late as the reign of King Richard, we find to be above eight, near ten times lower than the present. Is not this the true inference, from comparing these facts, that, in all uncivilized nations, cattle, which propagate of themselves, bear always a lower price than corn, which requires more art and stock to render it plentiful than those nations are possessed of? It is to be remarked that Henry's assize of corn was copied from a preceding assize established by King John; consequently, the prices which we have here compared of corn and cattle may be looked on as contemporary, and they were drawn, not from one particular year, but from an estimation of the middling prices for a series of years. It is true, the prices assigned by the assize of Richard were meant as a standard for the accompts of sheriffs and escheators; and, as considerable profits were allowed to these ministers, we may naturally suppose that the common value of cattle was somewhat higher. Yet still, so great a difference between the prices of corn and cattle as that of four to one compared to the present rates affords important reflections concerning the very different state of industry and tillage in the two periods.

Interest had in that age amounted to an enormous height, as might be expected from the barbarism of the times, and men's ignorance of commerce. Instances occur at fifty per cent. paid for money.[169] There is an edict of Philip Augustus near this period, limiting the Jews in France to forty-eight per cent.[170] Such profits tempted the Jews to remain in the kingdom, notwithstanding the grievous oppressions to which, from the prevalent bigotry and rapine of the age, they were continually exposed. It is easy to imagine how precarious their state must have been under an indigent prince, somewhat restrained in his tyranny over his native

[169] Matt. Paris. p.586.   [170] Brussel, Traité des Fiefs, vol. i. p. 756.

subjects, but who possessed an unlimited authority over the
Jews, the sole proprietors of money in the kingdom, and
hated on account of their riches, their religion, and their
usury. Yet will our ideas scarcely come up to the extortions which, in fact, we find to have been practised upon
them. In the year 1241, twenty thousand marks were exacted of them.[171] Two years after, money was again extorted, and one Jew alone, Aaron of York, was obliged to
pay above four thousand marks.[172] In 1250, Henry renewed
his oppressions, and the same Aaron was condemned to pay
him thirty thousand marks upon an accusation of forgery.[173]
The high penalty imposed upon him, and which, it seems,
he was thought able to pay, is rather a presumption of his
innocence than of his guilt. In 1255, the king demanded
eight thousand marks from the Jews, and threatened to hang
them if they refused compliance. They now lost all patience, and desired leave to retire with their effects out of the
kingdom. But the king replied, "How can I remedy the
oppressions you complain of? I am myself a beggar. I am
spoiled, I am stripped of all my revenues. I owe above two
hundred thousand marks, and if I had said three hundred
thousand, I should not exceed the truth. I am obliged to
pay my son, Prince Edward, fifteen thousand marks a year.
I have not a farthing, and I must have money, from any hand,
from any quarter, or by any means." He then delivered
over the Jews to the Earl of Cornwall, that those whom the
one brother had flayed, the other might embowel, to make
use of the words of the historian.[174] King John, his father,
once demanded ten thousand marks from a Jew of Bristol,
and, on his refusal, ordered one of his teeth to be drawn
every day till he should comply. The Jew lost seven teeth,
and then paid the sum required of him.[175] One talliage paid
upon the Jews in 1243 amounted to sixty thousand marks[176]
—a sum equal to the whole yearly revenue of the crown.

To give a better pretence for extortions, the improbable
and absurd accusation, which has been at different times
advanced against that nation, was revived in England that
they had crucified a child in derision of the sufferings of
Christ. Eighteen of them were hanged at once for this
crime[177]—though it is nowise credible that even the antipathy borne them by the Christians, and the oppressions under

---

171 Matt. Paris, p. 372.   172 Matt. Paris, p. 410.   173 Matt. Paris, p. 525.
174 Matt. Paris, p. 606.   175 Matt. Paris, p. 160.   176 Madox, p. 152.
177 Matt. Paris, p. 613.

which they labored, would ever have pushed them to be guilty of that dangerous enormity. But it is natural to imagine that a race exposed to such insults and indignities both from king and people, and who had so uncertain an enjoyment of their riches, would carry usury to the utmost extremity, and by their great profits make themselves some compensation for their continual perils.

Though these acts of violence against the Jews proceeded much from bigotry, they were still more derived from avidity and rapine. So far from desiring in that age to convert them, it was enacted by law in France that if any Jew embraced Christianity, he forfeited all his goods, without exception, to the king or his superior lord. These plunderers were careful lest the profits accruing from their dominion over that unhappy race should be diminished by their conversion.[178]

Commerce must be in a wretched condition where interest was so high, and where the sole proprietors of money employed it in usury only, and were exposed to such extortion and injustice. But the bad police of the country was another obstacle to improvements, and rendered all communication dangerous, and all property precarious. The Chronicle of Dunstable says [179] that men were never secure in their houses, and that whole villages were often plundered by bands of robbers, though no civil wars at that time prevailed in the kingdom. In 1249, some years before the insurrection of the barons, two merchants of Brabant came to the king at Winchester, and told him that they had been spoiled of all their goods by certain robbers whom they knew, because they saw their faces every day in his court; that like practices prevailed all over England, and travellers were continually exposed to the danger of being robbed, bound, wounded, and murdered; that these crimes escaped with impunity, because the ministers of justice themselves were in a confederacy with the robbers; and that they, for their part, instead of bringing matters to a fruitless trial by law, were willing, though merchants, to decide their cause with the robbers by arms and a duel. The king, provoked at these abuses, ordered a jury to be enclosed, and to try the robbers. The jury, though consisting of twelve men of property in Hampshire, were found to be also in a confederacy with the felons, and acquitted them. Henry, in a rage, committed the jury to prison, threatened them with severe punishment, and ordered a new jury to be enclosed, who, dreading the fate of their fellows, at last found a verdict against the criminals. Many of the king's own household were discovered to have participated in the guilt and they said for their excuse that they received no wages from him, and were obliged to rob for a maintenance.[180] " Knights and esquires," says the Dictum of Kenilworth, " who were robbers, if they have no land, shall pay the half of their goods, and find sufficient security to keep henceforth the peace of the kingdom." Such were the manners of the times!

One can the less repine, during the prevalence of such manners, at the frauds and forgeries of the clergy; as it gives less disturbance to society to take men's money from them with their own consent, though by deceits and lies, than to ravish it by open force and violence. During this reign the papal power was at its summit, and was even beginning insensibly to decline, by reason of the immeasurable avarice and extortions of the court of Rome, which disgusted the clergy as well as laity, in every kingdom of Europe. England itself, though sunk in the deepest abyss of ignorance and superstition, had seriously entertained thoughts of shaking off the papal yoke,[181] and the Roman pontiff was obliged to think of new expedients for riveting it faster upon the Christian world. For this purpose, Gregory IX. published his decretals,[182] which are a collection of forgeries favorable to the court of Rome, and consist of the supposed decrees of popes in the first centuries. But these forgeries are so gross, and confound so palpably all language, history, chronology, and antiquities, matters more stubborn than any speculative truths whatsoever, that even that Church, which is not startled at the most monstrous contradictions and absurdities, has been obliged to abandon them to the critics. But in the dark period of the thirteenth century they passed for undisputed and authentic; and men entangled in the mazes of this false literature, joined to the philosophy, equally false, of the times, had nothing wherewithal to defend themselves but some small remains of common-sense, which passed for profaneness and impiety, and the indelible regard to self-interest, which, as it was the sole motive in the priests for framing these impostures, served also, in some degree, to protect the laity against them.

Another expedient devised by the Church of Rome, in

[180] Matt. Paris, p. 509.   [181] Matt. Paris, p. 421.   [182] Trivet, p. 191.

this period, for securing her power, was the institution of new religious orders, chiefly the Dominicans and Franciscans, who proceeded with all the zeal and success that attend novelties; were better qualified to gain the populace than the old orders, now become rich and indolent; maintained a perpetual rivalship with each other in promoting their gainful superstitions; and acquired a great dominion over the minds, and consequently over the purses, of men by pretending a desire of poverty and a contempt for riches. The quarrels which arose between these orders, lying still under the control of the sovereign pontiff, never disturbed the peace of the Church, and served only as a spur to their industry in promoting the common cause; and though the Dominicans lost some popularity by their denial of the immaculate conception—a point in which they unwarily engaged too far to be able to recede with honor—they counterbalanced this disadvantage by acquiring more solid establishments, by gaining the confidence of kings and princes, and by exercising the jurisdiction assigned them, of ultimate judges and punishers of heresy. Thus, the several orders of monks became a kind of regular troops or garrisons of the Roman Church; and though the temporal interests of society, still more the cause of true piety, were hurt by their various devices to captivate the populace, they proved the chief supports of that mighty fabric of superstition, and, till the revival of true learning, secured it from any dangerous invasion.

The trial by ordeal was abolished in this reign by order of council—a faint mark of improvement in the age.[183]

Henry granted a charter to the town of Newcastle, in which he gave the inhabitants a license to dig coal. This is the first mention of coal in England. We learn from Madox [184] that this king gave, at one time, one hundred shillings to Master Henry, his poet. Also, the same year, he orders this poet ten pounds.

It appears from Selden that, in the forty-seventh of this reign, a hundred and fifty temporal and fifty spiritual barons were summoned to perform the service due by their tenures.[185] In the thirty-fifth of the subsequent reign, eighty-six temporal barons, twenty bishops, and forty-eight abbots were summoned to a Parliament convened at Carlisle.[186]

---

[183] Rymer, vol. i. p. 228. Spell. p. 326.
[184] P. 268.
[185] Titles of Honor, part ii. ch. 3.
[186] Parl. Hist. vol. i. p. 151.

CHAPTER XIII.

EDWARD I.

CIVIL ADMINISTRATION OF THE KING.—CONQUEST OF WALES.
—AFFAIRS OF SCOTLAND.—COMPETITORS FOR THE CROWN
OF SCOTLAND.—REFERENCE TO EDWARD.—HOMAGE OF
SCOTLAND.—AWARD OF EDWARD IN FAVOR OF BALIOL.—
WAR WITH FRANCE.—DIGRESSION CONCERNING THE CON-
STITUTION OF PARLIAMENT.—WAR WITH SCOTLAND.—
SCOTLAND SUBDUED.—WAR WITH FRANCE.—DISSENSIONS
WITH THE CLERGY.—ARBITRARY MEASURES.—PEACE WITH
FRANCE.—REVOLT OF SCOTLAND.—THAT KINGDOM AGAIN
SUBDUED—AGAIN REVOLTS—IS AGAIN SUBDUED.—ROBERT
BRUCE.—THIRD REVOLT OF SCOTLAND.—DEATH AND
CHARACTER OF THE KING.—MISCELLANEOUS TRANSAC-
TIONS OF THIS REIGN.

THE English were as yet so little inured to obedience
under a regular government that the death of almost every
king since the Conquest had been attended with disorders;
and the council, reflecting on the recent civil wars, and on
the animosities which naturally remain after these great
convulsions, had reason to apprehend dangerous consequences
from the absence of the son and successor of Henry. They
therefore hastened to proclaim Prince Edward, to swear
allegiance to him, and to summon the states of the kingdom,
in order to provide for the public peace in this important
conjuncture.[1] Walter Gifford, Archbishop of York, the
Earl of Cornwall, son of Richard, king of the Romans, and
the Earl of Gloucester were appointed guardians of the
realm, and proceeded peaceably to the exercise of their authority, without either meeting with opposition from any of
the people or being disturbed with emulation and faction
among themselves. The high character acquired by Edward
during the late commotions, his military genius, his success
in subduing the rebels, his moderation in settling the kingdom had procured him great esteem, mixed with affection,

[1] Rymer, vol. ii. p. 1.   Walsing. p. 43.   Trivet, p. 239.

among all orders of men; and no one could reasonably entertain hopes of making any advantage of his absence, or of raising disturbance in the nation. The Earl of Gloucester himself, whose great power and turbulent spirit had excited most jealousy, was forward to give proofs of his allegiance; and the other malcontents, being destitute of a leader, were obliged to remain in submission to the government.

Prince Edward had reached Sicily, in his return from the Holy Land, when he received intelligence of the death of his father; and he discovered a deep concern on the occasion. At the same time he learned the death of an infant son, John, whom his princess, Eleanor of Castile, had borne him at Acre, in Palestine; and as he appeared much less affected with that misfortune, the king of Sicily expressed a surprise at this difference of sentiment, but was told by Edward that the death of a son was a loss which he might hope to repair; the death of a father was a loss irreparable.[2]

[1273.] Edward proceeded homeward; but as he soon learned the quiet settlement of the kingdom, he was in no hurry to take possession of the throne, but spent near a year in France before he made his appearance in England. In his passage by Chalons, in Burgundy, he was challenged by the prince of the country to a tournament which he was preparing; and as Edward excelled in those martial and dangerous exercises, the true image of war, he declined not the opportunity of acquiring honor in that great assembly of the neighboring nobles. But the image of war was here, unfortunately, turned into the thing itself. Edward and his retinue were so successful in the jousts that the French knights, provoked at their superiority, made a serious attack upon them, which was repulsed, and much blood was idly shed in the quarrel.[3] This rencounter received the name of the petty battle of Chalons.

Edward went from Chalons to Paris, and did homage to Philip for the dominions which he held in France.[4] He thence returned to Guienne, and settled that province, which was in some confusion. He made his journey to London through France; in his passage he accommodated at Montreuil, a difference with Margaret, Countess of Flanders, heiress of that territory.[5] He was received with joy-

---

[2] Walsing. p. 44.   Trivet, p. 240.
[3] Walsing. p. 44.   Trivet, p. 241.   Matt. West. p. 402.
[4] Walsing. p. 45.   [5] Rymer, vol. ii. pp. 32, 33.

ful acclamations by his people, and was solemnly crowned at Westminster by Robert, Archbishop of Canterbury.

The king immediately applied himself to the re-establishment of his kingdom, and to the correcting of those disorders which the civil commotions and the loose administration of his father had introduced into every part of government. The plan of his policy was equally generous and prudent. He considered the great barons both as the immediate rivals of the crown and oppressors of the people; and he purposed, by an exact distribution of justice and a rigid execution of the laws, to give at once protection to the inferior orders of the state, and to diminish the arbitrary power of the great, on which their dangerous authority was chiefly founded. Making it a rule in his own conduct to observe, except on extraordinary occasions, the privileges secured to them by the great charter, he acquired a right to insist upon their observance of the same charter towards their vassals and inferiors, and he made the crown be regarded, by all the gentry and commonalty of the kingdom, as the fountain of justice and the general asylum against oppression. [1275.] Besides enacting several useful statutes, in a Parliament which he summoned at Westminster, he took care to inspect the conduct of all his magistrates and judges, to displace such as were either negligent or corrupt, to provide them with sufficient force for the execution of justice, to extirpate all bands and confederacies of robbers, and to repress those more silent robberies which were committed either by the power of the nobles or under the countenance of public authority. By this rigid administration, the face of the kingdom was soon changed, and order and justice took place of violence and oppression; but amidst the excellent institutions and public-spirited plans of Edward, there still appears somewhat both of the severity of his personal character and of the prejudices of the times.

As the various kinds of malefactors—the murderers, robbers, incendiaries, ravishers, and plunderers—had become so numerous and powerful that the ordinary ministers of justice, especially in the western counties, were afraid to execute the laws against them, the king found it necessary to provide an extraordinary remedy for the evil; and he erected a new tribunal, which, however useful, would have been deemed in times of more regular liberty a great stretch of illegal and arbitrary power. It consisted of commissioners, who were empowered to inquire into disorders and crimes of all kinds, and to inflict the proper punishments upon them. The officers charged with this unusual commission made their circuits throughout the counties of England most infested with this evil, and carried terror into all those parts of the kingdom. In their zeal to punish crimes, they did not sufficiently distinguish between the innocent and guilty: the smallest suspicion became a ground of accusation and trial; the slightest evidence was received against criminals; prisons were crowded with malefactors, real or pretended; severe fines were levied for small offences; and the king, though his exhausted exchequer was supplied by this expedient, found it necessary to stop the course of so great rigor; and after terrifying and dissipating, by this tribunal, the gangs of disorderly people in England, he prudently annulled the commission,[6] and never afterwards renewed it.

Among the various disorders to which the kingdom was subject, no one was more universally complained of than the adulteration of the coin; and as this crime required more art than the English of that age, who chiefly employed force and violence in their iniquities, were possessed of, the imputation fell upon the Jews.[7] Edward also seems to have indulged a strong prepossession against that nation; and this ill-judged zeal for Christianity being naturally augmented by an expedition to the Holy Land, he let loose the whole rigor of his justice against that unhappy people. Two hundred and eighty of them were hanged at once for this crime in London alone, besides those who suffered in other parts of the kingdom.[8] The houses and lands (for the Jews had of late ventured to make purchases of that kind), as well as the goods of great multitudes, were sold and confiscated; and the king, lest it should be suspected that the riches of the sufferers were the chief part of their guilt, ordered a moiety of the money raised by these confiscations to be set apart and bestowed upon such as were willing to be converted to Christianity. But resentment was more prevalent with them than any temptation from their poverty; and very few of them could be induced, by interest, to embrace the religion of their persecutors. The miseries of this people did not here terminate. Though the arbitrary talliages and exactions levied upon them had yielded a

---

[6] Spellman's Gloss. in verbo Trailbaston. But Spellman was either mistaken in placing this commission in the fifth year of the king, or it was renewed in 1305. See Rymer, vol. ii. p. 960. Trivet, p. 338. Matt. West. p. 450.

[7] Walsing p. 48. Heming. vol. i. p. 6.   [8] T. Wykes, p. 107.

constant and considerable revenue to the crown, Edward, prompted by his zeal and his rapacity, resolved some time after[9] to purge the kingdom entirely of that hated race, and to seize to himself at once their whole property as the reward of his labor.[10] He left them only money sufficient to bear their charges into foreign countries, where new persecutions and extortions awaited them ; but the inhabitants of the Cinque Ports, imitating the bigotry and avidity of their sovereign, despoiled most of them of this small pittance, and even threw many of them into the sea—a crime for which the king, who was determined to be the sole plunderer in his dominions, inflicted a capital punishment upon them. No less than fifteen thousand Jews were at this time robbed of their effects, and banished the kingdom. Very few of that nation have since lived in England ; and as it is impossible for a nation to subsist without lenders of money, and none will lend without a compensation, the practice of usury, as it was then called, was thenceforth exercised by the English themselves upon their fellow-citizens, or by Lombards and other foreigners. It is very much to be questioned whether the dealings of these new usurers were equally open and unexceptionable with those of the old. By a law of Richard it was enacted that three copies should be made of every bond given to a Jew: one to be put into the hands of a public magistrate, another into those of a man of credit, and a third to remain with the Jew himself.[11] But as the canon law, seconded by the municipal, permitted no Christian to take interest, all transactions of this kind must, after the banishment of the Jews, have become more secret and clandestine, and the lender, of consequence, be paid both for the use of his money and for the infamy and danger which he incurred by lending it.

The great poverty of the crown, though no excuse, was probably the cause of this egregious tyranny exercised against the Jews ; but Edward also practised other more honorable means of remedying that evil. He employed a strict frugality in the management and distribution of his revenue ; he engaged the Parliament to vote him a fifteenth of all movables ; the pope to grant him the tenth of all ecclesiastical revenues for three years ; and the merchants to consent to a perpetual imposition of half a mark on every sack of wool exported, and a mark on three hundred skins.

---

9 In the year 1290.
10 Walsing. p. 54. Heming. vol. i. p. 20. Trivet, p. 266.   11 Trivet, p. 128.

He also issued commissions to inquire into all encroachments on the royal demesne; into the value of escheats, forfeitures, and wardships; and into the means of repairing or improving every branch of the revenue.[12] The commissioners, in the execution of their office, began to carry matters too far against the nobility, and to question titles to estates which had been transmitted from father to son for several generations. Earl Warrenne, who had done such eminent service in the late reign, being required to show his titles, drew his sword, and subjoined that William the Bastard had not conquered the kingdom for himself alone; his ancestor was a joint adventurer in the enterprise; and he himself was determined to maintain what had from that period remained unquestioned in his family. The king, sensible of the danger, desisted from making farther inquiries of this nature.

But the active spirit of Edward could not long remain without employment. [1276.] He soon after undertook an enterprise more prudent for himself and more advantageous to his people. Llewellyn, Prince of Wales, had been deeply engaged with the Montfort faction; had entered into all their conspiracies against the crown; had frequently fought on their side; and till the battle of Evesham, so fatal to that party, had employed every expedient to depress the royal cause, and to promote the success of the barons. In the general accommodation made with the vanquished, Llewellyn had also obtained his pardon; but as he was the most powerful, and therefore the most obnoxious, vassal of the crown, he had reason to entertain anxiety about his situation, and to dread the future effects of resentment and jealousy in the English monarch. For this reason he determined to provide for his security by maintaining a secret correspondence with his former associates; and he even made his addresses to a daughter of the Earl of Leicester, who was sent to him from beyond sea, but being intercepted in her passage near the isles of Scilly, was detained in the court of England.[13] This incident increasing the mutual jealousy between Edward and Llewellyn, the latter, when required to come to England and do homage to the new king, scrupled to put himself into the hands of an enemy, desired a safe-conduct from Edward, insisted upon having the king's son and other noblemen delivered to him as hos-

---

[12] Annal. Waverl. p. 235.
[13] Walsing. pp. 46, 47. Heming. vol. i. p. 5. Trivet, p. 248

tages, and demanded that his consort should previously be set at liberty.[14] The king, having now brought the state to a full settlement, was not displeased with this occasion of exercising his authority and subduing entirely the principality of Wales. He refused all Llewellyn's demands except that of a safe-conduct; sent him repeated summonses to perform the duty of a vassal; levied an army to reduce him to obedience; obtained a new aid of a fifteenth from Parliament; and marched out with certain assurance of success against the enemy. [1277.] Besides the great disproportion of force between the kingdom and the principality, the circumstances of the two states were entirely reversed; and the same intestine dissensions which had formerly weakened England now prevailed in Wales, and had even taken place in the reigning family. David and Roderic, brothers to Llewellyn, dispossessed of their inheritance by that prince, had been obliged to have recourse to the protection of Edward, and they seconded with all their interest, which was extensive, his attempts to enslave their native country. The Welsh prince had no resource but in the inaccessible situation of his mountains, which had hitherto, through many ages, defended his forefathers against all attempts of the Saxon and Norman conquerors; and he retired among the hills of Snowdon, resolved to defend himself to the last extremity. But Edward, equally vigorous and cautious, entering by the north with a formidable army, pierced into the heart of the country, and, having carefully explored every road before him and secured every pass behind him, approached the Welsh army in its last retreat. He here avoided the putting to trial the valor of a nation proud of its ancient independence and inflamed with animosity against its hereditary enemies, and he trusted to the slow but sure effects of famine for reducing that people to subjection. The rude and simple manners of the natives, as well as the mountainous situation of their country, had made them entirely neglect tillage, and trust to pasturage alone for their subsistence—a method of life which had hitherto secured them against the irregular attempts of the English, but exposed them to certain ruin when the conquest of the country was steadily pursued and prudently planned by Edward. Destitute of magazines, cooped up in a narrow corner, they, as well as their cattle, suffered all the rigors of famine; and Llewellyn, without

<hr>

[14] Rymer, vol. ii. p. 68. Walsing, p. 46. Trivet, p. 247.

being able to strike a blow for his independence, was at last obliged to submit at discretion, and receive the terms imposed upon him by the victor.[15] He bound himself to pay to Edward fifty thousand pounds, as a reparation of damages; to do homage to the crown of England; to permit all the other barons of Wales, except four near Snowdon, to swear fealty to the same crown; to relinquish the country between Cheshire and the river Conway; to settle on his brother Roderic a thousand marks a year, and on David five hundred; and to deliver ten hostages as security for his future submission.[16]

Edward, on the performance of the other articles, remitted to the Prince of Wales the payment of the fifty thousand pounds [17] which were stipulated by treaty, and which it is probable the poverty of the country made it absolutely impossible for him to levy. But notwithstanding this indulgence, complaints of iniquities soon arose on the side of the vanquished: the English, insolent on their easy and bloodless victory, oppressed the inhabitants of the districts which were yielded to them; the lords marchers committed with impunity all kinds of violence on their Welsh neighbors; new and more severe terms were imposed on Llewellyn himself; and Edward, when the prince attended him at Worcester, exacted a promise that he would retain no person in his principality who should be obnoxious to the English monarch.[18] There were other personal insults which raised the indignation of the Welsh, and made them determine rather to encounter a force which they had already experienced to be so much superior than to bear oppression from the haughty victors. Prince David, seized with the national spirit, made peace with his brother, and promised to concur in the defence of public liberty. The Welsh flew to arms; and Edward, not displeased with the occasion of making his conquest final and absolute, assembled all his military tenants, and advanced into Wales with an army which the inhabitants could not reasonably hope to resist. The situation of the country gave the Welsh at first some advantage over Luke de Tany, one of Edward's captains, who had passed the Menau with a detachment; [19] but Llewellyn, being surprised by Mortimer, was defeated and slain in an action, and two thousand of his followers were

15 T. Wykes, p. 105.
16 Rymer, vol. ii. p. 88. Walsing. p. 47. Trivet, p. 251. T. Wykes, p. 106.
17 Rymer, p. 92.   18 Dr. Powell's Hist. of Wales, pp. 344, 345.
19 Walsing. p. 50. Heming. vol. i. p. 9. Trivet, p. 258. T. Wykes, p. 120.

put to the sword.[20] [1283.] David, who succeeded him in
the principality, could never collect an army sufficient to
face the English; and being chased from hill to hill, and
hunted from one retreat to another, was obliged to conceal
himself under various disguises, and was at last betrayed in
his lurking-place to the enemy. Edward sent him in chains
to Shrewsbury, and bringing him to a formal trial before all
the peers of England, ordered this sovereign prince to be
hanged, drawn, and quartered, as a traitor, for defending
by arms the liberties of his native country, together with
his own hereditary authority.[21] All the Welsh nobility
submitted to the conqueror; the laws of England, with the
sheriffs and other ministers of justice, were established in
that principality; and though it was long before national
antipathies were extinguished and a thorough union attained between the people, yet this important conquest,
which it had required eight hundred years fully to effect,
was at last, through the abilities of Edward, completed by
the English.

[1284.] The king, sensible that nothing kept alive the
ideas of military valor and of ancient glory so much as the
traditional poetry of the people, which, assisted by the
power of music and the jollity of festivals, made deep impression on the minds of the youth, gathered together all
the Welsh bards, and, from a barbarous though not absurd
policy, ordered them to be put to death.[22]

There prevails a vulgar story, which, as it well suits the
capacity of the monkish writers, is carefully recorded by
them : that Edward, assembling the Welsh, promised to
give them a prince of unexceptionable manners, a Welshman by birth, and one who could speak no other language.
On their acclamations of joy and promise of obedience, he
invested in the principality his second son, Edward, then an
infant, who had been born at Carnarvon. The death of
his eldest son, Alphonso, soon after, made young Edward
heir of the monarchy ; the principality of Wales was fully
annexed to the crown, and henceforth gives a title to the
eldest son of the kings of England.

[1286.] The settlement of Wales appeared so complete
to Edward that, in less than two years after, he went abroad
in order to make peace between Alphonso, king of Arragon,

20 Heming. vol. i. p. 11.   Trivet, p. 257.   Annal. Waverl. p. 235.
21 Heming. vol. i. p. 12.   Trivet, p. 259.   Annal. Waverl. p. 238.   T. Wykes, p.
111.   Matt. West. p. 411.   22 Sir J. Wynne, p. 15.

and Philip the Fair, who had lately succeeded his fath[er]
Philip the Hardy, on the throne of France.[23]   The differen[ces]
between these two princes had arisen about the kingdom o[f]
Sicily, which the pope, after his hopes from England failed
him, had bestowed on Charles, brother to St. Lewis, and
which was claimed upon other titles by Peter, king of
Arragon, father to Alphonso. Edward had powers from
both princes to settle the terms of peace, and he succeeded
in his endeavors; but as the controversy nowise regards
England, we shall not enter into a detail of it. He stayed
abroad above three years, and on his return found many
disorders to have prevailed, both from open violence and
from the corruption of justice.

Thomas Chamberlain, a gentleman of some note, had assembled several of his associates at Boston, in Lincolnshire,
under pretence of holding a tournament—an exercise practised by the gentry only—but in reality with a view of
plundering the rich fair of Boston and robbing the merchants.
To facilitate his purpose, he privately set fire to the town;
and while the inhabitants were employed in quenching the
flames, the conspirators broke into the booths and carried
off the goods. Chamberlain himself was detected and
hanged, but maintained so steadily the point of honor to his
accomplices that he could not be prevailed on, by offers or
promises, to discover any of them. Many other instances
of robbery and violence broke out in all parts of England;
though the singular circumstances attending this conspiracy
have made it alone be particularly recorded by historians.[24]

[1289.] But the corruption of the judges, by which the
fountains of justice were poisoned, seemed of still more
dangerous consequence. Edward, in order to remedy this
prevailing abuse, summoned a Parliament, and brought the
judges to a trial, where all of them, except two, who were
clergymen, were convicted of this flagrant iniquity, were
fined and deposed. The amount of the fines levied upon
them is alone a sufficient proof of their guilt, being above
one hundred thousand marks—an immense sum in those
days, and sufficient to defray the charges of an expensive
war between two great kingdoms. The king afterwards
made all the new judges swear that they would take no
bribes; but his expedient of deposing and fining the old ones
was the more effectual remedy.

We now come to give an account of the state of affairs

[23] Rymer, vol. ii. pp. 149, 150, 174.   [24] Heming. vol. i. pp. 16, 17.

in Scotland, which gave rise to the most interesting transactions of this reign, and of some of the subsequent; though the intercourse of that kingdom with England, either in peace or war, had hitherto produced so few events of moment that, to avoid tediousness, we have omitted many of them, and have been very concise in relating the rest. If the Scots had, before this period, any real history worthy of the name, except what they glean from scattered passages in the English historians, those events, however minute, yet being the only foreign transactions of the nation, might deserve a place in it.

Though the government of Scotland had been continually exposed to those factions and convulsions which are incident to all barbarous and to many civilized nations, and though the successions of their kings, the only part of their history which deserves any credit, had often been disordered by irregularities and usurpations, the true heir of the royal family had still in the end prevailed, and Alexander III., who had espoused the sister of Edward, probably inherited, after a period of about eight hundred years, and through a succession of males, the sceptre of all the Scottish princes who had governed the nation since its first establishment in the island. This prince died in 1286, by a fall from his horse at Kinghorn,[25] without leaving any male issue, and without any descendant, except Margaret, born of Eric, king of Norway, and of Margaret, daughter of the Scottish monarch. This princess, commonly called the Maid of Norway, though a female, and an infant, and a foreigner, yet being the lawful heir of the kingdom, had, through her grandfather's care, been recognized successor by the states of Scotland;[26] and on Alexander's death, the dispositions which had been previously made against that event appeared so just and prudent that no disorders, as might naturally be apprehended, ensued in the kingdom. Margaret was acknowledged Queen of Scotland; five guardians, the Bishops of St. Andrew's and Glasgow, the Earls of Fife and Buchan, and James, Steward of Scotland, entered peaceably upon the administration; and the infant princess, under the protection of Edward, her great-uncle, and Eric, her father, who exerted themselves on this occasion, seemed firmly seated on the throne of Scotland. [1290.] The English monarch was naturally led to build mighty projects on this incident; and having lately, by force of arms, brought Wales under sub-

---

jection, he attempted, by the marriage of Margaret with his eldest son, Edward, to unite the whole island into one monarchy, and thereby to give it security both against domestic convulsions and foreign invasions. The amity which had of late prevailed between the two nations, and which even in former times, had never been interrupted by any violent wars or injuries, facilitated extremely the execution of this project, so favorable to the happiness and grandeur of both kingdoms; and the states of Scotland readily gave their assent to the English proposals, and even agreed that their young sovereign should be educated in the court of Edward. Anxious, however, for the liberty and independence of their country, they took care to stipulate very equitable conditions ere they intrusted themselves into the hands of so great and so ambitious a monarch. It was agreed that they should enjoy all their ancient laws, liberties, and customs; that in case young Edward and Margaret should die without issue, the crown of Scotland should revert to the next heir, and should be inherited by him free and independent; that the military tenants of the crown should never be obliged to go out of Scotland in order to do homage to the sovereign of the united kingdoms, nor the chapters of cathedral, collegiate, or conventual churches, in order to make elections; that the Parliaments summoned for Scottish affairs should always be held within the bounds of that kingdom; and that Edward should bind himself, under the penalty of one hundred thousand marks, payable to the pope for the use of the holy wars, to observe all these articles.[27] It is not easy to conceive that two nations could have treated more on a footing of equality than Scotland and England maintained during the whole course of this transaction; and though Edward gave his assent to the article concerning the future independency of the Scottish crown, with a *saving of his former rights*, this reserve gave no alarm to the nobility of Scotland, both because these rights, having hitherto been little heard of, had occasioned no disturbance, and because the Scots had so near a prospect of seeing them entirely absorbed in the rights of their sovereignty.

[1291.] But this project, so happily formed and so amicably conducted, failed of success by the sudden death of the Norwegian princess, who expired on her passage to Scotland,[28] and left a very dismal prospect to the kingdom. Though disorders were for the present obviated by the

[27] Rymer, vol. ii. p. 482.   [28] Heming. vol. i. p. 30. Trivet, p. 268.

authority of the regency formerly established, the succession itself of the crown was now become an object of dispute; and the regents could not expect that a controversy which is not usually decided by reason and argument alone would be peaceably settled by them, or even by the states of the kingdom, amid so many powerful pretenders. The posterity of William, King of Scotland, the prince taken prisoner by Henry II., being all extinct by the death of Margaret of Norway, the right to the crown devolved on the issue of David, Earl of Huntingdon, brother to William, whose male line being also extinct, left the succession open to the posterity of his daughters. The Earl of Huntingdon had three daughters: Margaret, married to Alan, Lord of Galloway; Isabella, wife of Robert Brus or Bruce, Lord of Annandale; and Adama, who espoused Henry Lord Hastings. Margaret, the eldest of the sisters, left one daughter, Devergilda, married to John Baliol, by whom she had a son of the same name, one of the present competitors for the crown; Isabella, the second, bore a son, Robert Bruce, who was now alive, and who also insisted on his claim; Adama, the third, left a son, John Hastings, who pretended that the kingdom of Scotland, like many other inheritances, was divisible among the three daughters of the Earl of Huntingdon, and that he, in right of his mother, had a title to a third of it. Baliol and Bruce united against Hastings in maintaining that the kingdom was indivisible; but each of them, supported by plausible reasons, asserted the preference to his own title. Baliol was sprung from the elder branch; Bruce was one degree nearer the common stock. If the principle of representation was regarded, the former had the better claim; if propinquity was considered, the latter was entitled to the preference.[29] The sentiments of men were divided: all the nobility had taken part on one side or the other; the people followed implicitly their leaders; the two claimants themselves had great power and numerous retainers in Scotland; and it is no wonder that, among a rude people, more accustomed to arms than inured to laws, a controversy of this nature, which could not be decided by any former precedent among them, and which is capable of exciting commotions in the most legal and best established governments, should threaten the state with the most fatal convulsions.

Each century has its peculiar mode in conducting busi-

[29] Heming. vol. i. p. 36.

ness; and men, guided more by custom than by reason, follow without inquiry the manners which are prevalent in their own time. The practice of that age, in controversies between states and princes, seems to have been to choose a foreign prince as an equal arbiter, by whom the question was decided, and whose sentence prevented those dismal confusions and disorders inseparable at all times from war, but which were multiplied a hundred-fold, and dispersed into every corner, by the nature of the feudal governments. It was thus that the English king and barons, in the preceding reign, had endeavored to compose their dissensions by a reference to the King of France; and the celebrated integrity of that monarch had prevented all the bad effects which might naturally have been dreaded from so perilous an expedient. It was thus that the kings of France and Arragon, and afterwards other princes, had submitted their controversies to Edward's judgment; and the remoteness of their states, the great power of the princes, and the little interest which he had on either side, had induced him to acquit himself with honor in his decisions. The Parliament of Scotland, therefore, threatened with a furious civil war, and allured by the great reputation of the English monarch, as well as by the present amicable correspondence between the kingdoms, agreed in making a reference to Edward; and Fraser, Bishop of St. Andrew's, with other deputies, was sent to notify to him their resolution, and to claim his good offices in the present dangers to which they were exposed.[30] His inclination, they flattered themselves, led him to prevent their dissensions, and to interpose with a power which none of the competitors would dare to withstand. When this expedient was proposed by one party, the other deemed it dangerous to object to it; indifferent persons thought that the imminent perils of a civil war would thereby be prevented; and no one reflected on the ambitious character of Edward, and the almost certain ruin which must attend a small state, divided by faction, when it thus implicitly submits itself to the will of so powerful and encroaching a neighbor.

The temptation was too strong for the virtue of the English monarch to resist. He purposed to lay hold of the present favorable opportunity, and if not to create, at least to revive, his claim of a feudal superiority over Scotland— a claim which had hitherto lain in the deepest obscurity,

[30] Heming. vol. i. p. 31.

and which, if ever it had been an object of attention, or had been so much as suspected, would have effectually prevented the Scottish barons from choosing him for an umpire. He well knew that if this pretension were once submitted to, as it seemed difficult, in the present situation of Scotland, to oppose it, the absolute sovereignty of that kingdom (which had been the case with Wales) would soon follow; and that one great vassal, cooped up in an island with his liege lord, without resource from foreign powers, without aid from any fellow-vassals, could not long maintain his dominions against the efforts of a mighty kingdom, assisted by all the cavils which the feudal law afforded his superior against him. In pursuit of this great object, very advantageous to England, perhaps in the end no less beneficial to Scotland, but extremely unjust and iniquitous in itself, Edward busied himself in searching for proofs of his pretended superiority; and instead of looking into his own archives, which, if his claim had been real, must have afforded him numerous records of the homages done by the Scottish princes, and could alone yield him any authentic testimony, he made all the monasteries be ransacked for old chronicles and histories written by Englishmen, and he collected all the passages which seemed anywise to favor his pretensions.[31] Yet even in this method of proceeding, which must have discovered to himself the injustice of his claim, he was far from being fortunate. He began his proofs from the time of Edward the Elder, and continued them through all the subsequent Saxon and Norman times, but produced nothing to his purpose.[32] The whole amount of his authorities during the Saxon period, when stripped of the bombast and inaccurate style of the monkish historians, is that the Scots had sometimes been defeated by the English, had received peace on disadvantageous terms, had made submissions to the English monarch, and had even, perhaps, fallen into some dependence on a power which was so much superior, and which they had not at that time sufficient force to resist. His authorities from the Norman period, were, if possible, still less conclusive: the historians indeed make frequent mention of homage done by the northern potentate, but no one of them says that it was done for his kingdom, and several of them declare, in express terms, that it was relative only to the fiefs which he enjoyed south of the

Tweed,[33] in the same manner as the King of England himself swore fealty to the French monarch for the fiefs which he inherited in France. And to such scandalous shifts was Edward reduced that he quotes a passage from Hoveden [34] where it is asserted that a Scottish king had done homage to England; but he purposely omits the latter part of the sentence, which expresses that this prince did homage for the lands which he held in England.

When William, King of Scotland, was taken prisoner in the battle of Alnwick, he was obliged, for the recovery of his liberty, to swear fealty to the victor for his crown itself. The deed was performed according to all the rites of the feudal law; the record was preserved in the English archives, and is mentioned by all the historians; but as it is the only one of the kind, and as historians speak of this superiority as a great acquisition gained by the fortunate arms of Henry II.,[35] there can remain no doubt that the kingdom of Scotland was, in all former periods, entirely free and independent. Its subjection continued a very few years. King Richard, desirous, before his departure for the Holy Land, to conciliate the friendship of William, renounced that homage which, he says in express terms, had been extorted by his father; and he only retained the usual homage which had been done by the Scottish princes for lands which they held in England.

But though this transaction rendered the independence of Scotland still more unquestionable than if no fealty had ever been sworn to the English crown, the Scottish kings, apprised of the point aimed at by their powerful neighbors, seemed for a long time to have retained some jealousy on that head, and, in doing homage, to have anxiously obviated all such pretensions. When William, in 1200, did homage to John at Lincoln, he was careful to insert a salvo for his royal dignity;[36] when Alexander III. sent assistance to his father-in-law, Henry III., during the wars of the barons, he previously procured an acknowledgment that this aid was granted only from friendship, not from any right claimed by the English monarch;[37] and when that same prince was invited to assist at the coronation of this very Edward, he declined attendance till he received a like acknowledgment.[38]

But as all these reasons (and stronger could not be pro-

[33] Hoveden, pp. 492, 662. Matt. Paris, p. 109. Matt. West. p. 256.
[34] P. 662.   [35] Neubr. lib. ii. cap. iv. Knyghton, p. 2392.
[36] Hoveden, p. 811.   [37] Rymer, vol. ii. p. 844.
[38] See note [T] at the end of the volume.

duced) were but a feeble rampart against the power of the sword, Edward, carrying with him a great army, which was to enforce his proofs, advanced to the frontiers, and invited the Scottish Parliament and all the competitors to attend him in the castle of Norham, a place situated on the southern banks of the Tweed, in order to determine that cause which had been referred to his arbitration. But though this deference seemed due to so great a monarch, and was no more than what his father and the English barons had, in similar circumstances, paid to Lewis IX., the king, careful not to give umbrage, and determined never to produce his claim till it should be too late to think of opposition, sent the Scottish barons an acknowledgment that, though at that time they had passed the frontiers, this step should never be drawn into precedent, or afford the English kings a pretence for exacting a like submission in any future transaction.[39] When the whole Scottish nation had thus unwarily put themselves in his power, Edward opened the conferences at Norham. He informed the Parliament, by the mouth of Roger le Brabançon, his chief justiciary, that he was come thither to determine the right among the competitors to their crown; that he was determined to do strict justice to all parties; and that he was entitled to this authority, not in virtue of the reference made to him, but in quality of superior and liege lord of the kingdom.[40] He then produced his proofs of this superiority, which he pretended to be unquestionable, and he required of them an acknowledgment of it—a demand which was superfluous if the fact were already known and avowed, and which plainly betrays Edward's consciousness of his lame and defective title. The Scottish Parliament were astonished at so new a pretension, and answered only by their silence. But the king, in order to maintain the appearance of free and regular proceedings, desired them to remove into their own country, to deliberate upon his claim, to examine his proofs, to propose all their objections, and to inform him of their resolution; and he appointed a plain at Upsettleton, on the northern banks of the Tweed, for that purpose.

When the Scottish barons assembled in this place, though moved with indignation at the injustice of this unexpected claim, and at the fraud with which it had been conducted, they found themselves betrayed into a situation

[39] Rymer, vol. ii. p. 539, 845.   Walsing. p. 56.
[40] Rymer, vol. ii. p. 543.   See note [U] at the end of the volume.

in which it was impossible for them to make any defence for the ancient liberty and independence of their country. The King of England, a martial and politic prince, at the head of a powerful army, lay at a very small distance, and was only separated from them by a river fordable in many places. Though by a sudden flight some of them might themselves be able to make their escape, what hopes could they entertain of securing the kingdom against his future enterprises? Without a head, without union among themselves, attached all of them to different competitors, whose title they had rashly submitted to the decision of this foreign usurper, and who were thereby reduced to an absolute dependence upon him, they could only expect, by resistance, to entail on themselves and their posterity a more grievous and more destructive servitude. Yet, even in this desperate state of their affairs, the Scottish barons, as we learn from Walsingham,[41] one of the best historians of that period, had the courage to reply that, till they had a king, they could take no resolution on so momentous a point. The journal of King Edward says that they made no answer at all;[42] that is, perhaps, no *particular* answer or objection to Edward's claim ; and by this solution it is possible to reconcile the journal with the historian. The king, therefore, interpreting their silence as consent, addressed himself to the several competitors, and, previously to his pronouncing sentence, required their acknowledgment of his superiority.

It is evident, from the genealogy of the royal family of Scotland, that there could only be two questions about the succession, that between Baliol and Bruce on the one hand, and Lord Hastings on the other, concerning the partition of the crown ; and that between Baliol and Bruce themselves, concerning the preference of their respective titles supposing the kingdom indivisible. Yet there appeared on this occasion no less than nine claimants besides : John Comyn, or Cummin, Lord of Badenoch, Florence, Earl of Holland, Patrick Dunbar, Earl of March, William de Vescey, Robert de Pynkeni, Nicholas de Soules, Patrick Galythly, Roger de Mandeville, Robert de Ross ; not to mention the King of Norway, who claimed as heir to his daughter Margaret.[43] Some of these competitors were descended from more remote branches of the royal family ; others were even sprung

---

[41] Page 56. Matt. West. p. 436. It is said by Hemingford, vol. i. p. 33, that the king menaced violently the Scottish barons, and forced them to compliance, at least to silence.

[42] Rymer, vol. ii. p. 548.   [43] Walsing. p. 58.

from illegitimate children ; and as none of them had the
least pretence of right, it is natural to conjecture that Edward had secretly encouraged them to appear in the list of
claimants, that he might sow the more division among the
Scottish nobility, make the cause appear the more intricate,
and be able to choose, among a great number, the most obsequious candidate.

But he found them all equally obsequious on this occasion.[44]   Robert Bruce was the first that acknowledged Edward's right of superiority over Scotland, and he had so far
foreseen the king's pretensions that even in his petition,
where he set forth his claim to the crown, he had previously
applied to him as liege lord of the kingdom—a step which
was not taken by any of the other competitors.[45]   They all,
however, with seeming willingness, made a like acknowledgment when required; though Baliol, lest he should
give offence to the Scottish nation, had taken care to be absent during the first days ; and he was the last that recognized the king's title.[46]   Edward next deliberated concerning the method of proceeding in the discussion of this great
controversy.   He gave orders that Baliol, and such of the
competitors as adhered to him, should choose forty commissioners ; Bruce and his adherents forty more ; to these the
king added twenty-four Englishmen.   He ordered these
hundred and four commissioners to examine the cause deliberately among themselves, and make their report to
him,[47] and he promised in the ensuing year to give his determination.   Meanwhile he pretended that it was requisite
to have all the fortresses of Scotland delivered into his
hands, in order to enable him, without opposition, to put
the true heir in possession of the crown ; and this exorbitant demand was complied with, both by the states and by
the claimants.[48]   The governors also of all the castles immediately resigned their command, except Umfreville, Earl
of Angus, who refused, without a formal and particular acquittal from the Parliament and the several claimants, to
surrender his fortresses to so domineering an arbiter, who
had given to Scotland so many just reasons of suspicion.[49]
Before this assembly broke up, which had fixed such a mark
of dishonor on the nation, all the prelates and barons there
present swore fealty to Edward ; and that prince appointed

  [44] Rymer, vol. ii. pp. 529, 545.   Walsing. p. 56.   Heming. vol. i. p. 33, 34.   Trivet, p. 260.   Matt. West. p. 415.   [45] Rymer, vol. ii. pp. 577, 578, 579.
  [46] Rymer, vol. ii. p. 546.   [47] Rymer, vol. ii. pp. 555, 556.
  [48] Rymer, vol. ii. p. 529.   Walsing. pp. 56, 57.   [49] Rymer, vol. ii. p. 531.

commissioners to receive a like oath from all the other barons and persons of distinction in Scotland.[50]

The king, having finally made, as he imagined, this important acquisition, left the commissioners to sit at Berwick and examine the titles of the several competitors who claimed the precarious crown, which Edward was willing for some time to allow the lawful heir to enjoy. He went southwards, both in order to assist at the funeral of his mother, Queen Eleanor, who died about this time, and to compose some differences which had arisen among the principal nobility. Gilbert, Earl of Gloucester, the greatest baron of the kingdom, had espoused the king's daughter; and being elated by that alliance, and still more by his own power, which, he thought, set him above the laws, he permitted his bailiffs and vassals to commit violence on the lands of Humphrey Bohun, Earl of Hereford, who retaliated the injury by like violence. But this was not a reign in which such illegal proceedings could pass with impunity. Edward procured a sentence against the two earls, committed them both to prison, and would not restore them to their liberty till he had exacted a fine of one thousand marks from Hereford, and one of ten thousand from his son-in-law.]

[1292.] During this interval the titles of John Baliol and of Robert Bruce, whose claims appeared to be the best founded among the competitors for the crown of Scotland, were the subject of general disquisition, as well as of debate among the commissioners. Edward, in order to give greater authority to his intended decision, proposed this general question both to the commissioners and to all the celebrated lawyers in Europe : Whether a person descended from the eldest sister, but farther removed by one degree, were preferable, in the succession of kingdoms, fiefs, and other indivisible inheritances, to one descended from the younger sister, but one degree nearer to the common stock? This was the true state of the case ; and the principle of representation had now gained such ground everywhere that a uniform answer was returned to the king in the affirmative. He therefore pronounced sentence in favor of Baliol; and when Bruce, upon this disappointment, joined afterwards Lord Hastings, and claimed a third of the kingdom, which he now pretended to be divisible, Edward, though his interest seemed more to require the partition of Scotland, again pronounced sentence in favor of Baliol. That competitor, upon renewing his oath of fealty to England, was put in possession of the kingdom ;[51] all his fortresses were restored to him ;[52] and the conduct of Edward, both in the deliberate solemnity of the proceedings and in the justice of the award, was so far unexceptionable.

[1293.] Had the king entertained no other view than that of establishing his superiority over Scotland, though the iniquity of that claim was apparent, and was aggravated by the most egregious breach of trust, he might have fixed his pretensions, and have left that important acquisition to his posterity; but he immediately proceeded in such a manner as made it evident that, not content with this usurpation, he aimed also at the absolute sovereignty and dominion of the kingdom. Instead of gradually inuring the Scots to the yoke, and exerting his rights of superiority with moderation, he encouraged all appeals to England; required King John himself, by six different summonses on trivial occasions, to come to London ;[53] refused him the privilege of defending his cause by a procurator ; and obliged him to appear at the bar of his Parliament as a private person.[54] These humiliating demands were hitherto quite unknown to a King of Scotland ; they are, however, the necessary consequence of vassalage by the feudal law ; and as there was no preceding instance of such treatment submitted to by a prince of that country, Edward must, from that circumstance alone, had there remained any doubt, have been himself convinced that his claim was altogether an usurpation.[55] But his intention plainly was to enrage Baliol by these indignities, to engage him in rebellion, and to assume the dominion of the state as the punishment of his treason and felony. Accordingly Baliol, though a prince of a soft and gentle spirit, returned into Scotland highly provoked at this usage, and determined at all hazards to vindicate his liberty ; and the war which soon after broke out between France and England gave him a favorable opportunity of executing his purpose.

The violence, robberies, and disorders to which that age was so subject were not confined to the licentious barons and their retainers at land : the sea was equally infested with piracy ; the feeble execution of the laws had

---

[51] Rymer, vol. ii. pp. 590, 591, 593, 600.   [52] Rymer, vol. ii. p. 590.
[53] Rymer, vol. ii. pp. 603, 605, 606, 608, 615, 616.
[54] Ryley's Placit. Parl. pp. 152, 153.   [55] See note (X) at the end of the volume.

given license to all orders of men, and a general appetite for rapine and revenge, supported by a false point of honor, had also infected the merchants and mariners; and it pushed them, on any provocation, to seek redress by immediate retaliation upon the aggressors. A Norman and an English vessel met off the coast near Bayonne; and both of them having occasion for water, they sent their boats to land, and the several crews came at the same time to the same spring. There ensued a quarrel for the preference: a Norman, drawing his dagger, attempted to stab an Englishman, who, grappling with him, threw his adversary on the ground, and the Norman, as was pretended, falling on his own dagger, was slain.[56] This scuffle between two seamen about water soon kindled a bloody war between the two nations, and involved a great part of Europe in the quarrel. The mariners of the Norman ship carried their complaints to the French king. Philip, without inquiring into the fact, without demanding redress, bade them take revenge, and trouble him no more about the matter.[57] The Normans, who had been more regular than usual in applying to the crown, needed but this hint to proceed to immediate violence. They seized an English ship in the channel; and hanging, along with some dogs, several of the crew on the yard-arm, in presence of their companions, dismissed the vessel,[58] and bade the mariners inform their countrymen that vengeance was now taken for the blood of the Norman killed at Bayonne. This injury, accompanied with so general and deliberate an insult, was resented by the mariners of the Cinque Ports, who, without carrying any complaint to the king or waiting for redress, retaliated by committing like barbarities on all French vessels without distinction. The French, provoked by their losses, preyed on the ships of all Edward's subjects, whether English or Gascon. The sea became a scene of piracy between the nations; the sovereigns, without either seconding or repressing the violence of their subjects, seemed to remain indifferent spectators; the English made private associations with the Irish and Dutch seamen, the French with the Flemish and Genoese;[59] and the animosities of the people on both sides became every day more violent and barbarous. A fleet of two hundred Norman vessels set sail to the south for wine and other commodities, and, in their passage, seized all the English

[56] Walsing. p. 58. Heming. vol. i. p. 39.
[57] Walsing p. 58.
[58] Heming. vol. i. p. 40. Matt. West. p. 419
[59] Heming. vol. i. p. 40.

ships which they met with, hanged the seamen, and seized the goods. The inhabitants of the English seaports, informed of this incident, fitted out a fleet of sixty sail, stronger and better manned than the others, and awaited the enemy on their return. After an obstinate battle, they put them to rout, and sunk, destroyed, or took the greater part of them.[60] No quarter was given, and it is pretended that the loss of the French amounted to fifteen thousand men ; which is accounted for by this circumstance, that the Norman fleet was employed in transporting a considerable body of soldiers from the south.

The affair was now become too important to be any longer overlooked by the sovereigns. On Philip's sending an envoy to demand reparation and restitution, the king despatched the Bishop of London to the French court, in order to accommodate the quarrel. He first said that the English courts of justice were open to all men ; and if any Frenchman were injured, he might seek reparation by course of law.[61] He next offered to adjust the matter by private arbiters, or by a personal interview with the King of France, or by a reference either to the pope or the college of cardinals, or any particular cardinals agreed on by both parties.[62] The French, probably the more disgusted as they were hitherto losers in the quarrel, refused all these expedients ; the vessels and the goods of merchants were confiscated on both sides ; depredations were continued by the Gascons on the western coast of France, as well as by the English in the channel ; Philip cited the king, as Duke of Guienne, to appear in his court at Paris and answer for these offences ; and Edward, apprehensive of danger to that province, sent John St. John, an experienced soldier, to Bordeaux, and gave him directions to put Guienne in a posture of defence.[63]

That he might, however, prevent a final rupture between the nations, the king despatched his brother, Edmond, Earl of Lancaster, to Paris ; [1294.] and as this prince had espoused the Queen of Navarre, mother to Jane, Queen of France, he seemed, on account of that alliance, the most proper person for finding expedients to accommodate the difference. Jane pretended to interpose with her good offices ; Mary, the queen dowager, feigned the same amicable disposition ; and these two princesses told Edmond that

[60] Walsing. p. 60. Trivet,   274. Chron. Dunst. vol. ii. p. 609.
[61] Trivet, p. 275.   [62] Ibid.   [63] Trivet, p. 276.

the circumstance the most difficult to adjust was the point of honor with Philip, who thought himself affronted by the injuries committed against him by his sub-vassals in Guienne; but if Edward would once consent to give him seisin and possession of that province, he would think his honor fully repaired, would engage to restore Guienne immediately, and would accept of a very easy satisfaction for all the other injuries. The king was consulted on the occasion; and as he then found himself in immediate danger of war with the Scots, which he regarded as the more important concern, this politic prince, blinded by his favorite passion for subduing that nation, allowed himself to be deceived by so gross an artifice.[64] He sent his brother orders to sign and execute the treaty with the two queens. Philip solemnly promised to execute his part of it, and the king's citation to appear in the court of France was accordingly recalled. But the French monarch was no sooner put in possession of Guienne than the citation was renewed; Edward was condemned for non-appearance, and Guienne, by a formal sentence, was declared to be forfeited and annexed to the crown.[65]

Edward, fallen into a like snare with that which he himself had spread for the Scots, was enraged; and the more so, as he was justly ashamed of his own conduct in being so egregiously overreached by the court of France. Sensible of the extreme difficulties which he should encounter in the recovery of Gascony, where he had not retained a single place in his hands, he endeavored to compensate that loss by forming alliances with several princes, who, he projected, should attack France on all quarters and make a diversion of her forces. Adolphus de Nassau, King of the Romans, entered into a treaty with him for that purpose,[66] as did also Amadæus, Count of Savoy, the Archbishop of Cologne, the Counts of Gueldre and Luxembourg, the Duke of Brabant and Count of Barre, who had married his two daughters, Margaret and Eleanor; but these alliances were extremely burdensome to his narrow revenues, and proved in the issue entirely ineffectual. More impression was made on Guienne by an English army, which he completed by emptying the jails of many thousand thieves and robbers who had been confined there for their crimes. So low had the profession

[64] Rymer, vol. ii. pp. 619, 620. Walsing. p. 61. Heming. vol. i. pp. 42, 43. Trivet, p. 277.   [65] Rymer, vol. ii. pp. 620, 622. Walsing. p 61. Trivet, p. 278.   [66] Heming. vol. i. p. 51.

of arms fallen, and so much had it degenerated from the estimation in which it stood during the vigor of the feudal system!

The king himself was detained in England, first by contrary winds,[67] then by his apprehension of a Scottish invasion, and by a rebellion of the Welsh, whom he repressed and brought again under subjection.[68] [1295.] The army which he sent to Guienne was commanded by his nephew, John de Bretagne, Earl of Richmond, and under him by St. John, Tibetot, De Vere, and other officers of reputation,[69] who made themselves masters of the town of Bayonne, as well as of Bourg, Blaye, Reole, St. Severe, and other places, which straitened Bordeaux, and cut off its communication both by sea and land. The favor which the Gascon nobility bore to the English government facilitated these conquests, and seemed to promise still greater successes; but this advantage was soon lost by the misconduct of some of the officers. Philip's brother, Charles de Valois, who commanded the French armies, having laid siege to Podensac, a small fortress near Reole, obliged Giffard, the governor, to capitulate; and the articles, though favorable to the English, left all the Gascons prisoners at discretion, of whom about fifty were hanged by Charles as rebels—a policy by which he both intimidated that people and produced an irreparable breach between them and the English.[70] That prince immediately attacked Reole, where the Earl of Richmond himself commanded; and as the place seemed not tenable, the English general drew his troops to the waterside, with an intention of embarking with the greater part of the army. The enraged Gascons fell upon his rear, and at the same time opened their gates to the French, who, besides making themselves masters of the place, took many prisoners of distinction. St. Severe was more vigorously defended by Hugh de Vere, son of the Earl of Oxford, but was at last obliged to capitulate. The French king, not content with these successes in Gascony, threatened England with an invasion; and, by a sudden attempt, his troops took and burnt Dover,[71] but were obliged soon after to retire. And in order to make a greater diversion of the English force, and engage Edward in dangerous and important wars, he formed a secret alliance with John Baliol, King of Scot-

[67] Chron. Dunst. vol. ii. p. 622.
[68] Walsing. p. 62. Heming. vol. i. p. 55. Trivet, p. 282. Chron. Dunst. vol. ii. p. 622. [69] Trivet, p, 279.
[70] Heming. vol. i, p. 49. [71] Trivet, p. 284 Chron. Dunst. vol. ii. p. 642.

land, the commencement of that strict union which, during so many centuries, was maintained, by mutual interests and necessities, between the French and Scottish nations. John confirmed this alliance by stipulating a marriage between his eldest son and the daughter of Charles de Valois.[72]

The expenses attending these multiplied wars of Edward and his preparations for war, joined to alterations which had insensibly taken place in the general state of affairs, obliged him to have frequent recourse to parliamentary supplies, introduced the lower orders of the state into the public councils, and laid the foundations of great and important changes in the government.

Though nothing could be worse calculated for cultivating the arts of peace, or maintaining peace itself, than the long subordination of vassalage from the king to the meanest gentleman, and the consequent slavery of the lower people (evils inseparable from the feudal system), that system was never able to fix the state in a proper warlike posture, or give it the full exertion of its power for defence, and still less for offence, against a public enemy. The military tenants, unacquainted with obedience, unexperienced in war, held a rank in the troops by their birth, not by their merits or services; composed a disorderly and consequently a feeble army; and, during the few days which they were obliged by their tenures to remain in the field, were often more formidable to their own prince than to foreign powers against whom they were assembled. The sovereigns came gradually to disuse this cumbersome and dangerous machine, so apt to recoil upon the hand which held it; and, exchanging the military service for pecuniary supplies, enlisted forces by means of a contract with particular officers (such as those the Italians denominate *Condottieri*), whom they dismissed at the end of the war.[73] The barons and knights themselves often entered into these engagements with the prince, and were enabled to fill their bands both by the authority which they possessed over their vassals and tenants, and from the great numbers of loose, disorderly people whom they found on their estates, and who willingly embraced an opportunity of gratifying their appetite for war and rapine.

Meanwhile the old Gothic fabric, being neglected, went gradually to decay. Though the conqueror had divided all the lands of England into sixty thousand knight's-fees, the

[72] Rymer, vol. ii. pp. 680, 681, 695, 697. Heming. vol. i. p. 76. Trivet, p. 285.
[73] Cotton's Abr. p. 11.

number of these was insensibly diminished by various artifices; and the king at last found that, by putting the law in
execution, he could assemble a small part only of the ancient
force of the kingdom. It was an usual expedient, for men
who held of the king or great barons by military tenure, to
transfer their land to the Church, and receive it back by
another tenure, called frankalmoigne, by which they were
not bound to perform any service.[74] A law was made against
this practice; but the abuse had probably gone far before it
was attended to, and probably was not entirely corrected by
the new statute, which, like most laws of that age, we may
conjecture to have been but feebly executed by the magistrate against the perpetual interest of so many individuals.
The constable and mareschal, when they mustered the armies,
often in a hurry, and for want of better information, received the service of a baron for fewer knight's-fees than
were due by him; and one precedent of this kind was held
good against the king, and became ever after a reason for
diminishing the service.[75] The rolls of knight's-fees were
inaccurately kept, no care was taken to correct them before
the armies were summoned into the field;[76] it was then too
late to think of examining records and charters, and the service was accepted on the footing which the vassal himself
was pleased to acknowledge, after all the various subdivisions
and conjunctions of property had thrown an obscurity on the
nature and extent of his tenure.[77] It is easy to judge of the
intricacies which would attend disputes of this kind with
individuals, when even the number of military fees belonging
to the Church, whose property was fixed and unalienable, became the subject of controversy; and we find, in particular,
that when the Bishop of Durham was charged with seventy
knight's-fees for the aid levied on occasion of the marriage
of Henry II.'s daughter to the Duke of Saxony, the prelate
acknowledged ten and disowned the other sixty.[78] It is not
known in what manner this difference terminated; but had
the question been concerning an armament to defend the
kingdom, the bishop's service would have probably been received without opposition for ten fees; and this rate must
also have fixed all his future payments. Pecuniary scutages,
therefore, diminished as much as military services.[79] Other

---

[74] Madox's Baronia Anglica, p. 114.   [75] Madox's Baronia Anglica, p. 115.
[76] We hear only of one king, Henry II., who took this pains; and the record
called Liber Niger Scaccarii was the result of it.
[77] Madox's Baronia Anglica, p. 116.
[78] Madox's Baronia Anglica, p. 122. Hist. of Exch. p. 404.
[79] In order to pay the sum of one hundred thousand marks, as King Richard's

methods of filling the exchequer, as well as the armies, must be devised. New situations produced new laws and institutions; and the great alterations in the finances and military power of the crown, as well as the private property, were the source of equal innovations in every part of the legislature or civil government.

The exorbitant estates conferred by the Norman on his barons and chieftains remained not long entire and unimpaired. The landed property was gradually shared out into more hands; and those immense baronies were divided either by provisions to younger children, by partitions among coheirs, by sale, or by escheating to the king, who gratified a great number of his courtiers by dealing them out among them in smaller portions. Such moderate estates, as they required economy and confined the proprietors to live at home, were better calculated for duration, and the order of knights and small barons grew daily more numerous, and began to form a very respectable rank or order in the state. As they were all immediate vassals of the crown by military tenure, they were, by the principles of the feudal law, equally entitled with the greatest barons to a seat in the national or general councils; and this right, though regarded as a privilege which the owners would not entirely relinquish, was also considered as a burden, which they desired to be subjected to on extraordinary occasions only. Hence it was provided in the charter of King John that, while the great barons were summoned to the national council by a particular writ, the small barons, under which appellation the knights were also comprehended, should only be called by a general summons of the sheriff. The distinction between great and small barons, like that between rich and poor, was not exactly defined, but, agreeably to the inaccurate genius of that age, and to the simplicity of ancient government, was left very much to be determined by the discretion of the king and his ministers. It was usual for the prince to require, by a particular summons, the attendance of a baron in one Parliament, and to neglect him in future Parliaments; [80] nor was this uncertainty ever complained of as an injury. He attended when required; he was better pleased,

---

ransom, twenty shillings were imposed on each knight's-fee. Had the fees remained on the original footing as settled by the Conqueror, this scutage would have amounted to ninety thousand marks, which was nearly the sum required. But we find that other grievous taxes were imposed to complete it—a certain proof that many frauds and abuses had prevailed in the roll of knight's-fees.

[80] Chancellor West's Inquiry into the Manner of creating Peers, pp. 43, 46, 47, 55.

on other occasions, to be exempted from the burden, and as he was acknowledged to be of the same order with the greatest barons, it gave them no surprise to see him take his seat in the great council, whether he appeared of his own accord or by a particular summons from the king. The barons by *writ*, therefore, began gradually to intermix themselves with the barons by *tenure;* and as Camden tells us [81] from an ancient manuscript now lost, that after the battle of Evesham a positive law was enacted, prohibiting every baron from appearing in Parliament who was not invited thither by a particular summons, the whole baronage of England held thenceforward their seat by writ, and this important privilege of their tenures was in effect abolished. Only where writs had been regularly continued for some time in one great family, the omission of them would have been regarded as an affront, and even as an injury.

A like alteration gradually took place in the order of earls, who were the highest rank of barons. The dignity of an earl, like that of a baron, was anciently territorial and official; [82] he exercised jurisdiction within his county; he levied the third of the fines to his own profit; he was at once a civil and military magistrate; and though his authority, from the time of the Norman conquest, was hereditary in England, the title was so much connected with the office that, where the king intended to create a new earl, he had no other expedient than to erect a certain territory into a county or earldom, and to bestow it upon the person and his family. [83] But as the sheriffs, who were the vicegerents of the earls, were named by the king and removable at pleasure, he found them more dependent upon him, and endeavored to throw the whole authority and jurisdiction of the office into their hands. This magistrate was at the head of the finances, and levied all the king's rents within the county; he assessed at pleasure the talliages of the inhabitants in royal demesne; he had usually committed to him the management of wards, and often of escheats; he presided in the lower courts of judicature; and thus, though inferior to the earl in dignity, he was soon considered, by this union of the judicial and fiscal powers, and by the confidence reposed in him by the king, as much superior to him in authority, and undermined his influence within his own

---

[81] In Britann. p. 122.   [82] Spellm. Gloss. *in voce* Comes.
[83] Essays on British Antiquities. This practice, however, seems to have been more familiar in Scotland and the kingdoms on the continent than in England.

jurisdiction.[84] It became usual, in creating an earl, to give him a fixed salary, commonly about twenty pounds a year, in lieu of his third of the fines. The diminution of his power kept pace with the retrenchment of his profit; and the dignity of earl, instead of being territorial and official, dwindled into personal and titular. Such was the mighty alterations which already had fully taken place, or were gradually advancing, in the House of Peers, that is, in the Parliament, for there seems anciently to have been no other house.

But though the introduction of barons by writ, and of titular earls, had given some increase to royal authority, there were other causes which counterbalanced those innovations, and tended in a higher degree to diminish the power of the sovereign. The disuse into which the feudal militia had in a great measure fallen made the barons almost entirely forget their dependency on the crown. By the diminution of the number of knight's-fees, the king had no reasonable compensation when he levied scutages, and exchanged their service for money; the alienations of the crown lands had reduced him to poverty; and, above all, the concession of the great charter had set bounds to royal power, and had rendered it more difficult and dangerous for the prince to exert any extraordinary act of arbitrary authority. In this situation it was natural for the king to court the friendship of the lesser barons and knights, whose influence was nowise dangerous to him, and who, being exposed to oppression from their powerful neighbors, sought a legal protection under the shadow of the throne. He desired, therefore, to have their presence in Parliament, where they served to control the turbulent resolutions of the great. To exact a regular attendance of the whole body would have produced confusion, and would have imposed too heavy a burden upon them. To summon only a few by writ, though it was practised, and had a good effect, served not entirely the king's purpose; because these members had no farther authority than attended their personal character, and were eclipsed by the appearance of the more powerful nobility. He therefore dispensed with the attendance of the most of the lesser barons in Parliament; and in return for this indulgence (for such it was then esteemed) required them to choose in each county a certain number of their own body.

---

[84] There are instances of princes of the blood who accepted of the office of Sheriff. Spellman, *in voce* Vicecomes.

whose charges they bore, and who, having gained the confidence, carried with them, of course, the authority of the whole order. This expedient had been practised at different times in the reign of Henry III.,[85] and regularly during that of the present king. The number sent up by each county varied at the will of the prince.[86] They took their seat among the other peers, because by their tenure they belonged to that order.[87] The introducing of them into that house scarcely appeared an innovation; and though it was easily in the king's power, by varying their number, to command the resolutions of the whole Parliament, this circumstance was little attended to in an age when force was more prevalent than laws, and when a resolution, though taken by the majority of a legal assembly, could not be executed if it opposed the will of the more powerful minority.

But there were other important consequences which followed the diminution and consequent disuse of the ancient feudal militia. The king's expense, in levying and maintaining a military force for every enterprise, was increased beyond what his narrow revenues were able to bear. As the scutages of his military tenants, which were accepted in lieu of their personal service, had fallen to nothing, there were no means of supply but from voluntary aids granted him by the Parliament and clergy, or from the talliages which he might levy upon the towns and inhabitants in royal demesne. In the preceding year Edward had been obliged to exact no less than the sixth of all movables from the laity, and a moiety of all ecclesiastical benefices,[88] for his expedition into Poictou and the suppression of the Welsh; and this distressful situation, which was likely often to return upon him and his successors, made him think of a new device, and summon the representatives of all the boroughs to Parliament. This period, which is the twenty-third of his reign, seems to be the real and the true epoch of the House of Commons, and the faint dawn of popular government in England. For the representatives of the counties were only deputies for the smaller barons and lesser nobility; and the former precedent of representatives from the boroughs, who were summoned by the Earl of Leicester, was regarded as the act of a violent usurpation, had been discontinued in

---

[85] Rot. Claus. 38 Hen. III. m. 7. and 12. d ; as also Rot. Claus. 42 Hen. III. m. 1. d.   Prynne's Pref. to Cotton's Abridgment.

[86] Brady's Answer to Petyt, from the Records, p. 151.

[87] Brady's Treatise of Boroughs, App. No. 13.

[88] Brady's Treatise of Boroughs, App. No. 13, p. 31, from the Records. Heming. vol. i. p. 52.   Matt. West. p. 422.   Ryley, p. 462.

all the subsequent Parliaments, and if such a measure had not become necessary on other accounts, that precedent was more likely to blast than give credit to it.

During the course of several years the kings of England, in imitation of other European princes, had embraced the salutary policy of encouraging and protecting the lower and more industrious orders of the state, whom they found well disposed to obey the laws and civil magistrate, and whose ingenuity and labor furnished commodities requisite for the ornament of peace and support of war. Though the inhabitants of the country were still left at the disposal of their imperious lords, many attempts were made to give more security and liberty to citizens, and make them enjoy unmolested the fruits of their industry. Boroughs were erected by royal patent within the demesne lands; liberty of trade was conferred upon them; the inhabitants were allowed to farm, at a fixed rent, their own tolls and customs; [89] they were permitted to elect their own magistrates; justice was administered to them by these magistrates, without obliging them to attend the sheriff or county court; and some shadow of independence, by means of these equitable privileges, was gradually acquired by the people.[90] The king, however, retained still the power of levying talliages or taxes upon them at pleasure; [91] and though their poverty and the customs of the age made these demands neither frequent nor exorbitant, such unlimited authority in the sovereign was a sensible check upon commerce, and was utterly incompatible with all the principles of a free government. But when the multiplied necessities of the crown produced a greater avidity for supply, the king, whose prerogative entitled him to exact it, found that he had not power sufficient to enforce his edicts, and that it was necessary, before he imposed taxes, to smooth the way for his demand, and to obtain the previous consent of the boroughs by solicitations, remonstrances, and authority. The inconvenience of transacting this business with every particular borough was soon felt; and Edward became sensible that the most expeditious way of obtaining supply was to assemble the deputies of all the boroughs, to lay before them the necessities of the state, to discuss the matter in their presence, and to require their

<hr/>

[89] Madox, Firma Burgi, p. 21.   [90] Brady of Boroughs, App. No. 1, 2, 3.

[91] The king had not only the power of talliating the inhabitants within his own demesnes, but that of granting to particular barons the power of talliating the inhabitants within theirs. See Brady's Answer to Petyt, p. 118. Madox's Hist. of the Exchequer, p. 518.

consent to the demands of their sovereign. For this reason he issued writs to the sheriffs, enjoining them to send to Parliament, along with two knights of the shire, two deputies from each borough within their county,[92] and these provided with sufficient powers from their community to consent, in their name, to what he and his council should require of them. "As it is a most equitable rule," says he, in his preamble to this writ, "that what concerns all should be approved by all, and common dangers be repelled by united efforts"[93]—a noble principle, which may seem to indicate a liberal mind in the king, and which laid the foundation of a free and equitable government.

After the election of these deputies by the aldermen and common council, they gave sureties for their attendance before the king and Parliament. Their charges were respectively borne by the borough which sent them; and they had so little idea of appearing as legislators, a character extremely wide of their low rank and condition,[94] that no intelligence could be more disagreeable to any borough than to find that they must elect, or to any individual than that he was elected, to a trust from which no profit or honor could possibly be derived.[95] They composed not, properly speaking, any essential part of the Parliament; they sat apart both from the barons and knights,[96] who disdained to mix with such mean personages; after they had given their consent to the taxes required of them, their business being then finished, they separated, even though the Parliament still continued to sit, and to canvass the national business;[97] and as they all consisted of men who were real burgesses of the place from which they were sent, the sheriff, when he found no person of abilities or wealth sufficient for the office, often used the freedom of omitting particular boroughs in his returns; and as he received the thanks of the people for this indulgence, he gave no displeasure to the court, who

[92] Writs were issued to about one hundred and twenty cities and boroughs.

[93] Brady of Boroughs, pp. 25, 33, from the Records. The writs of the Parliament immediately preceding remain, and the return of knights is there required, but not a word of the boroughs—a demonstration that this was the very year in which they commenced. In the year immediately preceding the taxes were levied by a seeming free consent of each particular borough, beginning with London. Id. pp. 31, 32, 33, from the Records. Also his answers to Petyt, pp. 40, 41.

[94] Reliquia Spellm. p. 64. Prynne's Preface to Cotton's Abridgment, and the Abridg. passim.   [95] Brady of Boroughs, pp. 59, 60.

[96] Brady of Boroughs, pp. 37, 38. from the Records, and Appendix, p. 19. Also his Appendix to his Answer to Petyt, Record ; and his Gloss. *in verb*. Communitas Regn. p. 33.

[97] Ryley's Placit. Parl. pp. 241, 242, &c.   Cotton's Abridgment, p. 14.

levied on all the boroughs, without distinction, the tax agreed to by the majority of deputies.[98]

The union, however, of the representatives from the boroughs gave gradually more weight to the whole order; and it became customary for them, in return for the supplies which they granted, to prefer petitions to the crown for the redress of any particular grievance of which they found reason to complain. The more the king's demands multiplied, the faster these petitions increased both in number and authority; and the prince found it difficult to refuse men whose grants had supported his throne, and to whose assistance he might so soon be obliged again to have recourse. The Commons, however, were still much below the rank of legislators.[99] Their petitions, though they received a verbal assent from the throne, were only the rudiments of laws. The judges were afterwards intrusted with the power of putting them into form; and the king, by adding to them the sanction of his authority, and that sometimes without the assent of the nobles, bestowed validity upon them. The age did not refine so much as to perceive the danger of these irregularities. No man was displeased that the sovereign, at the desire of any class of men, should issue an order which appeared only to concern that class; and his predecessors were so near possessing the whole legislative power that he gave no disgust by assuming it in this seemingly inoffensive manner. But time and farther experience gradually opened men's eyes, and corrected these abuses. It was found that no laws could be fixed for one order of men without affecting the whole, and that the force and efficacy of laws depended entirely on the terms employed in wording them. The House of Peers, therefore, the most powerful order in the state, with reason expected that their assent should be expressely granted to all public ordinances;[100] and in the reign of Henry V. the Commons re-

---

[98] Brady of Boroughs, p. 52, from the Records. There is even an instance in the reign of Edward III. when the king named all the deputies. Id. Answ. to Petyt, p. 161. If he fairly named the most considerable and creditable burgesses, little exception would be taken; as their business was not to check the king, but to reason with him, and consent to his demands. It was not till the reign of Richard II. that the sheriffs were deprived of the power of omitting boroughs at pleasure. See Stat. at large, 5th Richard II. cap. 4.

[99] See note [Y] at the end of the volume.

[100] In those instances found in Cotton's Abridgment where the king appears to answer of himself the petitions of the Commons, he probably exerted no more than that power, which was long inherent in the crown, of regulating matters by royal edicts or proclamations. But no durable or general statute seems ever to have been made by the king from the petitions of the Commons alone, without the assent of the Peers. It is more likely that the Peers alone, without the Commons, would enact statutes.

quired that no laws should be framed merely upon their petitions, unless the statutes were worded by themselves, and had passed their House in the form of a bill.[101]

But as the same causes which had produced a partition of property continued still to operate, the number of knights and lesser barons, or what the English call the gentry, perpetually increased, and they sunk into a rank still more inferior to the great nobility. The equality of tenure was lost in the great inferiority of power and property; and the House of Representatives from the counties was gradually separated from that of the Peers, and formed a distinct order in the state.[102] The growth of commerce meanwhile augmented the private wealth and consideration of the burgesses; the frequent demands of the crown increased their public importance; and as they resembled the knights of shires in one material circumstance, that of representing particular bodies of men, it no longer appeared unsuitable to unite them together in the same house, and to confound their rights and privileges.[103] Thus the third estate, that of the Commons, reached at last its present form; and as the country gentlemen made thenceforwards no scruple of appearing as deputies from the boroughs, the distinction between the members was entirely lost, and the Lower House acquired thence a great accession of weight and importance in the kingdom. Still, however, the office of this estate was very different from that which it has since exercised with so much advantage to the public. Instead of checking and controlling the authority of the king, they were naturally induced to adhere to him as the great fountain of law and justice, and to support him against the power of the aristocracy, which at once was the source of oppression to themselves and disturbed him in the execution of the laws. The king, in his turn, gave countenance to an order of men so useful and so little dangerous; the Peers also were obliged to pay them some consideration; and by this means the third estate, formerly so abject in England, as well as in all other European nations, rose, by slow degrees, to their present importance, and, in their progress, made arts and commerce, the necessary attendants of liberty and equality, flourish in the kingdom.[104]

What sufficiently proves that the commencement of the

[101] Brady's Answer to Petyt, p. 85, from the Records.
[102] Cotton's Abridgment, p. 18.   [103] See note [Z] at the end of the volume.
[104] See note [AA] at the end of the volume.

house of burgesses, who are the true Commons, was not an affair of chance, but arose from the necessities of the present situation, is that Edward, at the very same time, summoned deputies from the inferior clergy, the first that ever met in England,[105] and he required them to impose taxes on their constituents for the public service. Formerly the ecclesiastical benefices bore no part of the burdens of the state. The pope, indeed, of late had often levied impositions upon them; he had sometimes granted this power to the sovereign.[106] The king himself had in the preceding year exacted, by menaces and violence, a very grievous tax of half the revenues of the clergy; but as this precedent was dangerous, and could not easily be repeated in a government which required the consent of the subject to any extraordinary resolution, Edward found it more prudent to assemble a lower house of convocation, to lay before them his necessities, and to ask some supply. But on this occasion he met with difficulties. Whether that the clergy thought themselves the most independent body in the kingdom or were disgusted by the former exorbitant impositions, they absolutely refused their assent to the king's demand of a fifth of their movables; and it was not till a second meeting that, on their persisting in this refusal, he was willing to accept of a tenth. The barons and knights granted him, without hesitation, an eleventh; the burgesses, a seventh. But the clergy still scrupled to meet on the king's writ, lest by such an instance of obedience they should seem to acknowledge the authority of the temporal power; and this compromise was at last fallen upon, that the king should issue his writ to the archbishop, and that the archbishop should, in consequence of it, summon the clergy, who, as they then appeared to obey their spiritual superior, no longer hesitated to meet in convocation. This expedient, however, was the cause why the ecclesiastics were separated into two houses of convocation under their several archbishops, and formed not one estate, as in other countries of Europe, which was at first the king's intention.[107] We now return to the course of our narration.

Edward, conscious of the reasons of disgust which he had given to the King of Scots, informed of the dispositions of that people, and expecting the most violent effects of their

<hr/>

[105] Archbishop Wake's State of the Church of England, p. 235. Brady of Boroughs, p. 34. Gilbert's Hist. of the Exch. p. 46.
[106] Annal. Waverl. pp. 227, 228. T. Wykes, pp. 99, 120.
[107] Gilbert's Hist. of Exch. pp. 51, 54.

resentment, which he knew he had so well merited, employed the supplies granted him by his people in making preparations against the hostilities of his northern neighbor. When in this situation, he received intelligence of the treaty secretly concluded between John and Philip; and though uneasy at this concurrence of a French and Scottish war, he resolved not to encourage his enemies by a pusillanimous behavior, or by yielding to their united efforts. He summoned John to perform the duty of a vassal, and to send him a supply of forces against an invasion from France, with which he was then threatened; he next required that the fortresses of Berwick, Jedborough, and Roxborough should be put into his hands as a security during the war; [108] he cited John to appear in an English Parliament to be held at Newcastle; and when none of these successive demands were complied with, he marched northward with numerous forces, thirty thousand foot and four thousand horse, to chastise his rebellious vassal. The Scottish nation, who had little reliance on the vigor and abilities of their prince, assigned him a council of twelve noblemen, in whose hands the sovereignty was really lodged, [109] and who put the country in the best posture of which the present distractions would admit. A great army, composed of forty thousand infantry, though supported only by five hundred cavalry, advanced to the frontiers, and, after a fruitless attempt upon Carlisle, marched eastwards to defend those provinces which Edward was preparing to attack. But some of the most considerable of the Scottish nobles, Robert Bruce, the father and son, the Earls of March and Angus, prognosticating the ruin of their country from the concurrence of intestine divisions and a foreign invasion, endeavored here to ingratiate themselves with Edward by an early submission; and the king, encouraged by this favorable incident, led his army into the enemy's country, and crossed the Tweed without opposition at Coldstream. [1296.] He then received a message from John, by which that prince, having now procured for himself and his nation Pope Celestine's dispensation from former oaths, renounced the homage which had been done to England, and set Edward at defiance. [110] This bravado was but ill supported by the military operations of the Scots. Berwick was already taken by assault; Sir William

---

[108] Rymer, vol. ii. p. 692. Walsing. p. 64. Heming, vol. i. p. 84. Trivet, p. 286. [109] Heming, vol. i. p. 75.
[110] Rymer, vol. ii. p. 607. Walsing. p. 66. Heming. vol. p. 82.

Douglas, the governor, was made prisoner; above seven thousand of the garrison were put to the sword; and Edward, elated by this great advantage, despatched Earl Warrenne, with twelve thousand men, to lay siege to Dunbar, which was defended by the flower of the Scottish nobility.

The Scots, sensible of the importance of the place, which, if taken, laid their whole country open to the enemy, advanced with their main army, under the command of the Earls of Buchan, Lenox, and Marre, in order to relieve it. Warrenne, not dismayed at the great superiority of their number, marched out to give them battle. He attacked them with great vigor; and as undisciplined troops, when numerous. are but the more exposed to a panic upon any alarm, he soon threw them into confusion, and chased them off the field with great slaughter. The loss of the Scots is said to have amounted to twenty thousand men. The castle of Dunbar, with all its garrison, surrendered next day to Edward, who, after the battle, had brought up the main body of the English, and who now proceeded with an assured confidence of success. The castle of Roxborough was yielded by James, Steward of Scotland; and that nobleman, from whom is descended the royal family of Stuart, was again obliged to swear fealty to Edward. After a feeble resistance, the castles of Edinburgh and Stirling opened their gates to the enemy. All the southern parts were instantly subdued by the English; and to enable them the better to reduce the northern, whose inaccessible situation seemed to give them some more security, Edward sent for a strong reinforcement of Welsh and Irish, who, being accustomed to a desultory kind of war, were the best fitted to pursue the fugitive Scots into the recesses of their lakes and mountains. But the spirit of the nation was already broken by their misfortunes; and the feeble and timid Baliol, discontented with his own subjects and overawed by the English, abandoned all those resources which his people might yet have possessed in this extremity. He hastened to make his submissions to Edward; he expressed the deepest penitence for his disloyalty to his liege lord; and he made a solemn and irrevocable resignation of his crown into the hands of that monarch.[111] Edward marched northwards to Aberdeen and Elgin without meeting an enemy; no Scotch-

[111] Rymer vol. ii. p. 718. Walsing. p. 67. Heming. vol. i. p. 99. Trivet, p. 292.

man approached him but to pay him submission and do him homage; even the turbulent Highlanders, ever refractory to their own princes and averse to the restraint of laws, endeavored to prevent the devastation of their country by giving him early proofs of obedience ; and Edward, having brought the whole kingdom to a seeming state of tranquillity, returned to the south with his army.   There was a stone to which the popular superstition of the Scots paid the highest veneration; all their kings were seated on it when they received the right of inauguration.   An ancient tradition assured them that wherever this stone was placed their nation should always govern; and it was carefully preserved at Scone as the true palladium of their monarchy, and their ultimate resource amidst all their misfortunes.   Edward got possession of it, and carried it with him to England.[112]   He gave orders to destroy the records and all those monuments of antiquity which might preserve the memory of the independence of the kingdom and refute the English claims of superiority.   The Scots pretend that he also destroyed all the annals preserved in their convents ; but it is not probable that a nation so rude and unpolished should be possessed of any history which deserves much to be regretted.   The great seal of Baliol was broken ; and that prince himself was carried prisoner to London, and committed to custody in the Tower.   Two years after he was restored to liberty, and submitted to a voluntary banishment in France, where, without making any farther attempts for the recovery of his royalty, he died in a private station.   Earl Warrenne was left governor of Scotland ;[113] Englishmen were intrusted with the chief offices ; and Edward, flattering himself that he had attained the end of all his wishes, and that the numerous acts of fraud and violence which he had practised against Scotland had terminated in the final reduction of that kingdom, returned with his victorious army into England.

An attempt which he made about the same time for the recovery of Guienne was not equally successful.   He sent thither an army of seven thousand men, under the command of his brother, the Earl of Lancaster.   That prince gained at first some advantages over the French at Bordeaux ; but he was soon after seized with a distemper, of which he died at Bayonne.   The command devolved on the Earl of Lin-

112 Walsing. p. 68.   Trivet, p. 299.
113 Rymer, vol. ii. p. 726.   Trivet, p. 295.

coln, who was not able to perform anything considerable during the rest of the campaign.[114]

But the active and ambitious spirit of Edward, while his conquests brought such considerable accessions to the English monarchy, could not be satisfied so long as Guienne, the ancient patrimony of his family, was wrested from him by the dishonest artifices of the French monarch. Finding that the distance of that province rendered all his efforts against it feeble and uncertain, he purposed to attack France in a quarter where she appeared more vulnerable; and with this view he married his daughter Elizabeth to John, Earl of Holland, and at the same time contracted an alliance with Guy, Earl of Flanders, stipulated to pay him the sum of seventy-five thousand pounds, and projected an invasion, with their united forces, upon Philip, their common enemy.[115] He hoped that when he himself, at the head of the English, Flemish, and Dutch armies, reinforced by his German allies, to whom he had promised or remitted considerable sums, should enter the frontiers of France and threaten the capital itself, Philip would at last be obliged to relinquish his acquisitions, and purchase peace by the restitution of Guienne. But, in order to set this great machine in movement, considerable supplies were requisite from the Parliament; and Edward, without much difficulty, obtained from the barons and knights a new grant of a twelfth of all their movables, and from the boroughs that of an eighth. The great and almost unlimited power of the king over the latter enabled him to throw the heavier part of the burden on them; and the prejudices which he seems always to have entertained against the Church, on account of the former zeal of the clergy for the Montfort faction, made him resolve to load them with still more considerable impositions, and he required of them a fifth of their movables. But he here met with an opposition which for some time disconcerted all his measures, and engaged him in enterprises that were somewhat dangerous to *him*, and would have proved fatal to any of his predecessors.

Boniface VIII., who had succeeded Celestine in the papal throne, was a man of the most lofty and enterprising spirit; and, though not endowed with that severity of manners which commonly accompanies ambition in men of his order, he was determined to carry the authority of the tiara and his dominion over the temporal power to as great a

114 Heming. vol. i. pp. 72, 73, 74.   115 Rymer, vol. ii. p. 761. Walsing. p. 68.
38

height as it had ever attained in any former period. Sensible that his immediate predecessors, by oppressing the Church in every province of Christendom, had extremely alienated the affections of the clergy, and had afforded the civil magistrate a pretence for laying like impositions on ecclesiastical revenues, he attempted to resume the former station of the sovereign pontiff, and to establish himself as the common protector of the spiritual order against all invaders. For this purpose he issued, very early in his pontificate, a general bull prohibiting all princes from levying, without his consent, any taxes upon the clergy, and all clergymen from submitting to such impositions; and he threatened both of them with the penalties of excommunication in case of disobedience.[116] This important edict is said to have been procured by the solicitation of Robert de Winchelsea, Archbishop of Canterbury, who intended to employ it as a rampart against the violent extortions which the Church had felt from Edward, and the still greater which that prince's multiplied necessities gave them reason to apprehend. When a demand, therefore, was made on the clergy of a fifth of their movables—a tax which was probably much more grievous than a fifth of their revenue, as their lands were mostly stocked with their cattle and cultivated by their villeins—the clergy took shelter under the bull of Pope Boniface, and pleaded conscience in refusing compliance.[117] The king came not immediately to extremities on this repulse; but, after locking up all their granaries and barns, and prohibiting all rent to be paid them, he appointed a new synod, to confer with him upon his demand. The primate, not dismayed by these proofs of Edward's resolution, here plainly told him that the clergy owed obedience to two sovereigns, their spiritual and their temporal, but their duty bound them to a much stricter attachment to the former than to the latter; they could not comply with his commands (for such, in some measure, the requests of the crown were then deemed), in contradiction to the express prohibition of the sovereign pontiff.[118]

[1297.] The clergy had seen, in many instances, that Edward paid little regard to those numerous privileges on which they set so high a value. He had formerly seized, in an arbitrary manner, all the money and plate belonging to

---

[116] Rymer, vol. ii. p. 706. Heming. vol. i. p. 104.
[117] Heming. vol. i. p. 107. Trivet, p. 296. Chron. Dunst. vol. ii. p. 652.
[118] Heming. vol. i. p. 107.

the churches and convents, and had applied them to the public service; [119] and they could not but expect more violent treatment on this sharp refusal, grounded on such dangerous principles. Instead of applying to the pope for a relaxation of his bull, he resolved immediately to employ the power in his hands; and he told the ecclesiastics that, since they refused to support the civil government, they were unworthy to receive any benefit from it, and he would accordingly put them out of the protection of the laws. This vigorous measure was immediately carried into execution.[120] Orders were issued to the judges to receive no cause brought before them by the clergy; to hear and decide all causes in which they were defendants; to do every man justice against them; to do them justice against nobody.[121] The ecclesiastics soon found themselves in the most miserable situation imaginable. They could not remain in their own houses or convents, for want of subsistence. If they went abroad in quest of maintenance, they were dismounted, robbed of their horses and clothes, abused by every ruffian, and no redress could be obtained by them for the most violent injury. The primate himself was attacked on the highway, was stripped of his equipage and furniture, and was at last reduced to board himself, with a single servant, in the house of a country clergyman.[122] The king meanwhile remained an indifferent spectator of all these violences; and without employing his officers in committing any immediate injury on the priests, which might have appeared invidious and oppressive, he took ample vengeance on them for their obstinate refusal of his demands. Though the archbishop issued a general sentence of excommunication against all who attacked the persons or property of ecclesiastics, it was not regarded; while Edward enjoyed the satisfaction of seeing the people become the voluntary instruments of his justice against them, and inure themselves to throw off that respect for the sacred order by which they had so long been overawed and governed.

The spirits of the clergy were at last broken by this harsh treatment. Besides that the whole province of York, which lay nearest the danger that still hung over them from the Scots, voluntarily, from the first, voted a fifth of their movables; the Bishops of Salisbury, Ely, and some others

[119] Walsing. p. 65. Heming. vol. i. p. 51.
[120] Walsing. p. 69. Heming. vol. i. p. 107.
[121] Matt. West. p. 429.
[122] Heming. vol. i. p. 109.

made a composition for the secular clergy within their dioceses; and they agreed not to pay the fifth, which would have been an act of disobedience to Boniface's bull, but to deposit a sum equivalent in some church appointed them, whence it was taken by the king's officers.[123] Many particular convents and clergymen made payment of a like sum, and received the king's protection.[124] Those who had not ready money entered into recognizances for the payment; and there was scarcely found one ecclesiastic in the kingdom who seemed willing to suffer, for the sake of religious privileges, this new species of martyrdom, the most tedious and languishing of any, the most mortifying to spiritual pride, and not rewarded by that crown of glory which the Church holds up with such ostentation, to her devoted adherents.

But as the money granted by Parliament, though considerable, was not sufficient to supply the king's necessities, and that levied by compositions with the clergy came in slowly, Edward was obliged, for the obtaining of farther supply, to exert his arbitrary power, and to lay an oppressive hand on all orders of men in the kingdom. He limited the merchants in the quantity of wool allowed to be exported, and at the same time forced them to pay him a duty of forty shillings a sack, which was computed to be above the third of the value.[125] He seized all the rest of the wool, as well as all the leather of the kingdom, into his hands, and disposed of these commodities for his own benefit.[126] He required the sheriffs of each county to supply him with two thousand quarters of wheat, and as many of oats, which he permitted them to seize wherever they could find them. The cattle and other commodities necessary for supplying his army were laid hold of without the consent of the owners;[127] and though he promised to pay afterwards the equivalent of all these goods, men saw but little probability that a prince who submitted so little to the limitations of law could ever, amidst his multiplied necessities, be reduced to a strict observance of his engagements. He showed, at the same time, an equal disregard to the principles of the feudal law, by which all the lands of his kingdom were held. In order to increase his army, and enable him to support that great effort which he intended to make against

[123] Heming. vol. i. pp. 108, 109.   Chron. Dunst. p. 653.
[124] Chron. Dunst. vol. ii. p. 654.   [125] Walsing. p. 69.   Trivet, p. 296.
[126] Heming. vol. i. pp. 52, 110.   [127] Heming. vol. i. p. 111.

France, he required the attendance of every proprietor of land possessed of twenty pounds a year, even though he held not of the crown, and was not obliged by his tenure to perform any such service.[128]

These acts of violence and of arbitrary power, notwithstanding the great personal regard generally borne to the king, bred murmurs in every order of men, and it was not long ere some of the great nobility, jealous of their own privileges as well as of national liberty, gave countenance and authority to these complaints. Edward assembled on the seacoast an army which he purposed to send over to Gascony, while he himself should in person make an impression on the side of Flanders; and he intended to put these forces under the command of Humphrey Bohun, Earl of Hereford, the Constable, and Roger Bigod, Earl of Norfolk, the Mareschal of England. But these two powerful earls refused to execute his commands, and affirmed that they were only obliged by their office to attend his person in the wars. A violent altercation ensued; and the king, in the height of his passion, addressing himself to the constable, exclaimed, "Sir earl, by God, you shall either go or hang!" "By God, sir king," replied Hereford, "I will neither go nor hang!"[129] And he immediately departed with the mareschal and above thirty other considerable barons.

Upon this opposition, the king laid aside the project of an expedition against Guienne, and assembled the forces which he himself purposed to transport into Flanders. But the two earls, irritated in the contest and elated by impunity, pretending that none of their ancestors had ever served in that country, refused to perform the duty of their office in mustering the army.[130] The king, now finding it advisable to proceed with moderation, instead of attainting the earls, who possessed their dignities by hereditary right, appointed Thomas de Berkeley and Geoffrey de Geyneville to act, in that emergence, as constable and mareschal.[131] He endeavored to reconcile himself with the Church; took the primate again into favor;[132] made him, in conjunction with Reginald de Grey, tutor to the prince, whom he intended to appoint guardian of the kingdom during his absence; and he even assembled a great number of the nobility in Westminster-hall, to whom he deigned to make an apology for his past

[128] Walsing. p. 69. [129] Heming. vol. i. p. 112.
[130] Rymer, vol. ii. p. 783. Walsing. p. 70. [131] Matt. West. p. 430.
[132] Heming. vol. i. p. 113. [133] Heming. vol. i. p. 114. Matt. West. p. 430.

conduct. He pleaded the urgent necessities of the crown; his extreme want of money; his engagements from honor, as well as interest to support his foreign allies; and he promised, if ever he returned in safety, to redress all their grievances, to restore the execution of the laws, and to make all his subjects compensation for the losses which they had sustained. Meanwhile he begged them to suspend their animosities; to judge of him by his future conduct, of which, he hoped, he should be more master; to remain faithful to his government, or, if he perished in the present war, to preserve their allegiance to his son and successor.[183]

There were certainly, from the concurrence of discontents among the great and grievances of the people, materials sufficient in any other period to have kindled a civil war in England; but the vigor and abilities of Edward kept every one in awe; and his dexterity, in stopping on the brink of danger, and retracting the measures to which he had been pushed by his violent temper and arbitrary principles, saved the nation from so great a calamity. The two great earls dared not to break out into open violence; they proceeded no farther than framing a remonstrance, which was delivered to the king at Winchelsea, when he was ready to embark for Flanders. They there complained of the violations of the great charter and that of forests; the violent seizures of corn, leather, cattle, and, above all, of wool, a commodity which they affirmed to be equal in value to half the lands of the kingdom; the arbitrary imposition of forty shillings a sack on the small quantity of wool allowed to be exported by the merchants; and they claimed an immediate redress of all these grievances.[184] The king told them that the greater part of his council were now at a distance, and without their advice he could not deliberate on measures of so great importance.[135]

But the constable and mareschal, with the barons of their party, resolved to take advantage of Edward's absence, and to obtain an explicit assent to their demands. When summoned to attend the Parliament at London, they came with a great body of cavalry and infantry, and, before they would enter the city, required that the gates should be put into their custody.[136] The primate, who secretly favored all their pretensions, advised the council to comply; and thus they

134 Walsing. p. 72.   Heming. vol. i. p. 115.   Trivet, p. 302.
135 Walsing. p. 72.   Heming. vol. i. p. 117.   Trivet, p. 304.
136 Heming. vol. i. p. 138.

became masters both of the young prince and of the resolutions of Parliament. Their demands, however, were moderate, and such as sufficiently justify the purity of their intentions in all their past measures: they only required that the two charters should receive a solemn confirmation ; that a clause should be added to secure the nation forever against all impositions and taxes without consent of Parliament ; and that they themselves and their adherents, who had refused to attend the king into Flanders, should be pardoned for the offence, and should be again received into favor.[137] The Prince of Wales and his council assented to these terms; and the charters were sent over to the king in Flanders, to be there confirmed by him. Edward felt the utmost reluctance to this measure, which, he apprehended, would for the future impose fetters on his conduct, and set limits to his lawless authority. On various pretences he delayed three days giving any answer to the deputies; and when the pernicious consequences of this refusal were represented to him, he was at last obliged, after many internal struggles, to affix his seal to the charters, as also to the clause that bereaved him of the power, which he had hitherto assumed, of imposing arbitrary taxes upon the people.[138]

That we may finish at once this interesting transaction concerning the settlement of the charters, we shall briefly mention the subsequent events which relate to it. The constable and mareschal, informed of the king's compliance, were satisfied; and not only ceased from disturbing the government, but assisted the regency with their power against the Scots, who had risen in arms, and had thrown off the yoke of England.[139] But being sensible that the smallest pretence would suffice to make Edward retract these detested laws, which, though they had often received the sanction both of king and Parliament, and had been acknowledged during three reigns, were never yet deemed to have sufficient validity, they insisted that he should again confirm them on his return to England, and should thereby renounce all plea which he might derive from his residing in a foreign country, when he formerly affixed his seal to them.[140] It appeared that they judged aright of Edward's character and intentions: he delayed his confirmation as long as possible ; and when the fear of worse consequences

[137] Walsing. p. 73.   Heming. vol. i. pp. 138, 139, 140, 141.   Trivet, p. 308.
[138] Walsing. p. 74.   Heming. ol.
[139] Heming. vol. i. p. 143.   [140] Heming. vol. i. p. 159.

obliged him again to comply, he expressly added a salvo for his royal dignity or prerogative, which in effect enervated the whole force of the charters.[141] The two earls and their adherents left the Parliament in disgust; and the king was constrained, on a future occasion, to grant to the people, without any subterfuge, a pure and absolute confirmation of those laws [142] which were so much the object of their passionate affection. Even farther securities were then provided for the establishment of national privileges. Three knights were appointed to be chosen in each county, and were invested with the power of punishing, by fine and imprisonment, every transgression or violation of the charters [143]—a precaution which, though it was soon disused, as encroaching too much on royal prerogative, proves the attachment which the English in that age bore to liberty, and their well-grounded jealousy of the arbitrary disposition of Edward.

The work, however, was not yet entirely finished and complete. In order to execute the lesser charter, it was requisite, by new perambulations, to set bounds to the royal forests, and to disafforest all land which former encroachments had comprehended within their limits. Edward discovered the same reluctance to comply with this equitable demand; and it was not till after many delays on his part, and many solicitations and requests, and even menaces of war and violence,[144] on the part of the barons, that the perambulations were made, and exact boundaries fixed, by a jury in each county, to the extent of his forests.[145] Had not his ambitious and active temper raised him so many foreign enemies, and obliged him to have recourse so often to the assistance of his subjects, it is not likely that those concessions could ever have been extorted from him.

But while the people, after so many successful struggles, deemed themselves happy in the secure possession of their privileges, they were surprised, in 1305, to find that Edward had secretly applied to Rome, and had procured from that mercenary court an absolution from all the oaths and engagements, which he had so often reiterated, to observe both the charters. There are some historians [146] so credulous as

141 Heming. vol. i. pp. 167, 168.   142 Heming, vol. i. p. 168.
143 Heming. vol. i. p. 170.
144 Walsing. p. 80.   We are told by Tyrrel, vol. ii. p. 145, from the chronicle of St. Alban's, that the barons, not content with the execution of the charter of forests, demanded of Edward as high terms as had been imposed on his father by the Earl of Leicester; but no other historian mentions this particular.
145 Heming. vol. i. p. 171.   Matt. West. pp. 431, 433.
146 Brady, vol. ii. p. 84.   Carte, vol. ii. p. 292.

to imagine that this perilous step was taken by him for no other purpose than to acquire the merit of granting a new confirmation of the charters, as he did soon after; and a confirmation so much the more unquestionable as it could never after be invalidated by his successors, on pretence of any force or violence which had been imposed upon him. But besides that this might have been done with a better grace if he had never applied for any such absolution, the whole tenor of his conduct proves him to be little suscepti- ble of such refinements in patriotism; and this very deed itself, in which he anew confirmed the charters, carries on the face of it a very opposite presumption. Though he ratified the charters in general, he still took advantage of the papal bull so far as to invalidate the late perambulations of the forests, which had been made with such care and atten- tion, and to reserve to himself the power, in case of favor- able incidents, to extend as much as formerly those arbi- trary jurisdictions. If the power was not in fact made use of, we can only conclude that the favorable incidents did not offer.

Thus, after the contests of near a whole century, and these ever accompanied with violent jealousies, often with public convulsions, the great charter was finally established; and the English nation have the honor of extorting, by their perseverance, this concession from the ablest, the most war- like, and the most ambitious of all their princes.[147] It is computed that above thirty confirmations of the charter were at different times required of several kings, and granted by them in full Parliament—a precaution which, while it dis- covers some ignorance of the true nature of law and gov- ernment, proves a laudable jealousy of national privileges in the people, and an extreme anxiety lest contrary prece- dents should ever be pleaded as an authority for infringing them. Accordingly we find that, though arbitrary practices often prevailed, and were even able to establish themselves into settled customs, the validity of the great charter was never afterwards formally disputed; and that grant was still regarded as the basis of English government, and the sure rule by which the authority of every custom was to be tried and canvassed. The jurisdiction of the Star-chamber, martial

[147] It must, however, be remarked that the king never forgave the chief actors in this transaction; and he found means afterwards to oblige both the constable and mareschal to resign their offices into his hands. The former received a new grant of it; but the office of mareschal was given to Thomas of Brotherton, the king's second son.

law, imprisonment by warrants from the privy council, and
other practices of a like nature, though established for several centuries, were scarcely ever allowed by the English
to be parts of their constitution ; the affection of the nation
for liberty still prevailed over all precedent, and even all
political reasoning. The exercise of these powers, after
being long the source of secret murmurs among the people,
was, in fulness of time, solemnly abolished as illegal, at least
as oppressive, by the whole legislative authority.

To return to the period from which this account of the
charters has led us. Though the king's impatience to appear at the head of his armies in Flanders made him overlook all considerations, either of domestic discontents or of
commotions among the Scots, his embarkation had been so
long retarded by the various obstructions thrown in his way
that he lost the proper season for action, and, after his
arrival, made no progress against the enemy. The King of
France, taking advantage of his absence, had broken into
the Low Countries ; had defeated the Flemings in the battle
of Furnes ; had made himself master of Lisle, St. Omer,
Courtrai, and Ypres ; and seemed in a situation to take full
vengeance on the Earl of Flanders, his rebellious vassal.
But Edward, seconded by an English army of fifty thousand
men (for this is the number assigned by historians [148]), was
able to stay the career of his victories ; and Philip, finding all
the weak resources of his kingdom already exhausted, began
to dread a reverse of fortune, and to apprehend an invasion
of France itself. The King of England, on the other hand,
disappointed of assistance from Adolph, King of the Romans, which he had purchased at a very high price, and
finding many urgent calls for his presence in England, was
desirous of ending, on any honorable terms, a war which
served only to divert his force from the execution of more
important projects. This disposition in both monarchs soon
produced a cessation of hostilities for two years, and engaged them to submit their differences to the arbitration of
Pope Boniface.

[1298.] Boniface was among the last of the sovereign
pontiffs that exercised an authority over the temporal jurisdiction of princes ; and these exorbitant pretensions, which
he had been tempted to assume from the successful example
of his predecessors, but of which the season was now past,
involved him in so many calamities, and were attended with

[148] Heming. vol. p. 146.

so unfortunate a catastrophe, that they have been secretly abandoned, though never openly relinquished, by his successors in the apostolic chair. Edward and Philip, equally jealous of papal claims, took care to insert in their reference that Boniface was made judge of the difference, by their consent, as a private person, not by any right of his pontificate , and the pope, without seeming to be offended at this mortifying clause, proceeded to give a sentence between them in which they both acquiesced.[149] He brought them to agree that their union should be cemented by a double marriage; that of Edward himself, who was now a widower, with Margaret, Philip's sister, and that of the Prince of Wales with Isabella, daughter of that monarch.[150] Philip was likewise willing to restore Guienne to the English, which he had, indeed, no good pretence to detain; but he insisted that the Scots and their king, John Baliol, should, as his allies, be comprehended in the treaty, and should be restored to their liberty. Their difference, after several disputes, was compromised by their making mutual sacrifices to each other. Edward agreed to abandon his ally, the Earl of Flanders, on condition that Philip should treat in like manner his ally, the King of Scots. The prospect of conquering these two countries, whose situation made them so commodious an acquisition to the respective kingdoms, prevailed over all other considerations; and though they were both finally disappointed in their hopes, their conduct was very reconcilable to the principles of an interested policy. This was the first specimen which the Scots had of the French alliance, and which was exactly conformable to what a smaller power must always expect when it blindly attaches itself to the will and fortunes of a greater. That unhappy people, now engaged in a brave though unequal contest for their liberties, were totally abandoned by the ally in whom they reposed their final confidence, to the will of an imperious conqueror.

Though England, as well as other European countries, was, in its ancient state, very ill qualified for making, and still worse for maintaining, conquests, Scotland was so much inferior in its internal force, and was so ill situated for receiving foreign succors, that it is no wonder Edward, an ambitious monarch, should have cast his eye on so tempting an acquisition, which brought both security and greatness to

[149] Rymer, vol. ii. p. 817. Heming. vol. i. p. 149. Trivet, p. 310.
[150] Rymer, vol. ii. p. 823.

his native country.   But the instruments whom he employed to maintain his dominion over the northern kingdom were not happily chosen, and acted not with the requisite prudence and moderation in reconciling the Scottish nation to a yoke which they bore with such extreme reluctance. Warrenne, retiring into England on account of his bad state of health, left the administration entirely in the hands of Ormesby, who was appointed justiciary of Scotland, and Cressingham, who bore the office of treasurer ; and a small military force remained to secure the precarious authority of those ministers.   The latter had no other object than the amassing of money by rapine and injustice ; the former distinguished himself by the rigor and severity of his temper ; and both of them, treating the Scots as a conquered people, made them sensible, too early, of the grievous servitude into which they had fallen.   As Edward required that all the proprietors of land should swear fealty to him, every one who refused or delayed giving this testimony of submission was outlawed and imprisoned, and punished without mercy ; and the bravest and most generous spirits of the nation were thus exasperated to the highest degree against the English government.[151]

There was one William Wallace, of a small fortune, but descended of an ancient family in the west of Scotland, whose courage prompted him to undertake, and enabled him finally to accomplish, the desperate attempt of delivering his native country from the dominion of foreigners. This man, whose valorous exploits are the object of just admiration, but have been much exaggerated by the traditions of his countrymen, had been provoked by the insolence of an English officer to put him to death ; and finding himself obnoxious, on that account, to the severity of the administration, he fled into the woods, and offered himself as a leader to all those whom their crimes, or bad fortune, or avowed hatred of the English, had reduced to a like necessity.   He was endowed with gigantic force of body, with heroic courage of mind, with disinterested magnanimity, with incredible patience, and ability to bear hunger, fatigue, and all the severities of the seasons ; and he soon acquired, among those desperate fugitives, that authority to which his virtues so justly entitled him.   Beginning with small attempts, in which he was always successful, he gradually proceeded to more momentous enterprises ; and he dis-

151 Walsing. p. 70.   Heming. vol. i. p. 118.   Trivet, p. 299.

covered equal caution in securing his followers, and valor in annoying the enemy. By his knowledge of the country he was enabled, when pursued, to insure a retreat among the morasses, or forests, or mountains; and again collecting his dispersed associates, he unexpectedly appeared in another quarter, and surprised, and routed, and put to the sword the unwary English. Every day brought accounts of his great actions, which were received with no less favor by his countrymen than terror by the enemy. All those who thirsted after military fame were desirous to partake of his renown; his successful valor seemed to vindicate the nation from the ignominy into which it had fallen by its tame submission to the English; and though no nobleman of note ventured as yet to join his party, he had gained a general confidence and attachment, which birth and fortune are not alone able to confer.

Wallace, having, by many fortunate enterprises, brought the valor of his followers to correspond to his own, resolved to strike a decisive blow against the English government; and he concerted the plan of attacking Ormesby, at Scone, and of taking vengeance on him for all the violence and tyranny of which he had been guilty. The justiciary, apprised of his intentions, fled hastily into England; all the other officers of that nation imitated his example. Their terror added alacrity and courage to the Scots, who betook themselves to arms in every quarter. Many of the principal barons, and among the rest Sir William Douglas,[152] openly countenanced Wallace's party. Robert Bruce secretly favored and promoted the same cause; and the Scots, shaking off their fetters, prepared themselves to defend, by an united effort, that liberty which they had so unexpectedly recovered from the hands of their oppressors.

But Warrenne, collecting an army of forty thousand men in the north of England, determined to re-establish his authority; and he endeavored, by the celerity of his armament and of his march, to compensate for his past negligence, which had enabled the Scots to throw off the English government. He suddenly entered Annandale, and came up with the enemy at Irvine, before their forces were fully collected, and before they had put themselves in a posture of defence. Many of the Scottish nobles, alarmed with their dangerous situation, here submitted to the English, renewed their oaths of fealty, promised to deliver hostages

152 Walsing. p. 70. Heming. vol. i. p. 118.

for their good behavior, and received a pardon for past of-fences.[153] Others who had not yet declared themselves, such as the Steward of Scotland and the Earl of Lenox, joined, though with reluctance, the English army, and waited a fa-vorable opportunity for embracing the cause of their dis-tressed countrymen. But Wallace, whose authority over his retainers was more fully confirmed by the absence of the great nobles, persevered obstinately in his purpose; and finding himself unable to give battle to the enemy, he marched northwards with an intention of prolonging the war, and of turning to his advantage the situation of that mountainous and barren country. When Warrenne ad-vanced to Stirling, he found Wallace encamped at Cam-buskenneth, on the opposite banks of the Forth; and being continually urged by the impatient Cressingham, who was actuated both by personal and national animosities against the Scots,[154] he prepared to attack them in that position, which Wallace, no less prudent than courageous, had chosen for his army.[155] In spite of the remonstrances of Sir Rich-ard Lundy, a Scotchman of birth and family, who sincerely adhered to the English, he ordered his army to pass a bridge which lay over the Forth; but he was soon convinced, by fatal experience, of the error of his conduct. Wallace, al-lowing such numbers of the English to pass as he thought proper, attacked them before they were fully formed, put them to rout, pushed part of them into the river, destroyed the rest by the edge of the sword, and gained a complete victory over them.[156] Among the slain was Cressingham himself, whose memory was so extremely odious to the Scots that they flayed his dead body, and made saddles and girths of his skin.[157] Warrenne, finding the remainder of his army much dismayed by this misfortune, was obliged again to evacuate the kingdom and retire into England. The castles of Roxburgh and Berwick, ill fortified and feebly defended, fell soon after into the hands of the Scots.

Wallace, universally revered as the deliverer of his country, now received, from the hands of his followers, the dignity of regent or guardian under the captive Baliol; and finding that the disorders of war, as well as the unfavorable seasons, had produced a famine in Scotland, he urged his army to march into England to subsist at the expense of

[153] Heming. vol. i. pp. 121, 122.
[154] Heming. vol. i. p. 127.   [155] On the 11th of September, 1297.
[156] Walsing. p. 73.   Heming. vol. i. pp. 127, 128, 129.   Trivet, p. 307.
[157] Heming. vol. i. p. 130.

the enemy, and to revenge all past injuries by retaliating on that hostile nation. The Scots, who deemed every thing possible under such a leader, joyfully attended his call. Wallace, breaking into the northern counties during the winter season, laid every place waste with fire and sword; and after extending on all sides, without opposition, the fury of his ravages as far as the bishopric of Durham, he returned, loaded with spoils and crowned with glory, into his own country.[158] The disorders which at that time prevailed in England, from the refractory behavior of the constable and mareschal, made it impossible to collect an army sufficient to resist the enemy, and exposed the nation to this loss and dishonor.

But Edward, who received in Flanders intelligence of these events, and had already concluded a truce with France, now hastened over to England, in certain hopes, by his activity and valor, not only of wiping off this disgrace, but of recovering the important conquest of Scotland, which he always regarded as the chief glory and advantage of his reign. He appeased the murmurs of his people by concessions and promises; he restored to the citizens of London the election of their own magistrates, of which they had been bereaved in the latter part of his father's reign; he ordered strict inquiry to be made concerning the corn and other goods which had been violently seized before his departure, as if he intended to pay the value to the owners;[159] and, making public professions of confirming and observing the charters, he regained the confidence of the discontented nobles. Having, by all these popular arts, rendered himself entirely master of his people, he collected the whole military force of England, Wales, and Ireland, and marched with an army of near a hundred thousand combatants to the northern frontiers.

Nothing could have enabled the Scots to resist but for one season so mighty a power, except an entire union among themselves; but as they were deprived of their king, whose personal qualities, even when he was present, appeared so contemptible, and had left among his subjects no principle of attachment to him or his family, factions, jealousies, and animosities unavoidably arose among the great, and distracted all their councils. The elevation of Wallace, though purchased by so great merit and such eminent services, was the object of envy to the nobility, who repined to see a private

[159] Rymer, vol. ii. p. 813.   [158] Heming. vol. i. pp. 131, 132, 133.

gentleman raised above them by his rank, and still more by his glory and reputation. Wallace himself, sensible of their jealousy, and dreading the ruin of his country from those intestine discords, voluntarily resigned his authority, and retained only the command over that body of his followers who, being accustomed to victory under his standard, refused to follow into the field any other leader. The chief power devolved on the Steward of Scotland and Cummin of Badenoch, men of eminent birth, under whom the great chieftains were more willing to serve in defence of their country. The two Scottish commanders, collecting their several forces from every quarter, fixed their station at Falkirk, and purposed there to abide the assault of the English. Wallace was at the head of a third body, which acted under his command. The Scottish army placed their pikemen along their front; lined the intervals between the three bodies with archers; and, dreading the great superiority of the English in cavalry, endeavored to secure their front by pallisadoes tied together with ropes.[160] In this disposition they expected the approach of the enemy.

The king, when he arrived in sight of the Scots, was pleased with the prospect of being able, by one decisive stroke, to determine the fortune of the war; and, dividing his army also into three bodies, he led them to the attack. The English archers, who began about this time to surpass those of other nations, first chased the Scottish bowmen off the field; then pouring in their arrows among the pikemen, who were cooped up within their intrenchments, threw them into disorder, and rendered the assault of the English pikemen and cavalry more easy and successful. The whole Scottish army was broken, and chased off the field with great slaughter; which the historians, attending more to the exaggerated relations of the populace than to the probability of things, make amount to fifty or sixty thousand men.[161] It is only certain that the Scots never suffered a greater loss in any action, nor one which seemed to threaten more inevitable ruin to their country.

In this general rout of the army, Wallace's military skill and presence of mind enabled him to keep his troops entire; and, retiring behind the Carron, he marched leisurely along the banks of that small river, which protected him from the

---

[160] Walsing. p. 75. Heming. vol. i. p. 163.
[161] Walsing. p. 76. T. Wykes, p. 127. Heming. vol. i. pp. 163,164, 165. Trivet, p. 313, says only twenty thousand. Matt. West. p. 431, says forty thousand.

enemy. Young Bruce, who had already given many proofs of his aspiring genius, but who served hitherto in the English army, appeared on the opposite banks ; and distinguishing the Scottish chief, as well by his majestic port as by the intrepid activity of his behavior, called out to him, and desired a short conference. He here represented to Wallace the fruitless and ruinous enterprise in which he was engaged, and endeavored to bend his inflexible spirit to submission under superior power and superior fortune. He insisted on the unequal contest between a weak state, deprived of its head and agitated by intestine discord, and a mighty nation, conducted by the ablest and most martial monarch of the age, and possessed of every resource either for protracting the war or for pushing it with vigor and activity. If the love of his country were his motive for perseverance, his obstinacy tended only to prolong her misery ; if he carried his views to private grandeur and ambition, he might reflect that, even if Edward should withdraw his armies, it appeared from past experience that so many haughty nobles, proud of the pre-eminence of their families, would never submit to personal merit, whose superiority they were less inclined to regard as an object of admiration than as a reproach and injury to themselves. To these exhortations Wallace replied that, if he had hitherto acted alone as the champion of his country, it was solely because no second or competitor, or, what he rather wished, no leader, had yet appeared to place himself in that honorable station ; that the blame lay entirely on the nobility, and chiefly on Bruce himself, who, uniting personal merit to dignity of family, had deserted the post which both nature and fortune, by such powerful calls, invited him to assume ; that the Scots, possessed of such a head, would, by their unanimity and concord, have surmounted the chief difficulty under which they now labored, and might hope, notwithstanding their present losses, to oppose successfully all the power and abilities of Edward ; that Heaven itself could not set a more glorious prize before the eyes either of virtue or ambition than to join, in one object, the acquisition of royalty with the defence of national independence ; and that, as the interests of his country, more than those of a brave man, could never be sincerely cultivated by a sacrifice of liberty, he himself was determined, as far as possible, to prolong, not her misery, but her freedom, and was desirous that his own life, as well as the existence of the nation, might terminate when they could not otherwise be preserved than by receiving the chains of a haughty victor. The gallantry of these sentiments, though delivered by an armed enemy, struck the generous mind of Bruce. The flame was conveyed from the breast of one hero to that of another. He repented of his engagements with Edward, and, opening his eyes to the honorable path pointed out to him by Wallace, secretly determined to seize the first opportunity of embracing the cause, however desperate, of his oppressed country.[162]

The subjection of Scotland, notwithstanding this great victory of Edward, was not yet entirely completed. [1299.] The English army, after reducing the southern provinces, was obliged to retire for want of provisions, and left the northern counties in the hands of the natives. The Scots, no less enraged at their present defeat than elated by their past victories, still maintained the contest for liberty; but, being fully sensible of the great inferiority of their force, they endeavored, by applications to foreign courts, to procure to themselves some assistance. The supplications of the Scottish ministers were rejected by Philip, but were more successful with the court of Rome. [1300.] Boniface, pleased with an occasion of exerting his authority, wrote a letter to Edward exhorting him to put a stop to his oppressions in Scotland, and displaying all the proofs, such as they had probably been furnished him by the Scots themselves, for the ancient independence of that kingdom.[163] Among other arguments hinted at above, he mentioned the treaty, conducted and finished by Edward himself, for the marriage of his son with the heiress of Scotland—a treaty which would have been absurd had he been superior lord of the kingdom, and had possessed, by the feudal law, the right of disposing of his ward in marriage. He mentioned several other striking facts which fell within the compass of Edward's own knowledge; particularly that Alexander, when he did homage to the king, openly and expressly declared in his presence that he swore fealty, not for his crown, but for the lands which he held in England; and the pope's letter might have passed for a reasonable one had he not subjoined his own claim to be liege lord of Scotland—a claim which had not once been heard of, but which, with a singular confidence, he asserted to be full, entire, and derived from the most

162 This story is told by all the Scotch writers; though it must be owned tha Trivet and Hemingford, authors of good credit, both agree that Bruce was not at that time in Edward's army.   163 Rymer, vol. ii. p. 844.

remote antiquity. The affirmative style, which had been so successful with him and his predecessors in spiritual contests, was never before abused after a more egregious manner in any civil controversy.

[1301.] The reply which Edward made to Boniface's letter contains particulars no less singular and remarkable.[164] He there proves the superiority of England by historical facts deduced from the period of Brutus, the Trojan, who, he said, founded the British monarchy in the age of Eli and Samuel. He supports his position by all the events which passed in the island before the arrival of the Romans; and, after laying great stress on the extensive dominions and heroic victories of King Arthur, he vouchsafes at last to descend to the time of Edward the Elder, with which, in his speech to the states of Scotland, he had chosen to begin his claim of superiority. He asserts it to be a fact, *notorious and confirmed by the records of antiquity,* that the English monarchs had often conferred the kingdom of Scotland on their own subjects, had dethroned these vassal kings when unfaithful to them, and had substituted others in their stead. He displays, with great pomp, the full and complete homage which William had done to Henry II., without mentioning the formal abolition of that *extorted* deed by King Richard, and the renunciation of all future claims of the same nature. Yet this paper he begins with a solemn appeal to the Almighty, the searcher of hearts, for his own firm persuasion of the justice of his claim ; and no less than a hundred and four barons, assembled in Parliament at Lincoln, concur in maintaining before the pope, under their seals, the validity of these pretensions.[165] At the same time, however, they take care to inform Boniface that, though they had justified their cause before him, they did not acknowledge him for their judge : the crown of England was free and sovereign; they had sworn to maintain all its royal prerogatives, and would never permit the king himself, were he willing, to relinquish its independence.

[1302.] That neglect, almost total, of truth and justice which sovereign states discover in their transactions with each other is an evil universal and inveterate ; is one great source of the misery to which the human race is continually exposed ; and it may be doubted whether, in many in-

[164] Rymer, vol. ii. p. 863.
[165] Rymer, vol. ii. p. 873. Walsing. p. 85. Heming. vol. i. p. 186. Trivet, p. Matt. West. p. 443.

stances, it be found in the end to contribute to the interests
of those princes themselves who thus sacrifice their integrity
to their politics.   As few monarchs have lain under stronger
temptations to violate the principles of equity than Edward
in his transactions with Scotland, so never were they violated with less scruple and reserve; yet his advantages
were hitherto precarious and uncertain; and the Scots,
once roused to arms and inured to war, began to appear a
formidable enemy even to this military and ambitious
monarch.   They chose John Cummin for their regent; and,
not content with maintaining their independence in the
northern parts, they made incursions into the southern
counties, which Edward imagined he had totally subdued.
John de Segrave, whom he had left guardian of Scotland,
led an army to oppose them; and, lying at Roslin, near
Edinburgh, sent out his forces, in three divisions, to provide
themselves with forage and subsistence from the neighborhood.   [1303.]   One party was suddenly attacked by the
regent and Sir Simon Fraser, and, being unprepared, was
immediately routed and pursued with great slaughter.   The
few that escaped, flying to the second division, gave warning of the approach of the enemy.   The soldiers ran to
their arms, and were immediately led on to take revenge
for the death of their countrymen.   The Scots, elated with
the advantage already obtained, made a vigorous impression
upon them.   The English, animated with a thirst of vengeance, maintained a stout resistance.   The victory was
long undecided between them, but at last declared itself entirely in favor of the former, who broke the English, and
chased them to the third division, now advancing with a
hasty march to support their distressed companions.   Many
of the Scots had fallen in the two first actions; most of
them were wounded, and all of them extremely fatigued by
the long continuance of the combat.   Yet were they so
transported with success and military rage that, having sud-
·denly recovered their order, and arming the followers of
their camp with the spoils of the slaughtered enemy, they
drove with fury upon the ranks of the dismayed English.
The favorable moment decided the battle, which the Scots,
had they met with a steady resistance, were not long able
to maintain.   The English were chased off the field.   Three
victories were thus gained in one day;[166] and the renown of
these great exploits, seconded by the favorable dispositions

166 Heming. vol. i. p. 197.

of the people, soon made the regent master of all the fortresses in the south; and it became necessary for Edward to begin anew the conquest of the kingdom.

The king prepared himself for this enterprise with his usual vigor and abilities. He assembled both a great fleet and a great army; and, entering the frontiers of Scotland, appeared with a force which the enemy could not think of resisting in the open field. The English navy, which sailed along the coast, secured the army from any danger of famine; Edward's vigilance preserved it from surprises; and by this prudent disposition they marched victorious from one extremity of the kingdom to the other, ravaging the open country, reducing all the castles,[167] and receiving the submissions of all the nobility, even those of Cummin, the regent. The most obstinate resistance was made by the castle of Brechin, defended by Sir Thomas Maule; and the place opened not its gates till the death of the governor, by discouraging the garrison, obliged them to submit to the fate which had overwhelmed the rest of the kingdom. Wallace, though he attended the English army in their march, found but few opportunities of signalizing that valor which had formerly made him so terrible to his enemies.

[1304.] Edward, having completed his conquest, which employed him during the space of near two years, now undertook the more difficult work of settling the country, of establishing a new form of government, and of making his acquisition durable to the crown of England. He seems to have carried matters to extremity against the natives. He abrogated all the Scottish laws and customs;[168] he endeavored to substitute the English in their place; he entirely razed or destroyed all the monuments of antiquity; such records or histories as had escaped his former search were now burnt or dispersed; and he hastened, by too precipitate steps, to abolish entirely the Scottish name, and to sink it finally in the English.

[1105.] Edward, however, still deemed his favorite conquest exposed to some danger so long as Wallace was alive; and, being prompted both by revenge and policy, he employed every art to discover his retreat and become master of his person. At last that hardy warrior, who was determined, amidst the universal slavery of his countrymen, still to maintain his independence, was betrayed into Ed-

---

[167] Heming. vol. i. p. 205.

[168] Ryley, p. 506.

ward's hands by Sir John Monteith, his friend, whom he had made acquainted with the place of his concealment. The king, whose natural bravery and magnanimity should have induced him to respect like qualities in an enemy, enraged at some acts of violence committed by Wallace during the fury of war, resolved to overawe the Scots by an example of severity. He ordered Wallace to be carried in chains to London, to be tried as a rebel and traitor, though he had never made submissions or sworn fealty to England and to be executed on Tower-hill. This was the unworthy fate of a hero who, through a course of many years, had with signal conduct, intrepidity, and perseverance, defended, against a public and oppressive enemy, the liberties of his native country.

But the barbarous policy of Edward failed of the purpose to which it was directed. The Scots, already disgusted at the great innovations introduced by the sword of a conqueror into their laws and government, were farther enraged at the injustice and cruelty exercised upon Wallace; and all the envy which, during his lifetime, had attended that gallant chief being now buried in his grave, he was universally regarded as the champion of Scotland, and the patron of her expiring independency. The people, inflamed with resentment, were everywhere disposed to rise against the English government; and it was not long ere a new and more fortunate leader presented himself, who conducted them to liberty, to victory, and to vengeance.

[1306.] Robert Bruce, grandson of that Robert who had been one of the competitors for the crown, had succeeded, by his grandfather's and father's death, to all their rights; and the demise of John Baliol, together with the captivity of Edward, eldest son of that prince, seemed to open a full career to the genius and ambition of this young nobleman. He saw that the Scots, when the title to their crown had expired in the males of their ancient royal family, had been divided into parties nearly equal between the houses of Bruce and Baliol, and that every incident which had since happened had tended to wean them from any attachment to the latter. The slender capacity of John had proved unable to defend them against their enemies. He had meanly resigned his crown into the hands of the conqueror; he had, before his deliverance from captivity, reiterated that resignation in a manner seemingly voluntary; and had, in that deed, thrown out many reflections extremely dishonorable to his ancient subjects, whom he publicly called traitors, ruffians, and rebels, and with whom he declared he was determined to maintain no farther correspondence.[169] He had, during the time of his exile, adhered strictly to that resolution ; and his son, being a prisoner, seemed ill qualified to revive the rights, now fully abandoned, of his family. Bruce therefore hoped that the Scots, so long exposed, from the want of a leader, to the oppressions of their enemies, would unanimously fly to his standard, and would seat him on the vacant throne to which he brought such plausible pretensions. His aspiring spirit, inflamed by the fervor of youth and buoyed up by his natural courage, saw the glory alone of the enterprise, or regarded the prodigious difficulties which attended it as the source only of farther glory. The miseries and oppressions which he had beheld his countrymen suffer in this unequal contest, the repeated defeats and misfortunes which they had undergone, proved to him so many incentives to bring them relief and conduct them to vengeance against the haughty victor. The circumstances which attended Bruce's first declaration are variously related ; but we shall rather follow the account given by the Scottish historians—not that their authority is in general anywise comparable to that of the English, but because they may be supposed sometimes better informed concerning facts which so nearly interested their own nation.

Bruce, who had long harbored in his breast the design of freeing his enslaved country, ventured at last to open his mind to John Cummin, a powerful nobleman, with whom he lived in strict intimacy. He found his friend, as he imagined, fully possessed with the same sentiments ; and he needed to employ no arts of persuasion to make him embrace the resolution of throwing off, on the first favorable opportunity, the usurped dominion of the English. But on the departure of Bruce, who attended Edward to London, Cummin, who had either all along dissembled with him, or began to reflect more coolly in his absence on the desperate nature of the undertaking, resolved to atone for his crime in assenting to rebellion by the merit of revealing the secret to the King of England. Edward did not immediately commit Bruce to custody, because he intended, at the same time, to seize his three brothers, who resided in Scotland ; and he contented himself with secretly setting spies upon him, and ordering all his motions to be strictly watched. A nobleman of Edward's court, Bruce's intimate friend, was apprised of his danger; but not daring, amidst so many jealous eyes, to hold any conversation with him, he fell on an expedient to give him warning that it was full time he should make his escape. He sent him, by his servant, a pair of gilt spurs and a purse of gold, which he pretended to have borrowed from him, and left it to the sagacity of his friend to discover the meaning of the present. Bruce immediately contrived the means of his escape; and as the ground was at that time covered with snow, he had the precaution, it is said, to order his horses to be shod with their shoes inverted, that he might deceive those who should track his path over the open fields or cross-roads through which he purposed to travel. He arrived in a few days at Dumfries in Annandale, the chief seat of his family interest; and he happily found a great number of the Scottish nobility there assembled, and, among the rest, John Cummin, his former associate.

The noblemen were astonished at the appearance of Bruce among them, and still more when he discovered to them the object of his journey. He told them that he was come to live or die with them in defence of the liberties of his country, and hoped, with their assistance, to redeem the Scottish name from all the indignities which it had so long suffered from the tyranny of their imperious masters; that the sacrifice of the rights of his family was the first injury which had prepared the way for their ensuing slavery, and by resuming them, which was his firm purpose, he opened to them the joyful prospect of recovering from the fraudulent usurper their ancient and hereditary independence; that all past misfortunes had proceeded from their disunion, and they would soon appear no less formidable than of old to their enemies, if they now deigned to follow into the field their rightful prince, who knew no medium between death and victory; that their mountains and their valor, which had, during so many ages, protected their liberty from all the efforts of the Roman empire, would still be sufficient, were they worthy of their generous ancestors, to defend them against the utmost violence of the English tyrant; that it was unbecoming men born to the most ancient independence known in Europe to submit to the will of any masters, but fatal to receive those who, being irritated by such persevering resistance, and inflamed with the highest animosity, would never deem themselves secure in their usurped dominion but by exterminating all the ancient nobility, and even all the ancient inhabitants; and that, being reduced to this desperate extremity, it were better for them at once to perish like brave men, with swords in their hands, than to dread long, and at last undergo, the fate of the unfortunate Wallace, whose merits in the brave and obstinate defence of his country were finally rewarded by the hands of an English executioner.

The spirit with which this discourse was delivered, the bold sentiments which it conveyed, the novelty of Bruce's declaration, assisted by the graces of his youth and manly deportment, made deep impression on the minds of his audience, and roused all those principles of indignation and revenge with which they had long been secretly actuated. The Scottish nobles declared their unanimous resolution to use the utmost efforts in delivering their country from bondage, and to second the courage of Bruce in asserting his and their undoubted rights against their common oppressors. Cummin alone, who had secretly taken his measures with the king, opposed this general determination; and by representing the great power of England, governed by a prince of such uncommon vigor and abilities, he endeavored to set before them the certain destruction which they must expect if they again violated their oaths of fealty and shook off their allegiance to the victorious Edward.[170] Bruce, already apprised of his treachery, and foreseeing the certain failure of all his own schemes of ambition and glory from the opposition of so potent a leader, took immediately his resolution, and, moved partly by resentment, partly by policy, followed Cummin on the dissolution of the assembly, attacked him in the cloisters of the Gray Friars, through which he passed, and running him through the body, left him for dead. Sir Thomas Kirkpatric, one of Bruce's friends, asking him soon after if the traitor was slain, "I believe so," replied Bruce. "And is that a matter," cried Kirkpatric, "to be left to conjecture? I will secure him." Upon which he drew his dagger, ran to Cummin, and stabbed him to the heart. This deed of Bruce and his associates, which contains circumstances justly condemned by our present manners, was regarded in that age as an effort of manly vigor and just policy. The family of Kirkpatric took for the crest of their arms, which they still wear, a hand with a bloody dagger, and chose for their motto these words: " I will secure him "

170 Matt. West. p. 453.

—the expression employed by their ancestor when he executed that violent action.

The murder of Cummin affixed the seal to the conspiracy
of the Scottish nobles. They had now no resource left but
to shake off the yoke of England, or to perish in the attempt.
The genius of the nation roused itself from its present de-
jection; and Bruce, flying to different quarters, excited his
partisans to arms, attacked with success the dispersed bodies
of the English, got possession of many of the castles, and,
having made his authority be acknowledged in most parts
of the kingdom, was solemnly crowned and inaugurated in
the abbey of Scone by the Bishop of St. Andrew's, who had
zealously embraced his cause. The English were again
chased out of the kingdom, except such as took shelter in
the fortresses that still remained in their hands; and Edward
found that the Scots, twice conquered in his reign, and often
defeated, must yet be anew subdued. Not discouraged
with these unexpected difficulties, he sent Aymer de Valence
with a considerable force into Scotland, to check the progress
of the malcontents; and that nobleman, falling unexpectedly
upon Bruce at Methven in Perthshire, threw his army into
such disorder as ended in a total defeat.[171] Bruce fought
with the most heroic courage; was thrice dismounted in the
action, and as often recovered himself; but was at last
obliged to yield to superior fortune, and take shelter, with a
few followers, in the western isles. The Earl of Athol, Sir
Simon Fraser, and Sir Christopher Seton, who had been
taken prisoners, were ordered by Edward to be executed as
rebels and traitors.[172] [1307.] Many other acts of rigor were
exercised by him; and that prince, vowing revenge against
the whole Scottish nation, whom he deemed incorrigible
in their aversion to his government, assembled a great army,
and was preparing to enter the frontiers, secure of success,
and determined to make the defenceless Scots the victims of
his severity, when he unexpectedly sickened and died near
Carlisle: enjoining, with his last breath, his son and successor to prosecute the enterprise, and never to desist till he
had finally subdued the kingdom of Scotland. He expired
in the sixty-ninth year of his age and the thirty-fifth of his
reign, hated by his neighbors, but extremely respected and
revered by his own subjects.

The enterprises finished by this prince, and the projects

---

[171] Walsing. p. 91. Heming. vol. i. pp. 222, 223. Trivet, p. 344.
[172] Heming. vol. i. p. 223. Matt. West. p. 456.

which he formed and brought near to a conclusion, were more prudent, more regularly conducted, and more advantageous to the solid interests of his kingdom than those which were undertaken in any reign either of his ancestors or his successors. He restored authority to the government, disordered by the weakness of his father; he maintained the laws against all the efforts of his turbulent barons; he fully annexed to his crown the principality of Wales; he took many wise and vigorous measures for reducing Scotland to a like condition; and though the equity of this latter enterprise may reasonably be questioned, the circumstances of the two kingdoms promised such certain success, and the advantage was so visible of uniting the whole island under one head, that those who give great indulgence to reasons of state in the measures of princes will not be apt to regard this part of his conduct with much severity. But Edward, however exceptionable his character may appear on the head of justice, is the model of a politic and warlike king; he possessed industry, penetration, courage, vigilance, and enterprise; he was frugal in all expenses that were not necessary; he knew how to open the public treasures on a proper occasion; he punished criminals with severity; he was gracious and affable to his servants and courtiers; and being of a majestic figure, expert in all military exercises, and in the main well proportioned in his limbs, notwithstanding the great length and the smallness of his legs, he was as well qualified to captivate the populace by his exterior appearance as to gain the approbation of men of sense by his more solid virtues.

But the chief advantage which the people of England reaped, and still continue to reap, from the reign of this great prince was the correction, extension, amendment, and establishment of the laws, which Edward maintained in great vigor and left much improved to posterity; for the acts of a wise legislator commonly remain, while the acquisitions of a conqueror often perish with him. This merit has justly gained to Edward the appellation of the English Justinian. Not only the numerous statutes passed in his reign touch the chief points of jurisprudence, and, according to Sir Edward Coke,[173] truly deserve the name of establishments, because they were more constant, standing, and durable laws than any made since, but the regular order maintained in his administration gave an opportunity to the common law to refine

[173] Institute, p. 156.

itself, and brought the judges to a certainty in their determinations, and the lawyers to a precision in their pleadings.
Sir Matthew Hale has remarked the sudden improvement
of English law during this reign, and ventures to assert that,
till his own time, it had never received any considerable increase.[174] Edward settled the jurisdiction of the several
courts; first established the office of justice of peace; abstained from the practice, too common before him, of inter-
rupting justice by mandates from the privy council; [175] repressed robberies and disorders; [176] encouraged trade by
giving merchants an easy method of recovering their debts; [177]
and, in short, introduced a new face of things by the vigor
and wisdom of his administration. As law began now to
be well established, the abuse of that blessing began also
to be remarked. Instead of their former associations for
robbery and violence, men entered into formal combinations
to support each other in lawsuits; and it was found requisite
to check this iniquity by act of Parliament.[178]

There happened in this reign a considerable alteration in
the execution of the laws. The king abolished the office of
chief justiciary, which he thought possessed too much power,
and was dangerous to the crown; [179] he completed the division
of the court of exchequer into four distinct courts, which
managed each its several branch, without dependence on
any one magistrate; and as the lawyers afterwards invented
a method, by means of their fictions, of carrying business
from one court to another, the several courts became rivals
and checks to each other—a circumstance which tended
much to improve the practice of the law in England.

But though Edward appeared thus, throughout his whole
reign, a friend to law and justice, it cannot be said that he
was an enemy to arbitrary power; and in a government
more regular and legal than was that of England in his age,
such practices as those which may be remarked in his administration would have given sufficient ground of complaint,
and sometimes were, even in his age, the object of general

---

[174] History of the English Law, pp. 158, 163.

[175] Articuli super Cart. cap. 6. Edward enacted a law to this purpose, but it
is doubtful whether he ever observed it. We are sure that scarcely any of his successors did. The multitude of these letters of protection were the ground of a
complaint by the Commons in the third of Edward II. See Ryley, p. 525. This
practice was declared illegal by the statute of Northampton, pa-sed in the second
of Edward III., but is still continued like many other abuses. There are instances
of it so late as the reign of Queen Elizabeth.

[176] Statute of Winton.   [177] Statute of Acton Burnel.

[178] Statute of Conspirators.

[179] Spellman, Gloss. *in verbo* Justiciarius. Gilbert's Hist. of the Exchequer,
p. 8.

displeasure. The violent plunder and banishment of the Jews; the putting of the whole clergy at once, and by an arbitrary edict, out of the protection of the law; the seizing of all the wool and leather of the kingdom; the heightening of the impositions on the former valuable commodity; the new and illegal commission of Trailbaston; the taking of all the money and plate of monasteries and churches even before he had any quarrel with the clergy; the subjecting of every man possessed of twenty pounds a year to military service, though not bound to it by his tenure; his visible reluctance to confirm the great charter, as if that concession had no validity from the deeds of his predecessors; the captious clause which he at last annexed to his confirmation; his procuring of the pope's dispensation from the oaths which he had taken to observe that charter; and his levying of talliages at discretion even after the statute, or rather charter, by which he had renounced that prerogative—these are so many demonstrations of his arbitrary disposition, and prove with what exception and reserve we ought to celebrate his love of justice. He took care that his subjects should do justice to each other; but he desired always to have his own hands free in all his transactions, both with them and with his neighbors.

The chief obstacle to the execution of justice in those times was the power of the great barons; and Edward was perfectly qualified, by his character and abilities, for keeping these tyrants in awe and restraining their illegal practices. This salutary purpose was accordingly the great object of his attention; yet was he imprudently led into a measure which tended to increase and confirm their dangerous authority. He passed a statute which, by allowing them to entail their estates, made it impracticable to diminish the property of the great families, and left them every means of increase and acquisition.[180]

Edward observed a contrary policy with regard to the Church. He seems to have been the first Christian prince that passed a statute of mortmain, and prevented by law the clergy from making new acquisitions of lands, which, by the ecclesiastical canons, they were forever prohibited from alienating. The opposition between his maxims, with regard to the nobility and to the ecclesiastics, leads us to conjecture that it was only by chance he passed the beneficial statute of mortmain, and that his sole object was to main-

---

[180] Brady of Boroughs, p. 25, from the Records.

tain the number of knight's-fees, and to prevent the superiors from being defrauded of the profits of wardship, marriage, livery, and other emoluments arising from the feudal tenures. This is indeed the reason assigned in the statute itself, and appears to have been his real object in enacting it. The author of the Annals of Waverley ascribes this act chiefly to the king's anxiety for maintaining the military force of the kingdom, but adds that he was mistaken in his purpose; for that the Amalekites were overcome more by the prayers of Moses than by the sword of the Israelites.[181] The statute of mortmain was often evaded afterwards by the invention of *uses*.

Edward was active in restraining the usurpations of the Church; and excepting his ardor for crusades, which adhered to him during his whole life, seems in other respects to have been little infected with superstition, the vice chiefly of weak minds. But the passion for crusades was really in that age the passion for glory. As the pope now felt himself somewhat more restrained in his former practice of pillaging the several churches in Europe, by laying impositions upon them, he permitted the generals of particular orders who resided at Rome to levy taxes on the convents subjected to their jurisdiction, and Edward was obliged to enact a law against this new abuse. It was also become a practice of the court of Rome to provide successors to benefices before they became vacant. Edward found it likewise necessary to prevent by law this species of injustice.

The tribute of one thousand marks a year to which King John, in doing homage to the pope, had subjected the kingdom had been pretty regularly paid since his time, though the vassalage was constantly denied, and indeed, for fear of giving offence, had been but little insisted on. The payment was called by a new name of *census*, not by that of tribute. King Edward seems always to have paid this money with great reluctance, and he suffered the arrears at one time to run on for six years,[182] at another for eleven;[183] but as princes in that age stood continually in need of the pope's good offices for dispensations of marriage and for other concessions, the court of Rome always found means, sooner or later, to catch the money. The levying of first-fruits was also a new device, begun in this reign, by which his holiness thrust his fingers very frequently into the purses

[181] P. 234. See also Matt. West. p. 409.
[182] Rymer, vol. ii. pp. 77, 107.   [183] Rymer, vol. ii. p. 862.

of the faithful; and the king seems to have unwarily given
way to it.

In the former reign the taxes had been partly scutages,
partly such a proportional part of the movables as was
granted by Parliament; in this, scutages were entirely
dropped, and the assessment on movables was the chief
method of taxation. Edward in his fourth year had a fifteenth granted him; in his fifth year, a twelfth; in his
eleventh year, a thirtieth from the laity, a twentieth from
the clergy; in his eighteenth year, a fifteenth; in his twenty-
second year, a tenth from the laity, a sixth from London
and other corporate towns, half of their benefices from the
clergy; in his twenty-third year, an eleventh from the barons and others, a tenth from the clergy, a seventh from the
burgesses; in his twenty-fourth year, a twelfth from the barons and others, an eighth from the burgesses (from the
clergy nothing, because of the pope's inhibition); in his
twenty-fifth year, an eighth from the laity, a tenth from the
clergy of Canterbury, a fifth from those of York; in his
twenty-ninth year, a fifteenth from the laity, on account of
his confirming the perambulations of the forests (the clergy
granted nothing); in his thirty-third year, first a thirtieth
from the barons and others, and a twentieth from the burgesses, then a fifteenth from all his subjects; in his thirty-
fourth year, a thirtieth from all his subjects for knighting
his eldest son.

These taxes were moderate; but the king had also duties
upon exportation and importation granted him from time to
time: the heaviest were commonly upon wool. Poundage,
or a shilling a pound, was not regularly granted the kings
for life till the reign of Henry V.

In 1296 the famous mercantile society called the "Merchant Adventurers" had its first origin; it was instituted
for the improvement of the woollen manufacture, and the
vending of the cloth abroad, particularly at Antwerp,[184] for
the English at this time scarcely thought of any more distant commerce.

This king granted a charter or declaration of protection
and privileges to foreign merchants, and also ascertained
the customs or duties which those merchants were in return
to pay on merchandise imported and exported. He promised them security; allowed them a jury on trials, consisting half of natives, half of foreigners; and appointed them

[184] Anderson's History of Commerce, vol. i. p. 137.

a justiciary in London for their protection. But notwithstanding this seeming attention to foreign merchants, Edward did not free them from the cruel hardship of making one answerable for the debts, and even for the crimes, of another that came from the same country.[185] We read of such practices among the present barbarous nations. The king also imposed on them a duty of two shillings on each tun of wine imported, over and above the old duty; and forty pence on each sack of wool exported, besides half a mark, the former duty.[186]

In the year 1303 the exchequer was robbed, and of no less a sum than one hundred thousand pounds, as is pretended.[187] The abbot and monks of Westminster were indicted for this robbery, but acquitted. It does not appear that the king ever discovered the criminals with certainty; though his indignation fell on the society of Lombard merchants, particularly the Frescobaldi, very opulent Florentines.

The pope having, in 1307, collected much money in England, the king enjoined the nuncio not to export it in specie, but in bills of exchange [188]—a proof that commerce was but ill understood at that time.

Edward had by his first wife, Eleanor of Castile, four sons; but Edward, his heir and successor, was the only one that survived him. She also bore him eleven daughters, most of whom died in their infancy. Of the surviving, Joan was married, first, to the Earl of Gloucester, and, after his death, to Ralph de Monthermer; Margaret espoused John, Duke of Brabant; Elizabeth espoused, first, John, Earl of Holland, and afterwards the Earl of Hereford; Mary was a nun at Ambresbury. He had by his second wife, Margaret of France, two sons and a daughter: Thomas, created Earl of Norfolk and Mareschal of England; and Edmond, who was created Earl of Kent by his brother when king. The princess died in her infancy.

---

[185] Anderson's History of Commerce, vol. i. p. 146.
[186] Rymer, vol. iv. p. 361. It is the charter of Edward I. which is there confirmed by Edward III.   [187] Rymer, vol. ii. p. 930.
[188] Rymer, vol. ii. p. 1092.

NOTES.

NOTE [A], p. 33.

THIS question has been disputed with as great zeal, and even acrimony, between the Scotch and Irish antiquaries, as if the honor of their respective countries were the most deeply concerned in the decision. We shall not enter into any detail on so uninteresting a subject, but shall propose our opinion in a few words. It appears more than probable, from the similitude of language and manners, that Britain either was originally peopled, or was subdued, by the migration of inhabitants from Gaul, and Ireland from Britain : the position of the several countries is an additional reason that favors this conclusion. It appears also probable that the migration of that colony of Gauls or Celts who peopled or subdued Ireland was originally made from the northwest parts of Britain ; and this conjecture (if it do not merit a higher name) is founded both on the Irish language, which is a very different dialect from the Welsh and from the language anciently spoken in South Britain, and on the vicinity of Lancashire, Cumberland, Galloway, and Argyleshire to that island. These events, as they passed long before the age of history and records, must be known by reasoning alone, which in this case seems to be pretty satisfactory ; Cæsar and Tacitus, not to mention a multitude of other Greek and Roman authors, were guided by like inferences. But besides these primitive facts, which lie in a very remote antiquity, it is a matter of positive and undoubted testimony that the Roman province of Britain, during the time of the Lower empire, was much infested by bands of robbers or pirates, whom the provincial Britons called Scots or Scuits— a name which was probably used as a term of reproach, and which these banditti themselves did not acknowledge or assume. We may infer from two passages in Claudian, and from one in Orosius and another in Isidore, that the chief seat of these Scots was in Ireland. That some part of the Irish freebooters migrated back to the northwest parts of Britain, whence their ancestors had probably been derived in a more remote age, is positively asserted by Bede, and implied in Gildas. I grant that neither Bede nor Gildas are Cæsars or Tacituses; but such as they are, they remain the sole testimony on the subject, and therefore must be relied on for want of better. Happily, the frivolousness of the question corresponds to the weakness of the authorities; not to mention that if any part of the traditional history of a barbarous people can be relied on, it is the genealogy of nations, and even sometimes that of families. It is in vain to argue against these facts from the supposed warlike disposition of the Highlanders, and unwarlike of the ancient Irish. Those arguments are still much weaker than the authorities. Nations change very quickly in these particulars. The Britons were unable to resist the Picts and Scots, and invited over the Saxons for their defence, who repelled those invaders ; yet the same Britons valiantly resisted for one hundred and fifty years, not only this victorious band of Saxons, but infinite numbers more, who poured in upon them from all quarters. Robert Bruce, in 1322, made a peace, in which England, after many defeats, was constrained to acknowledge the independence of his country ; yet in no more distant period than ten years after, Scotland was totally subdued by a small handful of English, led by a few private noblemen. All history is full of such events. The Irish Scots, in the course of two or three centuries, might find time and opportunities sufficient to settle in North Britain, though we can neither assign the period nor causes of that revolution. Their barbarous manner of life rendered them much fitter than the Romans for subduing these mountaineers. And, in a word, it is clear from the language of the two countries that the Highlanders and the Irish are the same people, and that the one are a colony from the other. We have positive evidence, which, though from neutral persons, is not perhaps the best that may be wished for, that the former, in the third or fourth century, sprang from the latter : we have no evidence at all that the latter sprang from the former. I shall add that the name of Erse, or Irish, given by the low-country Scotch to the language of the Scotch Highlanders is a certain proof of the traditional opinion delivered from father to son that the latter people came originally from Ireland.

NOTE [B], p. 112.

There is a seeming contradiction in ancient historians with regard to some circumstances in the story of Edwy and Elgiva. It is agreed that this prince had a violent passion for his second or third cousin, Elgiva, whom he married, though within the degrees prohibited by the canons. It is also agreed that he was dragged from a lady on the day of his coronation, and that the lady was afterwards treated with the singular barbarity above mentioned. The only difference is, that Osberne and some others call her his strumpet, not his wife, as she is said to be by Malmesbury. But this difference is easily reconciled, for if Edwy married her contrary to the canons, the monks would be sure to deny her to be his wife, and would insist that she could be nothing but his strumpet ; so that, on the whole, we may esteem this representation of the matter as certain — at least, as by far the most probable. If Edwy had only kept a mistress, it is well known that there are methods of accommodation with the Church which would have prevented the clergy from proceeding to such extremities against him ; but his marriage contrary to the canons was an insult on their authority, and called for their highest resentment.

NOTE [C], p. 113.

Many of the English historians make Edgar's ships amount to an extravagant number—to three thousand, or three thousand six hundred (see Hoveden, p. 426 ; Flor. Wigorn. p. 607 ; Abbas Rieval. p. 360). Brompton, p. 869, says that Edgar had four thousand vessels. How can these accounts be reconciled to probability, and to the state of the navy in the time of Alfred ? W. Thorne makes the whole number amount only to three hundred, which is more probable. The fleet of Ethelred, Edgar's son, must have been short of one thousand ships ; yet the Saxon Chronicle, p. 137, says it was the greatest navy that ever had been seen in England.

NOTE [D], p. 130.

Almost all the ancient historians speak of this massacre of the Danes as if it had been universal, and as if every individual of that nation throughout England had been put to death. But the Danes were almost the sole inhabitants in the kingdoms of Northumberland and East Anglia, and were very numerous in Mercia. This representation, therefore, of the matter is absolutely impossible. Great resistance must have been made, and violent wars ensued, which was not the case. This account given by Wallingford, though he stands single, must be admitted as the only true one. We are told that the name *Lurdane, lord Dane*, for an idle, lazy fellow who lives at the other people's expense, came from the conduct of the Danes, who were put to death. But the English princes had been entirely masters for several generations, and only supported a military corps of that nation. It seems probable, therefore, that it was these Danes only that were put to death.

NOTE [E], p. 150.

The ingenious author of the article GODWIN, in the Biographia Britannica, has endeavored to clear the memory of that nobleman upon the supposition that all the English annals had been falsified by the Norman historians after the Conquest. But that this supposition has not much foundation appears hence, that almost all these historians have given a very good character to his son Harold, whom it was much more the interest of the Norman cause to blacken.

NOTE [F], p. 158.

The whole story of the transactions between Edward, Harold, and the Duke of Normandy is told so differently by the ancient writers that there are few important passages of the English history liable to so great uncertainty. I have followed the account which appeared to me the most consistent and probable. It does not seem likely that Edward ever executed a will in the duke's favor, much less that he got it ratified by the states of the kingdom, as is affirmed by some. The will would have been known to all, and would have been produced by the

Conqueror, to whom it gave so plausible and really so just a title ; but the doubtful and ambiguous manner in which he seems always to have mentioned it
proves that he could only plead the known intentions of that monarch in his
favor, which he was desirous to call a will. There is indeed a charter of the Conqueror preserved by Dr. Hickes, vol. i , where he calls himself *rex hereditarius*,
meaning heir by will ; but a prince possessed of so much power, and attended
with so much success, may employ what pretence he pleases : it is sufficient to
refute his pretences to observe that there is a great difference and variation
among historians with regard to a point, which, had it been real, must have been
agreed upon by all of them.

Again, some historians, particularly Malmesbury and Matthew of Westminster, affirm that Harold had no intention of going over to Normandy, but
that, taking the air in a pleasure-boat on the coast, he was driven over, by stress
of weather, to the territories of Guy, Count of Ponthieu. But besides that this
story is not probable in itself, and is contradicted by most of the ancient historians, it is contradicted by a very curious and authentic monument lately discovered. It is a tapestry, preserved in the ducal palace of Rouen, and supposed
to have been wrought by orders of Matilda, wife to the emperor; at least it is of
very great antiquity. Harold is there represented as taking his departure from
King Edward in execution of some commission, and mounting his vessel with a
great train. The design of redeeming his brother and nephew, who were hostages, is the most likely cause that can be assigned ; and is accordingly mentioned
by Eadmer, Hoveden, Brompton, and Simeon of Durham. For a further account of this piece of tapestry, see Histoire de l'Académie de Littérature, tom.
ix. p. 535.

NOTE [G], p. 175.

It appears from the ancient translations of the Saxon annals and laws, and
from King Alfred's translation of Bede, as well as from all the ancient historians,
that *comes* in Latin, *alderman* in Saxon, and *earl* in Dano-Saxon were quite
synonymous. There is only a clause in a law of King Athelstan's (see Spell.
Conc. p. 406) which has stumbled some antiquaries, and has made them imagine
that an earl was superior to an alderman. The weregild, or the price of an earl's
blood, is there fixed at fifteen thousand thrimsas, equal to that of an archbishop;
whereas that of a bishop and alderman is only eight thousand thrimsas. To
solve this difficulty we must have recourse to Selden's conjecture (see his Titles
of Honor, ch. v. pp. 603, 604), that the term of earl was in the age of Athelstan
just beginning to be in use in England, and stood at that time for the atheling,
or prince of the blood—heir to the crown. This he confirms by a law of Canute,
§ 55, where an atheling and an archbishop are put upon the same footing. In
another law of the same Athelstan, the weregild of the prince, or atheling, is said
to be fifteen thousand thrimsas (see Wilkins, p. 71). He is therefore the same
who is called earl in the former law.

NOTE [H], p. 213.

There is a paper or record of the family of Sharneborn, which pretends that
that family, which was Saxon, was restored upon proving its innocence, as well
as other Saxon families which were in the same situation. Though this paper
was able to impose on such great antiquaries as Spellman (see Gloss. *in verbo*
Drenges), and Dugdale (see Baron. vol. i. p. 118), it is proved by Dr. Brady (see
Answ. to Petyt. pp. 11, 12) to have been a forgery, and is allowed as such by Tyrrel,
though a pertinacious defender of his party notions (see his Hist. vol. ii. introd.
pp. 51, 73). Ingulf, p. 70, tells us that very early Hereward, though absent during
the time of the Conquest, was turned out of all his estate, and could not obtain
redress. William even plundered the monasteries (Flor. Wigorn. p. 636 ; Chron.
Abb. St. Petri de Burgo, p. 48 ; Matt. Paris, p. 5 ; Sim. Dun. p. 200 ; Diceto, p.
482 ; Brompton, p. 967 ; Knyghton, p. 2344 ; Alur. Beverl. p. 130). We are told
by Ingulf that Ivo de Taillebois plundered the monastery of Croyland of a great
part of its land, and no redress could be obtained.

NOTE [I], p. 213.

The obliging of all the inhabitants to put out their fires and lights at certain
hours, upon the sounding of a bell called the *courfeu*, is represented by Polydore
Vergil, lib. 9, as a mark of the servitude of the English. But this was a law of
police, which William had previously established in Normandy (see Du Moulin,
Hist. de Normandie, p. 160). The same law had place in Scotland (Leges Burgor.
cap. 86).

NOTE [K], p. 219.

What these laws were of Edward the Confessor which the English, every reign during a century and a half, desire so passionately to have restored, is much disputed by antiquaries, and our ignorance of them seems one of the greatest defects in the ancient English history. The collection of laws in Wilkins which pass under the name of Edward are plainly a posterior and an ignorant compilation. Those to be found in Ingulf are genuine; but so imperfect, and contain so few clauses favorable to the subject, that we see no great reason for their contending for them so vehemently. It is probable that the English meant the *common law* as it prevailed during the reign of Edward, which we may conjecture to have been more indulgent to liberty than the Norman institutions. The most material articles of it were afterwards comprehended in Magna Charta.

NOTE [L], p. 237.

Ingulph. p. 70; H. Hunting, pp. 370, 372; Matt. West. p. 225; Gul. Neub. p. 357; Alur. Beveri. p. 124; De Gest. Angl. p. 333; Matt. Paris, p. 4; Sim. Dun. p. 206; Brompton, pp. 962, 980, 1161; Gervase Tilb. lib. 1, cap. 16; Textus Roffensis apud Seld. Spicileg. ad Eadm. p. 179; Gul. Pict. p. 206; Ordericus Vitalis, pp. 521, 666, 853; Epist. St. Thom. p. 801; Gul. Malm. pp. 52, 57; Knyghton, p. 2354; Eadmer, p. 110; Thom. Rudborne in Anglia Sacra, vol. i. p. 248; Monach. Roff. in Anglia Sacra, vol. ii. p. 276; Girald. Camb. in eadem, vol. ii. p. 413; Hist. Elyensis, p. 516. The words of this last historian, who is very ancient, are remarkable, and worth transcribing: "Rex itaque factus Willielmus, quid in principes Anglorum, qui tantæ cladi superesse poterant, fecerit, dicere, cum nihil prosit, omitto. Quid enim prodesset, si nec unum in toto regno de illis dicerem pristina potestate uti permissum, sed omnes aut in gravem paupertatis ærumnam detrusos, aut exhæredatos, patria pulsos, aut effossis oculis, vel cæteris amputatis membris, opprobrium hominum factos, aut certe miserrime afflictos, vita privatos? Simili modo utilitate carere existimo dicere quid in minorem populum, non solum ab eo, sed a suis actum sit, cum id dictu sciamus difficile, et ob immanem crudelitatem, fortassis incredibile."

NOTE [M], p. 280.

Henry, by the feudal customs, was entitled to levy a tax for the marrying of his eldest daughter, and he exacted three shillings a hide on all England (H. Hunting. p. 379). Some historians (Brady, p. 270, and Tyrrel, vol. ii. p. 182) heedlessly make this sum amount to about eight hundred thousand pounds of our present money, but it could not exceed one hundred and thirty-five thousand. Five hides, sometimes less, made a knight's-fee, of which there were about sixty thousand in England—consequently near three hundred thousand hides; and at the rate of three shillings a hide the sum would amount to forty-five thousand pounds, or one hundred and thirty-five thousand of our present money (see Rudborne, p. 257). In the Saxon times, there were only computed two hundred and forty-three thousand six hundred hides in England.

NOTE [N], p. 283.

The legates *à latere*, as they were called, were a kind of delegates who possessed the full power of the pope in all the provinces committed to their charge, and were very busy in extending as well as exercising it. They nominated to all vacant benefices, assembled synods, and were anxious to maintain ecclesiastical privileges, which never could be fully protected without encroachments on the civil power. If there were the least concurrence or opposition, it was always supposed that the civil power was to give way. Every deed which had the least pretence of holding of anything spiritual—as marriages, testaments, promissory oaths—was brought into the spiritual court, and could not be canvassed before a civil magistrate. These were the established laws of the Church; and where a legate was sent immediately from Rome, he was sure to maintain the papal claims with the utmost rigor; but it was an advantage to the king to have the Archbishop of Canterbury appointed legate, because the connections of that prelate with the kingdom tended to moderate his measures.

NOTE [O], p. 308.

William of Newbridge, p. 383 (who is copied by later historians), asserts that Geoffrey had some title to the counties of Maine and Anjou. He pretends that Count Geoffrey, his father, had left him these dominions by a secret will, and had ordered that his body should not be buried till Henry should swear to the observance of it, which he, ignorant of the contents, was induced to do. But, besides that this story is not very likely in itself and savors of monkish fiction, it is found in no other ancient writer, and is contradicted by some of them, particularly the monk of Marmouuier, who had better opportunities than Newbridge of knowing the truth (see Vita Gauf. Duc. Norman. p. 103).

NOTE [P], p. 310.

The sum scarcely appears credible, as it would amount to much above half the rent of the whole land. Gervase is indeed a contemporary author; but churchmen are often guilty of strange mistakes of that nature, and are commonly but little acquainted with the public revenues. This sum would make five hundred and forty thousand pounds of our present money. The Norman Chronicle, p. 995, says that Henry raised only sixty Angevin shillings on each knight's-fee in his foreign dominions; this is only a fourth of the sum which Gervase says he levied on England—an inequality nowise probable. A nation may, by degrees, be brought to bear a tax of fifteen shillings in the pound; but a sudden and precarious tax can never be imposed to that amount without a very visible necessity, especially in an age so little accustomed to taxes. In the succeeding reign the rent of a knight's-fee was computed at four pounds a year. There were sixty thousand knight's-fees in England.

NOTE [Q], p. 312.

Fitz-Stephen, p. 18. This conduct appears violent and arbitrary, but was suitable to the strain of administration in those days. His father, Geoffrey, though represented as a mild prince, set him an example of much greater violence. When Geoffrey was master of Normandy the chapter of sees presumed, without his consent, to proceed to the election of a bishop; upon which he ordered all of them, with the bishop elect, to be castrated, and made all their testicles be brought him in a platter (Fitz-Stephen, p. 44). In the war of Toulouse Henry laid a heavy and an arbitrary tax on all the churches within his dominions (see Epist. St. Thom. p. 232).

NOTE [R], p. 323.

I follow here the narrative of Fitz-Stephen, who was secretary to Becket, though no doubt he may be suspected of partiality towards his patron. Lord Lyttleton chooses to follow the authority of a manuscript letter, or rather manifesto, of Folliot, Bishop of London, which is addressed to Becket himself at the time when the bishop appealed to the pope from the excommunication pronounced against him by his primate. My reasons why I give the preference to Fitz-Stephen are, (1) If the friendship of Fitz-Stephen might render him partial to Becket, even after the death of that prelate, the declared enmity of the bishop must, during his lifetime, have rendered him more partial on the other side. (2) The bishop was moved by interest as well as enmity to calumniate Becket. He had himself to defend against the sentence of excommunication, dreadful to all, especially to a prelate; and no more effectual means than to throw all the blame on his adversary. (3) He has actually been guilty of palpable calumnies in that letter. Among these I reckon the following: He affirms that when Becket subscribed the Constitutions of Clarendon, he said plainly to all the bishops of England, " It is my master's pleasure that I should forswear myself, and at present I submit to it, and do resolve to incur a perjury and repent afterwards as I may." However barbarous the times, and however negligent zealous churchmen were then of morality, these are not words which a primate of great sense and of much seeming sanctity would employ in an assembly of his suffragans; he might act upon these principles, but never, surely, would publicly avow them. Folliot also says that all the bishops were resolved obstinately to oppose the Constitutions of Clarendon, but the primate himself betrayed them from timidity, and led the way to their subscribing. This is contrary to the testimony of all the historians, and directly contrary to Becket's character, who surely was not destitute either of courage or of zeal for ecclesiastical immunities. (4) The violence and injustice of Henry, ascribed to him by Fitz-Stephen, are of a piece with the rest of the prosecution. Nothing could be more iniquitous than, after two years' silence, to make a sudden and unprepared demand upon Becket to the amount of forty-four thousand marks (equal to a sum of near a million in our time), and not allow him the least interval to bring in his accounts. If the king was so palpably oppressive in one article, he may be presumed to be equally so in the rest. (5) Though Folliot's letter, or rather manifesto, be addressed to

Becket himself, it does not acquire more authority on that account. We know not what answer was made by Becket : the collection of letters cannot be supposed quite complete. But that the collection was not made by one (whoever he were) very partial to that primate, appears from the tenor of them, where there are many passages very little favorable to him ; insomuch that the editor of them at Brussels, a Jesuit, thought proper to publish them with great omissions, particularly of this letter of Folliot's. Perhaps Becket made no answer at all, as not deigning to write to an excommunicated person, whose very commerce would contaminate him ; and the bishop, trusting to this arrogance of his primate, might calumniate him the more freely. (6) Though the sentence pronounced on Becket by the great council implies that he had refused to make any answer to the king's court, this does not fortify the narrative of Folliot ; for if his excuse was rejected as false and frivolous, it would be treated as no answer. Becket submitted so far to the sentence of confiscation of goods and chattels that he gave surety, which is a proof that he meant not at that time to question the authority of the king's courts. (7) It may be worth observing that both the author of Historia Quadripartita, and Gervase, contemporary writers, agree with Fitz-Stephen ; and the latter is not usually very partial to Becket. All the ancient historians give the same account.

NOTE [S], p. 406.

Madox, in his Baronia Anglica, cap. 14, tells us that, in the thirtieth of Henry II. thirty-three cows and two bulls cost but eight pounds seven shillings—money of that age ; five hundred sheep, twenty-two pounds ten shillings, or about ten pence three farthings per sheep ; sixty-six oxen, eighteen pounds three shillings ; fifteen breeding-mares, two pounds twelve shillings and sixpence ; and twenty-two hogs, one pound two shillings. Commodities seem then to have been about ten times cheaper than at present—all except the sheep—probably on account of the value of the fleece. The same author, in his Formulare Anglicanum, p. 17, says that in the tenth year of Richard I. mention is made of ten per cent. paid for money ; but the Jews frequently exacted much higher interest.

NOTE [T], p. 569.

Rymer, vol. ii. pp. 216, 845. There cannot be the least question that the homage usually paid by the kings of Scotland was not for their crown, but for some other territory. The only question remains, what that territory was. It was not always for the earldom of Huntingdon, nor the honor of Penryth ; because we find it sometimes done at a time when these possessions were not in the hands of the kings of Scotland. It is probable that the homage was performed in general terms, without any particular specification of territory ; and this inaccuracy had proceeded either from some dispute between the two kings about the territory, and some opposite claims, which were compromised by the general homage, or from the simplicity of the age, which employed few words in every transaction. To prove this we need but look into the letter of King Richard, where he resigns the homage of Scotland, reserving the usual homage. His words are, "Sæpedictus W. Rex ligius homo noster deveniat de omnibus terris de quibus antecessores sui antecessorum nostrorum ligii homines fuerunt, et nobis atque hæredibus nostris fidelitatem jurarunt" (Rymer, vol. i. p. 65). These general terms were probably copied from the usual form of the homage itself.

It is no proof that the kings of Scotland possessed no lands or baronies in England, because we cannot find them in the imperfect histories and records of that age. For instance, it clearly appears, from another passage in this very letter of Richard, that the Scottish king held lands both in the county of Huntingdon and elsewhere in England, though the earldom of Huntingdon itself was then in the person of his brother David ; and we know at present of no other baronies which William held. It cannot be expected that we should now be able to specify all his fees which he either possessed or claimed in England, when it is probable that the two monarchs themselves, and their ministers, would at that very time have differed in the list ; the Scottish king might possess some to which his right was disputed, he might claim others which he did not possess ; and neither of the two kings was willing to resign his pretensions by a particular enumeration.

A late author of great industry and learning, but full of prejudices, and of no penetration, Mr. Carte, has taken advantage of the undefined terms of the Scottish homage, and has pretended that it was done for Lothian and Galloway ; that is, all the territories of the country now called Scotland, lying south of the Clyde and Forth ; but to refute this pretension at once, we need only consider that if these territories were held in fee of the English kings, there would, by the nature of the feudal law as established in England, have been continual appeals from them to the courts of the lord paramount, contrary to all the histories and records of that age. We find that as soon as Edward really established his superiority, appeals immediately commenced from all parts of Scotland: and that king, in his writ to the king's bench, considers them as a necessary consequence of the feudal tenure. Such large territories also would have supplied a considerable p rt of the English armies, which never could have escaped all the historians; not to mention that there is not any instance of a Scotch prisoner of war being tried as a rebel, in the frequent hostilities between the kingdoms, where the Scottish armies were chiefly filled from the southern counties.

Mr. Carte's notion with regard to Galloway, which comprehends, in the language of that age, or rather in that of the preceding, most of the southwest counties of Scotland—his notion, I say, rests on so slight a foundation, that it scarcely merits being refuted. He will have it (and merely because he will have it) that the Cumberland yielded by King Edmund to Malcolm I. meant not only the county in England of that name, but all the territory northwards to the Clyde. But the case of Lothian deserves some more consideration.

It is certain that in very ancient language Scotland means only the country north of the friths of Clyde and Forth. I shall not make a parade of literature to prove it, because I do not find that this point is disputed by the Scots themselves. The southern country was divided into Galloway and Lothian, and the latter comprehended all the southeast counties. This territory was certainly a part of the ancient kingdom of Northumberland, and was entirely peopled by Saxons, who afterwards received a great mixture of Danes among them. It appears from all the English histories, that the whole kingdom of Northumberland paid very little obedience to the Anglo-Saxon monarchs, who governed after the dissolution of the Heptarchy; and the northern and remote parts of it seem to have fallen into a kind of anarchy, sometimes pillaged by the Danes, sometimes joining them in their ravages upon other parts of England. The kings of Scotland, lying nearer them, took at last possession of the country, which had scarcely any government: and we are told by Matthew of Westminster (p. 193) that King Edgar made a grant of the territory to Kenneth III.; that is, he resigned claims which he could not make effectual, without bestowing on them more trouble and expense than they were worth; for these are the only grants of provinces made by kings; and so ambitious and active a prince as Edgar would never have made presents of any other kind. Though Matthew of Westminster's authority may appear small with regard to so remote a transaction, yet we may admit it in this case, because Ordericus Vitalis, a good authority, tells us (p. 701) that Malcolm acknowledged to William Rufus that the Conqueror had confirmed to him the former grant of Lothian. But it follows not, because Edgar made this species of grant to Kenneth, that therefore he exacted homage for that territory. Homage and all the rites of the feudal law were very little known among the Saxons, and we may also suppose that the claim of Edgar was so antiquated and weak, that, in resigning it, he made no very valuable concession; and Kenneth might well refuse to hold, by so precarious a tenure, a territory which he at present held by the sword. In short, no author says he did homage for it.

The only color, indeed, of authority for Mr. Carte's notion is, that Matthew Paris, who wrote in the reign of Henry III., before Edward's claim of superiority was heard of, says that Alexander III. did homage to Henry III. "pro Laudiano et aliis terris" (see p. 555). This word seems naturally to be interpreted Lothian. But, in the first place, Matthew Paris's testimony, though considerable, will not outweigh that of all the other historians, who say that the Scotch homage was always done for lands in England. Secondly, if the Scotch homage was done in general terms (as has been already proved), it is no wonder that historians should differ in their account of the object of it, since it is probable the parties themselves were not fully agreed. Thirdly, there is reason to think that *Laudianum*, in Matthew Paris, does not mean the Lothians now in Scotland. There appears to have been a territory which anciently bore that or a similar name in the north of England. For (1.) The Saxon Chronicle (p. 197) says that Malcolm Kenmure met William Rufus in Lodene in England. (2.) It is agreed by all historians that Henry II. only reconquered from Scotland the northern counties of Northumberland, Cumberland, and Westmoreland (see Newbriggs, p. 383; Wykes, p. 30; Hemingford, p. 492). Yet the same country is called by other historians Loidis, comitatus Lodonensis, or some such name (see Matt. Paris, p. 68; Matt. West, p. 247; Annal. Waverl. p. 159, and Diceto, p. 531). (3.) This last-mentioned author, when he speaks of Lothian in Scotland, calls it Loheneis (p. 574), though he had called the English territory Loidis.

I thought this long note necessary, in order to correct Mr. Carte's mistake, an author whose diligence and industry have given light to many passages of the more ancient English history.

NOTE [U], p. 570.

Rymer, vol. ii. p. 543. It is remarkable that the English chancellor spoke to the Scotch Parliament in the French tongue. This was also the language commonly made use of by all parties on that occasion (ibid. passim). Some of the most considerable among the Scotch, as well as almost all the English barons, were of French origin ; they valued themselves upon it, and pretended to despise the language and manners of the island. It is difficult to account for the settlement of so many French families in Scotland, the Bruces, Baliols, St. Clairs, Montgomeries, Somervilles, Gordons, Frasers, Cummins, Colvilles, Umfrevilles, Mowbrays, Hays, Maules, who were not supported there, as in England, by the power of the sword. But the superiority of the smallest civility and knowledge over total ignorance and barbarism is prodigious.

NOTE [X], p. 574.

See Rymer, vol. ii. p. 533, where Edward writes to the king's bench to receive appeals from Scotland. He knew the practice to be new and unusual, yet he establishes it as an infallible consequence of his superiority. We learn also from the same collection (p. 603) that immediately upon receiving the homage, he changed the style of his address to the Scotch king, whom he now calls "dilecto et fideli," instead of "fratri dilecto et fideli," the appellation which he had always before used to him (see pp. 109, 124, 168, 280, 1064). This is a certain proof that he himself was not deceived, as was scarcely indeed possible, but that he was conscious of his usurpations. Yet he solemnly swore afterwards to the justice of his pretensions when he defended them before Pope Boniface.

NOTE [Y], p. 587.

Throughout the reign of Edward I. the assent of the Commons is not once expressed in any of the enacting clauses : nor in the reigns ensuing, till the 9 Edw. III., nor in any of the enacting clauses of 16 Rich. II. Nay, even so low as Henry VI., from the beginning till the 8th of his reign, the assent of the Commons is not once expressed in any enacting clause (see preface to Ruffhead's edition of the Statutes, p. 7). If it should be asserted that the Commons had really given their assent to these statutes, though they are not expressly mentioned, this very omission, proceeding if you will, from carelessness, is a proof how little they were respected. The Commons were so little accustomed to transact public business, that they had no speaker till after the Parliament 6 Edw. III. (see Prynne's Preface to Cotton's Abridgment); not till the first of Richard II. in the opinion of most antiquaries. The Commons were very unwilling to meddle in any state affairs, and commonly either referred themselves to the Lords, or desired a select committee of that House to assist them, as appears from Cotton (5 Edw. III. n. 5 ; 15 Edw. III. n. 17 ; 21 Edw. III. n. 5 ; 47 Edw. III. n. 5 ; 50 Edw. III. n. 10 ; 51 Edw. III. n. 18 ; 1 Rich. II. n. 12 ; 2 Rich. II. n 12 ; 5 Rich. II. n. 14 ; 2 Parl. 6 Rich. II. n. 14 : Parl. 2, 6 Rich II. n. 8, etc.).

NOTE [Z], p. 588.

It was very agreeable to the maxims of all the feudal governments, that every order of the state should give their consent to the acts which more immediately concern them ; and as the notion of a political system was not then so well understood, the other orders of the state were often not consulted on these occasions. In this reign, even the merchants, though no public body, granted the king impositions on merchandise, because the first payments came out of their pockets. They did the same in the reign of Edward III., but the Commons had then observed that the people paid these duties, though the merchants advanced them ; and they therefore remonstrated against this practice (Cotton's Abridg. p. 39). The taxes imposed by the knights on the counties were always lighter than those which the burgesses laid on the boroughs—a presumption that, in voting those taxes, the knights and burgesses did not form the same house (see Chancellor West's Inquiry into the manner of creating Peers, p. 8). But there are so many proofs that those two orders of representatives were long separate, that it is needless to insist on them. Mr. Carte, who had carefully perused the rolls of Parliament, affirms that they never appear to have been united till the 16 Edw. III. (see Hist. vol. ii. p. 451). But it is certain that this union was not even then final ; in 1372 the burgesses acted by themselves, and voted a tax after the knights were dismissed (see Tyrrel, Hist. vol. iii. p. 734, from Rot. Claus. 46

Edw. III. n. 9). In 1376 they were the knights alone who passed a vote for the removal of Alice Pierce from the king's person, if we may credit Walsingham, p. 189. There is an instance of a like kind in the reign of Richard II. (Cotton, p. 193). The different taxes voted by those two branches of the Lower Houses naturally kept them separate ; but as their petitions had mostly the same object, namely, the redress of grievances, and the support of law and justice, both against the crown and the barons, this cause as naturally united them, and was the reason why they at last joined in one house for the despatch of business. The barons had few petitions ; their privileges were of more ancient date : grievances seldom affected them ; they were themselves the chief oppressors.

In 1333 the knights by themselves concurred with the bishops and barons in advising the king to stay his journey into Ireland. Here was a petition which regarded a matter of state, and was supposed to be above the capacity of the burgesses. The knights, therefore, acted a part in this petition (see Cotton's Abridg. p. 13). Chief Baron Gilbert thinks that the reason why taxes always began with the Commons or burgesses was, that they were limited by the instructions of their boroughs (see Hist. of the Exchequer, p. 37).

NOTE [AA], p. 588.

The chief argument from ancient authority for the opinion that the representatives of boroughs preceded the 49th of Henry III. is the famous petition of the borough of St. Alban's, first taken notice of by Selden, and then by Petyt, Brady, Tyrrel, and others. In this petition, presented to the Parliament in the reign of Edward II., the town of St. Alban's asserts that though they held *in capite* of the crown, and owed only, for all other service, their attendance in Parliament, yet the sheriff had omitted them in his writs ; whereas both in the reign of the king's father, and all his predecessors, they had always sent members. Now, say the defenders of this opinion, if the commencement of the House of Commons were in Henry III.'s reign, this expression could not have been used. But Madox, in his History of the Exchequer, pp. 522, 523, 524, has endeavored, and with great reason, to destroy the authority of this petition for the purpose alleged. He asserts, first, that there was no such tenure in England as that of holding by attendance in Parliament, instead of all other service ; secondly, that the borough of St. Alban's never held of the crown at all, but was always demesne land of the abbot. It is no wonder, therefore, that a petition which advances two falsehoods should contain one historical mistake, which indeed amounts only to an inaccurate and exaggerated expression ; no strange matter in ignorant burgesses of that age. Accordingly, St. Alban's continued still to belong to the abbot. It never held of the crown till after the dissolution of the monasteries. But the assurance of these petitioners is remarkable. They wanted to shake off the authority of their abbot, and to hold of the king, but were unwilling to pay any services even to the crown ; upon which they framed this idle petition, which later writers have made the foundation of so many inferences and conclusions. From the tenor of the petition it appears that there was a close connection between holding of the crown and being represented in Parliament ; the latter had scarcely ever place without the former ; yet we learn from Tyrrel's Appendix, vol. iv., that there were some instances to the contrary. It is not improbable that Edward followed the roll of the Earl of Leicester, who had summoned, without distinction, all the considerable boroughs of the kingdom, among which there might be some few that did not hold of the crown. Edward also found it necessary to impose taxes on all the boroughs in the kingdom without distinction. This was a good expedient for augmenting his revenue. We are not to imagine, because the House of Commons have since become of great importance, that the first summoning of them would form any remarkable and striking epoch, and be generally known to the people even seventy or eighty years after. So ignorant were the generality of men in that age, that country burgesses would readily imagine an innovation, seemingly so little material, to have existed from time immemorial, because it was beyond their own memory, and perhaps that of their father. Even the Parliament in the reign of Henry V. say that Ireland had, from the beginning of time, been subject to the crown of England (see Brady). And surely if any thing interests the people above all others, it is war and conquests, with their dates and circumstances.